DATE DUE

PRINTED IN U.S.A.

SOMETHING ABOUT THE AUTHOR

R

ISSN 0276-816X

0667462

SOMETHING ABOUT THE AUTHOR

**Facts and Pictures about Authors
and Illustrators of Books for Young People**

EDITED BY
DONNA OLENDORF

VOLUME 67

 **Gale Research Inc.** • *DETROIT* • *LONDON*

STAFF

Editor: Donna Olendorf

Associate Editor: James F. Kamp

Senior Editor: Hal May

Sketchwriters: Marilyn K. Basel, Sonia Benson, Barbara Carlisle Bigelow, Suzanne M. Burgoin, Elizabeth A. Des Chenes, Kathleen J. Edgar, Katherine Huebl, Janice E. Jorgensen, Denise E. Kasinec, Thomas Kozikowski, Sharon Malinowski, Margaret Mazurkiewicz, Susan Reicha, Mary K. Ruby, Edward G. Scheff, Kenneth R. Shepherd, Diane Telgen, Polly A. Vedder, and Thomas Wiloch

Research Manager: Victoria B. Cariappa

Research Supervisor: Mary Rose Bonk

Editorial Associates: Jane A. Cousins, Andrew Guy Malonis, and Norma Sawaya

Editorial Assistants: Mike Avolio, Patricia Bowen, Reginald A. Carlton, Clare Collins, Catherine A. Coulson, Theodore J. Dumbrigue, Shirley Gates, Sharon McGilvray, and Tracy Head Turbett

Production Manager: Mary Beth Trimper

External Production Assistant: Shanna P. Heilveil

Art Director: Arthur Chartow

Keyliner: C. J. Jonik

This book is printed on acid-free paper that meets the minimum requirements of American National Standard for Information Sciences—Permanence Paper for Printed Library Materials, ANSI Z39.48-1984. ∞™

This book is printed on recycled paper that meets Environmental Agency standards.

Copyright © 1992
Gale Research Inc.
835 Penobscot Bldg.
Detroit, MI 48226-4094

Library of Congress Catalog Card Number 72-27107

ISBN 0-8103-2277-3
ISSN 0276-816X

Printed in the United States

Published simultaneously in the United Kingdom
by Gale Research International Limited
(An affiliated company of Gale Research Inc.)

Contents

Introduction

Something about the Author (SATA) is an ongoing reference series that deals with the lives and works of authors and illustrators of children's books. *SATA* includes not only well-known authors and illustrators whose books are widely read, but also those less prominent people whose works are just coming to be recognized. This series is often the only readily available information source for emerging writers or artists. You'll find *SATA* informative and entertaining whether you are a student, a librarian, an English teacher, a parent, or simply an adult who enjoys children's literature for its own sake.

What's Inside SATA

SATA provides detailed information about authors and illustrators who span the full time range of children's literature, from early figures like John Newbery and L. Frank Baum to contemporary figures like Judy Blume and Richard Peck. Authors in the series represent primarily English-speaking countries, particularly the United States, Canada, and the United Kingdom. Also included, however, are authors from around the world whose works are available in English translation. The writings represented in *SATA* include those created intentionally for children and young adults as well as those written for a general audience and known to interest younger readers. These writings cover the entire spectrum of children's literature, including picture books, humor, folk and fairy tales, animal stories, mystery and adventure, science fiction and fantasy, historical fiction, poetry and nonsense verse, drama, biography, and nonfiction.

Obituaries are also included in *SATA* and are intended not only as death notices but as concise views of people's lives and work. Additionally, each edition features newly revised and updated entries for a selection of *SATA* listees who remain of interest to today's readers and who have been active enough to require extensive revision of their earlier biographies.

Two Convenient Indexes

In response to suggestions from librarians, *SATA* indexes no longer appear in each volume, but are included in alternate (odd-numbered) volumes of the series, beginning with Volume 57.

SATA continues to include two indexes that cumulate with each alternate volume: the Illustrations Index, arranged by the name of the illustrator, gives the number of the volume and page where the illustrator's work appears in the current volume as well as all preceding volumes in the series; the Author Index gives the number of the volume in which a person's Biographical Sketch or Obituary appears in the current volume as well as all preceding volumes in the series.

These indexes also include references to authors and illustrators who appear in Gale's *Yesterday's Authors of Books for Children, Children's Literature Review*, and the *Something about the Author Autobiography Series*.

Easy-to-Use Entry Format

Whether you're already familiar with the *SATA* series or just getting acquainted, you will want to be aware of the kind of information that an entry provides. In every *SATA* entry the editors attempt to give as complete a picture of the person's life and work as possible. A typical entry in *SATA* includes the following clearly labeled information sections:

● *PERSONAL:* date and place of birth and death, parents' names and occupations, name of spouse, date of marriage, and names of children, educational institutions attended, degrees received, religious and political affiliations.

● *ADDRESSES:* complete home, office, and agent's address.

● *CAREER:* name of employer, position, and dates for each career post; military service.

● *MEMBER:* memberships and offices held in professional and civic organizations.

● *AWARDS, HONORS:* literary and professional awards received.

● *WRITINGS:* title-by-title chronological bibliography of books written and/or illustrated, listed by genre when known; lists of other notable publications, such as plays, screenplays, and periodical contributions.

● *WORK IN PROGRESS:* description of projects in progress.

● *SIDELIGHTS:* a biographical portrait of the author's development, either directly from the person—and often written specifically for the *SATA* entry—or gathered from diaries, letters, interviews, or other published sources.

● *FOR MORE INFORMATION SEE:* references for further reading.

● *EXTENSIVE ILLUSTRATIONS:* photographs, movie stills, manuscript samples, book covers, and other interesting visual materials supplement the text.

How a SATA Entry Is Compiled

A *SATA* entry progresses through a series of steps. If the biographee is living, the *SATA* editors try to secure information directly from him or her through a questionnaire. From the information that the biographee supplies, the editors prepare an entry, filling in any essential missing details with research and/or telephone interviews. When necessary, the author or illustrator is sent a copy of the entry to check for accuracy and completeness.

If the biographee is deceased or cannot be reached by questionnaire, the *SATA* editors examine a wide variety of published sources to gather information for an entry. Biographical and bibliographic sources are consulted, as are book reviews, feature articles, published interviews, and material sometimes obtained from the biographee's family, publishers, agent, or other associates. Entries compiled entirely from secondary sources are marked with an asterisk (*).

We Welcome Your Suggestions

We invite you to examine the entire *SATA* series, starting with this volume. Please write and tell us if we can make *SATA* even more helpful to you. Send comments and suggestions to: The Editor, *Something about the Author*, Gale Research Inc., 835 Penobscot Bldg., Detroit, Michigan 48226.

Acknowledgments

Grateful acknowledgment is made to the following publishers, authors, and artists whose works appear in this volume.

VICTOR APPLETON. Cover of *Tom Swift and His Motorcycle*, by Victor Appleton. Pocket Books, 1910. Copyright (c) 1919, 1938 by Stratemeyer Syndicate. Reprinted by permission of Pocket Books, a division of Simon & Schuster, Inc./ Cover of *Tom Swift and His Television Detector*, by Victor Appleton. Pocket Books, 1933. Copyright (c) 1933, 1962 by Stratemeyer Syndicate. Reprinted by permission of Pocket Books, a division of Simon & Schuster, Inc./ Endpapers from *Tom Swift and His Flying Lab*, by Victor Appleton II. Grosset & Dunlap, 1954. Copyright (c) 1954, 1982 by Grosset & Dunlap. Illustrations by Graham Kaye. Reprinted by permission of Simon & Schuster, Inc./ Cover of *Tom Swift and His Electronic Retroscope*, by Victor Appleton. Pocket Books, 1959. Copyright (c) 1987 by Simon & Schuster, Inc. Reprinted by permission of Pocket Books, a division of Simon & Schuster, Inc./ Cover of *Tom Swift in the Jungle of the Mayas*, by Victor Appleton II. Tempo Books Edition, 1972. Copyright (c) 1987 by Simon & Schuster, Inc. Cover illustration by Graham Kaye. Reprinted by permission of Simon & Schuster, Inc./ Cover of *Tom Swift: The Black Dragon*, by Victor Appleton. Pocket Books, 1991. Copyright (c) 1991 by Simon & Schuster, Inc. Reprinted by permission of Pocket Books, a division of Simon & Schuster, Inc.

JOHN ARCHAMBAULT. Cover and illustration by Ted Rand from *The Ghost-Eye Tree*, by Bill Martin, Jr. and John Archambault. Holt, 1985. Copyright (c) 1985 by Bill Martin, Jr. and John Archambault. Illustrations copyright (c) 1985 by Ted Rand. Reprinted by permission of Henry Holt and Company, Inc.

BRENT ASHABRANNER. Jacket of a *A Grateful Nation: The Story of Arlington Cemetery,* by Brent Ashabranner. G.P. Putnam's Sons,1990. Jacket photograph (c) 1990 by Jennifer Ashabranner. Jacket design by Joy Taylor. Reproduced by permission of Brent Ashabranner./Jacket of *The Times of My Life,* by Brent Ashabranner. Cobblehill Books. 1990. Jacket design by Charlotte Straub. Reproduced by permission of Brent Ashabranner./ Photograph by Jennifer Ashabranner.

WILBERT VERE AWDRY. Photograph courtesy of Heinemann Young Books.

PATRICIA BARNES-SVARNEY. Photograph courtesy of Patricia Barnes-Svarney.

GRAEME BASE. Photograph (c) Moshe Dinor, courtesy of Harry N. Abrams, Inc.

JAMES BERRY. Photograph courtesy of Hamish Hamilton.

VAL BIRO. Photograph courtesy of Val Biro. Illustration by Val Biro from **100 Bible Stories**, retold by Norman J. Ball. Copyright (c) 1980 by Hamlyn Publishing Group, Ltd. Reprinted by permission of Hamlyn Publishing Group, Ltd.

STEPHEN BOWKETT. Photograph courtesy of Stephen Bowkett.

PAT BRISSON. Cover of *Kate Heads West,* by Pat Brisson. Bradbury Press, 1990. Text copyright (c) 1990 by Pat Brisson. Illustrated by Rick Brown. Illustrations (c) 1990 by Rick Brown. Reprinted by permission of Bradbury Press, an affiliate of Macmillan, Inc./ Photograph by Emil Brisson, courtesy of Pat Brisson.

RICHARD A. BROWNE. Illustrations by Dik Browne from his *Hagar the Horrible on the Rack.* Reprinted by permission of King Features Syndicate./ Illustrations by Dik Browne from *Hi and Lois: Trixie a la Mode,* by Mort Walker. Copyright (c) 1986 by King Features Syndicate, Inc. World rights Reserved. Reprinted by permission of King Features Syndicate./ Illustrations by Dik Browne from his *Sack Time.* Reprinted by permission of King Features Syndicate./ Photographs courtesy of Richard A. Browne.

RUTH CALIF. Photograph courtesy of Ruth Calif.

ALDEN CARTER. Jacket of *Sheila's Dying,* by Alden Carter. Copyright (c) 1987 by Alden R. Carter. Jacket illustration by Jacqueline Garrick. Reprinted by permission of G.P. Putnam's Sons./ Jacket of *Up Country,* by Alden R. Carter, G.P. Putnams's Sons, 1989. Copyright (c) 1989 by Alden R. Carter. Jacket art copyright (c) 1989 by Ellen Thompson. Reprinted by permission of G.P. Putnam's Sons./ Jacket of *RoboDad,* by Alden R. Carter. G.P. Putnam's Sons, 1990. Copyright (c) 1990 by Alden R. Carter. Jacket art copyright (c) 1990 by Jacqueline Garrick. Reprinted by permission of G.P. Putnam's Son./ Photograph courtesy of Alden R. Carter.

SOMETHING ABOUT THE AUTHOR

ADAMS, John Anthony 1944-

PERSONAL: Born March 12, 1944, in San Bernardino, CA; son of Frank Lowell (a citrus field foreman) and Jean (an artist and homemaker; maiden name, Cooley) Adams. *Education:* Pomona College, B.A. (magna cum laude), 1966; Claremont Graduate School, M.A., 1968; University of California at Riverside, Ph.D., 1975. *Politics:* Independent. *Religion:* Protestant.

CAREER: Bureau of Land Management, United States Department of the Interior, Riverside, CA, soil scientist, 1975-82; writer. News editor and consultant, Rialto Historical Society. Member of historical survey advisory committee, Rialto, CA. Speaker for numerous organizations and groups.

MEMBER: Rialto Historical Society, Phi Beta Kappa.

AWARDS, HONORS: Honored for civic historical work with Rialto Historical Society.

WRITINGS:

Dirt, Texas A & M University Press, 1986.
Dangling from the Golden Gate Bridge, and Other Narrow Escapes, Ballantine, 1988.

Contributor to scientific journals.

WORK IN PROGRESS: A book of historical anecdotes and an examination of southern California's "much reduced citrus industry," tentatively titled *The Disappearing Orange;* a book tracing the origin and evolution of various sports.

SIDELIGHTS: John Anthony Adams told *SATA* that he wrote *Dangling from the Golden Gate Bridge, and Other Narrow Escapes* because he "is fascinated by unusual true incidents when an apparently doomed person survives impending death and can tell his feelings of the experience." He also "had an urge to collect the very best of these stories for a book. This presented the challenges of not only assembling all of these special incidents, but presenting them in the form of a logically connected narrative.

"As the book took shape, I realized that many of these precarious and potentially fatal situations had, in retrospect, a rather humorous twist. In fact, some of them became almost slapstick in nature. However, the serious information and explanations create a balanced and interesting educational dimension."

Adams said he wrote *Dirt* "because, as a soil scientist, I felt there was a definite need for an enjoyable and readable book with accurate information about soil. With such books abounding on the oceans, the deserts, the stars, plants and animal life, and all the rest of nature, nothing had been written to show the surprising and unexpected aspects (as well as the many misconceptions) about the most basic part of our planet."

*　　*　　*

ALGER, Horatio, Jr.
See STRATEMEYER, Edward L.

1

APPLETON, Victor
[Collective pseudonym]

WRITINGS:

"DON STURDY" SERIES

Don Sturdy on the Desert of Mystery; or, Autoing in the Land of Caravans, Grosset & Dunlap, 1925.
Don Sturdy with the Big Snake Hunters; or, Lost in the Jungles of the Amazon, Grosset & Dunlap, 1925.
Don Sturdy in the Tombs of Gold; or, The Old Egyptian's Great Secret, Grosset & Dunlap, 1925.
Don Sturdy across the North Pole; or, Cast Away in the Land of Ice, Grosset & Dunlap, 1925.
Don Sturdy in the Land of Volcanoes; or, The Trail of the Ten Thousand Smokes, Grosset & Dunlap, 1925.
Don Sturdy in the Port of Lost Ships; or, Adrift in the Sargasso Sea, Grosset & Dunlap, 1926.
Don Sturdy among the Gorillas; or, Adrift in the Great Jungle, Grosset & Dunlap, 1927.
Don Sturdy Captured by Head Hunters; or, Adrift in the Wilds of Borneo, Grosset & Dunlap, 1928.
Don Sturdy in Lion Land; or, The Strange Clearing in the Jungle, Grosset & Dunlap, 1929.
Don Sturdy in the Land of Giants; or, Captives of the Savage Patagonians, Grosset & Dunlap, 1930.
Don Sturdy on the Ocean Bottom; or, The Strange Cruise of the Phantom, Grosset & Dunlap, 1931.

Cover from the very first "Tom Swift" title, published in 1910.

Tom's ingenuity is captured in a 1933 cover.

Don Sturdy in the Temples of Fear; or, Destined for a Strange Sacrifice, Grosset & Dunlap, 1932.
Don Sturdy Lost in Glacier Bay; or, The Mystery of the Moving Totem Poles, Grosset & Dunlap, 1933.
Don Sturdy Trapped in the Flaming Wilderness; or, Unearthing Secrets in Central Asia, Grosset & Dunlap, 1934.
Don Sturdy with the Harpoon Hunters; or, The Strange Cruise of the Whaling Ship, Grosset & Dunlap, 1935.

"MOTION PICTURE CHUMS" SERIES

The Motion Picture Chums' First Venture; or, Opening a Photo Playhouse in Fairlands (also see below), Grosset & Dunlap, 1913.
The Motion Picture Chums at Seaside Park; or, The Rival Photo Theatres of the Boardwalk (also see below), Grosset & Dunlap, 1913.
The Motion Picture Chums on Broadway; or, The Mystery of the Missing Cash Box (also see below), Grosset & Dunlap, 1914.
The Motion Picture Chums' Outdoor Exhibition; or, The Film That Solved a Mystery (also see below), Grosset & Dunlap, 1914.
The Motion Picture Chums' New Idea; or, The First Educational Photo Playhouse (also see below), Grosset & Dunlap, 1914.
The Motion Picture Chums at the Fair; or, The Greatest Film Ever Exhibited (also see below), Grosset & Dunlap, 1915.

The Motion Picture Chums' War Spectacle; or, The Film That Won the Prize (also see below), Grosset & Dunlap, 1916.

"MOVING PICTURE BOYS" SERIES

The Moving Picture Boys; or, The Perils of a Great City Depicted (also see below), Grosset & Dunlap, 1913.

The Moving Picture Boys in the West; or, Taking Scenes among the Cowboys and Indians (also see below), Grosset & Dunlap, 1913.

The Moving Picture Boys on the Coast; or, Showing the Perils of the Deep (also see below), Grosset & Dunlap, 1913.

The Moving Picture Boys in the Jungle; or, Stirring Times among the Wild Animals (also see below), Grosset & Dunlap, 1913.

The Moving Picture Boys in Earthquake Land; or, Working amid Many Perils (also see below), Grosset & Dunlap, 1913.

The Moving Picture Boys and the Flood; or, Perilous Days on the Mississippi (also see below), Grosset & Dunlap, 1914.

The Moving Picture Boys at Panama; or, Stirring Adventures along the Great Canal (also see below), Grosset & Dunlap, 1915.

The Moving Picture Boys under the Sea; or, The Treasure of the Lost Ship (also see below), Grosset & Dunlap, 1916.

The Moving Picture Boys on the War Front; or, The Hunt for the Stolen Army Film (also see below), Grosset & Dunlap, 1918.

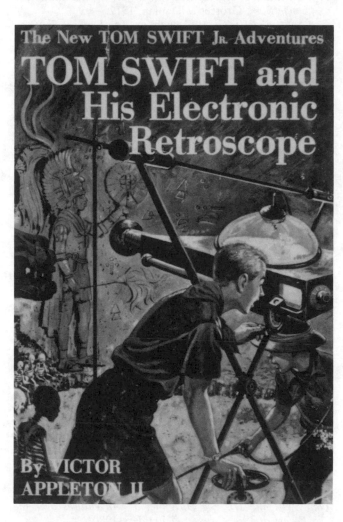

This 1959 title by Victor Appleton II reflects Tom Jr.'s technological progress.

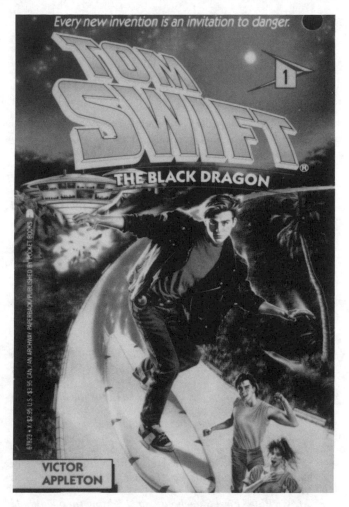

Sporting a stylish new hairdo and a California address, Tom has been reborn as a teen for the nineties in this 1991 Archway edition by Victor Appleton II.

The Moving Picture Boys on French Battlefields; or, Taking Pictures for the U.S. Army (also see below), Grosset & Dunlap, 1919.

The Moving Picture Boys' First Showhouse; or, Opening up for Business in Fairlands (originally published as *The Motion Picture Chums' First Venture; or, Opening a Photo Playhouse in Fairlands*), Grosset & Dunlap, 1921.

The Moving Picture Boys at Seaside Park; or, The Rival Photo Theatres of the Boardwalk (originally published as *The Motion Picture Chums at Seaside Park; or, The Rival Photo Theatres of the Boardwalk*), Grosset & Dunlap, 1921.

The Moving Picture Boys on Broadway; or, The Mystery of the Missing Cash Box (originally published as *The Motion Picture Chums on Broadway; or, The Mystery of the Missing Cash Box*), Grosset & Dunlap, 1921.

The Moving Picture Boys' Outdoor Exhibition; or, The Film That Solved a Mystery (originally published as *The Motion Picture Chums' Outdoor Exhibition; or, The Film That Solved a Mystery*), Grosset & Dunlap, 1922.

The Moving Picture Boys' New Idea (originally published as *The Motion Picture Chums' New Idea; or, The First Educational Photo Playhouse*), Grosset & Dunlap, 1922.

"MOVIE BOYS" SERIES

The Movie Boys on Call; or, Filming the Perils of a Great City (originally published as *The Moving Picture Boys; or, The Perils of a Great City Depicted*), Garden City, 1926.

The Movie Boys in the Wild West; or, Stirring Days among the Cowboys and Indians (originally published as *The Moving Picture Boys in the West; or, Taking Scenes among the Cowboys and Indians*), Garden City, 1926.

The Movie Boys and the Wreckers; or, Facing the Perils of the Deep (originally published as *The Moving Picture Boys on the Coast; or, Showing the Perils of the Deep*), Garden City, 1926.

The Movie Boys in the Jungle; or, Lively Times among the Wild Beasts (originally published as *The Moving Picture Boys in the Jungle; or, Stirring Times among the Wild Animals*), Garden City, 1926.

The Movie Boys in Earthquake Land; or, Filming Pictures amid Strange Perils (originally published as *The Moving Picture Boys in Earthquake Land; or, Working amid Many Perils*), Garden City, 1926.

The Movie Boys and the Flood; or, Perilous Days on the Mighty Mississippi (originally published as *The Moving Picture Boys and the Flood; or, Perilous Days on the Mississippi*), Garden City, 1926.

The Movie Boys in Peril; or, Strenuous Days along the Panama Canal (originally published as *The Moving Picture Boys at Panama; or, Stirring Adventures along the Great Canal*), Garden City, 1926.

The Movie Boys under the Sea; or, The Treasure of the Lost Ship (originally published as *The Moving Picture Boys under the Sea; or, The Treasure of the Lost Ship*), Garden City, 1926.

The Movie Boys under Fire; or, The Search for the Stolen Film (originally published as *The Moving Picture Boys on the War Front; or, The Hunt for the Stolen Army Film*), Garden City, 1926.

The Movie Boys under Uncle Sam; or, Taking Pictures for the Army (originally published as *The Moving Picture Boys on French Battlefields; or, Taking Pictures for the U.S. Army*), Garden City, 1926.

The Movie Boys' First Showhouse; or, Fighting for a Foothold in Fairlands (originally published as *The Motion Picture Chums' First Venture; or, Opening a Photo Playhouse in Fairlands*), Garden City, 1926.

The Movie Boys at Seaside Park; or, The Rival Photo Houses of the Boardwalk (originally published as *The Motion Picture Chums at Seaside Park; or, The Rival Photo Theatres of the Boardwalk*), Garden City, 1926.

The Movie Boys on Broadway; or, The Mystery of the Missing Cash Box (originally published as *The Motion Picture Chums on Broadway; or, The Mystery of the Missing Cash Box*), Garden City, 1926.

The Movie Boys' Outdoor Exhibition; or, The Film That Solved a Mystery (originally published as *The Motion Picture Chums' Outdoor Exhibition; or, The Film That Solved a Mystery*), Garden City, 1927.

The Movie Boys' New Idea; or, Getting the Best of Their Enemies (originally published as *The Motion Picture Chums' New Idea; or, The First Educational Photo Playhouse*), Garden City, 1927.

The Movie Boys at the Big Fair; or, The Greatest Film Ever Exhibited (originally published as *The Motion Picture Chums at the Fair; or, The Greatest Film Ever Exhibited*), Garden City, 1927.

The Movie Boys' War Spectacle; or, The Film That Won the Prize (originally published as *The Motion Picture Chums' War Spectacle; or, The Film That Won the Prize*), Garden City, 1927.

"TOM SWIFT" SERIES

Tom Swift and His Motor Cycle; or, Fun and Adventures on the Road, Grosset & Dunlap, 1910.

Tom Swift and His Motor Boat; or, The Rivals of Lake Carlopa, Grosset & Dunlap, 1910.

Tom Swift and His Airship; or, The Stirring Cruise of the Red Cloud, Grosset & Dunlap, 1910.

Tom Swift and His Submarine Boat; or, Under the Ocean for Sunken Treasure, Grosset & Dunlap, 1910.

Tom Swift and His Electric Runabout; or, The Speediest Car on the Road, Grosset & Dunlap, 1910.

Tom Swift and His Wireless Message; or, The Castaways of Earthquake Island, Grosset & Dunlap, 1911.

Tom Swift among the Diamond Makers; or, The Secret of Phantom Mountain, Grosset & Dunlap, 1911.

Tom Swift in the Caves of Ice; or, The Wreck of the Airship, Grosset & Dunlap, 1911.

Tom Swift and His Sky Racer; or, The Quickest Flight on Record, Grosset & Dunlap, 1911.

Tom Swift and His Electric Rifle; or, Daring Adventures in Elephant Land, Grosset & Dunlap, 1911.

Tom Swift in the City of Gold; or, Marvelous Adventures Underground, Grosset & Dunlap, 1912.

Tom Swift and His Air Glider; or, Seeking the Platinum Treasure, Grosset & Dunlap, 1912.

Tom Swift in Captivity; or, A Daring Escape by Airship, Grosset & Dunlap, 1912.

Tom Swift and His Wizard Camera; or, The Perils of Moving Picture Taking, Grosset & Dunlap, 1912.

Tom Swift and His Great Searchlight; or, On the Border for Uncle Sam, Grosset & Dunlap, 1912.

Tom Swift and His Giant Cannon; or, The Longest Shots on Record, Grosset & Dunlap, 1913.

Tom Swift and His Photo Telephone; or, The Picture That Saved a Fortune, Grosset & Dunlap, 1914.

Tom Swift and His Aerial Warship; or, The Naval Terror of the Seas, Grosset & Dunlap, 1915.

Tom Swift and His Big Tunnel; or, The Hidden City of the Andes, Grosset & Dunlap, 1916.

Tom Swift in the Land of Wonders; or, The Underground Search for the Idol of Gold, Grosset & Dunlap, 1917.

Tom Swift and His War Tank; or, Doing His Bit for Uncle Sam, Grosset & Dunlap, 1918.

Tom Swift and His Air Scout; or, Uncle Sam's Mastery of the Sky, Grosset & Dunlap, 1919.

Tom Swift and His Undersea Search; or, The Treasure on the Floor of the Atlantic, Grosset & Dunlap, 1920.

Tom Swift among the Fire Fighters; or, Battling with Flames from the Air, Grosset & Dunlap, 1921.

Tom Swift and His Electric Locomotive; or, Two Miles a Minute on the Rails, Grosset & Dunlap, 1922.

Tom Swift and His Flying Boat; or, The Castaways of the Giant Iceberg, Grosset & Dunlap, 1923.

Tom Swift and His Great Oil Gusher; or, The Treasure of Goby Farm, Grosset & Dunlap, 1924.

Tom Swift and His Chest of Secrets; or, Tracing the Stolen Inventions, Grosset & Dunlap, 1925.

Tom Swift and His Airline Express; or, From Ocean to Ocean by Daylight, Grosset & Dunlap, 1926.

Tom Swift Circling the Globe; or, The Daring Cruise of the Air Monarch, Grosset & Dunlap, 1927.

Tom Swift and His Talking Pictures; or, The Greatest Invention on Record, Grosset & Dunlap, 1928.

Tom Swift and His House on Wheels; or, A Trip to the Mountain of Mystery, Grosset & Dunlap, 1929.

Tom Swift and His Big Dirigible; or, Adventures over the Forest of Fire, Grosset & Dunlap, 1930.

Tom Swift and His Sky Train; or, Overland through the Clouds, Grosset & Dunlap, 1931.

*Tom Swift and His Giant Magnet; or, Bringing up the Lost
   Submarine,* Grosset & Dunlap, 1932.
*Tom Swift and His Television Detector; or, Trailing the Secret
   Plotters,* Grosset & Dunlap, 1933.
*Tom Swift and His Ocean Airport; or, Foiling the Haargoland-
   ers,* Grosset & Dunlap, 1934.
*Tom Swift and His Planet Stone; or, Discovering the Secret of
   Another World,* Grosset & Dunlap, 1935.
Tom Swift and His Giant Telescope, Whitman, 1939.
Tom Swift and His Magnetic Silencer, Whitman, 1941.

OTHER

(Contributor) Stephen Dunning and Henry B. Maloney,
   editors, *A Superboy, Supergirl Anthology: Selected
   Chapters from the Earlier Works of Victor Appleton,
   Franklin W. Dixon, and Carolyn Keene,* Scholastic Book
   Services, 1971.

ADAPTATIONS: Barry Kirk Productions and Twentieth
Century-Fox designed a film based on the "Tom Swift" series
that was never produced. Twentieth Century-Fox also
planned a musical based on Tom's life, but the project was
shelved. Barry Kirk Productions and Levy-Gardner-Laven
Productions mapped out a Tom Swift television series that
never materialized.

SIDELIGHTS: Victor Appleton was the pseudonym used by
Edward Stratemeyer for the "Tom Swift" series. "Of all the
characters created by Stratemeyer," states J. Randolph Cox
in his introduction to John Dizer's *Tom Swift & Company:
"Boys' Books" by Stratemeyer and Others,* "probably none
arouses more affection than Tom Swift. His adventures serve
as a symbol of American ingenuity and technological progress, one part of that American Dream." Aided and abetted
by a large cast of characters—including his father, retired
inventor Barton Swift, his chum and accountant Ned Newton, his blushing sweetheart Mary Nestor, his eccentric companion Mr. Wakefield Damon, his faithful black hired hand
Eradicate Sampson, and his giant servant Koku—and hin-
dered by a wide assortment of villains—the red-haired,
squinting bully Andy Foger, the shyster lawyers Smeak &
Katch, and the unspeakable Hankinshaw—Tom overcame
all obstacles and emerged as one of the best-selling series
heroes of all time. Estimated sales of the series suggest that
children bought well over fifteen million "Tom Swift" volumes in the years between 1910 and 1941. Arthur Prager
reports in an *American Heritage* article that in 1926 "a survey
of 36,750 school children in thirty-four representative cities
revealed that 98 per cent of them were reading Stratemeyer
series books, and that most of them liked Tom Swift best."

Although some enthusiasts have seen Thomas Edison and
aircraft engineer Glenn Curtiss as prototypes for the hero of
this early science fiction series, Prager declares that the
author based Tom "nearly 100 per cent [on] Stratemeyer's
own idol, Henry Ford. In 1910 Edison was a deaf old man in
his sixties, and hardly a figure with whom a teen-ager could
identify. Ford, on the other hand, was in his vigorous prime,
and in the news almost every day. Boys could . . . marvel at
his Model T, introduced in 1908 and not unlike Tom Swift's
own 'runabout.'" Like Ford, Prager adds, Tom had a
distaste for labor unions, and he eventually formed his own
version of Ford's automotive empire: the Swift Construction
Company, located on the shores of Lake Carlopa near the
town of Shopton, New York, manufactured many of Tom's
inventions.

The youthful inventor's scientific ingenuity attracted
readers. "Tom, in his private laboratory, casually solved
problems that had stumped the world since Newton," states

Russel B. Nye in his survey *The Unembarrassed Muse: The
Popular Arts in America.* "What he invented was always
almost plausible, just far enough around the corner to be
visionary, not quite far enough to be absurd; many of his
inventions, in fact, were only a year or so ahead of their real-
life counterparts." "His color television was twenty years
ahead of its time," reports Prager. "His electric rifle, first
produced in Tom's Shopton laboratory in 1911, anticipated
the first Browning machine rifle by five years. Although
Tom's rifle fired a charge of electricity instead of a bullet, it
was similar to Browning's 1916 rapid-fire repeater," he adds.
"Tom's 'wizard camera,' which was constructed in 1912, was
eleven years ahead of Victor's original portable motion-
picture camera. His electric locomotive was in service two
years before the New Jersey Central ran its first diesel electric,
and his photo telephone was eleven years ahead of the Bell
Laboratories' first successful phototelegraphy process,"
Prager declares. Even his famous "house on wheels" pre-
ceded the first camper-trailer by a year.

Tom's faith in technology's ability to solve all problems made
him truly a twentieth-century hero, Nye reports. Money was
not important to Tom in the way it had been to Horatio
Alger's heroes, the critic adds: "What mattered was Tom's
success at breaking through the barriers of the unknown. His
books were filled, in their naive way, with the excitement of a
conquest of matter and space, the thrill of accomplishing with
one's own brain and hands what others had hoped to do." "It
was not Rockefeller or Carnegie, Honus Wagner or Eddie
Plank who were the implied heroes of the Swift books," Nye
continues, "but the Wright brothers, Steinmetz, Tesla,
Edison, and the others who were pushing back the frontiers
of knowledge and invention." "Whereas Alger's boys faced
the problems of an urbanized, acquisitive society, and the
Merriwells the ethics of the competitive contest, Tom Swift
grasped the technology of the machine age and brought it
under control," the critic concludes. "He made scientific
discovery exciting and technological advance adventurous,
and most of all he made both seem useful and optimistic."

While the Tom Swift books were undeniably popular, some
critics see them as lacking in literary qualities. For instance,
Selma Lanes, in *Down the Rabbit Hole: Adventures and
Misadventures in the Realm of Children's Literature,* calls
them "decidedly regressive so far as literary or human content are concerned," and states that "they play subtly upon
the restlessness and idealism of older children, perhaps even
staving off adolescent depression with their pure fantasies of
the power of youth and the glory of the life of action." Prager
points out that the series occasionally made disparaging
remarks about Jews, foreigners, and blacks, although he adds
that "these references were later expunged in revised editions." Editor Neil Barron, writing in *Anatomy of Wonder: A
Critical Guide to Science Fiction,* calls the writing in the Tom
Swift books wooden, and maintains that they "emphasize
rapidity of incident and stereotypical characterization."
Other reviewers disagree; although allowing for the defects of
series fiction, they see Tom as a cut above the rest. Nye
asserts, "The best of the Stratemeyer books was the *Tom
Swift* series," and Prager declares that "the books are as
much fun to read as they ever were, anachronisms and
prejudices notwithstanding; one can always put them in the
context of their times."

Though his adventures have been out of print for many years,
Tom remains a prime favorite among readers. Prager explains the attraction his exploits hold in his 1971 book
Rascals at Large; or, The Clue in the Old Nostalgia: "They
gave us a taste of power, of the thrill of invention, the dim

rattle of a foreign land in the earphones of a homemade radio, the trembling of a joystick in the treacherous updrafts of the Rockies, the excitement of a technological breakthrough in the backyard lab." He continues, "The recent landings on the moon were anticlimactic compared with some of Tom Swift's adventures. After all, the astronauts simply got into their capsule, went to the moon, and came back again. No bullies dropped bolts into the machinery. No unscrupulous inventors tried to steal their mortgaged homes. No one was kidnaped or locked in a burning barn. They were all married. Not one of them was a gallant teen-ager." "Good luck to those brave astronauts," Prager concludes, "but if I had not known Edward Stratemeyer was dead these thirty years I would have sworn he was writing their dialogue. One Great Leap Forward for Mankind indeed. How he would have loved that line."

Victor Appleton was also the pseudonym used for the "Don Sturdy" books, featuring a young man whose adventures took him into all sorts of exotic locales, and various stories about boys who make, produce and show motion pictures. Tom Swift himself has passed into the realm of literary immortality through the "Tom Swifties" jokes that play on the Stratemeyer Syndicate's liberal use of adverbs: for example, "That's the last time I try to feed a lion," Tom said offhandedly. Edward Stratemeyer and Howard R. Garis both worked on the Tom Swift series, although sources differ on the exact amount of their individual involvement. Harriet S. Adams also contributed some of the later volumes in the series. In 1954, Adams and her partner Andrew E. Svenson introduced the "Tom Swift Jr." adventure series, featuring the exploits of Tom's son, and Simon & Schuster continue to publish Tom, Jr.'s adventures. See the *SATA* index for more information on Harriet S. Adams, Howard R. Garis, Andrew E. Svenson, and Edward Stratemeyer.

WORKS CITED:

Barron, Neil, editor, *Anatomy of Wonder: A Critical Guide to Science Fiction,* 2nd edition, Bowker, 1981, p. 343.
Cox, J. Randolph, "Introduction," *Tom Swift & Company: "Boys' Books" by Stratemeyer and Others,* by John T. Dizer, Jr., McFarland & Co., 1982, pp. vi-viii.
Lanes, Selma G., *Down the Rabbit Hole: Adventures and Misadventures in the Realm of Children's Literature,* Atheneum, 1971.
Nye, Russel B., "For It Was Indeed He: Books for the Young," *The Unembarrassed Muse: The Popular Arts in America,* Dial, 1970, pp. 60-87.
Prager, Arthur, "Peril: The Mother of Invention," *Rascals at Large; or, The Clue in the Old Nostalgia,* Doubleday, 1971, pp. 127-65.
Prager, Arthur, "Bless My Collar Button, if It Isn't Tom Swift, the World's Greatest Inventor," *American Heritage,* December, 1976, pp. 64-75.

FOR MORE INFORMATION SEE:

BOOKS

Dictionary of Literary Biography, Volume 42: *American Writers for Children before 1900,* Gale, 1985.
Garis, Roger, *My Father Was Uncle Wiggily,* McGraw-Hill, 1966.
Johnson, Deidre, editor and compiler, *Stratemeyer Pseudonyms and Series Books: An Annotated Checklist of Stratemeyer and Stratemeyer Syndicate Publications,* Greenwood Press, 1982.

Moskowitz, Sam, *Strange Horizons: The Spectrum of Science Fiction,* Scribner, 1976.

PERIODICALS

Art Journal, fall, 1983.
Children's Literature, Volume 7, 1978.
Hobbies, August, 1985.
New Yorker, March 20, 1954.
Saturday Review, July 10, 1971.
Time, June 30, 1980.

*   *   *

APPLETON, Victor II
[Collective pseudonym]

WRITINGS:

"TOM SWIFT JR. ADVENTURES" SERIES

Tom Swift and His Flying Lab, Grosset & Dunlap, 1954, reprinted, Tempo, 1977.
Tom Swift and His Jetmarine, Grosset & Dunlap, 1954, reprinted, Tempo, 1977.
Tom Swift and His Rocket Ship, Grosset & Dunlap, 1954, reprinted, Tempo, 1977.
Tom Swift and His Giant Robot, Grosset & Dunlap, 1954, reprinted, Tempo, 1977.
Tom Swift and His Atomic Earth Blaster, Grosset & Dunlap, 1954.
Tom Swift and His Outpost in Space, Grosset & Dunlap, 1955, published as *Tom Swift and His Sky Wheel,* Tempo, 1977.
Tom Swift and His Diving Seacopter, Grosset & Dunlap, 1956.
Tom Swift in the Caves of Nuclear Fire, Grosset & Dunlap, 1956, reprinted, Tempo, 1977.
Tom Swift on the Phantom Satellite, Grosset & Dunlap, 1957.
Tom Swift and His Ultrasonic Cycloplane, Grosset & Dunlap, 1957.
Tom Swift and His Deep-Sea Hydrodome, Grosset & Dunlap, 1958.
Tom Swift in the Race to the Moon, Grosset & Dunlap, 1958.
Tom Swift and His Space Solartron, Grosset & Dunlap, 1958.
Tom Swift and His Electronic Retroscope, Grosset & Dunlap, 1959, published as *Tom Swift in the Jungle of the Mayas,* Tempo, 1972.
Tom Swift and His Spectromarine Selector, Grosset & Dunlap, 1960, published as *Tom Swift and the City of Gold,* Tempo, 1973.
Tom Swift and the Cosmic Astronauts, Grosset & Dunlap, 1960.
Tom Swift and the Visitor from Planet X, Grosset & Dunlap, 1961.
Tom Swift and the Electronic Hydrolung, Grosset & Dunlap, 1961.
Tom Swift and His Triphibian Atomicar, Grosset & Dunlap, 1962.
Tom Swift and His Megascope Space Prober, Grosset & Dunlap, 1962.
Tom Swift and the Asteroid Pirates, Grosset & Dunlap, 1963.
Tom Swift and His Repelatron Skyway, Grosset & Dunlap, 1963.
Tom Swift and His Aquatomic Tracker, Grosset & Dunlap, 1964.
Tom Swift and His 3-D Telejector, Grosset & Dunlap, 1964.
Tom Swift and His Polar-Ray Dynasphere, Grosset & Dunlap, 1965.
Tom Swift and His Sonic Boom Trap, Grosset & Dunlap, 1965.

Endpapers from the 1954 edition of *Tom Swift and His Flying Lab*. (Illustration by Graham Kaye.)

Tom Swift and His Subocean Geotron, Grosset & Dunlap, 1966.

Tom Swift and the Mystery Comet, Grosset & Dunlap, 1966.

Tom Swift and the Captive Planetoid, Grosset & Dunlap, 1967.

Tom Swift and His G-Force Inverter, Grosset & Dunlap, 1968.

Tom Swift and His Dyna-4 Capsule, Grosset & Dunlap, 1969.

Tom Swift and His Cosmotron Express, Grosset & Dunlap, 1970.

Tom Swift and the Galaxy Ghosts, Grosset & Dunlap, 1971.

"TOM SWIFT" ADVENTURES

Tom Swift: The City in the Stars, Wanderer, 1981.
Tom Swift: Terror on the Moons of Jupiter, Wanderer, 1981.
Tom Swift: The Alien Probe, Wanderer, 1981.
Tom Swift: The War in Outer Space, Wanderer, 1981.
Tom Swift: The Space Fortress, Wanderer, 1981.
Tom Swift: The Rescue Mission, Wanderer, 1981.
Tom Swift: Ark Two, Wanderer, 1982.
Tom Swift: Crater of Mystery, Wanderer, 1983.
Tom Swift: Gateway to Doom, Wanderer, 1983.
Tom Swift: The Invisible Force, Wanderer, 1983.
Tom Swift: Planet of Nightmares, Wanderer, 1984.
Tom Swift: Chaos on Earth, Wanderer, in press.

NEW "TOM SWIFT" SERIES

The Black Dragon, Archway, 1991.
The Negative Zone, Archway, 1991.

Cyborg Kickboxer, Archway, 1991.
The DNA Disaster, Archway, 1991.
Monster Machine, Archway, 1991.
Aquatech Warriors, Archway, 1991.

ADAPTATIONS: "The Tom Swift and Linda Craig Mystery Hour" was produced by Paramount and aired by ABC-TV on July 3, 1983. It starred Willie Aames as Tom and Lori Loughlin as Linda.

SIDELIGHTS: The last Stratemeyer Syndicate book featuring Tom Swift, hero of one of the best-selling juvenile series of all time, appeared in 1941. In 1954 the Stratemeyer Syndicate attempted to recreate Tom's success with a new series starring his son, Tom Jr. Harriet Adams, head of the Syndicate, explained to the *New Yorker* some of the chief differences between the old and new series: "We use a more up-to-date brand of humor. You won't find any stammerers in the Tom, Jr., series. As far as inventing goes, Tom, Jr., is more prolific. He's invented Tomasite Plastic, to encase nuclear reactors. It absorbs radiation more effectively than lead. And a Damonscope, which is really a photometer with nonabsorptive prisms to detect fluorescence from a distance and record its density on photographic film. And a Swift Spectrograph, which, not to go into too much detail, analyzes anything in a split second."

Readers familiar with the old series may note the loss of many familiar characters. Barton Swift, Mr. Damon, and Eradicate Sampson have all passed away. But several familiar faces remain: Tom, Sr., his wife, Mary Nestor, and Ned Newton, now manager of the Swift Construction Company. And many new characters are introduced, including Tom and Mary's daughter Sandra, Ned's daughter Phyllis, Chow Winkler, the cowboy chef, and Tom Jr.'s sidekick Bud Barclay—described by Neal Rubin in the *Detroit Free Press* as "the Ed McMahon of juvenile fiction, the perpetual second banana."

Tom Jr.'s adventures differ from his father's; instead of being primarily adventure stories with a science background, they tend to concentrate on real science. The *New Yorker* states that the Syndicate "consulted with jet experts, rocket experts, TV experts, and physicists" while creating the series. Writers had to have some background in science; Stratemeyer author Jim Lawrence explains to *Yellowback Library* interviewer Geoffrey S. Lapin, "You had to have at least some smattering of science to begin to even wing it in that stuff." The young inventor's exploits filled thirty-three volumes before Grosset & Dunlap stopped publishing the series in 1971.

Several titles in the "Tom Swift" series were renamed and repackaged to update their image, including this 1972 edition, originally published as *Tom Swift and His Electronic Retroscope* in 1959. (Illustration by Graham Kaye.)

"But Tom Swift lives," declares Rubin. In 1981, Simon & Schuster began producing new stories of Tom's adventures, which Rubin views with some trepidation: Tom, he says, "has become a man of the '80s. Phyllis, his all-but-mute girlfriend of decades past, has evolved into Anita Thorwald, a brilliant co-worker with a bionic leg. Bud is a computer hacker named Benjamin Walking Eagle." "Tom probably has taken to styling his hair and drinking Perrier," he concludes, "but progress always has its price."

Simon & Schuster acquired the Stratemeyer Syndicate in 1984 and revised Tom Swift Jr. once again in 1991. Inspired by the success of the "Back to the Future" film series starring Michael J. Fox, the new volumes are published in pocket-sized paperback editions like the bestselling "Hardy Boys Case Files" and "Nancy Drew Files." Other changes are also apparent: "this Tom," writes *Wall Street Journal* contributor Cynthia Crossen, "is a teen for the '90s. He lives in Southern California instead of New York state; he invents superconductive surfboards instead of telescopes; he'd rather be rocking at a beach party than saving the world with aerial warships; and his girlfriend's brother says things like, 'Hey, babe, there are two choices here. We could go swimming together or I could rub tanning oil on that lovely bod.'" Harriet Adams and Andrew Svenson originally conceived the "Tom Swift Jr." series, and Stratemeyer Syndicate writer Jim Lawrence actually wrote many of the volumes in the years between 1954 and 1967. See the *SATA* index for more information on Harriet S. Adams and Andrew E. Svenson.

WORKS CITED:

Crossen, Cynthia, "Gone Are the Days When Tom Swift Was a Serious Nerd," *Wall Street Journal,* April 16, 1991, pp. A1-A4.

Lapin, Geoffrey S., interview with Jim Lawrence, *Yellowback Library,* January/February, 1986.

Rubin, Neal, "Storybook Heroes Too Good to Ring True Today," *Detroit Free Press,* November 25, 1984, p. 3C.

"Tom, Jr.," *New Yorker,* March 20, 1954, pp. 26-27.

FOR MORE INFORMATION SEE:

BOOKS

Barron, Neil, editor, *Anatomy of Wonder: A Critical Guide to Science Fiction,* 2nd edition, Bowker, 1981.

Dizer, John T., *Tom Swift & Company: "Boys' Books" by Stratemeyer and Others,* McFarland & Co., 1981.

Johnson, Deidre, editor and compiler, *Stratemeyer Pseudonyms and Series Books: An Annotated Checklist of Stratemeyer and Stratemeyer Syndicate Publications,* Greenwood Press, 1982.

Moskowitz, Sam, *Strange Horizons: The Spectrum of Science Fiction,* Scribner, 1976.

Prager, Arthur, *Rascals at Large; or, The Clue in the Old Nostalgia,* Doubleday, 1971.

PERIODICALS

American Heritage, December, 1976.
Children's Literature, Volume 7, 1978.
Entertainment Weekly, June 21, 1991.
Publishers Weekly, April 5, 1991.

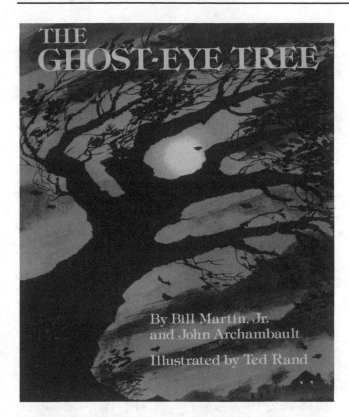

THE GHOST-EYE TREE

By Bill Martin, Jr.
and John Archambault

Illustrated by Ted Rand

A boy confronts his fears in *The Ghost-Eye Tree,* one of several books John Archambault wrote with Bill Martin, Jr. (Cover illustration by Ted Rand.)

ARCHAMBAULT, John

PERSONAL: Born in Pasadena, CA. *Education:* Attended Columbia Teacher's College; University of California, B.A., 1981; graduate study at University of California, Riverside.

ADDRESSES: Home—5616 Glen Haven Ave., Riverside, CA 92506.

CAREER: Poet, storyteller, and journalist.

AWARDS, HONORS: The Ghost-Eye Tree was named an Irma Simonton Black Honor Book by the Bank Street College of Education, 1985; *The Ghost-Eye Tree* and *Barn Dance!* were named Children's Choice Books by the International Reading Association and the Children's Book Council, 1986 and 1987, respectively; *Knots on a Counting Rope* was named a Notable Children's Trade Book in the field of social studies by the Children's Book Council and the National Council on the Social Studies, 1987.

WRITINGS:

FOR CHILDREN; WITH BILL MARTIN, JR.

"Little Seashore Books" series (contains *A Harvest of Oysters, The Irritable Alligator, The Loggerhead Turtle Crawls Out of the Sea, The Night-Hunting Lobster, A River of Salmon, The Seafaring Seals, The Silent Wetlands Hold Back the Sea, The Singing Whale, A Skyway of Geese,* and *The Sooty Shearwater Flies over the Sea*), Encyclopaedia Britannica Educational Corporation, 1982.
The Ghost-Eye Tree, illustrated by Ted Rand, Holt, 1985.

Barn Dance!, illustrated by Rand, Holt, 1986.
White Dynamite and Curly Kidd, illustrated by Rand, Holt, 1986.
Knots on a Counting Rope (originally published by Martin with illustrations by Joe Smith as part of the "Young Owl Books Social Studies Series," Holt, 1966), illustrated by Rand, Holt, 1987.
Here Are My Hands, illustrated by Rand, Holt, 1987.
Listen to the Rain, illustrated by James Endicott, Holt, 1988.
Up and Down on the Merry-Go-Round, illustrated by Rand, Holt, 1988.
The Magic Pumpkin, illustrated by Robert J. Lee, Holt, 1989.
Chicka Chicka Boom Boom, illustrated by Lois Ehlert, Simon & Schuster, 1989.

OTHER

Counting Sheep (for children), illustrated by John Rombola, Holt, 1989.

Also author of poetry and educational books.

ADAPTATIONS: Three videotapes of Archambault and Martin's poems and stories have been produced by DLM Publishers; *Barn Dance!* and *Knots on a Counting Rope* were featured selections on Public Broadcasting Service (PBS-TV) series, *Reading Rainbow,* 1989.

SIDELIGHTS: John Archambault, a children's writer dedicated to making reading comfortable, stimulating, and above all, fun for young readers, was an eager reader and writer himself as a child. His professional writing career began when, as a sophomore in high school, he took a part-time job at the Pasadena *Star,* a local newspaper. His good work was quickly rewarded with a full-time position as a reporter, a job he maintained throughout his high school years. He carried his interest in writing and journalism into college as the editor of his campus newspaper. When he was a graduate student at the University of California at Riverside, Archambault met Dr. Bill Martin, a children's writer and educator who had been working on books and educational techniques for children for many years. In the mid-1980s, the two men began working together on children's picture books designed for new readers aged four and up. Since then, Archambault and Martin have enjoyed a productive and successful collaboration. They share a strong common interest in the art of storytelling and create books that are meant to be seen and heard, as well as read. They have also combined their efforts in designing innovative ways to help children discover the sheer joy of reading. *Los Angeles Times Book Review* contributor Kristiana Gregory called Archambault and Martin "a valuable duo with much to offer" young readers.

Ghost-Eye Tree was the first publication written by Archambault and Martin with Ted Rand as illustrator—a trio that would go on to produce several popular juvenile books. *Ghost-Eye Tree* is the story of a boy and his sister sent out by their mother for a pail of milk on a dark, windy night. In order to get to the milkman's farm, the children have to go past an old oak tree that the little boy fears is haunted. On their way back, both the boy and his sister (who has been teasing him for being afraid), see the ghost of the tree and flee home. The story "emphasizes the bonds of love and friendship that develop between a brother and sister as they face their fears together," according to *Washington Post Book World* contributor John Cech. Critics praised *Ghost-Eye Tree* for its imaginatively spooky story, its rhythmic readability, and its effective illustrations. *Ghost-Eye Tree* is "a top-notch hair-raiser," noted a reviewer for the *Bulletin of the Center for*

Children's Books, who added that "it's poetry, too, the kind that reaches out to grab you." The illustrations, according to Ann A. Flowers of *Horn Book,* are "strong, striking, very dark, with highlights of moonlight and lantern light that cast a spooky, scary spell." Flowers concluded that *Ghost-Eye Tree* is perfect for reading aloud.

In their 1986 book *Barn Dance!* Archambault, Martin, and Rand again present a child's adventures in the night. A little boy, lying awake in a sleeping farmhouse, hears the unmistakable pluck of a violin. Following his ears to the barn, he finds a scarecrow playing the fiddle and the farm animals dancing. He joins them and dances until dawn. Read aloud, this book sounds like a square dance. With upbeat words and rhythms—"a hummin' an' a-yeein' an' a-rockin' an' a-sockin,'" or "Let's begin! Grab yourself a partner and jump right in!"—the authors mimic the lively music and dance.

The energy of *Barn Dance!* is more than matched by the spiritedness of the trio's *White Dynamite and Curly Kidd,* the story of a girl watching her rodeo star father ride White Dynamite, "the meanest bull in the whole United States." Once again, the rhythm and tone of the poetry match the frenzied pace of the rodeo: "Oh! Dad's in the rocker now . . . floppin' back and forth! His head's goin' south! Bull's goin' north . . . twistin' like a corkscrew straight down the right-away. His middle name's Doomsday! U!S!A!" Gregory summarized that the story "is rousing as a pep rally and meant to be yelled aloud so GET READY."

Knots on a Counting Rope, Archambault, Martin, and Rand's 1987 best-seller, scored a resounding success with both readers and critics. It is the story of a blind Indian boy who repeatedly asks to hear the tale of his birth and upbringing from his grandfather. The grandfather tells the boy of two

great blue horses that looked upon him when he was a weak newborn baby, giving him strength. The elder also relates how the blind child learned to ride his horse by memorizing trails—and even took part in a horse race. Each time he tells the story, the grandfather ties another knot in his rope, assuring his grandson that when the counting rope is filled with knots, the boy will know the story of his own birth by heart. *Los Angeles Times Book Review* contributor Barbara Karlin summarized that the aging grandfather "is telling his grandson that he will not always be there to tell the tale, even though his love for the child will last forever." *Knots on a Counting Rope* reflects the passing on of identity, love, and strength through the spoken word. This "dialogue between generations" observed *Los Angeles Times Book Review* contributor Richard Peck, demonstrates the power of "the oral tradition, the link best forged by families."

With their later collaborations, Archambault and Martin continue to make reading fun for children by dramatizing familiar experiences in appealing ways. In her *Horn Book* critique of *Up and Down on the Merry-Go-Round,* Ellen Fader found Archambault and Martin to be supremely successful in capturing the motion and joy of riding a carousel. The coauthors' 1989 publication, *Chicka Chicka Boom Boom,* also received enthusiastic reviews. "Rap comes to alphabet books," said *School Library Journal* critic John Philbrook of the book's "engaging rhyme" and "restless, exciting rhythms." And Mary M. Burns, writing in *Horn Book,* called *Chicka Chicka Boom Boom* "one of the liveliest, jazziest alphabet books on record . . . Tongue-tingling, visually stimulating . . . Absolutely irresistible. Join in, snap your fingers, listen to the beat, let yourself go—and have fun."

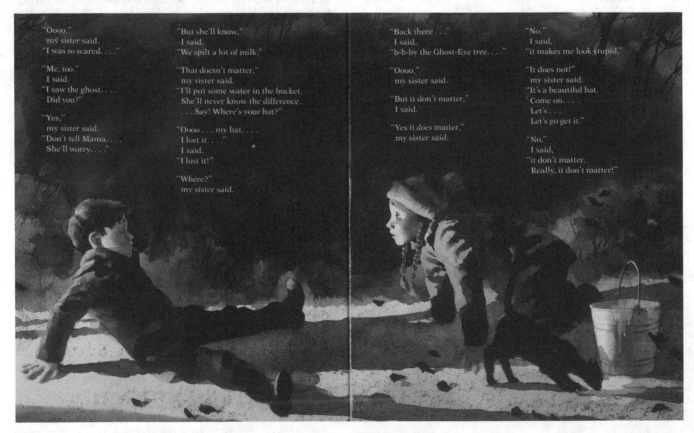

(From *The Ghost-Eye Tree,* by Archambault and Martin, Jr., illustrated by Ted Rand.)

WORKS CITED:

Archambault, John, and Bill Martin, Jr., *Barn Dance!,* Holt, 1986.

Archambault, John, and Bill Martin, Jr., *White Dynamite and Curly Kidd,* Holt, 1986.

Bulletin of the Center for Children's Books, February, 1986, p. 114.

Burns, Mary M., review of *Chicka Chicka Boom Boom, Horn Book,* January/February, 1990, p. 54.

Cech, John, "A Palette of Picture Books," *Washington Post Book World,* November 10, 1985, p. 19.

Fader, Ellen, review of *Up and Down the Merry-Go-Round, Horn Book,* July/August, 1988, p. 483.

Flowers, Ann A., *Horn Book,* January/February, 1986, p. 51.

Gregory, Kristiana, review of *White Dynamite and Curly Kidd, Los Angeles Times Book Review,* June 15, 1986, p. 7.

Karlin, Barbara, review of *Knots on a Counting Rope, Los Angeles Times Book Review,* December 6, 1987, p. 7.

Peck, Richard, "Birds, Deserts, Space Insects and a Navajo Grandfather," *Los Angeles Times Book Review,* March 27, 1988, p. 12.

Philbrook, John, review of *Chicka Chicka Boom Boom, School Library Journal,* November, 1989, p. 89.

FOR MORE INFORMATION SEE:

PERIODICALS

Bulletin of the Center for Children's Books, February, 1987.
Junior Literary Guild, October, 1986/March, 1987.
Los Angeles Times Book Review, November 22, 1987, p. 6.
New York Times Book Review, March 15, 1987, p. 29.
School Library Journal, December, 1989, p. 86.
Tribune Books (Chicago), October 4, 1987, p. 4; November 15, 1987, p. 6; November 12, 1989. p. 7.

See also *MARTIN, Bill, Jr.*

Sketch by Sonia Benson

*   *   *

ASHABRANNER, Brent (Kenneth) 1921-

PERSONAL: Born November 3, 1921, in Shawnee, OK; son of Dudley (a pharmacist) and Rose Thelma (Cotton) Ashabranner; married Martha White, August 9, 1941; children: Melissa Lynn, Jennifer Ann. *Education:* Oklahoma State University, B.S., 1948, M.A., 1951; additional study at University of Michigan, 1955, and Boston University and Oxford University, 1959-60. *Hobbies and other interests:* Tennis, African and Asian traditional art.

ADDRESSES: Home and office—15 Spring W., Williamsburg, VA 23185.

CAREER. Oklahoma State University, Stillwater, instructor in English, 1952-55; Ministry of Education, Technical Cooperation Administration, Addis Ababa, Ethiopia, educational materials adviser, 1955-57; International Cooperation Administration, Tripoli, Libya, chief of Education Materials Development Division, 1957-59; Agency for International Development, Lagos, Nigeria, education program officer, 1960-61; Peace Corps, Washington, DC, acting director of program in Nigeria, 1961-62, deputy director of program in India, 1962-64, director of program in India, 1964-66, director of Office of Training, 1966-67, deputy director of Peace Corps, 1967-69; Harvard University, Center for Studies in Education and Development, Cambridge, MA, research associate, 1969-70; Pathfinder Fund, Boston, MA, director of Near East-South Asia Population Program, 1970-71; director of project development for World Population International Assistance Division, Planned Parenthood, 1971-72; Ford Foundation, New York City, associate representative and population program officer, 1972-80, deputy representative to Philippines, 1972-75, deputy representative to Indonesia, 1975-80; writer, 1980—. *Military service:* U.S. Navy, 1942-45.

AWARDS, HONORS: National Civil Service League career service award, 1968; Notable Children's Trade Book in the Field of Social Studies, 1982, and Carter G. Woodson Book Award, National Council for the Social Studies, 1983, both for *Morning Star, Black Sun: The Northern Cheyenne Indians and America's Energy Crisis;* Notable Children's Trade Book in the Field of Social Studies, American Library Association (ALA) Notable Book, and Books for the Teen Age, New York Public Library, all 1983, all for *The New Americans: Changing Patterns in U.S. Immigration;* Notable Children's Trade Book in the Field of Social Studies, 1984, ALA Best Book for Young Adults, 1984, and Carter G. Woodson Book Award, 1985, all for *To Live in Two Worlds: American Indian Youth Today;* Notable Children's Book in the Field of Social Studies and ALA Notable Book, both 1984, both for *Gavriel and Jemal: Two Boys of Jerusalem;* ALA Notable Book, 1985, *Boston Horn-Globe* Honor Book, 1986, and Carter G. Woodson Book Award, 1986, all for *Dark Harvest: Migrant Farmworkers in America;* ALA Notable Book and *School Library Journal* Best Book of the Year, both 1986, both for *Children of the Maya: A Guatemalan Indian Odyssey;* Notable Children's Trade Book in the Field of Social Studies,

BRENT ASHABRANNER

School Library Journal Best Book of the Year, ALA Notable Book, and Christopher Award, all 1987, all for *Into a Strange Land: Unaccompanied Refugee Youth in America;* Notable Children's Trade Book in the Field of Social Studies, 1987, for *The Vanishing Border: A Photographic Journey along Our Frontier with Mexico;* ALA Notable Book and ALA Best Book for Young Adults, both 1988, both for *Always to Remember: The Story of the Vietnam Veterans Memorial; Born to the Land: An American Portrait, Counting America: The Story of the United States Census, People Who Make a Difference,* and *The Times of My Life: A Memoir* were named Books for the Teen Age by New York Public Library.

WRITINGS:

FOR JUVENILES

(With Russell Davis) *The Lion's Whiskers,* Little, Brown, 1959.

(With Davis) *Point Four Assignment: Stories from the Records of Those Who Work in Foreign Fields for the Mutual Security of Free Nations,* Little, Brown, 1959.

(With Davis) *Ten Thousand Desert Swords,* Little, Brown, 1960.

(With Davis) *The Choctaw Code,* McGraw, 1961.

(With Davis) *Chief Joseph: War Chief of the Nez Perce,* McGraw, 1962.

(With Davis) *Land in the Sun: The Story of West Africa,* Little, Brown, 1963.

(With Davis) *Strangers in Africa,* McGraw, 1963.

Morning Star, Black Sun: The Northern Cheyenne Indians and America's Energy Crisis (Junior Literary Guild selection), Dodd, 1982.

The New Americans: Changing Patterns in U.S. Immigration (Junior Literary Guild selection), Dodd, 1983.

To Live in Two Worlds: American Indian Youth Today (Junior Literary Guild selection), Dodd, 1984.

Gavriel and Jemal: Two Boys of Jerusalem (Junior Literary Guild selection), Dodd, 1984.

Dark Harvest: Migrant Farmworkers in America, Dodd, 1985.

Children of the Maya: A Guatemalan Indian Odyssey, photographs by Paul Conklin, Dodd, 1986.

(With daughter, Melissa Ashabranner) *Into a Strange Land: Unaccompanied Refugee Youth in America* (Junior Literary Guild selection), Dodd, 1987.

The Vanishing Border: A Photographic Journey along Our Frontier with Mexico (Junior Literary Guild selection), Dodd, 1987.

Always to Remember: The Story of the Vietnam Veterans Memorial, photographs by daughter, Jennifer Ashabranner, Dodd, 1988.

Born to the Land: An American Portrait (Junior Library Guild selection), photographs by Paul Conklin, Putnam, 1989.

I'm in the Zoo, Too!, illustrated by Janet Stevens, Cobblehill Books, 1989.

(With daughter, Melissa Ashabranner) *Counting America: The Story of the United States Census* (Junior Library Guild selection), Putnam, 1989.

People Who Make a Difference, Cobblehill Books, 1989.

A Grateful Nation: The Story of Arlington National Cemetery (Junior Literary Guild selection), Putnam, 1990.

The Times of My Life: A Memoir, Dutton, 1990.

Crazy about German Shepherds, Dutton, 1990.

An Ancient Heritage: The Arab-American Minority, Harper, 1991.

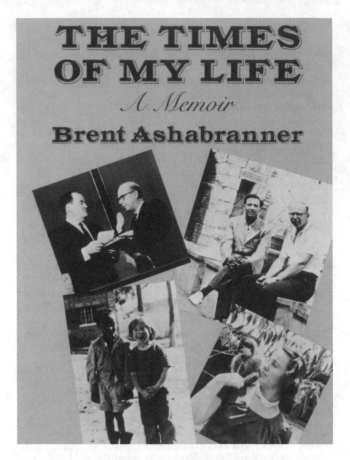

Ashabranner's 1990 memoir, *The Times of My Life,* covers his boyhood in Oklahoma during the Depression up through his involvement in the Peace Corps during the 1960s.

OTHER

(Editor) *The Stakes Are High,* Bantam, 1954.

(With Judson Milburn and Cecil B. Williams) *A First Course in College English* (textbook), Houghton, 1962.

A Moment in History: The First Ten Years of the Peace Corps, Doubleday, 1971.

Contributor of articles and short stories to periodicals.

WORK IN PROGRESS: A book about the Lincoln Memorial, for Putnam; a book about the United States as a multicultural country, for Cobblehill Books.

SIDELIGHTS: A former Peace Corps director, Brent Ashabranner writes informative books for children about the social issues facing a variety of cultures in the United States and other countries. The author has been praised for his knowledge of the customs and lifestyles of many groups of people. He is delicate but frank in his treatment of a wide range of topics, including the plight of American Indians and migrant workers. Ashabranner once commented to *SATA* about his collaboration with Russell Davis on such books as *The Choctaw Code* and *Land in the Sun: The Story of West Africa:* "Russ and I have lived and worked in many countries—Ethiopia, Libya, Nigeria, India, Nicaragua—and have travelled in dozens of others. Most of our books are about these countries, their people, their colorful legends, and about Americans who live and work overseas. In other words, we write about what we know and have experienced—which is good advice for anyone who wants to be an author."

Since his joint efforts with Davis, Ashabranner has penned young adult books on his own for which he has won several awards. Among his titles are *To Live in Two Worlds: American Indian Youth Today,* a Junior Literary Guild selection that presents the concerns of American Indian youth in the 1980s, and *Gavriel and Jemal: Two Boys of Jerusalem,* an account of the experiences of a Jewish boy and an Arab boy, both residing with their families in the ethnically diverse city of Jerusalem, Israel. The author also drew on the knowledge he gained as deputy director of the Peace Corps in the late 1960s to write *A Moment in History: The First Ten Years of the Peace Corps,* a well-received chronicle of the inception and development of the organization.

Ashabranner told *SATA:* "I started out as a fiction writer when I was eleven years old. I loved to read adventure books set in foreign places. Under the spell of a novel called *Bomba the Jungle Boy* I started writing a novel called *Barbara the Jungle Girl.* That wasn't very original, but at least I was, like Robert Louis Stevenson, 'playing the sedulous ape' to a writer I admired. By page three, I was hopelessly bogged down in the plot of my jungle story and never finished it; but that was a start, and I never stopped writing after that. I sold my first story when I was twenty and went on to publish scores of magazine short stories.

"I began nonfiction writing during the 1950s and 1960s when I was working overseas in the foreign aid program and the Peace Corps. The experiences I was having in Ethiopia, India, and other countries seemed more interesting than

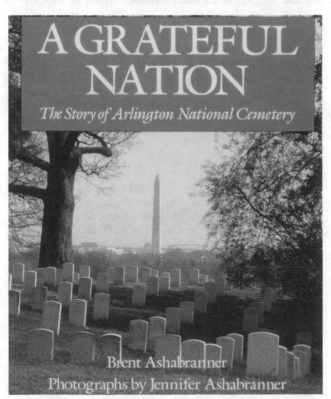

Dustjacket from Ashabranner's *A Grateful Nation,* a Junior Literary Guild selection that charts the history of the Arlington National Cemetery since its inception in 1864.

anything I could invent. I liked the nonfiction medium and have stayed with it. I began writing for children and young adults during my overseas years. The things I felt I was learning about other cultures and about people of different cultures understanding each other seemed worth sharing with young readers. Before, I wrote only for adults. Now, I write almost exclusively for children and young adults.

"I write mostly about rather complex social issues and problems; finding ways to make these subjects interesting and understandable to young readers is a challenging task I never tire of. I firmly believe that we do our most important reading when we are young; to try to engage young minds on worthwhile subjects is a great satisfaction.

"I do a great deal of field research and library research. In most cases I cover a lot of territory, talking with and sometimes living with the people I'm writing about. I think there is no other way to make my subjects interesting to young readers. But library research is vital to my full understanding of a subject. In the course of writing a book, I will consult many books, articles, government reports, and scholarly studies. The most important of these I put in a bibliography. I live only three hours from the Library of Congress, and I spend a good deal of time there."

FOR MORE INFORMATION SEE:

BOOKS

Abrahamson, Richard F., and Betty Carter, *From Delight to Wisdom: Nonfiction for Young Adults,* Oryx, 1990.
Contemporary Authors New Revision Series, Volume 27, Gale, 1989.

PERIODICALS

Horn Book, September/October, 1984; September/October, 1986.
Library Journal, August, 1971.
Los Angeles Times, October 17, 1987.
New York Times Book Review, August 5, 1962; April 4, 1971.
School Library Journal, January, 1985; June/July, 1987.
School Library Media Activities Monthly, April, 1991.
Voice of Youth Advocates, October, 1987.
Washington Post Book World, June 8, 1986.

*   *   *

AWDRY, Christopher Vere 1940-

PERSONAL: Born July 2, 1940; son of Wilbert Vere (an ordained priest of Church of England and writer) and Margaret Emily (Wale) Awdry. *Education:* St. Chad's, University of Durham. *Religion:* Church of England. *Hobbies and other interests:* Reading, music, theater, cricket.

ADDRESSES: Home—9 Neue View, Oundle, Peterborough PE 8 4LY, England.

CAREER: Writer.

MEMBER: Society of Authors, Railway and Canal Historical Society, Railway and Correspondence Travel Society.

WRITINGS:

Really Useful Engines, Heinemann, 1983.

James and the Diesel Engines, Heinemann, 1984.
Great Little Engines, Heinemann, 1985.
More About Thomas the Tank Engine, Heinemann, 1986.
Gordon, the High-Speed Engine, Heinemann, 1987.
Percy and the Postman: Sticker Book, Heinemann, 1988.
Thomas and the Evil Diesel, Heinemann, 1988.
Thomas and the Lost Cat: Sticker Book, Heinemann, 1988.
Thomas and the Missing Christmas Tree, Heinemann, 1988.
Toby, Trucks and Trouble, Kaye, 1988.
Up and Down with Percy, Heinemann, 1989.
Percy, the Seaside Train, Heinemann, 1989.
Thomas and the Twins, Heinemann, 1989.
Henry Pulls the Express Train, Heinemann, 1989.
James and the Rescue Train, Heinemann, 1989.
Trouble for Thomas and Other Stories, Random House, 1989.
Thomas's Book of Colours, Heinemann, 1989.
Thomas's Big Book of Games and Puzzles, Heinemann, 1989.
Thomas and the Good Train, Heinemann, 1989.
Meet Thomas the Tank Engine and His Friends, Random House, 1989.
Thomas Gets Tricked and Other Stories, Random House, 1989.
Thomas the Tank Engine and the Great Race, Random House, 1989.
Thomas the Tank Engine's Noisy Trip, Random House, 1989.
Thomas the Tank Engine's ABC's, McKay, 1990.
Breakfast Time for Thomas, McKay, 1990.
Jock the New Engine, Heinemann, 1990.
Catch Me, Catch Me!, McKay, 1990.
Happy Birthday, Thomas!, McKay, 1990.
Henry and the Elephant, McKay, 1990.
Encyclopedia of British Railway Companies, P. Stephens, 1990.
Thomas Visits a Farm, Random House, 1991.
Thomas and the Great Railway Show, Heinemann, 1991.

WORK IN PROGRESS: Over the Summit; Little Trains of Britain.

SIDELIGHTS: Christopher Vere Awdry told *SATA* that he "wanted to be a writer since my schooldays. I began writing for magazines in 1977." Awdry also remarked that he wrote his first book for his two-and-a-half year old son.

Awdry's father, Wilbert Vere Awdry, is the author of the popular "Railway" series of books for children. After his father retired from writing, Awdry continued writing stories with the same railway theme and engine characters that his father originated in 1945. Awdry has also written numerous other tales for children.

*   *   *

AWDRY, Wilbert Vere 1911-

PERSONAL: Born in June, 1911, at Ampfield, near Romsey, Hampshire, England; son of Vere (a vicar) and Lucy Louisa (a teacher; maiden name, Bury) Awdry; married Margaret Emily Wale, August, 1938; children: Christopher, Veronica, Hilary Margaret. *Education:* St. Peter's College, Oxford, B.A., 1932, M.A., 1936; Wycliffe Hall, Oxford, diploma in theology, 1933.

ADDRESSES: Home—Sodor, 30 Rodborough Ave., Stroud, Gloucestershire GL5 3RS, England.

WILBERT VERE AWDRY

CAREER: Ordained priest of Church of England, 1937; schoolmaster at boys' school in Jerusalem, 1933-36; curate of Odiham, England, 1936-39, West Lavington, England, 1939-40, and King's Norton, Birmingham, England, 1940-46; rector of Elsworth and Knapwell, England, 1946-53; vicar of Emneth, England, 1953-65; licenced to officiate in Diocese of Gloucester, 1965—.

WRITINGS:

Our Child Begins to Pray, E. Ward, 1951.
Belinda the Beetle, Brockhampton Press, 1958.
Belinda Beats the Band, Brockhampton Press, 1961.
Map of the Island of Sodor, Kaye & Ward, 1971, revised edition, 1987.
(With Peter J. Long) *The Birmingham and Gloucester Railway,* A. Sutton, 1987.
(With G. Awdry) *The Island of Sodor: Its People, History, and Railways,* Kaye & Ward, 1987.

"RAILWAY" SERIES; ALL PUBLISHED BY KAYE & WARD

The Three Railway Engines, 1945.
Thomas the Tank Engine, 1946.
James the Red Engine, 1948.
Tank-Engine Thomas Again, 1949.
Troublesome Engines, 1950.
Henry the Green Engine, 1951.
Toby the Tram Engine, 1952.
Gordon the Big Engine, 1953.
Edward the Blue Engine, 1954.
Four Little Engines, 1955.

Percy the Small Engine, 1956.
Eight Famous Engines, 1957.
Duck and the Diesel Engine, 1958.
The Little Old Engine, 1959.
The Twin Engines, 1960.
Branch Line Engines, 1961.
Gallant Old Engine, 1962.
Stepney, the Blueball Engine, 1963.
Mountain Engines, 1964.
Very Old Engines, 1965.
Main Line Engines, 1966.
The Small Railway Engines, 1967.
Enterprising Engines, 1968.
Oliver the Western Engine, 1969.
Duke the Lost Engine, 1970.
Thomas the Tank Engine's Surprise Packet, 1972.
Tramway Engines, 1972.

EDITOR

Industrial Archaeology in Gloucestershire, Gloucester Community Council, 1973, 3rd edition, Gloucestershire Society for Industrial Archaeology, 1983.
(With Christopher Cook) *A Guide to the Steam Railways of Great Britain,* Pelham Books, 1979, revised edition (with Roger Crombleholme), 1984.

SIDELIGHTS: Wilbert Vere Awdry told *SATA:* "Now eighty, I am writing no more. My son, Christopher, now writes the series of 'Engine Books,' which I began for him in 1945."

*   *   *

BARNES-SVARNEY, Patricia L(ou) 1953-

PERSONAL: Born May 10, 1953, in Binghamton, NY; daughter of William E. (an urbanist) and Helen M. (an artist; maiden name, Sherba) Barnes; married Thomas E. Svarney (an engineer), January 8, 1977. *Education:* Catawba College, B.A., 1975; State University of New York, M.A., 1983. *Hobbies and other interests:* Astronomy, rock collecting, weight training, cross country skiing, motorcycling, and biking.

ADDRESSES: Home—2603 Smith Dr., Endwell, NY, 13760. *Agent*—Barbara Kouts, P.O. Box 558, Bellport, NY 11713.

CAREER: Science writer, 1985—. Professional photographer, lecturer, and consulting editor to several major corporations and publishing companies; worked variously as a geochemist, astronomer, and physical oceanographer.

MEMBER: American Society of Journalists and Authors, American Geophysical Union, National Association of Science Writers, Gamma Theta Upsilon.

WRITINGS:

The National Science Foundation (part of the "Know Your Government" series), Chelsea House, 1989.
Zimbabwe (part of the "People and Places of the World" series), Chelsea House, 1989.
Clocks in the Rocks: Learning about Earth's Past (part of the "Earth Processes" series), Enslow Publishers, 1990.

Born of Heat and Pressure: Mountains and Metamorphic Rocks (part of the "Earth Processes" series), Enslow Publishers, 1991.
Fossils: Stories from Bones and Stones (part of the "Earth Processes" series), Enslow Publishers, 1991.

Author of test units for the American College Testing (ACT) program. Contributor to magazines, including *Astronomy, Cobblestone, Odyssey, Omni, Popular Astronomy, Ranger Rick,* and *Supercomputing Review.*

WORK IN PROGRESS: Middle readers book on science and technology; editorial work on an astronomy book.

SIDELIGHTS: Patricia L. Barnes-Svarney told *SATA:* "I was born in Binghamton and grew up in Endwell, New York. My parents were instrumental in helping me love reading and writing. When I was very young, they would read the classics to me—books like *Peter Rabbit* and *Charlotte's Web*—as well as the poetry and stories of famous authors, such as Rudyard Kipling and Robert Louis Stevenson. When I was old enough to read, I was shown the library.

"Though we had hundreds of books at home, I still found there was something special about choosing books from the library shelf, standing in line, and having the librarian date stamp the books. It seemed so official! The librarians were always helpful, and many of them talked to me about books

PATRICIA L. BARNES-SVARNEY

they enjoyed reading. They even suggested books they thought I would like to read. Some old habits do not die. Even today, one of my favorite places to go is the library, searching the stacks, reading the jackets for interesting sounding books, and checking books out. When I travel for my writing, I always try to stop at the local public or university library.

"My interest in science and writing grew as I grew. I first started out collecting pretty rocks. I wanted to know about the rocks, and I ended up in the library searching for books on rock collecting. My parents would also take me out into the backyard at night where we would sit on lawn chairs talking about the constellations. The stars fascinated me, and again, I ended up in the library, searching for information on the stars and planets.

"I was very lucky to grow up near a university. When I was in high school, I took courses in science, was in the science club, and joined the local community geology and astronomy clubs. One night, a geologist spoke to our club—and I was hooked! After talking to her, I decided I wanted to become a geologist. (In fact, she became my adviser when I went to graduate school!)

"In the meantime, I loved to write and read about space and geology. But I also wrote poetry, short stories, song lyrics, and a few pieces for the high school newspaper because it was fun. In addition, I took as many creative writing classes as possible. Even in college, I read, wrote, and took courses in English.

"How did I go from geology and astronomy to writing? No matter what job I had after college, I always enjoyed editing and helping people write papers or articles. After I received my master's degree, I decided I wanted to try writing my own stories and articles. I started by writing what I know: science. My first published paper was based on my research from graduate school, but I soon learned that writing magazine articles for the general public was fun and rewarding.

"Today, I write articles for numerous magazines. My research takes me into many fields. I write articles mainly about science, including subjects about space and the environment. I write about computers, health, women, and nature. I also take photographs of my subject for some magazine articles.

"My most favorite writing projects have been articles and books for children—especially middle readers. I am a regular writer for *Odyssey*, the young reader's astronomy magazine, and occasionally for many other young reader's science magazines. My first book, *The National Science Foundation*, was assigned to me because of my background in science. I was able to visit the National Science Foundation (NSF) in Washington, D.C., and talk to scientists who worked on projects for the foundation. I wanted to tell readers that there were many ways to fund science—but the NSF was one of the top ways that scientists fund their basic research.

"My second book is on Zimbabwe, a country in the southern portion of Africa. I did not get to visit the country, but I was able to obtain a great deal of information from several Zimbabweans. They taught me a lot about the culture and thoughts of another country located halfway around the globe from the United States.

"My latest three books are part of a series on the Earth. The first, *Clocks in the Rocks: Learning about Earth's Past*, tells about geologic time and what the world has been like since the Earth was formed. *Born of Heat and Pressure: Mountains and Metamorphic Rocks* allowed me to explore the inside and outside of our restless Earth. The latest book, *Fossils: Stories from Bones and Stones*, tells about how big and little fossils have helped us to understand the many creatures that have lived on the Earth since the beginning of life.

"I love writing for young readers, especially middle readers. I often lecture to students between fourth and ninth grade. Many are very interested in science and writing. Many of them ask, 'Has everything been discovered already?' (I say no.) 'Can we cure the common cold?' 'Is there other life in the solar system?' Or, 'Is there a better way to launch a rocket into space?' There is so much we do not know!

"Writing has led me to understand more about the world around me. I write because I never stop asking questions. I want to know about how the Sun shines. I want to know what it is like to be an astronaut. I want to know why a squirrel buries a nut just before the winter. And I want to help everyone else to understand."

FOR MORE INFORMATION SEE:

PERIODICALS

Children's Book Review Service, March, 1990.
Science Books and Films, September, 1989.

*   *   *

BARNUM, Richard
[Collective pseudonym]

WRITINGS:

"KNEETIME ANIMAL STORIES" SERIES

Squinty, the Comical Pig: His Many Adventures, Barse & Hopkins, 1915.
Slicko, the Jumping Squirrel: Her Many Adventures, Barse & Hopkins, 1915.
Mappo, the Merry Monkey: His Many Adventures, Barse & Hopkins, 1915.
Tum Tum, the Jolly Elephant, Barse & Hopkins, 1915.
Don, a Runaway Dog, Barse & Hopkins, 1915.
Dido, the Dancing Bear: His Many Adventures, Barse & Hopkins, 1916.
Blackie, a Lost Cat: Her Many Adventures, Barse & Hopkins, 1916.
Flop Ear, the Funny Rabbit, Barse & Hopkins, 1916.
Tinkle the Trick Pony: His Many Adventures, Barse & Hopkins, 1917.
Lightfoot, the Leaping Goat: His Many Adventures, Barse & Hopkins, 1917.
Chunky, the Happy Hippo, Barse & Hopkins, 1918.
Sharp Eyes, the Silver Fox: His Many Adventures, Barse & Hopkins, 1918.
Nero, the Circus Lion: His Many Adventures, Barse & Hopkins, 1919.
Tamba, the Tame Tiger, Barse & Hopkins, 1919.
Toto, the Bustling Beaver: His Many Adventures, Barse & Hopkins, 1920.
Shaggo, the Mighty Buffalo: His Many Adventures, Barse & Hopkins, 1921.
Winkie, the Wily Woodchuck, Barse & Hopkins, 1922.

SIDELIGHTS: The "Kneetime Animal Stories" series, written under the pseudonym Richard Barnum, was one of only two Stratemeyer Syndicate series to feature animals rather than people as main characters. These stories were intended for children from four to nine years old. See the *SATA* index for more information on Harriet S. Adams, Edward L. Stratemeyer, and Andrew E. Svenson.

FOR MORE INFORMATION SEE:

BOOKS

Johnson, Deidre, editor and compiler, *Stratemeyer Pseudonyms and Series Books: An Annotated Checklist of Stratemeyer and Stratemeyer Syndicate Publications,* Greenwood Press, 1982.

*   *   *

BARTON, May Hollis
[Collective pseudonym]

WRITINGS:

(Contributor) *Mystery and Adventure Stories for Girls* (includes *Two Girls and a Mystery;* also see below), Cupples & Leon, 1934.
Favorite Stories for Girls: Four Complete Books in One Volume (contains *Kate Martin's Problem, Charlotte Cross and Aunt Deb, The Girl from the Country,* and *Hazel Hood's Strange Discovery;* also see below), Cupples & Leon, 1937.

"BARTON BOOKS FOR GIRLS"

The Girl from the Country; or, Laura Mayford's City Experiences, Cupples & Leon, 1926.
Three Girl Chums at Laurel Hall; or, The Mystery of the School by the Lake, Cupples & Leon, 1926.
Nell Grayson's Ranching Days; or, A City Girl in the Great West, Cupples & Leon, 1926.
Four Little Women of Roxby; or, The Queer Old Lady Who Lost Her Way, Cupples & Leon, 1926.
Plain Jane and Pretty Betty; or, The Girl Who Won Out, Cupples & Leon, 1926.
Little Miss Sunshine; or, The Old Bachelor's Ward, Cupples & Leon, 1928.
Hazel Hood's Strange Discovery; or, The Old Scientist's Treasure Vault, Cupples & Leon, 1928.
Two Girls and a Mystery; or, The Old House in the Glen, Cupples & Leon, 1928.
The Girls of Lighthouse Island; or, The Strange Sea Chest, Cupples & Leon, 1929.
Kate Martin's Problem; or, Facing the Wide World, Cupples & Leon, 1929.
The Girl in the Top Flat; or, The Daughter of an Artist, Cupples & Leon, 1930.
The Search for Peggy Ann; or, A Mystery of the Flood, Cupples & Leon, 1930.
Sallie's Test of Skill; or, Winning the Trophy, Cupples & Leon, 1931.
Charlotte Cross and Aunt Deb; or, The Queerest Trip on Record, Cupples & Leon, 1931.
Virginia's Venture; or, Strange Business at the Tea House, Cupples & Leon, 1932.

SIDELIGHTS: See the *SATA* index for more information on Harriet S. Adams, Edward L. Stratemeyer and Andrew E. Svenson.

FOR MORE INFORMATION SEE:

BOOKS

Johnson, Deidre, editor and compiler, *Stratemeyer Pseudonyms and Series Books: An Annotated Checklist of Stratemeyer and Stratemeyer Syndicate Publications,* Greenwood Press, 1982.

*   *   *

BASE, Graeme (Rowland) 1958-

PERSONAL: Born April 6, 1958, in Amersham, England; immigrated to Australia, 1966; Australian citizen; son of Geoffrey Donald (a civil engineer) and Elizabeth Enid (Philips) Base; married Robyn Anne Paterson (an artist), August 1, 1981; children: James Geoffrey. *Education:* Swinburne Institute of Technology, diploma of art, 1978. *Politics:* None. *Religion:* Church of England. *Hobbies and other interests:* Listening to and writing music.

ADDRESSES: Home—Australia. *Agent*—c/o Penguin Books Australia Ltd., 487 Maroondah Highway, P.O. Box 257, Ringwood, Victoria 3134, Australia.

CAREER: Worked in advertising at design studios, including The Art Producers, Stannard Patten Samuelson, and Paul Pantelis & Partners, 1979-80; keyboard player in band Riki-Tiki-Tavi, with wife, 1980-85; author and illustrator of books for children.

MEMBER: Australian Society of Book Illustrators.

AWARDS, HONORS: Australian Children's Book Award, Children's Book Council of Australia, Picture Book Honor, 1987, for *Animalia,* and Picture Book of the Year, 1989, for *The Eleventh Hour: A Curious Mystery;* Book Design Award high commendation, Australian Book Publishers' Association, 1988, and Young Australian Best Book Award, 1989, both for *The Eleventh Hour: A Curious Mystery;* Kids Own Australia Literature awards, Secondary, 1988, for *Animalia,* and Infants/Primary, 1989, for *The Eleventh Hour: A Curious Mystery.*

WRITINGS:

SELF-ILLUSTRATED BOOKS FOR CHILDREN

My Grandma Lived in Gooligulch, Nelson Australia, 1983.
Animalia, Abrams, 1986.
The Eleventh Hour: A Curious Mystery, Viking Kestrel, 1988, Abrams, 1989.
The Sign of the Seahorse, Abrams, in press.

ILLUSTRATOR

Max Dann, *Adventures with My Best Worst Friend,* Oxford University Press, 1982.
(With Betty Greenhatch) Susan Burke, *The Island Bike Business,* Oxford University Press, 1982.
Lewis Carroll, *Jabberwocky: From "Through the Looking Glass,"* Macmillan, 1985, Abrams, 1987.

OTHER

Also coauthor, with Craig Christie, of contemporary opera *Tutankhamun,* based on the death of an Egyptian king. Composer of instrumental music.

GRAEME BASE

SIDELIGHTS: An innovative writer and illustrator of children's books, Graeme Base is known for his sense of humor, intricate and colorful drawings, and use of wordplay. His best-selling alphabet book, *Animalia,* received widespread acclaim from critics and the public, despite difficult captions such as "Horrible hairy hogs hurrying homeward on heavily harnessed horses." Base packed each page with items whose names begin with the featured letter. In a competition, one eagle-eyed reader listed twenty-four hundred of them. The artist also hid drawings of himself as a boy throughout the work. Base's next book, *The Eleventh Hour: A Curious Mystery,* also encourages young readers to look closely at image-packed pages. A story in verse about the disappearance of an elephant's party feast, it contains a variety of codes, puzzles, and other hidden clues to help the reader identify the culprit.

Base told *SATA:* "Everyone is influenced by his childhood. The things I write about and illustrate come from a vast range of inputs, some from the earliest impressions of a little child, others from things I saw yesterday, and still others from completely out of the blue, though no doubt they owe their arrival to some stimulus, albeit unconscious. I have a great love of wildlife, inherited from my parents, which shows through in my subject matter, though always with a view to the humorous—not as a commercial device but as a reflection of my own fairly happy nature.

"For me, the relationship between text and illustration is the very essence of producing a good picture book. Because I write the books I illustrate, I have the luxury of being able to refine the text as the illustration ideas emerge. Through the whole life of a project (and it can take several years sometimes), I constantly revise the relationship of the two parts, looking for unnecessary duplication of information, mistakes in continuity, and ways of improving what I have come

up with to date. I started off in the publishing business illustrating other people's texts and found it very frustrating, mainly because the text was considered sacred and unchangeable, putting ridiculous restrictions on the eventual harmony of word and picture.

"My style is tightly controlled and quite linear, although I use strong colors, largely instinctively, having only a vivid mental image of what I hope the picture will look like as a guide. The paintings are done on hot press illustration board with watercolors and transparent inks, using brushes, pencils, technical drawing pens, and a scalpel (for scratching). I also use an airbrush for skies and mist and breath from horses' mouths.

"When it gets around to finished artwork I work on only one illustration at a time, and on one part of that illustration. After a few weeks most of the board is covered with image, and I then go through a process of balancing the whole, bringing all the individual parts together. This is slow work, finishing only when every picture is complete. I live with my pictures in quite an obsessive way during the time it takes to create a book, thinking of nothing else, totally involved in the images. The actual production of a book is a task taken on by several specialized trades—a photographic studio to make transparencies of the artwork; a separator to make the film; a supplier of appropriate paper; a printer to print the sheets that make up the book; a binder to collate all the sheets, endpapers, covers, and jackets and stitch the books together; and a publisher to oversee the whole process and distribute the books to the bookshops. In this long chain are countless opportunities for things to go wrong. I insist on being very involved in all these stages to ensure that the quality of the finished book is as high as possible. It would be a great pity to spend months or years on a project and, for the want of a few more months of effort, allow the end result to be a lesser creation than were possible.

"The graphic design course at Swinburne Institute of Technology was, when I went through, very much geared for a career in advertising. As a result I worked in a few design studios after I graduated and generally hated it, but I am certain the training in spatial dynamics, typography, and meeting deadlines I received at Swinburne and in the advertising industry was tremendously important—you can spend all the time in the world on technique and detail, but if the design is flawed the illustration will never work out satisfactorily.

"I aim my books primarily at myself. Although I would have to be a fool to totally disregard the eventual marketplace, my most important audience is *me.* After I am happy with a verse or an illustration, I let other people see it and hope they will share my enjoyment, finding the same stimulation of the imagination as I have experienced creating it. I *never* talk down to kids, for this is fatal. Much better to aim over their heads and allow some subtleties to go unnoticed than to earn their scorn by serving up 'kiddie fare.' This makes people think I direct my work at all those parents out there, but I don't—I direct it at a certain hybrid, part adult, part child, that is in all probability the basis of all well-balanced happy people. An adult who cannot allow himself to be childlike is lacking something somewhere.

"Australian picture books were for a long time very parochial and self-consciously Australian in their content but are now, due to the much greater availability and influence of overseas input, often quite universal in their themes and styles. This is a good thing. The public awareness of the importance of good picture books is greater now than ever before, making it possible to describe the recent years as a renaissance for children's book publishing in Australia, recognizing and embracing the role of picture books as central and vital to the teaching and development of children."

FOR MORE INFORMATION SEE:

PERIODICALS

Books for Keeps, November, 1989.
Magpies, September, 1989.
Publishers Weekly, March 24, 1989.
Reading Time, Volume 31, number 1, 1987; Volume 34, number 1, 1990.

*   *   *

BERRY, James 1925-

PERSONAL: Born in 1925 in Jamaica; came to England in 1948.

ADDRESSES: Agent—c/o Hamish Hamilton, 27 Wright's Lane, London W8, England.

CAREER: Writer and editor. Has worked as an educator and conductor of writing workshops for children in the British school system, 1977.

JAMES BERRY

AWARDS, HONORS: Grand Prix Smarties Prize, 1987, and Coretta Scott King award honor book, 1988, both for *A Thief in the Village and Other Stories; Signal* Poetry Award, 1989, for *When I Dance.*

WRITINGS:

(Editor) *Bluefoot Traveller: An Anthology of Westindian Poets in Britain,* Limestone Publications, 1976, revised edition published as *Bluefoot Poetry by West Indians in Britain,* Harrap, 1981.
Fractured Circles (poetry), New Beacon Books, 1979.
Cut-Away Feelins; Loving; [and] *Lucy's Letters,* Strange Lime Fruit Stone, 1981.
Lucy's Letters [and] *Loving,* New Beacon Books, 1982.
(Editor) *Dance to a Different Drum: Brixton Festival Poetry 1983,* Brixton Festival, 1983.
(Editor) *News for Babylon: The Chatto Book of West Indian-British Poetry*(anthology of Westindian poetry), Chatto & Windus, 1984
Chain of Days, Oxford University Press, 1985.
A Thief in the Village and Other Stories, Hamish Hamilton, 1987, Orchard Watts, 1988.
Anancy-Spiderman, illustrations by Joseph Olubo, Walker, 1988, published as *Spiderman-Anancy,* Holt, 1989.
When I Dance: Poems, Hamish Hamilton, 1988.
(Contributor) Grace Nichols, *Black Poetry,* Blackie, 1989.

Also author of *The Girls and Yanga Marshall,* 1987.

SIDELIGHTS: The stories collected in James Berry's *A Thief in the Village and Other Stories* are told from a Jamaican child's point of view. Berry was happy to present them in book form to Jane Nissen, an editor at Hamish Hamilton, because he sees the need for more children's books about black life. He noticed there were few books available on the subject while he was working in the British school system in 1977. "Those stories were straight out of my own childhood and later observations," Berry told a *Publishers Weekly* interviewer. "In the Caribbean, we were the last outpost of the Empire. No one has reported our stories, or the way we saw things. It's the function of writers and poets to bring in the left-out side of the human family."

Berry's *A Thief in the Village and Other Stories* won the Grand Prix Smarties Prize in 1987 and was named a Coretta Scott King award honor book in 1988. Berry feels his success is partly due to changing attitudes about cultural and ethnic differences. People of all cultures are more accepting and appreciative of the ethnic differences that exist between people, especially in the larger nations. As more and more writers celebrate their ethnic heritage in poems and stories, the entire world benefits, he said in *Publishers Weekly.* "It's so important to me to use authentic voices—readers need to learn to appreciate black people's voices."

He believes this is especially important for Caribbeans since language plays such a central role in the preservation of their culture, with dialect or "national language" being taught as well as traditional history in stories and poems spoken or performed for children by their elders. He said, "Sounds are community. We may damage children by putting down something so closely knitted to their early years. Life has given us a rich variety of language. And if we celebrate one language over the many, we are deprived. When people share, they are joyful and enriched." Eva Gillies comments in the *Times Literary Supplement* that the language in *A Thief in the Village* makes it "ideal for reading aloud. Both language and stories form a good introduction to West Indian culture."

Unlike stories written in the United States and Britain, the West Indian stories do not always resolve problems or complete actions. Though many reviewers feel this is a weakness in the stories, it reflects the unique way in which Caribbean children see the world. Gillies points out that children from all cultures, however, will recognize the experiences described, including wishing for a bicycle, the cruelty of children against an outcast, a boy's curiosity about his long-absent father, and the fight to save a banana crop from damaging weather.

In *The Girls and Yanga Marshall,* the title story about a young man's adventures at school and on the streets brings another aspect of Caribbean life into focus. Readers can perceive the two kinds of history he learns and the difference between how he feels about others and the way they regard him. In another story of identity, a young man endures a conflict with the traditional ways of his father by strengthening his relationship with his sister. Each of the four stories in the book says something about the desire to resolve conflicts, which is not a quick or easy task.

Anancy-Spiderman introduces a crafty character from the Caribbean people's West African past. According to tradition, the spiderman is a sly superman who outwits his opponents and escapes punishment. An inspiration to children, he is also said to whisper stories in the night that give a kind of guidance for daily life. Listeners who have heard the Creole tales about this trickster will notice a British cast to Berry's retelling, as sometimes the spiderman resembles the fox of British fairy tales more than its African forebears, John Figueroa remarks in the *Times Educational Supplement.* A reviewer for the *Bulletin of the Center for Children's Books* praises the "musical appeal" of Berry's language and the illustrations by Joseph Olubo, concluding, "There's no question that this is a living tradition."

The poems in *When I Dance* are in Berry's Caribbean dialect, "but they exclude no one," John Mole observes in a *Times Educational Supplement* review. Critics like its insights into teen life as well as its language, which is rhythmic and energetic. A reviewer for *Junior Bookshelf* calls the poems "relaxed and humorous as well as wise," adding that the poet's control of rhythm teaches that "it's the ear, not the eye, that governs understanding" for the Jamaican. These are balanced poems that tell much about daily life, regarding both injustice and goodness "with more warmth than anger." They celebrate the possibility of fun and discovery even in difficult times, Jan Mark and Aidan Chambers relate in *Signal.* Many of them delight in the uniqueness of individuals, as one poems states: "Nobody can get into my clothes for me / or feel my fall for me, or do my running. / Nobody hears my music for me, either." Matching this awareness of personality is the invitation to reach out and make connections to the rich opportunities in the world—even though some poems acknowledge that racial barriers exist and not all reaching out is rewarded. Further enriching the prize-winning volume is a section of Jamaican proverbs, expressed in both the difficult-to-understand Creole and English translations. For example, "De tick wha flog de black dog wi whip de white" becomes "The same stick that flogs the black dog will also flog the white one." The book won the *Signal* Poetry Award in 1989. Mark and Chambers conclude, "If Berry did nothing more than give us a voice for our times, his book would be worthy of the [*Signal*] award, but it seems to me that he is also offering a lifeline back to a language that most of his

readers will never have seen, and all the vigour and frankness that went with it."

WORKS CITED:

Berry, James, *When I Dance,* Hamish Hamilton, 1989.
Figueroa, John, "Afro-Caribbean folktales: Travelling Trickster," *Times Educational Supplement,* June 3, 1988, p. 48.
"Flying Starts: New Faces of 1988," *Publishers Weekly,* December 23, 1988, pp. 27-28.
Gillies, Eva, review of *A Thief in the Village and Other Stories, Times Literary Supplement,* July 8, 1988, p. 765.
Mark, Jan and Aidan Chambers, "The Signal Poetry Award," *Signal,* May, 1989, pp. 75-92.
Mole, John, "Rap, Pap and Poetry," *Times Educational Supplement,* November 11, 1988, p. 51.
Review of *Spiderman Anancy, Bulletin of the Center for Children's Books,* December, 1989, p. 78.
Review of *When I Dance, Junior Bookshelf,* April, 1989, p. 78.

FOR MORE INFORMATION SEE:

BOOKS

Children's Literature Review, Volume 22, Gale, 1989.

PERIODICALS

British Book News, July, 1985.
Horn Book, May, 1988.
London Review of Books, September 6, 1984.
New York Times Book Review, May 8, 1988.
Observer, August 11, 1985.
School Librarian, November, 1987.
Times Literary Supplement, June 20, 1986; June 12, 1987; March 3, 1989.*

*   *   *

BIRO, B(alint) S(tephen) 1921-
(B. Biro, Val Biro)

PERSONAL: Val is Biro's translation of his Hungarian given name, Balint; surname is pronounced "*beer*-oh"; born October 6, 1921, in Hungary; son of Balint (a lawyer) and Margaret (Gyulahazi) Biro; married Vivien Woolley, April 14, 1946 (marriage ended); married Marie Louise Ellaway, September 25, 1970; children: (first marriage) Melissa. *Education:* Cistercian School, Budapest, Hungary, Baccaloreat, 1939; attended Central School of Art, London, England, 1939-42. *Politics:* Liberal Conservative. *Religion:* Roman Catholic.

ADDRESSES: Home and studio—Bridge Cottage, Brook Ave., Bosham, West Sussex PO18 8LQ, England.

CAREER: Sylvan Press Ltd., London, England, studio manager, 1944-46; C. & J. Temple Ltd., London, production manager, 1946-48; John Lehmann Ltd., London, art director, 1948-53; free-lance artist and illustrator, 1953—. Urban district councillor, 1966-70; governor of Amersham College of Art and Design and Berkshire College of Art and Design; designer of silver medals for collectors and of illustrations for engraving on glass; regular illustrator for *Radio Times,* London.

Val Biro and "Gumdrop," his 1926 Austin Clifton.

MEMBER: Society of Authors, Society of Industrial Artists and Designers (fellow), Vintage Sports Car Club.

AWARDS, HONORS: Awarded a prize from the Spanish publishers of *Hungarian Folk-Tales*, 1991, for having sold over 100,000 copies in Spain.

WRITINGS:

"GUMDROP" SERIES; SELF-ILLUSTRATED; UNDER NAME VAL BIRO

Gumdrop: The Adventures of a Vintage Car, Brockhampton Press, 1966, Follett, 1967.

Gumdrop and the Farmer's Friend, Brockhampton Press, 1967, Follett, 1968.

Gumdrop on the Rally, Brockhampton Press, 1968, Follett, 1969.

Gumdrop on the Move, Brockhampton Press, 1969, Follett, 1970.

Gumdrop Goes to London, Brockhampton Press, 1971.

Gumdrop Finds a Friend, Hodder & Stoughton, 1973, 2nd edition, Pan Books, 1978, Children's Book Co., 1982.

Gumdrop in Double Trouble, Brockhampton Press, 1975, Children's Book Co., 1982.

Gumdrop and the Steamroller, Hodder & Stoughton, 1976, Childrens Press, 1977.

Gumdrop on the Brighton Run, Hodder & Stoughton, 1976.

Gumdrop Posts a Letter, Knight Books, 1976, Childrens Press, 1977, published in the United States as *Gumdrop and the Birthday Surprise*, Stevens, 1986.

Gumdrop Has a Birthday, Hodder & Stoughton, 1977, Children's Book Co., 1982.

Val Biro's Gumdrop Annual, Purnell, 1979.

Gumdrop Gets His Wings, Hodder & Stoughton, 1979, Chidren's Book Co., 1982.

Gumdrop Finds a Ghost, Hodder & Stoughton, 1980, Children's Book Co., 1982.

Gumdrop and the Secret Switches, Hodder & Stoughton, 1981, Children's Book Co., 1982.

Gumdrop and Horace, Hodder & Stoughton, 1982.

Gumdrop Makes a Start, Hodder & Stoughton, 1982.

Gumdrop Races a Train, Hodder & Stoughton, 1982, Stevens, 1986.

Gumdrop at Sea, Hodder & Stoughton, 1983.

Gumdrop Goes to School, Hodder & Stoughton, 1983, Stevens, 1986.

Gumdrop at the Zoo, Hodder & Stoughton, 1983, Stevens, 1985.

Gumdrop Gets a Lift, Hodder & Stoughton, 1983, Stevens, 1986.

Gumdrop in a Hurry, Hodder & Stoughton, 1983, published in the United States as *Gumdrop Beats the Clock,* Stevens, 1986.

Gumdrop's Magic Journey, Hodder & Stoughton, 1984.

Gumdrop Goes Fishing, Hodder & Stoughton, 1984.

Gumdrop Has a Tummy-Ache, Hodder & Stoughton, 1984.

Gumdrop Is the Best Car, Hodder & Stoughton, 1984, published in the United States as *Gumdrop Is the Best,* Stevens, 1985.

Gumdrop on the Farm, Hodder & Stoughton, 1984.

Gumdrop and the Monster, Hodder & Stoughton, 1985.

Gumdrop and the Farmyard Caper, Stevens, 1985.

Gumdrop and the Great Sausage Caper, Stevens, 1985.

Gumdrop Catches a Cold, Stevens, 1985.

Gumdrop Floats Away, Stevens, 1985.

Gumdrop to the Rescue, Hodder & Stoughton, 1986.

Gumdrop For Ever!, Hodder & Stoughton, 1987.

Gumdrop and the Dinosaur, Hodder & Stoughton, 1988.

The Bumper Gumdrop Omnibus, Hodder & Stoughton, 1989.

Gumdrop and the Pirates, Hodder & Stoughton, 1989.

Gumdrop and the Elephant, Hodder & Stoughton, 1990.

Gumdrop and the Bulldozer, Hodder & Stoughton, 1991.

SELF-ILLUSTRATED; UNDER NAME VAL BIRO

(With Arnold Baines) *Val Biro's Discovering Chesham,* Shire Publications, 1968.

The Honest Thief: A Hungarian Folktale, Brockhampton Press, 1972, Holiday House, 1973.

Hungarian Folk-Tales, Oxford University Press, 1980.

The Magic Doctor, Oxford University Press, 1982.

Hansel and Gretel, Macmillan, 1983.

The Pied Piper of Hamelin, Silver Burdett, 1985.

The Hobyahs, Oxford University Press, 1985.

Tales from Hans Christian Andersen, four volumes, Wright Group, 1986.

Fables from Aesop, twelve volumes, Wright Group, 1986.

The Donkey That Sneezed, Oxford University Press, 1986.

Drango Dragon, Ladybird Books, 1989.

Jack and the Beanstalk, Oxford University Press, 1989.

Tobias and the Dragon, Blackie, 1989, Peter Bedrick, 1990.

Miranda's Umbrella, Peter Bedrick, 1990.

The Three Little Pigs, Oxford University Press, 1990.

Rub-a-Dub-Dub: Val Biro's 77 Favourite Nursery Rhymes, Blackie, 1991.

The Three Billy Goats Gruff, Oxford University Press, 1991.

ILLUSTRATOR; UNDER NAME B. BIRO

S. J. Totton, *The Story of Canada,* Benn, 1960.

L. Frank Baum, *The Wonderful Wizard of Oz,* Dent, 1965.

William Wise, *The Terrible Trumpet,* Hamish Hamilton, 1966, Norton, 1969.

ILLUSTRATOR; UNDER NAME B. S. BIRO

Lord Tweedsmuir, *One Man's Happiness,* Hale, 1968.

Donald Bisset, *Kangaroo Tennis,* Benn, 1968.

Eric Shipton, *That Untravelled World: An Autobiography,* Hodder & Stoughton, 1969.

Jean Plaidy, *The Third George,* Hale, 1969.

Boswell Taylor, editor, *Picture Reference Book of the Georgians,* Brockhampton Press, 1969.

L. Frank Baum, *The Marvellous Land of Oz,* Dent, 1969.

A. Elliott-Cannon, *Man Discovers America,* Hamish Hamilton, 1969.

L. A. Hill, *A First Reading Book,* Oxford University Press, 1969.

Wilson Stevens, editor, *"The Field" Bedside Book,* 2nd edition, Collins, 1969.

Dora Thatcher, *Tommy and the Spanish Galleon,* Brockhampton Press, 1969.

Ted Humphris, *Garden Glory,* Collins, 1969.

J. H. B. Peel, *Country Talk,* Hale, 1970.

Thatcher, *Henry and the Traction Engine,* Brockhampton Press, 1970.

Thatcher, *Tommy and the Yellow Submarine,* Brockhampton Press, 1971.

Helen Steiner Rice, *Lovingly: Poems for All Seasons,* Hutchinson, 1971.

Hill, adaptor, *The Boy in the Moon,* Oxford University Press, 1971.

Joan Drake, *Mr. Bubbus and the Apple-Green Engine,* Brockhampton Press, 1971.

Donald Sutherland, *See, Hear and Speak* (teacher's edition), Oxford University Press, 1971.

Plaidy, *Victoria in the Wings,* Hale, 1972.

Bisset, *Les dix kangourous,* Benn, 1972.

Peel, *More Country Talk,* Hale, 1973.

Rosemary Weir, *What a Lark,* White Lion, 1974.

Peel, *New Country Talk,* Hale, 1975.

Thatcher, *Hovering with Henry,* Hodder & Stoughton, 1976.

Plaidy, *The Prince and the Quakeress,* Pan Books, 1976.

Drake, *Mr. Bubbus and the Railway Smugglers,* Hodder & Stoughton, 1976.

Taylor, editor, *Georgians,* Knight Books, 1978.

ILLUSTRATOR; UNDER NAME VAL BIRO

Pamela Sykes, *Air Day for the Brownies,* Brockhampton Press, 1968.

Sykes, *Brownies at the Zoo,* Brockhampton Press, 1969.

Donald Bisset, *Benjie the Circus Dog,* Benn, 1969.

Fanny and Johnnie Cradock, *The Cook Hostess' Book,* Collins, 1970.

Joan Drake, *James and Sally Again,* Hutchinson, 1970.

Edmund Bohan, *The Writ of Green Wax,* Hutchinson, 1970.

Geoffrey Morgan and W. A. Lasocki, *Soldier Bear,* Collins, 1970.

Sykes, *The Brownies and the Fire,* Brockhampton Press, 1970.

James Glennon, *Making Friends with Music,* Foulsham, 1971.

James L. Dow, editor, *American Wit and Wisdom,* Collins, 1971.

Christopher Driver, editor, *The Good Food Guide,* Consumers' Association/Hodder & Stoughton, 1971.

Dorian Williams, *Kingdom for a Horse,* Dent, 1971.

(With Judith Trevelyan and Ernest Papps) Dawn Bowker, Myrtle Simpson, and Barbara McPhail, *The Dinghy Stories,* Methuen, 1972.

Mimi Irving, *Mr. Purpose,* Cape, 1972.

Dora Thatcher, *Henry in the Mountains,* Brockhampton Press, 1972.

Helen Solomon, *The Jazz Band,* Macmillan, 1972.

D. Macer Wright, *A Fish Will Rise,* David & Charles, 1972.

Jane MacMichael, *Tales of the Circus: Two Stories,* Blackie, 1972.

L. A. Hill, *A Reading Book,* two volumes, Oxford University Press, 1972, also published as *A First Reading Book,* 1973.

Richard Parker, *The Penguin Goes Home,* Chivers, 1973.

Michael Pollard, *The Reporter,* Macmillan, 1973.

Gladys Williams, *Garry the Goblin, and Five More Spooky Stories,* Blackie, 1973.

Language in Action, Macmillan, Level 1: *Buster is Lost,* 1974, Level 0: *A Dog and His Bone,* 1975, Level 3: *Roy and the Pointon Express,* 1976.

Stephen Andrews, *Cubs Away,* Brockhampton Press, 1974.

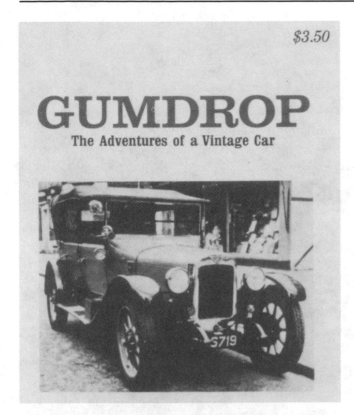

$3.50

GUMDROP
The Adventures of a Vintage Car

Cover from the first of dozens of books in Biro's self-illustrated series "Gumdrop."

Thatcher, *Tommy in the Caribbean*, Brockhampton Press, 1974.

(With others) J. D. Bevington, *Stories for Today*, Ginn, 1974.

Robert Carrier, *The Robert Carrier Cookery Course*, W. H. Allen, 1974.

Peter John Stephens, *Faster Than Anything*, Benn, 1974.

Beverley Nichols, *Down the Kitchen Sink*, W. H. Allen, 1974.

E. W. Hildick, *Dolls in Danger*, Brockhampton Press, 1974.

H. E. Todd, *The Sick Cow*, Brockhampton Press, 1974, Childrens Press, 1976.

Daniel Green, *Food and Drink from Your Garden*, Standfast Press, 1975.

Enid Blyton, *Br'er Rabbit and the Wonderful Tar-Baby*, Knight Books, 1975.

Blyton, *Br'er Rabbit Is Trapped*, Knight Books, 1975.

Helen Steiner Rice, *Thankfully: Including the "Christmas Guest" and Other Poems*, Hutchinson, 1975.

John Denton, *Machines on the Farm*, Puffin, 1975.

Green, *The Rough Shoot*, J. Bartholomew, 1975.

Hildick, *The Case of the Condemned Cat: A McGurk Mystery*, Hodder & Stoughton, 1975.

Hildick, *The Menaced Midget: A McGurk Mystery*, Brockhampton Press, 1975.

Hildick, *The Great Rabbit Robbery: A McGurk Mystery*, Hodder & Stoughton, 1976.

Andrews, *Cubs on Saturday*, Hodder & Stoughton, 1976.

Dorothy Figueroa, editor, *Colibri Readers*, Ginn, Introductory Book: *En nuestra casa*, 1976, Book 1: *La familia Gomez*, 1977, Book 3: *Cuentos para gozar*, 1979.

David Scott Daniell, *Hideaway Johnny*, White Lion, 1976.

Richard Sharp, *The Best Games People Play*, Ward Lock, 1976.

Blyton, *Br'er Rabbit and the Alligator*, Knight Books, 1976.

Blyton, *Br'er Rabbit Saves Br'er Terrapin*, Knight Books, 1976.

Hildick, *The Case of the Nervous Schoolboy*, Hodder & Stoughton, 1976.

Christina Hole, *British Folk Customs*, Hutchinson, 1976.

Fanny Cradock, editor, *The Sherlock Holmes Cook Book*, W. H. Allen, 1976.

Sykes, *The Brownies Throw a Party*, Hodder & Stoughton, 1976.

Todd, *George the Fire Engine*, Hodder & Stoughton, 1976, Childrens Press, 1978.

Hildick, *The Case of the Nervous Newsboy: A McGurk Mystery*, Hodder & Stoughton, 1976.

Hildick, *A Cat Called Amnesia*, D. White, 1976.

Hildick, *The Case of the Invisible Dog: A McGurk Mystery*, Hodder & Stoughton, 1977.

Delia Huddy, *Catch the Plane!*, Benn, 1977.

Andrews, *Cubs at Play*, Hodder & Stoughton, 1977.

H. J. B. Peel, *Country Talk Again*, R. Hale, 1977.

Edna Jenkins, *Yn yr ardd*, Macmillan, 1978.

Hazel Townson, *The Barley Sugar Ghosts*, Beaver Books, 1978.

Todd, *Changing of the Guard* (also see below), Hodder & Stoughton, 1978.

Hildick, *The Case of the Secret Scribbler: A McGurk Mystery*, Hodder & Stoughton, 1978.

Edward Ramsbottom and Joan Redmayne, *Out of an Egg*, Macmillan, 1978.

Clive King, *The Devil's Cut*, Hodder & Stoughton, 1978.

Todd, *The Roundabout Horse*, Hodder & Stoughton, 1978, Childrens Press, 1980.

Todd, *The Very Very Very Long Dog*, Carousel Books, 1978.

Alison Winn, *Charlie's Iron Horse*, Hodder & Stoughton, 1979.

Andrews, *Cubs Ahoy!*, Hodder & Stoughton, 1979.

Peter J. Davies, *The Sign of the Smiling Lion*, Hodder & Stoughton, 1979.

Hildick, *The Case of the Phantom Frog: A McGurk Mystery*, Hodder & Stoughton, 1979.

Todd, *King of Beasts*, Hodder & Stoughton, 1979.

Todd, *Here Comes Wordman!*, Carousel Books, 1979.

Hildick, *The Nose Knows: A McGurk Mystery*, Dragon Books, 1979.

Hildick, *The Case of the Treetop Treasure: A McGurk Mystery*, Hodder & Stoughton, 1980.

Norman J. Bull, *100 Bible Stories*, Hamlyn, 1980, Abingdon, 1982.

Lindsay Brown, *The Treasure of Duberry Castle*, Piccolo, 1980.

Todd, *The Big Sneeze*, Hodder & Stoughton, 1980.

(With others) *My Gold Storybook*, Hamlyn, 1981.

Todd, *The Crawly, Crawly Caterpillar*, Carousel Books, 1981.

Todd, *Jungle Silver*, Hodder & Stoughton, 1981.

Todd, *The Dial-a-Story Book*, Puffin, 1981.

Maggie Prince, *Dragon in the Drainpipe*, Hodder & Stoughton, 1981.

Bull, *100 New Testament Stories*, Hamlyn, 1981, Abingdon, 1984.

Doreen Coates, *Where Are You Going?*, Ginn, 1981.

Blyton, *Bumblebee Stories*, Hamlyn, 1981.

Blyton, *Buttercup Day and Other Stories*, Hamlyn, 1982.

Blyton, *Mike's Monkey and Other Stories*, Hamlyn, 1982.

Ruth McDonald, *Bad Cat-psst!*, Macmillan, 1982.

Todd, *The Tiny Tiny Tadpole*, Transworld Books, 1982.

Todd, *Changing of the Guard* [and] *Wallpaper Holiday*, Puffin, 1982.

K. H. Roberts, *Bingo Bones and the Boggart*, Hodder & Stoughton, 1982.

The St. Michael Book of Worzel Gummidge Stories, Marks & Spencer, 1982.

Biro's depiction of Moses and the burning bush from "God Calls Moses" in Norman J. Bull's *100 Bible Stories.*

Blyton, *The Runaway Cows and Other Stories,* Hamlyn, 1982.

Blyton, *Telltale Tommy and Other Stories,* Hamlyn, 1982.

Blyton, *The Forgotten Pets and Other Stories,* Hamlyn, 1983.

Blyton, *The Magic Mirror and Other Stories,* Hamlyn, 1983.

Blyton, *The Three Wishes and Other Stories,* Hamlyn, 1983.

Kenneth Grahame, *Tales from "The Wind in the Willows,"* Marks & Spencer, 1983.

David Gamble, *The Ivory Elephant's Orchard,* Hodder & Stoughton, 1983.

Todd, *The Scruffy, Scruffy Dog,* Hodder & Stoughton, 1983.

Blyton, *Dame Topple's Buns and Other Stories,* Hamlyn, 1983.

Todd, *The Tiger Who Couldn't Be Bothered,* Hodder & Stoughton, 1984.

Jill Bennett, *Jack and the Robbers,* Oxford University Press, 1984.

Sykes, *The Brownies in Hospital,* Beaver Books, 1984.

Andrews, *Cubs with a Difference,* Brockhampton Press, 1984.

Jean Chapman, *The Big Fib,* Macmillan, 1984.

Brown, *The Secret of the Silver Lockets,* Hale, 1984.

Grahame, *The Wind in the Willows,* Purnell, 1984.

Prince, *Dragon in the Family,* Hodder & Stoughton, 1985.

Todd, *The Clever Clever Cats,* Hodder & Stoughton, 1985.

Thatcher, *Lizzie the Lifeboat,* Hodder & Stoughton, 1985.

(With Jane Bottomley, Robina Smith, Leslie Smith, and Katy Sleight) Barbara Mitchelhill, *Little Books,* six volumes, Wright Group, 1986.

Bull and Reg Ferris, *The Day Yam Lifted the Sky and Jubok the Creator,* Basil Blackwell, 1986.

Bull and Ferris, *Maui of a Thousand Tricks* [and] *Quat Brings Right-Time to the Pacific Ocean,* Basil Blackwell, 1986.

Bull and Ferris, *Night and Day and the Milky Way,* Basil Blackwell, 1986.

The Giant's Footsteps (based on characters originally created by John Patience), Macdonald Purnell, 1986.

The Missing Ring (based on characters originally created by Patience), Macdonald Purnell, 1986.

The Mystery Voice (based on characters originally created by Patience), Macdonald Purnell, 1986.

Strangers in Town (based on characters originally created by Patience), Macdonald Purnell, 1986.

Jean Kenward, *Collected Tales from Aesop's Fables,* Blackie, 1986.

Prince, *Wishing Powder,* Hodder & Stoughton, 1986.

Roberts, *Bingo, Boggart and the Funny Cube,* Hodder & Stoughton, 1986.

The Three Billy Goats Gruff, Macmillan Education, 1987.

(With Ian Jackson) Pat Edwards, *Who Asked the Ants?,* Longman, 1987.

Grahame, *The Wind in the Willows: Home Sweet Home,* Wanderer Books, 1987.

Grahame, *The Wind in the Willows: The Open Road,* Wanderer Books, 1987.

Grahame, *The Wind in the Willows: The Wild Wood,* Wanderer Books, 1987.

Grahame, *The Wind in the Willows: The River Bank,* Wanderer Books, 1987.

Joy Cowley, *Mrs. Grindy's Shoes,* Wright Group, 1987.

Todd, *The Silly Silly Ghost,* Hodder & Stoughton, 1987.

Kenward, *The Hotchpotch Horse and Other Stories and Poems,* Hodder & Stoughton, 1987.

Rudyard Kipling, *The Jungle Book,* adapted by Sheila Lane and Marion Kemp, Ward Lock, 1987.

Edwards, *Poor Rabbit,* Longman, 1987.

Kenward, *The Odd Job Man and the Thousand Mile Boots,* Oxford University Press, 1987.

Sykes, *The Brownies and the Flood,* Hodder & Stoughton, 1987.

Todd, *Bobby Brewster's Jigsaw Puzzle,* Hodder & Stoughton, 1988.

Jill Eggleton, *I Dream,* Wright Group, 1988.

Kenward, *A Kettleful of Magic and Other Stories and Poems,* Hodder & Stoughton, 1988.

Linda Allen, *Crash, Bang, and Wallop,* Hodder & Stoughton, 1988.

Todd, *The Sleeping Policeman,* Hodder & Stoughton, 1988.

Helen Arnold, *The Hare and the Tortoise,* Pan Books, 1989.

Arnold, *The Crooked Man,* Pan Books, 1989.

William Shakespeare, *Much Ado about Nothing,* Macmillan, 1989.

Jean McKenzie, *Pedro and the Singing Dog,* Hodder & Stoughton, 1990.

Michael Rosen, *The Golem of Old Prague,* Deutsch, 1990.

Sybille Bedford, *A Visit to Don Otavio,* Folio Society, 1990.

Ken Adams, *When I Was Your Age,* Simon & Schuster, 1991.

A. H. Benjamin, *What's Up the Coconut Tree?,* Oxford University Press, 1991.

M. Christina Butler, *The Dinosaur's Egg,* Simon & Schuster, 1991.

Also illustrator of William Shepherd's *Balloons,* Wright Group, and Joy Cowley's "The Sunshine Series," Wright Group.

OTHER

Contributor to *Children's Literature Abstracts.*

ADAPTATIONS: Seven "Gumdrop" stories were adapted for video cassette and released as *The Adventures of Gumdrop, the Trusty Old Car* by Nutland Video, 1982; seven stories by Biro and Todd were adapted for video cassette and released as *Tales of Bobby Brewster and More Adventures of Gumdrop* by Nutland Video, 1982.

SIDELIGHTS: Primarily an illustrator, Val Biro began writing children's books at the suggestion of his publishers. Drawing on his personal interest in vintage cars, Biro created the character of Gumdrop after his own 1926 Austin Clifton, adding his black cocker spaniel to the series through the character of Horace. Once the "Gumdrop" series was under way, Biro began a different type of writing—the retelling of fables and fairy tales. Like the Gumdrop books, most of these books are self-illustrated and include some of Aesop's fables and such fairy tales as *Hansel and Gretel* and *Jack and the Beanstalk.*

The main character of the "Gumdrop" series is the car, but its driver, Mr. Oldcastle, plays an important role as well. In the first book of the series, *Gumdrop: The Adventures of a Vintage Car,* Mr. Oldcastle finds Gumdrop and restores him. A variety of boys and girls, including older boys, will enjoy "the fast-moving plot and humorous illustrations," writes Flossie Perkins in *Library Journal.* In many of Gumdrop's following adventures, Mr. Oldcastle and Horace become the heroes. *Gumdrop Finds a Friend* introduces Horace, who is able to assist Mr. Oldcastle in the capture a pair of smugglers. And in *Gumdrop and the Secret Switches,* Horace finds switches in Gumdrop that enable the car to fly and float on water. "The plots are thin, with a minimum of suspense, but this won't deter young listeners who will undoubtedly be cheering for Mr. Oldcastle, Horace, and Gumdrop," claims *School Library Journal* contributor Kathleen Brachmann.

Many of the books emphasize the maintenance of Gumdrop and his various parts. The first book even contains a double-page illustration of a detailed cross-section of the car; and Gumdrop becomes the safest and best-looking car available in *Gumdrop Gets His Wings.* Mr. Oldcastle gives Gumdrop up in *Gumdrop and the Farmer's Friend,* but tries to get him back when he finds out that the car is to be in a vintage car auction. Someone outbids Mr. Oldcastle, though, and Gumdrop goes through a series of owners, each one changing some of his parts before reselling him. An almost unrecognizable Gumdrop finally finds his way back to Mr. Oldcastle, who restores him and exhibits him proudly, writes *Library Journal* contributor Eleanor Glaser. "The colorful, detailed comic illustrations add zest to this humorous story that will be especially enjoyed by young car-minded readers," concludes Glaser.

In *Hungarian Folk-Tales,* Biro retells tales that are similar to familiar western European stories, "yet different enough to be uniquely rewarding," maintains Katharyn F. Crabbe in the *School Library Journal.* The usual tales about young handsome princes who must complete several clever tasks in order to win the princess can be found in such tales as "The Thieving Goblins" and "The Honest Thief." And in addition to these heroic tales, Biro has also included some trickster tales, in which the heroes triumph over the unwise and arrogant. "This is a first-rate collection in which the tales, the retellings and the illustrations all work together well," concludes Crabbe; and a *School Librarian* contributor finds the stories, "in essence, delightful."

Biro, who speaks Hungarian, English, German, and French, and travels mainly in England and Europe to sketch and paint, once commented on the relationship between his writing and illustrating: "I write so as to give my alter-ego a good chance for drawing pictures, though I find that the story I invent tends to run away with itself, leaving me, the illustrator, behind! Each story tends to be based on personal experience and, equally, each tends to grow out of that into the imagination. Each book seems to take a few months to gestate, and then I write it in one long day (or night)."

WORKS CITED:

Brachmann, Kathleen, review of *Gumdrop and the Secret Switches, Gumdrop Finds a Friend, Gumdrop Finds a Ghost, Gumdrop Gets His Wings, Gumdrop Has a Birthday,* and *Gumdrop in Double Trouble, School Library Journal,* March, 1983, pp. 157-58.

Crabbe, Katharyn F., review of *Hungarian Folk-Tales, School Library Journal,* April, 1983.

Glaser, Eleanor, review of *Gumdrop on the Move, Library Journal,* January 15, 1971, p. 256.

Perkins, Flossie, review of *Gumdrop: The Adventures of a Vintage Car, Library Journal,* February 15, 1968, p. 857.

School Librarian, September, 1981, p. 230.

FOR MORE INFORMATION SEE:

PERIODICALS

Library Journal, July, 1973.

Publishers Weekly, March 19, 1973; December 12, 1986.

School Library Journal, April 15, 1973; May, 1977; October, 1985; March, 1986; October, 1986; August, 1990.

Times Educational Supplement, July 23, 1982; July 1, 1983; October 24, 1986.

Times Literary Supplement, September 18, 1981.

BIRO, B.
See BIRO, B(alint) S(tephen)

* * *

BIRO, Val
See BIRO, B(alint) S(tephen)

* * *

BJOERK, Christina 1938-

PERSONAL: Born July 27, 1938, in Stockholm, Sweden.

ADDRESSES: Home—Folkungagatan 78, 116 22 Stockholm, Sweden.

CAREER: Author, journalist, educator.

MEMBER: Swedish Authors Union, Swedish Journalists Union, Swedish Publicists Club.

AWARDS, HONORS: Swedish Authors Union scholarship for travel, 1975.

WRITINGS:

How to Build and Fly Kites, Bonniers, 1974.
Inning Instead of Outing, Bonniers, 1975.
Stop Spraying, Bonniers, 1975.
You Are in Love, Aren't You?, Bonniers, 1976.
Are You Crazy?, Bonniers, 1976.
Mimmi's Book, Prisma, 1976.
Fiffi and Birger and Left and Right, Prisma, 1976.
Linnea in Monet's Garden, Farrar, Straus, 1987.
Linnea's Windowsill Garden, Farrar, Straus, 1988.
Linea's Almanac, Farrar, Straus, 1990.
Elliot's Extraordinary Cookbook, Farrar, Straus, 1991.

OTHER

Also writer for Swedish television channels one and two. Contributor to the magazines *Dagens Nyheter, Vi,* and *Femina.*

SIDELIGHTS: Christina Bjoerk is best known for her three books about a little girl named Linnea. In each of these books Linnea's love of flowers leads her to learn about gardening, animals, and the seasons of the year. In the book *Linnea in Monet's Garden,* she learns about French Impressionist painter Claude Monet as well. A. R. Williams in *Junior Bookshelf* calls Linnea "a city girl who brings the countryside into her home and heart."

Linnea's name is derived from Carlos Linnaeus, a Swedish botanist of the eighteenth century who created the system of plant and animal classification we now call the science of botany. The Linnea books are designed to give the young reader a knowledge of plants and animals. *Linnea's Windowsill Garden* provides an "informative, accurate, comprehensive, clear and well-organized" introduction for the beginning gardener, as Zena Sutherland writes in the *Bulletin of the Center for Children's Books. Linnea's Almanac* gives recipes, craft projects, and nature lore suitable for each season of the year. The book is, according to Amy Adler in *School Library Journal,* "simultaneously instructive and entertaining."

WORKS CITED:

Adler, Amy, *School Library Journal,* April, 1990, p. 102.
Sutherland, Zena, *Bulletin of the Center for Children's Books,* December, 1988, p. 92.
Williams, A. R., *Junior Bookshelf,* February, 1990, pp. 21-22.

FOR MORE INFORMATION SEE:

BOOKS

Children's Literature Review, Volume 22, Gale, 1991.

PERIODICALS

Bulletin of the Center for Children's Books, February, 1988; December, 1988.
Children's Literature in Education, June, 1989.
Growing Point, March, 1990.
Junior Bookshelf, December, 1987; February, 1990.
Kirkus Reviews, October 1, 1988.
Publishers Weekly, September 30, 1988.
School Library Journal, February, 1988; November, 1988; April, 1990.
Times Literary Supplement, December 18-24, 1987.

* * *

BONEHILL, Captain Ralph
See STRATEMEYER, Edward L.

* * *

BOWKETT, Stephen 1953-
(Louis P. Garou)

PERSONAL: Born December 30, 1953, in South Wales; son of Ieuan (a plumber) and Winnifred (a homemaker; maiden name, Smith) Bowkett; married August 24, 1975; wife's name, Wendy Ann (a teacher). *Education:* Coventry College of Education, B.Ed., teaching certificate, 1975. *Politics:* "Left of center and environmentalist." *Religion:* "Still wondering."

ADDRESSES: Home—88A Northampton Rd., Market Harborough, Leicestershire LE16 9HF, England. *Agent*—Sheila Watson, Watson, Little Ltd., 12 Egbert St., London NW1 8LJ, England.

CAREER: Lutterworth High School, Leicestershire, England, teacher, 1976—; writer. Conductor of creative thinking workshops for children.

MEMBER: Greenpeace, Saint Club, Asthma Campaign.

WRITINGS:

Spellbinder, Gollancz, 1985.
The Copy Cat Plan (two plays), Basil Blackwell, 1986.
Gameplayers, Gollancz, 1986.
Dualists, Gollancz, 1987.
Catch and Other Stories, Gollancz, 1988.
Frontiersville High, Gollancz, 1990.
The Train, Macmillan, 1991.
The Run, Gollancz, 1991.

Also author of a short book for the six-plus age group, *The Paper Boy.* Contributor of a play to *Collections,* edited by

STEPHEN BOWKETT

David Eccles, Thomas Nelson, 1991. Contributor of short stories and poetry to numerous magazines. Several of Bowkett's short stories and poems were broadcast on British Broadcasting Corporation Radio Leicester, BRMB (Birmingham), and Radio Northampton.

WORK IN PROGRESS: Microids, a story of nanotechnology; an adult horror novel titled *Community,* under pseudonym Louis P. Garou; research on earthlights and earth mysteries.

SIDELIGHTS: Stephen Bowkett told *SATA:* "I was born and brought up in the Rhondda mining valleys of South Wales, a poor and depleted area of miners' houses arranged in drab terraces along the hillsides. Our village was overlooked by a huge slag-heap, up the spine of which, I remember, the tiny, insect-like slagtrucks used to crawl to tip their loads of unusable coke and slate. The place was claustrophobic, dirty, insular—but one of the most wonderful learning grounds for a young boy's mind that I can imagine.

"From somewhere (I don't know where), I developed an interest in the stars, space, what might be out there. I recall on one occasion watching a tiny light drifting across the heavens and telling my younger brother that this must have been a star that had broken loose from its moorings. It was months later that I learned it was one of the first artificial satellites in orbit around the Earth.

"The valley was also a good place for fossils. I used to go up to the quarries from which stone had been taken generations earlier to build the workers' houses. Up there, I came across beautiful specimens of ammonites, fern fronds, leaves, tree fern scales, and also quartz crystals. Lying in the long summer grass in those lonely places, I would imagine what the world was like millions of years before. It was easy to see dinosaurs bulking over the big boulders at the base of the quarry; easy too, to wonder why they weren't around now, or how things would be different if they were! Not so easy, of course, to discover the answers to these questions. I guess you could say that during this part of my life I developed a perspective of time and space and potential that has proved useful in the writing that followed.

"Moving from Wales when I was twelve years old coincided with a graduation from comics (*Batman, Superman,* et al, imported from America) to real novels. Not long before, the long-running science fiction serial *Doctor Who* started up on BBC television. I was captivated and began reading the few existing novelizations of those early stories. Engaging in that activity gave direction to my perspective and took me on a tour of the universe that has lasted to this day.

"I make a distinction between 'writing' and 'Writing' when I talk about my craft. My Writing career began soon after I moved to my new school in the midlands of England. Back in Wales I had been taking lessons in the Welsh language; in the school in Leicester, I was put in a French class and found myself three years behind the other students. Rather than fight a losing battle with me, the French teacher sat me in a corner by myself and told me 'to get on with something.' Simply to pass the time, I decided to try my hand at a story. It was a mixture of science fiction and wishful thinking, wherein I saved the Earth from an invasion by giant green blobs (GGB's to use the jargon!) and won the girl of my dreams (who was a member of my class but who I never got to date). I enjoyed myself so much that during every subsequent French lesson I wrote a story or a poem. Thus, inauspiciously and due entirely to a bit of serendipity, my Writing career began.

"Writing continued throughout school days and on into my college years. Even then I was a 'closet author,' keeping the work very private, not telling people that this inexpensive activity had become one of the passions of my life.

"Round about this time, I 'made the jump' to novels. Up until then my output had been entirely poems and short stories. In my late teens I realized that I wanted to do something more with Writing than just to keep it as a hobby, and I saw too that I'd stand much more chance of publication as a novelist. Since I was training as a schoolteacher, I decided to concentrate on the age-range of the children I would be teaching—early teens. And so college-course essays were interspersed with (largely abortive) early attempts at novels. I have never abandoned short stories, however. Indeed, one of my books, *Catch,* is a collection of some of my favorites. Quite frequently I will try a short story form to see if the idea will pan out to novel-length (I call this 'checking for mileage'), and also to vary the routine, since writing novels can be an energy-sapping process.

"To date, all of my prose work has drifted between the science fiction, fantasy, and horror genres, although I often use those genres' conventions in a metaphorical way, to explore themes that fascinate me. My preferred themes include the ideas that life is more than we perceive it to be; that behind this surface varnish there exists a larger reality; that individuals live equally on the inside and the outside, life being an interface between inner and outer space; that unexpected power changes people, and so on. I reckon there's material here to keep me going forever!

"The acceptance of my first book, *Spellbinder,* was, as I suppose it is with most authors, a mixture of perseverance and luck. I'd had some short horror stories for kids accepted by a local radio station in 1981 and that prompted me to submit work to publishing houses. I operated a kind of conveyor-belt system. I had about a dozen typescripts that I felt were reasonable and began sending these out to ten or so publishers who had children's fantasy lists. This went on for about two-and-a-half years before Victor Gollancz in London showed an interest in my work and, eventually, became my hardcover publisher.

"*Spellbinder* tells the story of a boy who develops magic powers as his voice breaks—unexpected power, again. I used to wonder (and still do!), what if I had the power of sorcery, or could become invisible, or could fly? That led me to wonder why the world is built as it is and why we have certain abilities and limitations. I have some education in science, and a great interest in it, but it's not science I'm talking about. I mean, why is the universe *like* this, and is it planned? Anyway, *Spellbinder* did well enough in hardback for Pan Books to buy the softback rights, as they did with the next three titles.

"My second book, *Gameplayers,* was brought out as a 'fantasy' book, but is really the story of a group of ordinary schoolkids and how playing 'Dungeons and Dragons' together changes their lives. Most of my stories feature real people and locations. The characters in *Gameplayers* are based closely on kids I knew; their dialogue and much of the story's action really happened. If my books have a subtext, then I suppose the one here is that a person's fantasy-life is vital to her/his 'real' life.

"I also wanted to address the problem of video and comic book violence influencing the minds of young people, knowing that 'Dungeons and Dragons' and similar activities had come in for much criticism from concerned parents and teachers. I concluded in my own mind, if not explicitly in the story, that in many cases fantasy violence does not spark off real violence. Indeed, fantasy violence can act as a safety valve to release tensions and anger. Nor does it necessarily desensitize kids to the horrors of the real world. Kids are not stupid; they know what's evil and what's not. I also feel that fantasy violence helps to 'rehearse' children in the concepts, logics, and moral dilemmas that accompany real violence. Besides all of this, if kids—or adults—want to get nasty, then they don't really need role playing games or films or comics as an excuse.

"On the other hand, I feel that the element of violence (like all threads in the weave of a children's story) needs to be handled with a sense of responsibility. However 'escapist' a kid's book might be, it still has an educative function insofar as it creates an impression that the reader will add to her/his world picture. For this reason, I was eager to show in *Gameplayers* that sheer brute force does not solve all problems and can create many more.

"The following novel, *Dualists,* came about after a holiday in Wales, which gave me the bleak beach location for the story. The central science-fictional idea of *Dualists* is 'slubber,' a substance that at first resembles an inert jelly; it feels a bit like slime, a bit like rubber—hence, 'slubber.' Early on in the story, the characters discover that anything immersed in slubber is duplicated, but never perfectly. Thus, a cup with 'Made in England' written on the bottom is replicated with the message changed to 'Mad in England,' and so on. The story is driven by the characters' differing responses to this unexpected power, but also by the fact that the slubber is not all that it seems. It too has a purpose and aims to ensure its own survival on Earth. So, while it bestows riches, it steals the will and freedom of the protagonists—you get nothing for nothing!

"I was able to use the idea in another story, *The Copy Cat Plan,* from the two-play collection of the same name. I suppose that *Dualists* is typical of my work, in postulating a 'what if' situation and then trying to answer it. The Walt Disney Company has just taken out a twelve-month option to film *Dualists.* So you never know, slubber might yet invade this planet more completely than I ever imagined!

"My next book *Catch,* a collection of nine short stories, is intended to show a range of styles and ideas. I did not want to be set in the mold of a 'children's fantasy author' whose books all have similar settings, characterizations, etc. I was keen to show what else I could do and to develop certain facets of my writing. Also, the short story format is very appealing, and I felt that some of my best work to date was contained within some of the stories that were eventually featured in *Catch.*

"*Frontiersville High* is my latest published book, more science fiction oriented than previous stories but continuing the exploration of my favorite themes. I have tried to strengthen female characters in one or two of the story segments, feeling that a wider viewpoint will benefit my writing and, hopefully, widen my readership.

"In conjunction with the actual writing, I enjoy visiting schools and libraries to talk about my books and running creative thinking workshops that provide for other aspiring writers a few springboards which I had to discover the slow way. To enhance these workshops, I have developed a number of individual and group activities that I have used across the age- range in a wide variety of circumstances.

"I enjoy teaching and working with kids, but in Britain the political interference with education—the bureaucratization of schools by putting systems before people—is becoming stifling. And so, in recent years, a kind of anger has driven my Writing and pushed me to diversify into other areas and age groups. I'm now writing for preteens and adults and hope to see some of this work published within the next couple of years."

*   *   *

BRISSON, Pat 1951-

PERSONAL: Born February 23, 1951, in Rahway, NJ; daughter of Thomas Francis (a plumber and foreman) and Jane Margaret (a homemaker; maiden name Gerity) McDonough; married Emil Girard Brisson (an administrator), May 29, 1971; children: Gabriel, Noah, Benjamin, Zachary. *Education:* Rutgers University, B.A., 1973, M.L.S., 1990. *Politics:* Democrat. *Religion:* Roman Catholic. *Hobbies and other interests:* Gardening, baking.

ADDRESSES: Home—94 Bullman St., Phillipsburg, NJ 08865. *Agent*—Liza Voges, Kirchoff/Wohlberg, 866 United Nations Plaza, New York, NY 10017.

PAT BRISSON

CAREER: St. Anthony of Padua School, Camden, NJ, elementary school teacher, 1973-75; Easton Area Public Library, Easton, PA, library clerk, 1981-88; Phillipsburg Free Public Library, Phillipsburg, NJ, library clerk, 1978-81, reference librarian, 1990—.

MEMBER: American Library Association, Society of Children's Book Writers.

AWARDS, HONORS: Kate Heads West was named American Booksellers Pick of the Lists selection, 1990.

WRITINGS:

Your Best Friend, Kate, illustrated by Rick Brown, Bradbury, 1989.
Kate Heads West, illustrated by Brown, Bradbury, 1990.
The Magic Carpet, illustrated by Amy Schwartz, Bradbury, 1991.
Kate on the Coast, Bradbury, in press.
Benny's Pennies, illustrated by Bob Barner, Doubleday, in press.

SIDELIGHTS: Pat Brisson told *SATA:* "I was born in New Jersey in 1951, the fourth and supposedly last child in the family. My father called me the caboose, a nickname I cherished, so it was quite a shock when I was five and my brother Kevin was born. Over the years I was able to forgive my brother for being born and complicating my life so much. But I also wrote a story in which I stayed the caboose forever—history the way it should have been, I like to call it. The unpublished story is called *The Star Blanket.*

"I don't remember having a lot of books as a child, but I remember loving a Golden Book, illustrated by Eloise Wilkin, and I thought it was a special bonus to have a parade of Golden Book characters marching across the back. I could almost feel myself sinking into the illustrations as I studied and studied the pictures. Art seemed a magical thing to me then and still does.

"Not having many books, I never thought about being a writer, and when I was in fifth grade and my father brought home an old manual typewriter from somewhere, it didn't occur to me to write stories. Instead, I did a little essay about why strawberries were named strawberries (because straw spelled backwards is warts and they have all those little bumps all over them that look like warts) and other burning issues and called the collection *Memoirs of a Potato Peeler.* I doubt that I had peeled more than a half dozen potatoes in my life so there was no reason for the name, except the unexpected fun of it.

"As a sophomore in high school, I took a course which was journalism one half of the year and creative writing the other half. The most significant thing that happened was that my creative writing teacher, Miss Martine, wrote 'good beginning for your first novel' on one of my papers. I was dumbstruck—here was someone suggesting that I had it in me to write a novel! It still hasn't happened, but it was and is very encouraging.

"In college, I took only one writing course—in poetry, the last semester of my senior year. My teacher, Frank McQuilkan, told me if he had known earlier I could write so well he would have nominated me for the writing prize at graduation. This meant a great deal to me. Even though I didn't consider myself a writer, it was there for encouragement later on when I decided to write for publication.

"I married Emil Brisson in 1971, and we lived for seven years in Haddonfield, New Jersey, where our first two sons, Gabriel and Noah, were born. In 1978 we moved to Phillipsburg, New Jersey, where we still live, and I discovered the picture book collection at the Phillipsburg Free Public Library. I brought home piles of them to read to my two young sons, who were soon joined by their two younger brothers, Benjamin and Zachary. By the time Zachary was born in 1982, I had decided to try writing some myself.

"I read all I could about getting published—every month's issues of *Writer's Digest* and *Writer*—and whatever books I could get my hands on. And somewhere I ran across advice which made a lot of sense to me and gave me some direction for my goals. The article said that it's easiest to get published in a newspaper because it comes out so frequently, magazines are harder because they're published less frequently, and books are hardest of all—especially picture books because they're so expensive to produce.

"So I decided to submit picture book manuscripts, because that's what I *really* wanted to write, but also to send things out to magazines. I also volunteered to write an article every other week for our weekly newspaper. These were reviews of books on a different topic each time (wood-burning stoves, crafts, car repairs); and, not only did I get to see my article (and name) in print, I also developed a distinct style and learned to write for a deadline—despite the fact that small children were climbing all over me as I typed.

"I sold the very first article I submitted to a magazine called *Religion Teachers' Journal.* The article was called 'Activities That Keep Them Interested,' and they paid me seventy-five dollars. I was on my way. I sold a few more articles to magazines and these kept me going, despite the rejections which kept coming back with my picture book manuscripts.

"Finally, in March of 1987, I sold *The Magic Carpet* to Bradbury Press. Amy Schwartz had agreed to illustrate it. The excitement was somewhat dampened by the fact that it wouldn't actually be published until 1991. (My mother, who was seventy-seven at the time, said she hoped she lived to see it.)

"I got very busy writing and sent off several more stories to my editor, Virginia Duncan, but she rejected all of them. I couldn't figure out what *The Magic Carpet* had that the others didn't, so I decided to ask her about it.

"'We really liked the geography angle,' she responded.

"Geography! So that was it. Well, I decided, if they wanted a geography story, I would write them a geography story. So I wrote *Your Best Friend, Kate,* and they bought it in July.

"But then it went through *major* revisions. I had written a very generic story because I hadn't been to any of the places I wrote about. But Virginia wrote away to all the cities I mention in the book and got piles of brochures sent to me and said, 'OK, they have to visit specific places in each city and make sure they're all different so the illustrator has something to work with.'

"I was overwhelmed at first and upset. But then I got to work and made a lot of phone calls to places to ask questions like, 'If I went on a glass-bottom boat ride, what could I expect to

by Pat Brisson • illustrations by Rick Brown

Kate goes on vacation with her best friend's family in *Kate Heads West,* **by Pat Brisson.** (Cover illustration by Rick Brown.)

see?' and finally it was done. And then Virginia wanted a few more smaller changes but eventually it really was finished.

"Rick Brown was chosen to do the illustrations and I was delighted with how well he captured the humor and emotions of the story. Part of the fun of being the author of picture books is seeing what the illustrator will do, and I felt very lucky to have the illustrations match my story so well.

"*Your Best Friend, Kate* came out in 1989, and then Virginia asked if I would like to write another 'Kate' book, but she stipulated that it needed a different premise. So instead of being on vacation with her family and writing to Lucy and fighting with her brother, Kate is on vacation with Lucy and Lucy's parents and writes to a variety of people. *Kate Heads West* came out in 1990, and a third 'Kate' book, *Kate on the Coast,* is in press.

"*Benny's Pennies* is also in press. It's written for younger children than the 'Kate' books and is closer to being poetry than any of my other books. Bob Barner is illustrating it in a cut paper style which I'm very excited about.

"Despite the fact that people kept telling me how well I was doing, the writing business seemed a rather unreliable source of income, so I went back to graduate school at Rutgers University and got my master of library service (M.L.S.) in 1990. Actually, this had been a long-time goal ever since 1978 when I had begun working part time in my local library.

"So now I work two days a week as a reference librarian at the Phillipsburg Free Public Library. Being a reference librarian means solving little puzzles all day long, and I enjoy it very much. And working part time means I still have time to write and visit schools to talk to kids about how picture books are made, and also to garden and bake and run my kids to doctor's appointments and baseball practices, and still have time to get together for tea with friends of mine who are writers and illustrators.

"I have recently written some board books, and I would like to try my hand at longer books although it is the picture book which I especially love. I hope to continue writing for a long, long time."

*   *   *

BROWNE, Dik
See BROWNE, Richard Arthur Allan

*   *   *

BROWNE, Richard Arthur Allan 1917-1989
(Dik Browne)

PERSONAL: Born August 11, 1917, in New York, NY; died of cancer, June 4, 1989, in Sarasota, FL; son of William Joseph (a cost accountant) and Mae (a wardrobe mistress; maiden name, Slattery) Browne; married Joan Marie Therese Hosey Haggerty Kelly (treasurer, Browne Creative Enterprises, Inc.), May 11, 1942 (died, 1986); children: Robert, Christopher, Sally. *Education:* Attended Cooper Union, 1934. *Politics:* Registered Democrat ("voted independent"). *Religion:* Roman Catholic.

ADDRESSES: Home—Sarasota, FL. *Offices*—King Features Syndicate, 235 E. 45th St., New York, NY 10017; and c/o Christopher Browne, Browne Creative Enterprises Studio, 7129 Curtiss Ave., Sarasota, FL 34231.

DIK BROWNE

CAREER: New York Journal-American, New York City, copyboy, staff artist, 1936-41; *Newsweek,* New York City, staff artist, 1941-42; Johnstone & Cushing Art Agents, New York City, advertising artist, 1946-54; comic strip artist, "Hi and Lois," 1954-89; comic strip artist and writer, "Hagar the Horrible," 1973-89. *Military service:* U.S. Army, 1942-46, became sergeant.

MEMBER: National Cartoonists Society (president, 1963-65), National Comics Council.

AWARDS, HONORS: Best Comic Strip Cartoonist, 1959, for "Hi and Lois," Reuben Award for best cartoonist in all categories, 1962, for "Hi and Lois," and 1973, for "Hagar the Horrible," Best Humor Strip Cartoonist, 1959, 1960, 1972, 1977, and 1985, all from National Cartoonists Society; Banshees Silver Lady Award, Banshees Press Club, 1962; Elzie Segar Award, 1975; Best Non-British International Cartoon Award, British Cartoonist Society, 1984, for "Hagar the Horrible"; Max und Moritz Preis for best comic artist, Comic Salon, Erlangen, West Germany, 1984, for "Hagar the Horrible."

WRITINGS:

SELF-ILLUSTRATED "HAGAR THE HORRIBLE" SERIES

The Wit and Wisdom of Hagar the Horrible, Windmill Press, 1974.
Hagar the Horrible, Ace, 1977.
Hagar the Horrible No. 2, Ace, 1978.
Have You Been Uptight Lately?, Berkley, 1980.
Big Bands Are Back, Berkley, 1981.
Hagar the Horrible and the Basilisk, Berkley, 1981.
The Best of Hagar the Horrible, Simon & Schuster, 1981.
Hagar the Horrible's Activity Book, Berkley, 1982.
Hagar the Horrible Puzzlers, Ace, 1982.
Midnight Munchies, Ace, 1982.
The Very Best of Hagar, Simon & Schuster, 1982.
Hagar and the Golden Maiden, Tor Books, 1983.
Hagar at Work, Tor Books, 1983.
Sacking Paris on a Budget, Tor Books, 1983.
Animal Haus, Ace, 1983.
Born Leader, Ace, 1983.
Bring 'Em Back Alive, Ace, 1983.
Hagar the Horrible: Tall Tales, Tor Books, 1983.
The Brutish Are Coming, Ace, 1983.
Helga's Revenge, Ace, 1983.
My Feet Are Really Drunk, Ace, 1983.
Hagar the Horrible on the Loose, Ace, 1983.
Hagar the Horrible on the Rack, Ace, 1983.
Hear No Evil, Tor Books, 1984.
Hagar: Room for One More, Tor Books, 1984.
Excuse Me!, Ace, 1984.
Hagar Hits the Mark, Ace, 1984.
Hagar's Knight Out, Ace, 1984.
Happy Hour, Ace, 1984.
The Simple Life, Ace, 1984.
Hagar the Horrible: All the World Loves a Lover, Tor Books, 1985.
Hagar on the Rocks, Ace, 1985.
Hagar the Horrible: Horns of Plenty, Tor Books, 1985.
Face Stuffer's Anonymous, Tor Books, 1985.
Sack Time, Ace, 1985.
Hagar the Horrible: Cang Wan, Tor Books, 1985.
Hagar the Horrible: Vikings Are Fun, Tor Books, 1985.
Hagar the Horrible's Very Nearly Complete Viking Handbook, Workman, 1985.
Hagar the Horrible: Gangway, Tor Books, 1985.

(From *Hi and Lois: Trixie a la Mode,* by Mort Walker, illustrated by Browne.)

Hagar the Horrible: Norse Code, Ace, 1986.
Roman Holiday, Ace, 1986.
Vikings Are Horrible Pillage Idiots, Tor Books, 1986.
Hagar the Horrible: Out on a Limb, Tor Books, 1986.
Hagar the Horrible: Hi Dear, Your Hair Looks Great, Jove, 1988.
Hagar the Horrible: Handyman Special, Jove, 1989.
Hagar the Horrible: Smotherly Love, Jove, 1989.
Hagar the Horrible: Look Sharp, Jove, 1989.
Hagar the Horrible: Strapped for Cash, Jove, 1989.
Hagar: Pillage Idiot, Tor Books, 1989.
Hagar the Horrible: Silly Sailing, Jove, 1990.
Hagar the Horrible: Start the Invasion without Me, Jove, 1990.

Also author and illustrator of *Hagar the Horrible: Spring Cleaning,* Jove.

ILLUSTRATOR; "HI AND LOIS" SERIES; ALL WRITTEN BY MORT WALKER

Trixie, Dell, 1960.
Hi and Lois: Beware, Children at Play, Putnam, 1968.
Hi and Lois: Family Ties, Ace, 1978.
Hi and Lois in Darkest Suburbia, Ace, 1978.
Suburban Cowboys, Ace, 1982.
Father Figure, Ace, 1983.
American Gothic, Ace, 1983.
Hi and Lois: Spring Dreams, Tor Books, 1983.
Hi and Lois: Home Sweat Home, Tor Books, 1983.
Hi and Lois: Hi Honey, I'm Home, Tor Books, 1984.
The Bright Stuff, Ace, 1984.
Mama's Home, Ace, 1984.
Is Dinner Ready?, Tor Books, 1984.
Mom, Where's My Homework?, Tor Books, 1984.
Hi and Lois: Saturday Night Fever, Tor Books, 1984.
Hi and Lois: How Do You Spell Dad?, Tor Books, 1985.

(From *Hi and Lois: Trixie a la Mode,* by Mort Walker, illustrated by Browne.)

Hi and Lois: Dawg Day Afternoon, Tor Books, 1986.
Hi and Lois: Good Housekeeping, Tor Books, 1986.
The Best of Hi and Lois, Holt, 1986.
Hi and Lois: Trixie a la Mode, Tor Books, 1986.
Hi and Lois: Sleepbusters, Tor Books, 1987.
Hi and Lois: Say Cheese, Tor Books, 1987.
Hi and Lois: House Calls, Tor Books, 1988.
Here Comes the Sun: A Hi And Lois Collection, Avon, 1990.

ILLUSTRATOR

Bishop Fulton J. Sheen, "Life Is Worth Living" (series), Doubleday, 1950-54.
Mort Walker, *Most* (juvenile), Windmill, 1971.
M. Walker, *Land of Lost Things* (juvenile), Windmill, 1973.

SIDELIGHTS: Dik Browne is best remembered as the creator of the laughable, pillaging viking in the comic strip "Hagar the Horrible." Created in 1973 to supplement

Browne's income as an illustrator for Mort Walker's "Hi and Lois" comic, "Hagar" quickly surpassed its expected appeal: It became the fastest-growing comic strip ever and is now featured in approximately seventeen hundred papers in fifty-eight countries. Browne died in 1989, but the strip has endured thanks to Dik's son Chris, who has written and illustrated "Hagar" since his father's death.

Reminiscing about his childhood, Dik Browne once told a *Cartoonist Profiles* interviewer: "When I was very young, I thought I would like to be a sculptor. . . . I loved the limestone yards where they carved the statues for the buildings in New York and Washington. But it didn't work out. I came of age during the Depression and we had to trim our sails to the prevailing winds. Unless you were terribly gifted, it was not a good time for fine arts. [My mother] was a wardrobe mistress on Broadway and I grew up. . . . back stage. I didn't know there was a front of the house! I didn't know there was an

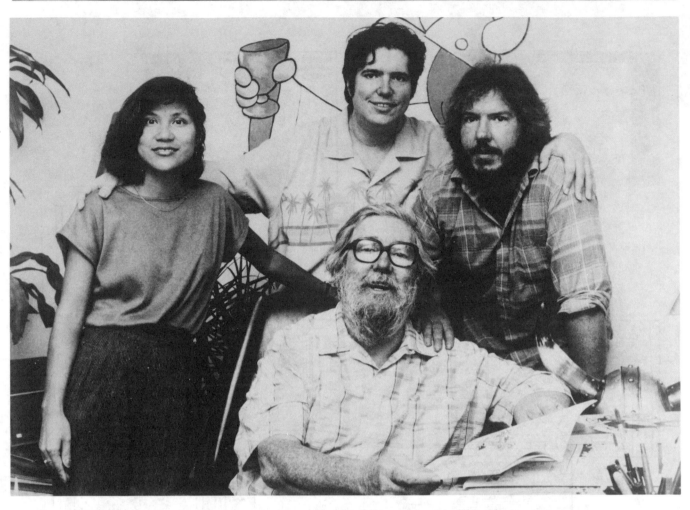

Browne with his children.

audience out there. I thought the actors were out there doing it for their own amusement."

The Depression had forced most people to make economic concessions during the early 1930s. Browne was no exception, managing to complete only one year at the Cooper Union Art School before he was forced to find work at a newspaper. In a *Hartford Courant* article, he shared his first impressions of journalism serving as a copyboy for the *New York Journal-American:* "Newspapers back in the mid-1930s were unbelievable.... When I entered the Journal's old office in lower Manhattan, I discovered a whole world I never knew existed. The city room was a mess with old newspapers thrown all over the floors. In the center sat the city editor and behind him was this big greasy guy cooking hot dogs at a grill. I couldn't believe it. Plus, there's this midget who used to run advance copy uptown to the Hearst offices buying a hot dog. And just as I walk in, the city editor takes a New York phone book, throws it across the room and decks a copy editor with whom he had been arguing. It was fantastic."

The future-cartoonist had vague ambitions of becoming a journalist, though, and soon decided his talents for drawing and caricature were better suited to the paper's art department. Browne's big break came when he was assigned to make courtroom sketches for a famous trial. "The gangster Lucky Luciano was a big story but all cameras were barred from the courtroom," Browne is quoted as saying in the *Hartford Courant*. "So the city editor began sending me to

cover the trial as the Journal's courtroom artist. . . . I got to meet some very interesting people on this assignment and in fact I was taught to foxtrot by 'Stoneface Peggy,' a madam of some renown, and her girls." It was during this period that Browne first attempted cartoon work, collaborating with another copyboy on an unpublished Yiddish strip called "Muttle the Gonif" ("Muttle the Thief"). Because of his success with courtroom assignments, Browne was quickly promoted to drawing maps and illustrations for World War II battle reports. The quality of his work attracted the attention of *Newsweek* magazine, who hired Browne at three times his previous salary.

In 1942, Browne was drafted into the U.S. Army Engineering Corps, where he performed largely the same tasks as in civilian life: drawing maps, charts and posters for the war effort. In his spare time, he worked on another unpublished comic strip, "Rembrandt," and created a character named "Ginny Jeep," whose cartoon adventures appeared in Army and Air Force newspapers. When the artist was discharged in March, 1946, he returned home to find his position at *Newsweek* had been eliminated.

Turning to advertising, Browne was hired by the Johnstone & Cushing agency, where a number of artists who would eventually be referred to as "The Connecticut School" also worked. Dik Browne's son and current "Hagar" illustrator, Chris Browne, told *Something about the Author:* "There were a lot of cartoonists right after World War II who didn't

(From *Hagar the Horrible on the Rack,* written and illustrated by Browne.)

(From *Sack Time,* written and illustrated by Browne.)

actually know they were cartoonists because they worked for New York advertising firms. My father worked for Johnstone & Cushing in a bullpen with about twenty other artists. He redesigned the Campbell Soup Kids, designed the Bird's Eye bird symbol and created Chiquita Banana. Mort Walker, who created 'Beetle Bailey,' had just bought a house in Connecticut, and when dad first started making money from cartoon work, we moved to Wilton, Connecticut. His buddies from Johnstone & Cushing would visit my father and Mort, and say 'this looks pretty good,' and before long there were about fifty cartoonists living in Fairfield County, and in fact most of them still do."

In the early fifties, with advertising work earning him professional esteem, Dik Browne at last began publishing cartoons, collaborating with Al Stenzel on "The Tracy Twins" for *Boy's Life.* The artist's association with Mort Walker began in 1954, when Walker saw one of Browne's signed drawings for Peter Paul Mounds candy. When Walker discussed his admiration for the piece with his editor, Sylvan Byck, he also learned of Browne's role with "The Tracy Twins." Byck and Walker decided to invite Browne to collaborate on "Hi and Lois," a family strip conceived as a spin-off of "Beetle Bailey."

With the Korean War over, Walker had hoped to shift "Beetle Bailey" from a military to a collegiate setting, but the artist encountered firm resistance from King Features Syndicate. As a compromise, Walker introduced Beetle's sister, Lois Flagston, and her family, into the cartoon. Readers protested the strip's move from Army life, however, and the syndicate encouraged Walker to create a separate strip for the suburban characters.

"The writing for 'Hi and Lois,'" according to Chris Browne, "was completely in the hands of Mort and his staff. But the graphic look, the feeling and the way that writing was interpreted was up to my father. He managed to achieve a very warm, wholesome 'It's a Wonderful Life' feeling with that strip. A lot of the pieces are standard family strip fare, but occasionally he would have a drawing that transcended what the strip was about and brought it to an emotional level that we're starting to see more of today in strips like 'Calvin and Hobbes.' There was a lot of heart in that strip, particularly in the Sunday pages where dad had more room to stretch and develop the emotions behind the characters.

"The early 'Hi and Lois' strips are very clever and the characters are somewhat goony, but as the strip developed, the characters are less polarized by their gooniness or their appearance; they become easier to relate to, and there's a little more warmth in some of the less wholesome characters, like Thirsty. He hit his stride with the strip in the middle '60s and early '70s. Some of the prettiest and warmest pieces are from that period. And though the earlier strips were rather stiff and 'designy,' his later work retained all the knowledge of inking and line work he developed, but spring-boards off those techniques into the human feelings under the surface.''

''Hi and Lois'' was eventually syndicated to over eleven hundred newspapers worldwide, and Browne continued drawing for it until his death. With steady work, his life had settled into a comfortable routine at last. Frequently, the artist would rise early to work, and then take an afternoon nap. Chris Browne recalled: ''My brother and sister and I would come home from school and my father would be getting up.... So he would come galloping down the stairs and all us kids would shout 'Here comes HAGAR THE HORRIBLE' because it sounded like somebody kicked a beer barrel downstairs. I don't know why it was Hagar. It just popped out of my head.''

This endearing nickname would remain a family joke until 1973. In that year, an extended series of medical emergencies and family tragedies culminated in a financial and emotional need for new creative ventures. ''My father had a terrible accident one winter in the '60s when he fell down from the top of a steep, icy driveway,'' Chris Browne told *SATA*. ''By the time he got to the bottom his left elbow was smashed to bits. The doctors patched him back together as best they could, but the main joint had to be rigged with a metal elbow that was set in a fixed position so that he couldn't really unbend it more than a few inches. Fortunately it wasn't the arm he drew with, but it was a devastating illness for him not only because of the physical pain, but also because he developed a staph infection which cropped up in his system every year, threatening to kill him.

''He once got so close to the edge that a priest performed last rites. My mother was told that dad would probably die in the next few days. We heard of a new antibiotic from England and made arrangements to fly some over. It saved his life. A few years later he broke his leg in a car accident and was once again beset with one thing after another. So he started thinking about our financial security in case something did happen to him, and he also wanted to prove to himself that he had a strip of his own in him.''

Within the same year, the artist's brother and father-in-law died, and his sister and mother-in-law became seriously ill. The final blow came just as ''Hagar'' debuted, when Browne suffered a detached retina. Chris Browne recalled his father's ordeal: ''We were going off on our first family vacation in a long time, driving down to Florida. We had gotten as far as the New Jersey Turnpike when it started snowing. I was sitting in the back seat with my sister when I saw my father lean over to my mother and whisper, 'When you see a place where there's a phone, pull over.' She asked what was wrong and he said, 'I've gone blind.' One of his eyes just went out, and we had to ride back to Connecticut in an ambulance.

''I got in the back of the ambulance with my father. On a stretcher, both eyes taped shut, he said to me, 'Is that you, Chris? Have you got your pad with you? Okay, let's make some good use of this time—let's write some gags.' He dictated gags to me not knowing if he'd ever see out of that eye again. His other eye had a cataract, and he had glaucoma, so there were three strikes against him. He had already been

saying that he was drawing by radar, but it was a shocking thing to have happen. It was a real turning point.

''Just about a year before, he had come up with the idea for the strip. He'd been talking about various concepts, such as a strip about a French cafe. There were other ideas, in fact he filled up whole sketch books with notes for different projects. Then one day he said to my mother, 'I'm going down to the basement [studio] and I'm going to come up with a comic strip idea.'

''He went down with a pad and came up with 'Hagar.' He had not only the first drawings for 'Hagar,' but the first month of gags, as well. He also had two strips of paper, one with this little Viking in different positions, running across the paper, like an animation test sheet in which each drawing advances further than the one before. On the other sheet he had two drawings of Hagar himself: a close-up of Hagar's face and a full figure drawing of the character. Those drawings depicted Hagar as a much meaner character than what now appears; originally he had a droopy, bulbous nose, almost like an eggplant, and dark circles under his eyes. The points on his helmet were also sharper, and he was not as cuddly as he is now. It was never intended to be an adventure strip, but from the first he was a gritty, tough, vulgar kind of character.''

Dik Browne revealed his intentions for the Hagar character in *Cartoonist Profiles:* ''I wanted a character that would be instantly recognizable ... universally recognizable.... Well, a Viking with a horned helmet seemed to fit ... those requirements. Better still, everybody loves a Viking ... they can get away with the most atrocious behavior.... Hagar almost drew himself. Once you draw the horned hat you need a nose. I made a few false starts here ... ended up with something between an orange and a grapefruit. The beard just naturally grew ... and just as naturally, I made him fat ... because thin just ain't funny!''

Essentially, ''Hagar the Horrible'' portrays the life of a sympathetic and naive, ninth-century Viking who considers his life of sacking and looting as natural as any other. Despite its archaic setting, the strip nonetheless reflected a number of deeply autobiographical themes for the artist. ''One of my father's few good childhood memories centers around a woman he referred to as a Swedish aunt,'' Chris Browne told *SATA*. ''She was probably a volunteer nanny or maybe a woman from his building who would tell him bedtime stories about Viking heroes.... That was a sweet spot for him, a golden childhood memory that rattled around in his head for a long time. But also, Hagar was my father. My dad was a six feet, 250-pound man of Irish descent with a big red beard who loved to eat and sing opera. He loved a good joke and was an imp and a gentle giant at the same time.

''My mother was a very wise, witty and patient woman. And although Helga [Hagar's wife] seems to be scowling a good deal, my mother would view dad with a sage eye, observing him as if he were a fascinating life form. Helga was based on my mother. My sister was the basis for Honey. Although my father toyed briefly with incorporating a Chinese character into the strip, he realized it was too fraught with difficulties to pull off, so he based her character on my sister's soul. My sister was a straight-'A' student and a 'let's-go-to-the-beach-and-party' type. So, like Honey, she's always been active and vibrant in everything she's done.

''At the start of the strip, my brother was a rock 'n' roll musician and my father incorporated him into the strip as

(From *Sack Time,* written and illustrated by Browne.)

(From *Sack Time,* written and illustrated by Browne.)

Lute, the wandering minstrel. He physically resembles my brother: tall, thin and always wearing a hat. The remaining character in the immediate family was Hamlet, who was based on me because in 1972 I was a vegetarian, very much against the war, and my father thought 'What could be better? I'll have a vegetarian peacenick as this Viking's son—the bane of his existence!'

"I often go back to the early strips to study them and see things I'd never noticed before that were quite autobiographical. My father didn't base every strip on what happened at home that day, and he didn't try to send us hidden messages through the strip, but he put a lot of depth in his work. Hagar's major strength over a lot of other strips about married couples was the undercurrent of affection between the two. Hagar would go out in the world and encounter nightmares and horrors because he loves his family. I think that's how dad was."

The artist initially hoped that one hundred newspapers would be attracted to the strip—it premiered in two hundred. By 1975, that figure had tripled, and three years later it passed the one thousand mark, making it the fastest-growing comic strip in history. Browne joined the ranks of Mort Walker and Charles Schulz as one of the three most widely syndicated

cartoonists of the seventies. In the United States alone, it has been estimated that the strip is seen by as many as 100 million readers daily.

Perhaps it was not surprising that a cartoon so rooted in positive family relationships would soon be produced as a collaborated family effort. Dik Browne said in *Cartoonist Profiles:* "Aside from financial reasons for starting the strip, I always dreamed of having a family business . . . a sort of 'cottage industry.' It's not an original idea, God knows. Every commuter in Connecticut has the same daydream . . . but . . . the great thing is . . . it worked! Chris is, of course, one helluva cartoonist. He's supplied some of the funniest gags. He's drawn 'Hi and Lois' from time to time. . . . Bob . . . is our resident designer. . . . Joan, who always had more faith in me than I had in myself, runs the business side . . . and supplies the witty one-liners. My daughter Sally . . . helps out with the filing and is a 'go-fer' on vacations. It's great, because I think we're even closer as a family because of this business we have going."

Chris Browne recalled some of his father's early influences: "My dad used to say, 'I'm not sure I'm a good artist'—I was sure he was a good artist—'but I am a good editor.' One of his big influences was Ernie Bushmiller, who did 'Nancy.'

'Nancy' was not the first thing I would turn to in the paper, but dad pointed out that it was a real departure from the cartoons that came before it in the 1940s. Ernie Bushmiller used to say, 'boil it down'—boil the gags down to something very simple. I would say Bushmiller, with his indefatigable sense of simplicity, was a big influence on my father and a lot of other cartoonists of the Connecticut School. . . . Another of my father's big influences was an art teacher named Kimon Nicolaides. His book, *The Natural Way to Draw,* shaped dad's whole approach to drawing. He was very big on drawing, very big on knowing the rules before you break them. So when I started working with him, my first assignment wasn't gag writing, it was life drawing lessons.

"My father always made sure that his characters had weight to them. If you look at the characters in Hagar, it's a subtle distinction, but they do have more of a sense that they are rounded figures than a lot of other comics. Finding ways to achieve that contoured feeling is one of the problems I still wrestle with when I draw Hagar. Hagar gives the impression that you could reach into the page and put your hand around him; it's wonderful to look at, but very elusive to draw.

"Another influence on my father was a younger artist named Robert Crumb. When dad started Hagar, he infused the strip with more of the old-time cartooning style, where the characters look like they've got a few too many pounds of air in them. They have an inflated, spongy look, and that was part of Crumb's influence, because at the same time he was also reviving interest in that period. My father especially admired Crumb as a craftsman; he thought Crumb was a little off the wall, and as far as content is concerned, it wouldn't be his first choice of reading material, but he loved the way that guy drew.

"Humor strips in the early seventies were for the most part very simply drawn. Prior to that, the trend went toward a lot of beautifully drawn strips like Fred Lazwell's 'Snuffy Smith,' but at that point they began to resemble greeting card art. These newer strips weren't poorly drawn—some of them were quite striking—but you didn't necessarily have to go to art school to produce them.

"While this aesthetic trend was developing, there was also a newspaper shortage, so that editors had to fit two or three pages of comics on to one page, sometimes sharing space with the horoscope and a game. While the physical size of the comics was shrinking, artists with an editorial bent like Gary Trudeau, or nowadays Berke Breathed, were using more and more words to make their point. 'Hagar' went against that trend and brought back a simpler, more graphically-oriented style."

Dik Browne once discussed this style in the *Hartford Courant.* In particular, he stressed his desire to achieve a harmony between technique and subject matter: "In 'Hi and Lois,' the line is clean and round, and that somehow suits a clean, round, tight, warm family. . . . When you get to someone as raunchy as Hagar, I like the line a lot cruder and bolder." From a creative perspective, "Hagar" afforded the artist full control of a strip for the first time in his career. Chris Browne explained: "He got more of a charge, a greater amount of satisfaction doing 'Hagar' because he could choose the images he wanted to draw. He loved working on 'Hi and Lois,' but only in occasional dream or fantasy sequences could he ever draw anything as flamboyant as a dragon.

"Once the strip started, there were a couple of instances in which we decided to alter its focus, but there were never any insurmountable problems with the characters or the way we handled them. Two key issues do come to mind, though. Early on, we had a Sunday page in which we showed a battle scene with Hagar carrying off a maiden. We never thought of it as anything more than a funny Viking cliche, but of course, there's nothing funny about rape. This was a time when the media was just beginning to touch on that issue, and there was enough controversy that dad decided from then on to have him carry off pizzas.

"The second instance occurred in the mid-eighties, when we started to weed out more and more of the drinking jokes. Previously, we had a lot of gags about getting sloppy, vulgar drunk and hallucinating flying angels and things. At that point, dad began to reflect on his own father's on-again, off-again drinking problem, and he realized that for a lot of people these jokes wouldn't be funny at all. We've tried not to tone Hagar down too much because we're not trying to educate people, but we certainly aren't trying to offend anyone, either.

"I think the accessibility of the strip was ultimately what made it so popular. People seem to identify with the characters, especially Hagar and Helga. I would say that 80 percent of our mail comes from women who say that Hagar is just like their husband or their father. I suppose that means there are a lot of people in America who like to eat and who come home tired in the evening. I think it also means that there are a lot of people who, like Hagar, feel their job, or what they do in life, isn't completely understood by anybody around them."

WORKS CITED:

Browne, Christopher, interview conducted by Marc Caplan for *Something about the Author.*
Crouch, Bill, Jr., "Comic Strip Superstar," *Hartford Courant,* November 10, 1974, pp. 66-67.
Walker, Mort, "Mort Walker Converses with Dik Browne," *Cartoonist Profiles,* March, 1979, pp. 12-27.

FOR MORE INFORMATION SEE:

BOOKS

Contemporary Graphic Artists, Volume 1, Gale, 1986.
Encyclopedia of Twentieth-Century Journalists, Garland, 1986.
The World Encyclopedia of Comics, Chelsea House Publishers, New York, 1976.

PERIODICALS

American Artist, Volume 1, number 1, 1984.
Cartoonist Profiles, December, 1977.
Christian Science Monitor, May 2, 1973.
Comics Journal, December, 1986.
Editor & Publisher, February 27, 1988.
People Weekly, December 11, 1978.
Sarasota Herald Tribune, May 11, 1980.

OBITUARIES:

PERIODICALS

Chicago Tribune, June 5, 1989.
Comics Journal, July, 1989.
Newsweek, June 19, 1989.

(From *Hagar the Horrible on the Rack,* written and illustrated by Browne.)

New York Daily News, June 5, 1989.
New York Times, June 5, 1989.
Time, June 19, 1989.
Washington Post, June 6, 1989.

*   *   *

CALIF, Ruth 1922-

PERSONAL: Surname is pronounced "kay-lif"; born June 16, 1922, in St. Louis, MO; daughter of Edward (an engineer) and Gertrude (a homemaker; maiden name, Gunther) Lammert; married Clarence W. Calif (a rancher), March 14, 1941; children: Gary Lee. *Education:* Attended Brown's Business College, 1939, and Santa Rosa College, 1973. *Politics:* "Survival." *Religion:* Christian. *Hobbies and other interests:* Designing toys.

ADDRESSES: Home and office—Route #1, Box 1128, Dunnegan, MO 65640. *Agent*—Lloyd Jones, 4301 Hidden Creek, Arlington, TX 76016.

CAREER: Missouri Valley Commission Co., St. Louis, MO, partner, 1942-62; Cactus Creek Kennels, Bellflower, MO, partner, 1962-72; Calif Enterprises, Dunnegan, MO, and Sebastopol, CA, chief executive officer, 1973—.

MEMBER: Missouri Writers' Guild.

AWARDS, HONORS: Best Book awards, Missouri Writers' Guild, first place, 1989, for *The Over-the-Hill Ghost,* second place, 1991, for *The Over-the-Hill Witch.*

WRITINGS:

Garden of Evil (fiction), Major, 1977.
(With Bev Buckingham) *Nurse at Orchard Hill,* Bouregy, 1978.
Rust (fiction), Manor Books, 1981.
The World on Wheels (nonfiction), Cornwall, 1983.
Shadow Mansion (fiction), Zebra Books, 1985.

The Over-the-Hill Ghost (novel), illustrations by Joan Holub, Pelican Publishing (Gretna, LA), 1988.
Mistress of Falcon Court (fiction), Zebra Books, 1989.
The Over-the-Hill Witch (novel), illustrations by Holub, Pelican Publishing, 1990.

Contributor to periodicals, including *Silver Eclectic.*

SIDELIGHTS: Ruth Calif told *SATA:* "After six months of total leisure, retirement, even in California, became boring. I

RUTH CALIF

went to a writing class at Santa Rosa College to learn how to put together a kennel-management manual and discovered I could write. I wrote for local newspapers and for magazines, then made a new discovery, thanks to a great teacher—I could write whole novels! During the next four years I wrote a dozen (various categories), seven of which have been published. I think the world needs humor these days, so I add it to whatever I write. Our young people need to read more, and the only way to get them interested is with plots that move as fast as *Miami Vice* and similar television programs, and with an occasional laugh. After all, 'entertainment' means to amuse and give pleasure to an audience.

"My husband spent four years in the army during World War II, and when he was released we bought a ranch while I continued with my commission business in St. Louis. It was a long commute, 125 miles each way, but it was a time I used for planning. Ten years later, after our son was born, we bought a farm on the prairie. Thirty years later we 'retired' to California in a ranch house on the second range of hills from the Pacific Ocean near Sebastopol. We both tired of leisure, so when I returned to school my husband got a job driving workers to the Geysers, and he also did an occasional turn driving Disney stars to the site of the latest production. He and other members of his motorcycle club appeared in *Mr. Billions* for just an instant, but it was fun. When he had to stop driving a bus because of a damaged knee, I paused in my novel writing and began designing items for craft magazines so I could do it while watching movies with him. When California became overcrowded we sold our home and retired to Crawford County to a house and eighteen acres just across the highway from our first 600-acre ranch. When our son and his family returned from California and settled near Springfield, we decided to do the same. We now live on ten acres in a comfortable home close enough to our family that we can see them often and watch our grandchildren grow."

FOR MORE INFORMATION SEE:

PERIODICALS

Abilene Reporter-News, September 4, 1988.
Booklist, July, 1988.
School Library Journal, December, 1988; August, 1990.

* * *

CARTER, Alden R(ichardson) 1947-

PERSONAL: Born April 7, 1947, in Eau Claire, WI; son of John Kelley and Hilda Small Richardson Carter; married Carol Ann Shadis (a social worker), September 14, 1974; children: Brian Patrick, Siri Morgan. *Education:* University of Kansas, B.A., 1969; Montana State University, teaching certificate, 1976. *Politics:* Democrat. *Hobbies and other interests:* Canoeing, camping, hiking, reading.

ADDRESSES: Home and office—1113 West Onstad Dr., Marshfield, WI 54449. *Agent*—Lazear Agency, 430 First Ave. N., Suite 416, Minneapolis, MN 55401.

CAREER: Writer. Taught high school English and journalism for four years in Marshfield, WI. Speaker at workshops, including ALAN Workshop on Young Adult Literature and National Council of Teachers of English. *Military service:* U.S. Navy, 1969-74; became lieutenant senior grade.

MEMBER: Council on Wisconsin Writers, Society of Children's Book Writers, Society of Midland Authors, Sierra Club.

AWARDS, HONORS: Best Book for Young Adults citation, American Library Association (ALA), 1984, for *Growing Season;* Best Book for Young Adults citations, ALA, New York Public Library, Los Angeles Public Library, and the Child Study Association, Best Book for Reluctant Readers citation, ALA Young Adult Services Committee, all 1985, all for *Wart, Son of Toad;* Best Book for Young Adults citations, ALA and Los Angeles Public Library, and Best Book for the Teenage citation, New York Public Library, all 1987, all for *Sheila's Dying;* Best Book citation, ALA, and Best Book for the Teenage citation, New York Public Library, both 1989, both for *Up Country;* Best Book for the Teenage citation, 1990, and Best Children's Fiction Book of the Year citation, Society of Midland Authors, both 1990, both for *RoboDad.*

WRITINGS:

YOUNG ADULT NONFICTION

(With Wayne Jarome LeBlanc) *Supercomputers,* F. Watts, 1985.
Modern China, with photographs by Carol S. and Alden R. Carter, F. Watts, 1986, revised edition, 1992.
(With LeBlanc) *Modern Electronics,* F. Watts, 1986.
Radio: From Marconi to the Space Age, F. Watts, 1987.
Illinois, F. Watts, 1987.
The Shoshoni, F. Watts, 1989.
Last Stand at the Alamo, F. Watts, 1990.
Battle of Gettysburg, F. Watts, 1990.
The Civil War, F. Watts, 1992.
The Spanish-American War, F. Watts, 1992.
Clashes in the Wilderness: The Colonial Wars, F. Watts, 1992.
The War of 1812, F. Watts, 1992.
The Mexican War, F. Watts, 1992.

"THE AMERICAN REVOLUTION" SERIES

Colonies in Revolt, F. Watts, 1988.
The Darkest Hours, F. Watts, 1988.
At the Forge of Liberty, F. Watts, 1988.
Birth of the Republic, F. Watts, 1988.

YOUNG-ADULT FICTION

Growing Season, Coward-McCann, 1984.
Wart, Son of Toad, Putnam Pacer Books, 1985.
Sheila's Dying, Putnam, 1987.
Up Country, Putnam, 1989.
RoboDad, Putnam, 1990.

WORK IN PROGRESS: Nonfiction for young adults, including *The Monitor and the Merrimack.* Fiction for young adults, including, *You're My Brother Not My Keeper, Dogwolf, I Was a Teenage Kangaroo.* A middle-grade novel, *Crescent Moon,* an adult novel, *Blade Dancer,* and a scholarly book, *Delivered in Suffering*—a collection of letters by American missionaries killed at Paoting-fu, North China, in the Boxer Rebellion of 1900.

SIDELIGHTS: Alden R. Carter, a former naval officer and high school English and journalism teacher, has authored more than a dozen books about history and technology for young adults; but he is perhaps best recognized for his award-winning fiction. Praised especially for his mastery of characterization, Carter writes realistically about the personal

ALDEN R. CARTER

problems that young people sometimes face as they mature; and his books are recognized by the American Library Association for their excellence.

Carter's first novel, *Growing Season,* concerns family relationships and the contrasts between city and country life, and it elicited much positive critical response. For instance, in *Voice of Youth Advocates,* Mary K. Chelton praises its "superior characterizations." The novel is told from the perspective of Rick, a straight-arrow teenager whose senior year in high school is disrupted when his family leaves the city for a dairy farm in the country, and recounts his journey into maturity and responsibility. Calling *Growing Season* "a realistic chronicle of agricultural and family life," *Horn Book* contributor Ethel R. Twichell adds that "it intertwines closely the narrative about farm life with the theme of family relations." And describing it as "an honest and sincere portrait of human growth and change," Hope Bridgewater adds in a review for *School Library Journal* that "the human emotions and situations described are universal."

Carter's second novel, *Wart, Son of Toad,* is the story of the relationship between a father and his son whose family has been devastated by the accidental death of the mother and daughter. The father is an unpopular biology teacher whose students refer to him behind his back as Toad, and to his son as Wart, says a *Kirkus Reviews* contributor, who finds "dramatic power" in the scenes between the father and son. Both are unhappy and "can offer each other neither communica-

tion nor comfort," writes a *Wilson Library Bulletin* contributor, who thinks that Carter tells his tale with "just the right amount of humor and compassion." Calling it a "good performance," Robert Unsworth suggests in *School Library Journal* that "Carter is strong on characterization—readers can connect with any of his readily recognizable people."

Sheila's Dying, the story of a young girl diagnosed with a fatal form of uterine cancer, "is a deeply moving story of the illness and death of a young girl," says Janet Bryan in the *School Library Journal.* The story is narrated by Jerry, the basketball star who changes his mind about dumping Sheila in order to devote himself to her in her terminal illness. Praising the novel's "sturdy characterization and dialogue," Zena Sutherland adds in *Bulletin of the Center for Children's Books* that it "makes a statement about responsibility without moralizing." And according to Susan Ackler in *Voice of Youth Advocates,* "It is a memorable cast of characters who are believable and will remain with the reader long after the book is finished." As Stephanie Zvirin states in *Booklist,* "Carter has written a tough book." Or as a *Publishers Weekly* contributor suggests, one that "rings starkly true."

Called "a powerful story, memorably told" by a *Kirkus Reviews* contributor, *Up Country* looks at the troubled life of sixteen-year-old Carl Staggers, who "uses his talent with electronics both to shield himself from his mother's alcoholism and promiscuity and to try to make enough money repairing stolen stereos to get into engineering school later," explains Barbara Hutcheson in *School Library Journal,* who calls the book "a solid, unpreachy novel." When Carl's mother is arrested after she is involved in a hit-and-run accident, he is sent to live with relatives on a country farm, where he encounters "unquestioning acceptance," writes Nancy Vasilakis in *Horn Book.* "Gripping, satisfying, and heart-wrenching—another winner from a talented writer," remarks Stella Baker in *Voice of Youth Advocates.* Although finding the story "a trifle didactic," Sally Estes suggests that Carl's transformation is "convincing enough to sustain the story's power." And according to Betsy Hearne in *Bulletin for the Center of Children's Books,* Carter's character and situation will make young adult readers "think about the ways they solve whatever problems loom in their own lives."

More recently, in *RoboDad,* Carter writes about a chubby and disheveled young girl named Shar, who must contend with the physiological changes of puberty as well as the upheaval in her family because of her father's changed physical condition. Shar's father suffered a massive stroke in which an aneurysm ruptured an artery and cut off oxygen to his brain, transforming him from a loving father into an emotionless and sometimes menacing stranger. Considering *RoboDad* "a fine, sensitive book," Leone McDermott adds in *Booklist,* "Carter is extraordinarily, almost painfully, perceptive . . . and extends an unsentimental sympathy to all." A *Bulletin of the Center for Children's Books* contributor remarks, "Powerful and disturbing, the story told with compassion and honesty." Finding the ending "unsettling" but "refreshingly realistic," Laura L. Lent writes in *Voice of*

Carter's award-winning *Up Country* focuses on a troubled sixteen-year old who attempts to straighten out his life by moving in with his aunt and uncle in the country. (Jacket illustration by Ellen Thompson.)

Youth Advocates that the book "keeps one's attention and leaves an ending that one can muse over for days."

In an autobiographical sketch written for the Putnam Publishing Group, Carter explains the origins of his desire to become a writer. As a child, after hearing his mother singing a song, he wrote a story about a retired race horse named Percy who runs one last race. When his sister cried listening to the story, Carter knew that he had to be a writer. He also relates why he has chosen to write for young adults: "I find myself constantly impressed with their courage. Despite all the problems—both traditional and recently invented—that fill the teenage years, the vast majority not only survive, but triumph. Their stories are far more dramatic than the tales I once imagined about pirates, cowboys, and an ill-starred race horse named Percy."

WORKS CITED:

Ackler, Susan, *Voice of Youth Advocates,* June, 1987, p. 75.
Baker, Stella, *Voice of Youth Advocates,* August, 1989, p. 155.
Bridgewater, Hope, *School Library Journal,* September, 1984, p. 126.
Bulletin of the Center for Children's Books, February, 1991, pp. 138-39.
Bryan, Janet, *School Library Journal,* May, 1987, p. 108.

Praised for its believable characters, Carter's *Sheila's Dying* tells of a teenager's relationship with a girlfriend who has terminal cancer. (Jacket illustration by Jacqueline Garrick.)

Carter, Alden R., "Alden Carter in His Own Words," Put-nam Publishing Group, October, 1987.

Chelton, Mary K., *Voice of Youth Advocates,* October, 1984, p. 195.

Hearne, Betsy, *Bulletin of the Center for Children's Books,* July/August, 1989, p. 486.

Hutcheson, Barbara, *School Library Journal,* June, 1989, p. 121.

Kirkus Reviews, November 1, 1985, p. 1197; June 15, 1989, p. 915.

Lent, Laura L., *Voice of Youth Advocates,* December, 1990, p. 277.

McDermott, Leone, *Booklist,* November 15, 1990, p. 653.

Publishers Weekly, May 8, 1987, p. 72.

Sutherland, Zena, *Bulletin of the Center for Children's Books,* July/August, 1987.

Twichell, Ethel R., *Horn Book,* August, 1984, pp. 473-74.

Unsworth, Robert, *School Library Journal,* February, 1986, pp. 93-94.

Vasilakis, Nancy, *Horn Book,* July/August, 1989, p. 486.

Wilson Library Bulletin, November, 1985, p. 47.

Zvirin, Stephanie, *Booklist,* June 1, 1987, pp. 1514-15.

FOR MORE INFORMATION SEE:

BOOKS

Children's Literature Review, Volume 22, Gale, 1991.

Carter's *Robodad* centers on the relationship between Shar, a slightly overweight adolescent, and her father, who has suffered a debilitating stroke. (Jacket illustration by Jacqueline Garrick.)

PERIODICALS

Booklist, July, 1984; May 1, 1985; November 15, 1985; June 1, 1986; December 1, 1988; October 1, 1989.

Booktalker, September, 1989.

English Journal, November, 1984; October, 1986; April, 1989.

Kirkus Reviews, October 1, 1988.

Los Angeles Times Book Review, November 20, 1988.

School Library Journal, August, 1985; August, 1986; March, 1988; May, 1988; May, 1989; November, 1989.

Voice of Youth Advocates, December, 1985; April, 1990.

*   *   *

CARTER, Nick
See STRATEMEYER, Edward L.

*   *   *

CHADWICK, Lester
[Collective pseudonym]

WRITINGS:

"BASEBALL JOE" SERIES

Baseball Joe of the Silver Stars; or, The Rivals of Riverside, Cupples & Leon, 1912.

Baseball Joe on the School Nine; or, Pitching for the Blue Banner, Cupples & Leon, 1912.

Baseball Joe at Yale; or, Pitching for the College Championship, Cupples & Leon, 1913.

Baseball Joe in the Central League; or, Making Good as a Professional Pitcher, Cupples & Leon, 1914.

Baseball Joe in the Big League; or, A Young Pitcher's Hardest Struggles, Cupples & Leon, 1915.

Baseball Joe on the Giants; or, Making Good as a Twirler in the Metropolis, Cupples & Leon, 1916.

Baseball Joe in the World Series; or, Pitching for the Championship, Cupples & Leon, 1917.

Baseball Joe around the World; or, Pitching on a Grand Tour, Cupples & Leon, 1918.

Baseball Joe, Home Run King; or, The Greatest Pitcher and Batter on Record, Cupples & Leon, 1922.

Baseball Joe Saving the League; or, Breaking up a Great Conspiracy, Cupples & Leon, 1923.

Baseball Joe, Captain of the Team; or, Bitter Struggles on the Diamond, Cupples & Leon, 1924.

Baseball Joe, Champion of the League; or, The Record That Was Worth While, Cupples & Leon, 1925.

Baseball Joe, Club Owner; or, Putting the Home Town on the Map, Cupples & Leon, 1926.

Baseball Joe, Pitching Wizard; or, Triumphs on and off the Diamond, Cupples & Leon, 1928.

"COLLEGE SPORTS" SERIES

The Rival Pitchers: A Story of College Baseball, Cupples & Leon, 1910.

A Quarterback's Pluck: A Story of College Football, Cupples & Leon, 1910.

Batting to Win: A Story of College Baseball, Cupples & Leon, 1911.

The Winning Touchdown: A Story of College Football, Cupples & Leon, 1911.

For the Honor of Randall: A Story of College Athletics, Cupples & Leon, 1912.

The Eight-Oared Victors: A Story of College Water Sports, Cupples & Leon, 1913.

SIDELIGHTS: Joe Matson, best known as "Baseball Joe," was the most popular sports figure featured in the books written under the Lester Chadwick pseudonym. The fourteen volumes in this series, according to to Arthur Prager in *Rascals at Large; or, The Clue in the Old Nostalgia,* chronicled Joe's rise "up the Stratemeyer ladder from sand-lot ball to the New York Giants and on to immortality breaking every extant record on the way." Joe ended his career as captain of the Giants, leading the National League in both pitching and hitting, and retired to his hometown of Riverside to manage a semi-professional ball club of his own. Publisher's advertisements sometimes carried the notice that " Mr. Chadwick has played on the diamond and on the gridiron himself."

Howard Garis and Edward Stratemeyer both used this pseudonym to produce sports stories. See the *SATA* index for more information on Harriet S. Adams, Howard R. Garis, Edward L. Stratemeyer, and Andrew E. Svenson.

WORKS CITED:

Johnson, Deidre, editor and compiler, *Stratemeyer Pseudonyms and Series Books: An Annotated Checklist of Stratemeyer and Stratemeyer Syndicate Publications,* Greenwood Press, 1982, p. 76.
Prager, Arthur, "The Saturday Heroes," *Rascals at Large; or, The Clue in the Old Nostalgia,* Doubleday, 1971, pp. 267-303.

FOR MORE INFORMATION SEE:

BOOKS

Garis, Roger, *My Father Was Uncle Wiggily,* McGraw-Hill, 1966.

PERIODICALS

Sports Illustrated, April 23, 1962.

*   *   *

CHAPMAN, Allen
[Collective pseudonym]

WRITINGS:

Bound to Rise; or, The Young Florists of Spring Hill [and] *Walter Loring's Career* (*Bound to Rise* originally serialized in *Bright Days,* 1896, under title "The Young Florists of Spring Hill; or, The New Heliotrope" by Albert Lee Ford; *Walter Loring's Career* originally serialized in *Bright Days,* 1896, under title "For Name and Fame; or, Walter Loring's Strange Quest"), Mershon, 1899.

"BOYS OF BUSINESS" SERIES

The Young Express Agent; or, Bart Stirling's Road to Success (also see below), Cupples & Leon, 1906, later published as part of the "Allen Chapman" series under title *Bart Stirling's Road to Success; or, The Young Express Agent* (also see below) by Goldsmith, and as part of the "Success" series under title *The Young Express Agent* by Donohue.
Two Boy Publishers; or, From Typecase to Editor's Chair (also see below), Cupples & Leon, 1906, later published as part of the "Allen Chapman" series under title *Working Hard to Win; or, Adventures of Two Boy Publishers* (also see below) by Goldsmith, and as part of the

Originally published in 1906, *The Young Express Agent* is the first in the "Boys of Business" series about young success stories.

"Success" series under title *Two Boy Publishers* by Donohue.
Mail Order Frank; or, A Smart Boy and His Chances (also see below), Cupples & Leon, 1907, later published as part of the "Allen Chapman" series under title *Bound to Succeed; or, Mail-Order Frank's Chances* (also see below) by Goldsmith.
A Business Boy; or, Winning Success (also see below), Cupples & Leon, 1908, later published as part of the "Allen Chapman" series under title *The Young Storekeeper; or, A Business Boy's Pluck* (also see below) by Goldsmith, and as part of the "Success" series under title *A Business Boy's Pluck* by Donohue.

"BOYS OF PLUCK" SERIES

The Young Express Agent; or, Bart Stirling's Road to Success, Cupples & Leon, 1906.
Two Boy Publishers; or, From Typecase to Editor's Chair, Cupples & Leon, 1906.
Mail Order Frank; or, A Smart Boy and His Chances, Cupples & Leon, 1907.
A Business Boy's Pluck; or, Winning Success, Cupples & Leon, 1908.
The Young Land Agent; or, The Secret of the Borden Estate, Cupples & Leon, 1911, later published as part of the "Allen Chapman" series under title *Nat Borden's Find;*

or, The Young Land Agent (also see below) by Goldsmith.

"BOY'S POCKET LIBRARY" SERIES

The Heroes of the School; or, The Darewell Chums through Thick and Thin (originally published as *The Darewell Chums; or, The Heroes of the School;* also see below), Cupples & Leon, 1917.

Ned Wilding's Disappearance; or, The Darewell Chums in the City (originally published as *The Darewell Chums in the City; or, The Disappearance of Nat Wilding;* also see below), Cupples & Leon, 1917.

Frank Roscoe's Secret; or, The Darewell Chums in the Woods (originally published as *The Darewell Chums in the Woods; or, Frank Roscoe's Secret;* also see below), Cupples & Leon, 1917.

Fenn Masterson's Discovery; or, The Darewell Chums on a Cruise (originally published as *The Darewell Chums on a Cruise; or, Fenn Masterson's Odd Discovery;* also see below), Cupples & Leon, 1917.

Bart Keene's Hunting Days; or, The Darewell Chums in a Winter Camp (originally published as *The Darewell Chums in a Winter Camp; or, Bart Keene's Best Shot;* also see below), Cupples & Leon, 1917.

Bart Stirling's Road to Success; or, The Young Express Agent, Cupples & Leon, 1917.

Working Hard to Win; or, Adventures of Two Boy Publishers, Cupples & Leon, 1917.

Bound to Succeed; or, Mail-Order Frank's Chances, Cupples & Leon, 1917.

The Young Storekeeper; or, A Business Boy's Pluck, Cupples & Leon, 1917.

Nat Borden's Find; or, The Young Land Agent, Cupples & Leon, 1917.

"DAREWELL CHUMS" SERIES

The Darewell Chums; or, The Heroes of the School, Cupples & Leon, 1908.

The Darewell Chums in the City; or, The Disappearance of Nat Wilding, Cupples & Leon, 1908, later published as part of the "Success" series under title *The Darewell Chums in the City* by Donohue.

The Darewell Chums in the Woods; or, Frank Roscoe's Secret, Cupples & Leon, 1908.

The Darewell Chums on a Cruise; or, Fenn Masterson's Odd Discovery, Cupples & Leon, 1909.

The Darewell Chums in a Winter Camp; or, Bart Keene's Best Shot, Cupples & Leon, 1911.

"FRED FENTON ATHLETIC SERIES"

Fred Fenton, the Pitcher; or, The Rivals of Riverport School, Cupples & Leon, 1913.

Fred Fenton in the Line; or, The Football Boys of Riverport School, Cupples & Leon, 1913.

Fred Fenton on the Crew; or, The Young Oarsmen of Riverport School, Cupples & Leon, 1913.

Fred Fenton on the Track; or, The Athletes of Riverport School, Cupples & Leon, 1913.

Fred Fenton, Marathon Runner; or, The Great Race at Riverport School, Cupples & Leon, 1915.

"RADIO BOYS" SERIES

The Radio Boys' First Wireless; or, Winning the Ferberton Prize, Grosset & Dunlap, 1922.

The Radio Boys at Ocean Point; or, The Message That Saved the Ship, Grosset & Dunlap, 1922.

The Radio Boys at the Sending Station; or, Making Good in the Wireless Room, Grosset & Dunlap, 1922.

The Radio Boys at Mountain Pass; or, The Midnight Call for Assistance, Grosset & Dunlap, 1922.

The Radio Boys Trailing a Voice; or, Solving a Wireless Mystery, Grosset & Dunlap, 1922.

The Radio Boys with the Forest Rangers; or, The Great Fire on Spruce Mountain, Grosset & Dunlap, 1923.

The Radio Boys with the Iceberg Patrol; or, Making Safe the Ocean Lanes, Grosset & Dunlap, 1924.

The Radio Boys with the Flood Fighters; or, Saving the City in the Valley, Grosset & Dunlap, 1925.

The Radio Boys on Signal Island; or, Watching for the Ships of Mystery, Grosset & Dunlap, 1926.

The Radio Boys in Gold Valley; or, The Mystery of the Deserted Mining Camp, Grosset & Dunlap, 1927.

The Radio Boys Aiding the Snowbound; or, Starvation Days at Lumber Run, Grosset & Dunlap, 1928.

The Radio Boys on the Pacific; or, Shipwrecked on an Unknown Island, Grosset & Dunlap, 1929.

The Radio Boys to the Rescue; or, The Search for the Barmore Twins, Grosset & Dunlap, 1930.

"RALPH OF THE RAILROAD" SERIES

Ralph of the Roundhouse; or, Bound to Become a Railroad Man (also see below), Mershon, 1906.

Ralph in the Switch Tower; or, Clearing the Track (also see below), Mershon, 1907.

Frontispiece from 1922 edition of *The Radio Boys' First Wireless*, the beginning of an adventure series featuring young radio enthusiasts.

Ralph on the Engine; or, The Young Fireman of the Limited Mail (also see below), Grosset & Dunlap, 1909.

Ralph on the Overland Express; or, The Trials and Triumphs of a Young Engineer (also see below), Grosset & Dunlap, 1910.

Ralph, the Train Dispatcher; or, The Mystery of the Pay Car, Grosset & Dunlap, 1911.

Ralph on the Army Train; or, The Young Railroader's Most Daring Exploit, Grosset & Dunlap, 1918.

Ralph on the Midnight Flyer; or, The Wreck at Shadow Valley, Grosset & Dunlap, 1923.

Ralph and the Missing Mail Pouch; or, The Stolen Government Bonds, Grosset & Dunlap, 1924.

Ralph on the Mountain Division; or, Fighting both Flames and Flood, Grosset & Dunlap, 1927.

Ralph and the Train Wreckers; or, The Secret of the Blue Freight Cars, Grosset & Dunlap, 1928.

Ralph on the Railroad: Four Complete Adventure Books for Boys in One Big Volume (contains *Ralph of the Roundhouse, Ralph in the Switch Tower, Ralph on the Engine,* and *Ralph on the Overland Express*), Grosset & Dunlap, 1933.

"TOM FAIRFIELD" SERIES

Tom Fairfield's School Days; or, The Chums of Elmwood Hall, Cupples & Leon, 1913.

Tom Fairfield at Sea; or, The Wreck of the Silver Star, Cupples & Leon, 1913.

Tom Fairfield in Camp; or, The Secret of the Old Mill, Cupples & Leon, 1913.

Tom Fairfield's Pluck and Luck; or, Working to Clear His Name, Cupples & Leon, 1913.

Tom Fairfield's Hunting Trip; or, Lost in the Wilderness, Cupples & Leon, 1915.

OTHER

Also pseudonym for *The Young Builders of Swiftdale,* for Chatterton Peck. Contributor to periodical *Bright Days.*

SIDELIGHTS: Two of the series produced under this pseudonym, the "Ralph of the Railroad" stories and the "Radio Boys" books, were based on mechanical and electronic inventions. Ralph Fairbanks was the hero of the "Ralph of the Railroad" series, which "centered around the Great Northern Railroad, a beleaguered line sorely beset with spies, 'sorehead strikers' and unscrupulous competitors who used every kind of skullduggery to wreck its schedules," according to Arthur Prager in *Rascals at Large; or, The Clue in the Old Nostalgia.* The Radio Boys were four young men, Bob Layton, Joe Atwood, Jimmy Plummer, and Herbert Fennington, all of whom evinced an interest in radio, encouraged by their local pastor Dr. Dale. "It wasn't easy to build thrills around stationary apparatus instead of zippy vehicles, but the boys did very well," says Prager. He continues, "Of course, there were chases and daring rescues, and attempts by infamous bullies to destroy the boys' apparatus, but the wonders of wireless, as explained by genial Dr. Dale, launched the boys on thirteen volumes of fun and adventure."

Some sources state that this pseudonym was used by Stratemeyer writer W. Bert Foster. See the *SATA* index for more information on Harriet S. Adams, Edward L. Stratemeyer, and Andrew E. Svenson.

WORKS CITED:

FOR MORE INFORMATION SEE:

Prager, Arthur, "Peril: The Mother of Invention," *Rascals at Large; or, The Clue in the Old Nostalgia,* Doubleday, 1971, pp. 127-65.

BOOKS

Dizer, John T., *Tom Swift & Company: "Boy's Books" by Stratemeyer and Others,* McFarland & Co., 1982.

Johnson, Deidre, editor and compiler, *Stratemeyer Pseudonyms and Series Books: An Annotated Checklist of Stratemeyer and Stratemeyer Syndicate Publications,* Greenwood Press, 1982.

McFarlane, Leslie, *Ghost of the Hardy Boys,* Two Continents, 1976.

*   *   *

CHAPPELL, Warren 1904-1991

OBITUARY NOTICE—See index for *SATA* sketch: Born July 9, 1904, in Richmond, VA; died of heart failure, March 26, 1991, in Charlottesville, VA. Graphic artist, illustrator, and author. Chappell's illustrations graced many books for both children and adults. With author John Updike, he produced books for children that retold stories from famous operas. He also designed the Lydian and Trajanus typefaces, and published several books on graphic design, including *The Anatomy of Lettering* and *A Short History of the Printed Word.* His later works include illustrations for Rainer Maria Rilke's *The Lay of the Love and Death of Cornet Christoph Rilke,* Robert Frost's *Stories for Lesley,* and Catherine Drinker Bowen's *Miracle at Philadelphia.*

OBITUARIES AND OTHER SOURCES:

BOOKS

Something about the Author Autobiography Series, Volume 10, Gale, 1990.

Who's Who in the World, 10th edition, Marquis, 1990.

PERIODICALS

Chicago Tribune, March 31, 1991, section 2, p. 7.
New York Times, March 29, 1991, p. D6.

*   *   *

CHARLES, Louis
See STRATEMEYER, Edward L.

*   *   *

CHILD, L. Maria
See CHILD, Lydia Maria

*   *   *

CHILD, Lydia Maria 1802-1880
(L. Maria Child, Mrs. Child)

PERSONAL: Born February 11, 1802, in Medford, MA; died October 20, 1880, in Wayland, MA; daughter of Convers (a baker and real-estate broker) and Susannah (a baker; maiden name, Rand) Francis; married David Lee Child (a

LYDIA MARIA CHILD

farmer, lawyer, legislator, writer, and editor), October 19, 1828 (died September 18, 1874). *Politics:* Abolitionist/Feminist.

CAREER: Schoolteacher, writer, and editor. Taught school in Gardiner, ME, 1820-21, Watertown, MA, 1826-27, and Dorchester Heights, MA, 1830.

WRITINGS:

Hobomok: A Tale of Early Times (novel; also see below), Cummings, Hilliard, 1824.

Evenings in New England: Intended for Juvenile Amusement and Instruction, Cummings, Hilliard, 1824.

The Rebels; or, Boston before the Revolution (novel), Cummings, Hilliard, 1825, revised edition, Phillips, Sampson, 1850.

Emily Parker; or, Impulse, Not Principle: Intended for Young Persons, Bowles & Dearborn, 1827.

(Editor and contributor) *The Juvenile Souvenir,* Putnam, 1827.

Biographical Sketches of Great and Good Men: Designed for the Amusement and Instruction of Young Persons, Putnam & Hunt, 1828.

The First Settlers of New-England; or, Conquest of the Pequods, Narragansets and Pokanokets: As Related by a Mother to Her Children, and Designed for the Instruction of Youth, by a Lady of Massachusetts, Charles S. Francis, 1829.

The Frugal Housewife (handbook), Carter & Hendee, 1829, published as *The American Frugal Housewife* beginning with the 8th edition, reprinted, Apple-Wood Books, 1985.

The Little Girl's Own Book (handbook), Carter, Hendee & Babcock, 1831, revised edition, Carter & Hendee, 1834, published as *Girls Own Book,* Apple-Wood Books, 1990.

The Mother's Book (handbook), Carter, Hendee & Babcock, 1831, revised edition, Charles S. Francis, 1844, reprinted, Apple-Wood Books, 1989.

The Coronal: A Collection of Miscellaneous Pieces, Written at Various Times, Carter & Hendee, 1832, enlarged edition with stories by Mary Howitt and Caroline Fry published as *The Mother's Story Book; or, Western Coronal: A Collection of Miscellaneous Pieces,* T. T. & J. Tegg, 1833.

The Biographies of Madame de Stael and Madame Roland (also see below), Carter & Hendee, 1832, reprinted in part as *The Biography of Madame de Stael,* Thomas Clark, 1836, revised and enlarged version of original 1832 edition published as *Memoirs of Madame de Stael and of Madame Roland,* Charles S. Francis, 1847.

The Biographies of Lady Russell and Madame Guyon (also see below), Carter & Hendee, 1832, reprinted in part as *The Biography of Lady Russell,* Thomas Clark, 1836.

Good Wives (also see below), Carter & Hendee, 1833, published as *Biographies of Good Wives,* Charles S. Francis, 1846, published as *Celebrated Women; or, Biographies of Good Wives,* Charles S. Francis, 1861, published as *Married Women: Biographies of Good Wives,* Charles S. Francis, 1871.

An Appeal in Favor of that Class of Americans Called Africans (essay), Allen & Ticknor, 1833, reprinted, Ayer Company, 1968.

(Editor and contributor) *The Oasis,* Allen & Ticknor, 1834.

The History of the Condition of Women in Various Ages and Nations (originally published as the fourth and fifth volumes of *The Ladies' Family Library;* also see below), two volumes, John Allen, 1835, reprinted as *Brief History of the Condition of Women in Various Ages and Nations,* two volumes, Charles S. Francis, 1845.

The Happy Grandmother [and] *The White Palfrey,* Darton & Clark, c. 1835.

Anti-Slavery Catechism, Charles Whipple, 1836.

Philothea: A Romance (novel), Otis, Broaders, 1836, published as *Philothea: A Grecian Romance,* Charles S. Francis, 1845.

The Evils of Slavery and the Cure of Slavery: The First Proved by the Opinions of Southerners Themselves, the Last Shown by Historical Evidence, Charles Whipple, 1836.

The Family Nurse; or, Companion of the Frugal Housewife, Charles J. Hendee, 1837.

(Editor) *Memoir of Benjamin Lay: Compiled from Various Sources,* American Anti-Slavery Society, 1842.

(Editor) *American Anti-Slavery Almanac,* American Anti-Slavery Society, 1843.

Letters from New-York (essays), Charles S. Francis, 1843, revised edition, 1844.

Flowers for Children (short stories and poetry; includes poem "Boy's Thanksgiving" [also see below]), three volumes, Charles S. Francis, 1844-1847, Volume 1 published separately as *The Christ-Child, and Other Stories,* D. Lothrop, 1869, Volume 2 published separately as *Good Little Mitty, and Other Stories,* D. Lothrop, 1869, Volume 3 published separately as *Making Something, and Other Stories,* D. Lothrop, 1869.

Letters from New-York: Second Series (essays), Charles S. Francis, 1845.

Fact and Fiction: A Collection of Stories, Charles S. Francis, 1846, reprinted as *The Children of Mt. Ida, and Other Stories,* 1871.

THE

AMERICAN

FRUGAL HOUSEWIFE.

DEDICATED TO

THOSE WHO ARE NOT ASHAMED OF ECONOMY.

BY MRS. CHILD,

AUTHOR OF "HOBOMOK," "THE MOTHER'S BOOK," EDITOR OF THE
"JUVENILE MISCELLANY," &c.

A fat kitchen maketh a lean will.—FRANKLIN.

"Economy is a poor man's revenue; extravagance a rich man's ruin."

TWELFTH EDITION.

ENLARGED AND CORRECTED BY THE AUTHOR.

BOSTON:
CARTER, HENDEE, AND CO.
1832.

Chock full of tips for economical household management, *The American Frugal Housewife* **was Child's most popular advice book, reprinted more than thirty times.**

Sketches from Real Life (contains "The Power of Kindness" and "Home and Politics"), Hazard & Mitchell, 1850, published as *The Power of Kindness, and Other Stories,* Willis P. Hazard, 1853.

Isaac T. Hopper: A True Life, John P. Jewett, 1853.

The Progress of Religious Ideas through Successive Ages (essays), three volumes, Charles S. Francis, 1855.

A New Flower for Children, Charles S. Francis, 1856.

Autumnal Leaves: Tales and Sketches in Prose and Rhyme, Charles S. Francis, 1857.

The Duty of Disobedience to the Fugitive Slave Act: An Appeal to the Legislators of Massachusetts, American Anti-Slavery Society, 1860.

(Compiler) *The Patriarchal Institution, as Described by Members of Its Own Family,* American Anti-Slavery Society, 1860.

(Editor and author of preface) Linda Brent (pseudonym of Harriet A. Jacobs) *Incidents in the Life of a Slave Girl,* privately published, 1861, published as *The Deeper Wrong; or, Incidents in the Life of a Slave Girl,* Tweedie, 1862, reprinted, Harcourt, 1973.

The Right Way, the Safe Way, Proved by Emancipation in the British West Indies and Elsewhere, [New York], 1860, reprinted, Ayer Company, 1969.

(Editor and contributor) *Looking toward Sunset, from Sources Old and New, Original and Selected,* Ticknor & Fields, 1865.

(Editor and contributor) *The Freedmen's Book,* Ticknor & Fields, 1865, reprinted, Ayer Company, 1968.

A Romance of the Republic (novel), Ticknor & Fields, 1867, published as *Rose and Flora,* two volumes, Routledge, 1867.

An Appeal for the Indians, William P. Tomlinson, 1868.

(Compiler and author of introduction) *Aspirations of the World: A Chain of Opals,* Roberts, 1878.

Letters of Lydia Maria Child, Houghton, 1883, reprinted, Ayer Company, 1969.

Over the River and through the Wood (adapted from Child's 1844 poem "Boy's Thanksgiving"), illustrated by Brinton Turkle, Coward, McCann & Geoghegan, 1974, revised edition, illustrated by Iris Van Rynbach, Little, Brown, 1989.

Lydia Maria Child: Selected Letters, 1817-1880 (part of the "New England Writers" series), edited by Milton

Meltzer and Patricia G. Holland, University of Massachusetts Press, 1982.

Hobomok and Other Writings on Indians (part of the "American Women Writers" series; includes short novel *Hobomok: A Tale of Early Times,* four short stories, and various letters and essays), edited with introduction by Carolyn L. Karcher, Rutgers University Press, 1986.

Some works published under names L. Maria Child and Mrs. Child. Also author of *The Ladies' Family Library* (includes *The Biographies of Lady Russell, and Madame Guyon, The Biographies of Madame de Stael and Madame Roland, Married Women: Biographies of Good Wives,* and *The History of the Condition of Women in Various Ages and Nations*), five volumes, 1832-1835. Presumed author of series of publications titled *Authentic Anecdotes of American Slavery,* and the book *The Childrens' Gems, The Brother and Sister, and Other Stories,* New Church Book Store, 1852. Contributor to books, including *The Legendary,* edited by Nathaniel P. Willis, Samuel G. Goodrich, 1828, and *The Liberty Bell,* Anti-Slavery Fair, 1843. Child's letters are included in the pamphlet *Correspondence between Lydia Maria Child and Gov. Wise and Mrs. Mason of Virginia,* American Anti-Slavery Society, 1860.

Founder and editor of *Juvenile Miscellany* (bimonthly magazine), 1826-34, and editor of *National Anti-Slavery Standard* during the 1840s. Contributor to periodicals, including *Atlantic Monthly, Columbian Lady's and Gentleman's Magazine,* and the *New York Tribune.*

Child's work has been translated into German.

SIDELIGHTS: A prolific writer for both children and adults, Lydia Maria Child is best remembered for her controversial work supporting vast social reforms. Child, unlike many women in the early to mid-nineteenth century, openly voiced her opinions in favor of the fair treatment of Native Americans, the abolition of slavery, and women's rights to vote and own property. Child's staunch stance on such issues, however, frequently affected her popularity as an author, since her views concerning civil rights were considered very liberal at the time. For example, she began writing abolitionist literature nearly thirty years before the start of the Civil War—an American conflict that arose between the northern and southern states, in part, over the issue of slavery. Today, Child is regarded as a woman who was ahead of her time, even though her success in her day was often marred by the public's disapproval of her politics.

Born in Medford, Massachusetts, in 1802 as Lydia Maria Francis, Child was raised in a family setting that stressed work and domesticity more than education. Child, who preferred to be called Maria, developed a fascination with books and school, much to the chagrin of her father. When she was twelve, Child was sent to live with her older sister, who had recently wed, after their mother died. Child's father hoped that a change in his young daughter's living environment would help her become more interested in homemaking. Such notions only fueled her enthusiasm for learning and reading. She also developed a belief in equality between men and women—principles that she would later weave into her writings.

Casting aside the idea of becoming a homemaker, Child aspired to become a schoolteacher. She obtained her first job as an educator in Gardiner, Maine, in 1820. But finding the small town lacking in the cultural offerings of the big city, she

moved to Watertown, Massachusetts, in 1822. There she resided with her brother Convers, who had broken family tradition by attending Harvard University. Convers had become a Unitarian minister and introduced his sister to his intellectual friends, including writers Ralph Waldo Emerson and John Greenleaf Whittier. Within several years, Child had written her first book, *Hobomok: A Tale of Early Times.*

The novel tells the story of an interracial marriage between a white woman and an Indian man. While other writers in the 1820s explored similar themes in their work, Child took a different approach—her characters did not suffer any adversity as a result of their forbidden love affair. A number of conservative reviewers at the time of *Hobomok*'s release were appalled by the story because it concerned love between people of different races. A *North American Review* critic noted, "To our minds there is a very considerable objection to . . . this story. . . . [The] train of events not only unnatural, but revolting, we conceive, to every feeling of delicacy in man or woman." However, Jared Sparks, also writing in the *North American Review,* reevaluated the book the following year. Although he noted his dislike of its controversial subject matter, he praised the writing in *Hobomok.* The positive review won Child acceptance in the literary world and helped her launch a writing career that spanned more than fifty years.

Child continued writing novels for adults, including 1825's *The Rebels; or, Boston before the Revolution.* She also found time to prepare stories for children. Her first book for younger audiences was 1824's *Evenings in New England: Intended for Juvenile Amusement and Instruction.* In 1826, Child began a magazine for children called *Juvenile Miscellany.* Child served as editor of the publication—the first of its kind in the United States—until 1834. While editing the periodical, she also wrote other volumes for children and prepared several handbooks for mothers and daughters. The most popular of these advice books was *The Frugal Housewife,* which was first published in 1829. The work contains tips for economical household management and has been reprinted more than thirty times.

In 1828, Child married fellow writer David Lee Child. By the early 1830s, she showed her feminist views in her work as she compiled biographies of notable women, including eighteenth-century French writer Anne-Louise-Germaine de Stael and eighteenth-century French revolutionary Jeanne-Marie Roland de la Platiere. She also authored *The History of the Condition of Women in Various Ages and Nations,* which was praised by numerous women's rights activists as it called for sexual equality. Modern critics have said that Child's introduction to the book was especially noteworthy since she argued against the common nineteenth-century notion that women were not as intelligent as men. She also criticized eighteenth-century English poet Lord Byron for the sexist attitudes he exhibited in his work. She wrote that Byron "would limit a woman's library to a Bible and a cookery book."

As Child wrote about women, she also became involved in the issue of slavery. Both Child and her husband believed slavery was immoral and should be abolished. Such views in the United States in the 1830s were controversial since slave labor was used extensively in the South, especially as a means to inexpensively harvest crops on plantations. The industrial North, however, had already abolished slavery and wanted the practice stopped in the South as well. The argument over slavery would become so intense by the 1860s that it would contribute to the beginning of the Civil War. Child's

First printed in 1844 as "The Boy's Thanksgiving," Child's *Over the River and through the Wood* **has become a classic Thanksgiving poem.** (Illustrated by Brinton Turkle.)

abolitionist stance in the 1830s alarmed many of her readers and negatively affected the sales of her books and magazines.

Child's first book devoted to the slavery issue was 1834's *An Appeal in Favor of that Class of Americans Called Africans.* The work called for immediate freedom and equality for slaves. Child was aware that her readership might be hesitant to accept her viewpoint and included the following statement in her preface: "I am fully aware of the unpopularity of the task I have undertaken, but though I *expect* ridicule and censure, it is not in my nature to *fear* them." The public response, however, was to boycott her work, including her well-received magazine, *Juvenile Miscellany.* As a result, Child turned over the editorship of the publication. The magazine eventually folded in 1836. Child had authored numerous anti-slavery articles for her children's magazine but had never experienced such public disapproval. The 1834 boycott of her work occurred only one year after G. Mellen praised Child's writings on behalf of the editors of *North American Review.* Asserting that Child was one of the best women writers in the country, Mellen noted that "this lady has long been before the public as an author, with much success. And she well deserves it,—for in all her work—we think that nothing can be found, which does not commend itself by its tone of healthy morality, and generally by its good sense."

In spite of the controversy, Child continued to stress the need for social reform in her books and articles. Her *Philothea: A Romance* of 1836 deals with feminist themes, while a number of her books maintain anti-slavery themes. She also penned various abolitionist tracks and pamphlets. In 1841, she moved to New York City and began editing the newspaper *National Anti-Slavery Standard.* She resigned, however, two years later after a disagreement with her publisher William Lloyd Garrison, who sought to end slavery through radical means. David Child then edited the publication for one year while his wife returned to writing literature. In 1843 she published *Letters from New-York,* a book containing articles she had written for the *Standard.* According to Carolyn L. Karcher in the *Dictionary of Literary Biography,* "Even today critics consider these freewheeling journalistic sketches, which launched a genre many women writers would adopt, to be Child's finest work." She published a second volume two years later.

Meanwhile, in 1844, Child wrote *Flowers for Children.* This work contains the poem "Boy's Thanksgiving," with the famous opening line "Over the river and through the wood." She then started the nonfictional *The Progress of Religious Ideas through Successive Ages,* which was published in 1855. During this time, she also cared for her ill father, who later died in 1856. In addition, Child and her husband remained active in their anti-slavery work and even helped fugitive slaves escape to freedom.

Child's correspondence with Virginia Governor Wise on behalf of radical abolitionist John Brown was published in 1860. Brown had been injured and sentenced to death after he led a raid on a federal arsenal in Harper's Ferry, Virginia. At the time of his arrest, he was attempting to capture the armory's weapons and lead a revolt of slaves. After Brown's capture, Child wrote the governor and asked if she could serve as his nurse. Their letters were published as *Correspondence between Lydia Maria Child and Gov. Wise and Mrs. Mason of Virginia.*

Just prior to the advent of the Civil War, Child helped fund the publication of slaves' autobiographies, including Linda Brent's *Incidents in the Life of a Slave Girl.* At the Civil War's conclusion in 1865, Child penned *The Freedmen's Book,* a guide to help former slaves adjust to life as free citizens. Since slavery was abolished, she again turned to writing about the fair treatment of the Indians who were being forced from their native lands by the government. Until her death in 1880, Child continued to fight for social reform, especially the right to vote for women and blacks. In a letter to friend Francis George Shaw, reprinted in *Dictionary of Literary Biography,* Child summed up her reasons for advocating social reforms in her writings, especially her 1867 novel *A Romance of the Republic:* "Having fought against slavery till I saw it go down ... I wanted to do something to undermine prejudice; and there is such a universal passion for novels, that more can be done in that way, than by the ablest arguments, and the most serious exhortations."

WORKS CITED:

Child, Lydia Maria, *An Appeal in Favor of that Class of Americans Called Africans,* Allen & Ticknor, 1833.
Child, Lydia Maria, *The History of the Condition of Women in Various Ages and Nations,* two volumes, John Allen, 1835.
Karcher, Carolyn L., "Lydia Maria Child," *Dictionary of Literary Biography,* Volume 74, *American Short-Story Writers before 1880,* Gale, 1988.
Mellen, G., "Works of Mrs. Child," *North American Review,* July, 1833, pp. 138-164.
North American Review, July, 1824, pp. 262-263.
Sparks, Jared, review of *Hobomok: A Tale of Early Times, North American Review,* July, 1825, pp. 86-95.

FOR MORE INFORMATION SEE:

BOOKS

Baer, Helene G., *The Heart Is Like Heaven: The Life of Lydia Maria Child,* University of Pennsylvania Press, 1964.
Blanck, Jacob, *Bibliography of American Literature,* Yale University Press, 1957.
Meltzer, Milton, editor, *Tongue of Flame: The Life of Lydia Maria Child,* Crowell, 1965.
Meltzer, Milton, and Patricia G. Holland, editors, *Lydia Maria Child: Selected Letters, 1817-1880,* University of Massachusetts Press, 1982.
Nineteenth-Century Literature Criticism, Volume 6, Gale, 1984.
Osborne, William S., *Lydia Maria Child,* Twayne, 1980.

PERIODICALS

AB Bookman Weekly, November 26, 1990.
Women' Studies International Forum, Volume 9, number 4, 1986.

Sketch by Kathleen J. Edgar

*   *   *

CHILD, Mrs.
See CHILD, Lydia Maria

COERR, Eleanor (Beatrice) 1922-
(Eleanor B. Hicks, Eleanor Page)

PERSONAL: Born May 29, 1922, in Kamsack Saskatchewan, Canada; daughter of William Thomas (a druggist) and Mabel (Selig) Page; married Wymberley De Renne Coerr (a diplomat and U.S. ambassador to South American Countries), June 10, 1965. *Education:* Attended University of Saskatchewan; graduated from Kadel Airbrush School, 1945; American University, B.Z. 1969; University of Maryland, M.L.S., 1971. *Religion:* Protestant.

CAREER: Edmonton Journal, Edmonton, Alberta, Canada, reporter and editor, 1944-49; *Advertiser-Journal,* Montgomery, AL, editorial post, 1953-58; *Manila Times,* Manila, Republic of the Philipines, editorial post, 1958-60; U.S. Information Service, Taipei, Taiwan, editor, 1960-62; Voice of America Special English Division, Washington, DC, contributing editor, 1963-65; Davis Memorial Library, Bethesda, MD, librarian, 1971-72; writer. Lecturer at Chapman and Monterey Peninsula colleges. Visiting author to schools, organizations, and reading councils in the United States and other countries.

AWARDS, HONORS: West Australia Book Award and OMAR Award, both 1982, both for *Sadako and the Thousand Paper Cranes.*

WRITINGS:

UNDER NAME ELEANOR PAGE; SELF-ILLUSTRATED

Snoopy, Institute of Applied Art, 1945.

UNDER NAME ELEANOR B. HICKS; SELF-ILLUSTRATED

Circus Day in Japan, Tuttle, 1954.

SELF-ILLUSTRATED

The Mystery of the Golden Cat, Tuttle, 1968.

ELEANOR COERR

Coerr's self-illustrated *The Mystery of the Golden Cat* depicts wooden houses on high stilts along both sides of a busy Oriental waterway.

PUBLISHED BY PUTNAM

Biography of a Giant Panda, illustrated by Kazue Mizumura, 1974.
Biography of a Kangaroo, illustrated by Linda Powell, 1976.
The Mixed-up Mystery Smell, illustrated by Tomie de Paola, 1976.
Biography of Jane Goodall, illustrated by Kees de Kiefte, 1976.
Sadako and the Thousand Paper Cranes, illustrated by Ronald Himler, 1977.
Waza Wins at Windy Gulch, illustrated by Janet McCaffery, 1977.
(With William E. Evans) *Gigi: A Baby Whale Borrowed for Science and Returned to the Sea,* 1980.

OTHER

Twenty-five Dragons, illustrated by Joann Daley, Follet, 1971.
The Big Balloon Race, illustrated by Carolyn Croll, Harper, 1981.
The Bell Ringer and the Pirates, illustrated by Joan Sandin, Harper, 1983.
The Josefina Story Quilt, illustrated by Bruce Degen, Harper, 1986.
Lady with a Torch: How the Statue of Liberty Was Born, illustrated by Oscar de Mejo, Harper, 1986.
Chang's Paper Pony, illustrated by Deborah K. Ray, Harper, 1989.

Contributor of articles to periodicals, including to the *Monterey Peninsula Herald;* editor of *CAT Bulletin* (travel magazine), 1958-60.

Sadako and the Thousand Paper Cranes has been translated into Swedish and German.

SIDELIGHTS: Eleanor Coerr once told *SATA:* "I have been interested in children's books since I read them as a child, and somehow the interest grew as the years rolled on. Producing short stories for youngsters satisfies my urge to write for about seven years, after which journeys to other parts of the world gave me the opportunity to gather information suitable for books about foreign countries. A total of nine years in the Orient supplied the material for *Circus Day in Japan, The Mystery of the Golden Cat,* and *Twenty-five Dragons.* In these books I have tried to give as much information as possible about the children who live in Japan, Thailand, and Taiwan, so that the reader might gain an authentic picture of life in the Orient.

"When my husband was Ambassador to Ecuador, I had the unique opportunity of establishing the first children's library in that country. I hope, if we go abroad again, to help put books in the hands of youngsters who might otherwise never know the joys a library has to offer."*

*   *   *

COLMAN, Warren (David) 1944-

PERSONAL: Born June 4, 1944 in St. Paul, MN; son of Maurice (an executive) and Judith (a homemaker; maiden name, Mogelson) Colman; married Barri Golbus (an accountant), August 21, 1967; children: Alison, Jocelyn, Dina. *Education:* Northwestern University, B.S.J., 1966, M.S.J., 1967.

WARREN COLMAN

ADDRESSES: Home and office—4137 Chester Dr., Glenview, IL 60025.

CAREER: Colman Communications Corp., president. Scriptwriter, producer, director, and author.

MEMBER: Authors Guild, Sigma Delta Chi.

WRITINGS:

The Constitution, Childrens Press, 1987.
The Bill of Rights, Childrens Press, 1987.
Understanding and Preventing AIDS, Childrens Press, 1988.
Understanding and Preventing Teen Suicide, Childrens Press, 1990.
Double Dutch and the Voodoo Shoes, Childrens Press, 1991.

Also author of scripts for motion pictures, videos, filmstrips, and industry and cable markets.

WORK IN PROGRESS: A fictional work, *A La Barca Bean in Brooklyn,* 1991; and an untitled screenplay.

SIDELIGHTS: Warren Colman told *SATA:* "I started writing books late in my career. For almost twenty years, I was a scriptwriter, producer, and director. I have always been fascinated with the relationship between words and pictures, and it has excited me to see my words come to life on the screen.

"To date, most of my work has been nonfiction, which requires more analytical thinking skills than imagination. As I grow older, however, I find nonfiction more and more confining. My first two fictional works have been extremely enjoyable to work on. For the first time, an important part of my personality—my imagination—has been allowed to come to the fore.

"I approach writing from two perspectives—one creative, the other business. To me, there's no purpose to writing unless a large number of people read (or hear or see) what you have to say. For that to happen, a publisher must decide to publish your manuscript. So if a writer wants to be published, he or she has to write about something that a publisher thinks people will want to read. In other words, the publisher has to be convinced a lot of people will buy the book. I write about things I believe lots of people will be interested in.

"The creative perspective is a lot more fun. Once my publisher and I decide on a topic, I try to write about it in a way people will find both enjoyable and interesting. How do I do that? I write about it in a way *I* find enjoyable and interesting. Hopefully, if it works for me, it will work for a lot of other people. Above all, I try to please myself. To do that, however, I have to be very tough on myself—I generally write five or six drafts before my editor looks at what I've written.

"The best thing about being a writer is that it allows you to come in contact with many different kinds of interesting people. I've conversed with presidents, diplomats, business leaders, scientists, actors and actresses, and common folk all over the world—in Asia, Europe, South America, and the Middle East. I've worked in palatial surroundings and in mud huts in Brazil.

"Writing is very hard work, but it does have its rewards."

OLGA COSSI

COSSI, Olga

PERSONAL: Name is pronounced "all-ga cah-see"; born in St. Helena, CA; daughter of Orlando (an olive oil manufacturer) and Filomena (a homemaker; maiden name, Micheli) Della Maggiora; married Don Cossi (in construction); children: Tamara Frishberg, Caren Franci, Donald. *Education:* Graduated from Palmer School of Authorship.

ADDRESSES: Home and office—800 H Ave., Coronado, CA 92118.

CAREER: Writer. Affiliated with "Meet the Author" program, San Diego County Schools, Authors' Fair, California Reading Association, and "Year of the Lifetime Reader" speakers' forum; teacher of writing workshops. Former staff correspondent and columnist for regional newspapers.

MEMBER: Society of Children's Book Writers, National Women's History Project, Gualala Arts, Inc., Gualala Community Center.

AWARDS, HONORS: Received honors at the California Media and Library Educators Association Authors Breakfast, 1990; *The Magic Box* was named one of the Books for the Teen Age, New York Public Library, 1991.

WRITINGS:

FOR JUVENILES

Robin Deer, Naturegraph, 1967.
Fire Mate, Independence Press, 1977, reissued, Council for Indian Education, 1988.
Gus the Bus, Scholastic, 1989.
Orlanda and the Contest of Thieves, Bookmakers Guild, 1989, Pelican, 1991.
The Wonderful Wonder-Full Donkey, Windswept House Publishers, 1989.
Harp Seals (nonfiction), Carolrhoda, 1990.
The Magic Box, Pelican Publishing, 1990.
The Great Getaway, Gareth Stevens, 1990.
Adventure on the Graveyard of the Wrecks, Pelican Publishing, 1991.

Contributor to periodicals, including *Christian Science Monitor, Young American,* and *Science Fiction Chronicle.*

WORK IN PROGRESS: On the Move, publication expected in 1991; *Fresh Water,* publication expected in 1991 or 1992; *Fat Girl,* publication expected in 1992; research on national water problems and waste treatment.

SIDELIGHTS: Olga Cossi told *SATA:* "As a native Californian, I grew up in the small town of St. Helena in the heart of Napa Valley. I always felt that I was different and that my independence was worth a price. I have been swimming upstream ever since.

"I can't remember when I didn't write. When I was in elementary school, my older sister talked me into reading all the books and doing all the book reports for her high school English class. One day she came home and told me I had to write a book. I tried to argue, but she was my big sister. So I went to work, choosing poetry as the form. My sister not only got an 'A' on the assignment, but the text was so well received it was made into a book, with her name as author, of course. She got the credit, but I got a solid background in good literature that turned out to be a wonderful gift. Even today, this sister continues to be a strong and important influence in my writing career.

"While still in school I worked on the local newspaper and discovered that I had printer's ink in my veins. I loved working with words, using them to make facts stand out clearly or weaving them together to form pictures.

"Later I managed to combine being a wife and mother with a job as a staff correspondent and columnist for the regional newspapers. This work and parenting gave me a rich collection of story ideas. Eventually I found time to write my first book, *Robin Deer.* By then, I was really into words and began a five-year study I called 'linguistic archeology.'

"For this study, I delved into the roots of words, especially key words on which great religions and nations were founded and great wars and civilizations carried forth. I literally dug through ancient Hebrew and Greek texts, using phonics as my basis, seeking the connection between the oral root or idea behind the word and the meaning that evolved. This study turned out to be a most exciting adventure. Sometimes I would work all night tracing a word to discover what it might have meant in the beginning. At the end of five years, I was ready to write my second book.

"*Fire Mate* was written on the beach at Mazatlan, using what I had learned about the phonetical connection of words to give the text a deeper meaning. I would carry my thesaurus, binders, and a stack of dictionaries with me and pile them on a towel spread on the sand. Within a few minutes, I was surrounded by native children as fascinated with me as I was with them. They taught me Spanish and I taught them English. Their eyes lit up when I showed them Spanish words in the unabridged dictionary that I took everywhere with me, especially when I let them touch the printed pages. How they loved and respected those books! So did I.

"When I got to the sad part in *Fire Mate,* I cried as I wrote, feeling deeply the emotions experienced by the main character, Yvonne, whose Indian name is Walakea. The children looked at me not understanding. How could I explain to them that my characters were real to me? I suffered and enjoyed with them. When a character comes into my mind, he or she takes over the story and tells it. I watch it happen, writing it down as I see it. I don't know exactly what a character will do next, what will happen next. Sometimes it is hard work to make the story go the way I want it to go.

"This independence of my characters makes writing exciting. It is like watching television. I am certain that my mind has a built-in television set. In fact, I am sure everyone has, especially children. As we grow up, we forget it's there or use it so little that it becomes rusty. But it is a very important part of

Cossi's *Magic Box* is about a girl's basketball team and its quest for a state championship.

our experiences. It is a way we can learn to program our lives by turning that built-in television set on or off and choosing what we view.

"For eleven years my family and I lived and traveled in a converted bus, crisscrossing the United States five times. We spent lots of time in Alaska as well as all of Mexico and parts of Canada. Everywhere I went, I attracted and was attracted to children. I wrote every morning, using my time with them to sharpen my imagination.

"When we finally settled down in Coronado, California, I began marketing my stories. Suddenly, within about two years I had six new books accepted for publication. In addition, *Fire Mate* was reissued in paperback by the Council for Indian Education. I was off and running.

"*Gus the Bus* is a fun-to-read story about a school bus that gets a set of heavy-duty radial tires and begins doing things it is not supposed to do. The idea came to me when we had our huge converted bus parked beside our house. The children who saw it couldn't get over the size of the tires. So Gus was born.

"*Orlanda and the Contest of Thieves* is my version of a story told to me by my father. He was a great storyteller. His name was Orlando, so I named the main character Orlanda and had a lot of fun writing about her, and the mayor's clever wife, and the crafty street thieves with their outrageous attempts to win the contest.

"*The Magic Box* is a young adult novel about girls' basketball. It is a strong story about the players and their friendships, their family relationships, and about the competition to win a State Championship trophy.

"*Adventure on the Graveyard of the Wrecks* is based on a real California adventure that took place on an isolated beach. The story has a dramatic climax involving a near drowning. Young readers will learn something about glass fishing floats that are found washed up on shore after a big storm. And they will also learn about Indian middens.

"*Harp Seals* is my only nonfiction to date. I worked twelve years on this story about the unique 'whitecoats' and life on the ice fields where they are born. The illustrations are actual photos and are so appealing.

"*The Great Getaway,* a fun-to-read picture book, is about two little sisters who run away from home. They make it all the way around the block before making a big discovery.

"I visit schools and libraries throughout California to spend time with young readers, hold writing workshops, or autograph books. So far, I have not charged for any of this time. It is my way of contributing to the children who will be running the United States in the near future. I want them to be as imaginative, open-minded, and responsive as possible. I want them to remain children at heart no matter how many birthdays they experience.

"Remaining a child at heart is the key to becoming a worthwhile adult. It is the spark of life that responds to others. It makes living fun, no matter what. I am fortunate that the child in me continues to imagine stories and to write."

RICHIE TANKERSLEY CUSICK

CUSICK, Richie Tankersley 1952-

PERSONAL: Born April 1, 1952, in New Orleans, LA; daughter of Dick (a petroleum engineer) and Louise (a homemaker; maiden name, Watts) Tankersley; married Rick Cusick (a book designer, calligrapher, and graphic artist), October 4, 1980. *Education:* University of Southwestern Louisiana, B.A., 1975. *Hobbies and other interests:* Animals, reading, watching movies, listening to music (country, ethnic, pop, soundtracks), collecting, travel.

ADDRESSES: Home and office—7501 Westgate, Lenexa, KS 66216. *Agent*—Mary Jack Wald Associates, Inc., Literary Representatives, 111 East 14th St., New York, NY 10003.

CAREER: Ochsner Foundation Hospital, New Orleans, LA, ward clerk, summers, 1970-72; Hallmark Cards, Inc., Kansas City, MO, writer, 1975-84; free-lance writer.

MEMBER: Humane Society of the United States, National Wildlife Federation, Doris Day Animal League.

AWARDS, HONORS: Children's Choice Award, IRA, 1989, for *The Lifeguard; Trick or Treat* was named a Book for the Teen Age by the New York Public Library, 1990.

WRITINGS:

HORROR NOVELS

Evil on the Bayou, Dell, 1984.
The Lifeguard, Scholastic, 1988.
Trick or Treat, Scholastic, 1989.
April Fools, Scholastic, 1990.
Scarecrow, Pocket Books, 1990.
Teacher's Pet, Scholastic, 1990.
Vampire, Pocket Books, 1991.
Fatal Secrets, Pocket Books, 1992.
Blood Roots, Pocket Books, 1992.

WORK IN PROGRESS: A young adult book and another book, both for Pocket Books, 1992 and 1993.

SIDELIGHTS: Richie Tankersley Cusick commented: "I've always believed in the supernatural, and I grew up with a ghost in my house. I've always loved scary books and movies—even though my parents didn't want me to watch horror films. I'd sometimes manage to sneak in and turn on the TV when my folks weren't in the room. In Girl Scouts I was the troop storyteller and would make up tales of haunted houses and murderers. Next to Christmas, Halloween is my favorite holiday, and I really decorate—including a hanged woman in our front hallway, a dead body laid out in our parlor, and tombstones around our front porch.

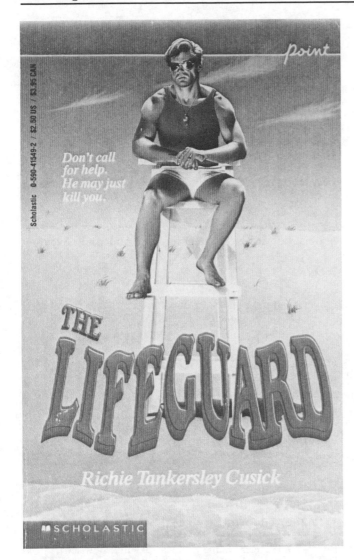

Richie Tankersley Cusick writes her horror novels, such as *The Lifeguard,* at a rolltop desk that belonged to a funeral director in the 1800s.

"I still feel my Southern roots deeply, even though my parents were originally from the Midwest. I was born and raised in New Orleans but spent summers and holidays with all my grandparents and great-grandparents in southern Missouri. At Great-Grandma Watts's house I would make up stories out loud to myself and accompany them with my own 'soundtracks,' which I would bang out on the piano (I couldn't play then, and I still can't). At Great-Grandma McClure's house I would make up stories and recite them aloud, even though she kept coming in and asking me who I was talking to. At Granny and Grandpa Watts's I would spend long summer days writing on the banks of the Gasconade River, fishing, exploring, and playing guitar and writing my own songs. At Grandma and Grandpa Tankersley's house I would write for hours in what I called my 'attic room'—which was really in the basement.

"I've always loved to write—being an only child, I found it a great way to entertain myself and invent friends and adventures. My best buddies and mentors were my dog and my grandmother Dereatha Tankersley. She has always been my biggest inspiration. She's young at heart and always open to new experiences. She has a way of looking at the world with total wonder and never takes anything for granted. She loves

to read and is a great writer. She always has time for kindness and encouragement, and she has always believed in me. She has the most beautiful heart and spirit. I will always cherish her.

"I was very fortunate as a child to be so encouraged to read. My father (and grandmother) made up stories, and my mother always made sure we had time set aside to just sit and enjoy our books together. Two of my uncles were songwriters. I'll always be grateful to my seventh-grade reading and spelling teacher, Maxwell Yerger, for being the very first outside my family to really encourage my creativity. It's so important to have teachers like that—those who make you realize your potential and encourage you to fulfill it.

"I love working at home. I'm happiest being with my husband and our cocker spaniel, Hannah (fondly referred to as the Dog from Hell). My studio is upstairs at the back of our house, and my favorite tree, Emily (yes, I name all our trees), stands guard outside my window. I love storms, rain, fog, and dark winter weather; my favorite part of the day is twilight, that dream state between dark and light. I love to watch the seasons change on Emily as I sit and write at my haunted rolltop desk, which belonged to a funeral director in the 1800s.

Cusick writes about one of her favorite holidays in her Halloween novel, *Trick or Treat.*

"The hardest part of writing is going up to my studio. Once I'm up there, I can lose myself in my research and writing and am very comfortable surrounded by all my clutter. But getting up there is the procrastination I'm best at—my husband refers to it as 'the long walk upstairs.'

"Writing is very important to me—being able to create people, adventures, worlds where readers can lose themselves for a little while. It's very hard work, but very rewarding. I hate it when a book ends and I have to tell my characters goodbye. I get so close to them that they linger in my own personality for days . . . and I guess when it comes right down to it, I never really lose them. They just become another part of me . . . or perhaps they were all along!"

FOR MORE INFORMATION SEE:

PERIODICALS

Kansas City Star, December 13, 1990.

* * *

DARLING, Sandra
See DAY, Alexandra

* * *

DAWSON, Elmer A.
[Collective pseudonym]

WRITINGS:

"BUCK AND LARRY" BASEBALL STORIES

The Pick-up Nine; or, The Chester Boys on the Diamond, Grosset & Dunlap, 1930.
Buck's Winning Hit; or, The Chester Boys Making a Record, Grosset & Dunlap, 1930.
Larry's Fadeaway; or, The Chester Boys Saving the Nine, Grosset & Dunlap, 1930.
Buck's Home Run Drive; or, The Chester Boys Winning against Odds, Grosset & Dunlap, 1931.
Larry's Speedball; or, The Chester Boys and the Diamond Secret, Grosset & Dunlap, 1932.

"GARRY GRAYSON" FOOTBALL STORIES

Garry Grayson's High Street Eleven; or, The Football Boys of Lenox, Grosset & Dunlap, 1926.
Garry Grayson at Lenox High; or, The Champions of the Football League, Grosset & Dunlap, 1926.
Garry Grayson's Football Rivals; or, The Secret of the Stolen Signals, Grosset & Dunlap, 1926.
Garry Grayson Showing His Speed; or, A Daring Run on the Gridiron, Grosset & Dunlap, 1927.
Garry Grayson at Stanley Prep; or, The Football Rivals of Riverview, Grosset & Dunlap, 1927.
Garry Grayson's Winning Kick; or, Battling for Honor, Grosset & Dunlap, 1928.
Garry Grayson Hitting the Line; or, Stanley Prep on a New Gridiron, Grosset & Dunlap, 1929.
Garry Grayson's Winning Touchdown; or, Putting Passmore Tech on the Map, Grosset & Dunlap, 1930.
Garry Grayson's Double Signals; or, Vanquishing the Football Plotters, Grosset & Dunlap, 1931.
Garry Grayson's Forward Pass; or, Winning in the Final Quarter, Grosset & Dunlap, 1932.

SIDELIGHTS: The sports stories produced under the pseudonym Elmer A. Dawson included the "Garry Grayson" series. Garry, described by Arthur Prager in *Rascals at Large; or, The Clue in the Old Nostalgia* as "an athletic male Nancy Drew, perfect and infallible," was about fourteen years old when the series began. The books themselves, continues Prager, were "long detailed chronicles like the games in [Lester Chadwick's] Baseball Joe series. Plot was unimportant, shoved in to give us a breather between halves. Most of the plots were lifted from other Stratemeyer series. There were frame-ups, missing money, fathers faced with ruin, abduction of stars before the game, and all the tried and true situations [found in other Stratemeyer Syndicate work]."

See the *SATA* index for more information on Harriet S. Adams, Edward L. Stratemeyer, and Andrew E. Svenson.

WORKS CITED:

Prager, Arthur, "The Saturday Heroes," *Rascals at Large; or, The Clue in the Old Nostalgia,* Doubleday, 1971, pp. 267-303.

FOR MORE INFORMATION SEE:

BOOKS

Johnson, Deidre, editor and compiler, *Stratemeyer Pseudonyms and Series Books: An Annotated Checklist of Stratemeyer and Stratemeyer Syndicate Publications,* Greenwood Press, 1982.

* * *

DAY, Alexandra
(Sandra Darling)

PERSONAL: Real name Sandra Darling; married Harold Darling; children: four. *Education:* Trained as an artist.

ADDRESSES: *Office*—Blue Lantern Studio, P.O. Box 8009, San Diego, CA 92102.

CAREER: Children's author and illustrator under pseudonym Alexandra Day. Green Tiger Press (children's book publishing company), San Diego, CA, founder and owner with husband, Harold Darling, 1970-86; Blue Lantern Studio, San Diego, owner with H. Darling. Designer of note cards and stationery.

AWARDS, HONORS: Children's Choice Award, International Reading Association and Children's Book Council, 1984, for *The Teddy Bears' Picnic;* Parents' Choice Award for Illustration, 1984, for *The Blue Faience Hippopotamus.*

WRITINGS:

SELF-ILLUSTRATED

Good Dog, Carl, Green Tiger, 1985.
Frank and Ernest, Scholastic Inc., 1988.
Carl Goes Shopping, Farrar, Straus, 1989.
Paddy's Pay-Day, Viking, 1989.
Frank and Ernest Play Ball, Scholastic Inc., 1990.
Carl's Christmas, Farrar, Straus, 1990.
River Parade, Viking, 1990.

Illustrator and author Sandra Darling is known to her readers as Alexandra Day.

ILLUSTRATOR

Jimmy Kennedy, *The Teddy Bears' Picnic* (book and record set), Green Tiger, 1983.

Joan Marshall Grant, *The Blue Faience Hippopotamus,* Green Tiger, 1984.

Cooper Edens, *Children of Wonder,* Volume 1: *Helping the Sun,* Volume 2: *Helping the Animals,* Volume 3: *Helping the Flowers,* Volume 4: *Helping the Night,* Green Tiger, 1987.

Ned Washington, *When You Wish upon a Star,* Green Tiger, 1987.

OTHER

(Editor with Welleran Poltarnees) *A. B. C. of Fashionable Animals,* Green Tiger, 1989.

SIDELIGHTS: Alexandra Day is recognized for her inventive animal stories and her lifelike, detailed illustrations. Born into a family of artists, Day trained in the profession from an early age. Later, as the mother of four children, she combined her artistic talent with, as her biographical note from Scholastic reads, "a special sensitivity to the themes that young people find amusing."

By 1984 Day had attained recognition in her field for illustrating the award-winning *Teddy Bears' Picnic* and *Blue Faience Hippopotamus.* A year later she wrote and illustrated *Good Dog, Carl,* the first of her books featuring a huge rottweiler that takes care of a baby while the mother is gone. In *Good Dog,* "Carl and the baby entertain themselves by wrecking the house," wrote Teresa Moore in the *Washington Post Book World.* Antics in 1989's *Carl Goes Shopping* include treks through various sections of a department store: in ladies' accessories Carl and the baby try on hats and gloves,

in the pet section they free all the animals, and in the book shop they look at *Rottweilers I Have Known.* Day uses little text in these books and relies on individual drawings to relate her stories. Her illustrations are "intensely realistic," declared *Horn Book*'s Ellen Fader, and offer "the most pinchable baby and pettable dog of the season."

In 1988 Day wrote and illustrated her first book about Frank and Ernest, a bear and an elephant that take care of various businesses while the owners are away. The animal pair's amusing ventures include running a diner in *Frank and Ernest* and managing a baseball team in *Frank and Ernest Play Ball.* Again reviewers praised Day's drawings and especially noted her eye for detail: in *Frank and Ernest,* for example, Day attaches a British flag to the top of an English muffin. Day also incorporates wordplay in the books—Frank and Ernest learn both "diner-ese" and baseball lingo. "Young readers will have fun with the language," noted Susan Stan in her *Five Owls* review of *Frank and Ernest Play Ball,* while Trev Jones in *School Library Journal* called *Frank and Ernest* "clever and original."

WORKS CITED:

Biographical note from Scholastic Inc.

Fader, Ellen, review of *Carl Goes Shopping, Horn Book,* January, 1990, p. 50.

Jones, Trev, review of *Frank and Ernest, School Library Journal,* August, 1988, p. 80.

Moore, Teresa, "Area Booksellers Name Their Favorite Titles," *Washington Post Book World,* May 8, 1988, p. 16.

Stan, Susan, "Play Ball!," *Five Owls,* May-June, 1990, p. 95.

In *Carl Goes Shopping,* Day portrays the escapades of an infant and the family Rottweiler in a department store. (Illustration by the author.)

FOR MORE INFORMATION SEE:

BOOKS

Children's Literature Review, Volume 22, Gale, 1991.

PERIODICALS

Booklist, January 1, 1990; May 1, 1990.
Bulletin of the Center for Children's Books, September, 1988;
    January, 1990.
Entertainment Weekly, June 1, 1990.
Kirkus Reviews, November 15, 1989.
Publishers Weekly, June 24, 1988; February 24, 1989.
School Library Journal, November, 1989; February, 1990.*

*   *   *

DIXON, Franklin W.
[Collective pseudonym]

WRITINGS:

"HARDY BOYS MYSTERY STORIES" SERIES

The Tower Treasure (also see below), Grosset & Dunlap,
    1927, revised edition, 1959, facsimile of original edition,
    Applewood Books, 1991.
The House on the Cliff (also see below), Grosset & Dunlap,
    1927, revised edition, 1959, facsimile of original edition,
    Applewood Books, 1991.
The Secret of the Old Mill (also see below), Grosset &
    Dunlap, 1927, revised edition, 1962, facsimile of original
    edition, Applewood Books, 1991.
The Missing Chums, Grosset & Dunlap, 1928, revised edi-
    tion, 1962.
Hunting for Hidden Gold, Grosset & Dunlap, 1928, revised
    edition, 1963.
The Shore Road Mystery, Grosset & Dunlap, 1928, revised
    edition, 1964.
The Secret of the Caves, Grosset & Dunlap, 1929, revised
    edition, 1965.
The Mystery of Cabin Island, Grosset & Dunlap, 1929,
    revised edition, 1966.
The Great Airport Mystery, Grosset & Dunlap, 1930, revised
    edition, 1965.
What Happened at Midnight, Grosset & Dunlap, 1931, re-
    vised edition, 1967.
While the Clock Ticked, Grosset & Dunlap, 1932, revised
    edition, 1962.
Footprints under the Window, Grosset & Dunlap, 1933, re-
    vised edition, 1965.
The Mark on the Door, Grosset & Dunlap, 1934, revised
    edition, 1967.
The Hidden Harbor Mystery, Grosset & Dunlap, 1935, re-
    vised edition, 1961.
The Sinister Signpost, Grosset & Dunlap, 1936, revised edi-
    tion, 1968.
A Figure in Hiding, Grosset & Dunlap, 1937, revised edition,
    1965.
The Secret Warning, Grosset & Dunlap, 1938, revised edi-
    tion, 1966.
The Twisted Claw, Grosset & Dunlap, 1939, revised edition,
    1969.
The Disappearing Floor, Grosset & Dunlap, 1940, revised
    edition, 1964.
The Mystery of the Flying Express, Grosset & Dunlap, 1941,
    revised edition, 1970.
The Clue of the Broken Blade, Grosset & Dunlap, 1942,
    revised edition, 1970.

**Teenage sleuths Frank and Joe Hardy remain popular
with readers more than sixty years after their creation.** (Frontispiece from *The House on the Cliff* by
Franklin W. Dixon.)

The Flickering Torch Mystery, Grosset & Dunlap, 1943,
    revised edition, 1971.
The Melted Coins, Grosset & Dunlap, 1944, revised edition,
    1970.
The Short-Wave Mystery, Grosset & Dunlap, 1945, revised
    edition, 1966.
The Secret Panel, Grosset & Dunlap, 1946, revised edition,
    1969.
The Phantom Freighter, Grosset & Dunlap, 1947, revised
    edition, 1970.
The Secret of Skull Mountain, Grosset & Dunlap, 1948,
    revised edition, 1966.
The Sign of the Crooked Arrow, Grosset & Dunlap, 1949,
    revised edition, 1970.
The Secret of the Lost Tunnel, Grosset & Dunlap, 1950,
    revised edition, 1968.
The Wailing Siren Mystery, Grosset & Dunlap, 1951, revised
    edition, 1968.
The Secret of Wildcat Swamp, Grosset & Dunlap, 1952,
    revised edition, 1969.
The Crisscross Shadow, Grosset & Dunlap, 1953, revised
    edition, 1969.
The Yellow Feather Mystery, Grosset & Dunlap, 1953, re-
    vised edition, 1971.
The Hooded Hawk Mystery, Grosset & Dunlap, 1954, revised
    edition, 1971.

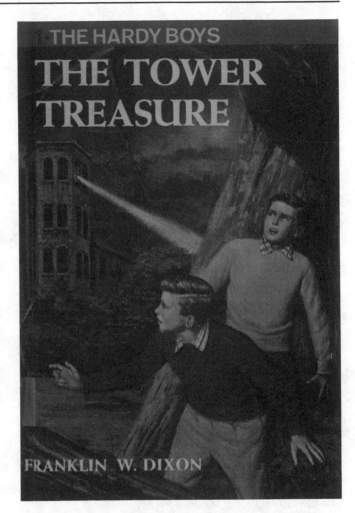

Sons of the world-famous detective Fenton Hardy, Frank and Joe help their father solve many thrilling cases after school hours. (Cover from *The Secret of the Lost Tunnel,* by Dixon.)

In *The Tower Treasure,* the Hardy Boys solve the mystery surrounding a dying criminal's loot in an old tower.

The Clue in the Embers, Grosset & Dunlap, 1955, revised edition, 1972.

The Secret of Pirates' Hill, Grosset & Dunlap, 1957, revised edition, 1972.

The Ghost at Skeleton Rock, Grosset & Dunlap, 1958, revised edition, 1966.

The Mystery at Devil's Paw, Grosset & Dunlap, 1959, revised edition, 1973.

The Mystery of the Chinese Junk, Grosset & Dunlap, 1960.

The Mystery of the Desert Giant, Grosset & Dunlap, 1961.

The Clue of the Screeching Owl, Grosset & Dunlap, 1962.

The Viking Symbol Mystery, Grosset & Dunlap, 1963.

The Mystery of the Aztec Warrior, Grosset & Dunlap, 1964.

The Haunted Fort, Grosset & Dunlap, 1965.

The Mystery of the Spiral Bridge, Grosset & Dunlap, 1966.

The Secret Agent on Flight 101, Grosset & Dunlap, 1967.

The Mystery of the Whale Tattoo, Grosset & Dunlap, 1968.

The Arctic Patrol Mystery, Grosset & Dunlap, 1969.

The Bombay Boomerang, Grosset & Dunlap, 1970.

Danger on Vampire Trail, Grosset & Dunlap, 1971.

The Masked Monkey, Grosset & Dunlap, 1972.

The Shattered Helmet, Grosset & Dunlap, 1973.

The Clue of the Hissing Serpent, Grosset & Dunlap, 1974.

The Mysterious Caravan, Grosset & Dunlap, 1975.

The Witchmaster's Key, Grosset & Dunlap, 1976.

The Jungle Pyramid, Grosset & Dunlap, 1977.

The Firebird Rocket, Grosset & Dunlap, 1978.

The Sting of the Scorpion, Grosset & Dunlap, 1979.

Night of the Werewolf, Wanderer, 1979.

Mystery of the Samurai Sword, Wanderer, 1979.

The Pentagon Spy, Wanderer, 1979.

The Apeman's Secret, Wanderer, 1980.

The Mummy Case, Wanderer, 1980.

Mystery of Smuggler's Cove, Wanderer, 1980.

The Stone Idol, Wanderer, 1981.

The Vanishing Thieves, Wanderer, 1981.

The Outlaw's Silver, Wanderer, 1981.

Deadly Chase, Wanderer, 1981.

The Four-Headed Dragon, Wanderer, 1981.

The Infinity Clue, Wanderer, 1981.

Track of the Zombie, Wanderer, 1982.

The Voodoo Plot, Wanderer, 1982.

The Billion Dollar Ransom, Wanderer, 1982.

Tic-Tac-Terror, Wanderer, 1982.

Trapped at Sea, Wanderer, 1982.

Game Plan for Disaster, Wanderer, 1982.

The Crimson Flame, Wanderer, 1983.

Cave-In!, Wanderer, 1983.

Sky Sabotage, Wanderer, 1983.

The Roaring River Mystery, Wanderer, 1984.

The Demon's Den, Wanderer, 1984.

The Blackwing Puzzle, Wanderer, 1984.

The Swamp Monster, Wanderer, 1985.

Revenge of the Desert Phantom, Wanderer, 1985.
The Skyfire Puzzle, Wanderer, 1985.
The Mystery of the Silver Star, Minstrel, 1987.
Program for Destruction, Minstrel, 1987.
Tricky Business, Minstrel, 1988.
The Sky Blue Frame, Minstrel, 1988.
Danger on the Diamond, Minstrel, 1988.
Shield of Fear, Minstrel, 1988.
The Shadow Killers, Minstrel, 1988.
The Serpent's Tooth Mystery, Minstrel, 1988.
Breakdown in Axeblade, Minstrel, 1989.
Danger on the Air, Minstrel, 1989.
Wipeout, Minstrel, 1989.
Cast of Criminals, Minstrel, 1989.
Spark of Suspicion, Minstrel, 1989.
Dungeon of Doom, Minstrel, 1989.
The Secret of the Island Treasure, Minstrel, 1990.
The Money Hunt, Minstrel, 1990.
Terminal Shock, Minstrel, 1990.
The Million Dollar Nightmare, Minstrel, 1990.
Tricks of the Trade, Minstrel, 1990.
The Smoke Screen Mystery, Minstrel, 1990.
Attack of the Video Villains, Minstrel, 1991.
Panic on Gull Island, Minstrel, 1991.
Fear on Wheels, Minstrel, 1991.
The Prime-Time Crime, Minstrel, 1991.
The Secret of Sigma Seven, Minstrel, 1991.
Three-Ring Terror, Minstrel, 1991.
The Demolition Mission, Minstrel, 1992.

"HARDY BOYS CASE FILES" SERIES

Dead on Target, Archway, 1986.
Evil, Inc., Archway, 1986.
Cult of Crime, Archway, 1986.
The Lazarus Plot, Archway, 1987.
Edge of Destruction, Archway, 1987.
The Crowning Terror, Archway, 1987.
Deathgame, Archway, 1987.
See No Evil, Archway, 1987.
The Genius Thieves, Archway, 1987.
Hostages of Hate, Archway, 1987.
Brother against Brother, Archway, 1988.
Perfect Getaway, Archway, 1988.
The Borgia Dagger, Archway, 1988.
Too Many Traitors, Archway, 1988.
Blood Relations, Archway, 1988.
Line of Fire, Archway, 1988.
The Number File, Archway, 1988.
A Killing in the Market, Archway, 1988.
Nightmare in Angel City, Archway, 1988.
Witness to Murder, Archway, 1988.
Street Spies, Archway, 1988.
Double Exposure, Archway, 1988.
Disaster for Hire, Archway, 1989.
Scene of the Crime, Archway, 1989.
The Borderline Case, Archway, 1989.
Trouble in the Pipeline, Archway, 1989.
Nowhere to Run, Archway, 1989.
Countdown to Terror, Archway, 1989.
Thick as Thieves, Archway, 1989.
The Deadliest Dare, Archway, 1989.
Without a Trace, Archway, 1989.
Blood Money, Archway, 1989.
Collision Course, Archway, 1989.
Final Cut, Archway, 1989.
The Dead Season, Archway, 1990.
Running on Empty, Archway, 1990.
Danger Zone, Archway, 1990.
Diplomatic Deceit, Archway, 1990.

Flesh and Blood, Archway, 1990.
Fright Wave, Archway, 1990.
Highway Robbery, Archway, 1990.
Last Laugh, Archway, 1990.
Strategic Moves, Archway, 1990.
Castle Fear, Archway, 1990.
In Self-Defense, Archway, 1990.
Foul Play, Archway, 1990.
Flight into Danger, Archway, 1991.
Rock 'n' Revenge, Archway, 1991.
Dirty Deeds, Archway, 1991.
Power Play, Archway, 1991.
Choke Hold, Archway, 1991.
Uncivil War, Archway, 1991.
Web of Horror, Archway, 1991.
Deep Trouble, Archway, 1991.
Beyond the Law, Archway, 1991.
Height of Danger, Archway, 1991.
Terror on Track, Archway, 1991.
Spiked!, Archway, 1991.
Open Season, Archway, 1992.
Deadfall, Archway, 1992.

"TED SCOTT FLYING STORIES" SERIES

Over the Ocean to Paris; or, Ted Scott's Daring Long Distance Flight, Grosset & Dunlap, 1927.
Rescued in the Clouds; or, Ted Scott, Hero of the Air, Grosset & Dunlap, 1927.
Over the Rockies with the Air Mail; or, Ted Scott Lost in the Wilderness, Grosset & Dunlap, 1927.
First Stop Honolulu; or, Ted Scott over the Pacific, Grosset & Dunlap, 1927.
The Search for the Lost Flyers; or, Ted Scott over the West Indies, Grosset & Dunlap, 1928.
South of the Rio Grande; or, Ted Scott on a Secret Mission, Grosset & Dunlap, 1928.
Across the Pacific; or, Ted Scott's Hop to Australia, Grosset & Dunlap, 1928.
The Lone Eagle of the Border; or, Ted Scott and the Diamond Smugglers, Grosset & Dunlap, 1929.
Flying against Time; or, Ted Scott Breaking the Ocean to Ocean Record, Grosset & Dunlap, 1929.
Over the Jungle Trails; or, Ted Scott and the Missing Explorers, Grosset & Dunlap, 1929.
Lost at the South Pole; or, Ted Scott in Blizzard Land, Grosset & Dunlap, 1930.
Through the Air to Alaska; or, Ted Scott's Search in Nugget Valley, Grosset & Dunlap, 1930.
Flying to the Rescue; or, Ted Scott and the Big Dirigible, Grosset & Dunlap, 1930.
Danger Trails of the Sky; or, Ted Scott's Great Mountain Climb, Grosset & Dunlap, 1931.
Following the Sun Shadow; or, Ted Scott and the Great Eclipse, Grosset & Dunlap, 1932.
Battling the Wind; or, Ted Scott Flying around Cape Horn, Grosset & Dunlap, 1933.
Brushing the Mountain Top; or, Aiding the Lost Traveler, Grosset & Dunlap, 1934.
Castaways of the Stratosphere; or, Hunting the Vanquished Balloonists, Grosset & Dunlap, 1935.
Hunting the Sky Spies; or, Testing the Invisible Plane, Grosset & Dunlap, 1941.
The Pursuit Patrol; or, Chasing the Platinum Pirates, Grosset & Dunlap, 1943.

WITH CAROLYN KEENE

Nancy Drew and the Hardy Boys: Super Sleuths! (short stories), Wanderer, Volume 1, 1981, Volume 2, 1984.

The first television adaptation of "The Hardy Boys," starring Tommy Kirk and Tim Considine, was aired on Walt Disney's "The Mickey Mouse Club Show" in 1956.

Parker Stevenson and Shaun Cassidy portrayed the sleuths in "The Hardy Boys/Nancy Drew Mysteries" which ran on ABC-TV from 1977 to 1979.

Nancy Drew and the Hardy Boys Camp Fire Stories, Wanderer, 1984.

Nancy Drew & the Hardy Boys Be a Detective Mystery Stories: The Secret of the Knight's Sword, edited by Betty Schwartz, Wanderer, 1984.

Nancy Drew & the Hardy Boys Be a Detective Mystery Stories: Danger on Ice, edited by Schwartz, Wanderer, 1984.

Nancy Drew & the Hardy Boys Be a Detective Mystery Stories: The Feathered Serpent, edited by Schwartz, Wanderer, 1984.

Nancy Drew & the Hardy Boys Be a Detective Mystery Stories: Secret Cargo, edited by Schwartz, Wanderer, 1984.

Nancy Drew & the Hardy Boys Be a Detective Mystery Stories: The Alaskan Mystery, edited by Diane Arico, Wanderer, 1985.

Nancy Drew & the Hardy Boys Be a Detective Mystery Stories: The Missing Money Mystery, edited by Arico, Wanderer, 1985.

Nancy Drew & the Hardy Boys Be a Detective Mystery Stories: Jungle of Evil, edited by Arico, Wanderer, 1985.

Nancy Drew & the Hardy Boys Be a Detective Mystery Stories: Ticket to Intrigue, edited by Arico, Wanderer, 1985.

The Hardy Boys are also featured in *The Nancy Drew/Hardy Boys Supermystery* series, published under the pseudonym Carolyn Keene.

OTHER

(With D. A. Spina) *The Hardy Boys' Detective Handbook* (short stories and police procedures), Grosset & Dunlap, 1959, revised edition, 1972.

The Tower Treasure, The House on the Cliff, [and] *The Secret of the Old Mill* (three-in-one reprint), Grosset & Dunlap, 1959.

(Contributor) Stephen Dunning and Henry B. Maloney, editors, *A Superboy, Supergirl Anthology: Selected Chapters from the Earlier Works of Victor Appleton, Franklin W. Dixon, and Carolyn Keene,* Scholastic Book Services, 1971.

The Hardy Boys and Nancy Drew Meet Dracula (based on episodes of "The Hardy Boys/Nancy Drew Mysteries"), Grosset & Dunlap, 1978.

The Haunted House and Flight to Nowhere (based on episodes of "The Hardy Boys/Nancy Drew Mysteries"; *Flight to Nowhere* adapted from *The Flickering Torch Mystery*), Grosset & Dunlap, 1978.

(With Sheila Link) *The Hardy Boys' Handbook: Seven Stories of Survival* (short stories), Wanderer, 1980.

The Hardy Boys' Who-Dunnit Mystery Book, Wanderer, 1980.

The Hardy Boys: Ghost Stories, edited by Schwartz, Wanderer, 1984.

Also author of *Hardy Boys Digest,* Pocket Books.

ADAPTATIONS: Walt Disney Productions filmed two Hardy Boys serials for the "Mickey Mouse Club Show." Both starred Tommy Kirk and Tim Considine as Frank and Joe Hardy: "The Hardy Boys," also known as "The Applegate Treasure," was loosely based on *The Tower Treasure,* and its first episode aired on October 1, 1956, on ABC-TV. An original story, not based on any of the series volumes, began September 30, 1957, on ABC; it was called "The Mystery of Ghost Farm." A pilot film, called "The Mystery of the Chinese Junk," and based on the series book of that title, was made for a series that never materialized. It was first broadcast on September 8, 1967, and starred Rick Gates as Frank and Tim Mathieson as Joe. Filmation Associates made an animated version of the Hardy Boys for the Saturday morning television market that starred the voices of Dallas McKennon, Jane Webb, and Byron Kane; the title of the show was "The Hardy Boys," and it ran on ABC from 1969-71. More recently, Parker Stevenson and Shaun Cassidy have portrayed the sleuths in "The Hardy Boys/ Nancy Drew Mysteries," which ran on ABC from 1977 to 1979, and then went into syndication.

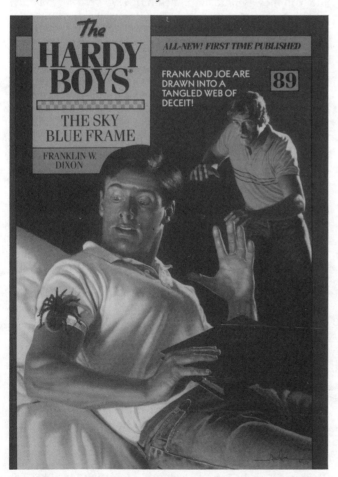

In the 1988 paperback original, *The Sky Blue Frame,* Frank and Joe are presented as savvy young men in a fast-paced world. (Cover illustration by Paul Bachem.)

The "Ted Scott Flying" series, based on the exploits of Charles Lindbergh, was another Dixon project launched in 1927. (Cover illustration by Walter S. Rogers.)

Three different Hardy Boys games have been published: *Walt Disney's Hardy Boys Treasure Game,* published by Walt Disney Productions and Parker Brothers in 1957; Milton Bradley's *The Hardy Boys Game,* linked to the Filmation series, 1969; and *The Secret of Thunder Mountain: The Hardy Boys Mystery Game,* published by Parker Brothers in 1978, and linked to the Parker Stevenson/Shaun Cassidy series. Recordings: Two original stories, "The Disco Conspiracy" and "The Mystery of the Missing Iceman," were recorded for Wonderland Records in 1978. The Cassette Book Company presently offers recordings of Frank and Joe's adventures, read by Eve Plumb.

Several comic books were released in conjunction with the Walt Disney serials. They were published by Dell from 1956 to 1959. Other comic books were published by Gold Key in 1970-71 in relation to the Filmation animated series. The Whitman Publishing Company brought out the first Hardy Boys coloring book in 1957; related to the Disney serial, it featured Tommy Kirk and Tim Considine on the cover. In 1977, at the time "The Hardy Boys/Nancy Drew Mysteries" were first broadcast, Grosset & Dunlap's imprint Treasure Books began publishing a variety of coloring and activity (puzzles, mazes, and word games) books featuring the Hardy Boys.

SIDELIGHTS: In 1927 Edward Stratemeyer, head of the productive literary syndicate that bore his name, proposed a new series to Leslie McFarlane, a Canadian journalist and free-lance writer who had worked for him on other titles. "He had observed . . . that detective stories had become very popular in the world of adult fiction. He instanced the works of S. S. Van Dine, which were selling in prodigious numbers as I was well aware," McFarlane reminisces in *Ghost of the Hardy Boys.* "It had recently occurred to him . . . that the growing boys of America might welcome similar fare." Stratemeyer enclosed an outline of the first volume in the new series, which he wanted McFarlane to write. "What Stratemeyer had in mind was a series of detective stories on the juvenile level, involving two brothers of high-school age who would solve such mysteries as came their way," McFarlane continues. "To lend credibility to their talents, they would be the sons of a professional private investigator, so big in his field that he had become a sleuth of international fame. His name—Fenton Hardy. His sons, Frank and Joe, would therefore be known as . . . The Hardy Boys!"

Thus began what is certainly one of the most popular series in the history of children's fiction, one written under the pseudonym Franklin W. Dixon. The Hardy Boys, their parents Fenton and Laura Hardy, as well as the inimitable Aunt Gertrude, their friends Chet Morton, Tony Prito, Biff Hooper, Phil Cohen, Callie Shaw and Iola Morton, are still going strong over sixty years after their creation and show no sign of stopping. "Reprinted, revised, and rewritten for more than half a century," states Jonathan Cott in *Esquire,* "works like *The Mystery at Devil's Paw, The Haunted Fort,* and *Hunting for Hidden Gold* still sell remarkably well; they are, in fact, the most popular boys' books of all time." Carol Billman, in her 1986 book *The Secret of the Stratemeyer Syndicate: Nancy Drew, the Hardy Boys, and the Million Dollar Fiction Factory,* reports that "over seventy million Hardy Boys novels have been purchased," and, she adds, "in the last three years over two and a half million paperback copies of their mysteries were sold."

Although earlier series had introduced the young-detective motif, the Hardys novels were innovative in introducing detection as their primary focus. "The essential ingredients of a Hardys title," says Billman, "are fast-paced investigative action and a large dollop of the conventional gimmickry of pulp magazine detection that began with Nick Carter: disguises, ciphers to be puzzled out, rude thugs to be put in their places, crime kits, secret messages, and passwords." Yet adventure—long a mainstay of children's fiction—also plays a significant role in the Hardys books. Billman sees them as "everyboy's fantasy adventure, the fantasy that explains in large part the thrill the fast-paced adventure genre has held for boys since the days of *Robinson Crusoe, The Coral Island,* and *Treasure Island.*" "The secret the Stratemeyer Syndicate hit upon in the Hardy Boys books," she continues, "was the *packing* of timeless adventure-story action into a distinctive, and repeatable, detective fiction pattern. Thus, the novel lure of the detective mystery had at last been thoroughly fused with the earlier adventure tale tradition."

Neither the Hardy Boys themselves nor the places they frequent are fully depicted in the books, and they do not develop as the series progresses. Billman recognizes that Bayport, the Hardys' home town, is "not a place that fires readers' imaginations, as settings so often do in literature for the young." "So different from the messy, unfragrant world depicted relentlessly in hard-boiled detective fiction," she concludes, "Bayport superficially looks like a real place but is

actually a fantasy island." "In Dixon's oeuvre, the characters do exactly the same things year after year," Billman declares. "They find another cave to explore, another international smuggling ring to smash open." Although crammed with criminals who are the Hardys' sworn enemies, Bayport remains to the reader a secure small town.

Yet this lack of depth seems to add, rather than subtract, from readers's enjoyment of the series. Cott recalls, "Still, what I *remembered* having liked about the Hardy Boys books was that paradoxical sense that the series had given me of living in a familiar, secure, protected world, in which one could imagine oneself being as curious, fearless, ingenious, risk-taking, courageous, and righteous as the Hardy Boys themselves—those two action-driven, brotherly ciphers, whose lack of interiority was in fact their most rewarding and positive attribute." A reader can identify with the boys; they are "paradoxically, average guys," says Billman, "'fellows like yourself' as the publicity went, even as they perform wondrous feats of detection. They can be likened to Wally and The Beaver or David and Ricky Nelson . . . average fellows from a town that is depicted as a quaint Everytown, U.S.A., right down to the smiling policemen and helpful shopkeepers. But *these* ordinary boys get mixed up in high-level detection and dangerous adventure."

Harriet Adams, Stratemeyer's daughter, continued the Hardy Boys series after her father's death in 1930. Many of the volumes—up to and including 1947's *The Phantom Freighter*—were written by Leslie McFarlane, the same man who originally created the characters for Stratemeyer. By the late 1950s, however, these earlier stories seemed dated to new readers. Volumes originally written in the 1920s did not reflect the faster paced postwar juvenile lifestyle. To eliminate this contrast, Adams and her co-workers modernized the Hardy Boys. Although they remained all-American and squeaky-clean, by the mid-1960s Frank and Joe were chasing around the world after international spies, rescuing American astronauts, and exhibiting a taste for rock music. In 1959, in order to reflect the changing times, the Stratemeyer Syndicate began to rewrite the earlier volumes of the series, bringing them up-to-date, and removing disparaging references to minority groups and other objectionable material.

Many readers of the original versions protested the changes Adams and her co-workers had made. "The leisurely pace, the sense of having world enough and time," says Cott, "—all of this had been excised or eviscerated in the flatter or more high-tech versions of recent times." "If anyone still doubts that the world is a profoundly different place than it was when we were children, consider this: Frank Hardy has encountered a groupie," declares Ed Zuckerman in *Rolling Stone.* "If word came that Abe Lincoln turned up on *Let's Make a Deal* dressed as a carrot, it could not be more unsettling." "The extent of this literary sacrilege is overwhelming," he asserts. "Every Hardy Boys book up to and including *The Mystery at Devil's Paw* (number 38) is not the same as it used to be. . . . The Hardy Boys have entered the new age." In response to this reaction, the publishers Applewood Books began to reprint facsimile editions of the early Hardy Boys volumes—with original text and illustrations—in 1991.

Frank and Joe were modernized once again when Simon & Schuster launched the "Hardy Boys Casefiles" in 1986. The new pocket-sized paperbacks offered grittier, more contemporary action; Frank and Joe now fought terrorists and drugdealers rather than smugglers and counterfeiters. Again, the changes upset some series followers. One irate reader complained to *Columbus Dispatch* columnist Mike Harden, "If I wanted Ian Fleming, I would buy Ian Fleming and read it." A more drastic alteration was the murder of Iola Morton, killed by a terrorist's bomb planted in the Hardys' car. The brutal realism of Iola's death shocked long-time Hardys fans. "In the old novels, girls were never killed, never even bruised," said John Corr in the *Chicago Tribune.* "They were just nice, slow people the Boys could be patient with and explain things to." Trying to understand the negative reaction, Harden explained, "There was something comfortable, even predictable, about the Hardy Boys. Evil never went unpunished. The good guys always prevailed. The innocent never died young. Though Frank and Joe kept the same girlfriends for 50 years . . . they remained—for all of their curiosity and sense of adventure—innocently celibate."

"But life has changed," Harden admits. "Hardy Boys' creator Edward Stratemeyer fashioned Frank and Joe's world the year Lindbergh flew the Atlantic. Bayport was a million miles from mass death at the hands of terrorists, the threat of nuclear annihilation. The world had yet to hear of crack addiction. Teen pregnancy was an exception, not an epidemic. It took something more than a Rambo or a Mad Max to earn a spot on youth's pedestal of idolatry." But for some the Hardys' attraction remains. In his book *Rascals at Large; or, The Clue in the Old Nostalgia* Arthur Prager remembers, "Rascals were at large, and the Hardys would fight on until the very last criminal was behind bars. The old readers are grown up and scattered now, and Stratemeyer has gone to whatever special Heaven exists for people who make children happy, but the boy detectives go on thrilling new generations, rewritten, brought 'up to date,' but still fearlessly making their dad proud of them."

Stratemeyer also used the pseudonym Franklin W. Dixon for another series launched in 1927: the "Ted Scott Flying Stories." "Ted Scott, intrepid airman, was a lanky, soft-spoken Middle-Westerner of twenty-one who had achieved world celebrity (and the nickname the 'Lone Eagle') by making the first flight across the Atlantic solo from New York to Paris," explains Prager. Based on Charles Lindbergh's exploits, the series progressed "with the aviation industry until it met the fate of most long-run series," Prager concludes. "Its little readers grew up and got involved in the apocalyptic events of the 1930s and 1940s and Ted Scott ceased to be an 'active property.'" Edward L. Stratemeyer, Andrew E. Svenson, Harriet S. Adams, and James Duncan Lawrence were among the authors who contributed to the "Hardy Boys" and "Ted Scott" series. See the *SATA* index for more information on Harriet S. Adams, Leslie McFarlane, Edward L. Stratemeyer, and Andrew E. Svenson.

WORKS CITED:

Billman, Carol, "The Hardy Boys: Soft-Boiled Detection," *The Secret of the Stratemeyer Syndicate: Nancy Drew, the Hardy Boys, and the Million Dollar Fiction Factory,* Ungar, 1986, pp. 79-96.

Corr, John, *Chicago Tribune,* July 5, 1987.

Cott, Jonathan, "Hale and Hardy," *Esquire,* June, 1986, p. 225-26.

Harden, Mike, "A Hardy Memory Is Blasted to Pieces," *Columbus Dispatch,* April 15, 1987, p. 1B.

McFarlane, Leslie, *Ghost of the Hardy Boys,* Two Continents, 1976.

Prager, Arthur, *Rascals at Large; or, The Clue in the Old Nostalgia,* Doubleday, 1971, pp. 97-124, 127-65.

Zuckerman, Ed, "The Great Hardy Boys Whodunnit," *Rolling Stone,* September 9, 1976, pp. 36-40.

FOR MORE INFORMATION SEE:

BOOKS

Johnson, Deidre, editor and compiler, *Stratemeyer Pseudonyms and Series Books: An Annotated Checklist of Stratemeyer and Stratemeyer Syndicate Publications,* Greenwood Press, 1982.

Nye, Russel B., *The Unembarrassed Muse: The Popular Arts in America,* Dial, 1970.

PERIODICALS

New Yorker, August 18, 1986.

People, August 5, 1991.

Publishers Weekly, March 5, 1979.

TV Guide, June 25, 1977.

Washington Post Book World, February 8, 1981.

Yellowback Library, May/June, 1983; July/August, 1987; February, 1988.

*   *   *

DOYLE, Brian 1935-

PERSONAL: Born August 12, 1935, in Ottawa, Ontario, Canada; son of Hulbert and Charlotte (Duff) Doyle; married December 26, 1960; wife's name, Jacqueline; children: Megan, Ryan. *Education:* Carleton University, B.J. and B.A., 1957.

ADDRESSES: Home—539 Rowanwood, Ottawa, Ontario, Canada K2A 3C9.

CAREER: High school English teacher at Glebe Collegiate, Ottawa, Ontario, and Ottawa Technical High School, Ottawa; children's writer. Worked variously as a journalist, waiter, taxi driver, bricklayer, and jazz singer.

BRIAN DOYLE

AWARDS, HONORS: Book of the Year awards, Canadian Library Association, 1983, for *Up to Low,* and 1989, for *Easy Avenue;* Vicky Metcalf Body of Work Award, Canadian Authors Association; Mr. Christie Book of the Year Award; three times runner up, Governor General's Award, Canadian Authors Association.

WRITINGS:

Hey Dad!, Groundwood Books, 1978.
You Can Pick Me Up at Peggy's Cove, Groundwood, 1979.
Up to Low, Groundwood Books, 1982.
Angel Square, Groundwood Books, 1984.
Easy Avenue, Groundwood Books, 1988.
Covered Bridge, Groundwood Books, 1990.

Also author of children's plays.

ADAPTATIONS: A film directed by Ann Wheeler was based on *Angel Square.*

SIDELIGHTS: "I've maintained for a long time that kids—just pre-puberty kids—are the smartest beings on earth," Brian Doyle said in an interview with *Something about the Author* (*SATA*). "Now they're not articulate and they don't add things up and make a lot of sense, but I think their instincts are the best of the species." According to many critics, Doyle's obvious regard for the clarity of children's insight radiates throughout his novels, inspiring him to "write up" rather than to "write down" to his readers. Doyle's works turn on timeless coming-of-age themes and feature poetically crafted prose, hefty doses of tragedy and comedy, and realistic representations that acknowledge the imperfections of contemporary human life without over-looking its goodness. Some observers credit Doyle's success to his use of child narrators, who, through their naive wisdom, find balance and meaning in the most frantic of situations. "There's a pretty decent difference between depth of insight and sophisticated insight," Doyle told *SATA*. "Kids at ten know a lot—they're very wise, although they're not slippery, not good enough liars yet. A ten-year-old boy or girl is as smart as she'll ever get or he'll ever get. So it's with that kind of belief I'm comfortable making the ten-year-old's insights as deep as I want."

Doyle's own keen memories of childhood—the settings, the people, and the atmosphere—figure prominently in his novels. As Doyle grew up, his family lived in two locations, winters in an ethnically divided section of Ottawa, Ontario, and summers in the Gatineau Hills north of town, in a log cabin where his great-grandfather Mickey Doyle had settled. Mickey Doyle provided the basis of one of the family's legends. "My great-grandfather was ten years old when he got off the boat in 1847; both his parents had died on the ship of cholera and so he wound up alone in a bush camp up north of Iowa." Mickey managed to survive, relocate to Canada, raise a family, and, according to a Children's Book Center pamphlet on Doyle, "to become a leader of the Gatineau's Irish settlers during one of Canada's lesser-known clashes, the Battle of Brennan's Hill."

Doyle credits his father and his grandfather with having planted the seeds of story-telling within him. "I loved sitting around listening to my father and my grandfather," Doyle told *SATA*. "Both of them were wonderful storytellers, and they didn't tell stories so much as they just talked. Neither of them were bookish. I never saw my grandfather read a book, but he was constantly reciting verse—songs and poems,

Doyle, a Canadian novelist, made his debut with *Hey Dad!,* a novel exploring a father-daughter relationship as it evolves during a summer vacation. (Cover illustration by Heather Collins.)

ballads mostly—about this adventure and that adventure. My father wasn't a literary person, although he was the best raconteur I ever met. If in my work there is a kind of sound, that's where it comes from, rhythms inherited from sitting around listening to my father's family exchanging their world vision. Those people were verbally very poetic. For me, listening to my father and grandfather was better than any entertainment—even going to the show on Saturdays."

Doyle's mother provided a very different influence on his development as a writer. "My mother was a literary person. She was not a verbal person at all. However, she wrote well and wrote privately. She was very private, but she'd show her poetry to me." Doyle's mother wrote the poem "Sea Savour" with which Doyle begins his second novel, *You Can Pick Me Up at Peggy's Cove.*

Doyle claims he "wasn't much of a student" until he reached college, but enjoyed reading books like *Heidi, Huck Finn,* and comic books. He began writing when he was about ten years old. "The first writing I did was in the snow," he recalled in the *SATA* interview, "I wrote 'Gerald is a bastard.' My father came out, and he brought me in the house, and he put a piece of paper down on the table and gave me a pencil. Then he said, 'Say some more, but don't write it in the snow because he'll see it.'" Looking back upon his childhood, Doyle explained: "I'm always surprised at how much I can feel, so I must have been the kind of kid that paid attention. I'm surprised at myself all the time at how much I can remember. I must have been all eyes and ears."

After graduating from Carleton University with a degree in journalism, Doyle quickly turned to what would be a thirty-three year career teaching high school English. He initially chose to work in the field of journalism because of his basic distaste for academic treatment of literature and writing. "I thought wrongly that a life of teaching would be a life surrounded by books and reading and discussing stuff, but that's when I was young and foolish. What I did find out teaching was that kids can write. Teenagers are in a sexual coma most of the time—they don't know anything—but, as opposed to most ten-year-olds who are very clear-minded, the teenagers can write. It turned out that my work as a teacher for thirty-three years had mostly to do with getting them to write."

As a teacher, Doyle has also been the force behind many school plays, most of which he wrote and produced himself. "The plays were an outlet for all the writing we were doing. Although I wrote the plays, they affected the kids' writing a lot. It would take seven or eight months of work, all home-grown—music and everything. Everybody was either in it or went to it. It was all local subjects—satirizing local things. We did take-offs on MacBeth, Chaucer's stuff, all kinds of crazy things. It was a lot of work—more work than football—involving 250 people to put the thing on, and lots of overtime and working through holidays, but it was worth it."

As a teacher and a writer, Doyle doesn't go along with the attitudes many contemporary children's authors seem to hold toward children. "I've often quarrelled with a lot of literature written for young people because adult writers have forgotten their Huck Finns and their Alice-in-Wonderlands. Those were smart people. In a lot of what is written these days, particularly targeted at these age groups, kids depicted by adult writers don't seem to have much wisdom. Well, my kids are smart because kids *are* smart. Good teachers who teach that age level are the ones who know that. Weak teachers are the ones who don't remember that and talk down to the kids, and the kids don't respect them."

Doyle not only objects to the way young people are often depicted in children's literature; he also finds much of the subject matter chosen by adults for children to be off-track. "There is a perception that young people are worried about menstruation, divorce, masturbation, hitchhiking—subjects that just carloads of kids' books are written about. These are not the concerns of young people at all as far as I'm concerned. They are the concerns of adults who have young people. Kids' concerns are classical concerns: Am I brave? Am I a hero? Am I honest? Do I love this person? Am I afraid? Am I admired? Am I weak? Am I strong? These are their concerns, and that's what I write about."

Doyle considers his teaching to be entirely separate from his writing. The knowledge of the inner workings of children's minds that is reflected in his novels began with his understanding of his own children and came later from somewhere inside himself. His first two books, *Hey Dad!* and *You Can Pick Me Up at Peggy's Cove,* were written for his children, Megan and Ryan, respectively. "I wrote them for them and, at the time, they were at that age—the good age, where I

thought I knew them really well, and in fact, I did. I don't think I ever knew anybody as well as I did my daughter when she was that age. I felt like I was right inside her skin. So writing *Hey Dad!* and *You Can Pick Me Up at Peggy's Cove* was an attempt to capture that knowledge before it went away. I did the same thing for my son a couple years later, when he got to be that age. I never could have gotten started without my own kids." While the first two novels are contemporary, Doyle's next four novels go back in time to the mid-twentieth-century, when Doyle himself was young. "My writing started with my daughter, then my son, and then I ran out of kids." So now, Doyle told *SATA,* "I find the kid inside of me, way back there."

Doyle's first novel, *Hey Dad!,* is, in its narrator Megan's words, "the story of how I hated my Dad for a while for some reason and how I loved him again for some reason and how I almost ruined a trip my family took to the Pacific Ocean and how all of a sudden I got independent for a while that summer when I was thirteen." After a thwarted attempt at running away from the family, watching her brother nearly fall off a mountain, and mistaking a dead man at the hot springs for her father, Megan grows beyond her childhood self-orienta-

Doyle's second novel is about a boy who hopes that getting into trouble will force his father, who has left home, to return. (Cover illustration of *You Can Pick Me Up at Peggy's Cove* by Paul Zwolak.)

tion and begins to worry about the instability of the world around her. She worries about strangers entering her life only to disappear forever, about the mysterious connection between love and death, and about ambiguities—even in the landscape. When Megan and her brother ask an Iroquois man they meet on the road how big the mountains are, he answers: "If they seem big to you from here, they won't seem as big when you get there. Everything is different than it looks to be."

Underneath Megan's strikingly familiar—and often very funny—teenage disgust at just about everything the family (but particularly her unconventional father) does, Doyle conveys a rather heroic struggle to grasp and cope with a confusing world. According to *In Review: Canadian Books for Children* contributor Irma McDonough, the family trip from Ottawa to Vancouver provides not only a "subliminally educational" rendering of Canada's geography, but also a vivid journey through some of the psychological pathways to maturity. The novel's two landscapes—internal and external—are related. In her *Canadian Children's Literature* review, Wendy R. Katz maintained that Doyle's child characters discover themselves through their relationships within the family, but also "in relation to people beyond the family, friends and strangers alike, to nature, and to the universe." Listening to the roar of the Athabaska River, Megan has a flash of comprehension illustrating the wonder and wisdom of an "unsophisticated" mind: "I was trying to stretch my mind so that I could think about how long an eon was. It was how long the Athabaska roared his deep roar. I stretched my mind. I grunted and held my breath and forced my mind to wrap around that long, long time. I thought of the summer and how long it was that I was in grade four and how long next year would be and then I thought of myself after Dad and Mum were dead and then after I was an old wrinkled lady and how *that* wouldn't be a century yet and then my mind kind of popped like a bubble gum bubble."

Before Canadian-based publishing house Groundwood Books saw *Hey, Dad!*'s potential and agreed to publish it, several publishers had turned it down, suggesting that children would not be able to appreciate the poetic prose and the depth of the novel. Doyle believes, to the contrary, that children appreciate good writing. He told *SATA:* "Kids would like the song, or they would like something, but they haven't got B.A.s in literature so they can't tell you why. So they might say, for instance, Read the part about this or that, and they're not quite sure that what they really like in there was the alliteration or the repetition or what wasn't said. They don't articulate why, but they do like stuff that's more than just plot. That's what the publisher and I had thought we would embark on, making sure that on every page in the writing there was more going on than just the events. People who wouldn't publish my stuff were saying that kids won't know that so much is there, and I was saying it doesn't matter, they'll feel it. And we proved it. They don't know it, but they feel it. They get it all. They laugh and they're sad, and they get it all. It's only the literary critics who go on and say why."

In *You Can Pick Me Up at Peggy's Cove,* the narrator Ryan is sent to stay with his aunt in the small, tourist-ridden Nova Scotia fishing town of Peggy's Cove when his father, who is suffering from the "C.O.L." (the change of life), runs away from home. "The C.O.L.," Ryan explains, "is when someone gets to be about forty-five years old and starts acting a little different because they start thinking about dying or getting old and all that. . . . The C.O.L. makes them do funny things. I guess the right word is unpredictable." Ryan, thinking that

if he gets into trouble his father will have to return to save him, becomes involved with stealing from tourists with the Drummer, the neglected son of a wealthy widow. Most mornings, however, Ryan goes out on a boat with the fisherman Eddie and his mute partner Wingding. With them he learns much about friendship, communication, heroism, and eventually, death. In the frenzy of events—some funny, some painfully sad—Ryan composes a letter to his father, hoping to hurt him or scare him into coming back.

The setting and the people in Peggy's Cove eventually orient Ryan to his own strange circumstances. While tourists frantically pursue perfect snapshots of the idyllic village life they expected to find in Peggy's Cove ("It would be a wonderful place to live," says one tourist. "It's so *realistic!*"), Ryan sees the town as it is, a place where everyone has his or her own peculiarities and accepts the peculiarities of others. Thus after Ryan and the Drummer are arrested for stealing, Ryan's friends, Eddie and Wingding accept him back into the fold, as he will in turn accept and forgive his father's "unpredictable" behavior and apparent betrayal. *World of Children's Books* contributor Jon C. Stott commended the "social realism" with which Doyle "sensitively explores the strengths and weaknesses of his characters and understands well the need of everyone for love."

Doyle's "realism" is a layered blend of different stylistic approaches. Stott, who called Doyle a "superb stylist," asserted that the novel's shifts in style—from straightforward to slapstick—are well suited to its great range of moods. Doyle told *SATA:* "The Peggy's Cove book is about friendship, and so what I try to do is treat that theme very realistically, as true as I can possibly make it. And then in the day to day—in the particulars, page to page where the whole thing is dealt with in all different ways—I'm dealing more in mythological kinds of views, the way I used to hear my father and grandfather depicting reality. I think if you want to apply realism to it, the themes are very realistic, and the emotions in them are as close to 'reality' as I can possibly get. Whereas the novel may be comic and kind of caricaturish, at the same time it's rooted in true feeling."

With a notable change in tone and style, Doyle's third novel, *Up to Low,* takes place in the mid-1900s in the Gatineau Hills, where the author spent his summers as a child. Its narrator, Tommy, travels up to the town of Low with his father and his father's friend, Frank—an alcoholic with a new car that he crashes every third or fourth mile. On the way to Low, the travelers stop at many taverns, where Tommy is treated, often involuntarily, to cokes and tavern talk. Everyone, but particularly Tommy's father, a very able storyteller, is talking about a man called Mean Hughie up in Low and how he disappeared after he got sick from cancer. As the novel proceeds, Mean Hughie's history unfolds through the larger-than-life story-telling of the men of Low. Tommy's attention is particularly engaged when the story of Mean Hughie's daughter, Baby Bridgette, is told. Years before, the story goes, Baby Bridgette got in the way of the binding machine and got her arm cut off. Mean Hughie slapped her for getting in the way of the machine before he bound up the wound with binder twine so she wouldn't bleed to death. Tommy confides to the reader that, on his last visit to Low, he fell in love with Baby Bridgette and her trillium-shaped green eyes. Upon reaching Low, Tommy re-establishes his relationship with her and together they embark on a healing journey to find the dying Mean Hughie. The strength of their love and forgiveness provides a steady light of clarity within an otherwise chaotic, but oddly lovable, world.

Doyle's *Up to Low,* a rural novel filled with dark humor, won Canadian Library Association's Book of the Year award in 1983. (Cover illustration by Paul Zwolak.)

Tommy's narration of the story is divided between the slapstick antics of daily life in Low and the subtle wonders he finds there. He reports in deadpan style on the drunken antics of Frank, who drives into walls and falls in cow pies; on Frank's nemesis, the compulsive Aunt Dottie, who sprays disinfectant on raspberries before eating them and often wears a surgical mask to protect herself from germs; on the teeming throng of indistinguishable red-headed Hendricks ("'Watch out you don't run down a Hendrick,' Dad was saying, 'you know it's unlucky.'"); and on the five indistinguishable chain-smoking uncles. Behind the comic portrayal of a static and somewhat nonsensical rural life, however, a steady lucidity emanates from Tommy. In creating Tommy, *Maclean's* reviewer Anne Collins commented, Doyle reverses the usual order of adult authority and teenage alienation, presenting "a sane and loving teenager who helps a slapstick and misfit world find its feet." While the townspeople, like the figures in their stories, remain largely the same, Tommy and Baby Bridgette move forward. They become acquainted, according to Carol Munro in her *Canadian Children's Literature* review, "with the power of a real affection for another person, and with the range of those natural human foibles which are better tolerated with good humor than railed

against." Sarah Ellis observed in her *Horn Book* review that *Up to Low,* with its elaborate plot and style, "takes a lot of risks." The reviewer added, however, that Doyle skillfully controls this "extravagant world" through the "voice of Tommy, whose quiet, observant, naive tone frames the whole rollicking crowded narrative in genuine human feeling."

Some critics have questioned the appropriateness of the humor in *Up to Low. Books in Canada* critic Mary Ainslie Smith, who praised *Up to Low* as Doyle's finest work, described some of Doyle's humor as "black, to say the least, and sometimes heavy, of the out-house and open-coffin variety." Munro, while applauding the life-affirming power of the book, commented that "a reader might take issue with some of the models presented" by the book's adult characters. The bar-hopping and drunk driving, according to Munro, "are perhaps examples not best set before the young reader." But Doyle believes that his place as an author is to set the world with all of its complexities before his readers. "As a child," Doyle told *SATA,* "I recall sitting around listening to the adults in my life talking away. They never left me out, and they didn't explain or anything either. I think that's how I would like to treat kids that are around me, put it out there, let them figure it out." Katz, observing this tendency, commended Doyle for not segregating his children from the adult world, as many children's authors have done. Doyle's child characters, she remarked, "are in close and occasionally oppressive proximity to adults and adult concerns. In this sense the books are unique, as are their fully-rounded adult characters."

The large issues faced in *Up to Low,* such as death, violence, love, forgiveness, and even alcohol addiction, cannot be satisfactorily resolved, according to Doyle. "I don't think there are any answers," he told *SATA.* "There are questions, though, that I hope my readers will ask the rest of their lives. The question is more important than the answer anyway. These things have to be asked and dealt with in some way if you're going to live a fulfilled existence." Comedy, in Doyle's view, is a way of dealing with these questions. "I don't think that kids read *Up to Low* and then become alcoholics. They may read *Up to Low* and then laugh, and that's important. Laughing at people who drink too much is very important. As a matter of fact, if you're looking for some kind of salutary effects of my books, that may be one. It seems to me that laughter and tears are the two most important reactions to life. They're essential for someone to live an ordinary existence. I was just brought up to take it for granted that if you weren't laughing, there was something wrong. There's far too much analysis and too many excuses going on already. People say, Let's study it, or Let's not do it, or Let's talk about it. But laughing and crying, for me anyway, are much more important than these scientific approaches to existence."

Tommy returns as narrator in *Angel Square,* Doyle's 1984 novel, this time back in his winter home in Ottawa's Lowertown. Every day Tommy must cross Angel Square, the site of three different schools, one attended by French Canadians, locally called Pea Soups, another attended by Irish Catholics, called Dogans, and Tommy's school, attended by Jewish kids, called Jews (although Tommy explains, "I'm not anything"). Hyperbolic descriptions of fighting among the factions in the square run intermittently throughout the novel, although no one seems to get hurt in the fights. Tommy reports on the furor nonchalantly, although in legendary proportions. "Over there, two Jews were tying a Dogan to a post. Over here, two Pea Soups were trying to tear off a Jew's arm. Over there, three Jews and a Dogan were torturing a Pea

Soup with bats. In the centre some Pea Soups were burying alive a Dogan in a deep hole in the snow."

But when anti-Semitism results in the beating and critical injury of the father of Tommy's best friend, Sammy Rosenberg, Tommy can no longer passively accept the irrational behavior of his community. He triumphs over bigotry by following in the footsteps of his radio hero, the Shadow, working through a network of Irish, Jewish, and French Canadian neighbors to find the culprit.

Bigotry is only one aspect of Tommy's life in the Lowertown community. Almost as concerned with buying Christmas presents as he is concerned with finding the assailant, Tommy's evocation of Lowertown at Christmastime achieves "special beauty," according to *Quill and Quire* contributor Paul Kropp. Whether invoking the sights, smells, and people at Woolworth's, conveying what a rubber duck means to his mentally handicapped sister, Pamela, "an angel who couldn't know anything," or showing the effects of a good teacher on his imagination, Tommy presents "a poignant message of tolerance and love," a *Children's Book News* reviewer remarked.

Tommy, the narrator in Doyle's *Up to Low*, returns in *Angel Square* and becomes involved in tensions between French Canadians, Irish Catholics, and Jews. (Cover illustration by Ron Berg.)

The novel's poignancy may have some particularly personal origins. Doyle told *SATA* that *Angel Square* was "very close to what my youth was, as I can conjure up anyway." He elaborated in *Canadian Books, Authors, and Illustrators*, "I started thinking of *Angel Square* when I was lying face down in the snow on my way home at lunch time one day with three or four people jumping up and down on my body. What I was thinking about was that somebody someday should write this down." But some of the memories are not easy for Doyle, as he told *SATA:* "I think that *Angel Square* was hard to relax with, because it touched on some pain. The mentally retarded sister was very hard for me to do, just to make sure it was right. When I was growing up, my playmate was my sister, who had Down's syndrome. She was two years older than me. I think I learned a lot from her, because she couldn't talk or anything. She died when she was fourteen. There's a little bit of her in each book—anybody who's handicapped in any way. I had trouble going all out with her memory, because it was painful, but some of it got in there in *Angel Square*."

Doyle's fifth book, *Easy Avenue,* was published in 1988. It shifts to a new narrator, Hubbo O'Driscoll, an orphan in the care of a very kind distant relative, known only as Mrs. O'Driscoll. In a state of poverty, Hubbo and Mrs. O'Driscoll have moved from Ottawa's Lowertown to the Uplands Emergency Shelter. There, both of them enter Glebe Collegiate Institute—Hubbo as a student and his foster-mother as the school's cleaning woman. They discover that in this part of town the division between rich and poor is pronounced—a division highlighted by Hubbo's descriptions of his daily bus ride. On the bus—an involuntary meeting place of the two classes—the rich people sit as far from the poor as they can, trying not to touch them and keeping "their noses pointed upwards so they wouldn't be breathing our air," Hubbo reports. Getting off the bus is a Doylesque frenzy. The poor people, who got on the bus first, have the window seats, and crawl over the rich people to get out. The rich people "couldn't get off first because there were piles of people, poor people, falling down the aisle and tumbling out the door and shoving and swearing and clawing their way out. . . . Everybody was touching the rich people now, putting their sticky hands on their nice coats, tromping all over their nice shiny shoes, breathing bad teeth right into their nice faces, bodies rubbing against their nice bodies, shoulders hitting shoulders, bony knees touching the backs of their nice fat legs."

Hubbo finds himself caught between factions. His real affections are with the people he knows at the shelter, especially Fleurette Fitchell Featherstone. Fleurette, Hubbo discovers, is the daughter of a prostitute. Back in Lowertown, Fleurette had a rather unsavory reputation, which she is intent on leaving behind. Hubbo likes her immediately. But, his aspirations to belong to an elite club at school lead him in another direction, causing him to pretend he doesn't know Mrs. O'Driscoll and to lie about his address. When Hubbo gets a job as a companion to a wealthy old woman and begins to receive money from a mysterious benefactor, he fabricates an identity for himself that is acceptable to the snobs in his school. The death of his employer and an estrangement from Fleurette activate Hubbo's natural generosity, and the affection of his friends helps him to resist the pull of this social world.

Easy Avenue is often compared by critics to classic novels for young readers. Its plot and "eccentric characters" parallel nineteenth-century British writer Charles Dickens's *Great Expectations,* according to Pamela Young in her *Maclean's* review. *Canadian Children's Literature* contributor Lionel Adley, also noting the similarities to *Great Expectations,* added that "the hero's laid-back ridicule of fools in office" recalls American author J. D. Salinger's well-known novel, *The Catcher in the Rye*. And Eva Martin in her *Books for Young People* review compared Fleurette Featherstone Fitchell's transformation to the story of "Cinderella." But reviewers agreed that although Doyle works with classical themes, his style is uniquely his own, and uniquely Canadian. Describing him as "regional yet universal," Martin commented that "Doyle's imagination is stimulated not by current social issues or middle-class fantasy worlds but by what the author has to say about himself and his community."

Doyle's next novel, *Covered Bridge,* continues Hubbo's story. The O'Driscolls have moved to a farm in the country, along with their newly-adopted dog, Nerves. For Hubbo, the well-deserved happiness that the makeshift family finds at the farm is represented by a nearby covered bridge—a symbol of the state of harmony that has existed for generations between nature and the human community. The bridge is also a memorial, to the romantic Hubbo, to the legend of two local lovers, Ophelia and Oscar. Years before, Ophelia, suffering gravely from a brain tumor, had jumped off the bridge to her death. Because of the suicide, Father Foley set her grave outside of the church cemetery. Her fiance Oscar makes daily visits to the site where she jumped, and Hubbo has seen her ghost there.

With its engaging mystery and good-natured satire, *Covered Bridge* depicts not only the effects of technological progress on the way of life in a rural Canadian town, but also the effects of the rural town upon progress. Hubbo plans to save the covered bridge, not in order to stop progress (a modern bridge is being built), but to keep the humanizing past alive in the rather intolerant and materialistic present. A petition, signed by the workers of the town, reads: "I, the undersigned, refuse to tear down the covered bridge. I would rather save it for Posterity. For, without a past, we have no future."

Covered Bridge, like so many of Doyle's novels, encompasses a large spectrum of contemporary problems within a framework of the old timeless questions yet manages to carry off a joke at the same time. Martin summarized that "Brian Doyle is one of the most daring and experimental writers of young-adult novels. He deals with the most sensitive of issues—racism, violence, anti-social activity of all sorts—with a tongue-in-cheek humor that never denigrates the human spirit."

Brian Doyle's novels have won several awards and continue to grow more and more popular in Canada, with movie producers and United States publishers now in the picture. For Doyle, success presents a new challenge. "Fame is something you want, but when you get it, you don't want it," he told *SATA*. "It's peculiar. I haven't got a lot of work done lately because of these two awards that just came in. If your head swells up, you can't really work. For me it is deadly; I have to wait for it to go away. I just want to get back to normal and start writing and not listen to anybody or anything."

Doyle spends a lot of his time writing and speaking. On the subject of writing, he believes that any good writer has to work regularly at his or her craft. "You just have to write every day, whether you like it or not. Make sure you never miss even if you don't have anything to say. That is the way you stay in shape. That is how I've been doing it." Writing, Doyle admitted, is not always fun. "I don't enjoy daily writing any more than an athlete enjoys going out and doing drills. You know, Shakespeare wrote his sonnets just as an

In Doyle's *Easy Avenue,* **narrator Hubbo O'Driscoll is torn between his poor but exciting family and friends and his rich but shallow classmates.** (Cover illustration by Paul Zwolak.)

exercise, although they are beautiful. He was always working on one because it kept him in shape. It's work."

But for Doyle, writing also has its rewards. "When it comes, and you go unconscious while you're writing, and you stop to check and see some pages filled up, that is great. And, you know that they are good because the time has gone and you haven't noticed. It's the same feeling as anything you do that you do well. You know that yourself. When you look at the clock and notice an hour has gone by, whatever you have done in that unconscious hour is good. The reverse is true as well. You write away and write away, then you look at the clock and four minutes have gone by."

Following his retirement from teaching in 1991, Doyle found himself in a state of transition. He reflected on this time of uncertainty in the deadpan manner of one of his narrators. "I'm right in the middle of a change of life here," he told *SATA*. "I don't know what you're supposed to do when you retire, other than that you are supposed to drop dead or something. But I don't think I'm going to do that just yet."

WORKS CITED:

Adley, Lionel, "Doyle for the Early Teens," *Canadian Children's Literature,* Number 54, 1989, pp. 71-72.

Children's Book Center, promotional pamphlet on Brian Doyle, 1983.

Children's Book News, review of *Angel Square,* December, 1984, p. 3.

Collins, Ann, "Tales for the Computer Generation," *Maclean's,* December 13, 1982, p. 56-58.

Doyle, Brian, *Hey, Dad!,* Groundwood Books, 1978.

Doyle, Brian, *You Can Pick Me Up at Peggy's Cove,* Groundwood Books, 1979.

Doyle, Brian, *Up to Low,* Groundwood Books, 1982.

Doyle, Brian, *Angel Square,* Groundwood Books, 1984.

Doyle, Brian, *Easy Avenue,* Groundwood Books, 1988.

Doyle, Brian, *Covered Bridge,* Groundwood Books, 1990.

Doyle, Brian, telephone interview with Sonia Benson for *Something about the Author,* conducted June 17, 1991.

Ellis, Sarah, "News from the North," *Horn Book,* February, 1984, pp. 99-103.

Katz, Wendy R., "Dying and Loving Somebody," *Canadian Children's Literature,* Number 22, 1981, pp. 47-50.

Kropp, Paul, "Growing Up Is Hard to Do: Leaving the Boy Behind," *Quill and Quire,* November, 1984, p. 18.

Martin, Eva, "*Easy Avenue* Is Vintage Doyle," *Books for Young People,* October, 1988, pp. 12 and 18.

Doyle probes the conflict between the past and present in the semi-satirical mystery *Covered Bridge*. (Cover illustration by Paul Zwolak.)

McDonough, Irma, review of *Hey, Dad!, In Review: Canadian Books for Children,* autumn, 1978, p. 57.

Munro, Carol, "Life and Growth and Change: Always a Journey," *Canadian Children's Literature,* Number 37, 1985, pp. 67-70.

"Our Choice/Your Choice," *Canadian Children's Books, Authors, and Illustrators,* 1985-86.

Smith, Mary Ainslie, review of *Up to Low, Books in Canada,* February, 1983, pp. 32-33.

Stott, Jon C., "A Second Baker's Dozen: Our Selection of the Best Canadian Books of 1980," *World of Children's Books,* 1981, pp. 27-33.

Young, Pamela, and others, "Tidings of Fun," *Maclean's,* December 26, 1988, p. 60.

FOR MORE INFORMATION SEE:

BOOKS

Landsberg, Michele, *Reading for the Love of It: Best Books for Young Readers,* Prentice-Hall, 1987.

Children's Literature Review, Volume 22, Gale, 1991.

PERIODICALS

In Review: Canadian Books for Children, August, 1980.

Quill and Quire, August, 1980; December, 1982.

Sketch by Sonia Benson

*   *   *

DRESCHER, Henrik 1955-

PERSONAL: Born December 15, 1955, in Denmark; immigrated to United States, 1967; married; wife's name, Lauren; children: Uli. *Education:* Studied illustrating at Boston Museum School.

CAREER: Writer and illustrator. Conducts workshops on bookmaking for children.

AWARDS, HONORS: The Strange Appearance of Howard Cranebill, Jr., 1982, *Simon's Book,* 1983, and *The Yellow Umbrella,* 1987, were named best illustrated books by the *New York Times Book Review; Simon's Book* received a Parents' Choice award and was selected for the Graphic Gallery showcase of books by *Horn Book* and for the television program *Reading Rainbow.*

WRITINGS:

AUTHOR AND ILLUSTRATOR

The Strange Appearance of Howard Cranebill, Jr., Lothrop, 1982.

Simon's Book, Lothrop, 1983.

(With Calvin Zeit) *True Paranoid Facts!,* Quill, 1983.

Looking for Santa Claus, Lothrop, 1984.

Look-alikes, Lothrop, 1985.

Whose Scaly Tail? African Animals You'd Like to Meet (nonfiction), Lippincott, 1987.

Whose Furry Nose? Australian Animals You'd Like to Meet (nonfiction), Lippincott, 1987.

The Yellow Umbrella, Bradbury, 1987.

ILLUSTRATOR

Harriet Ziefert, *All Clean!,* Harper, 1986.

Ziefert, *All Gone!,* Harper, 1986.

HENRIK DRESCHER

Ziefert, *Cock-a-Doodle-Doo!*, Harper, 1986.
Ziefert, *Run! Run!*, Harper, 1986.
Mark Dittrick and Diane Kender Dittrick, *Misnomers*, Collier Books, 1986.
Poems of A. Nonny Mouse, selected by Jack Prelutsky, Knopf, 1989.
Joel C. Harris and Eric Metaxas, editors, *Brer Rabbit and the Wonderful Tar Baby*, Picture Book Studio, 1990.

OTHER

Contributor of editorial illustrations to periodicals, including *New York Times Book Review* and *Rolling Stone*.

ADAPTATIONS: Simon's Book was adapted as a filmstrip by Random House.

SIDELIGHTS: Henrik Drescher is the author and illustrator of *The Strange Appearance of Howard Cranebill, Jr.* and *Simon's Book,* award-winning children's books known for their innovative illustrations. Born in Denmark, Drescher came to the United States with his family when he was an adolescent. Though he decided to be an artist at the age of fifteen, he did not pursue formal training, but instead opted to travel the world with a drawing notebook in hand. "I travel often," the author told Jim Roginski in *Parents' Choice.* "Notebooks are my way of keeping in touch with bookmaking. I draw in little theme books. This is where a lot of my ideas come from. All the squiggles, the lines, the textures—all graphic and sensual."

Beginning his career as a political illustrator, Drescher contributed editorial drawings to periodicals, including *Rolling Stone* and the *New York Times Book Review.* The author told Roginski that the inspiration for his first book, *The Strange Appearance of Howard Cranebill, Jr.,* came when "a friend who works in children's books as a designer . . . encouraged me to do children's books, or to try one anyway. I always put it off. Eventually I got to the point when I thought I had something in me. That was *Howard Cranebill.*"

The Strange Appearance of Howard Cranebill, Jr., was named a *New York Times* Best Illustrated Book of 1982; critics praised Drescher's pictures for their characteristic combination of squiggly lines, splotches of paint, and decorative borders. In creating his singular style, Drescher acknowledges that he was influenced by the artists of northern Europe. "Drawing is a cultural phenomenon there," he told Roginski, "it's all around you. My line quality, my spontaneity, my sensibility is northern European. I draw very heavily from their traditions and bookmaking."

In addition to their distinctive illustrations, Drescher's books are noted for their unique and delightful stories. The author pointed out to Roginski that "my purpose with children's books is to open the book up, engage the mind. That's if I have a 'Big Purpose' at all. My personal purpose is to make children's books *fun!*" In *Simon's Book,* for example, an artistic youn boy named Simon dreams one night that he is being pursued by a fearsome but ultimately friendly monster. Two pens and a bottle of ink come to life in order to draw Simon's way to safety. "Original, fresh, and engaging," commented Mary M. Burns in *Horn Book,* "the book is deliciously thrilling but never terrifying."

Whose Furry Nose? Australian Animals You'd Like to Meet and *Whose Scaly Tail? African Animals You'd Like to Meet,* two nonfiction books that teach children to identify some less familiar animals, are among Drescher's other self-illustrated titles.

WORKS CITED:

Burns, Mary M., review of *Simon's Book, Horn Book,* December, 1983, p. 699.
Roginski, Jim, interview with Henrik Drescher, *Parents' Choice,* autumn, 1985, pp. 11 and 26.

FOR MORE INFORMATION SEE:

BOOKS

Children's Literature Review, Volume 20, Gale, 1990.

PERIODICALS

New York Times Book Review, November 8, 1987.*

*   *   *

EDWARDS, Julia
See STRATEMEYER, Edward L.

EMERSON, Alice B.
[Collective pseudonym]

WRITINGS:

"RUTH FIELDING" SERIES

Ruth Fielding of the Red Mill; or, Jasper Parloe's Secret (also see below), Cupples & Leon, 1913.

Ruth Fielding at Briarwood Hall; or, Solving the Campus Mystery, Cupples & Leon, 1913.

Ruth Fielding at Snow Camp; or, Lost in the Backwoods, Cupples & Leon, 1913.

Ruth Fielding at Lighthouse Point; or, Nita, the Girl Castaway, Cupples & Leon, 1913.

Ruth Fielding at Silver Ranch; or, Schoolgirls among the Cowboys, Cupples & Leon, 1913.

Ruth Fielding on Cliff Island; or, The Old Hunter's Treasure Box, Cupples & Leon, 1915.

Ruth Fielding at Sunrise Farm; or, What Became of the Ruby Orphans, Cupples & Leon, 1915.

Ruth Fielding and the Gypsies; or, The Missing Pearl Necklace, Cupples & Leon, 1915.

Once a favorite among young female readers, the "Ruth Fielding" series faded in popularity when the title character—an orphan turned movie star and sleuth—married her longtime suitor and settled down to quiet family life.

Ruth Fielding in Moving Pictures; or, Helping the Dormitory Fund, Cupples & Leon, 1916.

Ruth Fielding Down in Dixie; or, Great Days in the Land of Cotton, Cupples & Leon, 1916.

Ruth Fielding at College; or, The Missing Examination Papers, Cupples & Leon, 1917.

Ruth Fielding in the Saddle; or, College Girls in the Land of Gold, Cupples & Leon, 1917.

Ruth Fielding in the Red Cross; or, Doing Her Best for Uncle Sam, Cupples & Leon, 1918.

Ruth Fielding at the War Front; or, The Hunt for the Lost Soldier, Cupples & Leon, 1918.

Ruth Fielding Homeward Bound; or, A Red Cross Worker's Ocean Perils, Cupples & Leon, 1919.

Ruth Fielding Down East; or, The Hermit of Beach Plum Point, Cupples & Leon, 1920.

Ruth Fielding in the Great Northwest; or, The Indian Girl Star of the Movies, Cupples & Leon, 1921.

Ruth Fielding on the St. Lawrence; or, The Queer Old Man of the Thousand Islands, Cupples & Leon, 1922.

Ruth Fielding Treasure Hunting; or, A Moving Picture That Became Real, Cupples & Leon, 1923.

Ruth Fielding in the Far North; or, The Lost Motion Picture Company, Cupples & Leon, 1924.

Ruth Fielding at Golden Pass; or, The Perils of an Artificial Avalanche, Cupples & Leon, 1925.

Ruth Fielding in Alaska; or, The Miners of Snow Mountain, Cupples & Leon, 1926.

Ruth Fielding and Her Great Scenario; or, Striving for the Motion Picture Prize, Cupples & Leon, 1927.

Ruth Fielding at Cameron Hall; or, A Mysterious Disappearance, Cupples & Leon, 1928.

Ruth Fielding Clearing Her Name; or, The Rivals of Hollywood, Cupples & Leon, 1929.

Ruth Fielding in Talking Pictures; or, The Prisoners of the Tower, Cupples & Leon, 1930.

Ruth Fielding and Baby June, Cupples & Leon, 1931.

Ruth Fielding and Her Double, Cupples & Leon, 1932.

Ruth Fielding and Her Greatest Triumph; or, Saving Her Company from Disaster, Cupples & Leon, 1933.

Ruth Fielding and Her Crowning Victory; or, Winning Honors Abroad, Cupples & Leon, 1934.

"BETTY GORDON" SERIES

Betty Gordon at Bramble Farm; or, The Mystery of a Nobody (also see below), Cupples & Leon, 1920.

Betty Gordon in Washington; or, Strange Adventures in a Great City, Cupples & Leon, 1920.

Betty Gordon in the Land of Oil; or, The Farm That Was Worth a Fortune, Cupples & Leon, 1920.

Betty Gordon at Boarding School; or, The Treasure of Indian Chasm, Cupples & Leon, 1921.

Betty Gordon at Mountain Camp; or, The Mystery of Ida Bellethorne, Cupples & Leon, 1922.

Betty Gordon at Ocean Park; or, School Chums on the Boardwalk, Cupples & Leon, 1923.

Betty Gordon and Her School Chums; or, Bringing the Rebels to Terms, Cupples & Leon, 1924.

Betty Gordon at Rainbow Ranch; or, Cowboy Joe's Secret, Cupples & Leon, 1925.

Betty Gordon in Mexican Wilds; or, The Secret of the Mountains, Cupples & Leon, 1926.

Betty Gordon and the Lost Pearls; or, A Mystery of the Seaside, Cupples & Leon, 1927.

Betty Gordon on the Campus; or, The Secret of the Trunk Room, Cupples & Leon, 1928.

Betty Gordon and the Hale Twins; or, An Exciting Vacation, Cupples & Leon, 1929.

"Oh, isn't she just perfect!" exclaimed Helen. (Frontispiece from *Ruth Fielding and Baby June*, by Alice B. Emerson.)

Betty Gordon at Mystery Farm; or, Strange Doings at Rocky Ridge, Cupples & Leon, 1930.
Betty Gordon on No-Trail Island; or, Uncovering a Queer Secret, Cupples & Leon, 1931.
Betty Gordon and the Mystery Girl; or, The Secret at Sundown Hall, Cupples & Leon, 1932.

OTHER

(Contributor) *Mystery and Adventure Stories for Girls* (includes *Betty Gordon at Bramble Farm*), Cupples & Leon, 1934.
(Contributor) *Popular Stories for Girls* (includes *Ruth Fielding of the Red Mill*), Cupples & Leon, 1934.

SIDELIGHTS: Alice B. Emerson was a collective pseudonym used by the Stratemeyer Syndicate, a writing house that produced children's fiction such as the popular "Nancy Drew," "Hardy Boys," and "Bobbsey Twins" series. "Edward Stratemeyer's Ruth Fielding," states Carol Billman in *The Secret of the Stratemeyer Syndicate*, "was the preeminent 'charity child' on the go." She is one of the best representative heroines of early twentieth-century girls' series fiction, Billman suggests, "because of her series' popularity and because of her own position as a pivotal figure in fiction for American girls. Ruth is the orphan, a carry-over from the nineteenth-century sentimental tradition, turned movie star

and sleuth, two new roles for fictional heroines of the 1900s." In her sleuthing capacity, Billman suggests, Ruth Fielding serves as a prototype for other female detectives, especially Nancy Drew.

Yet Nancy Drew is still published today, while the last Ruth Fielding volume appeared in 1934. Part of the reason the series' success diminished, Billman declares, is because Ruth was unable to balance her career and her domestic life successfully after her marriage to her long-time suitor, Tom Cameron. Ruth's marriage, says Billman, altered the nature of the series; it lost the adventure orientation it had once had. "Ruth Fielding settles down to a quiet family life imbued with the strength of her conquests and discoveries in the wide world, and the desire for more such excitement," Billman asserts. "And the result is unsettling, for both her and her readers, who had come to expect in a Fielding title the tale of an independent and glamorous supergirl."

Ruth's dilemma lies in the fact that she is trying to be a working executive, a wife, and a mother all at once. "In her youth Ruth had no . . . qualms [about her future life]," states Billman, "for she knew she would grow up to do exactly what she chose. But her later conflict as an adult woman demonstrated that even when enormous talent, strong character, and indomitable will are available, there was reason for girls to be unsure. 'Having it all'—interesting work, marriage, and children—didn't come easily."

Mildred Augustine Wirt Benson wrote the last seven volumes of the "Ruth Fielding" series at Edward Stratemeyer's request. Stratemeyer writer W. Bert Foster also worked under the pseudonym on both Ruth Fielding and the Betty Gordon books, a series that capitalized on Ruth's popularity. See the *SATA* index for more information on Harriet S. Adams, Mildred Benson, Edward L. Stratemeyer, and Andrew E. Svenson.

WORKS CITED:

Billman, Carol, "Ruth Fielding: Orphan Turned Hollywood Sleuth," *The Secret of the Stratemeyer Syndicate: Nancy Drew, the Hardy Boys, and the Million Dollar Fiction Factory*, Ungar, 1986, pp. 57-77.

FOR MORE INFORMATION SEE:

BOOKS

Dizer, John T., *Tom Swift & Company: "Boy's Books" by Stratemeyer and Others*, McFarland & Co., 1982.
Johnson, Deidre, editor and compiler, *Stratemeyer Pseudonyms and Series Books: An Annotated Checklist of Stratemeyer and Stratemeyer Syndicate Publications*, Greenwood Press, 1982.
Paluka, Frank, *Iowa Authors: A Bio-Bibliography of Sixty Native Writers*, Friends of the University of Iowa Libraries, 1967.

PERIODICALS

Books at Iowa, November, 1973.
New York Times Book Review, September 28, 1986.
People's Voice, December, 1974.
Yellowback Library, July, 1983, September, 1986.

GAROU, Louis P.
See BOWKETT, Stephen

*   *   *

GEISEL, Theodor Seuss 1904-1991
(Theo. LeSieg, Dr. Seuss; Rosetta Stone, a joint pseudonym)

OBITUARY NOTICE—See index for *SATA* sketch: Surname is pronounced "*Guy*-zel"; born March 2, 1904, in Springfield, MA; died of cancer, September 24, 1991, in La Jolla, CA. Publisher, illustrator, and author. Known to the world as "Dr. Seuss," Theodor Seuss Geisel was loved and respected by many as the leading children's author of the twentieth century. Winner of several major awards—including a Pulitzer Prize in 1984—Geisel endeared himself to readers young and old with fanciful drawings and rhyming couplets in classics like *The Cat in the Hat, Green Eggs and Ham, Horton Hears a Who,* and *Hop on Pop.* In all he wrote forty-seven books that sold more than 200 million copies worldwide. *The Cat in the Hat,* published in 1957, had perhaps the greatest impact of these works by providing an imaginative story line spiced with offbeat humor that appealed to beginning readers more than the conventional "Dick and Jane" books. The success of *The Cat in the Hat* prompted Seuss to establish Beginner Books, which published works for young readers, including books he wrote under the pseudonym Theo. LeSieg, such as *Wacky Wednesday,* and the joint pseudonym Rosetta Stone, such as *Because a Little Bug Went Ka-Choo!* Other widely popular Seuss books include *And to Think I Saw It on Mulberry Street,* Seuss's 1937 debut work that had been rejected by twenty-seven publishers; *How the Grinch Stole Christmas,* a 1957 offering that became a seasonal standard when Seuss adapted it into a television special in 1971; and Seuss's personal favorite, *The Lorax,* an environmental book about a mossy creature who tries to save the truffula trees from the ax of the dreaded Onceler. Seuss continued producing books through his eighties, writing *The Butter Battle Book* in 1984, *You're Only Old Once* in 1986, *I'm Not Going to Get Up Today* in 1987, and *Oh, the Places You'll Go,* in 1990.

OBITUARIES AND OTHER SOURCES:

PERIODICALS

Detroit Free Press, September 26, 1991; September 27, 1991.
Detroit News, September 26, 1991.

*   *   *

GREENE, Carla 1916-

PERSONAL: Born December 18, 1916, in Minneapolis, MN; daughter of William L. and Charlotte (Wunderman) Greene. *Education:* High school graduate. *Hobbies and other interests:* Ballet, theater, painting, music, lectures.

ADDRESSES: Office—8300 Sunset Blvd., Los Angeles, CA 90069. *Agent*—Toni Strassman, 130 E. 18th St., New York, NY 10003.

CAREER: Began as secretary in Minneapolis, MN; worked variously as a radio and magazine writer and an advertising copy writer for department stores in Detroit, MI, Chicago, IL, and New York City, 1932-52; children's book writer, 1952—. Lecturer on travel and children's reading.

MEMBER: PEN International, Authors League of America, Reading Is Fundamental, California Council on Children's Literature, Los Angeles County Museum, Los Angeles Music Center.

AWARDS, HONORS: Outstanding Book Award, Junior Science Teachers of America, 1972, for *How Man Began.*

WRITINGS:

"TRAVEL" SERIES

A Hotel Holiday, photography by William L. Hoffman, Melmont, 1954.
Holiday in a Trailer, photography by Harold L. Van Pelt, Melmont, 1955.
A Motor Holiday, photography by Van Pelt, Melmont, 1956.
A Trip on a Train, Lantern Press, 1956.
A Trip on a Plane, Lantern Press, 1957.
A Trip on a Ship, Lantern Press, 1958.
A Trip to Hawaii, Lantern Press, 1959.
A Trip on a Jet, Lantern Press, 1960.
A Trip to the Zoo, illustrated by Gloria Stevens, Lantern Press, 1962.
A Trip on a Bus, photography by Jack Warford, Lantern Press, 1964.
A Trip to the Aquarium, illustrated by Stevens, Lantern Press, 1967.

"I WANT TO BE" SERIES

I Want to Be an Animal Doctor, illustrated by Frances Eckart, Childrens Press, 1956.
I Want to Be a Baker, illustrated by Audrey Williamson, Childrens Press, 1956.
I Want to Be a Train Engineer, illustrated by Victor Havel, Childrens Press, 1956.
I Want to Be an Orange Grower, illustrated by Williamson, Childrens Press, 1956.
I Want to Be a Bus Driver, illustrated by Katherine Evans, Childrens Press, 1957.
I Want to Be a Coal Miner, illustrated by Williamson, Childrens Press, 1957.
I Want to Be a Dairy Farmer, illustrated by Eckart, Childrens Press, 1957.
I Want to Be a Fisherman, illustrated by Lucy and John Hawkinson, Childrens Press, 1957.
I Want to Be a Nurse, illustrated by Becky and Evans Krehbiel, Childrens Press, 1957.
I Want to Be a Pilot, illustrated by Richard Gates, Childrens Press, 1957.
I Want to Be a Teacher, illustrated by Vie Johnson, Childrens Press, 1957.
I Want to Be a Zoo Keeper, illustrated by Eckart, Childrens Press, 1957.
I Want to Be a Doctor, illustrated by Eckart, Childrens Press, 1958.
I Want to Be a News Reporter, illustrated by Eckart, Childrens Press, 1958.
I Want to Be a Policeman, illustrated by Carol Rogers, Childrens Press, 1958.
I Want to Be a Postman, illustrated by Evans, Childrens Press, 1958.
I Want to Be a Road Builder, illustrated by Irma Wilde and George Wilde, Childrens Press, 1958.
I Want to Be a Storekeeper, illustrated by Eckart, Childrens Press, 1958.

Oh! Oh! A traffic jam!

Honk! *Honk!* HOOONK!

Nothing moves.

Jack must wait until

the cars and trucks can go ahead.

It seems to take forever.

But in a few minutes

Jack's truck

is on its way again.

As he drives in the city

Jack sees many kinds

of trucks and drivers.

Carla Greene's *Truck Drivers* is part of her seven-book "What Do They Do" series, which provides information on careers while teaching youngsters to read. (Illustration by Leonard Kessler.)

I Want to Be a Telephone Operator, illustrated by Mary Gehr, Childrens Press, 1958.

I Want to Be a Truck Driver, illustrated by I. Wilde and G. Wilde, Childrens Press, 1958.

I Want to Be a Ballet Dancer, illustrated by Gehr, Childrens Press, 1959.

I Want to Be a Carpenter, illustrated by Eckart, Childrens Press, 1959.

I Want to Be a Farmer, illustrated by I. Wilde and G. Wilde, Childrens Press, 1959.

I Want to Be a Fireman, illustrated by I. Wilde and G. Wilde, Childrens Press, 1959.

I Want to Be a Mechanic, illustrated by Gehr, Childrens Press, 1959.

I Want to Be a Restaurant Owner, illustrated by Rogers, Childrens Press, 1959.

I Want to Be a Cowboy, illustrated by Janet LaSalle, Childrens Press, 1960.

I Want to Be a Dentist, illustrated by I. Wilde, Childrens Press, 1960.

I Want to Be a Librarian, illustrated by Eckart, Childrens Press, 1960.

I Want to Be an Airplane Hostess, illustrated by Eckart, Childrens Press, 1960.

I Want to Be a Baseball Player, illustrated by Eckart, Childrens Press, 1961.

I Want to Be a Homemaker, illustrated by Eckart, Childrens Press, 1961.

I Want to Be a Scientist, illustrated by LaSalle, Childrens Press, 1961.

I Want to Be a Space Pilot, Childrens Press, 1961.

I Want to Be a Musician, illustrated by Eckart, Childrens Press, 1962.

I Want to Be a Ship Captain, illustrated by Felix Palm, Childrens Press, 1962.

"WHAT DO THEY DO" SERIES

Policemen and Firemen, illustrated by Leonard Kessler, Harper, 1962.

Doctors and Nurses, illustrated by Kessler, Harper, 1963.

Soldiers and Sailors, illustrated by Kessler, Harper, 1963.

Railroad Engineers and Airplane Pilots, illustrated by Kessler, Harper, 1964.

Animal Doctors, illustrated by Kessler, Harper, 1967.

Truck Drivers, illustrated by Kessler, Harper, 1967.

Cowboys, illustrated by Kessler, Harper, 1972.

"LET'S LEARN ABOUT" SERIES

Where Does a Letter Go?, Harvey House, 1965.

Let's Meet the Chemist, illustrated by John J. Floherty, Jr., Harvey House, 1966.

Let's Learn about the Orchestra, illustrated by Anne Lewis, Harvey House, 1967.

Moses: The Great Lawgiver, illustrated by Lewis, Harvey House, 1968.

Let's Learn about Lighthouses, illustrated by Floherty, Harvey House, 1969.

"SCIENCE AND NATURAL HISTORY" SERIES

How to Know Dinosaurs, Bobbs-Merrill, 1966.

After the Dinosaurs, illustrated by Kyuzo Tsugami, Bobbs-Merrill, 1968.

Before the Dinosaurs, illustrated by Richard Cuffari, Bobbs-Merrill, 1970.

How Man Began, illustrated by Floherty, Bobbs-Merrill, 1972.

Our Living Earth: Its Origins and Ecology of Our Planet, illustrated by Floherty, Bobbs-Merrill, 1974.

Man and Ancient Civilizations, illustrated by Marika, Bobbs-Merrill, 1977.

OTHER

Charles Darwin (biography), illustrated by David Hodges, Dial, 1968.

Manuel: Young Mexican-American (fiction), illustrated by Haris Petie, Lantern Press, 1969.

Gregor Mendel (biography), illustrated by Cuffari, Dial, 1970.

(Editor) *Handbook of Adult Primary Care* (adult medical nonfiction), illustrated by Masako Herman, Wiley, 1987.

Contributor of articles to various periodicals.

Greene's *Truck Drivers,* a title in the "What Do They Do?" series, has been translated into Spanish.

SIDELIGHTS: Carla Greene has written more than sixty books for children aged five to twelve. Many of her works have sold more than one million copies. She began her book writing career in the early 1950s with a travel series based on

PENI R. GRIFFIN

her experiences as tourist. Continuing with the "I Want to Be" series in the mid-1950s and her "What Do They Do?" series in the early 1960s, she wrote about the duties and activities of men and women in professions like teaching, truck driving, firefighting, and baking. These books, while providing information on careers, were also designed to help youngsters learn how to read. In the late 1960s, Greene turned to writing science and natural history books for intermediate readers on subjects such as dinosaurs and early mankind. She also wrote biographies of famous men, including Bible prophet Moses, nineteenth-century English naturalist Charles Darwin, and nineteenth-century Austrian botanist Gregor Mendel.

Carla Greene commented: "I believe that today's youngsters are much more eager, alert, and knowledgeable than former generations. Bearing this in mind, I try to bring them information about their world in a way that excites the young reader and leads him or her to further investigation on a subject. Without underestimating their intelligence or assaulting the reader with boring statistics or trite facts, I try to bring them insight into the world around them, both modern and ancient."

FOR MORE INFORMATION SEE:

PERIODICALS

Booklist, December 1, 1977.

Kirkus Reviews, November 1, 1970.

Library Journal, March 15, 1969; June 15, 1971; February 15, 1973.

New York Times Book Review, November 5, 1967; September 14, 1969.

Publishers Weekly, March 10, 1969.

School Library Journal, October, 1977.

Times Literary Supplement, April 3, 1969.

*   *   *

GRIFFIN, Peni R(ae) 1961-

PERSONAL: Born July 11, 1961, in Harlingin, TX; daughter of William Jay (in the Air Force) and Sandra Sue (Roberts) Robinson; married Michael David Griffin (a collector), July 13, 1987; stepchildren: Morgan Leigh. *Education:* Attended Trinity University, 1979-80, and University of Texas at San Antonio, 1982-84. *Religion:* Agnostic.

ADDRESSES: Home—1123 West Magnolia Ave., San Antonio, TX 78201.

CAREER: City Public Service, San Antonio, TX, clerk, 1985-89; Manpower Temporary Services, San Antonio, temporary worker, 1990; writer.

AWARDS, HONORS: Third place, *Twilight Zone* magazine writing contest, 1986, for "Nereid"; second place, National Society for Arts and Letters (San Antonio branch) short story contest, 1988, for "The Truth in the Case of Eliza Mary Muller, by Herself."

WRITINGS:

Otto from Otherwhere (science fiction novel for children), Margaret K. McElderry, 1990.

A Dig in Time (science fiction novel for children), Margaret K. McElderry, 1991.

Hobkin, Margaret K. McElderry, in press.

Contributor of short stories to magazines, including *Dragon, Fantasy Macabre, Figment, Isaac Asimov's Science Fiction Magazine, Leading Edge, Magazine of Fantasy and Science Fiction, Pandora, Pulphouse, Space and Time,* and *Twilight Zone.*

WORK IN PROGRESS: Lifegame, a fantasy novel for adults; a juvenile mystery; research on parrots, hidden treasure, and *fin de siecle* America, especially Texas.

SIDELIGHTS: Peni R. Griffin told *SATA:* "I am one of the fortunate few who always knew what she wanted to do. This makes life simple. I'm told it also makes me arrogant, but that's all right, as it takes great gobs of arrogance to try to live by writing. I am technically unemployed just now and intend to remain so if I can.

"My husband gave me the idea for *Otto from Otherwhere* one foggy January. He worked near Woodlawn Lake, where the story happens, and he told me one day that that morning the fog had been so thick on the surface, it looked as if you could walk out across it into another world. I knew at once what people in that other world looked like. At first I began working it out as a short story, from the grandmother's point of view, but I soon realized that all the interesting things would be happening to the children. Children's books are, as a rule, so much better than adult books that I had assumed I wasn't good enough to write them, but I decided to give this a shot. I wrote it on my coffee breaks over a period of ten months, working out logically what would really happen in the situation, while leaving out the boring parts.

"The second book, *A Dig in Time,* came busting out of my head in about six months. I had been researching the past fifty years heavily for an adult book about comic collecting and time travel, and the plot and incidents of the children's book formed naturally underneath my main activity. One slow day at work I began fiddling with ideas that would allow me to use the name 'Utnapishtim' in a story, because I like the sound of it. The idea of two children having an archaeological dig in their back yard and literally digging up the past took hold of me and made me write it.

"I am still trying to write adult books, because I am still getting adult ideas, but compared to the children's books they take so long and come out so indifferently that I take them less and less seriously as time goes on.

"My advice to aspiring writers is to get life partners without literary ambitions and treat them well. They are useful not only for their paychecks but for their knack for passing on information, ideas, and observations that can turn into stories; for relieving you of housework; for providing chocolate during blue periods; and for keeping you in touch with the world outside your head."

*   *   *

GROSS, Ernie 1913-

PERSONAL: Given name is Ernest; born April 25, 1913, in Temesvar, Hungary (now Romania); son of Henry (in advertising) and Rose (Weinberg) Gross; married Helen H. Gross, August 1, 1939 (deceased); married Carolyn A. Boyce, December 12, 1967; children: Patricia Bresien, Richard Conklin, Terry Temescu, Eileen Orcutt. *Education:* University of Chicago, B.A., 1934; University of Nebraska, M.A., 1937. *Politics:* Independent. *Religion:* Protestant.

ADDRESSES: Home—Accomac, VA. *Office*—c/o Publicity Director, Neal-Schuman Publishers Inc., 23 Leonard St., New York, NY 10013.

CAREER: Writer. *Lincoln Star,* Lincoln, NB, reporter, 1937-41; *Buffalo Evening News,* Buffalo, NY, reporter, 1941-63; New York State Labor Department, Albany, NY, public relations director, 1963-64; U.S. Office of Economic Opportunity, Washington, DC, public relations director of job corps, 1964-67; U.S. Department of Housing and Urban Development, Washington DC, director of new services, 1967-75. President, Hospice Care of Eastern Shore, 1982-90; town councilman, Accomac, VA, 1990—. *Military service:* U.S. Army, 1943-46, became technical sergeant.

WRITINGS:

This Day in Religion, Neal-Schuman, 1990.
This Day in American History, Neal-Schuman, 1990.

SIDELIGHTS: Ernie Gross told *SATA:* "The only motivational advice I can offer is that if one confidently believes in their work, just keep trying to convince someone of the work's worth. The effort in itself is of great value."

FOR MORE INFORMATION SEE:

PERIODICALS

Booklist, April 1, 1990; November 15, 1990.
Library Journal, March 1, 1990.
Voice of Youth Advocates, August, 1990.
Wilson Library Bulletin, October, 1990.

*   *   *

GRUNEWALT, Pine
See KUNHARDT, Edith

*   *   *

GUTHRIE, A(lfred) B(ertram), Jr. 1901-1991

OBITUARY NOTICE—See index for *SATA* sketch: Born January 13, 1901, in Bedford, IN; died of lung failure, April 26, 1991, at home in Choteau, MT. Journalist, educator, screenwriter, and author. Pulitzer Prize-winner Guthrie was noted for his realistic depiction of Western life. He grew up in the Montana Rockies and graduated from the University of Montana in 1923. From 1926 to 1947, he served as reporter, city editor, editorial writer and executive editor on the *Lexington Leader* in Kentucky. In 1947, he published his most famous novel, *The Big Sky,* and began to teach creative writing at the University of Kentucky. His 1949 Western novel, *The Way West,* won the Pulitzer Prize for fiction. During the 1950s Guthrie also wrote screenplays, of which the most famous were *Shane,* which he adapted from Jack Schaefer's novel, and *The Kentuckian.* Many of his works had environmental themes, and in 1988 he published *Big Sky, Fair Land,* a collection of his environmental essays and excerpts from his novels. Guthrie's works also included mysteries, such as the 1989 novel *Murder in the Cotswolds,* and nonfiction, such as 1991's *A Field Guide to Writing Fiction.*

OBITUARIES AND OTHER SOURCES:

BOOKS

Who's Who in America, Supplement to 45th edition, Marquis, 1989.

PERIODICALS

Chicago Tribune, April 28, 1991, section 2, p. 10.
Los Angeles Times, April 27, 1991, p. A26.
New York Times, April 27, 1991, p. 13.
Times (London), April 30, 1991, p. 16.
Washington Post, April 27, 1991, p. B6.

*   *   *

GUTMAN, Bill

PERSONAL: Born in New York, NY; married; wife's name, Elizabeth. *Education:* Washington College, B.A., 1965; attended University of Bridgeport.

ADDRESSES: Home—Ridgefield, CT.

CAREER: Sportswriter. *Greenwich Time,* Greenwich, CT, reporter and sports editor during the late 1960s; has also worked in advertising.

WRITINGS:

NONFICTION

Great Quarterbacks, Grosset & Dunlap, Volume 1: *Staubach, Landry, Plunkett, Gabriel,* 1972, Volume 2: *Kilmer, Hale, Bradshaw, Phipps,* 1973, revised edition, 1974.
Pistol Pete Maravich: The Making of a Basketball Superstar, Grosset & Dunlap, 1972.
Hockey Explosion, Grosset & Dunlap, 1973.
World Series Classics, Random House, 1973.
Hank Aaron, Grosset & Dunlap, 1973, published as *Henry Aaron.*
Famous Baseball Stars, Dodd, Mead, 1973.
Gamebreakers of the NFL, Random House, 1973.
Jim Plunkett, Grosset & Dunlap, 1973.
Modern Baseball Superstars, Dodd, Mead, 1973.
At Bat, Grosset & Dunlap, 1973.
Great Running Backs, Grosset & Dunlap, Volume 1, 1973, Volume 2, 1974.
New Breed Heroes in Pro Baseball, Messner, 1973.
New Breed Heroes of Pro Football, Messner, 1974.
Great Linebackers, No. 1, Grosset & Dunlap, 1974.
Csonka, Grosset & Dunlap, 1974.
Modern Football Superstars, Dodd, Mead, 1974.
O. J., Grosset & Dunlap, 1974.
Griese Tarkenton, Grosset & Dunlap, 1974.
Jackson—Bench, Grosset & Dunlap, 1974.
Great Hockey Players, No. 1, Grosset & Dunlap, 1974.
Aaron—Murcer, Grosset & Dunlap, 1974.
At Bat, No. 2: Cedeno, Rose, Bonds, and Fish, Grosset & Dunlap, 1974.
Modern Basketball Superstars, Dodd, Mead, 1975.
Football Superstars of the '70s, Messner, 1975.
The Front Four, Grosset & Dunlap, 1975.
Giants of Baseball, Grosset & Dunlap, 1975.
Great Receivers of the NFL, Grosset & Dunlap, 1975.
New Ball Game, Grosset & Dunlap, 1975.
Modern Hockey Superstars, Dodd, Mead, 1976.
Pele, Grosset & Dunlap, 1976.
Munson, Garvey, Brock, Carew, Grosset & Dunlap, 1976.

Mark Fidrych, Grosset & Dunlap, 1977.
Modern Women Superstars, Dodd, Mead, 1977.
Harlem Globetrotters: Basketball's Funniest Team, Garrard, 1977.
Duke: The Musical Life of Duke Ellington, Random House, 1977.
Dr. J., Grosset & Dunlap, 1977.
Walton, Thompson, Lanier, Collins, Grosset & Dunlap, 1978.
Superstars of the Sports World, Messner, 1978.
The Picture Life of Reggie Jackson, Watts, 1978, published as *Reggie Jackson: The Picture Life,* Avon, 1978.
Great Basketball Stories: Today and Yesterday, Messner, 1978.
More Modern Baseball Superstars, Dodd, Mead, 1978.
Modern Soccer Superstars, Dodd, Mead, 1979.
Grand Slammers: Rice, Luzinski, Foster and Hisle, Grosset & Dunlap, 1979.
(Editor) Franklin Folsom, *Baseball,* revised edition (Gutman not associated with previous edition), Watts, 1979.
Great Sports Feats of the '70s, Messner, 1979.
Gridiron Greats: Campbell, Zorn, Swann, Grogan, Grosset & Dunlap, 1979.
More Modern Women Superstars, Dodd, Mead, 1979.
Pro Sports Champions, Messner, 1981.
The Signal Callers: Sipe, Jaworski, Ferguson, Bartowski, Grosset & Dunlap, 1981.
Baseball's Belters: Jackson, Schmidt, Parker, Brett, Grosset & Dunlap, 1981.
Baseball Stars of Tomorrow: An Inside Look at the Minor Leagues, Grosset & Dunlap, 1982.
Women Who Work with Animals, Dodd, Mead, 1982.
Flame Throwers: Carlton and Gossage, Ace Books, 1982.
Gridiron Superstars, Ace Books, 1983.
Summer Dreams, Avon, 1985.
Strange and Amazing Wrestling Stories, Pocket Books, 1986.
Refrigerator Perry and the Super Bowl Bears, Archway, 1987.
Sports Illustrated Great Moments in Pro Football, Archway, 1987.
Sports Illustrated Pro Football's Record Breakers, Archway, 1987.
Pictorial History of Basketball, Smith, 1988.
Great Sports Upsets, Pocket Books, 1988.
Sports Illustrated Baseball's Record Breakers, Archway, 1988.
Great World Series, Bantam, 1989.
Sports Illustrated Great Moments in Baseball, Pocket Books, 1989.
Sports Illustrated Strange and Amazing Football Stories, Pocket Books, 1989.
Great All-Star Games, Bantam, 1989.
Baseball's Hot New Stars, Pocket Books, 1989.
Sports Illustrated Growing Up Painfully, Simon & Schuster, 1990.
Pro Sports Champions, Pocket Books, 1990.
Sports Illustrated Baseball Records, Pocket Books, 1990.
(With Lee Heiman and Dave Weiner) *When the Cheering Stops: Ex-Major Leaguers Talk about Their Game and Their Lives,* Macmillan, 1990.
Sports Illustrated Strange and Amazing Baseball Stories, Pocket Books, 1990.
Bo Jackson, Pocket Books, 1991.
The Giants Win the Pennant! The Giants Win the Pennant!, Zebra Books, 1991.
Micro-League Championship Baseball: Official Field Guide and Disk, Bantam, 1991.

Also author of *Payton, Jones, Haden, Dorsett* and *Chairmen of the Boards,* 1980.

"START RIGHT AND PLAY WELL" SERIES; ILLUSTRATED BY BEN BROWN

Football: Start Right and Play Well, Grey Castle, 1989.
Volleyball: Start Right and Play Well, Pocket Books, 1989, published as *Volleyball for Boys and Girls: Start Right and Play Well*, Grey Castle, 1990.
Basketball for Boys and Girls: Start Right and Play Well, Grey Castle, 1990.
Field Hockey: Start Right and Play Well, Grey Castle, 1990.
Soccer for Boys and Girls: Start Right and Play Well, Grey Castle, 1990.
Softball for Boys and Girls: Start Right and Play Well, Grey Castle, 1990.
Tennis for Boys and Girls: Start Right and Play Well, Grey Castle, 1990.

"GO FOR IT!" SERIES; ILLUSTRATED BY BEN BROWN

Tennis, Grey Castle, 1989.
Softball, Grey Castle, 1989.
Basketball, Grey Castle, 1989.
Field Hockey, Grey Castle, 1989.
Wrestling, Grey Castle, 1989.
Track and Field, Grey Castle, 1989.
Ice Hockey, Grey Castle, 1989.
Football, Grey Castle, 1989.
Baseball, Grey Castle, 1989.
Soccer, Grey Castle, 1989.
Swimming, Grey Castle, 1989.
Volleyball, Grey Castle, 1989.

FICTION

"My Father, the Coach" and Other Sports Stories (contains the short stories "The Geek," "Smitty," "Shorty," "Gridiron Scholar," "The Trouble with Rusty," "The Quarterback Question," "Rocky's Hard Head," "Little Brother," and "Shortstop"), Messner, 1976.
Smitty, Turman, 1988.
Rookie Summer (novel), Turman, 1988.
Smitty II: The Olympics, Turman, 1990.

OTHER

Also contributor to *Boy's Life* and other magazines. Contributing editor, *Team!*

WORK IN PROGRESS: Books on sports, sports figures, and sports history.

SIDELIGHTS: Sportswriter Bill Gutman was born in New York City and grew up in Stamford, Connecticut. He planned to become a dentist, but instead he earned a bachelor's degree in English literature at Washington College in Chestertown, Maryland. Eventually he became a reporter and feature writer for the Greenwich, Connecticut, newspaper *Greenwich Time*. He worked briefly in advertising, then began to write nonfiction sports books full-time. Since 1972 he has written more than one hundred books about sports for readers of all ages.

Critics recommend Gutman's biographies of sports figures as accurate and interesting depictions of the men and women who have achieved fame in all the major sports. Beginning with *Pistol Pete Maravich: The Making of a Basketball Superstar*, Gutman's subjects include star performers from baseball, basketball, football, hockey, tennis, wrestling, and soccer. When they were first published, his books were the most complete sources of information available for several sports personalities including Greg Landry, Chris Evert,

Dorothy Hamill, and Nadia Comeneci. His books appeal to readers of all ages by combining descriptions of game action and sports facts.

Gutman and coauthors Lee Heiman and Dave Weiner asked professional baseball players about their lives for *When the Cheering Stops: Ex-Major Leaguers Talk about Their Game and Their Lives*. Mark Clayton observes in the *Christian Science Monitor*, "The authors seem to have asked each of the players similar questions, which could have been a bore. But the word-for-word statements are a surprisingly interesting and spontaneous recounting of what it is like to play in the shadow of the big guys, only occasionally holding the spotlight. The answers include their impressions, their gripes, the great players they remember, and what they've been doing since hanging up their spikes."

Modern Women Sports Superstars dispels some myths about women in professional sports and provides important statistics about their accomplishments. Gutman reports, for example, that Joan Joyce was the fastest pitcher alive in 1979, with the speed of one pitch measured at one hundred and sixteen miles per hour. Female stars of tennis, golf, auto and horse racing, swimming, and softball are featured in this book and in *More Modern Women Sports Superstars*.

Women Who Work with Animals looks at the careers of six women in jobs that have been dominated by men in the past. A horse trainer, two zoo workers, a show dog handler, a veterinarian, and a sea mammal trainer are featured in the book. These women tell Gutman and young readers how they became interested in working with animals and what kinds of education best prepared them for their work. They also offer advice for young women seeking similar careers. Diane Tuccillo remarks in the *High/Low Report*, "Reluctant readers who enjoy stories about animals may like this book. There is high-interest subject matter scattered throughout." For example, true stories about living with caged gorilla babies and overcoming allergies to animal hair make the book fascinating as well as readable.

Gutman turns his attention from sports figures to a famous name in the music world in *Duke Ellington: The Musical Life of Duke Ellington*. Giving more emphasis to the development of the jazz musician's musical style than to the details of his personal life, the biographer follows Ellington's rise from his beginning as a pianist to a jazz composer of international fame. He also explains many of the social and economic conditions faced by black musicians in the United States. Critics agree that readers can find this book a useful introductory history of American jazz presented in a format that is appealing to younger readers.

WORKS CITED:

Clayton, Mark, review of *When the Cheering Stops, Christian Science Monitor*, May 7, 1990, p. 13.
Tuccillo, Diane, review of *Women Who Work with Animals, High/Low Report*, October, 1982, p. 6.

FOR MORE INFORMATION SEE:

BOOKS

Authors of Books for Young People, supplement to the 2nd edition, Scarecrow, 1979.

PERIODICALS

Best Sellers, October, 1978.
Booklist, July 1, 1978; October 1, 1982.
High/Low Report, April, 1980.
School Library Journal, September, 1978.
Voice of Youth Advocates, December, 1982.*

* * *

HALL, Kirsten Marie 1974-

PERSONAL: Born October 14, 1974, in New York, NY; daughter of John R., Jr. (in research and development of children's toys) and Nancy Christensen (a children's book producer) Hall. *Education:* Attending Moses Brown High School. *Hobbies and other interests:* Sports, community service, music, art.

ADDRESSES: Home—86 Woodbury St., Providence, RI 02906.

AWARDS, HONORS: Hallmark Award, Rhode Island regional gold key award for art.

WRITINGS:

Bunny, Bunny, Childrens Press, 1990.
Who Says?, Childrens Press, 1990.
A Visit to France, Western Publishing, 1991.

SIDELIGHTS: Kirsten Marie Hall explains that she was inspired by her parents to write children's books. "My mother produces children's books," she states, "and my father does research and development of children's toys. I have always been encouraged to explore my own creativity."

Hall's first book, *Bunny, Bunny,* is part of an ongoing series of books produced for Childrens Press. Each of the books in the series tells a story using a vocabulary of only twenty-four words. Writing *Bunny, Bunny,* Hall found, was "more like doing a puzzle than writing a book." A couple of weeks after *Bunny, Bunny* was accepted for publication, Hall wrote *Who Says?*, another book in the series.

A Visit to France was inspired by a summer Hall spent living with a French family in the south of France. She named the two boys in the book after the French family's two little boys, Raphael and Lucas. It is "a very simple story," she says, "but a child who reads it could learn a lot about France."

Still attending high school in Rhode Island, Hall is unsure of her future career plans. "At this point I think I will probably pursue a career in some way related to publishing," she reveals, "but whatever I wind up doing some day, I know I will always keep writing stories for children."

* * *

HARDY, Alice Dale
[Collective pseudonym]

WRITINGS:

"FLYAWAYS" SERIES

The Flyaways and Cinderella, Grosset & Dunlap, 1925.
The Flyaways and Little Red Riding Hood, Grosset & Dunlap, 1925.
The Flyaways and Goldilocks, Grosset & Dunlap, 1925.

"RIDDLE CLUB" SERIES

The Riddle Club at Home: How the Club Was Formed, What Riddles Were Asked, and How the Members Solved a Mystery, Grosset & Dunlap, 1924.
The Riddle Club in Camp: How They Journeyed to the Lake, What Happened around the Campfire, and How a Forgotten Name Was Recalled, Grosset & Dunlap, 1924.
The Riddle Club through the Holidays: The Club and Its Doings, How the Riddles Were Solved, and What the Snowman Revealed, Grosset & Dunlap, 1924.
The Riddle Club at Sunrise Beach: How They Toured to the Shore, What Happened on the Sand, and How They Solved the Mystery of Rattlesnake Island, Grosset & Dunlap, 1925.
The Riddle Club at Shadybrook: Why They Went There, What Happened on the Way, and What Occurred during Their Absence from Home, Grosset & Dunlap, 1926.
The Riddle Club at Rocky Falls: How They Went up the River, What Adventures They Had in the Woods, and How They Solved the Mystery of the Deserted Hotel, Grosset & Dunlap, 1929.

SIDELIGHTS: Alice Dale Hardy was a pseudonym used by the Stratemeyer Syndicate, a writing house that produced such popular juvenile fiction as the "Nancy Drew," "Hardy Boys," and "Bobbsey Twins" series. The "Flyaways" books featured adventures with characters from classic fairytales, and was the only Stratemeyer fantasy series to feature human characters. The "Riddle Club" was formed by three boys and three girls; the books chronicled the adventures of the members. See the *SATA* index for more information on Harriet S. Adams, Edward L. Stratemeyer, and Andrew E. Svenson.

FOR MORE INFORMATION SEE:

BOOKS

Johnson, Deidre, editor and compiler, *Stratemeyer Pseudonyms and Series Books: An Annotated Checklist of Stratemeyer and Stratemeyer Syndicate Publications*, Greenwood Press, 1982.

* * *

HAWLEY, Mabel C.
[Collective pseudonym]

WRITINGS:

"FOUR LITTLE BLOSSOMS" SERIES

Four Little Blossoms at Brookside Farm, G. Sully, 1920, reprinted, Saalfield Publishing, 1938.
Four Little Blossoms at Oak Hill School, G. Sully, 1920, reprinted, Saalfield Publishing, 1938.
Four Little Blossoms and Their Winter Fun, G. Sully, 1920, reprinted, Saalfield Publishing, 1938.
Four Little Blossoms on Appletree Island, G. Sully, 1921, reprinted, Saalfield Publishing, 1938.
Four Little Blossoms through the Holidays, G. Sully, 1922.
Four Little Blossoms at Sunrise Beach, Cupples & Leon, 1929.
Four Little Blossoms Indoors and Out, Cupples & Leon, 1930.

SIDELIGHTS: The "Blossom" series was written under the collective pseudonym Mabel C. Hawley by writers for the Stratemeyer Syndicate, a writing house that produced children's fiction, including the popular "Nancy Drew," "Hardy

Boys," and "Bobbsey Twins" series. The Blossom siblings, Bobby, Meg, and the twins Twaddles and Dot, were the featured characters in this series for young children. See the *SATA* index for more information on Harriet S. Adams, Edward L. Stratemeyer, and Andrew E. Svenson.

FOR MORE INFORMATION SEE:

BOOKS

Johnson, Deidre, editor and compiler, *Stratemeyer Pseudonyms and Series Books: An Annotated Checklist of Stratemeyer and Stratemeyer Syndicate Publications,* Greenwood Press, 1982.

*   *   *

HEINE, Helme 1941-

PERSONAL: Born April 4, 1941, in Berlin, Germany.

ADDRESSES: Viktoriastrasse 2, 8000 Munich 40, Germany.

CAREER: Writer and illustrator.

HELME HEINE

WRITINGS:

IN ENGLISH TRANSLATION; SELF-ILLUSTRATED

The Pig's Wedding, Atheneum, 1979 (originally published as *Na Warte, sagte Schwarte,* Middlehauve, 1978).

Mr. Miller the Dog, Atheneum, 1980 (originally published as *Der Hund Herr Muller,* Unterhaching, 1979).

Friends, Atheneum, 1982 (originally published as *Freunde,* Middlehauve, 1981).

King Bounce the 1st, Neugebauer Press, 1982 (originally published as *Koenig Hupf der 1,* Middlehauve, 1981).

The Racing Car, Atheneum, 1985 (originally published as *Der Rennwagen,* Middlehauve, 1983).

The Most Wonderful Egg in the World, Aladdin, 1987 (originally published as *Das schoenste Ei der Welt,* Middlehauve, 1983).

The Alarm Clock, Atheneum, 1986 (originally published as *Der Wecker,* Middlehauve, 1983).

The Pearl, Dent, 1985 (originally published as *Die Perle,* Middlehauve, 1984).

The Visitor, Atheneum, 1985 (originally published as *Der Besuch,* Middlehauve, 1985).

One Day in Paradise, Atheneum, 1986 (originally published as *Samstag in Paradies,* Middlehauve, 1986).

Prince Bear, M. K. McElderry, 1989 (originally published as *Prinz Baer,* Middlehauve, 1988).

Seven Wild Pigs: Eleven Picture Book Fantasies, M. K. McElderry, 1988 (originally published as *Sieben Wilde Schweine,* Middlehauve, 1988).

IN ENGLISH; SELF-ILLUSTRATED

Superhare, Barron's, 1979.

Merry-Go-Round, Barron's, 1980.

OTHER

Uhren haben keine Bremse (humor), Diogenes, 1985.

Also author of untranslated children's books, including *Tante Nudel, Onkel Ruhe, und Herr Schlau: Ein Bilderbuch,* Middlehauve, 1979.

SIDELIGHTS: Author and illustrator Helme Heine is best known for creating picture books that are both thought-provoking and entertaining. While his work covers a wide range of subjects and themes, Heine specializes in retelling classic fables and fairytales from a humorous point of view. Many of Heine's books feature playful and inventive watercolor illustrations of animals and nature. Despite the often whimsical nature of his illustrations and stories, Heine tries to put a bit of seriousness in all his tales. "I like to put in something that continues to grow when the book is closed—a moral, or a different way to think about something," Heine told Margaret Carter in an interview for *Books for Your Children.* He added: "Language and illustration are after all two sides of the same coin. Language creates pictures but an illustrator shouldn't follow the author—it is his job to create between the lines—what the author has *not* written. . . . Language is the opposite—the picture builds up gradually word by word so that sometimes it isn't until the end of the story that you recognize the landscape."

WORKS CITED:

Carter, Margaret, "Helme Heine," *Books for Your Children,* spring, 1985, p. 9.

In *The Pearl*, a happy-go-lucky beaver dreams that he finds a great treasure that incites envy and anger among his friends. (Written and illustrated by Heine.)

FOR MORE INFORMATION SEE:

BOOKS

Children's Literature Review, Volume 18, Gale, 1989.

PERIODICALS

Hornbook, February, 1981.
Publishers Weekly, November 19, 1982; June 20, 1986.
Times Literary Supplement, March 26, 1982; September 17, 1982.
Wilson Library Bulletin, September, 1982; December, 1985.*

*   *   *

HICKS, Eleanor B.
See COERR, Eleanor (Beatrice)

*   *   *

HICKS, Harvey
See STRATEMEYER, Edward L.

*   *   *

HILL, Grace Brooks
[Collective pseudonym]

WRITINGS:

"CORNER HOUSE GIRLS" SERIES

The Corner House Girls: How They Moved to Milton, What They Found, and What They Did, Barse & Hopkins, 1915.
The Corner House Girls at School: How They Entered, Whom They Met, and What They Did, Barse & Hopkins, 1915.
The Corner House Girls under Canvas: How They Reached Pleasant Cove and What Happened Afterward, Barse & Hopkins, 1915.
The Corner House Girls in a Play: How They Rehearsed, How They Acted, and What the Play Brought In, Barse & Hopkins, 1916.
The Corner House Girls' Odd Find: Where They Made It, and What the Strange Discovery Led To, Barse & Hopkins, 1916.
The Corner House Girls on a Tour: Where They Went, What They Saw, and What They Found, Barse & Hopkins, 1917.
The Corner House Girls Growing Up: What Happened First, What Came Next, and How It Ended, Barse & Hopkins, 1918.
The Corner House Girls Snowbound: How They Went Away, What They Discovered, and How It Ended, Barse & Hopkins, 1919.
The Corner House Girls on a Houseboat: How They Sailed Away, What Happened on the Voyage, and What They Discovered, Barse & Hopkins, 1920.
The Corner House Girls among the Gypsies: How They Met, What Happened, and How It Ended, Barse & Hopkins, 1921.
The Corner House Girls on Palm Island: Looking for Adventure, How They Found It, and What Happened, Barse & Hopkins, 1922.
The Corner House Girls Solve a Mystery: What It Was, Where It Was, and Who Found It, Barse & Hopkins, 1923.
The Corner House Girls Facing the World: Why They Had to, How They Did It, and What Came of It, Barse & Hopkins, 1926.

SIDELIGHTS: Grace Brooks Hill was a collective pseudonym used by the Stratemeyer Syndicate, a writing house that produced such popular children's fiction as the "Nancy Drew," "Hardy Boys," and "Bobbsey Twins" series. The "Corner House Girls" series features four girls, aged eight to fourteen years, who were left an old house by a rich bachelor uncle. The books chronicled their adventures after they moved into the place. See the *SATA* index for more information on Harriet S. Adams, Edward L. Stratemeyer, and Andrew E. Svenson.

FOR MORE INFORMATION SEE:

BOOKS

Johnson, Deidre, editor and compiler, *Stratemeyer Pseudonyms and Series Books: An Annotated Checklist of Stratemeyer and Stratemeyer Syndicate Publications,* Greenwood Press, 1982.

*   *   *

HILL, Johnson
See KUNHARDT, Edith

*   *   *

HOPE, Laura Lee
[Collective pseudonym]

WRITINGS:

"BLYTHE GIRLS" SERIES

The Blythe Girls: Helen, Margy, and Rose; or, Facing the Great World, Grosset & Dunlap, 1925.
The Blythe Girls: Margy's Queer Inheritance; or, The Worth of a Name, Grosset & Dunlap, 1925.
The Blythe Girls: Rose's Great Problem; or, Face to Face with a Crisis, Grosset & Dunlap, 1925.
The Blythe Girls: Helen's Strange Boarder; or, The Girl from Bronx Park, Grosset & Dunlap, 1925.
The Blythe Girls: Three on a Vacation; or, The Mystery at Peach Farm, Grosset & Dunlap, 1925.
The Blythe Girls: Margy's Secret Mission; or, Exciting Days at Shadymore, Grosset & Dunlap, 1926.
The Blythe Girls: Rose's Odd Discovery; or, The Search for Irene Conroy, Grosset & Dunlap, 1927.
The Blythe Girls: The Disappearance of Helen; or, The Art Shop Mystery, Grosset & Dunlap, 1928.
The Blythe Girls: Snowbound in Camp; or, The Mystery at Elk Lodge, Grosset & Dunlap, 1929.
The Blythe Girls: Margy's Mysterious Visitor; or, Guarding the Pepper Fortune, Grosset & Dunlap, 1930.
The Blythe Girls: Rose's Hidden Talent, Grosset & Dunlap, 1931.
The Blythe Girls: Helen's Wonderful Mistake; or, The Mysterious Necklace, Grosset & Dunlap, 1932.

"BOBBSEY TWINS" SERIES

The Bobbsey Twins; or, Merry Days Indoors and Out, Mershon, 1904, new and enlarged edition, Grosset & Dunlap, 1928, published as *Laura Lee Hope's "The Bobbsey Twins,"* retold by Bennett Kline, Whitman, 1940, revised edition published as *The Bobbsey Twins* (also see below), Grosset & Dunlap, 1950, published as *Meet the Bobbsey Twins,* Wonder Books, 1954, published as *The Bobbsey Twins of Lakeport* (also see

The Bobbsey Twins at Meadow Brook

LAURA LEE HOPE

Along with Nancy Drew and the Hardy Boys, the Bobbsey Twins were among the most popular characters created by the Stratemeyer Syndicate. (Cover illustration by Howard Connolly.)

below), Grosset & Dunlap, 1961, reprinted, Wanderer, 1979.

The Bobbsey Twins in the Country (also see below), Mershon, 1904, revised edition, Grosset & Dunlap, 1950, published as *The Bobbsey Twins' Adventures in the Country* (also see below), reprinted, Wanderer, 1979.

The Bobbsey Twins at the Seashore (also see below), Chatterton-Peck, 1907, revised edition, Grosset & Dunlap, 1950, published as *The Bobbsey Twins' Secret at the Seashore* (also see below), Grosset & Dunlap, 1962, reprinted, Wanderer, 1979.

The Bobbsey Twins at School, Grosset & Dunlap, 1913, reprinted, 1941, revised edition published as *The Bobsey Twins' Mystery at School*, 1962.

The Bobbsey Twins at Snow Lodge, Grosset & Dunlap, 1913, revised edition published as *The Bobbsey Twins and the Mystery at Snow Lodge*, 1960.

The Bobbsey Twins on a Houseboat, Grosset & Dunlap, 1915, revised edition, 1955.

The Bobbsey Twins at Meadow Brook, Grosset & Dunlap, 1915, revised edition published as *The Bobbsey Twins' Mystery at Meadowbrook*, 1963.

The Bobbsey Twins at Home, Grosset & Dunlap, 1916, revised edition published as *The Bobbsey Twins' Big Adventure at Home*, 1960.

The Bobbsey Twins in a Great City, Grosset & Dunlap, 1917, revised edition published as *The Bobbsey Twins' Search in the Great City*, Grosset & Dunlap, 1960.

The Bobbsey Twins on Blueberry Island, Grosset & Dunlap, 1917, revised edition, 1959.

The Bobbsey Twins on the Deep Blue Sea, Grosset & Dunlap, 1918, revised edition published as *The Bobbsey Twins' Mystery on the Deep Blue Sea*, 1965.

The Bobbsey Twins in Washington, Grosset & Dunlap, 1919, revised edition published as *The Bobbsey Twins' Adventure in Washington*, 1963.

The Bobbsey Twins in the Great West, Grosset & Dunlap, 1920, revised edition published as *The Bobbsey Twins' Visit to the Great West*, 1966.

The Bobbsey Twins at Cedar Camp, Grosset & Dunlap, 1921, revised edition published as *The Bobbsey Twins and the Cedar Camp Mystery*, 1967.

The Bobbsey Twins at the County Fair, Grosset & Dunlap, 1922, revised edition published as *The Bobbsey Twins and the County Fair Mystery*, 1960.

The Bobbsey Twins Camping Out, Grosset & Dunlap, 1923, revised edition, 1955.

The Bobbsey Twins and Baby May, Grosset & Dunlap, 1924, revised edition published as *The Bobbsey Twins' Adventures with Baby May*, 1968.

The Bobbsey Twins Keeping House, Grosset & Dunlap, 1925, revised edition published as *The Bobbsey Twins and the Play House Secret*, 1968.

The Bobbsey Twins at Cloverbank, Grosset & Dunlap, 1926, revised edition published as *The Bobbsey Twins and the Four-Leaf Clover Mystery*, 1968.

The Bobbsey Twins at Cherry Corners, Grosset & Dunlap, 1927, revised edition published as *The Bobbsey Twins' Mystery at Cherry Corners*, 1971.

The Bobbsey Twins and Their Schoolmates, Grosset & Dunlap, 1928.

The Bobbsey Twins Treasure Hunting, Grosset & Dunlap, 1929.

The Bobbsey Twins at Spruce Lake, Grosset & Dunlap, 1930.

The Bobbsey Twins' Wonderful Secret, Grosset & Dunlap, 1931, revised edition published as *The Bobbsey Twins' Wonderful Winter Secret*, 1962.

The Bobbsey Twins at the Circus, Grosset & Dunlap, 1932, revised edition published as *The Bobbsey Twins and the Circus Surprise*, 1960.

The Bobbsey Twins on an Airplane Trip, Grosset & Dunlap, 1933.

The Bobbsey Twins Solve a Mystery, Grosset & Dunlap, 1934.

The Bobbsey Twins on a Ranch, Grosset & Dunlap, 1935.

The Bobbsey Twins in Eskimo Land, Grosset & Dunlap, 1936.

The Bobbsey Twins in a Radio Play, Grosset & Dunlap, 1937.

The Bobbsey Twins at Windmill Cottage, Grosset & Dunlap, 1938.

The Bobbsey Twins at Lighthouse Point, Grosset & Dunlap, 1939.

The Bobbsey Twins at Indian Hollow, Grosset & Dunlap, 1940.

The Bobbsey Twins at the Ice Carnival, Grosset & Dunlap, 1941.

The Bobbsey Twins in the Land of Cotton, Grosset & Dunlap, 1942.

The Bobbsey Twins in Echo Valley, Grosset & Dunlap, 1943.

The Bobbsey Twins on the Pony Trail, Grosset & Dunlap, 1944.

The Bobbsey Twins at Mystery Mansion, Grosset & Dunlap, 1945.

The Bobbsey Twins at Sugar Maple Hill, Grosset & Dunlap, 1946.

The Bobbsey Twins in Mexico, Grosset & Dunlap, 1947.

The Bobbsey Twins' Toy Shop, Grosset & Dunlap, 1948.

The Bobbsey Twins in Tulip Land, Grosset & Dunlap, 1949.

The Bobbsey Twins in Rainbow Valley, Grosset & Dunlap, 1950.

The Bobbsey Twins' Own Little Railroad, Grosset & Dunlap, 1951.

The Bobbsey Twins at Whitesail Harbor, Grosset & Dunlap, 1952.

The Bobbsey Twins and the Horseshoe Riddle, Grosset & Dunlap, 1953.

The Bobbsey Twins at Big Bear Pond, Grosset & Dunlap, 1954.

The Bobbsey Twins on a Bicycle Trip, Grosset & Dunlap, 1955.

The Bobbsey Twins' Own Little Ferryboat, Grosset & Dunlap, 1956.

The Bobbsey Twins at Pilgrim Rock, Grosset & Dunlap, 1957.

The Bobbsey Twins' Forest Adventure, Grosset & Dunlap, 1958.

The Bobbsey Twins at London Tower, Grosset & Dunlap, 1959.

The Bobbsey Twins in the Mystery Cave, Grosset & Dunlap, 1960.

The Bobbsey Twins are joined by their cousins, the Walter Twins, in this 1979 detective thriller set in the Cayman Islands.

The Bobbsey Twins in Volcano Land, Grosset & Dunlap, 1961.

The Bobbsey Twins and the Goldfish Mystery, Grosset & Dunlap, 1962.

The Bobbsey Twins and the Big River Mystery, Grosset & Dunlap, 1963.

The Bobbsey Twins and the Greek Hat Mystery, Grosset & Dunlap, 1964.

The Bobbsey Twins' Search for the Green Rooster, Grosset & Dunlap, 1965.

The Bobbsey Twins and Their Camel Adventure, Grosset & Dunlap, 1966.

The Bobbsey Twins' Mystery of the King's Puppet, Grosset & Dunlap, 1967.

The Bobbsey Twins and the Secret of Candy Castle, Grosset & Dunlap, 1968.

The Bobbsey Twins and the Doodlebug Mystery, Grosset & Dunlap, 1969.

The Bobbsey Twins and the Talking Fox Mystery, Grosset & Dunlap, 1970.

The Bobbsey Twins: The Red, White, and Blue Mystery, Grosset & Dunlap, 1971.

The Bobbsey Twins: Dr. Funnybone's Secret, Grosset & Dunlap, 1972.

The Bobbsey Twins and the Tagalong Giraffe, Grosset & Dunlap, 1973.

The Bobbsey Twins and the Flying Clown, Grosset & Dunlap, 1974.

The Bobbsey Twins on the Sun-Moon Cruise, Grosset & Dunlap, 1975.

The Bobbsey Twins: The Freedom Bell Mystery, Grosset & Dunlap, 1976.

The Bobbsey Twins and the Smoky Mountain Mystery, Grosset & Dunlap, 1977.

The Bobbsey Twins in a TV Mystery Show, Grosset & Dunlap, 1978.

The Bobbsey Twins: The Coral Turtle Mystery, Grosset & Dunlap, 1979.

The Bobbsey Twins: The Blue Poodle Mystery, Wanderer, 1980.

The Bobbsey Twins: The Secret in the Pirate's Cave, Wanderer, 1980.

The Bobbsey Twins: The Dune Buggy Mystery, Wanderer, 1980.

The Bobbsey Twins: The Missing Pony Mystery, Wanderer, 1981.

The Bobbsey Twins: The Rose Parade Mystery, Wanderer, 1981.

The Bobbsey Twins: The Camp Fire Mystery, Wanderer, 1982.

The Bobbsey Twins: Double Trouble, Wanderer, 1982.

The Bobbsey Twins: Mystery of the Laughing Dinosaur, Wanderer, 1983.

The Bobbsey Twins: The Music Box Mystery, Wanderer, 1983.

The Bobbsey Twins: The Ghost in the Computer, Wanderer, 1984.

The Bobbsey Twins: The Scarecrow Mystery, Wanderer, 1984.

The Bobbsey Twins: The Haunted House Mystery, Wanderer, 1985.

The Bobbsey Twins: Mystery of the Hindu Temple, Wanderer, 1985.

The Bobbsey Twins: The Grinning Gargoyle Mystery, Wanderer, 1986.

"NEW BOBBSEY TWINS" SERIES

The Secret of Jungle Park, Minstrel, 1987.

The Case of the Runaway Money, Minstrel, 1987.

The Clue That Flew Away, Minstrel, 1987.
The Secret in the Sand Castle, Minstrel, 1988.
The Case of the Close Encounter, Minstrel, 1988.
Mystery on the Mississippi, Minstrel, 1988.
Trouble in Toyland, Minstrel, 1988.
The Secret of the Stolen Puppies, Minstrel, 1988.
The Clue in the Classroom, Minstrel, 1988.
The Chocolate-Covered Clue, Minstrel, 1989.
The Case of the Crooked Contest, Minstrel, 1989.
The Secret of the Sunken Treasure, Minstrel, 1989.
The Case of the Crying Clown, Minstrel, 1989.
The Mystery of the Missing Mummy, Minstrel, 1989.
The Secret of the Stolen Clue, Minstrel, 1989.
The Case of the Missing Dinosaur, Minstrel, 1990.
The Case at Creepy Castle, Minstrel, 1990.
The Secret at Sleepaway Camp, Minstrel, 1990.
The Show and Tell Mystery, Minstrel, 1990.
The Weird Science Mystery, Minstrel, 1990.
The Great Skate Mystery, Minstrel, 1990.
The Super-Duper Cookie Caper, Minstrel, 1991.
The Monster Mouse Mystery, Minstrel, 1991.
The Case of the Goofy Game Show, Minstrel, 1991.
The Case of the Crazy Collections, Minstrel, 1991.
The Clue at Casper Creek, Minstrel, 1991.
The Big Pig Puzzle, Minstrel, 1991.
The Case of the Vanishing Video, Minstrel, 1992.

"BUNNY BROWN AND HIS SISTER SUE" SERIES

Bunny Brown and His Sister Sue, Grosset & Dunlap, 1916.
Bunny Brown and His Sister Sue on Grandpa's Farm, Grosset & Dunlap, 1916.
Bunny Brown and His Sister Sue Playing Circus, Grosset & Dunlap, 1916.
Bunny Brown and His Sister Sue at Camp Rest-A-While, Grosset & Dunlap, 1916.
Bunny Brown and His Sister Sue at Aunt Lou's City Home, Grosset & Dunlap, 1916.
Bunny Brown and His Sister Sue in the Big Woods, Grosset & Dunlap, 1917.
Bunny Brown and His Sister Sue on an Auto Tour, Grosset & Dunlap, 1917.
Bunny Brown and His Sister Sue and Their Shetland Pony, Grosset & Dunlap, 1918.
Bunny Brown and His Sister Sue Giving a Show, Grosset & Dunlap, 1919.
Bunny Brown and His Sister Sue at Christmas Tree Cove, Grosset & Dunlap, 1920.
Bunny Brown and His Sister Sue in the Sunny South, Grosset & Dunlap, 1921.
Bunny Brown and His Sister Sue Keeping Store, Grosset & Dunlap, 1922.
Bunny Brown and His Sister Sue and Their Trick Dog, Grosset & Dunlap, 1923.
Bunny Brown and His Sister Sue at a Sugar Camp, Grosset & Dunlap, 1924.
Bunny Brown and His Sister Sue on the Rolling Ocean, Grosset & Dunlap, 1925.
Bunny Brown and His Sister Sue on Jack Frost Island, Grosset & Dunlap, 1927.
Bunny Brown and His Sister Sue at Shore Acres, Grosset & Dunlap, 1928.
Bunny Brown and His Sister Sue at Berry Hill, Grosset & Dunlap, 1929.
Bunny Brown and His Sister Sue at Sky Top, Grosset & Dunlap, 1930.
Bunny Brown and His Sister Sue at the Summer Carnival, Grosset & Dunlap, 1931.

Frontispiece from the 1914 edition of *The Moving Picture Girls under the Palms,* **a Stratemeyer Syndicate novel written under Laura Lee Hope—one of the most productive Stratemeyer collective pseudonyms.**

"MAKE-BELIEVE STORIES" SERIES

The Story of a Sawdust Doll, Grosset & Dunlap, 1920.
The Story of a White Rocking Horse, Grosset & Dunlap, 1920.
The Story of a Lamb on Wheels, Grosset & Dunlap, 1920.
The Story of a Bold Tin Soldier, Grosset & Dunlap, 1920.
The Story of a Candy Rabbit, Grosset & Dunlap, 1920.
The Story of a Monkey on a Stick, Grosset & Dunlap, 1920.
The Story of a Calico Clown, Grosset & Dunlap, 1920.
The Story of a Nodding Donkey, Grosset & Dunlap, 1921.
The Story of a China Cat, Grosset & Dunlap, 1921.
The Story of a Plush Bear, Grosset & Dunlap, 1921.
The Story of a Stuffed Elephant, Grosset & Dunlap, 1922.
The Story of a Woolly Dog, Grosset & Dunlap, 1923.

"MOVING PICTURE GIRLS" SERIES

The Moving Picture Girls; or, First Appearances in Photo Dramas, Grosset & Dunlap, 1914.
The Moving Picture Girls at Oak Farm; or, Queer Happenings While Taking Rural Plays, Grosset & Dunlap, 1914.
The Moving Picture Girls Snowbound; or, The Proof on the Film, Grosset & Dunlap, 1914.
The Moving Picture Girls under the Palms; or, Lost in the Wilds of Florida, Grosset & Dunlap, 1914.
The Moving Picture Girls at Rocky Ranch; or, Great Days among the Cowboys, Grosset & Dunlap, 1914.

The Moving Picture Girls at Sea; or, A Pictured Shipwreck That Became Real, Grosset & Dunlap, 1915.

The Moving Picture Girls in War Plays; or, The Sham Battles at Oak Farm, Grosset & Dunlap, 1916.

"OUTDOOR GIRLS" SERIES

The Outdoor Girls of Deepdale; or, Camping and Tramping for Fun and Health, Grosset & Dunlap, 1913.

The Outdoor Girls at Rainbow Lake; or, The Stirring Cruise of the Motor Boat Gem, Grosset & Dunlap, 1913.

The Outdoor Girls in a Motor Car; or, The Haunted Mansion of Shadow Valley, Grosset & Dunlap, 1913.

The Outdoor Girls in a Winter Camp; or, Glorious Days on Skates and Iceboats, Grosset & Dunlap, 1913.

The Outdoor Girls in Florida; or, Wintering in the Sunny South, Grosset & Dunlap, 1913.

The Outdoor Girls at Ocean View; or, The Box That Was Found in the Sand, Grosset & Dunlap, 1915.

The Outdoor Girls on Pine Island; or, A Cave and What It Contained, Grosset & Dunlap, 1916.

The Outdoor Girls in Army Service; or, Doing Their Bit for the Soldier Boys, Grosset & Dunlap, 1918.

The Outdoor Girls at the Hostess House; or, Doing Their Best for the Soldiers, Grosset & Dunlap, 1919.

The Outdoor Girls at Bluff Point; or, A Wreck and a Rescue, Grosset & Dunlap, 1920.

Frontispiece from *The Outdoor Girls at Rainbow Lake*, one of the first of more than twenty titles in Hope's "Outdoor Girls" series.

The Outdoor Girls at Wild Rose Lodge; or, The Hermit of Moonlight Falls, Grosset & Dunlap, 1921.

The Outdoor Girls in the Saddle; or, The Girl Miner of Gold Run, Grosset & Dunlap, 1922.

The Outdoor Girls around the Campfire; or, The Old Maid of the Mountains, Grosset & Dunlap, 1923.

The Outdoor Girls at Cape Cod; or, Sally Ann of Lighthouse Rock, Grosset & Dunlap, 1924.

The Outdoor Girls at Foaming Falls; or, Robina of Red Kennels, Grosset & Dunlap, 1925.

The Outdoor Girls along the Coast; or, The Cruise of the Motor Boat Liberty, Grosset & Dunlap, 1926.

The Outdoor Girls at Spring Hill Farm; or, The Ghost of the Old Milk House, Grosset & Dunlap, 1927.

The Outdoor Girls at New Moon Ranch; or, Riding with the Cowboys, Grosset & Dunlap, 1928.

The Outdoor Girls on a Hike; or, The Mystery of the Deserted Airplane, Grosset & Dunlap, 1929.

The Outdoor Girls on a Canoe Trip; or, The Secret of the Brown Mill, Grosset & Dunlap, 1930.

The Outdoor Girls at Cedar Ridge; or, The Mystery of the Old Windmill, Grosset & Dunlap, 1931.

The Outdoor Girls in the Air; or, Saving the Stolen Invention, Grosset & Dunlap, 1932.

The Outdoor Girls in Desert Valley; or, Strange Happenings in a Cowboy Camp, Grosset & Dunlap, 1933.

"SIX LITTLE BUNKERS" SERIES

Six Little Bunkers at Grandma Bell's, Grosset & Dunlap, 1918.

Six Little Bunkers at Aunt Jo's, Grosset & Dunlap, 1918.

Six Little Bunkers at Cousin Tom's, Grosset & Dunlap, 1918.

Six Little Bunkers at Grandpa Ford's, Grosset & Dunlap, 1918.

Six Little Bunkers at Uncle Fred's, Grosset & Dunlap, 1918.

Six Little Bunkers at Captain Ben's, Grosset & Dunlap, 1920.

Six Little Bunkers at Cowboy Jack's, Grosset & Dunlap, 1921.

Six Little Bunkers at Mammy June's, Grosset & Dunlap, 1922.

Six Little Bunkers at Farmer Joel's, Grosset & Dunlap, 1923.

Six Little Bunkers at Miller Ned's, Grosset & Dunlap, 1924.

Six Little Bunkers at Indian John's, Grosset & Dunlap, 1925.

Six Little Bunkers at Happy Jim's, Grosset & Dunlap, 1928.

Six Little Bunkers at Skipper Bob's, Grosset & Dunlap, 1929.

Six Little Bunkers at Lighthouse Nell's, Grosset & Dunlap, 1930.

OTHER

Six Little Bunkers (four-in-one reprint), Grosset & Dunlap, 1933.

The Bobbsey Twins, The Bobbsey Twins in the Country, [and] *The Bobbsey Twins at the Seashore*, Donohue, ca. 1940.

The Bobbsey Twins Mystery Stories (contains *The Bobbsey Twins of Lakeport, The Bobbsey Twins' Adventures in the Country*, and *The Bobbsey Twins' Secret at the Seashore*), Grosset & Dunlap, ca. 1960.

SIDELIGHTS: In 1904 Edward Stratemeyer's new literary syndicate began to produce the "Bobbsey Twins." This first series produced by the new coalition was published under the house pseudonym Laura Lee Hope, "in the final analysis one of the most productive of all Stratemeyer Syndicate noms de plume," according to Carol Billman in *The Secret of the Stratemeyer Syndicate: Nancy Drew, the Hardy Boys, and the Million Dollar Fiction Factory*. The Bobbseys proved very popular, outselling all previous Stratemeyer series, and their popularity continues today with new adventures produced and old adventures rewritten for a modern juvenile audience. Glenn Collins, writing in the *New York Times* in 1987, described the series of more than 70 books for children seven to nine years old as having "sold more than 50 million copies worldwide." Each copy, adds Arthur Prager in *Saturday Review,* is "enjoyed by an average of two readers."

"The 'Bobbseys' were aimed at a younger market [than previous Stratemeyer series] and covered both male and female readers," explains Prager. "There were two sets of twins, Flossie and Freddie, who were four years old, and Nan and Bert, who were eight (they were later raised to six and twelve). They had a beloved dog, Snap, and a mischievous cat, Snoop." Their parents, Richard and Mary Bobbsey, the Bobbsey's cook and gardener, Dinah and Sam Johnson, and the bully Danny Rugg also figured in the books. But why twins? Bobbie Ann Mason, author of *The Girl Sleuth: A Feminist Guide,* suggests that "the Bobbsey Twins . . . are archetypal: they stroke the deepest longings of a child for a soulmate. The double theme is recurrent in children's literature, and the Bobbseys, more than others, have capitalized on this desire children have for a mirror-image that talks, sure proof that one has an identity."

Many of the earlier volumes chronicled the Bobbseys' adventures on vacation at various sites in and around the country. "Most of the excitement in the [earlier volumes of the] series was at the under-ten level," Prager continues. "Flossie saw a snake at a Sunday School picnic, but it turned out to be only an old dead stick. Mr. Bobbsey's wallet was stolen by a tramp. The littlest Bobbseys, however, were often caught in real danger: lost, caught in thunderstorms, trapped in a runaway balloon, or facing some similar peril." However, "at about the time the Hardy Boys and Nancy Drew first began their investigations," Billman observes, the Bobbsey Twins books "took on some of the traits of the mystery genre."

Some critics perceive unfortunate consequences in this trend. "The Bobbseys are now known as amateur detectives and there is a purpose to childhood after all," says Mason. She sees that purpose as a defense of the upper-middle-class values that she calls "Bobbsey Bourgeois." "There used to be a lot of simple fun in the childlike defense of innocence, but nowadays the twins are super-serious," she concludes. "They must defend that station-wagon scene like crazy." "Why don't the Bobbseys investigate some truly destructive social force, such as the David Letterman show?" complains Margot Dougherty of *People* magazine. In some of the most recent volumes the twins foil arsonists, shoplifters, kidnapping and blackmail, states Michael Kernan of the *Washington Post.* "It's one thing for Nancy Drew and the Hardy Boys and all the children on public TV to be detectives," he protests, "but somehow I didn't expect it from the Bobbseys."

Although the series has been undeniably popular, some readers consider the Bobbseys overly moralistic and sentimental. Russel Nye, for instance, writing in *The Unembarrassed Muse: The Popular Arts in America,* calls the books "surely the most syrupy" of their genre. Mason disagrees; she declares that the volumes "supplant sentiment with action. The characters are morally upright and the books end happily, but sloppy emotions and meaningful moralities are shunned in favor of zestful pursuits. The characterizations are so slim and the language so sparse it is hard to say that they are ever drippy." Mason detects other, more ominous defects in the books: "Models of authority are insisted upon in the Bobbsey Twins series, not only through

obvious sexism but through red-white-and-blue patriotism and through extensive racism." Gypsies and other racial minorities are frequently characterized as malign or threatening, but this, she feels, is a result of the milieu from which the stories came. "The racist assumptions are basic to most of the series books I read as a child," she concludes, "but the series stories were merely a barometer of society, rather than deliberate propaganda."

In the 1950s, the Stratemeyer Syndicate began to rewrite the "Bobbsey Twins" in order to eliminate some of these outdated racial and ethnic prejudices. In this, declares Mason, they were partly successful; but, she adds, they "could not remove the fundamental assumptions without abandoning the Bobbseys and starting over again." The stories were showing their age in other ways as well. Characters, plots, and settings, says Billman, "evoked an *earlier* era, and that was bad." In 1987, Simon & Schuster again updated the Bobbseys in a new paperback series that, according to Collins, "fast-forwarded" the family into the 1980s. Mrs. Bobbsey has a part-time job as a reporter for the *Lakeport News,* and Sam Johnson has become foreman at Mr. Bobbsey's lumber mill. Nan wears silver eyeshadow, a miniskirt, and purple lipstick, and she and Bert belong to a punk rock band. "But one character has hardly been touched: Danny Rugg," states an article in *Publishers Weekly.* "It seems that once a bully, always a bully, whether in 1904 or 1987."

Besides the "Bobbsey Twins," the pseudonym Laura Lee Hope was used on books intended for young children ("Make-Believe Stories," "Bunny Brown and His Sister Sue," "Six Little Bunkers") and teen-aged girls ("Blythe Girls," "Moving Picture Girls," "Outdoor Girls"). Harriet S. Adams, former Stratemeyer Syndicate partner Nancy Axelrad, Lilian and Howard R. Garis, James Duncan Lawrence, Edward L. Stratemeyer, and Andrew E. Svenson were among the authors who used this pseudonym to write "Bobbsey Twins" books and others. See the *SATA* index for more information on Harriet S. Adams, Howard R. Garis, Edward L. Stratemeyer, and Andrew Svenson.

WORKS CITED:

Billman, Carol, "Edward Stratemeyer: The Man and the Literary Machine," *The Secret of the Stratemeyer Syndicate: Nancy Drew, the Hardy Boys, and the Million Dollar Fiction Factory,* Ungar, 1986, pp. 17-35.
Collins, Glenn, *New York Times,* August 17, 1987.
Dougherty, Margot, "Picks & Pans," *People,* September 14, 1987, p. 22.
Kernan, Michael, *Washington Post,* September 5, 1987.
Mason, Bobbie Ann, "Bobbsey Bourgeois," *The Girl Sleuth: A Feminist Guide,* Feminist Press, 1975, pp. 29-47.
Nye, Russel B., "For It Was Indeed He: Books for the Young," *The Unembarrassed Muse: The Popular Arts in America,* Dial, 1970, pp. 60-87.
Prager, Arthur, "Edward Stratemeyer and His Book Machine," *Saturday Review,* July 10, 1971, pp. 15-53.
"Updated Bobbsey Twins Series Follows Nancy Drew, Hardy Boys," *Publishers Weekly,* August 28, 1987, p. 32.

FOR MORE INFORMATION SEE:

BOOKS

Garis, Roger, *My Father Was Uncle Wiggily,* McGraw-Hill, 1966.

Johnson, Deidre, editor and compiler, *Stratemeyer Pseudonyms and Series Books: An Annotated Checklist of Stratemeyer and Stratemeyer Syndicate Publications,* Greenwood Press, 1982.

PERIODICALS

New York Times Book Review, April 26, 1981.
Washington Post Book World, August 17, 1980.

*   *   *

HOWARD, Ellen 1943-

PERSONAL: Born May 8, 1943, in New Bern, NC; daughter of Gerald Willis Phillips (a salesman) and Betty Jeane Chord (a banker; maiden name, Slate); married Kermit W. Jensen, June 15, 1963 (divorced June 15, 1969); married Charles F. Howard, Jr. (a research administrator), June 29, 1975; children: (first marriage) Anna Elizabeth; stepchildren: Cynthia, Laurie, Shaley. *Education:* Attended University of Oregon, 1961-63; Portland State University, B.A. (with honors), 1979. *Politics:* Liberal Democrat. *Religion:* Unitarian-Universalist.

ADDRESSES: Home—2011 Waite Ave., Kalamazoo, MI 49008. *Agent*—Emilie Jacobson, Curtis Brown Ltd., 10 Astor Pl., New York, NY 10003.

CAREER: Writer. Worked in various libraries and offices for twenty-five years before working as a secretary at The Collins Foundation in Portland, OR, 1980-88.

MEMBER: Authors Guild, Society of Children's Book Writers (regional advisor, 1985-88).

AWARDS, HONORS: Golden Kite Honor Book Award, Society of Children's Book Writers, 1984, for *Circle of Giving; When Daylight Comes, Gillyflower,* and *Her Own Song* were named notable children's trade books in the field of social studies, 1985, 1986, and 1988, respectively; *Edith Herself* was named one of the "Best Books of 1987" by *School Library Journal;* Children's Middle Grade Award, International PEN USA Center West, 1989, for *Her Own Song; Sister* was named a notable children's book by the American Library Association, 1990.

WRITINGS:

Circle of Giving, Atheneum, 1984.
When Daylight Comes, Atheneum, 1985.
Gillyflower, Atheneum, 1986.
Edith Herself, Atheneum, 1987.
Her Own Song (Junior Library Guild selection), Atheneum, 1988.
Sister, Atheneum, 1990.
The Chickenhouse House, Atheneum, 1991.
The Big Seed, Simon & Schuster, in press.
The Cellar, Atheneum, in press.

Contributor to periodicals, including *The Lion and the Unicorn.*

SIDELIGHTS: In a speech given at various schools, Ellen Howard told children: "When I was a child, I was like someone you may know (or even be)—the person who hurries to finish her work so she can read her library book, the one who hides under the bleachers during physical

ELLEN HOWARD

education and memorizes poems, the one who reads at lunch time, and walking home from school. And I was a person with a dream. Someday, I dreamed, I was going to write books." It wasn't until she went back to college at the age of thirty-four that Howard even remembered that writing was what she really wanted to do; but on her fortieth birthday, Howard signed the contract for her first book—her dream of being a writer had finally become a reality.

Growing up in Portland, Oregon, Howard lived in a big house with her parents, grandparents, brother, and sister. There was always an adult there to listen to her, and Howard's mother and grandmother were storytellers—the house was the gathering place for all the storytelling relatives. Howard dreamed of being a writer, but in her speech she explains how this dream was discouraged by the adults: "There were a few people who encouraged my dream, but most of the grown-ups thought it was not a silly, but an impractical dream. People have to make a living, the grown-ups said, and everyone knew that only a very few writers earned enough money to live on. Also, the grown-ups said, lots of people write, but not very many are able to get what they write made into real books. Both those things are true: It is hard to get your writing published, and very few writers can make enough money to live on."

So, Howard stopped talking about her dream, and eventually stopped thinking about it too. By the time she entered college, Howard had decided to become a librarian. "Then I fell in love," remembers Howard in her speech. "That was the beginning of a life that involved family and work as a secretary (I didn't finish college so I couldn't be a librarian either), but that didn't include writing at all. Oh, once in a while, I'd think, '*That* would make a good story!' But I would shove the thought away. After all, mostly I was happy, and even when I wasn't, I was always busy, and my family—if not my work—filled my life."

It was when her family grew up that Howard finally remembered her dream of being a writer. Her kids didn't need her as much anymore, so Howard decided to go back to school. "College was something I had begun that I hadn't finished," explains Howard in her speech, adding: "I could feel that unfinished thing, like a hole, in my life. I thought I would feel better if I could close up that hole, if I could fill it with a little more knowledge." Howard began taking writing classes, and describes in her speech what her first attempts at writing revealed: "For me it was a wonderful feeling—saying things in writing. I found out that it helped me to think. I found out that often I didn't really *know* how I felt or thought about a thing until I wrote down my feelings and thoughts. Writing helped me to begin to know myself. Writing helped me to *become more* myself."

Howard began trying many different kinds of writing and sent her best pieces to publishers, only to receive many rejections. Finally, a small magazine published her first story, and in her speech, Howard says it was "the most exciting money I ever earned. Because many people could be a much better secretary than I was, but only *I* could have written that story. It was a good feeling." Eventually, Howard wrote her first story for children. The first publisher she sent it to said she liked it, but needed Howard to make some changes before

Cover art from *When Daylight Comes,* the story of an eleven-year-old girl taken captive by rebellious slaves on the island of St. John in 1733.

it could be published. The story wouldn't be the same if she made these changes, so Howard almost gave up. She sent the story to another publisher, though, who also asked for some changes, but not ones that would change the meaning of the story. *Circle of Giving* was published in 1984.

Like a few of her other books, Howard's third book, *Gillyflower,* deals with a sensitive issue—sexual abuse. It is the story of Gilly, a young girl who likes to make up stories about a beautiful princess to whom, unlike Gilly, nothing bad ever happens. Gilly's father is often out of work, and her mother works at night. Sometimes, when no one else is around, Gilly's father makes Gilly "keep him company," and this is when she is sexually abused. The story relates Gilly's pain and the courage she finally finds to tell others about it. "To this day, I don't really know, for sure, *why* I wrote my third book, *Gillyflower,*" states Howard in her speech, "but coming to grips with its difficult subject helped me to face what I call the dark side of human beings. I believe that it is only when we face that dark side of our own natures, that we can also find the goodness in ourselves." "It's a heavy, depressing subject deftly handled by author Ellen Howard, who wisely avoids graphic descriptions of the abuse while still providing a rare glimpse into the psyche of the tormented child," maintains Mary Ellin Arch in the Roanoke *Times & World News,* concluding that "only a few books deserve the adjective 'important'. . . . *Gillyflower* is an important young-

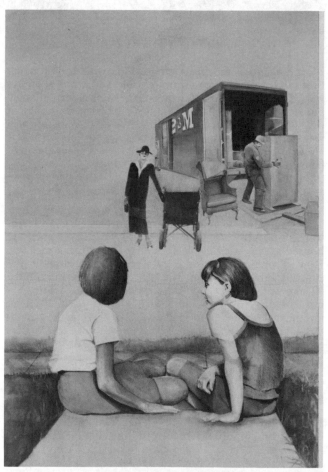

Cover art from *Circle of Giving,* **Howard's first children's book.**

adult book—one that deserves a spot in every school library and on every home bookshelf."

In an article in *The Lion and the Unicorn,* Howard says that it was while she was writing *When Daylight Comes* that she first became aware of the subject of child abuse. *When Daylight Comes* tells the story of Helena, an eleven-year-old girl who is taken captive by rebellious slaves on the Caribbean island of St. John in 1733. Howard recalls that in the back of her mind she realized that Helena would most likely be raped by her male captors, but she couldn't bring herself to put it in the book. Certain she had made the right decision, Howard says that she still feels like a liar to this day. "Here I suppose is where I made a decision about writing for children," observes Howard in *The Lion and the Unicorn.* "I decided I believe in telling children the truth, even when the truth is unpleasant. I believe that children have a right to know about their world. I believe they cannot learn to recognize and rise above evil if they are not taught it exists."

"I have sometimes said that writing a book is like having a baby," remarks Howard in her speech. "Both take time, some hurting, some work. But the joy of creating a book, like the joy of the birth of a baby, is indescribable. That joy goes on and on, as we watch our book go out into the world in the same way we watch our children grow up. Sometimes we doubt that we have done as well as we could have. Sometimes we feel so proud! But always we know that we have done something important. That is the thing about writing. It is an important thing to do." To potential storytellers like herself, in *Writers West* Howard gives this advice: "She must write her stories as well as she knows how. She must work to perfect that ability. She must believe that to do so is good. She must hope someday someone else will believe it too. But she cannot expect it; she cannot depend on it. She can only hope . . . and submit her stories . . . and write again and again and again." "As it turned out," comments Howard in her speech, "I was lucky. I have had both—a comfortable life and my dream. But now, looking back, I know that if I had to choose, the dream would be just as important, maybe more important than the comfortable life. I might not have remembered my dream so many years later—and if I had not, my life would not be so rich and rewarding as it is."

WORKS CITED:

Arch, Mary Ellin, review of *Gillyflower, Times & World News* (Roanoke), May 31, 1986.
Howard, Ellen, "Advice for a Story-Teller," *Writers West,* November, 1983, p. 14.
Howard, Ellen, "Facing the Dark Side in Children's Books," *Lion and the Unicorn,* December, 1988, pp. 7-11.
Howard, Ellen, text from a speech given at various schools.

FOR MORE INFORMATION SEE:

PERIODICALS

Horn Book, November, 1987; November, 1988; November/ December, 1990.
Publishers Weekly, August 22, 1986; February 13, 1987; September 9, 1988; September 28, 1990.
School Library Journal, August, 1984; November, 1985; October, 1986; April, 1987; May, 1988; September, 1988; August, 1989.

Times Educational Supplement, November 11, 1988; November 24, 1989.

Sketch by Susan M. Reicha

*   *   *

HUFF, Barbara A. 1929-

PERSONAL: Born July 2, 1929, in Los Angeles, CA; daughter of Robert H. (a securities professional) and Irene Lawton (a teacher) Huff. *Education:* University of California, Los Angeles, B.A., 1952. *Politics:* Independent. *Hobbies and other interests:* Ship travel, gardening, reading, baseball.

ADDRESSES: Home—One Christopher St., New York, NY 10014. *Office*—Bantam Doubleday Dell, 666 Fifth Ave., New York, NY 10103.

CAREER: Doubleday's Junior Literary Guild (now Junior Library Guild), New York City, 1954—, became managing editor. Has also worked at odd jobs including work at a television store and for a television service company.

MEMBER: Society of Children's Book Writers, Ocean Liner Museum, Steamship Historical Society, Association of Community Gardeners, MENSA.

WRITINGS:

Welcome Aboard!: Traveling on an Ocean Liner, Clarion, 1987.

BARBARA A. HUFF

Greening the City Streets: the Story of Community Gardens, Clarion, 1990.
Once Inside the Library, Little, Brown, 1990.

Also contributor of poems and articles to *Daily Bruin, New York Times* and *School Library Journal.*

WORK IN PROGRESS: Fiction and nonfiction for children of several age levels; research about ships, gardens, music, dogs, travel, and sports.

SIDELIGHTS: Barbara A. Huff commented, "Traveling as much as I have in the relaxed social setting of ocean liners, I'm used to answering two questions designed to get a handle on a new acquaintance: Where are you from? and What do you do? For some reason, no one says, Where do you live? So I have to explain that I'm from California, but have lived in New York City since I was in my twenties."

In answer to the second question, Huff said she reads and writes. "Part of my work at the Junior Library Guild is to research and write biographies of the authors and artists who create the eighty-four new books the Junior Library Guild sends each year to its library members. The total word count in the two Junior Library Guild catalogues I do each year is the equivalent of a substantial book, although I let my subjects speak for themselves as much as I can. My contacts with the amazing people who create children's books is a most pleasurable part of my job.

"The best definition of why my job seems so ideal came to me in a letter from an author named Gene Namovicz. She quoted Anne Tyler as saying, 'I write because I want more than one life.' Gene told me that she reads for the same reason, as a way of extending her life. How many people are lucky enough to spend their working days leading more than one life?

"Corresponding with the Junior Library Guild writers and artists, and then trying my best to convey what fascinating people they are, takes up about half my time. The rest of the year I read children's books scheduled for release by the leading publishers. We work well in advance, from six months to a year before publication, and we see the books in every stage from manuscript to early proofs. We often see original art, a big treat.

"Our staff includes the director, a first reader for the picture books, and one for the older books; I read across the seven age levels from preschool to young adult, and write reports on them for reference and to help in the final selection process. These days that's about five hundred reports a year; I'm up around twelve thousand since I was given the chance to evaluate submissions, early in my career with the Guild. I've read and written reports on numerous books I've since seen listed in the invaluable pages of these *Something About the Author* (*SATA*) volumes. *SATA* is a great reference source, and I get a kick out of being asked to be in it.

"I certainly didn't come to New York to get into children's books. I grew up in Los Angeles, in a house full of books. My mother read to me often, all the good stuff. I went to a fine prep school—Marlborough—and then got a B.A. at University of California at Los Angeles, where I remember working on the *Daily Bruin* and playing endless bridge.

"I wrote stories and feature columns for the *Bruin,* and anonymously I was class poet for a couple of literature courses: a sonnet on the sonnet, that sort of thing. Years later, I stopped by the professor's office and revealed my indentity.

"During my last year in college I worked at various odd, some very odd, jobs, and then spent a couple of years working for a television store and a TV service company. Finally, a friend from Marlborough who was working in New York suggested I chuck Los Angeles and come East. Good idea! It took nearly a year to save up, but in late '54 I arrived, ready for a life in some glamour area of the media. Recession had also arrived and the media was firing, not hiring. My tiny nest-egg was fading rapidly away and I had come face to face with applying at Woolworth's when I was offered a job as clerk/typist at the Junior Literary Guild (now called the Junior Library Guild).

"That the Guild was the oldest and most prestigious kids' book club meant little to me; I needed the money, such as it was. But overtime from reading manuscripts helped, staff changes over the years gave me the opportunity to turn the job into what it is now, the best job there is. I spend half my year reading and the other half getting to know, and writing about, the wonderful people who spend their years communicating with children. These writers and artists often tell me that they continue in awe of a profession that allows them to get paid for doing what they would do in any case. I know just how they feel.

"There's a continuity about my job that pleases me. The first Junior Literary Guild books were distributed in June of 1929, one month before I was, so to speak, distributed. I've met people who belonged to the Guild as children. I wrote recently to a man whose last Guild title was ten years ago. He was delighted to find my name on the letter; it suited his own sense of continuity.

"Aside from my on-the-job-writing, I've always written something or other: magazine verse, *New York Magazine* competition entries (I won it in the spring of 1991), trade magazine articles, a piece for the *New York Times* travel section on a double round trip I once made on the *France.* It was called 'Over and Back and Over and Back.' My unpublished work includes a dreadful adult mystery and various children's books I'll get published one day, wait and see. My three published books are described below. They reflect my main interests—ship travel, gardening, and reading. Another interest (obsession?) is baseball, as embodied by the New York Mets. To learn what an ocean liner had to do with Babe Ruth's leaving baseball, see my first book.

"*Welcome Aboard! Traveling on an Ocean Liner,* was published in 1987 by Clarion. With fifty transatlantic crossings in my wake, it's a wonder I didn't think of doing a book on the subject long ago. When it did occur to me, I queried Ann Troy about doing one for her list and in a short time we'd worked out a format. I had a great time researching the book aboard *Queen Elizabeth 2* and in London at such intriguing places as the Imperial War Museum. Ann was everything an editor should be and I'm still happy, at this remove, with the result."

About her second book, *Greening the City Streets: The Story of Community Gardens,* Huff said, "here was another subject I felt needed a book, and Ann agreed. Now I was in touch with a second group of interesting and dedicated and helpful people. Like ocean liner buffs, community gardeners are enthusiastic, caring, and can't do enough for another enthusiast. The book came out in 1990. Ann had done her usual fine job as its editor, working through illness calmly and efficiently. Sadly, she died before the book was published."

Huff's third book was *Once Inside the Library.* She recalled, "This book was pure serendipity. When I started at the Guild, the club's first editor, Helen Ferris, was putting together a collection of poetry for children. Called *Favorite Poems Old and New,* it continues in print and has become a classic. She asked me to write poems on libraries and modern grandmothers, subjects she hadn't been able to find. Since the collection was published in 1957, the poems have been widely reprinted, 'The Library' around fifty times. In 1989 I had a call from Little, Brown, asking what I would think about the library poem as text for a picture book. On rereading it I realized how well suited it was for the lavish, full-color pictures they had in mind. It was the artist, Iris Van Rynbach, who had brought the poem to them. Her editor sent me some of Iris's work, I loved it, and the whole project was on its way in a remarkably short time. The book was published in 1990."

* * *

JOHNSON, Rebecca L. 1956-

PERSONAL: Born April 10, 1956, in Sioux Falls, SD; married Leland Johnson, 1978; stepchildren: Michael, Julie, Franklin. *Education:* Augustana College, B.A., 1978, M.A., 1986.

ADDRESSES: Agent—c/o Publicity Director, Lerner Publications Company, 241 First Ave., Minneapolis, MN 55401.

CAREER: Free-lance writer and science illustrator, 1982—. Part-time instructor, Great Plains Zoo and Delbridge Museum of Natural History, Sioux Falls, SD.

MEMBER: Guild of Natural Science Illustrators, South Dakota Academy of Science, Archeological Society of South Dakota.

WRITINGS:

(With husband, Leland G. Johnson) *Essentials of Biology,* W. C. Brown, 1986.
The Secret Language: Pheromones in the Animal World, Lerner, 1989.
Diving into Darkness: A Submersible Explores the Sea, Lerner, 1989.
The Greenhouse Effect: Life on a Warmer Planet, Lerner, 1990.
The Great Barrier Reef: A Living Laboratory, Lerner, 1991.

WORK IN PROGRESS: A book on giant clams; a study of the ozone layer based on travels in the Antarctic as a member of the National Science Foundation's Antarctic Artist and Writers Program.

SIDELIGHTS: Rebecca L. Johnson has been interested in science since childhood. She told *SATA:* "Every summer my family spent two or three weeks in Chicago. Most of the time was taken up visiting relatives (we had lots!), but at least one entire day was always reserved for a trip to what was then one of my favorite places in the world: the Field Museum of Natural History. I could always be found in the same place, wandering the exhibits in the Ancient Egyptian collection. For hours at a time I would stand transfixed before mummies propped up against their elaborately painted sarcophagi, staring at the smoothly polished feet of dark granite statues of pharaohs, gods, and goddesses, or with my nose pressed against the glass cases filled with odd bits and pieces of

jewelry and other personal treasures. At the time, I thought there could be no more interesting way to spend one's life than exploring the tombs and temples of this once great civilization on the Nile.

"Despite my intentions, however, I didn't become an archaeologist. And although I've been to the African continent, I have yet to set foot in the land of the pharaohs that was the focus of so many of my childhood dreams. Instead, I became a writer. Writing was something I didn't seriously consider taking up as my vocation until I was in my mid-twenties. But I've never regretted leaving the archaeologist in me behind. That's because writing has made it possible for me to spend my life, not exploring tombs, but the infinitely more diverse and captivating worlds of science and nature.

"My first real exposure to book writing came when I met my husband, who at the time was in the middle of writing a college biology textbook. During the first few years of our marriage, I became immersed in book work. I quickly learned all about deadlines, reviewers, editors, layouts, galleys, and photo searches—everything that goes into the creative process of writing and putting together a book. I also learned that writing well is a challenging task; it's hard work that requires not just tireless creativity, but enormous dedication and discipline."

In 1986, Johnson began writing about science for young people. Her first book for children, *The Secret Language: Pheromones in the Animal World,* grew out of research Johnson had completed for her Master's degree. Johnson's next book was inspired by a visit with a group of marine biologists who worked with deep-diving research subs. In *Diving into Darkness: A Submersible Explores the Sea,* Johnson told the exciting story of her trip in one of these subs to a depth of more than 2000 feet. *The Greenhouse Effect* explored the environmental issues concerning the depletion of the ozone layer.

In the past few years, Johnson has become increasingly concerned with the future of science in America, specifically the fact that fewer young people are choosing science as a career. Johnson told *SATA:* "Part of the problem may lie in the fact that many children have little or no idea of what scientists, whatever their particular field, actually do on a day to day basis. This tends to make science a subject that doesn't have much connection with reality for them. I'm trying to address this problem more and more in my writing. If, through my writing, I can capture the interest of even just a few readers and increase their appreciation of science, I'll feel that I have succeeded in doing something very positive. For me, writing about science is the best of two worlds. I'm able to be an explorer and experience firsthand the excitement of many different kinds of scientific research, then turn around and have the fun of sharing it all with young people."

* * *

JONES, Terry 1942-
(Monty Python, a joint pseudonym)

PERSONAL: Full name is Terence Graham Parry Jones; born February 1, 1942, in Colwyn Bay, North Wales; son of Alick George Parry (a bank clerk) and Dilys Louisa (a homemaker; maiden name, Newnes) Jones; married Alison Telfer (a botanist), 1970; children: Sally, Bill. *Education:* Graduated from St. Edmund Hall, Oxford, 1964.

Terry Jones first earned fame as a member of the popular British comedy troupe, Monty Python.

ADDRESSES: Home—London, England. *Office*—c/o Python Pictures Ltd., 68A Delancey St., London NW1 7RY, England.

CAREER: Television scriptwriter and actor for British Broadcasting Corp., 1965-69, writing for and appearing in television series *The Frost Report,* 1965-67, *Do Not Adjust Your Set,* c. 1968, and *The Complete and Utter History of Britain,* 1969; writer and performer with Graham Chapman, John Cleese, Terry Gilliam, Eric Idle, and Michael Palin in Monty Python comedy troupe, beginning 1969, in television series *Monty Python's Flying Circus,* BBC-TV, 1969-74, in motion pictures *Pythons in Deutschland,* 1972, *And Now for Something Completely Different,* 1972, *Monty Python and the Holy Grail,* 1975, *Monty Python's Life of Brian,* 1979, *Monty Python Live at the Hollywood Bowl,* 1982, and *Monty Python's The Meaning of Life,* 1983, and in concert tours in England, Canada, and the United States. Actor in motion pictures, including *Jabberwocky,* 1977, and *Erik the Viking,* 1989; director of motion pictures, including *Personal Services,* 1987, and *Erik the Viking,* 1989. Cofounder of Prominent Features, a production company.

AWARDS, HONORS: Silver Rose, Montreux Television Festival, 1971, for *Monty Python's Flying Circus;* Best Television Comedy Show of 1977, from press critics in Britain, and British Academy of Film and Television Arts (BAFTA) Award for best light entertainment program, 1979, both for

Ripping Yarns; Cannes Grand Prix for feature length film, Cannes Film Festival, 1983, for *Monty Python's The Meaning of Life;* Children's Book Award, 1984, for *The Saga of Erik the Viking;* Michael Balcon Award for outstanding British contribution to cinema (with Monty Python), BAFTA, 1987.

WRITINGS:

(With Michael Palin) *The Complete and Utter History of Britain* (television series), London Weekend Television, 1969.
(With Palin) *Secrets* (teleplay), BBC-TV, 1973.
(With Palin) *Bert Fegg's Nasty Book for Boys and Girls,* Methuen, 1974, new revised edition published as *Dr. Fegg's Encyclopaedia of All World Knowledge,* Peter Bedrick, 1985.
(With Palin) *Their Finest Hours* (two short plays, *Underhill's Finest Hour* and *Buchanan's Finest Hour*), produced in Sheffield, England, 1976.
(With Palin) *Ripping Yarns* (television series; also see below), BBC-TV, 1976-77, and 1979.
(With Palin) *Ripping Yarns* (stories; adapted from the television series), Methuen, 1978, Pantheon, 1979.
(With Palin) *More Ripping Yarns* (stories; adapted from television series *Ripping Yarns*), Methuen, 1978, Pantheon, 1980.
Chaucer's Knight: The Portrait of a Medieval Mercenary (nonfiction), Louisiana State University Press, 1980.
Labyrinth (screenplay), Tri-Star, 1986.
Attacks of Opinion (essays), Penguin, 1988.
Erik the Viking (screenplay), Orion, 1989, published as *Erik the Viking: The Screenplay,* Applause Book Publishers, 1989.

FOR CHILDREN

Fairy Tales, illustrated by Michael Foreman, Schocken, 1981, published as *Terry Jones' Fairy Tales,* Puffin, 1986.
The Saga of Erik the Viking, illustrated by Foreman, Schocken, 1983.
Nicobobinus, illustrated by Foreman, Viking Kestrel, 1985.
The Goblins of Labyrinth (adapted from the film *Labyrinth*), illustrated by Brian Froud, Pavilion, 1986.
The Curse of the Vampire Socks (poetry), illustrated by Foreman, Pavilion, 1988.

COAUTHOR OF MONTY PYTHON SCREENPLAYS

And Now for Something Completely Different (adapted from *Monty Python's Flying Circus*), Columbia, 1972.
(And director with Gilliam) *Monty Python and the Holy Grail* (also see below), Cinema 5, 1975.
(And director) *Monty Python's Life of Brian* (also see below), Warner Brothers, 1979.
Monty Python Live at the Hollywood Bowl, Handmade Films/Columbia, 1982.
(And director) *Monty Python's The Meaning of Life* (also see below), Universal, 1983.

COAUTHOR OF MONTY PYTHON BOOKS

Monty Python's Big Red Book, edited by Eric Idle, Methuen, 1972, Warner Books, 1975.
The Brand New Monty Python Bok, edited by Idle, illustrations by Gilliam (under pseudonym Jerry Gillian) and Peter Brookes, Methuen, 1973, published as *The Brand New Monty Python Papperbok* (also see below), 1974.
Monty Python and the Holy Grail (also published as *Monty Python's Second Film: A First Draft*), Methuen, 1977.

Monty Python's Life of Brian [and] *Montypythonscrapbook,* edited by Idle, Grosset, 1979.

The Complete Works of Shakespeare and Monty Python: Volume One—Monty Python (contains *Monty Python's Big Red Book* and *The Brand New Monty Python Papperbok*), Methuen, 1981.

Monty Python's The Meaning of Life, Grove Press, 1983.

The Complete Monty Python's Flying Circus: All the Words, two volumes, Pantheon, 1989.

COAUTHOR OF OTHER MONTY PYTHON WORKS

Monty Python's Flying Circus (television series), BBC-TV, 1969-74, televised in United States, PBS-TV, 1974.

Pythons in Deutschland (television movie), Batavia Atelier, c. 1972.

Also coauthor of records *Monty Python's Flying Circus,* 1970, *Another Monty Python Record,* 1971, *Monty Python's Previous Record,* 1972, *Monty Python Matching Tie and Handkerchief,* 1973, *Monty Python Live at the Theatre Royal, Drury Lane,* 1974, *The Album of the Soundtrack of the Trailer of the Film of Monty Python and the Holy Grail* (film soundtrack, includes additional material), 1975, *Monty Python Live at City Center,* 1976, *The Worst of Monty Python,* 1976, *The Monty Python Instant Record Collection,* 1977, *Monty Python's Life of Brian* (film soundtrack), 1979, *Monty Python's Contractual Obligation Album,* 1980, *Monty Python's The Meaning of Life* (film soundtrack), 1983, and *Monty Python's the Final Ripoff* (compilation), 1988.

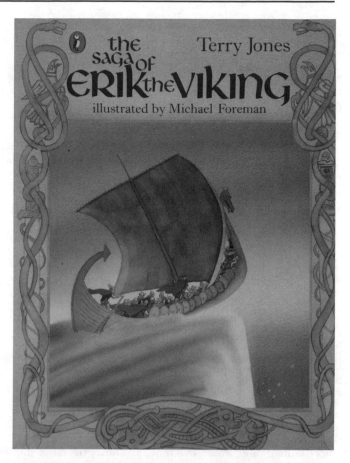

The Saga of Erik the Viking, which Jones wrote for his son, won the 1984 Children's Book Award. (Cover illustration by Michael Foreman.)

ADAPTATIONS: The film *Consuming Passions,* produced by Samuel Goldwyn and Euston Films in 1988, was based on Jones and Palin's teleplay *Secrets;* some of Jones's *Fairy Tales* have been adapted for television.

SIDELIGHTS: Terry Jones is known to millions as one of the six members of Monty Python, the popular British comedy troupe who created *Monty Python's Flying Circus.* Jones wrote and acted in the offbeat and satirical television show, and directed the group's three movies. Outside of Python, Jones brings the same peculiar sense of humor to several books for children. His fresh and imaginative handling of traditional fables and legends, such as in his *Fairy Tales* and *The Saga of Erik the Viking,* have led to a successful second career as an author for children.

Jones wrote *Fairy Tales* for his daughter because he found that many traditional fables "deal with violence in a way I don't approve of," he told Andrea Chambers of *People.* "One version of *Sleeping Beauty* ends with the wicked step-mother being made to put on these red-hot iron slippers and dance until she falls down dead." Jones was determined to create a series of satirical yet light-hearted tales appropriate for young children, so he began writing. Published in 1981, his *Fairy Tales* include the stories of a ferocious thousand-toothed beast who loses his teeth to sweets; a slightly deaf princess who is so beautiful the birds sing loudly to wake her up; and a little girl who turns a monster into a rabbit by standing up to it.

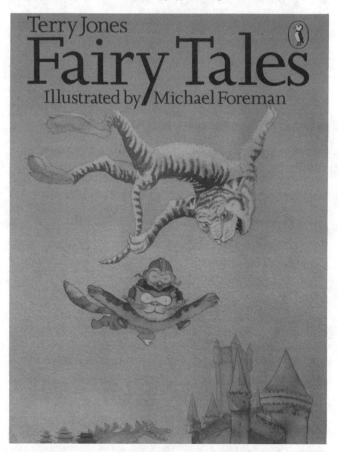

Jones's imaginative handling of traditional fables and legends have led him to a successful second career as an author for children. (Cover illustration by Michael Foreman.)

Brian Patten predicts that Jones's *Fairy Tales* "could conceivably become a 'modern classic,'" as he writes in *Spectator*. The old European fairy tales of the Brothers Grimm and Hans Christian Andersen are humorless, "dark and weird," according to Patten. In contrast, the critic finds Jones's stories "a joy." Jones's themes are "often as dark," Patten explains, "but his lunatic sense of humour makes them unique." Carol Van Strum of the *New York Times Book Review* likewise notes that Jones "springs from the tradition of Andersen and the brothers Grimm," but adds "new color and his own whacky sense of humor to the classic style and form of the fairy tale. As a storyteller, Mr. Jones is a wizard."

This time writing for his son, Jones created *The Saga of Erik the Viking*, a tale of a hero's search for "the land where the sun goes at night." *Times Literary Supplement* writer Andrew Wawn calls the book "an intriguing sequence of tales, . . . full of wit and invention." The reviewer also praises Jones for handling the book's moral without preaching. Instead, ideas such as "fear of the randomly destructive power of weaponry" and "sympathy for doing" are presented as part of the story. In her *New York Times Book Review* critique of *Erik*, Van Strum hails Jones for creating "the legend the Vikings forgot to leave us." Describing Erik's odyssey as "startlingly fresh," Van Strum notes that the Viking's adventures "carry echoes of timeless wisdom to the children of a nuclear age."

In *Nicobobinus*, Jones relates the adventures of a young boy who lived in Venice, Italy, many years ago. Inspired by his friend Rosie, who believes he can do anything, Nicobobinus sets out to find the Land of Dragons. Along the way he has one hand and both feet turned into gold, and he and Rosie meet kidnapping pirates, evil monks, a nasty doctor, a ship that steers itself, dragons, and a mysterious Basilcat. *Nicobobinus* is "an irreverent, parodic, often witty romp," says Beverly Lyon Clark in the *New York Times Book Review*. She adds that the book pokes fun at many types of stories: "the swashbuckling adventure tale, the Carrollian nonsense story, the descent to the inferno, the dragon fantasy. Even the conventions of storytelling are parodied." The result is "a fantasy tale of a high order," writes *Washington Post Book World* contributor Elizabeth Ward, who calls Jones "a leading English children's author."

"Aimed at the six to 11 market," a *Variety* critic observes, Jones's children's books are "really too good for such youngsters who should be satisfied with Mother Goose." *National Review*'s Kevin Lynch also praises Jones's work as "spellbinding," and suggests that "the English-reading world owes an incalculable debt to the daughter of Terry Jones" for inspiring her father to write. And even though he keeps busy writing and directing movies for adults, Jones does intend to continue writing for a younger audience. As he told Jean Ross in a *Contemporary Authors* interview, "I love writing the children's books; it's the thing that gives me the most pleasure."

WORKS CITED:

Chambers, Andrea, "The Mad, Mad World of Monty Python's Terry Jones Is Not for Adults Only," *People*, February 6, 1984, p. 103.
Clark, Beverly Lyon, review of *Nicobobinus, New York Times Book Review*, August 24, 1986, p. 21.
Contemporary Authors, Volume 116, Gale, 1986, pp. 238-242.
Lynch, Kevin, review of *The Saga of Erik the Viking, National Review*, December 23, 1983, p. 1628.
Patten, Brian, "Children's Books: Sam Jones's Selection," *Spectator*, December 19, 1981, pp. 33-34.
Van Strum, Carol, "Children's Books," *New York Times Book Review*, January 16, 1983, p. 22.
Van Strum, Carol, "Children's Books," *New York Times Book Review*, October 30, 1983, p. 26.
Variety, February 2, 1983.
Ward, Elizabeth, "Dragons and Rats," *Washington Post Book World*, January 11, 1987, pp. 11, 13.
Wawn, Andrew, "Excalibur and Exocet," *Times Literary Supplement*, November 25, 1983, p. 1310.

FOR MORE INFORMATION SEE:

BOOKS

Contemporary Literary Criticism, Volume 21, Gale, 1982.
Johnson, Kim Howard, *The First 200 Years of Monty Python*, St. Martin's, 1989.
Perry, George, *The Life of Python*, Pavilion, 1983.

PERIODICALS

Face, March, 1985.
New Republic, September 23, 1972; April 18, 1983.
Newsweek, September 3, 1979; July 12, 1982.
New Yorker, May 5, 1975; May 12, 1975.
New York Times, August 17, 1979; March 31, 1983; October 28, 1989.
People, August 2, 1982.
Rolling Stone, November 13, 1980.
Spectator, January 19, 1980.
Time, May 26, 1975; September 17, 1979; March 28, 1983.
Times Literary Supplement, February 15, 1980; February 14, 1986.
Variety, September 6-12, 1989.
Washington Post, April 4, 1983.*

*   *   *

KINGMAN, (Mary) Lee 1919-

PERSONAL: Born October 6, 1919, in Reading, MA; daughter of Leland W. (a businessman) and Genevieve (Bosson) Kingman; married Robert H. Natti (an educational administrator), September 22, 1945; children: Susanna, Peter. *Education:* Colby Junior College (now Colby-Sawyer College), A.A., 1938; Smith College, B.A., 1940.

ADDRESSES: Home—Box 7126, Lanesville Station, Gloucester, MA 01930.

CAREER: Writer, editor, textile designer, and printer. Worked as a switchboard operator and receptionist-secretary for an insurance company, 1940-42; Houghton-Mifflin Co. (publishers), Boston, MA, editorial assistant, 1943-44, juvenile editor, 1945-46. Former member of board of directors, Sawyer Free Library, Gloucester, MA, and Horn Book, Inc., Boston.

MEMBER: Authors Guild, Authors League of America.

WRITINGS:

Pierre Pidgeon, Houghton, 1943.
Ilenka, Houghton, 1945.
The Rocky Summer, Houghton, 1948.
The Best Christmas, Doubleday, 1949.
Phillippe's Hill, Doubleday, 1950.

LEE KINGMAN

Quarry Adventure, Doubleday, 1951.
Kathy and the Mysterious Statue, Doubleday, 1953.
Peter's Long Walk, Doubleday, 1953.
Mikko's Fortune, Farrar, Straus, 1955.
The Magic Christmas Tree, Farrar, Straus, 1955.
The Village Band Mystery, Doubleday, 1956.
Flivver, the Heroic Horse, Doubleday, 1958.
Ginny's First Secret, Phillips Publishing, 1958.
House of the Blue Horse, Doubleday, 1960.
The Saturday Gang, Doubleday, 1961.
Peter's Pony, Doubleday, 1963.
Sheep Ahoy, Houghton, 1963.
Private Eyes, Doubleday, 1964.
The Year of the Raccoon, Houghton, 1966.
Secret Journey of the Silver Reindeer, Doubleday, 1968.
The Peter Pan Bag, Houghton, 1970.
Georgina and the Dragon, Houghton, 1972.
The Meeting Post: A Story of Lapland, Crowell, 1972.
Escape from the Evil Prophecy, Houghton, 1973.
Break a Leg, Betsy Maybe!, Houghton, 1976.
Head Over Wheels, Houghton, 1978.
The Refiner's Fire, Houghton, 1981.
The Luck of the Miss L, Houghton, 1986.
Catch the Baby!, Viking, 1990.

EDITOR

Newbery and Caldecott Medal Books: 1956-1965, Horn Book, 1965.
(With others) *Illustrators of Children's Books: 1957-1966,* Horn Book, 1968.
Newbery and Caldecott Medal Books: 1966-1975, Horn Book, 1975.
(With others) *Illustrators of Children's Books: 1967-1976,* Horn Book, 1978.
The Illustrator's Notebook, Horn Book, 1978.
Newbery and Caldecott Medal Books: 1976-1985, Horn Book, 1986.

Contributor of children's plays to *Plays Magazine.*

*   *   *

KITUOMBA
   See ODAGA, Asenath (Bole)

*   *   *

KLINE, Suzy 1943-

PERSONAL: Born August 27, 1943, in Berkeley, CA; daughter of Harry C. (in real estate) and Martha S. (a substitute school teacher) Weaver; married Rufus O. Kline (a college teacher, newspaper correspondent, and children's author), October 12, 1968; children: Jennifer, Emily. *Education:* Attended Columbia University; University of California, Berkeley, B.A., 1966; California State College (now University), Hayward, Standard Elementary Credential, 1967. *Politics:* Democrat. *Religion:* Presbyterian. *Hobbies and other interests:* Camping, drawing, travel, sports, reading.

ADDRESSES: Home—124 Hoffman St., Torrington, CT 06790. *Office*—Southwest School, Torrington, CT.

CAREER: Elementary schoolteacher in Richmond, CA, 1968-71; Southwest School, Torrington, CT, elementary teacher and drama director, 1976—. Makes author visits to schools and conducts workshops for teachers.

MEMBER: Society of Children's Book Writers, PEN, New England Reading Association, Connecticut Education Association, Torrington Education Association.

AWARDS, HONORS: Herbie Jones was named one of the best books of 1985 by the *Christian Science Monitor* and received West Virginia Children's Book Award, 1988; *What's the Matter with Herbie Jones* was named a *Booklist* Editor's Choice Book for 1986; International Reading Association Children's Choice Awards, 1986, for *Herbie Jones,* 1987, for *What's the Matter with Herbie Jones?,* 1989, for *Horrible Harry in Room 2B,* 1990, for *Orp,* and 1991, for *Orp and the Chop Suey Burgers;* School District Teacher of the Year Award from state of Connecticut, 1987; Probus Educator of the Year Award, 1988.

WRITINGS:

SHHHH! (juvenile), illustrations by Dora Leder, Albert Whitman, 1984.
Herbie Jones (juvenile), illustrations by Richard Williams, Putnam, 1985.
Don't Touch! (juvenile), illustrations by Leder, Albert Whitman, 1985.
What's the Matter with Herbie Jones?, (Junior Library Guild selection), illustrations by Williams, Putnam, 1986.
OOOPS!, illustrations by Leder, Albert Whitman, 1987.
Herbie Jones and the Class Gift (Junior Library Guild selection), illustrations by Williams, Putnam, 1987.
Horrible Harry in Room 2B, illustrations by Frank Remkiewicz, Viking, 1988.
Herbie Jones and the Monster Ball (Junior Library Guild selection), illustrations by Williams, Putnam, 1988.
Herbie Jones and Hamburger Head, illustrations by Williams, Putnam, 1989.
The Hole Book, illustrations by Laurie Newton, Putnam, 1989.

SUZY KLINE

Orp (Junior Literary Guild selection), Putnam, 1989.

Horrible Harry and the Green Slime, illustrations by Remkiewicz, Viking, 1989.

Horrible Harry and the Ant Invasion, illustrations by Remkiewicz, Viking, 1989.

Horrible Harry's Secret, Viking, 1990.

Orp and the Chop Suey Burgers, Putnam, 1990.

Orp Goes to the Hoop, Putnam, 1991.

Horrible Harry and the Christmas Surprise, Viking, 1991.

Mary Marony and the Snake, illustrated by Blanche Sims, Putnam, 1992.

The Herbie Jones Reader's Theater, illustrated by Williams, Putnam, 1992.

Herbie Jones and the Dark Attic, illustrated by Williams, Putnam, 1992.

Who's Orp's Girlfriend?, Putnam, 1992.

Also author of plays for local elementary school. Contributor to *Instructor.*

WORK IN PROGRESS: Two short chapter books, *Mummy Girl* and *Garbage Girl;* a picture book, *The Boy Who Swallowed a Seed;* another Horrible Harry book; four musicals for middle grade school productions based on author's books: *Orp, Herbie and Raymond on the Bench, Orp and the Chop Suey Burgers,* and *Phoebe's Secret.*

SIDELIGHTS: Suzy Kline told *SATA:* "I enjoy being the drama director at our school. Each year we present a special,

original play. I write the script and lyrics, and a fellow teacher composes the music. I have been writing these musicals for five years now.

"My first serious writing began when I was eight. I wrote letters to my grandfather in Indiana, telling him what was happening at our house. It seemed to me that he missed his son—my dad—very much, and he would be interested in hearing about him. Our home in California was three thousand miles away. My aunt told me that my letters helped him live a little longer, which made me feel really good about writing.

"When I visit classrooms and talk to students about writing, I always bring my bag of rejections (or No Thank You's as I tell primary children). I also bring my box of flops, the stories no one wanted. But I tell the students how I still save them and how some ideas can be reworked—even my third grade poem! The children know that the first book I got published was *not* the first story I wrote.

"I think I could go on forever writing about Herbie Jones and Raymond and Annabelle Louisa Hodgekiss. To me, this series is about family, friendships, and the classroom, three things that are so close to my heart. Most of all, I am blessed

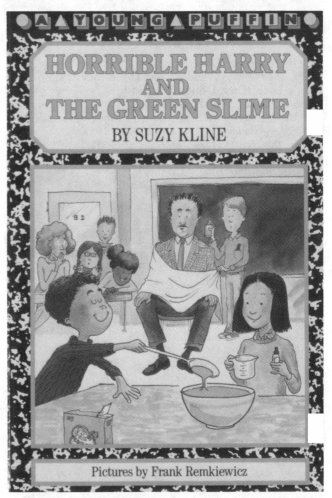

A collection of four stories by Kline, *Horrible Harry and the Green Slime* relates Harry's adventures in his second-grade classroom. (Cover illustration by Frank Remkiewicz.)

with a strong Christian faith, and that has made all the difference in my life."

*   *   *

KNAPP, Edward
See KUNHARDT, Edith

*   *   *

KODA-CALLAN, Elizabeth 1944-

PERSONAL: Born September 26, 1944, in Stamford, CT; daughter of Alexander John and Helen (Wojciehowski) Koda; married J. Michael Callan, August 14, 1971 (divorced, 1978); children: Jennifer Kristen. *Education:* University of Dayton, B.A., 1966; postgraduate study at School for Visual Arts, 1969-70, 1972-75. *Politics:* Democrat.

ADDRESSES: Home and office—792 Columbus Ave., Apt. 6D, New York, NY 10025.

CAREER: Conde Nast Publications, New York City, designer for *Glamour* magazine, 1967-69; Columbia Broadcasting System, New York City, designer and art director, 1969-70; *Mademoiselle* magazine, New York City, designer and illustrator, 1970-71; Visible Studio, New York City, assistant to illustrator, 1973-75; Scholastic Inc., New York City, designer, art editor, and associate art editor, 1975-81; Pushpin Lubalin Peckolick, New York City, illustrator, 1982—.

MEMBER: Graphic Artists Guild.

AWARDS, HONORS: Society of Illustrators award, 1975; Art Directors Show award, Art Directors Club, 1980; American Institute of Graphic Arts book design show award, 1982, for Early Childhood Program Teaching Guides; *Print* magazine award, 1982; New York Regional Show award, 1982; *Graphis Annual* award, 1983-84.

WRITINGS:

(Illustrator) *200 Years of American Illustration,* Random House, 1977.
The Magic Locket, Workman Publishing, 1988.
The Silver Slippers, Workman Publishing, 1989.
The Good Luck Pony, Workman Publishing, 1990.

Also designer and associate art director for Early Childhood Program Teaching Guides, Scholastic Inc., 1981.

*   *   *

KOSCIELNIAK, Bruce 1947-

PERSONAL: Born July 9, 1947, in Adams, MA; son of Edwin and Irene Koscielniak. *Education:* Vesper George School of Art, Boston, MA, degree in commercial art, 1969; Williams College, B.A., 1975.

ADDRESSES: Home—36 Summer St., Adams, MA 01220.

CAREER: U.S. Postal Service, Adams, MA, clerk, 1977—; writer and illustrator. *Military service:* U.S. Army, 1969-71.

BRUCE KOSCIELNIAK

WRITINGS:

FOR CHILDREN; SELF-ILLUSTRATED

Hector and Prudence, Knopf, 1990.
Hector and Prudence—All Aboard!, Knopf, 1990.
Euclid Bunny Delivers the Mail, Knopf, 1991.

*   *   *

KRUPINSKI, Loretta 1940-

PERSONAL: Born September 5, 1940, in Brooklyn, NY; daughter of Frederick (an executive with U.S. Steel) and Emma Vollmuth; married Joseph Krupinski (divorced); children: Jennifer. *Education:* Syracuse University, B.F.A., 1962.

ADDRESSES: Home and office—6 Coach Dr., Old Lyme, CT 06371.

CAREER: Illustrator. Worked for *Newsday* (newspaper), Long Island, NY, as editorial illustrator for eight years, for General Dynamics, Groton, CT, for seven years, and held various jobs relating to design and illustration until 1987; freelance children's book illustrator and marine art painter, 1987—.

MEMBER: American Society of Marine Artists (artist member and member of board of directors), Society of Children's Book Writers and Artists.

ILLUSTRATOR:

(And adaptor) Irving Bachelor, *Lost in the Fog,* Little, Brown, 1990.
Carol Greene, *The Old Ladies Who Loved Cats,* Harper/Collins, 1991.
M. C. Helldorfer, *Sailing to the Sea,* Viking, 1991.
Helen Jordan, *How a Seed Grows,* Harper/Collins, 1992.
(And adaptor) Celia Thaxter, *Celia's Island Journal,* Little, Brown, 1992.

WORK IN PROGRESS: Working on several manuscripts for picture books.

SIDELIGHTS: Loretta Krupinski writes, "I began drawing as a very young child and have never stopped. In this respect drawing has become a natural part of my life as much as eating, sleeping, and breathing.

"After graduating from Syracuse University in 1962, majoring in illustration and painting, I followed the responsible road to career success by working for other companies. My first job (and my favorite) was for *Newsday,* a large, successful New York newspaper, as an editorial illustrator. This limited my work to just black and white, but it was a good foundation, for my subject matter ran the gamut from humorous to serious art. Many moves and jobs later, now residing in Connecticut, I am living in an area surrounded by Long Island Sound, the Connecticut River, and a lake. The fine art part of me grew into the marine art field, where I am now a well-known realist painter of traditional classic wood boats, lighthouses and harbors, all endangered species stalked by the ravages of time.

Illustrator Loretta Krupinski specializes in painting marine art. (From *Sailing to the Sea,* by M. C. Helldorfer, illustrated by Krupinski.)

"When my only child, Jennifer, left to pursue her college career, I decided it was time to do what *I'd* been wanting to do for years: take a risk and leave the corporate world and its weekly paycheck and paid health insurance. I then began to pursue illustrating and writing children's picture books, and continued my marine art painting. I feel that all the rules and elements of painting—composition, color theory, and technique have definitely propelled me into doing the quality of illustrations I do today.

"Painting has been an excellent background for me in my commercial work. Painting deals with reality, and children's books deal with fantasy. It is enlightening and fun to step back and forth into each world. While my maritime background is a definite asset in my choice of children's books, I hope not to be typecast as a 'boat illustrator.' I like to do little soft fuzzy things as well!"

*   *   *

KUNHARDT, Edith 1937-
(Pine Grunewalt, Johnson Hill, Edward Knapp, Jessie Smith, Harry Coe Verr)

PERSONAL: Surname is pronounced "*coon*-heart"; born September 30, 1937, in New York, NY; daughter of Philip B. (a textile salesman) and Dorothy (a children's book writer and illustrator; maiden name, Meserve) Kunhardt; married Edward S. Davis (a lawyer), November 20, 1959 (divorced, 1971); children: Martha Knapp, Edward, Jr. *Education:* Bryn Mawr College, B.A., 1959. *Politics:* Democrat. *Religion:* Episcopalian.

ADDRESSES: Home—New York, NY. *Office*—c/o Greenwillow Books, William Morrow & Co. Inc., 1350 Avenue of the Americas, New York, NY 10019. *Agent*—Marilyn E. Marlow, Curtis Brown Ltd., 10 Astor Place, New York, NY 10003.

CAREER: Golden Books, New York City, assistant editor, 1974-76, associate editor, 1976-80, editor, 1980-83, and senior editor, 1983-86; children's book writer and illustrator; free-lance writer, 1986—.

MEMBER: Authors Guild, Society of Children's Book Writers.

WRITINGS:

The Mouse Family's New Home, illustrated by Diane Dawson, Western Publishing, 1981.
(Under pseudonym Edward Knapp) *What! No Spinach?: A Popeye Story,* illustrated by Manny Campana, Western Publishing, 1981.
Ned's Number Book, illustrated by Eugenie, Western Publishing, 1981.
Martha's House, illustrated by Carolyn Bracken, Western Publishing, 1982.
The Race to Pearl Peak: A Popeye Adventure, illustrated by Campana, Western Publishing, 1982.
Animal Quiz Book, illustrated by Kelly Oechsli, Western Publishing, 1983.
All Kinds of Trucks, illustrated by Art Seiden, Western Publishing, 1984.
Giant Sea Creatures, illustrated by Fiona Reid, Western Publishing, 1984.
(And illustrator) *Pat the Cat,* Western Publishing, 1984.

EDITH KUNHARDT

Grandma and Grandpa Smith, illustrated by Terri Super, Western Publishing, 1985.

(And illustrator) *Danny's Birthday*, Greenwillow, 1986.

(Under pseudonym Johnson Hill) *The Puppy Who Couldn't Remember* (a "Pound Puppy" story), illustrated by Pat Paris, Western Publishing, 1986.

Summer Vacation, illustrated by Kathy Allert, Western Publishing, 1986.

(Under pseudonym Jessie Smith) *Big Bird's Busy Day*, illustrated by Ellen Appleby, Western Publishing, 1987.

(Under pseudonym Edward Knapp) *How Speedy Is a Cheetah?: Fascinating Facts about Animals* (part of the "All Aboard Books" series), illustrated by Richard Roe, Putnam, 1987.

The Airplane Book, illustrated by Bracken, Western Publishing, 1987.

Kittens, Kittens, Kittens, illustrated by Kathy Mitchell, Western Publishing, 1987.

Danny's Mystery Valentine, Greenwillow, 1987.

Pompeii—Buried Alive!, illustrated by Michael Eagle, Random House, 1987.

(And illustrator) *Where's Peter?*, Greenwillow, 1988.

(Under pseudonym Jessie Smith) *Grover's Day at the Beach: A Counting Story*, illustrated by Tom Cooke, Western Publishing, 1988.

(Under pseudonym Jessie Smith) *Going Places: Featuring Jim Henson's Sesame Street Muppets*, illustrated by Joseph Ewers, Western Publishing, 1988.

Trick or Treat, Danny!, Greenwillow, 1988.

Danny and the Easter Egg, Greenwillow, 1989.

(And photographer) *I Want to Be a Farmer* (part of the "On the Job" series), Putnam, 1989.

(And photographer) *I Want to Be a Firefighter* (part of the "On the Job" series), Putnam, 1989.

Which One Would You Choose?, Greenwillow, 1989.

Danny's Christmas Star, Greenwillow, 1989.

Which Pig Would You Choose?, Greenwillow, 1990.

Also author of other books for children, including, under pseudonym Johnson Hill, *Alf: A Day at the Fair*, Macmillan; under pseudonym Harry Coe Verr, *Alf Summer Camp Adventure*, Macmillan; *Angel Bunny Count with Me*, Western Publishing; *Angel Bunny Off We Go*, Western Publishing; *Animal Homes*, Western Publishing; *Cinderella*, Western Publishing; *Disney Babies Name the Colors*, Western Publishing; *The Fox and the Hound: Lost and Found*, Western Publishing; *Go Fly a Kite, Charlie Brown*, Western Publishing; *The Good Morning Book*, Western Publishing; *The Good Night Book*, Western Publishing; under pseudonym Jessie Smith, *Grover's Sand Castle*, Western Publishing; *Hello and Bye-Bye*, Western Publishing; *How Do We Get There?*, Western Publishing; *Mickey Mouse and the Lucky Goose Chase*, Western Publishing; *Mrs. Brisby's Remembering Game*, Western Publishing; *My Alphabet*, Western Publishing; *My Things*, Western Publishing; *Pinocchio*, Western Publishing; *The Poky Little Puppy at the Fair*, Western Publishing; under pseudonym Pine Grunewalt, *Rainbow Brite and the Color Thieves*, Western Publishing; *Rainbow Brite and the Magic Belt*, Western Publishing; *Red Day, Blue Day*, Greenwillow; *A Sleep-over Visit*, Western Publishing; *The Taxi Book*, Western Publishing; *The Truck Book*, Western Publishing; *Where's Your Nose?*, Western Publishing.

Also adapting *Santabear's First Christmas* for book and videotape for Crown.

Kunhardt began her career as an illustrator when she created *Pat the Cat*, a companion to her mother's classic, *Pat the Bunny*, which also invites children to interact with the text.

Kunhardt's "Danny" series describes the exploits of a loveable-looking alligator. (From a postcard illustration of *Danny and the Easter Egg,* written and illustrated by Kunhardt.)

WORK IN PROGRESS: "A book about grief for adults, a novel about mothers and daughters, and various children's book projects—one about a sea otter and another about America's sixteenth president, Abraham Lincoln."

SIDELIGHTS: Edith Kunhardt told *SATA:* "I was born in New York City and grew up in Morristown, New Jersey. We lived in a house on a run-down estate on a steep hill that abounded with deer, foxes, and groundhogs. There were horses to ride and an ice-cold, spring-fed pool to swim in. I played football with my two big brothers (perfecting my spiral pass and a mean end run) and learned about astronomy from my beautiful big sister. My father loved the outdoors—climbing mountains, fishing, and hacking a rose garden out of the jungle of arborvitae on the hill in front of our house. My mother loved the indoors—pouring for hours over her research (she was a Civil War scholar) and her antique book and toy collections. She also was one of the most innovative children's book authors of her time, inventing a little book called *Pat the Bunny* for me in 1940. This book is currently an American best-seller, second only in the world to Beatrix Potter's *Peter Rabbit.* Some of her other highly acclaimed books were *Junket Is Nice, The Telephone Book,* and *Lucky Mrs. Ticklefeather.*

"My mother liked to do hands-on research, so to speak. She rode with garbagemen on their trucks and visited barbers at their school to watch them shave balloons for practice. And she was full of fascinating facts that she used in her books.

For example, elephant calves sometimes fall in their parents' footsteps and baby whales sometimes get jellyfish caught in their throats.

"Being a combination of my father and mother, I spent a lot of time roaming the hill in my blue jeans, a knife at my belt, sitting up in a tree reading books. I was an acrobat, cowboy, or Indian according to whether I'd been to the circus, rodeo, or seen a movie about Indians. I had discovered a hemlock where two branches crossed about twenty feet up, and I hauled books (and food, mostly Malomars) up there on a rope. I'll never forget the feeling of power and freedom I had, hidden in that tree. At that time my favorite books were the 'Freddy the Pig' series by Walter R. Brooks, *The Deerslayer* by James Fenimore Cooper, and books about Joan of Arc.

"I started drawing, of course, as soon as I could. (I have an early illustration—a drawing of our dalmatian dog, Hundred, named for the number of spots we thought he had—that I accomplished when I was three.) In fourth grade I had a wonderful teacher, Mrs. Harold Noling, who valued creativity of all kinds. In her class we made books, literally penning the words and drawing the illustrations and sewing and pasting the covers. (One of my stories was 'Mole and Friends.' A memorable line was, ' "Be eyes for me," said Mole.') I still have the books.

"At boarding school and college, I continued to write, but mainly in the context of a history of art major. When I married at age twenty-one, I think it was no accident that I married Edward S. Davis, the son of children's book writer Lavinia Davis (author of *Hobby Horse Hill, Island City,* and *Melody, Muttonbone, and Sam*). Yet I didn't believe that *I* could write children's books.

"After my divorce I started working in publishing and eventually became an editor. But it was not until my mother died in 1979 that the way to writing for children began to come clear. (In retrospect, I think I believed that *she* was the children's book author, and that was that!) I started writing in the early 1980s and have had fifty-six books published thus far. Ideas tumbled out—an alligator who watches videotapes, a boy who becomes invisible, and an ancient Egyptian who happens to be a hippopotamus. I began to be a hands-on researcher, too, traveling to the top of Colorado's Pike's Peak where my grandfather spent a year as a weather observer in 1880. I also counted grey whales on an expedition to Baja (215 in one day!), rode in a fire chief's car to fire drills, and chased a speeder in a police car—all in the name of writing. I also amassed and used facts about ninety-foot worms, potato harvesting, and the eruption of Pompeii's Mount Vesuvius in A.D. 79.

"I started illustrating when I created a companion to my mother's book *Pat the Bunny,* called *Pat the Cat,* which was published in 1984. I used my children as models. I often draw on their early childhoods, as well as my own, for experience and points of view. I am also a professional photographer."

FOR MORE INFORMATION SEE:

PERIODICALS

Booklist, March 15, 1989; February 15, 1990.
New York Times Book Review, February 10, 1985.
Kirkus Reviews, January 1, 1988.
Publishers Weekly, July 25, 1986; February 24, 1989.
School Library Journal, November, 1987.
Washington Post Book World, January 13, 1985.

LAMPTON, Christopher (F.)

PERSONAL: Education: Received degree in broadcast journalism.

ADDRESSES: Home—Maryland.

CAREER: Writer.

WRITINGS:

FOR YOUNG PEOPLE; UNDER NAME CHRISTOPHER LAMPTON, EXCEPT AS NOTED; PUBLISHED BY F. WATTS

Black Holes and Other Secrets of the Universe, 1980.
Meteorology: An Introduction, 1981.
Fusion: The Eternal Flame, 1982.
Planet Earth, 1982.
The Sun, 1982.
Dinosaurs and the Age of Reptiles, 1983.
DNA and the Creation of New Life, 1983.
Prehistoric Animals, 1983.
Programming in BASIC, 1983.
Space Sciences, illustrations by Anne Canevari Green, 1983.
Computer Languages, 1983.
Advanced BASIC, 1984.
BASIC for Beginners, 1984.
COBOL for Beginners, 1984.
FORTRAN for Beginners, 1984.
The Micro Dictionary, 1984.
Pascal for Beginners, 1984.
PILOT for Beginners, 1984.
Advanced BASIC for Beginners, 1984.
6502 Assembly-Language Programming for Apple, Commodore, and Atari Computers, 1985.
Forth for Beginners, 1985.
Graphics and Animation on the Commodore 64, 1985.
Z80 Assembly-Language: Programming for Radio Shack, Timex Sinclair, Adam, and CP/M Computers, 1985.
Graphics and Animation on the TRS-80: Models I, III, and 4, 1985.
Flying Safe?, 1986.
Graphics and Animation on the Apple II, II Plus, IIe and IIc, 1986.
Graphics and Animation on the Atari: 800, 400, 1200XL, and 600XL, 1986.
How to Create Adventure Games, 1986.
How to Create Computer Games, 1986.
Mass Extinctions: One Theory of Why the Dinosaurs Vanished, 1986.
Astronomy: From Copernicus to the Space Telescope, 1987.
The Space Telescope, 1987.
Star Wars, 1987.
CD-ROMS, 1987.
Endangered Species, 1988.
Rocketry: From Goddard to Space Travel, 1988.
Supernova!, 1988.
(Under name Christopher F. Lampton) *Thomas Alva Edison,* 1988.
Undersea Archaeology, 1988.
Wernher von Braun, 1988.
Stars and Planets: A Useful and Entertaining Tool to Guide Youngsters into the Twenty-First Century, illustrations by Ron Miller, 1988.

New Theories on the Dinosaurs, 1989.
New Theories on the Origins of the Human Race, 1989.
New Theories on the Birth of the Universe, 1989.
Predicting AIDS and Other Epidemics, 1989.
Predicting Nuclear and Other Technological Disasters, 1989.
Gene Technology: Confronting the Issues, 1990.
Telecommunications: From Telegraphs to Modems, 1991.

OTHER; UNDER NAME CHRISTOPHER LAMPTON, EXCEPT AS NOTED

(With David Bischoff) *The Seeker,* Laser Books, 1976.
(Under name Chris Lampton) *Gateway to Limbo* (science fiction novel), Doubleday, 1979.
(Under name Christopher F. Lampton) *Superconductors,* Enslow, 1989.
Bathtubs, Slides, Roller Coaster Rails: Simple Machines That Are Really Inclined Planes, illustrations by Carol Nicklaus, Millbrook, 1991.
Marbles, Roller Skates, Doorknobs: Simple Machines That Are Really Wheels, illustrations by Nicklaus, Millbrook, 1991.
Seesaws, Nutcrackers, Brooms: Simple Machines That Are Really Levers, illustrations by Nicklaus, Millbrook, 1991.
Simple Machines That Are Really Pulleys, Millbrook, 1991.
Blizzard Alert!, Millbrook, 1991.
Earthquake Alert!, Millbrook, 1991.
Forest Fire Alert!, Millbrook, 1991.
Hurricane Alert!, Millbrook, 1991.
Tornado Alert!, Millbrook, 1991.
Volcano Alert!, Millbrook, 1991.
Nintendo Action Games, Millbrook, 1991.
Nintendo Role-Playing Games, Millbrook, 1991.*

*   *   *

LEE, Sally 1943-

PERSONAL: Born March 13, 1943, in Denver, CO; daughter of Paul W. Forker (an attorney) and Marion Helen Davidson (a homemaker and secretary; maiden name, Fry); stepdaughter of Roy A. Davidson (an educator); married Stephen K. Lee (a petroleum engineer), June 9, 1968; children: Michael, Tracy. *Education:* University of Missouri, B.S., 1965. *Politics:* Republican. *Religion:* Methodist.

ADDRESSES: Office—3111 East Hickory Park, Sugar Land, TX 77479. *Agent*—c/o Franklin Watts, Inc., 387 Park Ave., New York, NY 10016.

CAREER: Special School District, St. Louis, MO, special education teacher, 1965-68; Spring Branch School District, Houston, TX, teacher, 1968-71; homemaker, 1971-90; Sugarland Properties, Inc., Sugar Land, TX, executive secretary, 1990—; writer.

MEMBER: Society of Children's Book Writers (Houston chapter; treasurer).

WRITINGS:

Donor Banks: Saving Lives with Organ and Tissue Transplants, F. Watts, 1988.
Predicting Violent Storms, F. Watts, 1989.
New Theories on Diet and Nutrition, F. Watts, 1990.
The Throwaway Society, F. Watts, 1990.
Pesticides, F. Watts, 1991.

Author of supplementary readers for C. E. Merrill. Contributor of short stories and articles to magazines, including *Cricket, Highlights for Children, Jack & Jill,* and *Teen.*

WORK IN PROGRESS: Hurricanes, for F. Watts; *San Antonio,* for Dillon.

SIDELIGHTS: Sally Lee told *SATA:* "Unlike most writers, I was not an avid reader as a child. I was much too busy climbing to the top of the lookout tower in my 'castle' (a grove of pine trees in a nearby park), or keeping Indians away from my 'fort' (a pile of sofa cushions), or riding my trusted horse (who just happened to have wheels and handlebars). Since we didn't get our first television set until I was ten, I had to rely on my imagination for fun. Thus the seeds of my writing career were planted.

"In 1961 I went to the University of Missouri to become a special education teacher. One of our required education courses was children's literature for elementary school teachers, affectionately known as 'Kiddy Lit.' Although I grumbled a lot about the hours spent in the library reading all the Newbery and Caldecott winners along with many classics, I came out of the course with a greater appreciation for good children's books.

SALLY LEE

"After teaching for five and a half years, I 'retired' in 1971 to raise my family. I loved being a full-time mother but felt there had to be more to life than soggy diapers and baby talk. I reactivated my brain by taking a correspondence course in writing for children from the Institute of Children's Literature. Our final assignment was to write a book. Since I was pregnant at the time, I must have felt some kinship with the Goodyear blimp stationed near our home. I decided to use it as the topic of my book. Goodyear graciously provided me with a blimp ride to gain some first-hand experience. A week before my daughter was born I lumbered onto the blimp for my ride. The trip was fun in spite of the concerned looks of the pilot and crew who undoubtedly wondered if they would be witnessing the first birth aboard a blimp in Goodyear's history. Although nothing ever came of my blimp story, the experience of getting to do something that the average person doesn't get to do made being a writer sound even more interesting.

"In the beginning my writing efforts met with far more rejections than acceptances. But I stuck with it and learned something from each thing I wrote. I came up through the ranks, writing short stories first for Sunday school magazines, then for better known publications such as *Jack & Jill, Highlights for Children,* and *Teen.* Three of my articles were published in *Cricket,* and all of them were reprinted in reading anthologies. I was slowly gaining more credibility as a writer.

"The topic for my first book came about by accident. In 1986 I attended a luncheon and sat next to the director of a bone bank. Never having heard of a bone bank, I immediately bombarded her with questions. I'm sure we ruined the appetites of our luncheon companions as we embarked on a lively discussion of how bones were harvested, freeze-dried like instant coffee, and kept in bottles and packages on a storeroom shelf until they were needed by doctors for use in certain types of surgery. I started thinking of all the other kinds of donor banks I had heard of, such as blood banks, eye banks, organ banks, and even skin banks. Suddenly, my lunchtime conversation had mushroomed into a book. I wrote my proposal and sent it to Franklin Watts, who agreed to publish it. In the spring of 1988 *Donor Banks: Saving Lives with Organ and Tissue Transplants* came out. After fifteen years of plugging away at writing short stories and articles for magazines, I was no longer just a writer. I was an *author!*

"The editors at Franklin Watts began giving me assignments. I became a temporary expert in a wide variety of subjects. I felt like a meteorologist as I wrote *Predicting Violent Storms,* a nutritionist as I wrote *New Theories on Diet and Nutrition,* and an environmentalist while writing *The Throwaway Society* and *Pesticides.* The months spent in researching these books may have been a drag for most people, but I loved it. To me, research is a treasure hunt filled with clues, dead ends, wild goose chases, and the delight of uncovering an obscure fact or a whole mother lode of information.

"In addition to writing books for Franklin Watts I have written some supplementary readers for the Charles Merrill Company. My first assignment was to write forty-eight one-page stories about a little boy named Carlos and his robot named Mish. I had a lot of fun thinking up ways that Mish could get Carlos into jams. I also learned about the restrictions inherent in the world of textbook publishing—no ghosts or witches, no religion, and (heaven forbid!) no sweets or other junk food. I felt sorry for textbook characters who couldn't have ice cream and cake at their birthday parties.

"A lot of people say they want to be writers but they quit at the first sight of a rejection slip. As in many fields, those who are successful are not necessarily the ones with the most talent, but the ones who refuse to give up."

*   *   *

LeSIEG, Theo.
See GEISEL, Theodor Seuss

*   *   *

LEVY, Marilyn 1937-

PERSONAL: Born August 23, 1937, in Youngstown, OH; daughter of Morris and Dorothy (maiden name, Shwartz) Lockshin; married Lawrence Levy (a producer/director), June, 1960; children: Lisa Levy Stromer, Samantha Levy Deutsch. *Education:* Northwestern University, B.S., 1959. *Politics:* Independent. *Religion:* Jewish.

ADDRESSES: Agent—Ellen Levine, Suite 1801, 15 East 26th St., New York, NY 10010.

CAREER: Beachwood Junior High, Beachwood, OH, English instructor, 1959-60; New Trier High School, Winnetka, IL, English instructor, 1960-61; Niles Township High School, Niles, IL, English instructor, 1962-63; Roosevelt University, Chicago, IL, instructor in speech, 1964-69; Roycemore School, Evanston, IL, English instructor, 1978-79; Crossroads School, Santa Monica, CA, English instructor, 1982-85; writer, 1985—. Precinct captain, Evanston, IL.

AWARDS, HONORS: American Library Association Award, 1989, for *Touching;* Utah Young Adult Book Award, 1991, for *No Way Home.*

WRITINGS:

JUVENILE

The Girl in the Plastic Cage, Fawcett, 1982.
Life Is Not a Dress Rehearsal, Fawcett, 1984.
Love Is a Long Shot, Fawcett, 1986.
Summer Snow, Fawcett, 1986.
Keeping Score, Fawcett, 1987.
Remember to Remember Me, Fawcett, 1988.
Touching, Fawcett, 1988.
Love Is Not Enough, Fawcett, 1989.
Putting Heather Together Again, Fawcett, 1989.
Sounds of Silence, Fawcett, 1989.
No Way Home, Fawcett, 1989.
Rumors and Whispers, Fawcett, 1989.
Is That Really Me in the Mirror?, Fawcett, 1991.
Fitting In, Fawcett, 1991.
The Last Good-bye, Fawcett, 1991.

OTHER

Also author of plays *Dangerous Perceptions* and *Breaking Windows.* Author of screenplays *Say Good-bye to Paradise, Sylvanie,* and *Hidden Room.*

WORK IN PROGRESS: Writing screenplays; a book on teens with Bruno Bettleheim.

SIDELIGHTS: Marilyn Levy has carved a niche for herself as a keen observer of young adult problems and concerns. In

MARILYN LEVY

books like *Summer Snow* and *Touching,* Levy's enlightened exploration of topics such as drug abuse and alcoholism is the direct result of contact with teens from all walks of life. Levy does not always offer a happy solution to the problems presented in her books, largely because she believes many issues are too complicated to lend themselves to simple answers. "If an idea strikes me, I like to go for it," Levy explained in an interview with *Something About the Author* (*SATA*). "I go with what strikes me, with what feels right, which probably isn't the best way to work, but that's the only way I know to write."

Levy was born into a middle-class Jewish family in Youngstown, Ohio. In many ways, her childhood was a very happy one. Levy was well-liked, popular, and heavily involved in school and extracurricular activities. Yet, despite her success at school and stability at home, Levy felt like an outsider. "I was always an outsider because I never thought the way other people thought," Levy admitted to *SATA*. Part of the problem was the nature of small-town living. Levy recalled: "It was a very small town mentality, not just in terms of population. There were certain ways to do things. There were certain groups one had to belong to, and it never seemed right to me. The rules were very rigid. I found it difficult to stay within the parameters of the group I was supposed to be in. In a small town, everybody noticed that."

Even though her refusal to live by a rigid set of rules made her feel isolated at times, Levy did not give in to her loneliness. She daydreamed a lot and wrote poetry. Her grandfather took her to museums and art galleries. They listened to opera together every Saturday afternoon. Levy's grandfather also introduced her to the world of literature. "He used to read adult books to me," Levy remembered. "He read Dostoyevsky and Chekov! No children's books."

As Levy grew older, she noticed that some of the most rigid small-town "rules" had social connotations. "There were fraternities and sororities at my high school," Levy recounted. "They broke up according to socioeconomics and religion, and all the kids I had been friendly with were suddenly in one group and I wasn't. I was invited to join a

Jewish sorority, but I chose not to because it felt too narrow and exclusive. As a result, I inhabited a lot of different worlds. I could never understand why choices had to be so limited."

Levy's choice of high school friends did not conform to the accepted social standard. "There were black students in my high school, and I chose to be friendly with them, which was something that no white person did at the time. I mean it simply was not done," she told *SATA*. "I remember going to parties with kids that were Italian and black, parties in very poor neighborhoods. I thought 'These people are real. They might live in very difficult circumstances, but they are more alive than the people I know.'"

Levy's favorite subject in school was English, and she read whenever possible. "If I could have, I would have just taken literature classes. In fact, in my other courses, I used to put novels behind my texts and read them!," Levy remarked in her *SATA* interview. Her writing skills were very good, but she did not take them very seriously. "Occasionally, if I ever had to write essays, I did very well," Levy disclosed. "I always wrote very quickly." Despite winning an essay contest as a high school senior, Levy was surprised when a college professor commented favorably on her work. She recalled that "it unnerved me because I never considered myself a writer, never wanted to be a writer. I thought writers lived outside the real world."

After graduating from high school, Levy left Youngstown to study acting in the speech department at Northwestern University. While she enjoyed her acting studies, Levy began to realize that acting was not the most stable of professions. Looking for something to fall back on that offered more security, she did some student teaching at New Trier High School in Winnetka. To her surprise, the experience was very rewarding. Levy found the school's curriculum challenging: "It was so different from my own high school experience because the classes were small and the teachers were very involved. Kids wrote all the time, and they studied things that were fascinating. It was wonderful to be part of that." Levy also discovered that her acting background was very helpful in the classroom. "It was like putting on a performance every day. I involved the kids in what I was doing. There was always give and take between my students and me. Every day was different; it was exciting," Levy remembered.

Levy continued teaching after graduating from college. She taught high school English for three years and speech at Roosevelt University in Chicago for one year. During this time, Levy also married a film producer and had two daughters. Her family lived in Europe for six months and on a moshav, or farm cooperative, in Israel for a year. In 1979, Levy and her family moved to California, where she began teaching at a private school. For Levy, teaching in California was very different from teaching in the Midwest. She noticed a severe lack of communication between many parents and students. Levy further described the problem for *SATA:* "I found many parents not only did not know what their kids were doing, they basically didn't care. I would often see problems with kids and call parents, and their reactions were basically 'Don't tell me. I really don't want to hear this.'"

Levy realized that some of this lack of communication stemmed from the way the members of her students' families interacted. She pointed out that "kids don't eat dinner with their families; if dinner is provided, somebody gets it together and people come in at different times and eat. There's no such thing as sitting down together and having a family meal."

Lack of family communication was a contributing factor in other problems Levy saw while teaching, such as drug and alcohol abuse. Levy found that while many young people were aware of the dangers facing them, few had anyone to go to with their concerns. Over time, Levy's belief in being honest with her students made many of them feel comfortable enough to discuss their problems with her.

Levy began writing young adult novels by accident. Her daughter Lisa had been in a brace from her chin to her mid hips for two years. After the brace was removed, Lisa was offered a part in a television commercial. A young adult novelist Levy met during the commercial shoot suggested Lisa's recovery might make an inspiring story. Levy agreed, and began work on what would become *The Girl in the Plastic Cage.* In her *SATA* interview, she described the experience of writing a novel based on personal circumstance as both fulfilling and somewhat painful. She explained: "It was both difficult and easier because I knew the situation so well, and because I knew her so well, but it was difficult reliving those memories and it was difficult for her when she read the book."

All Levy's books have some basis in fact; many, like *The Girl in the Plastic Cage,* are based on actual incidents or people. In many cases, Levy's characters are composites of former students. Levy told *SATA* how she begins to sketch a character: "If I want to write about a certain subject or a certain type of kid, I don't make it up out of my head; I search out that kid until I find someone that I think fits my general idea. I spend a lot of time with him or her. For example, when I wrote about a deaf boy, I found one boy that I could really connect with. And we spent a lot of time together. When I felt I really knew him and knew the way he thought and felt about things, I began the book (and only then invented the dramatic situation)." Levy also carefully researches the locations that will appear in her books in order to insure their authentic depiction.

Levy believes that it is very important for writers to be observant at all times. "All I have to do is keep my eyes and ears open, then allow my characters to be human and fun and funny, serious and devilish, smart about some things, not so smart about others, cocky and self-confident, and plagued by self-doubt—just like real kids," she told *SATA*. Levy admits that some young people prefer to read more escapist literature, but she also feels that books which offer realistic problems and situations fulfill an important need. Levy hopes that if "a kid reads one of my books, he or she will think before dismissing someone who's different, and perhaps they will come to understand and appreciate life outside their own limited world. I want a kid to be able to read one of my books and say 'There's another kid who's the most popular kid in school, but underneath it all has the same fears, the same needs, the same desires, the same insecurities I have' or 'Here's someone totally different from me, but we have so much in common.'"

Ultimately, Levy maintains that every teenager has a story, and she tries to find these stories in the young people she comes in contact with. "Some are more interesting than others, but each story is original in its own way," Levy pointed out, adding that "As long as I remain open enough to listen to kids without forming any judgements, hopefully kids will continue to talk to me, and I will have no problem filling up those blank pieces of paper."

WORKS CITED:

Levy, Marilyn, telephone interview for *Something About the Author* conducted by Elizabeth A. Des Chenes, June 26, 1991.

Sketch by Elizabeth A. Des Chenes

*   *   *

LEWIS, Linda (Joy) 1946-

PERSONAL: Born June 20, 1946, in New York, NY; daughter of Abraham and Shirley (Feinberg) Bierman; married Leonard Lewis, March 31, 1965; children: Joyce Lewis Kelson, Kenneth Lewis. *Education:* City College of the City University of New York, B.A., 1972; Florida Atlantic University, Ed.M., 1976. *Religion:* Jewish.

ADDRESSES: Home—4469 Poinciana St., Fort Lauderdale, FL 33308. *Office*—c/o Archway Simon & Schuster, 1230 Sixth Ave., New York, NY 10020.

CAREER: Broward County Schools, Fort Lauderdale, FL, school teacher, 1972-81; Simon & Schuster, New York City, writer, 1985—.

MEMBER: Authors Guild.

WRITINGS:

"LINDA" SERIES; PUBLISHED BY SIMON & SCHUSTER

We Hate Everything but Boys, 1985.
Is There Life after Boys?, 1987.
We Love Only Older Boys, 1988.
2 Young 2 Go 4 Boys, 1988.
My Heart Belongs to That Boy, 1989.
All for the Love of That Boy, 1989.
Want to Trade Two Brothers for a Cat?, 1989.
Dedicated to That Boy I Love, 1990.

LINDA LEWIS

Lewis's first book, *We Hate Everything but Boys,* **was so popular with readers that it led to a whole series of "Linda" stories.** (Cover illustration by Richard Lauter.)

Loving Two Is Hard to Do, 1990.
Tomboy Terror in Bunk 109, 1991.

WORK IN PROGRESS: A story about Linda's friend Darlene, tentatively titled *Preteen Means in Between;* a sequel, tentatively titled *Two Lips Met in a Daring Kiss.*

SIDELIGHTS: Linda Lewis told *SATA:* "I was born in New York City and grew up in the upper Manhattan neighborhood of Washington Heights. The street, park, and corner candy store provided a fertile social life for the teenagers of our neighborhood, and it was there, at age fourteen, that I started going with the boy who eventually was to become my husband.

"Ours was a turbulent relationship; we broke up and went back together thirteen times before we finally got married. And I faithfully recorded everything—the ups and downs, the feelings and emotions, the major and minor events—in the diaries I had been keeping since age eleven. For I always seemed to have a need to write, probably an extension of my love for reading. Reading expanded my mind, enabled me to use my imagination and to explore new and fascinating worlds, and exposed me to the ideas and knowledge of others. Writing also expanded my mind, helping me to understand and give order to my own world and ideas.

"Still, it took me a long time to consider writing on a professional basis. I was married at eighteen and within two years had my children, Joyce and Kenny. I finished college at night and became a teacher, working with children with physical and intellectual handicaps. In 1973 I moved to Florida, where I continued to teach, and I received my master's degree in special education. But as time went on I found myself increasingly unfulfilled by teaching. I longed for a career that would be more stimulating and that would better utilize my mind and talents.

"After much soul-searching I realized that what I really wanted to do was become a writer of children's books. That's when I turned to my diaries. Reading them brought me right back to that place and time, and I found myself reliving the feelings and emotions, the fun and the good times as well as the sad and seemingly tragic moments that all teenagers go through on the path to adulthood. I wanted to turn my experiences and what I had learned from them into lively, exciting, and fun stories that would have universal appeal. I hoped kids would see themselves and their friends in my books, that they would relate to the stories and the characters because they seemed so real.

"My first book, *We Hate Everything but Boys,* took two years to write—I was still teaching—and was finally published in 1985. The book was very popular, and I received numerous requests to continue Linda's story. So I did. The result is a series of ten books. *Want to Trade Two Brothers for a Cat?, Tomboy Terror in Bunk 109,* and *2 Young 2 Go 4 Boys* are about Linda when she was younger. *Is There Life after Boys?, We Love Only Older Boys, My Heart Belongs to That Boy, All for the Love of That Boy, Dedicated to That Boy I Love,* and *Loving Two Is Hard to Do* follow Linda's story as she grows older and falls in love. My fans inevitably enjoy finding out that the real Linda is still married to Lenny twenty-six years later.

"While my main purpose is to tell a story that is entertaining and fun to read, my books incorporate my philosophy that life presents a series of lessons which we see as problems, but which are actually opportunities to learn and grow. My goal is to help kids learn to deal with the lessons in their own lives as well as have them enjoy my books and develop the love of reading that I always had."

*   *   *

LINDSAY, Norman (Alfred William) 1879-1969

PERSONAL: Name originally Alfred William Norman Lindsay; born February 23 (some sources say February 22), 1879, in Creswick, Victoria, New South Wales, Australia; died November 21, 1969; son of a physician; married Kate Parkinson, 1900 (divorced, 1920); married Rose Soady, 1920; children: (first marriage) Jack, Phillip, Raymond; (second marriage) two daughters. *Education:* Attended schools in Creswick, Australia.

CAREER: Hawklet (sporting paper), Melbourne, Australia, illustrator, 1896-99; *Toscin,* Melbourne, illustrator, 1896-99; free-lance artist, 1899-1901; *Sydney Bulletin,* Sydney, Austra-

lia, cartoonist, illustrator, and writer, 1901-23 and 1932-58. Cosponsor of Endeavor Press; cofounder of *Vision,* 1924. *Exhibitions:* Artwork exhibited in one-man shows in Sydney, 1898 and 1968, Melbourne, 1898, Adelaide, 1924, London, 1925, and New Castle, New South Wales, 1969 and 1979; in group shows, including Exhibition of Australian Art, London, 1923; and in Norman Lindsay Gallery and Museum, Australia.

WRITINGS:

FOR CHILDREN; SELF-ILLUSTRATED

The Magic Pudding: Being the Adventures of Bunyip Bluegum and His Friends Bill Barnacle and Sam Sawnoff, Angus & Robertson, 1918.
The Flyaway Highway, Angus & Robertson, 1935.
Puddin' Poems: Being the Best of the Verse from "The Magic Pudding," Angus & Robertson, 1977.

OTHER

(Self-illustrated) *Norman Lindsay's Book,* two volumes, edited by Harold Burston, Bookstall, 1912-15.
(Self-illustrated) *A Curate in Bohemia* (fiction), Bookstall, 1913.
The Pen Drawings of Norman Lindsay, edited by Sydney Ure Smith and Bertram Stevens, Angus & Robertson, 1918 (also see below).
Creative Effort: An Essay in Affirmation, Cecil Palmer, 1924.
Pen Drawings, McQuitty, 1924.
The Etchings of Norman Lindsay, Constable, 1927.
(Self-illustrated) *Hyperborea: Two Fantastic Travel Sketches* (fiction), Fanfrolico Press, 1928.
Madam Life's Lovers: A Human Narrative Embodying a Philosophy of the Artist in Dialogue Form, Fanfrolico Press, 1929.

NORMAN LINDSAY

Redheap (first novel in trilogy), Faber, 1930, published as *Every Mother's Son,* Cosmopolitan, 1930.

Norman Lindsay's Pen Drawings (includes illustrations from *The Pen Drawings of Norman Lindsay*), Art in Australia, 1931.

Work of Eileen McGrath, privately printed, 1931.

(Self-illustrated) *The Cautious Amorist* (fiction), Farrar & Reinhart, 1932.

Miracles by Arrangement (fiction), Faber, 1932.

Mr. Gresham and Olympus (fiction), Farrar & Reinhart, 1932.

Pan in the Parlour (fiction), Farrar & Reinhart, 1933.

Saturdee (second novel in trilogy), Endeavor Press, 1933.

(Self-illustrated) *Age of Consent* (fiction), Farrar & Reinhart, 1938.

Norman Lindsay Water Colour Book: Eighteen Reproductions in Colour from Original Watercolours, with an Appreciation of the Medium, Springwood Press, 1939, published as *Norman Lindsay's Watercolours,* Ure Smith, 1969.

The Cousin from Fiji (fiction), Angus & Robertson, 1945, Random House, 1946.

(With Douglas Stewart) *Paintings in Oil,* Shepherd Press, 1945.

Halfway to Anywhere (third novel in trilogy), Angus & Robertson, 1947.

Dust or Polish? (fiction), Angus & Robertson, 1950.

(Compiler and author of introduction) Edward George Dyson, *The Golden Shanty: Short Stories,* Angus & Robertson, 1963.

Bohemians of the Bulletin, Angus & Robertson, 1965.

Norman Lindsay's Ship Models, Angus & Robertson, 1966.

The Scribblings of an Idle Mind, Lansdowne, 1966.

Rooms and Houses: An Autobiographical Novel, Ure Smith, 1968.

Selected Pen Drawings, Angus & Robertson, 1968, Bonanza, 1970.

Norman Lindsay: His Books, Manuscripts, and Autograph Letters, compiled by Harry F. Chaplin, Wentworth Press, 1969.

Pencil Drawings, Angus & Robertson, 1969.

Showdown at Iron Hill (fiction), New English Library, 1969.

My Mask: For What Little I Know of the Man Behind It (autobiography), Angus & Robertson, 1970.

Two Hundred Etchings, Angus & Robertson, 1973.

Norman Lindsay's Cats, edited by Douglas Stewart, Macmillan, 1975.

Siren and Satyr: The Personal Philosophy of Norman Lindsay, Sun, 1976.

Favorite Etchings, Angus & Robertson, 1977.

Letters of Norman Lindsay, edited by R. G. Howarth and W. Barker, Angus & Robertson, 1978.

Micomicana (illustrations), Melbourne University Press, 1979.

Norman Lindsay War Cartoons, 1914-1918, edited and with commentary by Peter Fullerton, Melbourne University Press, 1983.

Also author of forward of *Elioth Gruner: Twenty-Four Reproductions in Colour from Original Oil Paintings,* by Elioth Gruner, Shepherd Press, 1947; and of preface of *Poetry in Australia, 1923,* Vision Press, 1923.

ILLUSTRATOR

(With others) Arthur Hoey Davis, *This Is the Book of Our New Selection,* Bulletin Newspaper, 1903.

Petronius Arbiter, *Petronius,* privately printed, 1910.

Leon Gellert, *Songs of a Campaign,* 5th edition, Angus & Robertson, 1918.

Leon Gellert, *The Isle of San,* Art in Australia, 1919.

Hugh Raymond MacCrae, *Colombine,* Angus & Robertson, 1920.

W. C. Firebaugh, *The Inns of Greece and Rome,* F. M. Morris, 1923.

Jack Lindsay, *The Passionate Neatherd,* Fanfrolico Press, 1925.

Aristophanes, *Lysistrata,* translated by Jack Lindsay, Fanfrolico Press, 1926, World Publishing, 1942.

Petronius Arbiter, *The Complete Works of Gaius Petronius,* translated by Jack Lindsay, Fanfrolico Press, 1927, published as *The Satyricon, and Poems,* Elek Books, 1960.

Mad Tom, *Loving Mad Tom,* Fanfrolico Press, 1927.

Propertius, *Propertius in Love,* translated by Jack Lindsay, Fanfrolico Press, 1927.

Friedrich Wilhelm Nietzsche, *The Antichrist,* translated by P. R. Stephensen, Fanfrolico Press, 1928.

(And translator with Jack Lindsay) Sappho, *A Homage to Sappho,* Fanfrolico Press, 1928.

Hugh Raymond MacCrae, *Satyrs and Sunlight,* Fanfrolico Press, 1928.

Aristophanes, *Women in Parliament,* translated by Jack Lindsay, Fanfrolico Press, 1929.

John Donne, *A Defence of Women for Their Inconstancy and Their Paintings,* Fanfrolico Press, 1930.

Andrew Barton Paterson, *The Animals Noah Forgot,* Endeavor Press, 1933, reprinted, Lansdowne, 1970.

Douglas Alexander Stewart, *Elegy for an Airman,* Frank C. Johnson, 1940.

Douglas Alexander Stewart, *Ned Kelly,* Shepherd Press, 1946.

Charles Dickens, *Great Expectations,* Shepherd Press, 1947.

Francis Webb, *A Drum for Ben Boyd* (poem), Angus & Robertson, 1948.

Rachel Bidduoph Henning, *Letters,* Bulletin Newspaper, 1952, published as *The Letters of Rachel Henning,* Angus & Robertson, 1963.

Douglas Alexander Stewart, *Fisher's Ghost,* Wentworth Press, 1960.

Douglas Alexander Stewart, *The Garden of Ships,* Wentworth Press, 1962.

Marguerite d'Angouleme, *Tales from the Heptameron of Marguerite of Navarre,* Melbourne University Press, 1976.

Also illustrator of *The Outrageous Antics of Tadwag: The Little Satyr Who Disturbed the Smugness of the Universe,* by Hunter B. Shirley, Twenty First Century Books.

ADAPTATIONS: The Cautious Amorist was adapted for film and released as *Our Girl Friday* in England and *The Adventures of Sadie* in the United States.

SIDELIGHTS: A versatile author and illustrator, Norman Lindsay is remembered for his many contributions to Australian art and literature. His numerous novels for adults, three books for children, and illustrations in scores of other works secured Lindsay a permanent standing among Australia's finest artists. In all of his creative endeavors, the author employed a unique style, peppering his works with sarcasm and irony in order to express his dissatisfaction with certain social norms. Though he began his career as an artist and worked in a wide variety of mediums, including oil, watercolor, wood, cement, and ink, Lindsay's most notable life achievement is his self-illustrated children's book *The Magic Pudding: Being the Adventures of Bunyip Bluegum and His Friends Bill Barnacle and Sam Sawnoff.* The book was first

"That's where the Magic comes in," explained Bill. "The more you eats the more you gets." (From *The Magic Pudding*, written and illustrated by Lindsay.)

published in 1918 and is considered a classic of Australian children's literature prompting comparison among critics and readers to Lewis Carroll's *Alice in Wonderland.*

Lindsay was born in 1879 and grew up in the small mining town of Creswick in Victoria, New South Wales. When he was only sixteen years old, he began free-lance illustrating and went on to work as an editor for several newspapers in Melbourne. Soon after taking a position as a cartoonist for the *Sydney Bulletin,* Lindsay began producing books that often spurred controversy. The trilogy of novels *Redheap, Saturdee,* and *Halfway to Anywhere* about a boy maturing into adulthood, for example, expresses many of the author's liberal philosophies. *Redheap,* in fact, was banned in Australia as a reaction to the teenaged protagonist's experimentation with sex and alcohol. Nevertheless, the author's *Magic Pudding* and his subsequent *Puddin' Poems: Being the Best of the Verse from "The Magic Pudding"* remain widely accepted as valuable works of children's literature.

The Magic Pudding was written after Lindsay decided that, instead of a more typical topic such as fairies, food would be a more captivating subject for a children's book. Thus, the central figure of the book is Albert, an ever-replenishing supply of pudding who becomes the source of conflict for the other characters. Bunyip Bluegum, an adventuresome koala bear, and his newfound friends Bill Barnacle, a sailor, and Sam Sawnoff, a penguin, are the owners of the pudding. Though they enjoy Albert's delectable offerings, the companions are in constant danger of losing him to a possum and a wombat, a twosome with a greedy appetite for pudding. *The Magic Pudding* "is the epic tale of the taking and retaking of the puddin', a contest of wits and fists and speech-making in

which rules were laid down before the other side could think," noted Ellen Lewis Buell in the *New York Times Book Review.* The reviewer also commented that the book "is a gutsy, absurd saga, told in rolling, high-flown phrases," and she found the illustrations "as daft and delightful as the text."

WORKS CITED:

Buell, Ellen Lewis, review of *The Magic Pudding: Being the Adventures of Bunyip Bluegum and His Friends Bill Barnacle and Sam Sawnoff, New York Times Book Review,* September 13, 1936, p. 10.

FOR MORE INFORMATION SEE:

BOOKS

Bloomfield, Lin, *Norman Lindsay: Impulse to Draw,* Bay Books, 1984.
Children's Literature Review, Volume 8, Gale, 1985.
Contemporary Authors, Volume 102, Gale, 1981.
Hetherington, John Aikman, *Norman Lindsay,* second edition, Lansdowne Press, 1962.
A History of Australian Children's Literature, 1841-1941, Wentworth Books, 1969.
Lindsay, Norman, *My Mask: For What Little I Know of the Man behind It,* Angus & Robertson, 1970.
Lindsay, Rose, *Model Wife: My Life with Norman Lindsay,* Ure Smith, 1967.
The Singing Roads: A Guide to Australian Children's Authors and Illustrators, Part I, fourth edition, Wentworth Books, 1972.

LOPEZ, Barry (Holstun) 1945-

PERSONAL: Born January 6, 1945, in Port Chester, NY; son of Adrian Bernard and Mary (Holstun) Lopez; married Sandra Landers (a bookwright), June 10, 1967. *Education:* University of Notre Dame, A.B. (cum laude), 1966, M.A.T., 1968; University of Oregon, graduate study, 1969-70.

CAREER: Full-time writer, 1970—. Associate, Gannett Foundation Media Center, Columbia University, 1985—; Distinguished Visiting Writer, Eastern Washington University, 1985; Ida Beam Visiting Professor, University of Iowa, 1985; Distinguished Visiting Naturalist, Carleton College, 1986; Welch Visiting Professor of American Studies, University of Notre Dame, 1989.

AWARDS, HONORS: John Burroughs Medal for distinguished natural history writing, Christopher Medal for humanitarian writing, and Pacific Northwest Booksellers Award for excellence in nonfiction, all 1979, and American Book Award nomination, 1980, all for *Of Wolves and Men;* Distinguished Recognition Award, Friends of American Writers, 1981, for *Winter Count;* National Book Award in nonfiction, Christopher Book Award, Pacific Northwest Booksellers Award, National Book Critics Circle Award nomination, *Los Angeles Times* Book Award nomination, American Library Association notable book citation, *New York Times* "Best Books" citation, and American Library Association "Best Books for Young Adults" citation, all 1986, and Francis Fuller Victor Award in nonfiction, Oregon Institute of Literary Arts, 1987, all for *Arctic Dreams;* Award in Literature, American Academy and Institute of Arts and Letters, 1986, for body of work; Guggenheim fellow, 1987; D.H.L., Wittier College, 1988; Parents' Choice Award, 1990, for *Crow and Weasel;* Lannan Foundation Award in nonfiction, 1990, for body of work; Governor's Award, 1990; Best Geographic Educational Article, National Council for Geographic Education, 1990, for "The American Geographies."

WRITINGS:

Desert Notes: Reflections in the Eye of a Raven (fiction), Andrews & McMeel, 1976.
Giving Birth to Thunder, Sleeping with His Daughter: Coyote Builds North America (native American trickster stories), Andrews & McMeel, 1978.
Of Wolves and Men (nonfiction), Scribner, 1978.
River Notes: The Dance of Herons (fiction), Andrews & McMeel, 1979.
Desert Reservation (chapbook), Copper Canyon Press, 1980.
Winter Count (fiction), Scribner, 1981.
Arctic Dreams: Imagination and Desire in a Northern Landscape (nonfiction), Scribner, 1986.
Crossing Open Ground (essays), Scribner, 1988.
Crow and Weasel (fable), illustrated by Tom Pohrt, North Point Press, 1990.
The Rediscovery of North America (essay), University Press of Kentucky, 1991.

Contributor to anthologies, including *Resist Much, Obey Little,* 1985, *The Sophisticated Traveler,* 1986, *On Nature,* 1987, *Four Minute Fictions,* 1987, *Best American Essays 1987,* 1988, *This Incomperable Lande,* 1989, and *Openings: Original*

BARRY LOPEZ

Essays by Contemporary Soviet and American Writers (contains "The American Geographies"), 1990. Contributor of articles, essays, and short fiction to numerous periodicals, including *Harper's, North American Review, Orion Nature Quarterly, New York Times, Antaeus, National Geographic,* and *Outside.* Contributing editor, *North American Review,* 1977—, and *Harper's,* 1981-82 and 1984—; guest editor of special section, "The American Indian Mind," *Quest,* September/October, 1978; correspondent, *Outside,* 1982—.

ADAPTATIONS: Composer John Luther Adams consulted with Lopez and others to create a stage adaptation of *Giving Birth to Thunder,* which premiered at Dartmouth College in 1990; three stories from *River Notes* have been recorded with accompanying music by cellist David Darling; portions of *Desert Notes* and *Arctic Dreams* have been adapted for the stage by modern dance companies.

WORK IN PROGRESS: A work of nonfiction about landscapes remote from North America; essays, articles, and short fiction for magazines.

SIDELIGHTS: Barry Lopez is best known for his writings on natural history and the environment. In many of his works, including *Of Wolves and Men* and *Arctic Dreams,* Lopez uses his subjects to explore moral issues such as man's place on earth. While his work is directed towards an adult audience, it is frequently read and enjoyed by younger readers. For example, his illustrated fable *Crow and Weasel,* with its adolescent heroes, has become a bestseller among young adult readers.

Set in the time of American Indian legend, *Crow and Weasel* details the journey of two young men who travel north into lands unknown by their tribe. As they meet new people and overcome dangers, the two learn some valuable lessons, many involving "ideas about the relationships between imagination and landscape, people and environment," Elizabeth Ward comments in the *Washington Post Book World*. Although the plot is familiar, echoing many traditional quest tales, Lopez "gives it a style and setting that make it new," Patricia Lothrop states in *Library Journal*.

Another feature of the book is that Crow and Weasel appear in the illustrations as actual animals; so does the tribal elder Mountain Lion, and two others who aid the boys' quest, Badger and Grizzly Bear. This use of actual animals for the main characters "is done subtly and without cuteness," *Washington Post Book World* writer David Streitfeld says. A *Kirkus Reviews* critic similarly praises *Crow and Weasel* as "an Aesop's fable dipped in Native America dyes," and adds: "Given the teen-age heroes, the adventure plot, and the moral instruction, this seems geared to young adults."

But Lopez believes that *Crow and Weasel* is more "a book with a large crossover audience, rather than a children's book," he told *SATA*. "When I sat down to write, insofar as I had an audience in mind, it was not much different from the one I usually write for," the author explained to Streitfeld. "The fact it has found such a strong audience with younger readers is somewhat of a surprise to me. . . . The best way to say it is that this is a story that doesn't exclude children."

Whatever the story's intended audience, reviewers have found it especially suited for younger readers. A *Parents* magazine reviewer, for instance, notes that "children, just beginning their struggle with life's great questions, may gain

the most from this exceptional story." The reviewer adds that the book is "compelling" in its spirituality. *Crow and Weasel* will appeal to young adults with its story of a youthful rite of passage, Lothrop believes. But the critic also remarks that the quest of Crow and Weasel, with its discoveries about human and animal nature, will "also speak to the adult of what is truly important in life."

In all his work, Lopez tries to convey this childlike appreciation for nature to his audience. "It's important to me," Lopez told Jim Aton in a *Western American Literature* interview, to approach a story "with a capacity for wonder, where I know I can derive something 'wonder-full' and then bring this into that story so that a reader can feel it and say, 'I am an adult . . . but still I have wonder. I have been brought to a state of wonder by contact with something in a story.'" Lopez has succeeded in bringing this admiration for the natural world to children and adults with *Crow and Weasel*. As Faith McNulty of the *New Yorker* concludes, this "fable of inner discovery" is "an engrossing story."

WORKS CITED:

Aton, Jim, "An Interview with Barry Lopez," *Western American Literature,* spring, 1986, pp. 3-17.
Review of *Crow and Weasel, Kirkus Reviews,* August 15, 1990, p. 1121.
Review of *Crow and Weasel, Parents,* December, 1990, pp. 199-200.
Lothrop, Patricia, review of *Crow of Weasel, Library Journal,* December, 1990, p. 164.
McNulty, Faith, review of *Crow and Weasel, New Yorker,* November 26, 1990, p. 144.
Streitfeld, David, "Book Report: Beauty and the Beasts," *Washington Post Book World,* December 9, 1990, p. 19.
Ward, Elizabeth, "Twelve Books for Good Children," *Washington Post Book World,* December 2, 1990, p. 3.

FOR MORE INFORMATION SEE:

BOOKS

Lueders, Edward, editor, *Writing Natural History: Dialogues with Authors,* University of Utah Press, 1989.

PERIODICALS

Bloomsbury Review, January/February, 1990.
Chicago Tribune, March 30, 1986.
Harper's, December, 1984.
New York Times, February 12, 1986; March 29, 1986.
New York Times Book Review, November 19, 1978; June 14, 1981; February 16, 1986.
Seattle Review, fall, 1985.
Time, March 10, 1986.
Washington Post, November 18, 1986; November 24, 1986.

*   *   *

LUNN, Carolyn (Kowalczyk) 1960-

PERSONAL: Born June 26, 1960, in Raleigh, NC; daughter of Michael Richard (in the U.S. Air Force) and Geraldine Ann (a teacher; maiden name, Johnson) Kowalczyk; married Geoffrey Hugh Lunn (in business), October 5, 1985; children: Stephen Michael, Katherine Frances. *Education:* Attended University of Poitiers, 1981-82; University of Oregon, B.A., 1983.

Lopez's illustrated fable, *Crow and Weasel,* has become a children's bestseller. (Cover illustration by Tom Pohrt.)

Carolyn Lunn and her children, Stephen Michael and Katherine Frances.

ADDRESSES: Home—23 Holyrood, Great Holm, Milton Keynes MK8 9DR, England.

CAREER: Sunshine Language College, Tokyo, Japan, instructor in English, 1983-84; nanny in Frankfurt, Germany, 1984-85; writer.

WRITINGS:

Purple Is Part of a Rainbow, Childrens Press, 1985.
A Whisper Is Quiet, Childrens Press, 1988.
Bobby's Zoo, Childrens Press, 1989.
Spiders and Webs, Childrens Press, 1989.
A Buzz Is Part of a Bee, Childrens Press, 1990.

Contributor of poems to *Country Times.*

WORK IN PROGRESS: Don't Drink the Bathwater, a children's rhyme book.

SIDELIGHTS: Carolyn Lunn told *SATA:* " 'Don't let any fuddy-duddy stop you from writing. Love from your fuddy-duddy daddy.' That is what dear Dad wrote in my first *Writer's Market* book given to me. Dad was referring to the comments my fifth-grade teacher had written on my essay. I had written: 'In summertime sprinklers soggy the lawn.' I was near to tears in frustration to find 'THIS IS NOT A VERB'

written in big mean letters next to 'soggy.' Of course I *knew* it was not a verb. I was trying to be different. This was also the sort of teacher who thought poems had to rhyme. I was more mature than that! It was always Dad I went to with schoolwork, and he thought it was very creative and effective to use an adjective, 'soggy,' as a verb. He was even proud of me. It breaks my heart that my fuddy-duddy daddy died at the age of forty-nine and never saw one of my books published.

"The other person responsible for my writing success is my college professor who taught children's literature. I never knew such a course existed and only found out when I was in the university library checking out a chemistry book that was out of stock at the bookstore. I walked past a library classroom where a woman was reading a children's book with such expression in her voice I had to stop and listen. The next day I dropped Chemistry and enrolled in children's literature.

"Since elementary school I have written poems for family birthdays, Mother's Day, Father's Day, etc. (I wrote fairy tales, too, that no one saw), but it was after that first day in children's literature that I knew absolutely that I wanted to write children's books. My favorite age, the age I write for, is preschool children, because everything from a dried worm, to a puddle, to a full, bright moon fills them with wonder and delight. They are so curious you can easily capture their attention.

"As much as I love to write children's books, I inherited *none* of my mother's artistic talent. She paints oils, watercolors, and remarkable portraits. I am embarrassed if I have to even sketch a map for someone!

"It is my two young children, with their child's-eye view of the world, who inspire me now! Playground, zoo, sea-side, and picnic excursions give me fresh ideas for future books."

*   *   *

MAGORIAN, Michelle 1947-

PERSONAL: Born November 6, 1947, in Portsmouth, England; married in 1987; children: one son. *Education:* Rose Bruford College of Speech and Drama, diploma, 1969; London University, certificate in film studies, 1984; attended Ecole Internationale de Mime, 1969-70. *Hobbies and other interests:* Dancing, singing, reading, swimming.

ADDRESSES: Home—803 Harrow Rd., Wembley, Middlesex HA0 2LP, England. *Agent*—(literary) Patricia White, Rogers, Coleridge & White, 20 Powis Mews, London W11 1JN, England; (theatre) Bill Horne and Peter Walmsley, The Bill Horne Partnership, 15 Exmoor St., London W10 6BA, England.

CAREER: Writer and actress. Appeared in the several television programs and the film *McVicar.* Has performed mime shows and was a member of a repertory theatre group.

AWARDS, HONORS: Carnegie Medal commendation, 1981, for *Good Night, Mr. Tom;* children's book award, International Reading Association, American Library Association "best book for young adults," and British Guardian Award for Children's Literature, all 1982, all for *Good Night, Mr. Tom;* West Australian Young Readers' Book Award, Library Association of Australia, 1983, for *Good Night, Mr. Tom,* and 1987, for *Back Home; Back Home* was named a "best book for young adults" by the American Library Association, 1984.

MICHELLE MAGORIAN

WRITINGS:

Good Night, Mr. Tom, Harper, 1982.
Back Home, Harper, 1984.
Waiting for My Shorts to Dry (poetry), illustrated by Jean Baylis, Viking Kestrel, 1989.
Who's Going to Take Care of Me?, illustrated by James Graham Hale, HarperCollins, 1990.
A Little Love Song, Methuen, 1991.
Orange Paw Marks (poetry), illustrated by Baylis, Viking Kestrel, 1991.
Jump!, Walker Books, in press.

Also author of short stories appearing in books and periodicals.

WORK IN PROGRESS: "Work on a short story collection, tentatively titled *In Deep Water.*"

ADAPTATIONS: Back Home was adapted as a television film.

SIDELIGHTS: Michelle Magorian, a prize-winning British author of books for young adults, including *Good Night, Mr. Tom* and *Back Home,* began her literary career by writing short stories in her spare time. However, Magorian told *SATA* that it was not her ambition to become a writer. "I was too busy acting and dancing and daydreaming and reading plays and poetry which were not on our exam schedule. My ambition was to be an actress. I auditioned for and was offered a place at the Rose Bruford College of Speech and Drama. For three years I studied subjects including mime, dance, voice, speech, verse speaking, and phonetics. I read lots more plays and poetry and wrote and wrote and wrote! I then went to a mime school in Paris, France, for a year and

while there I continued writing poetry and began a journal. I do remember thinking then how lovely it would be to write for six months of the year and act for the remaining six months, but that seemed like a pipe dream. After I had finished my training I worked in touring and repertory theatre companies and continued scribbling in secret.

"In my mid twenties, I became interested in reading children's novels. I had already written a story which was over a hundred pages long in which one of the main characters was a twelve-year-old girl. It was while reading the children's books that I suddenly realized that I wanted to write one. I expected it to take me until I was eighty to write one that would be accepted for publication. I was stunned when it happened fifty years earlier."

Magorian's first book was *Good Night, Mr. Tom,* which was published in 1982. The author told *SATA* that the work is "set at the beginning of the Second World War and is about a nine-year-old boy called Willie who is evacuated from a slum area to the country. He is billeted with a man in his sixties who he comes to call Mister Tom. Willie is thin and pale with limp sandy hair and is, in Tom's words, like a 'frightened rabbit.' Mister Tom, who lives in a cottage at the end of the village graveyard, has kept to himself for forty or more years—ever since his wife died. The story is about how he and Willie both change through living together.

Magorian's award-winning first book, *Good Night, Mr. Tom,* took her four years to complete. (Cover art by Michael Garland.)

"*Good Night, Mr. Tom* took me four years; three years to write the first draft, and a year to re-write it. During the three years I was writing it, I was doing a lot of repertory theatre work which involves working six days and six nights a week—rehearsing one play during the day and performing another at night. I wrote on Sundays and in between acting jobs. Some of my time was also taken up with research as I knew very little about domestic life during the war years."

When performing research for *Good Night, Mr. Tom*, Magorian got the idea for her second book, *Back Home*. She told *SATA:* "I came across a photograph that had been taken in August, 1945, of a group of English children on an ocean liner returning to England after having lived in America for five years. The children looked totally Americanized. How, I wondered, had these children coped after five years and with the additional problem of having been separated form their parents?

"At first I tried to forget the photograph. I knew that if I wrote a book on this subject, not only would I have to carry out research on life in Britain immediately after the war, but I would also need to know what life was like in America in the 1940s. It seemed too daunting a task. But the photgraph refused to go away. It was as though the children were tapping me on the shoulder saying 'We're not going to leave you alone until you write about one of us.' As I read and listened and scribbled, the characters and scenes began to grow. One night, unable to sleep for a barrage of scenes, I switched on my light, made a large pot of tea, and wrote into the early hours nonstop. When I finished I had the framework of the book."

For Magorian, creating a framework is the first step in writing a book. She told *SATA:* "I have to have the rough framework before I begin and know how the story is going to end. The scenario may change slightly and, of course, there are many surprises along the way, but if I know where I'm going it gives me momentum. However, I don't write that framework down until I've done a lot of thinking and jotting down of ideas and scenes."

The author also attributed writing success to relying on imagination. "Daydreaming is an important part of creating fiction," she remarked. "When the characters begin popping into your head and speaking to one another, that's when it starts to get exciting. I have a picture in my head of what the people look like and an idea of their personalities and I make lists of names and see which ones feel right."

Magorian summed up her philosophy of writing for *SATA.* "You have to be persistent to write books. You have to live with a book for a long time. There will be many days when you will be tempted to throw away what you've written, but you need to keep plodding on."

*   *   *

MARGOLIS, Richard J(ules) 1929-1991

OBITUARY NOTICE—See index for *SATA* sketch: Born June 30, 1929, in St. Paul, MN; died of heart failure, April 22, 1991, in New Haven, CT. Columnist and author. Margolis was a free-lance writer known by many for his social-issues column in *New Leader* magazine. In addition to his numerous contributions to such periodicals as *Harper's, New Republic,* and *New York Times Magazine,* Margolis also wrote fiction and poetry for children. His writings for young readers include *Only the Moon and Me, The Upside-Down*

King, Homer the Hunter, Big Bear to the Rescue, and *Secrets of a Small Brother,* which won a Christopher Award in 1985. Many of his writings for adults deal with minorities such as the elderly, Indians, and migrant farm workers; *Homes of the Brave,* for example, is a report on the housing of the migrant farm workers. Margolis' other works include *Something to Build On, At the Crossroads: An Inquiry into Rural Post Offices and the Communities They Serve,* and *Risking Old Age in America,* which was published in 1990.

OBITUARIES AND OTHER SOURCES:

PERIODICALS

New York Times, April 23, 1991.
Washington Post, April 25, 1991.

*   *   *

MARLOWE, Amy Bell
[Collective pseudonym]

WRITINGS:

"AMY BELL MARLOWE'S BOOKS FOR GIRLS" SERIES

The Oldest of Four; or, Natalie's Way Out, Grosset & Dunlap, 1914.
The Girls of Hillcrest Farm; or, The Secret of the Rocks, Grosset & Dunlap, 1914.
A Little Miss Nobody; or, With the Girls of Pinewood Hall, Grosset & Dunlap, 1914.
The Girl from Sunset Ranch; or, Alone in a Great City, Grosset & Dunlap, 1914.
Wyn's Camping Days; or, The Outing of the Go-Ahead Club, Grosset & Dunlap, 1914.
Frances of the Ranges; or, The Old Ranchman's Treasure, Grosset & Dunlap, 1915.
The Girls of Rivercliff School; or, Beth Baldwin's Resolve (also see below), Grosset & Dunlap, 1916.
Sunset Ranch, Grosset & Dunlap, 1933.

"ORIOLE" SERIES

When Oriole Came to Harbor Light (also see below), Grosset & Dunlap, 1920.
When Oriole Travelled Westward (also see below), Grosset & Dunlap, 1921.
When Oriole Went to Boarding School (also see below), Grosset & Dunlap, 1927.
Oriole's Adventures: Four Complete Adventure Books for Girls in One Big Volume (contains *When Oriole Came to Harbor Light, When Oriole Travelled Westward, When Oriole Went to Boarding School,* and *The Girls of Rivercliff School*), Grosset & Dunlap, 1933.

SIDELIGHTS: Amy Bell Marlowe was a collective pseudonym used by the Statemeyer Syndicate, a writing house that produced such popular children's fiction as the "Nancy Drew," "Hardy Boys," and "Bobbsey Twins" series. The "Amy Bell Marlowe Books for Girls" series did not share the same characters or focus on a single theme, but were advertised by Grosset & Dunlap as a series. The publishers also described them as "somewhat of the style of Miss [Louisa May] Alcott," but brought up to date. See the *SATA* index for more information on Harriet S. Adams, Edward L. Stratemeyer, and Andrew E. Svenson.

WORKS CITED:

Johnson, Deidre, editor and compiler, *Stratemeyer Pseudonyms and Series Books: An Annotated Checklist of Stratemeyer and Stratemeyer Syndicate Publications,* Greenwood Press, 1982, p. 183.

*   *   *

MARTIN, Bill, Jr. 1916-
(Bill Martin)

PERSONAL: Full name is William Ivan Martin; born March 20, 1916, in Hiawatha, KS; son of William and Iva June (Lilly) Martin; married Betty Jeanne Buchmann, 1942 (divorced, 1979); children: Gary (deceased), Danielle. *Education:* Kansas State Teachers College (now Emporia State University), B.S., 1934; Northwestern University, M.A., 1957, Ph.D., 1961.

ADDRESSES: Home and office—230 West 55th St., 26F, New York, NY 10019.

CAREER: Children's author, 1945—. High school journalism, dramatics, and English teacher in St. John and Newton, KS, 1934-41; Crow Island Elementary School, Winnetka, IL, principal, 1955-61; Holt, Rinehart & Winston, Inc., New York City, editor and children's textbook and picture book series creator, 1960-67; free-lance writer, editor, and lecturer, 1967—. Producer of video and tape recordings; creator of television series *The Storyteller.* Visiting professor at universities and colleges throughout the United States. *Military service:* U.S. Air Force; served as newspaper editor, 1942-45.

WRITINGS:

ALL WRITINGS UNDER NAME BILL MARTIN, JR., EXCEPT AS NOTED

(With brother, Bernard Martin) *The Little Squeegy Bug,* Tell-Well Press, 1945, reprinted as part of the "Kin/Der Owl Books Literature Series," Holt, 1967 (also see below).

(With Bernard Martin) *Chicken Chuck,* Tell-Well Press, 1946.

(With Bernard Martin) *Rosy Nose,* Tell-Well Press, 1946.

(With Bernard Martin) *Smoky Poky,* Tell-Well Press, 1947, reprinted as part of the "Little Owl Books Social Studies Series," Holt, 1967 (also see below).

(With Bernard Martin) *Bunny's Easter Gift,* Tell-Well Press, 1948.

(With Bernard Martin) *Hook and Ladder No. 3,* Tell-Well Press, 1948.

(With Bernard Martin) *Lightning, A Cowboy's Colt,* Tell-Well Press, 1948.

(With Bernard Martin) *Christmas Puppy,* Tell-Well Press, 1949.

(With Bernard Martin) *Silver Stallion,* Tell-Well Press, 1949.

(With Bernard Martin) *Golden Arrow,* Tell-Well Press, 1950.

(With Bernard Martin) *Teach Me to Pray,* Tell-Well Press, 1950.

(With Bernard Martin) *Wild Horse Roundup,* Tell-Well Press, 1950.

(With Bernard Martin) *The Brave Little Indian,* illustrations by Charlene Bisch, Tell-Well Press, 1951, reissued with illustrations by Eric Carle as part of the "Kin/Der Owl Books Literature Series," Holt, 1967 (also see below).

(With Bernard Martin) *Five Little Rabbits,* Tell-Well Press, 1951.

(With Bernard Martin) *Palomino Pony,* Tell-Well Press, 1952.

(With Bernard Martin and Mary Adams) *Thank You, God,* Tell-Well Press, 1952.

(With Bernard Martin) *The Green-Eyed Stallion,* Tell-Well Press, 1953.

(With John Archambault) *The Ghost-Eye Tree,* illustrations by Ted Rand, Holt, 1985.

(With Archambault) *Barn Dance!,* illustrations by Ted Rand, Holt, 1986.

(With Archambault) *White Dynamite and Curly Kidd,* illustrations by Ted Rand, Holt, 1986.

(With Archambault) *Knots on a Counting Rope* (originally published with illustrations by Joe Smith as part of the "Young Owl Books Social Studies Series," Holt, 1966 [also see below]), illustrations by Ted Rand, Holt, 1987.

(With Archambault) *Here Are My Hands,* illustrations by Ted Rand, Holt, 1987.

(With Archambault) *Listen to the Rain,* illustrations by James Endicott, Holt, 1988.

(With Archambault) *Up and Down on the Merry-Go-Round,* illustrations by Ted Rand, Holt, 1988.

(With Archambault) *The Magic Pumpkin,* illustrations by Robert J. Lee, Holt, 1989.

(With Archambault) *Chicka Chicka Boom Boom,* Simon & Schuster, 1989.

Polar Bear, Polar Bear, What Do You Hear?, illustrations by Eric Carle, Holt, 1991.

JUVENILE; "BILL MARTIN INSTANT READERS" SERIES

Brown Bear, Brown Bear, What Do You See?, illustrations by Eric Carle, Holt, 1967, reprinted as part of the "Kin/Der Owl Books Language Series," 1971 (also see below).

(With Peggy Brogan, under name Bill Martin) *Bill Martin's Instant Readers* (teachers guides), four volumes, Holt, 1970-79.

The Eagle Has Landed, illustrations by Frank Aloise, Holt, 1970.

(Adaptor) *Fire! Fire! Said Mrs. McGuire,* illustrations by Ted Schroeder, Holt, 1970.

A Ghost Story, illustrations by Eric Carle, Holt, 1970.

The Happy Hippopotami, illustrations by Bob Velde, Holt, 1970.

The Haunted House, illustrations by Peter Lippman, Holt, 1970.

I Paint the Joy of a Flower, illustrations by Carolyn Jablonsky and others, Holt, 1970.

(Adaptor) Helen Baten and Barbara von Molnar, *I'm Going To Build a Supermarket One of These Days,* illustrations by Papas, Holt, 1970.

King of the Mountain, illustrations by Ivor Parry, Holt, 1970.

The Maestro Plays, illustrations by Sal Murdocca, Holt, 1970.

Monday, Monday, I Like Monday, illustrations by Dora Leder, Holt, 1970.

(Adaptor) Sano M. Galea'i Fa'apouli, *My Days Are Made of Butterflies,* Holt, 1970.

Old Devil Wind, illustrations by Robert J. Lee, Holt, 1970.

In *Barn Dance!* by Bill Martin, Jr., and John Archambault, a "skinny kid" stays up all night to see a magical dance of barnyard animals. (Cover illustration by Ted Rand.)

Old Mother Middle Muddle, illustrations by Don Madden, Holt, 1970.

(Adaptor) Annabelle Sumera, *Silly Goose and the Holidays,* illustrations by Leon Winik, Holt, 1970.

A Spooky Story, illustrations by Albert John Pucci, Holt, 1970.

Tatty Mae and Catty Mae, illustrations by Aldren A. Watson, Holt, 1970.

(Adaptor) *Ten Little Squirrels,* illustrations by Bernard Martin, 1970.

"Tricks or Treats?," illustrations by Jim Spanfeller, Holt, 1970.

The Turning of the Year, illustrations by Samuel Maitin, Holt, 1970.

Up the Down Escalator, illustrations by Kelly Oechsli, Holt, 1970.

Welcome Home, Henry, illustrations by Muriel Batherman, Holt, 1970.

When It Rains . . . It Rains, illustrations by Emanuele Luzzati, Holt, 1970.

What to Say and When to Say It, illustrations by Bob Shein, Holt, 1970.

Whistle, Mary, Whistle, illustrations by Emanuele Luzzati, Holt, 1970.

The Wizard, illustrations by Sal Murdocca, Holt, 1970.

JUVENILE; "SOUNDS OF LANGUAGE READERS" SERIES

(With Peggy Brogan) *Sounds of Language Readers,* eight volumes, Holt, 1966-67, Volume 1: *Sounds of Home,* Volume 2: *Sounds of Numbers,* Volume 3: *Sounds Around the Clock,* Volume 4: *Sounds of Laughter,* Volume 5: *Sounds of the Storyteller,* Volume 6: *Sounds of Mystery,* Volume 7: *Sounds of a Young Hunter,* Volume 8: *Sounds of a Distant Drum,* teachers edition, 1972.

(With Brogan) *Sounds After Dark,* Holt, 1970.

(With Brogan) *Sounds I Remember,* Holt, 1970.

(With Brogan) *Sounds of a Powwow,* Holt, 1970.

(With Brogan) *Sounds Freedom Ring,* Holt, 1973.

(With Brogan) *Sounds Jubilee,* Holt, 1973.

(With Brogan) *Sounds of a Hound Dog,* teacher's edition, Holt, 1974.

(With Brogan) *Sounds of Our Heritage,* Holt, 1981.

JUVENILE; "BILL MARTIN FREEDOM BOOKS" SERIES

Adam's Balm, illustrations by Michael Foreman, Bowmar/Noble, 1970.
America, I Know You, illustrations by Ted Rand, Bowmar/Noble, 1970.
Freedom's Apple Tree, illustrations by John Rombola, Bowmar/Noble, 1970.
(With Gene D. Shepherd) *Gentle, Gentle Thursday*, illustrations by Samuel Maitin, Bowmar/Noble, 1970.
I Am Freedom's Child, illustrations by Symeon Shimin, Bowmar/Noble, 1970.
I Reach Out to the Morning, illustrations by Henry Markowitz, Bowmar/Noble, 1970.
It's America for Me, illustrations by Lou Glanzman, Bowmar/Noble, 1970.
Once There Were Bluebirds, illustrations by Bernard Martin, Bowmar/Noble, 1970.
Poor Old Uncle Sam, illustrations by Sal Murdocca, Bowmar/Noble, 1970.
Spoiled Tomatoes, illustrations by Jay Ells, Bowmar/Noble, 1970.

JUVENILE; "WISE OWL BOOKS SCIENCE SERIES"

The Electric Eel, Holt, 1971.
The Frightened Hare, Holt, 1971.
Giant Fishes of the Open Sea, Holt, 1971.
Hawk in the Sky, Holt, 1971.
The Life of a Star, Holt, 1971.

JUVENILE; "WISE OWL BOOKS SOCIAL STUDIES SERIES"

The History of the Horse, Holt, 1971.
Horseshoe Nails, Holt, 1971.
A Race with the Wolves, Holt, 1971.
The River, Holt, 1971.
When Great Grandmother Was a Little Girl, Holt, 1971.

JUVENILE; "WISE OWL BOOKS ARITHMETIC SERIES"

Dr. Frick and His Fractions, Holt, 1971.
I've Got Your Number, John, Holt, 1971.
Millions of People, Holt, 1971.
Number Patterns Make Sense, Holt, 1971.
Optical Illusions, Holt, 1971.

JUVENILE; "WISE OWL BOOKS LITERATURE SERIES"

The Emperor's Nightingale, Holt, 1971.
Golden Crane, Holt, 1971.
The Proud Peacock, Holt, 1971.
Sandusky Sam, Holt, 1971.
The Selfish Giant, Holt, 1971.

JUVENILE; "LITTLE OWL BOOKS SCIENCE SERIES"

At Home on the Ice, Holt, 1971.
Baby Elephant, Holt, 1971.
Big Frogs, Little Frogs, Holt, 1971.
Birds in Wintertime, Holt, 1971.
Good Morning, Mr. Sun, Holt, 1971.
Joey Kangaroo, Holt, 1971.
The Sun Is a Star, Holt, 1971.
To Know a Tree, Holt, 1971.
Tulips, Holt, 1971.
You Can Find a Snail, Holt, 1971.

JUVENILE; "LITTLE OWL BOOKS SOCIAL STUDIES SERIES"

Smoky Poky, Tell-Well Press, 1947, reprinted, Holt, 1967 (also see above).
All Kinds of Neighbors, Holt, 1971.
Children of the World Say "Good Morning," Holt, 1971.

Daddy Is Home, Holt, 1971.
Here Comes Jimmy! Here Comes Jimmy's Dog, Holt, 1971.
Where Is My Shoe?, Holt, 1971.
Let's Talk About the World, Holt, 1971.
Mr. Jolly's Sidewalk Market, Holt, 1971.
My Little Brother, Holt, 1971.
The House Biter, Holt, 1971.

JUVENILE; "LITTLE OWL BOOKS ARITHMETIC SERIES"

Captain Murphy's Tugboats, Holt, 1971.
Five is 5, Holt, 1971.
Going Up, Going Down, Holt, 1971.
One, Two, Three, Four, Holt, 1971.
Poems for Counting, Holt, 1971.
Round Is a Pancake, Holt, 1971.
Ten Pennies for Candy, Holt, 1971.
This Is My Family, Holt, 1971.
Three Little Dachshunds, Holt, 1971.
What Is Big?, Holt, 1971.

JUVENILE; "LITTLE OWL BOOKS LITERATURE SERIES"

A Cat Story, Holt, 1971.
The Great Circus Parade, Holt, 1971.
The House That Jack Built, Holt, 1971.
Old Mother Goose, Holt, 1971.
The Old Woman and Her Pig, Holt, 1971.
Poems for Galloping, Holt, 1971.
Poems for Weather Watching, Holt, 1971.
The Three Billy-Goats Gruff, Holt, 1971.
What Is Pink?, Holt, 1971.

JUVENILE; "KIN/DER OWL BOOKS SCIENCE SERIES"

Buzz, Buzz, Buzzing Bees, Holt, 1971.
The Moon Tonight, Holt, 1971.
Good Morning, Good Night, Holt, 1971.
Working Wheels, Holt, 1971.

JUVENILE; "KIN/DER OWL BOOKS SOCIAL STUDIES SERIES"

David Was Mad, illustrations by Symeon Shimin, Holt, 1967.
Let's Eat, photos by Larry Nicholson and others, Holt, 1967.
Weather, illustrations by Fred Sweney, Holt, 1967.
My Schoolbook of Picture Stories, Holt, 1971.

JUVENILE; "KIN/DER OWL BOOKS ARITHMETIC SERIES"

Ten Little Caterpillars, illustrations by Gilbert Riswold, Holt, 1967.
It's Schooltime, Holt, 1971.
One, Two, Buckle My Shoe, Holt, 1971.
Surprise! Surprise!, Holt, 1971.

JUVENILE; "KIN/DER OWL BOOKS LITERATURE SERIES"

(With Bernard Martin) *The Little Squeegy Bug*, Tell-Well Press, 1945, reprinted with illustrations by Eric Carle, Holt, 1967 (also see above).
The Brave Little Indian, illustrations by Charlene Bisch, Tell-Well Press, 1951, reprinted with illustrations by Eric Carle, Holt, 1967 (also see above).
Little Princess Goodnight, illustrations by Joseph Domjan, Holt, 1967.
Let's Look at Letters, Holt, 1971.

JUVENILE; "KIN/DER OWL BOOKS LANGUAGE SERIES"

Which Do You Choose?, illustrations by Bill McKibben, Holt, 1967.
Brown Bear, Brown Bear, What Do You See?, illustrations by Eric Carle, Holt, 1971, also published as part of the "Bill Martin Instant Readers" series, 1967 (also see above).

In *White Dynamite and Curly Kidd,* a quiet rodeo rider shares the excitement of his work with his daughter, who also wants to ride bulls. (Cover illustration by Ted Rand.)

What Is Sour? What Is Sweet? A Book of Opposites, Holt, 1971.
Say with Me ABC Book, Holt, 1971.

JUVENILE; "YOUNG OWL BOOKS SCIENCE SERIES"

Care and Feeding of Animals, Holt, 1971.
Fox Story, Holt, 1971.
Gravity at Work and Play, Holt, 1971.
How Birds Keep Warm in Winter, Holt, 1971.
How to Be a Better Athlete, Holt, 1971.
Our Friend, the Sun, Holt, 1971.
Poetry for Young Scientists, Holt, 1971.
The Sun and Its Planets, Holt, 1971.
Why Satellites Stay in Orbit, Holt, 1971.
The Wonder of the Monarchs, Holt, 1971.

JUVENILE; "YOUNG OWL BOOKS SOCIAL STUDIES SERIES"

Knots on a Counting Rope, illustrations by Joe Smith, Holt, 1966, reissued with coauthor John Archambault, illustrations by Ted Rand, 1987 (also see above).
Growing Up, Growing Older, Holt, 1971.
Living in Pioneer Days, Holt, 1971.
Long Ago in Colonial Days, Holt, 1971.
My Turtle Died Today, Holt, 1971.
The Old Man on Our Block, Holt, 1971.
Our New Home in the City, Holt, 1971.
Paulossie, Holt, 1971.

Town Mouse, Country Mouse, Holt, 1971.
When Christmas Comes, Holt, 1971.

JUVENILE; "YOUNG OWL BOOKS ARITHMETIC SERIES"

Adding: A Poem, Holt, 1971.
Counting Lightly, Holt, 1971.
Delight in Numbers, Holt, 1971.
Eleven and Three Are Poetry, Holt, 1971.
Four Threes Are Twelve, Holt, 1971.
Fun with the Calendar, Holt, 1971.
If You Can Count to Ten, Holt, 1971.
A Maker of Boxes, Holt, 1971.
Stretching Numbers, Holt, 1971.
Twenty White Horses, Holt, 1971.

JUVENILE; "YOUNG OWL BOOKS LITERATURE SERIES"

The Burning Rice Fields, Holt, 1971.
The Caterpillar Man, Holt, 1971.
The Funny Old Man and the Funny Old Woman, Holt, 1971.
Good Old Kristie, Holt, 1971.
Little Red Cap, Holt, 1971.
Mother Meadowlark and Brother Snake: An Indian Legend, Holt, 1971.
Old Lucy Lindy, Holt, 1971.
Showtime with Hokey Horse, Holt, 1971.
The Steadfast Tin Soldier, Holt, 1971.
The Tiger, the Brahman, and the Jackal: An East Indian Legend, Holt, 1971.

JUVENILE; OTHER SERIES

"Noodles Instant Readers" series (contains *How to Catch a Ghost, Super Midnight Menu, False Face Detective, This Little Thing, Spooky Sounds, Where Do Ghosts Live, The Phantom Athlete,* and *The Night of the Ooley Bugs*), Holt, 1970.

"Little Nature Books" series (contains *A Hydra Goes Walking, A Mushroom Is Growing, Ants Underground, Butterflies Becoming, Frogs in a Pond, Germination, June Bugs, Messenger Bee, Moon Cycle,* and *Poppies Afield*), illustrations by Colette Portal, Encyclopaedia Britannica Educational Corporation, 1975.

"Little Woodland Books" series (contains *The Bears and the Bees, The Bird and the Snake, The Doe and the Fawn, The Earthworm and the Underground, The Fox and the Fleas, The Grey Squirrel and the Red Intruder, The Owl and the Mouse, The Rabbit and the Cat, The Skunk and Its Swoosher,* and *The Wild Turkey and Her Poults,*) Encyclopaedia Britannica Educational Corporation, 1979.

(With John Archambault) "Little Seashore Books" series (contains *A Harvest of Oysters, The Irritable Alligator, The Loggerhead Turtle Crawls Out of The Sea, The Night-Hunting Lobster, A River of Salmon, The Seafaring Seals, The Silent Wetlands Hold Back the Sea, The Singing Whale, A Skyway of Geese,* and *The Sooty Shearwater Flies over the Sea*), Encyclopaedia Britannica Educational Corporation, 1982.

ADULT

The Human Connection: Language and Literature, illustrations by Kelly Oechsli, National Education Association, 1967.

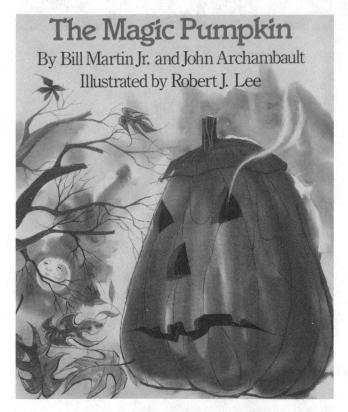

When he's not working with Archambault on children's books like *The Magic Pumpkin*, Martin, Jr., travels the country as a storyteller, folksinger, and lecturer. (Cover illustration by Robert J. Lee.)

ADAPTATIONS: The Night-Hunting Lobster, The Seafaring Seals, and *The Singing Whale* have been recorded on audio cassette by Encyclopaedia Britannica Educational Corporation, all 1985.

SIDELIGHTS: Known to elementary school teachers as Bill Martin, Jr., William Ivan Martin is the creator of numerous series of children's books. In his works, Martin told *Contemporary Authors,* he sets out to satisfy "children's appetite for language and their quest for meaning in whatever print they encounter." He encourages children to read better, faster, and more enjoyably by "giving them," Martin continued, "highly predictable stories for beginning readers." In addition to his work as an author and editor, Martin also works as a storyteller, folk singer, and lecturer; he travels extensively, conducting programs in which he conveys to both teachers and students the joy and importance of reading.

Growing up in Hobarth, Kansas, Martin lacked reading skills as a young boy. He was subsequently forced "to go the route of the 'hearing ear' to learning," Martin revealed in the *Claremont Reading Conference Yearbook.* "Oh, I could read a sentence—but never 15 connected sentences through which an idea or a concept emerged." Martin attests that a major source of comfort during his childhood was his storytelling grandmother. "She was a robust, sod-busting woman . . . who threaded the family history into story form to the continuous delight of the Martin children," Martin related to Nancy Larrick in *Language Arts.*

Despite Martin's poor reading ability, he managed to proceed through school with the help of several extraordinary teachers. Martin, for example, particularly admired his fifth grade teacher, who enriched his education by reading aloud to the class twice daily. This practice, according to Martin in the *Claremont Reading Conference Yearbook,* "neutralized me of the worldly confusions I brought into the classroom [and] depressurized me of the day's accumulation of scholastic anxieties."

Other teachers made an impression on Martin, including a high school drama teacher who introduced him to the plays of William Shakespeare. Still suffering from limited reading capabilities, Martin relished the spoken nature of drama. "People always ask: But how did you manage through high school and college without the reading skills?," Martin maintained in the *Claremont Reading Conference Yearbook.* "The times were in my favor. In those days, education was more genial, more respectful, more humble. We students had more of a chance to speak from our uniqueness than students do today, without being narrowly or arrogantly measured at every turn by test scores."

While he had difficulty reading, Martin nevertheless loved books. Admitted to the Kansas State Teachers College of Emporia without having to take a reading test, he was elated when he finally read a book from cover to cover during his freshman composition class. "It was a laborious but glorious undertaking," noted Martin in the *Claremont Reading Conference Yearbook.* Under the rigorous instruction of a college teacher, Martin improved his abilities to read and write. Martin maintained later in the *Claremont* article: "Through it all and even today, I have never lost touch with [certain of my teachers'] sensitivity. . . . They imprinted in my memory models of how a sentence runs its fluent course and carries with it an awareness of literary completeness."

After graduation Martin taught high school journalism, English, and drama, before serving in World War II in the U.S. Air Force as a newspaper editor. During this time he wrote his first children's book, *The Little Squeegy Bug,* illustrated by his brother Bernard. Its sales were meager until Martin personally visited bookstores and drugstores with the book, causing sales to increase considerably. Furthermore, when then first lady of the United States Eleanor Roosevelt mentioned *The Little Squeegy Bug* on the radio, the book sold more than half a million copies.

Martin and his brother continued collaborating on children's books; as a result, Martin's interest in children's learning and reading habits grew. He attended graduate school in education at Northwestern University and, while working on his M.A. and Ph.D., became principal of the Crow Island Elementary School in Winnetka, Illinois. "My years at Crow Island were the best learning years of my life," Martin expressed to Larrick. As an educator, he realized the significance of a child's first reading experience. "On the very first day of first grade," the author told Charlotte Cox in *Curriculum Review,* "the child should have some sort of 'whole book success'—the feeling of exhilaration that comes with the completion of an entire little book, even if it has only the smallest vocabulary—and be able to say, 'I did it! It was fun! Can I have another?'"

In 1960 Martin joined the publishing house of Holt, Rinehart & Winston, not only as editor but as creator of materials for elementary classrooms. During the late 1960s and 1970s Martin developed several reading series intended to help children learn to read and enjoy it. The "Sounds of Language" program was designed to help students from kindergarten through eighth grade relate sounds to the printed word.

Larrick described how Martin's books function: "Typographically, Bill Martin's books demonstrate his conviction that 'language works in chunks of meanings' and should be so presented to beginning readers. The jagged right margin of his books comes from breaking each line where there is a break in meaning, a break in rhythm. Thus the young reader learns from the beginning to focus on clusters of words which sing together and give meaning together."

Despite the popularity of his approach to teaching reading, Martin sometimes encounters a teacher who does not agree with his technique. "I believe that the way to teach is to trust students to respond," Martin disclosed to Jean F. Mercier in *Publishers Weekly.* "I had to convince [a doubting teacher] that whether the kids understood the *word* was unimportant, so long as they could assimilate the sounds, the music, the poet's vision."

In addition to his "Sounds of Language" books, Martin created the "Owl Books," four libraries totalling more than one hundred books ("Kin/Der Owl Books"; "Little Owl Books"; "Wise Owl Books"; and "Young Owl Books"). These works instruct children in social studies, science, literature, and arithmetic. Also, the "Bill Martin Instant Readers" series helps children expand their language and literature experience by encouraging them to read aloud. And the "Bill Martin Freedom Books" series teaches children the dynamics of democracy. In his interview with Cox, Martin stressed the importance of providing a variety of printed material to hold the interest of young readers: "We must find ways for the reluctant or nonreader to discover in print life-supporting reasons to read, whether it's in the sports pages, movie

reviews, pictorial magazines, specialty publications, or whatever."

In 1967 Martin left the Holt publishing company. Since then he has pursued a free-lance writing and editing career; he also lectures around the United States, inviting veteran teachers to regain their enthusiasm for teaching. "I think writing makes you a better writer, and reading makes you a better reader, and probably driving a truck makes you a better truck driver," Martin related in the *English Journal,* "but I think there is a point at which teaching does not make you a better teacher." Martin continued, "The trouble with many of us teachers is that we begin as professionals: questioning the assumptions, looking for theoretical support, and developing new ways to accomplish our goals. Soon, however, we become so good at the routine and predictable aspects of our jobs that we sink comfortably into reliance on our craft: perfecting our act, but not rethinking our role." Martin suggests that in order for teachers to improve, they must assume the role of a student. "By becoming students again we can come to realize more clearly than any stack of books could tell us what a good student is and what makes someone a good student. . . . By continuing to be students, . . . we will gain wisdom about learning and education and teaching. We *are* students. We can't help it. If we become *better* students, we will become better teachers."

WORKS CITED:

Contemporary Authors, Volume 130, Gale, 1990, pp. 301-05.
Cox, Charlotte, "The Love of Reading: Five Experts Speak Out," *Curriculum Review,* May/June, 1985, p. 9.
Larrick, Nancy, "Profile: Bill Martin, Jr.," *Language Arts,* Volume 59, number 5, May, 1982, p. 490-94.
Martin, Bill, Jr., "Booking for the Long Flight," *Claremont Reading Conference Yearbook,* Claremont Graduate School University Center, 1978, pp. 33-39.
Martin, "Becoming Students to Become Better Teachers," *English Journal,* April, 1988, pp. 41-44.
Mercier, Jean F., "Bill Martin: Holt's Writer in Residence Is Determined to Get Children to Read—Even If He Has to Print from Right to Left to Do It," *Publishers Weekly,* February 25, 1974, pp. 4-5.

FOR MORE INFORMATION SEE:

PERIODICALS

Library Association Record, October, 1984.
Los Angeles Times Book Review, November 22, 1987; March 27, 1988.
New York Times Book Review, March 15, 1987.
Times Literary Supplement, September 28, 1984.
Tribune Books, October 4, 1987; November 15, 1987.
Washington Post Book World, November 10, 1985.

*   *   *

MAZER, Anne 1953-

PERSONAL: Born April 2, 1953, in Schenectady, NY; daughter of Harry (a writer) and Norma (a writer; maiden name, Fox) Mazer; married Andrew Futterman (a clinical social worker), June, 1983; children: Max, Mollie. *Education:* Attended State University of New York at Binghamton, Syracuse University, and the Sorbonne.

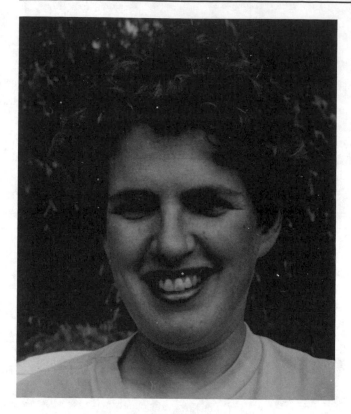

ANNE MAZER

ADDRESSES: Agent—Joanna Cole, Elaine Markson Literary Agency, 44 Greenwich Ave., New York, NY 10011.

CAREER: Free-lance writer, 1982—. Worked as an executive secretary at a real estate office and at various other jobs.

MEMBER: Authors Guild, Authors League of America.

WRITINGS:

Watch Me, illustrated by Stacey Schuett, Knopf, 1990.
The Yellow Button, illustrated by Judy Pedersen, Knopf, 1990.
The Salamander Room, illustrated by Steve Johnson, Knopf, 1991.
The Accidental Witch, Knopf, in press.

Also author of a children's book review column in the *River Reporter,* 1988-89.

WORK IN PROGRESS: Moose Street Stories, stories about a young Jewish girl growing up in a mostly Catholic neighborhood.

SIDELIGHTS: Anne Mazer told *SATA:* "I have always loved books. From the earliest age, I would devour anything that could be read—from sappy comic books to cereal boxes to encyclopedias, dictionaries, to just about any kind of fiction. I loved boys' books, girls' books, great books, simple books, educational books and just-for-thrills books. As a young girl, I stood in front of the shelves of books that lined our walls, and hungrily pulled out volumes. The same scene was repeated countless times in libraries, where I would wander among the stacks almost intoxicated by so many books. When I got older, I crept into my closet late at night, where I stuffed towels under the door and read 'til well past midnight.

"As a teenager, I disliked school and would often slip out after homeroom and walk four miles to the Syracuse Public Library or the Syracuse University Library, where I would spend the day reading. Though my parents had begun writing when I was five, I did not think of myself as a future writer. My love of books was somehow private and almost secret.

"After high school, I lived in many different cities and held many different jobs. But I wasn't happy. At the age of twenty-eight, I was working in a real estate office as an executive secretary. One day, a friend said to me, 'You are a misfit in an office.' 'I have always wanted to be a writer,' I replied. 'What's stopping you?' he asked. I didn't have any good answer to that, so that night I sat down to my typewriter and began to explore ideas for a novel. I haven't stopped working since.

"My first book was a novel for young adults, which was never published. After a few years of trial and error, I decided to try my hand at picture books. It was an instant fit. I love writing for small children. Though the text has to be done with the utmost simplicity, I find that I can express many complex and profound emotions such as joy, love and contentment. I also love the spareness of the picture book. There is no waste in a good picture book. Each word counts and each word must be placed exactly right.

"In the spring-summer of 1987, I wrote three picture books. I was sitting at my typewriter, casting about for ideas. My two-year-old son was tumbling on the bed in front of me. 'Look at me, Mom! Look at me!' I wrote the words on my blank piece of paper. In a few minutes 'look at me' had changed to 'watch me,' and I was off. *Watch Me* has a simple text that hides the fact that each verse was written hundreds of times. Some of the verses came out smoothly and easily, but most were the result of hours of trial and error. The phrase 'watch me' seemed such a universal theme for small children that I couldn't believe half a dozen people hadn't thought of it already.

"*The Yellow Button* was a completely different experience. When I was a small child, I often tried to encompass infinity within my own mind. I would dazzle myself with visions of unlimited space, and then return to my room, my self, my own small, but somehow newly expanded and enlivened reality. This mental game—a kind of contemplation really—used to give me great pleasure. One night I was sitting at the typewriter, when a picture popped into my mind of a button sitting in a pocket. As I wrote down the words, describing the picture I clearly saw, one image seemed to flow from another. In a very short time, the book was written—and I made few changes in it.

"My third book *The Salamander Room,* was triggered by a remark a little boy made while we were on a nature hike. I no longer remember the original conversation, but the boy wanted to bring a salamander home. From this, I got the idea of a boy who transforms his room to make a home for the salamander. I wrote several versions of *The Salamander Room* before I hit on its final form."

FOR MORE INFORMATION SEE:

PERIODICALS

Horn Book Guide, January, 1990.
School Library Journal, October, 1990.

*   *   *

MAZER, Harry 1925-

PERSONAL: Born May 31, 1925, in New York, NY; son of Sam (a dressmaker) and Rose (a dressmaker; maiden name, Lazevnick) Mazer; married Norma Fox (a novelist), February 12, 1950; children: Anne, Joseph, Susan, Gina. *Education:* Union College, B.A., 1948; Syracuse University, M.A., 1960.

ADDRESSES: Home and office—330 3rd Ave., New York, NY 10010. *Agent*—Marilyn Marlow, Curtis Brown Ltd., 10 Astor Pl., New York, NY 10003.

CAREER: Railroad brake man and switchtender for New York Central, 1950-55; New York Construction, Syracuse, NY, sheet metal worker, 1957-59; Central Square School, Central Square, NY, teacher of English, 1959-60; Aerofin Corp., Syracuse, welder, 1960-63; full-time writer, 1963—. *Military service:* U.S. Army Air Forces, 1943-45; became sergeant; received Purple Heart and Air Medal with four bronze oak leaf clusters.

HARRY MAZER

MEMBER: Authors Guild, Authors League of America, Society of Children's Book Writers, American Civil Liberties Union.

AWARDS, HONORS: American Library Association (ALA) Best of the Best Books list, 1970-73, for *Snowbound;* Kirkus Choice list, 1974, for *The Dollar Man;* (with Norma Fox Mazer) ALA Best Books for Young Adults list, 1977, and International Reading Association-Children's Book Council Children's Choice, 1978, both for *The Solid Gold Kid;* ALA Best Books for Young Adults list, and Dorothy Canfield Fisher Children's Book Award nomination, both 1979, both for *The War on Villa Street; New York Times* Best Books of the Year list, 1979, New York Public Library Books for the Teen Age list, 1980, ALA Best Books for Young Adults list, 1981, and ALA Best of the Best Books list, 1970-83, all for *The Last Mission; Booklist* Contemporary Classics list, 1984, and German "Preis der Lesseratten," both for *Snowbound;* Arizona Young Readers Award nomination, 1985, for *The Island Keeper;* ALA Best Books for Young Adults list, 1986, for *I Love You, Stupid!;* New York Library Books for the Teen Age list, 1986, and International Reading Association-Children's Book Council Young Adult Choice list, 1987, both for *Hey Kid! Does She Love Me?;* ALA Best Books for Young Adults list, 1987, Iowa Teen Award Master list, 1988, and West Australian Young Reader's Book Award, 1989, all for *When the Phone Rang;* ALA Best Books for Young Adults list, ALA Books for Young Adult Reluctant Readers list, 1988, and New York Public Library Books for the Teen Age list, 1988, all for *The Girl of His Dreams;* (with Norma Fox Mazer) New York Public Library Books for the Teen Age list, 1989, for *Heartbeat;* ALA Books for Young Adult Reluctant Readers list, 1989, for *City Light.*

WRITINGS:

JUVENILE NOVELS

Guy Lenny, Delacorte, 1971, reprinted, Avon, 1988.
Snow Bound, Delacorte, 1973.
The Dollar Man, Delacorte, 1974.
(With wife, Norma Fox Mazer) *The Solid Gold Kid,* Delacorte, 1977.
The War on Villa Street, Delacorte, 1978.
The Last Mission, Delacorte, 1979.
The Island Keeper: A Tale of Courage and Survival, Delacorte, 1981.
I Love You, Stupid!, Crowell Junior Books, 1981.
When the Phone Rang, Scholastic, Inc., 1985.
Hey Kid! Does She Love Me?, Crowell Junior Books, 1985.
Cave under the City, Crowell Junior Books, 1986.
The Girl of His Dreams, Crowell Junior Books, 1987.
City Light, Scholastic, Inc., 1988.
(With N. F. Mazer) *Heartbeat,* Bantam, 1989.
Someone's Mother Is Missing, Delacorte, 1990.

Snowbound and *The Last Mission* were recorded onto audiocassette by Listening Library, 1985.

ADAPTATIONS: Snowbound was produced as a National Broadcasting Company "After School Special" in 1978.

SIDELIGHTS: "A dream is made by real effort," writes Harry Mazer in an autobiographical essay in *Something about the Author Autobiography Series.* "I needed to play at writing. I needed to write badly before I could write well. It was years before I could write well. It was years before I knew enough to know this." Mazer was in his mid-thirties when he and his wife began to write every day; they wrote for the women's confession market, using the money to support the family. "My writing dismayed me," reveals Mazer in his essay, adding: "I had dark moments when I wondered why I was going on with this. I would write that, too. I wrote a lot about my feelings, interpreting my dreams, trying to keep myself together." In 1971, Mazer's "real effort" resulted in *Guy Lenny,* his first novel, and since then, many of his novels have been translated into German, French, Finnish, and Danish. Kenneth L. Donelson asserts in *Voice of Youth Advocates* that "Mazer writes about young people caught in the midst of moral crises, often of their own making. Searching for a way out, they discover themselves, or rather they learn that the first step in extricating themselves from their physical and moral dilemmas is self-discovery. Intensely moral as Mazer's books are," continues Donelson, "they present young people thinking and talking and acting believably," a characteristic which accounts for Mazer's popularity.

The son of hard-working Polish-Jewish immigrants, Mazer grew up in an apartment building in the Bronx. The building was a part of a two-block complex called the Coops, and Mazer remembers in his essay that "you could feel the optimistic spirit that built these houses—in the central courtyards with their gardens and fountains, in the library, the gymnasium, and the kindergarten. The Coops were special, an island, a community, a village in a great city built on a shared dream of cooperation and social justice." Mazer shared the bedroom of the two room apartment with his brother, while his parents slept in the living room, which was also the dining room and the kitchen. The halls and the stairs were Mazer's playground, and he says in his essay that he grew up between two worlds—the park and the street—both of which he uses in his novels. "The park was mine, so big it was limitless," recalls Mazer in his autobiographical essay. The many games that the street offered, such as marbles and chalk games, also appealed to Mazer, as did the huge fires built in empty lots after dark.

Lack of money was always a problem for Mazer during these years. In his autobiographical essay, Mazer says: "If I didn't have the nickel for the movies, I would get into the theater when the first show let out and the doors alongside the movie screen were opened to let people out." School was only two blocks away, and Mazer doesn't remember much about it. *The Gingerbread Man* and *Little Black Sambo* are the first books Mazer recalls, and in his essay he remarks that "reading was my greatest pleasure. . . . I read and ate. I used to lie on the couch with the book and a pile of apple cores on the floor." Mazer read everything from series books and adventure stories to the collected works of Charles Dickens. "Two of my all-time favorite books were *Robinson Crusoe,* the story of a man alone on a desert island, and *Tarzan of the Apes,*" states Mazer in his autobiographical essay.

The big changes in Mazer's life came when he was about to enter high school. It was at this time that he began asking himself what he was going to do with his life. Jobs were scarce at the time, and a lot of employers wouldn't hire Jews. If he had been a dutiful son, Mazer reflects in his essay, he would have become a teacher; "but I was in rebellion. I was impatient. I wanted to be great, famous. . . . My secret desire was to be a writer, but I knew nothing about how to make it happen. I had the idea that if I could only write it down, if I could only put all my feelings into words, I would finally figure everything out (whatever everything was)." Mazer took the competitive exam for the Bronx High School of

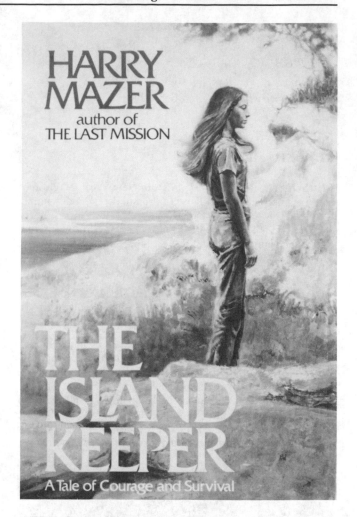

Winner of several awards, Harry Mazer was nominated for the Arizona Young Readers Award in 1985 for *The Island Keeper.*

Science and got in, but the courses that most interested him were English and history, and the questions concerning his future still lingered.

The war was on Mazer's mind at this time too. When he was seventeen, he passed the tests for the Army Air Force Cadets, but had to wait until he was eighteen to actually be called. "I prayed that the war didn't end before I got in," remembers Mazer in his autobiographical essay. While he waited, Mazer started college classes, only to quit after less than a week. The army finally called him, and Mazer served for two-and-a-half years. Starting out as an airplane mechanic, Mazer longed for combat and volunteered for aerial gunnery school, training as a ball-turret and waist gunner. After training, Mazer was assigned to a crew on a B-17 bomber. In December of 1941, the young crew headed for Europe, and flew their first mission two months later. Their last mission was flown in April when the plane was shot down over Czechoslovakia; only Mazer and one other crew member survived. "I remember thinking afterward that there had to be a reason why I had survived," remarks Mazer in his essay, adding: "I didn't think it was God. It was chance. Luck. But why me? Chance can't be denied as a factor in life, but I clung to the thought that there was a reason for my survival."

Mazer was discharged from the army in October of 1945, and was in a liberal arts college only a few days later. It was here that Mazer began writing, and in his essay he describes what it was like: "My writing at the time was too serious and self-conscious. I turned each word over in my head before I allowed it out into the open. . . . I wrote, but I was full of doubt, my standards were miles higher than my abilities. I suffered over what I wrote and didn't write any more than I had to." Graduating with a liberal arts degree, Mazer says that it was at this point in his life that he lost his way. He took a three-month course in welding and then a job in an auto-body shop, deciding to become a part of the working class. "I was dramatizing myself," recalls Mazer in his essay, "imagining myself a leader of the downtrodden, pointing the way to the future. . . . I was idealistic. I was unrealistic. Most of all I was avoiding the real issues of my life. I didn't have the belief or the nerve to say I was a writer, to begin writing and let everything else take care of itself."

Politics also interested Mazer during this period of his life, and it was while he was working on a campaign that he met Norma Fox for the second time. He had met her two years earlier when she was fifteen and he was twenty-one, but it was the second meeting that started their on-again off-again romance. A year later, Norma started college, and Mazer was pressing her to get married. "Norma said yes, we'd get married, then she said no," writes Mazer in his autobiographical essay. "When she was with me it was yes, but when she went back to school it was no again." They were finally married, and the couple settled in a tiny apartment in New York City, but soon moved back upstate to Schenectady, and then to Utica, finally settling in Syracuse. Mazer worked at various jobs, doing welding, sheet metal work, and track work for the railroad. In his essay, Mazer describes what the weekends were like: "Every Saturday I ran off to be by myself. I was moody and didn't talk and I wasn't nice to be around. I didn't know what was bothering me. I only knew I had to get out, move, walk off the mood. I'd walk along the railroad tracks and pick wild asparagus or I'd go to Three Rivers, where I'd sit under a tree and watch birds. I thought if I could only write down what I was feeling—if only I could put thought to paper—I'd know what I ought to do. But I didn't know how to start."

Ten years of factory work behind him, Mazer became a teacher, but something was still missing. Then one day, he and Norma talked and discovered that they both longed to be writers. It was at this point that they began writing every day. Mazer lost his teaching job and returned to factory work, taking paperbacks with him, trying to understand how a story worked. The insurance money from an accident finally enabled Mazer to quit his job and begin writing full-time; both Mazers began writing two confession stories a week. "These stories demanded that I develop a character, a plot, action that rose to a climax, and a satisfying ending. And I had to do it every week, week after week. It was a demanding school. I was being forced to write to stay out of the factory," says Mazer in his essay. Other forms of writing were also tried—television scripts and pieces for literary magazines among them. It was the Mazers' agent that suggested they try the children's field, and Mazer recalls that "these were the sixties and things were opening up in many areas. The protected world of children's books was giving way to a more realistic look at what children's lives were really like."

A piece in a "Dear Abby" column gave Mazer the idea for his first attempt at the children's market. It was about a boy who was concerned about an older girl he liked. She was going with someone else who was no good for her, and the boy wanted to know how he could break them up. "It was the germ that started my first book, *Guy Lenny*," reveals Mazer

in his essay. *Guy Lenny* is the story of a boy whose parents are divorced, a subject that children's books of the time did not deal with. His mother has left him, and he is living with his father when she returns to claim him. "It's a children's story because it's about a boy and is told from his point of view," explains Mazer in his autobiographical essay, adding that "it's also an adult story because it's about growing up and having to live with some of the hard, intractable things of life. And that's what made it a young-adult book, a new category of fiction that was still to be named." Norma was writing *I, Trissy* at the same time, and her book was accepted by the first editor that saw it. Mazer sent his book off reluctantly, expecting the worst. And when he received the call from his agent, he didn't believe that his book had actually been accepted. "There is no moment to equal the moment when your first book is taken," claims Mazer. "In my mind it stands with the moment my parachute opened and I knew I would live. It was like the moment after Norma and I had broken up and then were reunited. It's life ripping through death."

Mazer comments in his essay that many books later, he senses "the connection between them. It's almost as if one book guided the next book. There is a thread running through them, a link that joins them all." Many of Mazer's novels use characters from earlier books, and father and son relationships appear again and again. "I've gone about the work of writing like a bird building a nest each year with the bits of thread and paper I snatch up in the street, but also from the scraps of memory I weave together in book after book," states Mazer in his autobiographical essay. "I didn't have a plan, there was no agenda, no burning purpose, no passion about injustice," he continues. "There was passion, but it was a passion for the characters, for the world they lived in."

A *Publishers Weekly* contributor maintains that Mazer "creates credible characters . . . and incorporates splashes of humor while maintaining the established mood and tone." In *The Girl of His Dreams,* for example, Mazer relates the romance of Willis and Sophie, two ordinary young adults, with "a credibility apart from its fairy-tale ending," comments Marianne Gingher in the *Los Angeles Times,* a credibility due to the "dimensional characters." Willis is a factory worker and dedicated runner who thinks he knows exactly what the girl of his dreams should be like. Sophie does not fit this image, and their relationship develops slowly and awkwardly. "No run-of-the-mill boy meets girl story here," states Libby K. White in *School Library Journal,* adding that the novel "is romantic without being either mushy or explicitly sexual. Willis and Sophie are attractive characters who will interest and involve readers."

Snow Bound is another tale of two mismatched teens who are caught unprepared in a New York blizzard and, as Donelson points out, they must cooperate to survive. Tony is a spoiled rich kid who sets out to get revenge on his parents for not letting him keep a stray dog. He steals his mother's car and takes off in the middle of a snowstorm, adds Donelson, picking up a hitchhiker, Cindy, along the way. Aside from getting lost, Tony also wrecks the car in a desolate area, and he and Cindy must save themselves from the cold and a pack of wild dogs. "The relationship that develops between the two of them is sensitively handled, never foolishly romanticized, and will probably be an easy thing for young readers to identify with," maintains Tom Heffernan in *Children's Literature: Annual of the Modern Language Association Seminar on Children's Literature and the Children's Literature Association.* And *New York Times Book Review* contributor Cathleen Burns Elmer concludes that "the final measure of the book's capacity to enthrall lies in the *mature* reader's willingness to suspend disbelief. 'Snow Bound' is a crackling tale; Mazer tells it with vigor and authority."

The Last Mission, based in part on Mazer's own experiences in World War II, "represents an amazing leap in writing, far surpassing anything [the author] had written before," claims Donelson. Fifteen-year-old Jack Raab is Jewish and so desperate to fight against Hitler that he borrows his older brother's identification to enlist in the Army Air Forces. Jack is trained as a gunner, and he and his fellow crew members fly out of England on over twenty missions before being hit by enemy fire; Jack bails out and is the only one to survive—but he ends up a German prisoner of war. While war stories are much-explored, Donelson believes that *The Last Mission* "conveys better than any other young adult novel, and better than most adult novels, the feeling of war and the desolation it leaves behind. . . . This book is a remarkable achievement, both for its theme and its portrait of a young man who searches and acts and finds the search futile and the actions incoherent." And Paxton Davis concludes in the *New York Times Book Review:* "Harry Mazer is a prize-winning writer for young people. No wonder."

The main character in *I Love You, Stupid!* is faced with more common adolescent problems. A senior in high school, Marcus wants to be a writer and is obsessed with sex. *School Library Journal* contributor Kay Webb O'Connell points out that Marcus's erotic dreams include almost every young

In *I Love You, Stupid!,* Marcus is obsessed with sex but has trouble wooing Wendy, his pal from grade school who teaches him the importance of friendship.

female he meets—everyone but Wendy, a girl he knew in grade school. Marcus even goes so far as to babysit for a young divorced woman, hoping she'll become his lover. Wendy and Marcus finally make love, but Marcus, looking for a reason to do it every day, drives Wendy away. By the end of the book, they are back together, and Marcus realizes the importance of friendship and love. "It takes most of the book to get them together, but it's better that way; Marcus and Wendy are friends who become lovers," observes O'Connell, concluding that "they're honest and humorous; their conversations and adventures are fresh and funny."

"Mazer's characters are down to earth, very ordinary people who are flawed, inept, good. Their eccentricities, loneliness, and dreams are lightly touched with humor," observes Margaret A. Bush in *Horn Book.* And in his autobiographical essay Mazer concludes: "I think underlying all my writing has always been the belief that beneath the surface of our differences there is a current, a dark stream that connects all of us, readers and writers, parents and children, the young and the old. Despite the erosion of time the child in us never dies. The search for love never ends, the need for connection, the desire to know who we are, and the need to find someone of our own to love. How else do I keep writing for young readers?"

WORKS CITED:

Bush, Margaret A., review of *The Girl of His Dreams, Horn Book,* March-April, 1988, pp. 209-210.
Davis, Paxton, review of *The Last Mission, New York Times Book Review,* December 2, 1979, p. 41.
Donelson, Ken, "Searchers and Doers: Heroes in Five Harry Mazer Novels," *Voice of Youth Advocates,* February, 1983, pp. 19-21.
Elmer, Cathleen Burns, review of *Snow Bound, New York Times Book Review,* August 12, 1973, p. 8.
Gingher, Marianne, "A Boy Who Runs Meets a Girl Anxious to Catch Up," *Los Angeles Times,* March 12, 1988.
Heffernan, Tom, review of *Snow Bound, Children's Literature: Annual of the Modern Language Association Seminar on Children's Literature and the Children's Literature Association,* edited by Francelia Butler, Volume 4, Temple University Press, 1975, p. 206.
Mazer, Harry, *Something about the Author Autobiography Series,* Volume 11, Gale, 1991, pp. 223-240.
O'Connell, Kay Webb, review of *I Love You, Stupid!, School Library Journal,* October, 1981, p. 152.
Publishers Weekly, November 1, 1985, p. 65.
White, Libby K., review of *The Girl of His Dreams, School Library Journal,* January, 1988, pp. 86-87.

FOR MORE INFORMATION SEE:

BOOKS

Authors and Artists for Young Adults, Volume 5, Gale, 1990.
Children's Literature Review, Volume 16, Gale, 1989.
Dreyer, Sharon Spredemann, *The Bookfinder: A Guide to Children's Literature about the Needs and Problems of Youth Aged 2-15,* Volume 1, American Guidance Service, 1977.
Nilsen, Alleen Pace and Kenneth L. Donelson, *Literature for Today's Young Adults,* Scott, Foresman, 1985.
Sherrard-Smith, Barbara, *Children's Book of the Year: 1982,* Julia MacRae, 1983.
Wilkin, Binnie Tate, *Survival Themes in Fiction for Children and Young People,* Scarecrow, 1978.

PERIODICALS

English Journal, April, 1982.
Horn Book, August, 1977; February, 1980.
Kirkus Reviews, August 15, 1974; January 1, 1980; May 15, 1985; September 15, 1985; October 1, 1986.
New York Times, December 4, 1979.
New York Times Book Review, November 17, 1974; September 13, 1981; November 15, 1981.
Publishers Weekly, August 10, 1990.
School Library Journal, October, 1971; December, 1978; November, 1979; September, 1980; April, 1981; November, 1985; December, 1986.
Voice of Youth Advocates, October, 1984; August, 1985.
Washington Post Book World, July 10, 1977.*

Sketch by Susan M. Reicha

*   *   *

MAZER, Norma Fox 1931-

PERSONAL: Born May 15, 1931, in New York, NY; daughter of Michael and Jean (Garlen) Fox; married Harry Mazer (a novelist), February 12, 1950; children: Anne, Joseph, Susan, Gina. *Education:* Attended Antioch College, 1949-50, and Syracuse University, 1957-59. *Politics:* "I believe in people—despise institutions while accepting their necessity." *Religion:* "Jewish by birth, pantheistic by nature." *Hobbies and other interests:* Reading, racquetball, gardening.

ADDRESSES: Home and office—330 3rd Ave., New York, NY 10010. *Agent*—Elaine Markson, 44 Greenwich Avenue, New York, NY 10012; or, Abner Stein, 10 Roland Gardens, London SW7 3PH, England.

CAREER: Writer, 1964—. Worked previously as a secretary at a radio station, punch press operator, waitress, and cashier.

AWARDS, HONORS: National Book Award nomination, 1973, for *A Figure of Speech;* Lewis Carroll Shelf Award, University of Wisconsin, 1975, for *Saturday the Twelfth of October;* Christopher Award, *New York Times* Outstanding Books of the Year list, *School Library Journal* Best Books of the Year list, American Library Association (ALA) Best Books for Young Adults list, ALA Notable Book, Lewis Carroll Shelf Award, all 1976, all for *Dear Bill, Remember Me? and Other Stories;* (with Harry Mazer) ALA Best Books for Young Adults list, 1977, and Children's Book Council-International Reading Association Children's Choice, 1978, both for *The Solid Gold Kid;* ALA Best Books for Young Adults list, 1979, *School Library Journal* Best Books of the Year list, 1979, and ALA Best of the Best Books 1970-83 list, all for *Up in Seth's Room;* Austrian Children's Books list of honor, and German Children's Literature prize, both 1982, both for *Mrs. Fish, Ape, and Me, the Dump Queen;* Edgar Award, Mystery Writers of America, 1982, and California Young Readers Medal, 1985, both for *Taking Terri Mueller;* ALA Best Books for Young Adults list, 1983, for *Someone to Love;* ALA Best Books for Young Adults list, *New York Times* Outstanding Books of the Year list, and New York Public Library Books for the Teenage list, all 1984, all for *Downtown;* Iowa Teen Award, 1985-86, for *When We First Met;* Children's Book Council-International Reading Association Children's Choice, 1986, for *A, My Name Is Ami;* Newbery Honor Book, *School Library Journal* Best Books of the Year list, ALA Notable Book, ALA Best Books for

NORMA FOX MAZER

Young Adults list, Canadian Children's Books Council Choice, *Horn Book* Fanfare Book, and Association of Booksellers for Children Choice, all 1988, all for *After the Rain;* ALA Best Books for Young Adults list, 1989, Iowa Teen Award, 1990, and New York Public Library Books for the Teenage list, all for *Silver;* (with Harry Mazer) Children's Book Council-International Reading Association Children's Choice, and New York Public Library Books for the Teen Age list, both 1989, both for *Heartbeat;* New York Public Library Books for the Teenage list, 1989 and 1990, both for *Waltzing on Water;* American Bookseller's Pick of the Lists, and New York Public Library Books for the Teenage list, both 1990, both for *Babyface.*

WRITINGS:

JUVENILE NOVELS

I, Trissy, Delacorte, 1971.
A Figure of Speech (also see below), Delacorte, 1973.
Saturday, the Twelfth of October, Delacorte, 1975.
Dear Bill, Remember Me? and Other Stories, Delacorte, 1976.
(With husband, Harry Mazer) *The Solid Gold Kid,* Delacorte, 1977.
Up in Seth's Room, Delacorte, 1979.
Mrs. Fish, Ape, and Me, the Dump Queen, Dutton, 1980.
Taking Terri Mueller, Avon/Morrow, 1981.
When We First Met (sequel to *A Figure of Speech;* also see below) Four Winds, 1982.
Summer Girls, Love Boys, and Other Short Stories, Delacorte, 1982.
Someone to Love, Delacorte, 1983.

(Coauthor of script) *When We First Met* (film based on novel of same title), Home Box Office, 1984.

Downtown, Avon/Morrow, 1984.

Supergirl (screenplay novelization), Warner Books, 1984.

A, My Name Is Ami, Scholastic, Inc., 1986.

Three Sisters, Scholastic, Inc., 1986.

B, My Name Is Bunny, Scholastic, Inc., 1987.

After the Rain, Avon/Morrow, 1987.

Silver, Morrow, 1988.

(With H. Mazer) *Heartbeat,* Bantam, 1989.

C, My Name Is Cal, Scholastic, Inc., 1990.

Babyface, Morrow, 1990.

D, My Name Is Danita, Scholastic, Inc., 1991.

E, My Name Is Emily, Scholastic, Inc., 1991.

OTHER

(Editor, with Margery Lewis) *Waltzing on Water: Poetry by Women,* Dell, 1989.

Novels that have also been recorded on audiocassette and released by Listening Library include: *Taking Terri Mueller,* 1986, *Dear Bill Remember Me? and Other Stories,* 1987, and *After the Rain,* 1988. Contributor to books, including *Sixteen: Short Stories by Outstanding Writers for Young Adults,* edited by Donald R. Gallo, Delacorte, 1984; *Short Takes: A Short Story Collection for Young Readers,* edited by Elizabeth Segal, Lothrop, 1986; and *Visions: Nineteen Short*

A popular young adult writer, Norma Fox Mazer has garnered numerous awards, including a Lewis Carroll Shelf Award for *Saturday, the Twelfth of October.*

Stories by Outstanding Writers for Young Adults, edited by Gallo, Delacorte, 1987. Contributor of stories and articles to magazines, including *Jack and Jill, Ingenue, Calling All Girls, Child Life, Boys and Girls, Redbook, English Journal, Voice of Youth Advocates, Signal, Top of the News,* and *ALAN Review.*

WORK IN PROGRESS: Several novels; a short story.

SIDELIGHTS: Norma Fox Mazer has become one of the most popular young adult authors writing today. Her books present teenagers in ordinary surroundings, experiencing common problems. "At her best," observes Suzanne Freeman in the *Washington Post Book World,* "Mazer can cut right to the bone of teenage troubles and then show us how the wounds will heal. She can set down the everyday scenes of her characters' lives in images that are scalpel sharp.... What's apparent throughout all of this is that Mazer has taken great care to get to know the world she writes about. She delves into the very heart of it with a sure and practiced hand." It took many years of discipline for Mazer to become such a writer, and even longer for her to consider herself one; it wasn't until she was writing *Dear Bill, Remember Me? and Other Stories* that Mazer actually believed she was a real author. In an essay in *Something about the Author Autobiography Series,* she says that "during the months I spent working on the stories, I somehow lost the secret fear that I was only masquerading as a writer. For the first time, I began to believe fearlessly in the endless vitality of that mysterious source from which my imagination is constantly replenished."

Mazer grew up in Glens Falls, New York, the middle child of three girls. Her father was a route man, delivering such things as milk and bread, and the family lived in various apartments and houses. "The year we lived on Ridge Street, when I was eight," states Mazer in her autobiographical essay, "I learned to ride a two-wheeler, changed my name (briefly, because I kept forgetting I'd changed it) to the more glamorous Diane, made up triplet brothers in the Navy to impress my new girlfriend, and was caught stealing." School, reading, and boys were her childhood loves, and it was in a new apartment on First Street, recalls Mazer in her autobiographical essay, that she may have realized the possibilities of her imagination: "A girlfriend and I are playing near ... wooden steps. I have forgotten the game, although I made it up, but not her words. 'Norma Fox! What an imagination!' And perhaps it was precisely then that I realized that my imagination had some other function than to torment me with witches in doorknobs and lurking figures in the shadows of the stairs."

During Mazer's teen years, her family started calling her the "Cold One," and she began to live more and more in her own world. Feeling like an outsider, Mazer writes in her autobiographical essay that "were I to be asked to use one word to describe myself then and for years afterward, it would be—eyes. There's a picture of me around thirteen, sitting in a high-backed leather chair, looking out of the corner of my eyes, looking around, watching, a little frightened smile on my face. Along about then, it struck me, a bone-aching truth, that grown-ups—adults, these powerful mysterious people—were all play-acting; they weren't, in fact, any older, any more grown-up than I was."

The school newspaper gave Mazer her first opportunity to write for others, and it soon became the focus of her school existence. "But I wanted to write more than newspaper articles. There was a longing in me, vague, . . . but real, almost an ache," remembers Mazer in her autobiographical essay. It was when she was fifteen that Mazer met her future husband, Harry Mazer, for the first time. He was a friend of her older sister, and at the age of twenty-one, he seemed ancient to Mazer. Two years later, they met again, and a much more confident Mazer was determined that Harry should fall in love with her. Harry thought that Mazer was too young, though, and she had to work at making him notice her—the couple fell in and out of love and quarreled many times before finally getting married.

During the early part of their marriage, the Mazers worked at "boring" jobs and tried to learn how to cook. Three children soon became part of the family, and Mazer notes in her autobiographical essay: "I was Mommy; I had almost forgotten Norma. One day, looking around at the houseful of kids and listening to the never ending cries of Mommy! Mom! Mama!, it occurred to me that the day I'd been both putting off and waiting for—the day when I was all grown up—had arrived without my noticing. Indeed, it must have been here for quite a while. And that famous question 'What are you going to do when you grow up?' had not gone away." A serious talk with her husband followed, and both Mazers revealed a desire to be writers. It was decided that if they were really serious about this, then they had to begin writing every day. So, for three years, the Mazers spent an hour at the end of each day writing. It was money from an insurance settlement that finally enabled them to write full-time. "It was mildly terrifying," reveals Mazer in her autobiographical essay. "I had some days when I sat in front of the typewriter and shook because I couldn't think of what to write next."

To support the family, the Mazers wrote pulp fiction for the women's romance and confession market. These stories were all written in the first person, and were meant to make the reader think that the author had actually experienced the events being described. During the following years, the Mazers each wrote one of these 5,000-8,000 word stories every week, leaving little time to devote to the writing of novels. In 1970, Mazer managed to find the time to write *I, Trissy,* and it was published the following year. *A Figure of Speech* came two years later and received a National Book Award nomination. "I remember meeting a member of the National Book Award Committee some time after *A Figure of Speech* had received a . . . nomination and hearing him say to me, '. . . and you just came out of nowhere.' I laughed. My 'nowhere' had been the ten years I'd spent writing full time and learning the craft," writes Mazer in her autobiographical essay.

By the time that *Dear Bill, Remember Me? and Other Stories* was published, Mazer had been free-lancing for thirteen years and had every right to finally consider herself a writer. The children were growing up, and "after years of dreaming, we bought an old farmhouse for a weekend place. No windows, no plumbing, no heating, no electricity. Even the outhouse had fallen in on itself and was useless. We loved it. It took every cent we had to buy it, but we wanted it too much to care," declares Mazer in her autobiographical essay. The farmhouse was eventually fixed up, just in time for the Mazers to discover Canada. They sold the house and bought seventeen acres of woods and scrub on a cliff one hundred feet above a small lake in Canada. Many of Mazer's books involve memories of summers spent camping. "Each one, in its own way, took me over," claims Mazer in her essay. "I lived in the world I was creating; it became real to me. Sometimes I'm asked about 'writer's block.' I don't have it and I don't fear it. Those years of writing pulp fiction taught me that there are always more words. And writing my own novels taught me that there are things inside me waiting to come out that I hardly know are there."

Along with her novels, Mazer has also written two short story collections. The eight short stories in *Dear Bill, Remember Me? and Other Stories* all deal with young girls going through some sort of crisis. In "Up on Fong Mountain," Jessie strives to be accepted as something other than an extension of her boyfriend. And eighteen-year-old Louise in "Guess Whose Friendly Hands" knows she's dying of cancer, and merely wishes that her mother and sister would accept it as she has. The stories in this collection "are clearly broadcast on a young teenager's wavelength, with the signal unobtrusively amplified as in good YA novels," contends a *Kirkus Reviews* contributor. The stories in Mazer's second collection, *Summer Girls, Love Boys and Other Short Stories,* are connected by the setting of Greene Street. In "Do You Really Think It's Fair?," Sarah tells about the death of her younger sister and questions the existence of justice. Another story, "Amelia Earhart, Where Are You When I Need You?," relates the short vacation a young girl spends with her eccentric Aunt Clare. "Each story has a strength and a sharpness of vision that delights and surprises in its maturity," comments Ruth I. Gordon in the *New York Times Book Review,* adding that "Mazer has the skill to reveal the human qualities in both ordinary and extraordinary situations as young people mature."

While she has earned praise for her short stories, Mazer is especially recognized for her novels. *Taking Terri Mueller,* for example, earned Mazer an Edgar Award from the Mystery Writers of America although she had not intended it as a mystery. The book follows Terri Mueller and her father as they wander from town to town, never staying in one place for more than a year. Although Terri is happy with her father, she is old enough to wonder why he will never talk about her mother, who supposedly died ten years ago; an overheard discussion leads her to discover that she had been kidnapped by her father after a bitter custody battle. "Skillfully handling the deeply emotional situation, the author portrays Terri's conflicting feelings as well as the feelings of both her parents," remarks a *Horn Book* reviewer, adding: "The unfolding and the solution of the mystery are effectively worked; filled with tension and with strong characterization, the book makes compelling reading." Freeman concludes that "we believe in just about everything Terri does, because Mazer's writing makes us willing to believe. She wins us completely with this finely wrought and moving book."

In the novel *Babyface,* Mazer handles another parent/daughter relationship that is threatened by secrets. Toni Chessmore believes she has perfect parents and an ideal best friend. During Toni's fourteenth summer, though, her opinions begin to change when her father has a heart attack and she goes to stay with her sister in New York. She learns shocking secrets about her parents' past, and has a hard time dealing with them when she returns home. "Toni's inner growth and increasing awareness . . . are realistically portrayed," writes a *Publishers Weekly* contributor, adding that "Mazer offers a thorough, sensitive exploration of parent/teen relationships."

In both *A Figure of Speech* and *After the Rain,* Mazer deals with the relationship between a young girl and her grandfather. Jenny is the granddaughter in *A Figure of Speech,* explains Jill Paton Walsh in the *New York Times Book Review,* and feels like an outsider in her own family. The only one she relates to is her grandpa, who lives in an apartment in the basement, and who is neglected by the rest of the family.

NORMA FOX MAZER
BABYFACE

With her best friend in another city and at odds with her parents, Toni feels lost until she is told a shocking family secret that helps her discover who she is. (Jacket illustration for Norma Fox Mazer's *Babyface* by Michael Deas.)

When Jenny's older brother returns home with a young wife they look longingly at grandpa's apartment, continues Walsh, and the family decides to put him in a nursing home. Grandpa runs away, and Jenny goes with him, sharing the last days of his life. "The fine definition of all characters, the plausibility of the situations and the variety of insights into motivation make [the novel] almost too good to be true," Tom Heffernan asserts in *Children's Literature: Annual of the Modern Language Association Seminar on Children's Literature and the Children's Literature Association.*

In *After the Rain* Rachel's grandfather, Izzy, has cancer, so Rachel begins to go with him on his long afternoon walks. Izzy's crusty exterior, states a *Voice of Youth Advocates* contributor, has often prevented his family from getting close to him. Rachel is the youngest member of her family, half the age of her older brother, and her parents embarrass her and seem incredibly old. During the walks with her grandfather, observes Cynthia Samuels in the *Washington Post Book World,* Rachel manages to know and love him before he dies. And when he is gone, she is able to deal with the death and loss, and even teach her parents a few things. A *Kirkus Reviews* contributor says that the story is "beautifully and sensitively written, sounding the basic chords of the pleasures and pains of family relationships."

Mazer points out in her autobiographical essay that there's "a kind of mystery" in all of her books: "I write and my readers read to find out the answers to questions, secrets, problems, to be drawn into the deepest mystery of all—someone else's life." Freeman asserts that "in its sharpest moments, Mazer's writing can etch a place in our hearts," and in her *Top of the News* essay, Mazer declares: "I love stories. I'm convinced that everyone does, and whether we recognize it or not, each of us tells stories. A day doesn't pass when we don't put our lives into story. Most often these stories are . . . of the moment. They are the recognition, the highlighting of . . . our daily lives. . . . In my own life, it seems that events are never finished until I've either told them or written them."

WORKS CITED:

Freeman, Suzanne, "The Truth about the Teens," *Washington Post Book World,* April 10, 1983, p. 10.

Gordon, Ruth I., review of *Summer Girls, Love Boys and Other Short Stories, New York Times Book Review,* March 13, 1983, p. 29.

Heffernan, Tom, review of *A Figure of Speech, Children's Literature: Annual of the Modern Language Association Seminar on Children's Literature and the Children's Literature Association,* edited by Francelia Butler, Volume 4, Temple University Press, 1975, pp. 206-207.

Horn Book, April, 1983, pp. 172-173.

Kirkus Reviews, October 1, 1976, pp. 1101-1102; May 1, 1987, p. 723.

Mazer, Norma Fox, "Growing Up with Stories," *Top of the News,* winter, 1985, pp. 157-167.

Mazer, *Something about the Author Autobiography Series,* Volume 1, Gale, 1986, pp. 185-202.

Publishers Weekly, July 27, 1990, p. 235.

Samuels, Cynthia, a review of *After the Rain, Washington Post Book World,* May 10, 1987, p. 19.

Walsh, Jill Paton, a review of *A Figure of Speech, New York Times Book Review,* March 17, 1974, p. 8.

Voice of Youth Advocates, June, 1987, p. 80.

FOR MORE INFORMATION SEE:

BOOKS

Authors and Artists for Young Adults, Volume 5, Gale, 1990.

Contemporary Literary Criticism, Volume 26, Gale, 1983.

Holtze, Sally Holmes, editor, *Fifth Book of Junior Authors and Illustrators,* H. W. Wilson, 1983.

Holtze, *Presenting Norma Fox Mazer,* Twayne, 1987, Dell, 1989.

PERIODICALS

English Journal, February, 1986.

Horn Book, December, 1982; September, 1987.

Kirkus Reviews, January 1, 1986.

Los Angeles Times, September 12, 1987.

Los Angeles Times Book Review, July 5, 1987.

Nation, March 12, 1983.

New York Times, December 21, 1976.

New York Times Book Review, October 19, 1975; January 20, 1980; November 25, 1984.

Publishers Weekly, December 17, 1982.

School Library Journal, September, 1980; December, 1981; November, 1982; March, 1986; May, 1987.

Top of the News, January, 1976.

Washington Post Book World, July 10, 1977; January 20, 1980; October 14, 1984; March 9, 1986.

Sketch by Susan M. Reicha

*   *   *

McDONALD, Megan 1959-

PERSONAL: Born February 28, 1959, in Pittsburgh, PA; daughter of John (an ironworker) and Mary Louise (a social worker; maiden name, Ritzel) McDonald. *Education:* Oberlin College, B.A., 1981; University of Pittsburgh, M.L.S., 1986.

ADDRESSES: Home—Pittsburgh, PA.

CAREER: Carnegie Library, Pittsburgh, PA, children's librarian, 1986-1990; Minneapolis Public Library, Minneapolis, MN, children's librarian, 1990-91; Adams Memorial Library, Latrobe, PA, children's librarian, 1991—; children's writer. Free-lance book reviewer and storyteller.

MEMBER: American Library Association, Society of Children's Book Writers, National Association for the Preservation and Perpetuation of Storytelling.

AWARDS, HONORS: Children's Book Award, International Reading Association, for *Is This a House for Hermit Crab?;* Judy Blume Contemporary Fiction Award, Society of Children's Book Writers, for *The Bridge to Nowhere;* other awards include American Bookseller's Pick of the Lists and Best Books of the Year, *School Library Journal.*

WRITINGS:

Is This a House for Hermit Crab?, illustrated by S. D. Schindler, Orchard Books, 1990.
The Potato Man, illustrated by Ted Lewin, Orchard Books, 1991.

MEGAN McDONALD

Whoo-oo Is It?, illustrated by Schindler, Orchard Books, in press.

WORK IN PROGRESS: "A semi-autobiographical novel for ages eleven and older," tentatively titled *The Bridge to Nowhere,* publication by Orchard Books expected in 1992; a sequel to *The Potato Man,* illustrated by Lewin, publication by Orchard Books expected in 1993.

SIDELIGHTS: Megan McDonald told *SATA:* "Although I have worked as a park ranger, bookseller, museum guide, teacher, 'living history' interpreter, and storyteller, I have also worked in libraries since the age of fifteen. Connecting children with books has always been the centerpiece of my life's work. With rising rates of illiteracy, this is important now more than ever.

"*Is This a House for Hermit Crab?* grew out of a story told with puppets to children at the library. Its alliterative sounds, its rhythm and repetition worked so well with young children that I decided to write it as a picture book, in hopes that the story would find a wider audience. *The Potato Man* is based on a story my father used to tell me about growing up in Pittsburgh before the Depression. The potato man was a huckster who would ride down the street in a horse-drawn wagon, calling out a strange cry that sounded like 'Abba-no-potata-man.' When the children heard the cry, they became frightened and ran away. Because the story has its roots in the oral tradition of my own family, I tried to capture the feel, the setting, the language as I imagined it when the story was told to me as a young girl.

"Story can come from memory or experience. It seems to come from everywhere, and out of nowhere. In everything there is story—a leaf falling, the smell of cinnamon, a dog that looks both ways before crossing the street. The idea, the seed of a story is implicit in everything—but requires paying attention, watching, seeing, listening, smelling, eavesdropping. As a writer, I am a keen observer, always on the lookout.

"To be a writer, I must write. To be a writer for children, I must continue to believe in the transformative power of story that connects children with books."

FOR MORE INFORMATION SEE:

PERIODICALS

Booklist, March 1, 1990.
Horn Book, March/April, 1990.
School Library Journal, April, 1990.
Publishers Weekly, December 15, 1990.

*   *   *

McGRAW, Eloise Jarvis 1915-

PERSONAL: Born December 9, 1915, in Houston, TX; daughter of Loy Hamilton (a merchant) and Genevieve (Scoffern) Jarvis; married William Corbin McGraw (a writer and filbert-grower), January 29, 1940; children: Peter Anthony, Lauren Lynn. *Education:* Principia College, B.A., 1937; graduate study in painting and sculpture, Oklahoma University, 1938, and Colorado University, 1939; additional study at Museum Art School, Portland, Ore., 1970-78. *Politics:* Moderate. *Hobbies and other interests:* Dressmak-

ELOISE JARVIS McGRAW

ing, bread baking, printmaking (etchings, woodcuts, wood-engraving), drawing, reading.

ADDRESSES: Home and office—1970 Indian Trail, Lake Oswego, OR 97034. *Agent*—Curtis Brown Ltd., 10 Astor Pl., New York, NY 10003.

CAREER: Oklahoma City University, Oklahoma City, OK, instructor in portrait and figure painting, 1943-44; writer, 1949—. Voluntarily corrected and graded English compositions for local district high school, 1961-62; teacher of adult education fiction writing classes, Lewis & Clark College, 1965-66; teacher at University of Oregon Haystack conference, manuscript clinic, summers, 1965-67, fiction writing, summers, 1971-78. Has directed juvenile workshops in Portland, OR, Seattle, WA, La Jolla, CA, and elsewhere; speaks frequently on writing at schools and literary gatherings. Featured in writers' "Teleconferences," broadcast on educational channels.

MEMBER: Authors Guild, Authors League of America.

AWARDS, HONORS: Crown Fire named an honor book in *New York Herald Tribune Children's Book Festival,* 1951; *Moccasin Trail* named Newbery Honor Book, 1952, and received Lewis Carroll Shelf Award, 1963; *The Golden Goblet* named Newbery Honor Book, 1962; William Allen White Award nominations, 1973, for *Master Cornhill* and 1983, for *The Money Room;* Edgar Award, Mystery Writers of America, for best juvenile mystery of the year, 1978, for *A Really Weird Summer;* Mark Twain Award, Sequoyah Award, and

Bluebonnet Award nominations, all 1983, all for *The Money Room;* Western Writers Golden Spur Award nomination, 1983-84, for *Hideaway;* Iowa Children's Choice Award, Tennessee Volunteer State Book Award nomination, and West Virginia Children's Book Award, all 1990-91, all for *The Seventeenth Swap.*

WRITINGS:

Sawdust in His Shoes (Junior Literary Guild selection), Coward, 1950, included in *Four Complete Teenage Novels,* compiled by J. A. Nunn, Globe, 1963.
Crown Fire, Coward, 1951.
Moccasin Trail (Junior Literary Guild selection), Coward, 1952, reprinted, Viking, 1986.
Mara, Daughter of the Nile, Coward, 1953, reprinted, Viking, 1985.
Pharaoh (adult novel), Coward, 1958.
Techniques of Fiction Writing, Writer, 1959.
The Golden Goblet, Coward, 1961, reprinted, Viking, 1986.
Steady, Stephanie (one-act play), Dramatic Publishing, 1962.
(With daughter, Lauren McGraw Wagner) *Merry Go Round in Oz,* Reilly & Lee, 1963, reprinted, Books of Wonder, 1989.
Greensleeves, Harcourt, 1968.
Master Cornhill (juvenile), Atheneum, 1973, reprinted, Viking, 1986.
A Really Weird Summer (juvenile), Atheneum, 1977.
Joel and the Great Merlini (Junior Literary Guild Selection), Pantheon, 1979.
The Forbidden Fountain of Oz, International Wizard of Oz Club, 1980.
The Money Room (Junior Literary Guild Selection), Atheneum, 1981.
Hideaway (Junior Literary Guild Selection), Atheneum, 1983.
The Seventeenth Swap (Junior Literary Guild Selection), Atheneum, 1986.
The Trouble with Jacob (Junior Literary Guild selection), Macmillan, 1988.
The Striped Ships, Macmillan, 1991.

Contributor to *Cricket, Jack and Jill, Childcraft, Parents' Magazine,* and *Writer.*

ADAPTATIONS: Moccasin Trail and *Golden Goblet* were both recorded and made into filmstrips by Miller-Brody Productions in 1975.

WORK IN PROGRESS: A novel for young people, tentatively entitled *Investigating Kelsey.*

SIDELIGHTS: Eloise McGraw writes that throughout her adult life her interests have ranged in intensity from minor hobbies to all-out obsessions and included drawing, painting and printmaking, dancing, stagecraft, acting, directing, puppetry, ceramics, enamel-on-metal work, drill-team horseback riding, and studying ancient Egyptian history and customs. Since 1949, however, her major—and only—vocation has been writing, always her dominant interest. She decided she wanted to be an author about the time she wrote her first story at the age of eight.

McGraw explained, "Writing is my natural gesture, as necessary to my well-being as breathing or eating. I never have a more specific purpose in mind than writing another book, exploring some character and situation that have captured my interest. But I have only to read the book later to realize that I have also been exploring my own emotions, clarifying my attitudes, sometimes resolving an inner conflict and coming to terms with a problem in my own life.

"For me, a story always starts with a character. I may have a small ember of a plot idea from which sparks occasionally fly up, but until I have the character, the fire won't start. Once it does, and the general shape and mood of the story begin to come clear, craftsmanship takes over for a while as I work out the plot in tentative form. It always grows and changes as the writing progresses.

"The writing itself is a curious process I can only describe as listening. I turn an inward ear to what my characters are saying, and how they're saying it, and to the sound and rhythm of the next sentence. Then I write down what I've heard, as nearly as I've been able to catch it. The trouble is, my hearing is imperfect, and often the voices are so exasperatingly soft that I catch myself wanting to snap, 'Speak up!' None of it is as simple as it sounds. Of course the craftsman must frequently intrude, and bustle about with his blue pencil and scissors and new broom, as well as his architect's tools; but I try to keep him out as much as I can until the first draft's finished. His turn comes then.

"My working habits have changed considerably over the years. For a long time I made meticulous outlines, attempting to envision each chapter clearly while still leaving myself room for spontaneity and added details. I always had to change these outlines as I went along—sometimes a little, sometimes a lot. At about chapter six or seven they finally settled down and I really did see clearly to the end. But at some point all this changed. As I remember, I caught myself one day being bored stiff with the outline I was trying to work out. It suddenly struck me that I was belaboring my idea, maybe killing it by trying to hold it too still. Why insist on pinning something down that was going to keep changing on me anyway, as it grew and developed and finally assumed its final form?

"So I quit that. When a book idea comes to me, it is usually just a notion—something I can put into one sentence. I write that sentence on a file card and put it in a box. As questions about the idea arise in my mind, I write them on other cards, and add the answers when I have them. Similarly, I note down other ideas that seem to want to join up with the first one, bits of scenes or dialogue, plans for characters and setting, facts I need to know. The book grows in this way while I may be doing other things, even writing a different book; my subconscious is doing most of the work. It is ever so much more relaxing than beating my conscious mind into producing a good and thorough outline—and it's more successful, too. Almost always, after the book is written, I can look back at that very first idea card (which I may have forgotten all about) and find that the essence of the completed story was right there in that one sentence.

"As to my working hours, they, too, have changed. Instead of trying to maintain an all-day, nine-to-five—and necessarily much interrupted—schedule, I have adopted a long half-day. I get up at six and go immediately to my desk, taking a cup of coffee with me. I stop at about eight to dress and eat breakfast, go back to work from nine until twelve or one. By then I am written out for the day; in the afternoons I do other things. This schedule produces just as many pages per day as the old one, and sometimes more. I find those first two early morning hours the most productive of all.

"My husband and I celebrated our fifty-first anniversary in 1991, and can no longer claim to be in the prime of life. However, we have not slowed down much and have no plans for doing so. We both have books coming out in fall '91; we're both currently at work on the next ones. I branched out in a slightly new direction by doing the jacket-drawing for *The Striped Ships.* I may try that again.

"We have enjoyed a good many rambling trips abroad over the years, some with our children, several with a grandchild in tow, and they have been strenuous but rewarding. For instance, the idea for *The Striped Ships* came to me in Normandy in 1985 as I stood looking at the Bayeux Tapestry for the first time. Work on the manuscript made a perfect excuse for going back in 1989 to look at it again. But that polar flight seems longer, as well as more claustrophobic, than it used to, little hotel rooms chillier and foreign beds harder. It is probably time to curtail our free-form traveling.

"Anyway, our five grandchildren are all grown now and out of college, though three are still in graduate school. They all live near us, as do our son and daughter. It gives us a good strong motive to just stay and write."

FOR MORE INFORMATION SEE:

BOOKS

Something about the Author Autobiography Series, Volume 6, Gale, 1988.

*   *   *

MONTY PYTHON
See JONES, Terry and PALIN, Michael

*   *   *

MUELLER, Joerg 1942-

PERSONAL: Born October 11, 1942, in Lausanne, Switzerland. *Education:* Attended Arts and Crafts School, Biel, Switzerland.

ADDRESSES: Office—c/o Verlag Sauerlaender, Laurenzenvorstadt 89, CH-5001 Aarau, Switzerland.

CAREER: Affiliated with advertising agencies in Paris, France, and Zurich and Berne, Switzerland. Illustrator.

AWARDS, HONORS: Special honorable mention for nonbook illustration, *Boston Globe-Horn Book* Awards, 1977, for *The Changing City* and *The Changing Countryside; The Changing City* and *The Changing Countryside* were named notable books by the American Library Association, and notable trade books in the field of social studies by the Children's Book Council and the National Council on the Social Studies, all 1977; Mildred L. Batchelder Award, 1979, for *Rabbit Island;* Young Critics Award, International Children's Book Fair in Bologna, Italy, 1986, for *Peter and the Wolf; Peter and the Wolf* was named Children's Choice Book by the Children's Book Council and the International Reading Association, 1987; Deutscher Jugend-literaturpreis, Sparte Bilderbuch, 1990, for *The Animal Rebellion.*

The wolf snarled, "You dare to tease *me*!" And he came nearer...and nearer...

Joerg Mueller's illustrations for *Peter and the Wolf,* a musical fairy tale by Sergey Prokofiev, are laid out in comic book form.

WRITINGS:

SELF-ILLUSTRATED

The Changing Countryside (juvenile), Atheneum, 1977 (published in German as *Alle Jahre wieder saust der Presslufthammer nieder,* Sauerlaender, 1973).

The Changing City (juvenile), Atheneum, 1977 (published in German as *Hier faullt ein Haus, dort steht ein Kran und ewig droht der Baggerzahn, oder Die Veraenderung der Stadt,* Sauerlaender, 1977).

(With Joerg Steiner) *The Sea People* (juvenile), Schocken, 1982 (published in German as *Die Menschen im Meer,* Sauerlaender, 1981).

ILLUSTRATOR

Sergey Prokofiev, *Peter and the Wolf: A Musical Fairy Tale* (juvenile book and cassette package), retold by Loriot, Knopf, 1986 (originally produced for children's theater as *Petya i volk,* Moscow, 1936).

Steiner, *The Bear Who Wanted to Be a Bear* (juvenile; adapted from an idea by Frank Tashlin), translated by Anthea Bell, Atheneum, 1977 (published in German as *Der Baer, der ein Baer bleiben wollte,* Sauerlaender, 1976).

Steiner, *Rabbit Island,* translated by Ann Conrad Lammers, Harcourt, 1978 (published in German as *Die Kanincheninsel,* Sauerlaender, 1977).

Hermann Rauber, *Altstadt Aarau* (photographs), AT-Verlag, 1981.

Steiner, *Der Eisblumenwald* (novel), Sauerlaender, 1983.

Steiner, *Der Mann vom Barengraben,* Sauerlaender, 1987.

Steiner, *The Animal's Rebellion,* translated by Susan Leubuscher and Tadzio Koelb, Atheneum, 1990, (published in German as *Aufstand der Tiere oder Die neuen Stadtmusikanten,* Sauerlaender, 1989).

SIDELIGHTS: Joerg Mueller's picture books have gained popularity and acclaim in the United States as well as in Mueller's native Switzerland for their powerful, though often wordless, stories about contemporary life. His 1977 publications *The Changing City* and *The Changing Countryside,* in fact, are considered by some observers to be art portfolios rather than books because of their lack of text. Yet the pictures in these works tell a distinct story about history and progress. *The Changing City* begins with a portrait of a European city neighborhood in 1953, followed by pictures of the same location at three year intervals through 1976. Modern roads, neon lights, and big, dreary buildings gradually destroy the old world charm of the neighborhood. Similarly, *The Changing Countryside* depicts the replacement of an isolated farmhouse in the country by suburban shopping centers, highways, and even a factory. Mueller did extensive research in order to represent the different time periods in his paintings with historically accurate details, including "children playing with hula hoops, new car styles,

In *The Bear Who Wanted to Be a Bear*, **a hibernating bear wakes up and wanders into a factory that has been built above his den. But no one notices that he is not human.** (Written by Joerg Steiner; illustrated by Mueller.)

advertisements for products" and other assorted items, according to a reviewer for the *Bulletin of the Center for Children's Books*. Calling *The Changing City* and *The Changing Countryside* series "a startlingly dramatic short history," *New York Times Book Review* contributor Karla Kuskin raved that "these two practically wordless books have so much to say that they make far wordier volumes seem inarticulate."

In 1977 Mueller also illustrated Joerg Steiner's *The Bear Who Wanted to Be a Bear*. In this story, a factory is built near the winter den of a hibernating bear. When the bear wakes up in the spring and wanders into the factory, the workers are so numbed by their dull routine that no one notices he is not human. Against his will, the bewildered bear is put to work on the assembly line. According *Wilson Library Bulletin* critics Olga Richard and Donnarae MacCann, Mueller's illustrations draw a sharp contrast between nature and industry by depicting the industrial setting in unbending sharp angles and the natural landscape in softer and less imposing strokes. Like *The Changing City* and *The Changing Countryside, The Bear Who Wanted to Be a Bear* reflects Mueller's longstanding concerns about the dehumanizing effect of industrial progress on individuals and their environment. Richard and MacCann further noted that although the story has a happy ending, a young reader may be left saddened by its view of a modern world in which machines and factory jobs overpower personal identity.

Mueller and Steiner spent "months of planning, sketching, and building models and puppets," according to *Washington Post Book World* contributor Alice Digilio, in preparation for their 1982 publication *The Sea People*, the story of two

islands with very different cultures. Greater Island has a king, stone buildings, organized farming, and a social class system. On Lesser Island, where there are no social classes, people fish for food, live in wigwams, and spend most of their time singing and dancing. Peace between the islands is disturbed by a mysterious shower of gold. The people of Greater Island become greedy, stealing land and even slaves from Lesser Island. The threat that the "civilized" society of Greater Island poses to the happy, carefree life on Lesser Island raises many questions about modern attitudes toward progress, money, working, and success. This point is brought across in Mueller's illustrations of the peace and beauty of the natural world before civilization moves in. *Times Literary Supplement* contributor Elaine Moss, describing a picture in *The Sea People* in which "a lemon dawn rises over seas, rock, olive trees, ramparts—each ripple, stone, leaf, rope in full focus," hailed Mueller's paintings as "truly breathtaking."

Mueller's 1986 award-winning publication, *Peter and the Wolf: A Musical Fairy Tale,* is a unique rendering of Russian composer Sergey Prokofiev's classic tale about a young boy who, despite his grandfather's warnings to the contrary, goes off to the forest and captures a wolf. A cassette provides Prokofiev's well-beloved symphony along with a narration of the story, as it is retold by Loriot. Mueller's accompanying illustrations are laid out in comic book form, with the characters' thoughts and dialogue appearing in balloons within the paintings. Although the comic book format gives the piece a slightly humorous effect, according to Betsy Hearne in her *Bulletin of the Center for Children's Books* review, the drama is heightened by this intersection of pictures and dialogue. Mueller's contrasting of viewpoints has an additional dramatic effect. Patricia Dooley of *School Library Journal* observed that Mueller makes the difference between the two main characters' outlooks and personalities visually apparent, without words, by painting the forest twice—first through the eyes of Peter's "youthful optimism," and then through the grandfather's more cautious perspective. Hearne applauded Mueller's "meticulously rendered paintings" for making this version of *Peter and the Wolf* "an absorbing work of art."

WORKS CITED:

Bulletin of the Center for Children's Books, September, 1977, p. 22.
Digilio, Alice, review of *The Sea People, Washington Post Book World,* September 12, 1982, p. 7.
Dooley, Patricia, review of *Peter and the Wolf, School Library Journal,* November, 1986, p. 82.
Hearne, Betsy, review of *Peter and the Wolf, Bulletin of the Center for Children's Books,* January, 1987, p. 96.
Kuskin, Karla, review of *The Changing Countryside* and *The Changing City, New York Times Book Review,* July 3, 1977, p. 11.
MacCann, Donnarae, and Olga Richard, review of *The Bear Who Wanted to Be a Bear, Wilson Library Bulletin,* June, 1986, p. 65.

FOR MORE INFORMATION SEE:

PERIODICALS

Time, November 21, 1977, p. 66; December 20, 1982, p. 80.
Times Literary Supplement, November 26, 1982, p. 1305.*

*   *   *

MULLER, Jorg
See MUELLER, Joerg

*   *   *

NEWTON, David E(dward) 1933-

PERSONAL: Born June 18, 1933, in Grand Rapids, MI; son of Edward T. (a truck driver) and Mildred M. (a homemaker; maiden name, Hammond) Newton. *Education:* University of Michigan, B.S. (with high distinction), 1955, M.Ed., 1961; Harvard University, Ed.D., 1971. *Hobbies and other interests:* Pets, gardening, hiking.

ADDRESSES: Office—Instructional Horizons, 297 Addison St., San Francisco, CA 94131.

CAREER: Grand Rapids Board of Education, Grand Rapids, MI, secondary school teacher, 1955-67; Misawa Dependent School, Misawa, Japan, high school teacher, 1962-63; Harvard-Boston summer school, Roxbury, MA, master teacher, 1966; Harvard-Newton summer school, Newton, MA, master teacher, 1967-68; Salem State College, Salem, MA, assistant professor, 1969-72, associate professor, 1972-76, professor of chemistry and physics, 1976-83; writer. Western Washington University, visiting professor of science education, 1980-87; University of San Francisco, adjunct professor of professional studies, 1983—. Grand Rapids Public Schools, chair of committee for reorganization of junior high school science curriculum, 1959-62; Greater Grand Rapids Science Teachers Organization, president, 1961-62 and 1963-64; Michigan Science Teachers Association, treasurer, and Grand Rapids Education Associa-

tion, member of board of directors, both 1963-65; International Science Education Program, member of planning committee, 1974-78; Massachusetts Association of Biology Teachers, chair of conference on social issues in biology, Bridgewater State College, member of compact accrediting team, and National Science Teachers Association national convention, member of program planning committee, all 1975; member of Faculty Senate Executive Board, 1975-76; Association for the Education of Teachers in Science (AETS), member of committee on needs, 1976, and international science education committee, 1978-82; AETS/Peace Corps conference on international science education, convener and chair, 1978. Guest lecturer at University of Saskatchewan, 1975, and National Science Teachers Association conventions. Peace Corps, PRO traveler to Ghana, Togo, and Sierra Leone, 1978, and consultant on recruiting strategies, 1978-79. Presenter of papers at conferences.

MEMBER: National Association of Science Writers, National Science Teachers Association, American Association for the Advancement of Science, Phi Beta Kappa, Phi Kappa Phi, Phi Lambda Upsilon, Delta Pi Alpha.

AWARDS, HONORS: Science Teaching Achievement Recognition (Star) Award, National Science Teachers Association, 1960; Shell Merit fellow, 1964; named Outstanding Young Science Educator of the Year, Association for the Education of Teachers in Science, 1968.

WRITINGS:

PUBLISHED BY J. WESTON WALCH, EXCEPT AS NOTED

Man and the Physical World, 1959.
Science Skills, 1961.
Chemistry Problems, 1962.
Guidelines in Chemistry, 1965.
(With Fletcher G. Watson) *The Research on Science Education Survey,* Harvard University Press, 1968.
Nutrition Today, 1973.
Understanding Venereal Disease, 1973.
Science and Society, Holbrook Press, 1974.
General Science Casebook, 1974.
Biological Science Casebook, 1974.
Math in Everyday Life, 1975.
Student Activity Guide to the Boston Museum of Science, Creative Dimensions, 1979.
(With Irwin Slesnick, A. LaVon Blazar, Alan McCormack, and Fred Rasmussen) *Scott Foresman Biology,* Scott, Foresman, 1980.
The Chemistry of Carbon, 1980.
Basic Skills in Science, 1983.
Science and Social Issues, 1983.
Consumer Math Survival Kit, 1983.
Nutrition for You, 1984.
Sexual Questions, 1984.
Basic Skills in Chemistry, 1984.
Biology Updated, 1984.
Chemistry Updated, 1985.
An Introduction to Molecular Biology, 1986.
Sexual Health, 1987.
The Comprehensive Data Book, 1987.
Science Ethics, Watts, 1987.
Refresher Math for Basic Science Classes, 1987.
U.S. and Soviet Space Programs, Watts, 1988.
Physics Updated, 1988.
Particle Accelerators, Watts, 1989.
Biology for the Allied Health Sciences, 1990.
Taking a Stand against Environmental Pollution, Watts, 1990.

David E. Newton and his dog Dolly.

Land Use, Enslow Publishers, 1991.

Also author, with Irwin Slesnick, of *Wetlands Interpretive Program,* 1982. Contributor to books, including *AETS Yearbook,* 1977; *Scott Foresman Physical Science* and *Scott Foresman Earth Science,* both Scott, Foresman, 1982; *The Sexual Abuse of Children: Theory, Research and Therapy,* by James Geer and William O'Donohue, Lawrence Erlbaum, 1991; and *Energy* (handbook). Author of study guides, instructor's manuals, activity packages, curriculum projects and units, surveys, science and math games, and poster, slide, tape, and activity sets. Contributor of numerous articles to journals, including *School Science and Mathematics, School Paperback Journal, High School Journal, Science Education, Life and Health, Adolescence, Journal of Homosexuality,* and *Appraisal.* Reviewer for Children's Science Book Review committee, 1973—, and American Association for the Advancement of Science (AAAS) Film Review, 1976-83.

WORK IN PROGRESS: Books for Watts, tentatively titled *Hunting, Earthquakes,* and *Scientific Equipment;* books for Enslow Publishers, tentatively titled *Population* and *Issues of the AIDS Epidemic;* a book for Houghton, tentatively titled *Physical Science;* a book for Walch, tentatively titled *Environmental Chemistry;* a book for New Discovery, tentatively titled *Cities at War: Tokyo.*

SIDELIGHTS: David E. Newton told *SATA:* "My hobby is spending time with my animals. I have two cats, Shearman and Sterling, and a dog, Dolly. I'm also a foster parent for the San Francisco Society for the Prevention of Cruelty to Animals (SPCA). That means taking care of very young kittens and puppies. Sometimes kittens and puppies as young as three or four weeks are brought into the SPCA. But they are too young to be adopted. So I keep them until they are eight weeks old. Sometimes it's hard to give the kittens and puppies back. That's how I got to keep Dolly! But it's usually not too difficult since I know they are going to good homes."

*　　*　　*

NICHOLS, Janet (Louise) 1952-

PERSONAL: Born October 3, 1952, in Sacramento, CA; daughter of William R. (a refrigeration engineer) and Lena (a homemaker; maiden name, Graifemberg) Nichols; married Timothy Lynch (a composer and college music instructor), June 30, 1984; children: Caitlin Grace, Sean Nichols. *Education:* California State University, Sacramento, B.A., 1974; Arizona State University, M.M., 1976. *Politics:* Democrat. *Hobbies and other interests:* Bicycling.

ADDRESSES: Home—123 S. Cottonwood Ct., Visalia, CA 93291. *Agent*—Diana Finch, Ellen Levine Literary Agency, 15 E. 26th St., Suite 1801, New York, NY 10010.

CAREER: Pianist, 1970—; private piano teacher, 1972-1990; writer, 1979—. De Anza College, Cupertino, CA, instructor in music, 1980-90; Skyline College, San Bruno, CA, instructor in music, 1981-90. Member of the Tulare County Symphony Programming Committee; adjudicator for the Guild of Piano Teachers national auditions.

MEMBER: National Guild of Piano Teachers, Society of Children's Book Writers, Tulare County Peace Coalition.

JANET NICHOLS

WRITINGS:

American Music Makers, Walker & Co., 1990.
Women Music Makers, Walker & Co., in press.

Contributor to various sports journals and other periodicals, including *Highlights for Children, Jack and Jill, New Yorker,* and *Seventeen.*

WORK IN PROGRESS: Writing *Zinger,* a young adult novel about bicycle racing in the United States, and *I Am a Musician,* an adult novel about a pianist/activist. Also researching the Tour de France bicycle race, American bicycling champion Greg LeMond, surrogate mothers, and black, Hispanic, and twentieth-century composers.

SIDELIGHTS: Janet Nichols told *SATA:* "Ever since I was very young, I wanted to be a great pianist. I started taking piano lessons when I was seven, and I hated to practice. That is mostly because I was bored, because I didn't know how to practice. Learning how to practice is the hardest thing about learning to play an instrument. I would tiptoe into the kitchen and turn the clock ahead five or ten minutes so that my mother would think that my practice time was over before it was supposed to be.

"Also, as a young girl, I was a terrible liar. I felt very guilty about lying and I really wanted to tell the truth, but every time I opened my mouth to tell about something that had happened, I changed the facts just the tiniest bit to make them

more interesting. Then, as I went along, I changed things more and more until pretty soon what I was saying didn't have anything to do with the truth. Actually, if I just admitted I was a storyteller, then I wouldn't have had to be a liar, but I thought no one would listen to me if I didn't try to pass my stories off as things that really happened.

"In my childhood I was very interested in amazing things that really happened. For instance, I hated the ending of the 1939 movie *The Wizard of Oz* because Dorothy wakes up and her journey to Oz was only a dream. It was very important to me that Dorothy *REALLY* went to Oz. I have always been a big reader, and I was disappointed by most movies or television programs that dramatized books I had read. The shows always left some of the very best stuff out or made the characters act in a way they would not have in the book.

"Ever since I can remember, words have poured out of me. Writing was a part of the way I played as a child. I wrote plays and made my schoolmates act them out. I wrote textbooks to play school with the neighborhood kids. I wrote to pen pals and in my journals. I made up stories and gave some of them to my friends in weekly installments. At eighteen, I wrote all the words and the music for a musical. It wasn't very good. By age twenty-three, I had written five hundred poems—enough to know that I would never be a poet. All this time, I never thought of myself as a writer. I was a musician. Writing was fun. More than that, it was a compulsion. I thought everyone used writing like I did—to set their heads straight.

"I also did a lot of jock things as a kid. I water-skied and snow-skied; played tennis, golf, softball, and volleyball; rode my bike; and swam competitively. I didn't get good grades in school unless I was interested in the subject, or the teacher made the subject interesting to me. When it came time for me to go to college, of course, still wanting to be a great pianist, I majored in music, and then I did get good grades. I learned how to practice, and sometimes I would work at it six or more hours a day. I thought it was absolutely wonderful that I could play and listen and learn about music all day long and pass it off as going to school.

"In college I decided I also wanted to be a great bicycle racer. One day in graduate school I raced my bike twenty-five miles in the morning and competed in a piano concerto competition at night. In the bike race I went slow because I was afraid I would fall and break my wrist and be unable to play the piano that night. During the concerto competition, I couldn't put too much energy into my performance, because I was too tired from racing my bike. This is called being a jack-of-all-trades and master of none. Actually, I wouldn't have won the bike race or the concerto competition no matter what I did, because there were always people around who rode faster and played better than I.

"In fact, it became apparent to me early on that I would not be a great pianist. Sometimes that made me very sad. But I decided being a pretty good pianist was better than not being one at all, so I kept practicing. I also liked learning everything I could about music, especially about the music that I played.

"At the end of six years of college, when I was handed a piece of paper that said I was a master of music, I must admit I was very disappointed. I didn't know then that a 'master's degree' was just words people made up to call a secondary degree something. I know now to be a master of anything you have to spend your whole life working very hard at it. Back then, though, I truly thought I would be able to play the piano like a master and, since I couldn't, I thought all my hard work had come to nothing. I changed directions in life. I still raced bikes and I still played and taught piano, but I also began trying to write for publication. My first articles were about bike racing and were published in *Competitive Cycling, Bike World,* and *Bicycling.*

"I tried to write a novel and it turned out terrible. Then I tried to write another novel and it was terrible, too. And then I wrote another novel that was just awful, not quite terrible. Since then, I've fixed it up some. All of this was okay by me. To be a good writer you have to be a terrible one first. Just like everything else, writing takes practice. When I was writing my fourth novel, I made part of it into a short story that was published by the *New Yorker.* A few of my other stories were published, too, in *Seventeen* and other magazines.

"I married a composer, Timothy Lynch, and I had two babies. I found I couldn't write stories and take care of babies at the same time because to write fiction you have to build an imaginary world all around you and leave the real one behind. It's easy to lose track of time that way. I was afraid while I was in my imaginary world one of my babies might drown in the toilet—babies do that, you know, if their legs get stuck up in the air. So I kept checking on them to make sure they were okay. When I did that, my imaginary world would dissolve. After that happened about six times in twenty minutes, it got frustrating.

"I sort of gave up writing for a while then. I missed it terribly, but I kept telling myself I could get back to it when my kids

In books such as *American Music Makers,* Nichols combines the two things she loves most—music and writing.

were old enough to go to school. I played with them, and I read to them a lot. I got so interested in children's books that I started reading ahead—books that my children weren't old enough to sit still for. I started reading books about music; then I decided to write one. Nonfiction is something I can pick up and put down easily. In between sentences, I can change a diaper, get a glass of juice, read a child a book, and never have to worry that I'm going to forget what I was going to write next because, unlike the imaginary world, facts don't go away when I stop thinking about them.

"This is the way a most wonderful and amazing thing accidentally happened to me. Music, the thing I love the most, and writing, the thing that comes most naturally to me, came together in one career. I never dreamed I could be so lucky or so happy as an adult. I thought for sure it was all downhill after age thirteen.

"One of my books, *American Music Makers,* about American composers, has been published. I'm working on my second one, *Women Music Makers,* which will be published in 1992. I want to write many more books about music for children—I'm sticking with kids on this because adults don't bother to read such things. I'd also like to write more stories for all ages, as soon as this lump of baby snoozing on my lap grows big enough to trudge off to kindergarten."

*   *   *

NORDTVEDT, Matilda 1926-

PERSONAL: Born November 27, 1926, in Bellingham, WA; daughter of Sven (a mill worker) and Ethel (a homemaker; maiden name, Hansen) Kivley; married Tom Nordtvedt (a pastor and real estate agent), April 29, 1949; children: Tim, Joel, Mark. *Education:* Attended Prairie Bible Institute. *Religion:* Lutheran Brethren.

CAREER: Teacher and missionary in Japan, 1951-59; freelance writer, 1962—.

MEMBER: Washington Christian Writers' Fellowship.

AWARDS, HONORS: Special recognition award from Warm Beach Christian Writers and Speakers Conference, 1984.

WRITINGS:

All Things, Even Frisky (juvenile), Moody, 1973.
Take a Break (juvenile), Moody, 1973.
The Vanishing Act and Other Stories (juvenile), Moody, 1974.
Defeating Despair and Depression, Moody, 1975, reprinted as *How to Overcome Depression,* 1986.
Fat Alfie and the Feather Caper (juvenile), Moody, 1975.
No Longer a Nobody (juvenile), Moody, 1976.
Jeff and the Case of the Missing Uncle, Moody, 1978.
Living Beyond Depression, Bethany House, 1978.
(With Pearl Steinkuehler) *Showers of Blessing,* Moody, 1980.
(With Steinkuehler) *Something Old, Something New,* Moody, 1981.
(With Steinkuehler) *Something Borrowed, Something Blue,* Moody, 1981.
Daddy Isn't Coming Home (juvenile), Zondervan, 1981.
(With Steinkuehler) *Women's Programs for Every Season,* Moody, 1982.

(With Steinkuehler) *Ideas for Junior High Leaders,* Moody, 1983.
(With Steinkuehler) *Programs for Special Occasions,* Moody, 1984.
The Family Idea Book, Moody, 1984.
Ladybugs, Bees, and Butterfly Trees (juvenile), Bethany House, 1985.
Pilgrim Boy (juvenile), A Beka Books, 1987.
Secret in the Maple (juvenile), A Beka Books, 1987.
Read and Think Skill Sheets (juvenile), A Beka Books, 1987.

Columnist for *Gospel Herald.* Contributor of more than two thousand articles and stories to magazines.

FOR MORE INFORMATION SEE:

BOOKS

Contemporary Authors, Volume 124, Gale, 1988.

* * *

NYSTROM, Carolyn 1940-

PERSONAL: Born May 22, 1940, in West Union, OH; daughter of Wilbur N. (a factory worker) and Ada (a homemaker; maiden name, Musser) Abbott; married J. Roger Nystrom (a junior high school mathematics teacher), August 26, 1961; children: Sheri, Lori, Randy, Craig. *Education:* Wheaton College, B.A., 1962. *Politics:* Independent. *Religion:* Evangelical Presbyterian. *Hobbies and other interests:* Quilting, gardening.

ADDRESSES: Home—38 West 566 Sunset, St. Charles, IL 60174. *Office*—Curtis Bruce Agency, 3015 Evergreen Dr., Plover, WI 54467.

CAREER: Ohio Soldiers' and Sailors' Orphans' Home, Xenia, part-time house parent and playground supervisor, 1958-62; teacher of second grade at public elementary schools in Glendale Heights, IL, 1962-67, and Elmhurst, IL, 1970-73; writer, 1974—.

AWARDS, HONORS: What Happens When We Die? was named best children's book of the year by Christian Booksellers Association, 1982; *Mike's Lonely Summer* was named best children's book of the year by Christian Bookseller's Convention, 1987.

WRITINGS:

FOR CHILDREN

I Learn about the Bible, Creation House, 1977.
Before I Was Born, illustrated by Dwight Walles, Crossway, 1984.
I Learn to Trust God (part of "Christian Character Builder" series), Moody, 1990.
I Learn to Tell the Truth (part of "Christian Character Builder" series), Moody, 1990.
I Learn to Obey Rules (part of "Christian Character Builder" series), Moody, 1990.
I Learn to Love My Enemies (part of "Christian Character Builder" series), Moody, 1990.
The Lark Who Had No Song, illustrated by Lori McElrath-Eslick, Lion, 1991.

CAROLYN NYSTROM

"CHILDREN'S BIBLE BASICS" SERIES; ILLUSTRATED BY WAYNE HANNA; PUBLISHED BY MOODY, EXCEPT AS NOTED

Angels and Me, Creation House, 1978, revised edition, Moody, 1984.
Who Is God?, 1980.
Who Is Jesus?, 1980.
The Holy Spirit in Me, 1980.
What Is Prayer?, 1980.
Why Do I Do Things Wrong?, 1981.
What Is a Christian?, 1981.
What Is the Church?, 1981.
What Happens When We Die?, 1981.
What Is the Bible?, 1982.
Growing Jesus' Way, 1982.
Jesus Is No Secret, 1983.

FOR CHILDREN; "LION CARE" SERIES; PUBLISHED BY LION

Mike's Lonely Summer: A Child's Guide through Divorce, illustrated by Ann Baum, 1986.
Mario's Big Question: Where Do I Belong; A Child's Guide through Adoption, illustrated by A. Baum, 1987.
Jenny and Grandpa: What Is It Like to Be Old?, illustrated by Shirley Bellwood, 1988.
The Trouble with Josh: What Is It Like to Be Different?, illustrated by Gary Rees, 1989.
Emma Says Goodbye, 1990.

FOR TEENS; "YOUNG FISHERMAN" SERIES; WORKBOOKS, WITH TEACHER'S GUIDES; PUBLISHED BY HAROLD SHAW

Mark: God on the Move, 1978.
Acts 1-12: Church on the Move, 1979.

(With Margaret Fromer) *Acts: Missions Accomplished,* 1979.
Romans: Christianity on Trial, 1980.
(With M. Fromer) *James: Roadmap for Down-to-Earth Christians,* 1982.
At the Starting Line: Beginning New Life, 1985.
(With Matthew Floding) *Relationships: Face to Face,* 1986.
(With M. Floding) *Who Am I? A Look in the Mirror,* 1987.
(With M. Floding) *Sexuality: God's Good Idea,* 1988.

FOR ADULTS

Compass for a Dark Road: Letters of Peter and Jude (part of "LifeGuide" series), Inter-Varsity Press, 1991.
Sharing Your Faith (part of "Discipleship" series), Zondervan, in press.
Knowing Scripture (part of "Discipleship" series), Zondervan, in press.

FOR ADULTS; "WORKSHOP" SERIES; PUBLISHED BY ZONDERVAN, EXCEPT AS NOTED

(With M. Fromer) *A Woman's Workshop on James: With Suggestions for Leaders,* 1980.
A Woman's Workshop on Romans (student's guide and leader's manual), 1981, student's guide published as *Workshop on Romans,* 1991.
A Woman's Workshop on David and His Psalms: With Helps for Leaders, 1982, published as *Workshop on David and His Psalms,* 1989.
New Life: A Woman's Workshop on Salvation with Helps for Leaders, Zondervan, 1983, revised edition published as *Basic Beliefs: A Woman's Workshop on the Christian Faith,* Lamplighter Books, 1986, published as *Workshop on the Christian Faith,* 1989.

In books such as *Angels and Me*, Nystrom hopes to show readers the connection between life and faith. (Cover illustration by Wayne A. Hanna.)

Characters and Kings: A Woman's Workshop on the History of Israel; Parts 1 and 2, 1985.
(With M. Fromer) *People in Turmoil: A Woman's Workshop on First Corinthians; With Helps for Leaders,* 1985, published as *Workshop on First Corinthians,* 1991.
Behold Your Christ: A Woman's Workshop on Jesus; With Helps for Leaders, 1986.
Who Is Jesus? A Woman's Workshop on the Gospel of Mark, 1987, published as *Workshop on Mark,* 1989.
Workshop on the Gospel of John, 1989.

FOR ADULTS; "CHRISTIAN CHARACTER" SERIES; PUBLISHED BY INTER-VARSITY PRESS

Loving God, in press.
Living in the World, in press.
Finding Contentment, in press.
Loving Each Other, in press.
Seeking Holiness, in press.

OTHER

Forgive Me If I'm Frayed around the Edges, Moody, 1977, published as *Fostering No Illusions,* Scripture Union, 1979.
Lord, I Want to Have a Quiet Time: Learning to Study the Bible for Yourself, Christian Herald, 1981, revised edition published by Harold Shaw, 1984, revised edition published as *Meeting with God,* 1991.
Borning Chamber, Inter-Varsity Press, in press.

Some of Carolyn Nystrom's works have been translated into Afrikaans, Chinese, Finnish, German, Japanese, Malay, Norwegian, Spanish, and Swedish.

WORK IN PROGRESS: Three books, tentatively titled *End Times and Heaven, New Testament Characters,* and *Loving the World.*

SIDELIGHTS: Carolyn Nystrom told *SATA:* "I first began writing when my husband and I became foster parents. For two years we took in young children, often babies, who were the victims of child abuse. I felt frustrated, angry, and often helpless—not to mention busy (we took three babies at a time added to our own two school-age girls). Between babies, I began to jot on paper this mixture of feelings along with some of what I was learning. These jottings, originally a longish letter to my mother, became my first book: *Forgive Me If I'm Frayed around the Edges.*

"Once things quieted down a bit—we adopted two of the babies who were not able to go back home—I took up writing as a part-time job that mixes well with home and family. So I work part time during the school year—about twenty hours a week. But summer is a favorite time for all of us. My husband, Roger, takes over the housework, complete with laundry, cooking, and chauffeuring, while I hole up in the air-conditioned quiet of a library study room generously provided by Wheaton College. There I accomplish half of my work schedule for the entire year.

"Why do I write for children? Like my first book, my children's books grew, at first, out of my own needs. I once called our son Craig, 'my small boy with big questions.' When he asked, 'How can God see in the dark? Does God speak English or Spanish? What will happen to me when I die?' I sputtered through answers I sort of knew—but I knew them in seminary language. Other parents must hear the same questions, I thought, and they need to treat those questions with the respect they deserve. So I wrote the Moody Press twelve-book series on basic doctrines of the Christian faith—in a child's language.

"Why do I write about religious subjects? I believe that faith, properly lived out, pervades all of life. If God is sovereign over all creation, as Scripture teaches, and if Jesus is *Lord* of His people, then no area of life remains untouched from that influence. I hope, in my writing, to help readers forge links between faith and all of life."

*   *   *

ODAGA, Asenath (Bole) 1938-
(Kituomba)

PERSONAL: Born July 5, 1938, in Rarieda, Kenya; daughter of Blasto Akumu Aum (a farmer and catechist) and Patricia Abuya Abok (a farmer); married James Charles Odaga (a manager), January 27, 1957; children: Odhiambo Odongo, Akelo, Adhiambo, Awuor. *Education:* University of Nairobi, B.A. (with honors) and Dip.Ed., both 1974, M.A., 1981. *Religion:* Protestant. *Hobbies and other interests:* Reading, photography, music, cooking, walking, painting, collecting traditional costumes and other artifacts of Kenyan people.

ADDRESSES: Home and office—P.O. Box 1743, Kisumu, Kenya.

CAREER: Church Missionary Society's Teacher Training College, Ngiya, Kenya, teacher, 1957; Kambare School, Kenya, teacher, 1957-58; Butere Girls School, Kakamega, Kenya, 1959-60; Nyakach Girls School, Kisumu district, Kenya, headmistress, 1961-63; Kenya Railways, Nairobi, Kenya, assistant secretary, 1964; Kenya Dairy board, Nairobi, assistant secretary, 1965-66; Kenya Library Services, Nairobi, secretary, 1967; *East African Standard,* Nairobi, advertising assistant, 1968; Kerr Downey and Selby Safaris, Nairobi, office manager, 1969-70; Christian Churches Educational Association, Nairobi, assistant director of curriculum development, 1974-75; University of Nairobi, Institute of African Studies, Nairobi, research fellow, 1976-81; free-lance researcher, writer, and editor, 1982-91. Manager of Thu Tinda Bookshop and Lake Publishers and Enterprises Ltd., both 1982-91; affiliated with Odaga & Associates (consulting firm), 1984-91. Chairperson of the board of governors of Nyakach Girls High School; Museum Management Committee, Kisumu, member and vice-chairperson, 1984-90.

MEMBER: International Board on Books for Young People (member of executive committee, 1990-92), Writers' Association of Kenya (founding member and member of executive committee, 1990-91), Children's Literature Association of Kenya (chairperson, 1988—), Kenya Women's Literature Group (chairperson, 1987-91), Kenya Association of University Women (chairperson of Kisumu chapter, 1983-87), Kenya Business and Professional Women's Club (past chairperson), Rarieda Women's Group, Akala Women's Group (patron).

AWARDS, HONORS: Best Story award, *Voice of Women* magazine, 1967, for short story, "The Suitor," and play, *Three Brides in an Hour.*

WRITINGS:

FOR CHILDREN

The Secret of Monkey the Rock, illustrated by William Agutu, Thomas Nelson, 1966.

ASENATH ODAGA

Jande's Ambition, illustrated by Adrienne Moore, East African Publishing, 1966.

The Diamond Ring, illustrated by A. Moore, East African Publishing, 1967.

The Hare's Blanket and Other Tales, illustrated by A. Moore, East African Publishing, 1967.

The Angry Flames, illustrated by A. Moore, East African Publishing, 1968.

Sweets and Sugar Cane, illustrated by Beryl Moore, East African Publishing, 1969.

The Villager's Son, illustrated by Shyam Varma, Heinemann Educational (London), 1971.

Kip on the Farm, illustrated by B. Moore, East African Publishing, 1972.

(Editor with David Kirui and David Crippen) *God, Myself, and Others* (Christian religious education), Evangel, 1976.

Kip at the Coast, illustrated by Gay Galsworthy, Evans, 1977.

Kip Goes to the City, illustrated by Galsworthy, Evans, 1977.

Poko Nyar Mugumba (title means "Poko Mugumba's Daughter"), illustrated by Sophia Ojienda, Foundation, 1978.

Thu Tinda: Stories from Kenya, Uzima, 1980.

The Two Friends (folktales), illustrated by Barrack Omondi, Bookwise (Nairobi), 1981.

Kenyan Folk Tales, illustrated by Margaret Humphries, Humphries (Caithness, Scotland), 1981.

(With Kenneth Cripwell) *Look and Write Book One,* Thomas Nelson, 1982.

(With Cripwell) *Look and Learn Book Two,* Thomas Nelson, 1982.

Ange ok Tel (title means "Regret Never Comes First"), illustrated by Joseph Odaga, Lake Publishers & Enterprises (Kisumu), 1982.

My Home Book One, Lake Publishers & Enterprises, 1983.

Ogilo Nungo Piny Kirom (title means "Ogilo, the Arms Can't Embrace the Earth's Waist"), illustrated by Henry Kirui Koske, Heinemann Educational (Nairobi), 1983.

Nyamgondho Whuod Ombare (title means "'Nyamgondho, the Son of Ombare' and Other Stories"), illustrated by J. Odaga, Lake Publishers & Enterprises, 1986.

Munde and His Friends, illustrated by Peter Odaga, Lake Publishers & Enterprises, 1987.
The Rag Ball, illustrated by J. Odaga, Lake Publishers & Enterprises, 1987.
Munde Goes to the Market, illustrated by P. Odaga, Lake Publishers & Enterprises, 1987.
Weche, Sigendi gi Timbe Luo Moko (title means "Stories and Some Customs of the Luo"), Lake Publishers & Enterprises, 1987.
Story Time (folktales), Lake Publishers & Enterprises, 1987.
The Silver Cup, Lake Publishers & Enterprises, 1988.
A Night on a Tree, Lake Publishers & Enterprises, 1991.
Ogilo and the Hippo, Heinemann, 1991.

OTHER

Nyathini Koa e Nyuolne Nyaka Higni Adek (title means "Your Child from Birth to Age Three"), Evangel, 1976.
Miaha (five-act play; title means "The Bride"), first produced in Nairobi, 1981.
(With S. Kichamu Akivaga) *Oral Literature: A School Certificate Course,* Heinemann Educational (Nairobi), 1982.
Simbi Nyaima (four-act play; title means "The Sunken Village"; first produced in Kisumu, 1982), Lake Publishers & Enterprises, 1983.
Nyamgondho (four-act play), first produced in Kisumu, 1983.
Yesterday's Today: The Study of Oral Literature, Lake Publishers & Enterprises, 1984.
The Shade Changes (fiction), Lake Publishers & Enterprises, 1984.
The Storm, Lake Publishers & Enterprises, 1985.
Literature for Children and Young People in Kenya, Kenya Literature Bureau (Nairobi), 1985.
Between the Years (fiction), Lake Publishers & Enterprises, 1987.

Rapemo quietly explained to the dwarfs how he had come to their home. (From *The Diamond Ring,* by Odaga, illustrated by Adrienne Moore.)

A Bridge in Time (fiction), Lake Publishers & Enterprises, 1987.
Riana (fiction), Lake Publishers & Enterprises, 1987.
A Taste of Life, Lake Publishers & Enterprises, 1988.
Love Potion, A Reed on the Roof, Block Ten, with Other Stories, Lake Publishers & Enterprises, 1988.
(Contributor) Woffram Frommlet, editor, *African Radio Plays,* Nomos, 1991.

Contributor, sometimes under the name Kituomba, to periodicals, including *Women's Mirror* and *Viva.* Member of editorial committee of Western Kenya branch of Wildlife Society.

WORK IN PROGRESS: Wat Ng'ue, a book of fiction in Luo; a Luo-English dictionary; an African recipe book; research on women in oral literature, women's groups and their economic role in the advancement of women's powers, Luo oral literature, and Luo sayings.

SIDELIGHTS: Asenath Odaga told *SATA:* "I love and enjoy writing for children because, through my writing, I'm able to escape with them into the simple make believe world I create in their books. I also love to share my thoughts and experience with my younger readers, especially when I go out to meet and talk to them.

"'Please tell us something about your childhood which you still remember clearly,' I often get asked. Well, I remember a host of things from my childhood, which was a very happy one. I recall the warm moon-bathed nights when we sat around the fire and listened to our grandmother's stories, or when we sat around the fire after supper, sang, and laughed as we shelled groundnut or maize for our parents. I remember, too, when I became top of my class, and my teacher made my classmates carry me around our classroom two times. That was all the reward I ever received for taking first position all those years! There was also that morning I woke up late and found that a pack of hungry hyenas had broken into Baba's sheep pen and had killed over thirty sheep! And I had slept through it all! I never wanted to fall asleep again!

"When I write for children I always set loose my imagination and allow it to run wild, creating a secret make believe world into which I love to roam with my young readers."

*   *   *

OLSON, Arielle North 1932-

PERSONAL: Born January 11, 1932, in Chicago, IL; daughter of Sterling (an author and literary editor) and Gladys (an editor; maiden name, Buchanan) North; married Clarence E. Olson (a literary editor), September 4, 1954; children: Randall, Christina, Jens. *Education:* Swarthmore College, B.A., 1953.

ADDRESSES: Home—236 North Elm Ave., Webster Groves, MO 63119.

CAREER: Morristown Daily Record, Morristown, NJ, feature writer, 1953-54; *St. Louis Post-Dispatch,* St. Louis, MO, children's book reviewer, 1969—; writer. Free-lance editor of manuscripts.

MEMBER: Sterling North Society, Ltd. (board member).

ARIELLE NORTH OLSON

AWARDS, HONORS: Second place in juvenile division, Friends of American Writers, 1988, for *The Lighthouse Keeper's Daughter.*

WRITINGS:

Hurry Home, Grandma!, illustrated by Lydia Dabcovich, Dutton, 1984.
The Lighthouse Keeper's Daughter, illustrated by Elaine Wentworth, Little, Brown, 1987.

Hurry Home, Grandma! has been published in France, Italy, Spain, and Great Britain.

WORK IN PROGRESS: A book about Noah's ark, illustrated by Barry Moser, publication by Orchard expected in 1992.

SIDELIGHTS: Arielle North Olson told *SATA:* "I can remember going to sleep at night with the clickety-clack of typewriter keys down the hall. My dad, Sterling North, was the literary editor of the *Chicago Daily News,* but evenings and weekends he wrote his own books—and that's what I wanted to do when I grew up. He encouraged me to make up stories long before I entered school. Then he typed them and put them in a notebook, so I felt as if I were writing books, too. And the stories he told us at bedtime—they were wonderful—particularly the ones about the pet raccoon he had when he was a child. In later years, he retold those stories in *Rascal,* a runner-up for the Newbery Medal.

"So there I was, growing up in a household centered on books. They overflowed our bookcases. They were discussed at the dinner table. And they sprang forth from my dad's typewriter.

"After college I began writing feature stories for a newspaper—and my dad took me under his wing. Within months he taught me more about writing than I had learned in all my years in school. He was a tough but loving mentor, encouraging me to red-pencil my copy as vigorously as he did. At first I didn't appreciate his intensity. But I soon realized how deeply he cared about my writing—and how much I had to learn.

"My dad's help was invaluable—particularly his insistence on rewriting. As a child I was amazed when my dad rewrote a difficult chapter twenty-seven times—from scratch! But now that I'm an author, I realize the importance of setting standards you can barely attain, of forcing yourself to the very limits of your capability.

"In *The Green and Burning Tree: On the Writing and Enjoyment of Children's Books,* the renowned Eleanor Cameron pinpoints three essential qualities for an author: 'Purpose (which engenders self-discipline), giftedness and energy.' I would like to add to that list. A writer also needs courage—the courage to continue writing, day after day, despite publishers' rejections—the courage to face his own inadequacies and grow when given constructive criticism.

"One of my chief regrets is that my dad died before I wrote my first book, *Hurry Home, Grandma!* But his influence continues. I can still feel his presence over my shoulder, urging me on. My dad would have called *Hurry Home, Grandma!* 'a finger exercise'—something that comes easily and quickly. As soon as I decided to write about a grandmother having trouble getting home for Christmas, the rest fell into place—even the characterization of the grandmother. I patterned her after all the spunky women in my own family. (Though I must admit that none of them ever got stuck in a jungle.)

"My second book was partly inspired by something my dad read aloud years ago. He was reading about the coast of Maine and shared a few paragraphs with us—about a rocky island where winter storms washed away every speck of dirt. But the lighthouse keeper wanted to plant a garden, so each spring fishermen brought fresh soil to tuck into the cracks and crevices. Just imagine having to replace the dirt each year! I remembered this for decades.

"Then I came across an exciting snippet of history—about a girl who lived in a wave-swept lighthouse in the mid-1800s. And I realized I had the framework for *The Lighthouse Keeper's Daughter.* I immersed myself in books about lighthouses, storms at sea, life in Maine more than a century ago—and I remembered anecdotes about my own ancestors. Research supplied authentic details. Then I let my imagination run free, filling in the unknowns with elements of my own experience.

"Our family's love of books was balanced by our love of nature—listening for bird songs, picking up agates on Lake Superior beaches, hiking in the woods, watching deer on the hillside above our new home in New Jersey—it was a rich and wonderful childhood. And when I grew up, I was lucky to find another kindred spirit, my husband, Clarence Olson. He, too, is a literary editor of a newspaper, and he, too, loves the outdoors. Recently, we have been backpacking in the Rocky

Mountains—hiking just far enough to leave civilization behind. Even in mid-summer, a second spring awaits us at the high altitudes. We set up camp by cool mountain streams, delight in the aerial acrobatics of hummingbirds, and marvel at the profusion of wildflowers that take root in little pockets of soil between the rocks. The flowers remind me of those grown by Miranda in *The Lighthouse Keeper's Daughter*—such beauty blossoming forth from mere handfuls of soil.

"The clickety-clack of typewriters is no longer heard in our house—just muted clicks, as my husband and I write at our computers. But the family tradition continues down through the generations, with our three children and our three grandchildren equally appreciative of books and the natural world. Will they become authors, too, someday? I wouldn't be the least bit surprised."

*　　*　　*

OPTIC, Oliver
　　See STRATEMEYER, Edward L.

*　　*　　*

OTTO, Svend
　　See SOERENSEN, Svend Otto

*　　*　　*

PAGE, Eleanor
　　See COERR, Eleanor (Beatrice)

*　　*　　*

PALIN, Michael (Edward) 1943-
　　(Monty Python, a joint pseudonym)

PERSONAL: Born May 5, 1943, in Sheffield, Yorkshire, England; son of Edward (an engineer) and Mary Palin;

Michael Palin, who first earned fame as a Monty Python member, with one of his sons.

married Helen M. Gibbins, 1966; children: Tom, William, Rachel. *Education:* Brasenose College, Oxford, B.A. (second class honors), 1965. *Hobbies and other interests:* Reading, running, railways.

ADDRESSES: Office—c/o Python Pictures Ltd., 68A Delancey St., London NW1 7RY, England.

CAREER: Writer and performer for British Broadcasting Corp. (BBC), England, 1965-69, including in programs *The Frost Report,* beginning 1965, *Do Not Adjust Your Set,* c. 1968, and *The Complete and Utter History of Britain,* 1969; writer and performer, with Graham Chapman, John Cleese, Terry Gilliam, Eric Idle, and Terry Jones, in Monty Python comedy troupe, beginning 1969, in television series *Monty Python's Flying Circus,* 1969-74, in motion pictures *And Now for Something Completely Different,* 1972, *Monty Python and the Holy Grail,* 1975, *Monty Python's Life of Brian,* 1979, *Monty Python Live at the Hollywood Bowl,* 1982, and *Monty Python's The Meaning of Life,* 1984, and in concert tours in Britain, Canada, and the United States. Actor in films, including *Time Bandits,* 1981, *The Missionary,* 1982, *A Private Function,* 1984, *The Dress* (short film), 1984, *Brazil,* 1985, and *A Fish Called Wanda,* 1988, and on television programs, including *Ripping Yarns,* 1976-79, and *Saturday Night Live.*

AWARDS, HONORS: Silver Rose, Montreux Television Festival, 1971, for *Monty Python's Flying Circus;* Best Television Comedy Show of 1977, from press critics in Britain, and British Academy of Film and Television Arts (BAFTA) Award for Best Light Entertainment Program, 1979, both for *Ripping Yarns;* Grand Prix Special du Jury award, Cannes Film Festival, 1983, for *Monty Python's The Meaning of Life;* Michael Balcon Award for Outstanding British Contribution to Cinema (with Monty Python), BAFTA, 1987; BAFTA Award for best supporting actor, 1988, for *A Fish Called Wanda.*

WRITINGS:

(With Terry Jones) *The Complete and Utter History of Britain* (television series), London Weekend Television, 1969.
(With Jones) *Secrets* (teleplay), BBC-TV, 1973.
(With Jones) *Bert Fegg's Nasty Book for Boys and Girls,* Methuen, 1974, new revised edition published as *Dr. Fegg's Encyclopaedia of All World Knowledge,* Peter Bedrick, 1985.
(With Jones) *Their Finest Hours* (two short plays, *Underhill's Finest Hour* and *Buchanan's Finest Hour*), produced in Sheffield, England, 1976.
(With Jones) *Ripping Yarns* (television series; also see below), BBC-TV, 1976-77, 1979.
(With Jones) *Ripping Yarns* (stories; adapted from the television series), artwork by Walter Junge, photographs by Amy Lune and Bertrand Polo, Methuen, 1978, Pantheon, 1979.
(With Jones) *More Ripping Yarns* (stories; adapted from television series *Ripping Yarns*), Methuen, 1978, Pantheon, 1980.
(With Terry Gilliam) *Time Bandits,* Avco Embassy, 1981, published as *Time Bandits: The Movie Script,* Doubleday, 1981.
Small Harry and the Toothache Pills (for children), illustrated by Caroline Holden, Methuen, 1981.
The Missionary (screenplay), Handmade Films, 1982, published by Methuen, 1983.

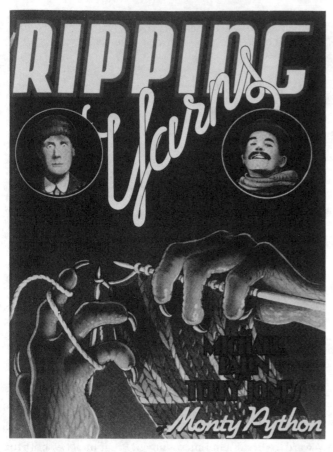

Ripping Yarns, by Palin and Terry Jones, is a collection of stories adapted from the television series of that name. (Cover illustration by Walter Junge.)

"Confessions of a Train-Spotter," *Great Railway Journeys of the World,* BBC-TV, 1983, published by Dutton, 1983.

Limericks (for children), illustrated by Tony Ross, Hutchinson, 1985, Random House, 1987.

(With Richard Seymour) *The Mirrorstone: A Ghost Story with Holograms* (for children), illustrations by Alan Lee, Knopf, 1986.

Cyril and the House of Commons (for children), illustrated by Holden, Pavilion, 1986.

Cyril and the Dinner Party (for children), illustrated by Holden, Pavilion, 1986.

East of Ipswich, BBC-TV, 1987.

Number 27, BBC-TV, 1988.

Around the World in Eighty Days? (travel documentary), BBC-TV, 1989, companion volume published by BBC Books, 1989.

Also contributor of articles to *New York* and *Esquire.*

CO-AUTHOR OF MONTY PYTHON SCREENPLAYS

And Now for Something Completely Different (adapted from *Monty Python's Flying Circus*), Columbia, 1972.

Monty Python and the Holy Grail (also see below), Cinema 5, 1975.

Monty Python's Life of Brian (also see below), Warner Brothers, 1979.

Monty Python Live at the Hollywood Bowl, Handmade Films/Columbia, 1982.

Monty Python's The Meaning of Life (also see below), Universal, 1983.

CO-AUTHOR OF MONTY PYTHON BOOKS

Monty Python's Big Red Book, edited by Eric Idle, Methuen, 1972, Warner Books, 1975.

The Brand New Monty Python Bok, edited by Idle, illustrations by Terry Gilliam (under pseudonym Jerry Gillian) and Peter Brookes, Methuen, 1973, published as *The Brand New Monty Python Papperbok,* Methuen, 1974.

Monty Python and the Holy Grail (also published as *Monty Python's Second Film: A First Draft*), both by Methuen, 1977.

Monty Python's Life of Brian [and] *Montypythonscrapbook,* edited by Idle, Grosset, 1979.

The Complete Works of Shakespeare and Monty Python: Volume One—Monty Python (contains *Monty Python's Big Red Book* and *The Brand New Monty Python Papperbok*), Methuen, 1981.

Monty Python's The Meaning of Life, Grove Press, 1983.

The Complete Monty Python's Flying Circus: All the Words, two volumes, Pantheon, 1989.

CO-AUTHOR OF OTHER MONTY PYTHON WORKS

Monty Python's Flying Circus (television series), BBC-TV, 1969-74, televised in United States, PBS-TV, 1974.

Pythons in Deutschland (television movie), Batavia Atelier, c. 1972.

Also co-author of scripts for records, including *Monty Python's Flying Circus,* 1970, *Another Monty Python Record,* 1971, *Monty Python's Previous Record,* 1972, *Monty Python Matching Tie and Handkerchief,* 1973, *Monty Python Live at the Theatre Royal, Drury Lane,* 1974, *The Album of the Soundtrack of the Trailer of the Film of Monty Python and the Holy Grail* (film soundtrack, includes additional material),

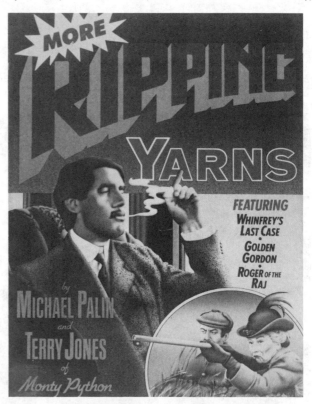

Like the first collection, the follow-up series, ***More Ripping Yarns,*** features satrirical stories of British pluck and adventure. (Cover illustration by Irving Freeman.)

1975, *Monty Python Live at City Center,* 1976, *The Worst of Monty Python,* 1976, *The Monty Python Instant Record Collection,* 1977, *Monty Python's Life of Brian* (film soundtrack), 1979, *Monty Python's Contractual Obligation Album,* 1980, *Monty Python's The Meaning of Life* (film soundtrack), 1983, and *Monty Python's the Final Ripoff* (compilation), 1988.

ADAPTATIONS: The film *Consuming Passions,* produced by Samuel Goldwyn and Euston Films in 1988, was based on the teleplay *Secrets* by Palin and Jones.

SIDELIGHTS: While best known as a founding member of the Monty Python comedy troupe, Michael Palin has also made a name for himself as an actor, screenwriter, and author of children's books. With the Pythons, Palin wrote and acted in the popular comedy television series *Monty Python's Flying Circus,* as well as three Python movies. He has brought the same unique sense of humor to his own books, television shows, and films as well. Some of these projects have involved working with individual members of Monty Python. He has written several television programs and plays with Terry Jones, and he co-starred in John Cleese's popular 1988 film *A Fish Called Wanda.*

One of Palin's most successful partnerships was *Time Bandits,* a film especially for children. Palin teamed up with another fellow-Python, Terry Gilliam, to write the script; he also had several cameos in the film. According to *New York Times* critic Vincent Canby, *Time Bandits* is "a cheerfully irreverent lark" about Kevin, a young boy whose bedroom is invaded by six time-travelling dwarfs. Using a map showing the holes in the universe, Kevin joins the bandits on a trip through time in search of riches and adventure. Along the way the group meets historical figures, such as Agamemnon, Robin Hood and Napoleon, and fantastic creatures, including an ogre, a giant, and the embodiment of Evil. This fantasy, says *Newsweek's* David Ansen, "is a teeming and original stew that stirs in many genres and moods," including "a childlike innocence" and "an earthy, satirical edge."

Other critics have also applauded the film. Gary Arnold of the *Washington Post* finds it "a sumptuous new classic in the tradition of time-travel and fairy-tale adventure." Comparing it to a children's classic, *Film Comment* writer Anne Thompson calls *Time Bandits* "the closest thing to a delicious fairy tale since *The Wizard of Oz.*" "*Time Bandits* is true invention, a [fertile] imagination at play," Ansen concludes in *Newsweek.* The film "is at once sophisticated and childlike in its magical but emotionally cool logic. . . . 'Time Bandits' is a wonderful wild card in the fall movie season." *Time Bandits* was the surprise hit of 1981, becoming one of the top-grossing films in the United States that year.

In 1981 Palin also published his first book for younger readers, *Small Harry and the Toothache Pills;* he has also written a volume of limericks. But in 1986 Palin brought out a truly unique children's book, *The Mirrorstone.* The book includes holograms—silvery, laser-created pictures that seem to move—among its illustrations. The story follows the adventures of Paul, a young boy who falls through his bathroom mirror into another world. There he is captured by an evil wizard, who forces him to journey under the sea to find a magic mirror. Paul's adventures "are fantastic enough to hold the interest of any child—even those who adore Indiana Jones and expect all stories to hold a thrill a minute," Edward Sorel comments in the *New York Times Book Review.* And while the holograms are attention-grabbing, "the

book is quite good enough not to need its gimmick," *Times Literary Supplement* reviewer Lachlan Mackinnon remarks. In addition, the critic notes, Palin's tale of Paul's journey and rescue is both "engrossing" and "emotionally engaging."

Palin has since written two more books for children, each featuring Cyril, a boy who can transform people into things just by looking at them. The actor and writer explained his interest in juvenile literature to Pat H. Broeske of the Hollywood *Drama-Logue:* "I've got three kids of my own. I'm also fairly childlike in my attitudes. I don't regard myself as a total grownup at all."

WORKS CITED:

Ansen, David, "A Merry, Scary Chase," *Newsweek,* November 9, 1981, p. 92.
Arnold, Gary, review of *Time Bandits, Washington Post,* November 6, 1981.
Broeske, Pat H., "Monty Python's Michael Palin," *Drama-Logue* (Hollywood), December 9-15, 1982, p. 17.
Canby, Vincent, review of *Time Bandits, New York Times,* November 6, 1981, section 3, p. 8.
Lodge, Sally A., "Michael Palin," *Publishers Weekly,* March 26, 1979, pp. 6-7.
Mackinnon, Lachlan, "Exotic Excursions," *Times Literary Supplement,* December 26, 1986, p. 1458.
Sorel, Edward, review of *The Mirrorstone, New York Times Book Review,* December 7, 1986, p. 77.
Thompson, Anne, *Film Comment,* November-December, 1981, pp. 49-54.

FOR MORE INFORMATION SEE:

BOOKS

Contemporary Literary Criticism, Volume 21, Gale, 1982.
Johnson, Kim Howard, *The First 200 Years of Monty Python,* St. Martin's, 1989.
Perry, George, *Life of Python,* Little, Brown, 1983.

PERIODICALS

America, September 15, 1979.
Chicago Tribune, September 21, 1979; April 1, 1983.
Face, March, 1985.
Globe and Mail (Toronto), December 13, 1986.
New Republic, Mary 24, 1975; November 29, 1982.
Newsweek, November 8, 1982.
New York, November 8, 1982.
New York Times, September 10, 1972; May 1, 1977; May 6, 1977; November 5, 1982; November 12, 1982.
New York Times Magazine, April 18, 1976.
Time, March 28, 1983.
Times (London), March 4, 1983.
Village Voice, May 5, 1975.*

*   *   *

PARADIS, Adrian A(lexis) 1912-

PERSONAL: Born November 3, 1912, in Brooklyn, NY; son of Adrian Frederick (a businessman) and Marjorie (Bartholomew) Paradis; married Grace Dennis, October 8, 1938; children: Steven, Joel, Andrea. *Education:* Dartmouth College, A.B., 1934; Columbia University, B.S., 1942. *Politics:* Democrat. *Hobbies and other interests:* Writing, mountain climbing.

ADRIAN A. PARADIS

ADDRESSES: Home—P.O. Box 653, Sugar Hill, NH 03585.

CAREER: In the hotel business, 1935-39. Chadbourne, Wallace, Parke & Whiteside, New York City, law librarian, 1940-42; American Airlines, Inc., New York City, assistant secretary, 1942-68; Ottaqueche Regional Planning Commission, VT, executive secretary, 1969-73, chairman, 1974-75; Phoenix Publishing Co., Sugar Hill, NH, editor, 1972—. Westchester County, NY, deputy director of Civil Defense, 1952-56.

MEMBER: American Society of Corporate Secretaries, American Personnel and Guidance Association, Authors League.

WRITINGS:

(With wife, Grace D. Paradis) *Grow in Grace* (daily spiritual readings), Abingdon, 1958.
Labor in Action: The Story of the American Labor Movement, Messner, 1963, revised edition, 1974.
Government in Action: How Our Federal Government Works, Messner, 1965.
Toward a Better World: The Growth and Challenge of Social Service, illustrations by Genia, McKay, 1966.
The Research Handbook: A Guide to Reference Sources, Funk, 1966.
Economics in Action Today, Messner, 1967.
The Hungry Years: The Story of the Great Depression, Chilton, 1967.
The Bulls and the Bears: How the Stock Exchange Works, illustrations by Alan Moyler, Hawthorn, 1967.
(With G. D. Paradis) *Your Life, Make It Count: A Guide for Young Americans,* Funk & Wagnalls, 1968.

Trade, the World's Lifeblood, illustrations by Moyler, Messner, 1969.
Gold: King of Metals, illustrations by Lorence F. Bjorklund, Hawthorn, 1970.
From Trails to Superhighways: The Story of America's Roads, illustrations by Russell Hoover, Messner, 1971.
How Money Works: The Federal Reserve System, Hawthorn, 1972.
The Labor Reference Book, Chilton, 1972.
International Trade in Action, Messner, 1973.
Inflation in Action, Messner, 1974.
(With Robert H. Wood) *Social Security in Action,* Messner, 1975.
(With G. D. Paradis) *The Labor Almanac,* Libraries Unlimited, 1983.
The Small Business Information Source Book, Betterway Publications, 1987.

VOCATIONAL GUIDES

75 Ways for Boys to Earn Money, Greenburg, 1950, revised edition published as *Dollars for You: 150 Ways for Boys to Earn Money,* illustrations by Genia, McKay, 1958.
Never Too Young to Earn: 101 Part Time Jobs for Girls, McKay, 1954.
For Immediate Release: Careers in Public Relations, McKay, 1955.
From High School to a Job, illustrations by Genia, McKay, 1956.
Americans at Work, illustrations by Genia, McKay, 1958.
Librarians Wanted: Careers in Library Service, McKay, 1959.
The New Look in Banking: Careers for Young Women in Finance, McKay, 1961.
Business in Action, Messner, 1962.
(With Betsy Burke) *The Life You Save: Your Career in Health,* McKay, 1962.
You and the Next Decade, illustrations by Genia, McKay, 1965.
Jobs to Take You Places—Here and Abroad: A Guide to Vocational Opportunities in Each of the Fifty States and Positions in Business, Government, and Voluntary Agencies Abroad, illustrations by Genia, McKay, 1968.
Job Opportunities for Young Negroes, illustrations by Genia, McKay, 1969.
Two Hundred Million Miles a Day, Chilton, 1969.
The Economics Reference Book, Chilton, 1970.
Reclaiming the Earth: Jobs That Help Improve the Environment, McKay, 1971.
Opportunities in Banking, Vocational Guidance Manuals (VGM) Career Horizons, 1980.
Opportunities in Airline Careers, VGM Career Horizons, 1981.
Opportunities in Transportation, VGM Career Horizons, 1983.
Planning Your Military Career, VGM Career Horizons, 1984.
Opportunities in Your Own Service Business, VGM Career Horizons, 1985.
Job Opportunities in the Twenty-first Century, VGM Career Horizons, 1986.
Planning Your Career of Tomorrow, VGM Career Horizons, 1986.
Opportunities in Part-Time and Summer Jobs, VGM Career Horizons, 1987.
Opportunities in Vocational and Technical Careers, VGM Career Horizons, 1987.
Opportunities in Transportation Careers, VGM Career Horizons, 1988.

Opportunities in Military Careers, VGM Career Horizons, 1989.
Opportunities in Cleaning Services Careers, VGM Career Horizons, 1992.

BIOGRAPHY

The Problem Solvers, Putnam, 1964.
Gail Borden: Resourceful Boy, illustrations by Nate Goldstein, Bobbs-Merrill, 1965.
Henry Ford, illustrations by Paul Frame, Putnam, 1967.
Harvey S. Firestone: Young Rubber Pioneer, illustrations by Fred M. Irvin, Bobbs-Merrill, 1968.
Ida Tarbell: Pioneer Woman Journalist and Biographer, Children's Press, 1985.

OTHER

(Editor) *PR Blue Book,* PR Publishing, 1970.
(Editor) *Who's Who in Public Relations,* PR Publishing, 1972.
(Editor, with G. D. Paradis) *International Stock and Commodity Exchange Directory,* Phoenix Publishing, 1974.

Contributor of articles to church publications and juvenile periodicals. Editor and consultant, public relations publications.

WORK IN PROGRESS: Where to Find It: A Guide to Locating and Gathering Information.

SIDELIGHTS: Adrian A. Paradis, whose mother Marjorie Paradis wrote children's books and taught writing courses, has written numerous books for young people on research, social studies, personal and vocational guidance, in addition to having penned the biographies of several important American business or historical figures. He once told *SATA:* "I dreamed that I was writing a book for boys on how to earn money. When I woke up I made a note of the idea and that day checked in the library to see if such a book had been done. It had not and so I wrote *75 Ways for Boys to Earn Money,* sent it to a publisher and a few weeks later learned that I was an author!. Because I was riding ninety miles a day on the train commuting to New York, I then decided to spend all my travel time writing for young people. . . . Before I choose a subject I try to discover what information young people need to help them with their choice of a career or in the preparation of their courses at school. Once I have chosen the topic, I check to make certain there are no other books on the subject. Then I do an outline and if a publisher agrees to give me a contract for the book, go to work."

In an essay for *Something about the Author Autobiography Series,* Paradis offers advice to prospective writers. First, he says, "Write, write, write. If you find you have a real urge but it seems impossible to express yourself properly on paper, wait until you are ready." Second, he adds, "Learn all you can about the type of writing you have chosen. You do this by obtaining appropriate books written by experts in your chosen field." And third, "Don't try at first to use your writing skills as a means of making a living. Keep it a hobby while you are learning. Then as you gradually place manuscripts with magazines or book publishers, take your time, keep a relaxed attitude. If you try too soon to make a livelihood from this craft, you may find you are not ready and that you destroy your muse."

WORKS CITED:

Something about the Author, Gale, Volume 1, 1971, p. 175.

Something about the Author Autobiography Series, Gale, Volume 8, 1989, pp. 211-225.

FOR MORE INFORMATION SEE:

PERIODICALS

Booklist, Novermber 1, 1967; November 15, 1967; December 15, 1967; March 15, 1969; April 15, 1971; July 15, 1971; May 1, 1972; November 15, 1972; April 15, 1973; October 15, 1973; January 15, 1974; May 15, 1975; November 15, 1975; September 1, 1984; March 15, 1986; July 1, 1986; July 1, 1987; September 1, 1987; November 15, 1987.
Library Journal, April 15, 1967; May 15, 1967; November 15, 1968; February 15, 1969; December 15, 1969; March 15, 1970; May 15, 1970; October 15, 1971; February 15, 1972; March 15, 1974; September 15, 1974; January, 1988.
New York Times Book Review, June 25, 1967.
Saturday Review, January 11, 1969.

*   *   *

PEARCE, Ann Philippa
See PEARCE, Philippa

*   *   *

PEARCE, Philippa 1920-
(Ann Philippa Pearce)

PERSONAL: Born 1920 in Great Shelford, Cambridgeshire, England; daughter of Ernest Alexander (a flour miller and corn merchant) and Gertrude Alice (Ramsden) Pearce; married Martin Christie (a fruitgrower), May 9, 1963 (died, 1965); children: Sarah. *Education:* Girton College, Cambridge, B.A., M.A. (with honors), 1942.

ADDRESSES: Home—Cambridge, England. *Office*—c/o Kestrel Books, Penguin Books Ltd., 536 King's Rd., London SW10 0UH, England.

CAREER: Writer, 1967—. Temporary civil servant, 1942-45; British Broadcasting Corp. (BBC), London, England, script writer and producer in school broadcasting department, 1945-58; Clarendon Press, Oxford, England, editor in educational department, 1959-60; Andre Deutsch Ltd., London, editor of children's books, 1960-67. Part-time radio producer, BBC, 1960-63.

MEMBER: Society of Authors.

AWARDS, HONORS: Carnegie Commendation, Library Association (England), 1956, for *Minnow on the Say,* 1978, for *The Shadow-Cage and Other Tales of the Supernatural,* and 1979, for *The Battle of Bubble and Squeak;* International Board on Books for Young People honour list selection, 1956, for *Minnow on the Say,* 1960, for *Tom's Midnight Garden,* and 1974, for *What the Neighbours Did and Other Stories;* Lewis Carroll Shelf Award, 1959, for *The Minnow Leads to Treasure,* and 1963, for *Tom's Midnight Garden;*

PHILIPPA PEARCE

Carnegie Medal, Library Association, 1959, for *Tom's Midnight Garden; New York Herald Tribune* Children's Spring Book Festival Award, 1963, for *A Dog So Small;* Whitbread Award, 1978, for *The Battle of Bubble and Squeak.*

WRITINGS:

UNDER NAME ANN PHILIPPA PEARCE

Minnow on the Say, Oxford University Press, 1954, reprinted under name Philippa Pearce, Puffin, 1979, published as *The Minnow Leads to Treasure,* World Publishing, 1958.
Tom's Midnight Garden, Lippincott, 1958, reprinted under name Philippa Pearce, Dell, 1979.
Still Jim and Silent Jim, Basil Blackwell, 1960.

UNDER NAME PHILIPPA PEARCE

Mrs. Cockle's Cat, Lippincott, 1961.
A Dog So Small, Constable, 1962, Lippincott, 1963.
(With Harold Scott) *From Inside Scotland Yard* (juvenile adaptation of Scott's *Scotland Yard*), Deutsch, 1963, Macmillan, 1965.
The Strange Sunflower, Thomas Nelson (London), 1966.
(With Brian Fairfax-Lucy) *The Children of the House,* Lippincott, 1968.
The Elm Street Lot, British Broadcasting Corp., 1969, enlarged hardcover edition, Kestrel, 1979.
The Squirrel Wife, Longman, 1971, Crowell, 1972.
(Adapter) *Beauty and the Beast,* Crowell, 1972.
(Editor and author of preface) *Stories from Hans Christian Andersen,* Collins, 1972.

What the Neighbours Did and Other Stories, Longman, 1972, published as *What the Neighbors Did and Other Stories,* Crowell, 1973.
Return to Air, Penguin, 1975.
The Shadow-Cage and Other Tales of the Supernatural, Crowell, 1977.
The Battle of Bubble and Squeak, Deutsch, 1978.
(Adapter) *Wings of Courage,* Kestrel, 1982.
A Picnic for Bunnykins, Viking, 1984.
Two Bunnykins Out to Tea, Viking, 1984.
Bunnykins in the Snow, Viking, 1985.
Lion at School and Other Stories, Greenwillow Books, 1985.
The Way to Sattin Shore, Viking, 1985.
Tooth Ball, Deutsch, 1987.
Fresh, Creative Education, 1987.
Who's Afraid?, and Other Strange Stories, Greenwillow Books, 1987.
Emily's Own Elephant, Macrae Books, 1987.
Freddy, Deutsch, 1988.
Old Belle's Summer Holiday, Deutsch, 1989.
Children of Charlecote, Gollancz, 1989.

OTHER

Editor of the first fourteen books in "People of the Past" social history series, 1961-64. Work is represented in anthologies, including *Another Six,* Basil Blackwell, 1959, *The Friday Miracle and Other Stories,* Puffin, 1969, and *Baker's Dozen,* Ward, Lock, 1974. Contributor of short stories to "Listening and Reading" radio series, BBC. Contributor of book reviews to periodicals.

SIDELIGHTS: Philippa Pearce enjoys a reputation as one of England's leading writers for children. Her novel *Tom's Midnight Garden* has been especially praised. John Rowe Townsend, speaking of *Tom's Midnight Garden* in his study *Written for Children: An Outline of English Children's Literature,* claims: "I have no reservations about it. If I were asked to name a single masterpiece of English children's literature since the last war . . . it would be this outstandingly beautiful and absorbing book." Similarly, W. L. Webb of the *Manchester Guardian* calls the novel "a rare, moving story, beautifully written, and true in every way that matters. . . . a modern classic."

Tom's Midnight Garden tells the story of a young boy who must spend the summer with his aunt and uncle in the country. At first bored with his surroundings, he soon learns that at midnight the backyard transforms into the Victorian garden that it was many years before. Every night in his dreams he explores the garden. One night he meets a little girl named Hatty and the two of them begin a series of explorations of the vast garden. Hatty begins to grow older while Tom remains the same age. At story's end, he discovers that the elderly woman who lives in the flat above his aunt and uncle is the girl Hatty he played with in the garden of her childhood.

The garden where Tom and Hatty meet is based on the garden Pearce played in as a girl. Her father was a miller and she lived in a mill house with a walled garden. "It is a beautiful early nineteenth-century house," Pearce tells Roni Natov and Geraldine DeLuca in *The Lion and the Unicorn.* "You see houses like it everywhere in East Anglia, farm houses and mill houses that correspond to a period of great agricultural prosperity, probably during the Napoleonic wars. My father was born in that house because my grandfather was also a miller. We moved in when I was very small; my grandfather died and we took over. This is the house and the garden with its sundial on the wall in *Tom's Midnight Garden.* The garden was absolutely the image of that walled garden in the book." Pearce now lives in a cottage across the street from the mill house.

The idea that characters can meet each other across time came to Pearce from a book by J. W. Dunne, *Experiment in Time.* Dunne theorizes that there are many times co-existing and yet able to blend together. "I never really understood it properly," Pearce admits in *Books for Keeps,* "but it was a sort of theoretical base for the book."

The story was meant to say something about the relationships between the young and the old too. Pearce tells Natov and DeLuca: "*Tom's Midnight Garden* was an attempt to reconcile childhood and old age, to bring them together." Speaking in *Books for Keeps,* she says the real impulse behind the book was "the feeling of time passing, people becoming old. Even though I wasn't old I could see that if you were old you hadn't been old forever."

Eventually Tom is unable to revisit the garden because he has grown too old for it. Hatty, too, cannot return. But when

***Tom's Midnight Garden* is a haunting story of time travel, embodying the idea that characters can meet each other across time.** (Cover illustration by Susan Einzig.)

Tom meets his aunt and uncle's neighbor, it is clear to him that she is Hatty grown up. For a brief moment the two friends are reunited. Townsend found "a profound, mysterious sense of time" in the story. Writing in *A Critical History of Children's Literature,* Ruth Hill Viguers claims that in *Tom's Midnight Garden,* "the idea that time has no barriers was embodied in nearly perfect literary form."

Much of Pearce's other fiction is also based on her own childhood. She writes in *Cricket:* "I was the youngest of four children. . . . We lived in a big, shabby, beautiful mill house by the river. We swam, fished, boated, skated. We always had a dog, and sometimes a cat—the business cat from the mill, who would knock off from catching rats and mice to visit us. When I grew up and went to London to work, I took with me all the places that I had loved. They turned up in the stories I was beginning to write. . . . I think there is no story I have ever written that didn't start from something in my own life."

Pearce works out the plots of her stories in her head. "I never write things down," she explains to Natov and DeLuca. "I don't keep a folder. I have never in my life kept a note of anything. I let ideas mill around in my head. Things begin to settle out like muddy water. Perhaps if I had kept notes I would have written more, I don't know." She does write down the story as it comes to her, though: "I do believe it is very useful to write down the actual words you think of. When I wake up in the night with just the right words, I write them down so as not to lose them."

WORKS CITED:

Books for Keeps, November, 1983, pp. 14-15.
Cricket, August, 1976, p. 35.
Natov, Roni and Geraldine DeLuca, "An Interview with Philippa Pearce," *The Lion and the Unicorn,* Volume 9, 1985, pp. 75-88.
Townsend, John Rowe, "The New Fantasy," *Written for Children: An Outline of English Children's Literature,* Lothrop, 1967, p. 128.
Viguers, Ruth Hill, "Golden Years and Time of Tumult: 1920-1967," *A Critical History of Children's Literature,* revised edition, Macmillan, 1969, pp. 477.
Webb, W. L., review of *Tom's Midnight Garden, Manchester Guardian,* December 5, 1958, p. 7.

FOR MORE INFORMATION SEE:

BOOKS

Blishen, Edward, editor, *The Thorny Paradise: Writers on Writing for Children,* Kestrel, 1975.
Butts, Dennis, editor, *Good Writers for Young Readers,* Hart-Davis, 1977.
Cameron, Eleanor, *The Green and Burning Tree: On the Writing and Enjoyment of Children's Books,* Little, Brown, 1969.
Children's Literature Review, Volume 9, Gale, 1985.
Crouch, Marcus, *Treasure Seekers and Borrowers: Children's Books in Britain, 1900-1960,* Library Association, 1962.
Crouch, Marcus, *The Nesbit Tradition: The CHildren's Novel in England, 1945-1970,* Ernest Benn Limited, 1972.
Eyre, Frank, *British Children's Books in the Twentieth Century,* revised edition, Dutton, 1973.
Fisher, Margery, *Intent Upon Reading: A Critical Appraisal of Modern Fiction for Children,* Hodder & Stoughton, 1961.

Rees, David, *The Marble in the Water: Essays on Contemporary Writers of Fiction for Children and Young Adults,* Horn Book, 1980.
Storr, Catherine, editor, *On Children's Literature,* Allen Lane, 1973.
Townsend, John Rowe, *A Sense of Story: Essays on Contemporary Writers for Children,* Lippincott, 1971.

PERIODICALS

Book World, May 7, 1972.
Children's Literature in Education, March, 1971; autumn, 1981.
Commonweal, May 23, 1958.
Growing Point, November, 1983; March, 1986; July, 1987.
Horn Book, April, 1958; April, 1978; June, 1984; May/June, 1987.
Kirkus, July 15, 1959.
New Statesman, November 15, 1958; May 18, 1962.
New York Herald Tribune Book Review, March 9, 1958; November 1, 1959.
New York Herald Tribune Books, May 12, 1963.
New York Times, May 4, 1958.
New York Times Book Review, November 1, 1959; March 12, 1972.

Saturday Review, August 23, 1958; May 11, 1963.
Signal, January, 1973; September, 1984.
Times Educational Supplement, September 30, 1983.
Times Literary Supplement, June 1, 1962; October 22, 1971; December 8, 1972; July 15, 1977; March 14, 1986.
The Use of English, spring, 1970.

*   *   *

PENNER, Fred (Ralph Cornelius) 1946-

PERSONAL: Born November 6, 1946, in Winnipeg, Manitoba, Canada; son of Edward William (an accountant) and Lydia (a homemaker; maiden name, Winter) Penner; married Odette Graziella Heyn (a homemaker, dancer, and choreographer), August 23, 1981; children: four. *Education:* University of Winnipeg, B.A., 1970. *Hobbies and other interests:* "Devoted husband and father," raising four children, photography, racquetball, skiing, canoeing.

ADDRESSES: Office—Oak Street Music, Suite 108, 93 Lombard Ave., Winnipeg, Manitoba, Canada R3B 3B1.

CAREER: Children's entertainer and television performer. Worked in residential treatment centers for children, 1969-72; toured with Kornstock (musical-comedy troupe), during 1970s; performed with Manitoba Theatre Workshop (now Prairie Theatre Exchange) and Rainbow Stage in numerous musicals and dramas, including *Pippin* in 1977, *The King and I* in 1978, *Death of a Salesman* in 1978, and *Hello, Dolly!* in 1979; resident-musician with wife, Odette Heyn-Penner, in Sundance (children's dance theatre company), 1977-79; host of *Fred Penner's Place* (filmed in Vancouver, British Columbia, Canada, and Winnipeg, Manitoba, Canada), Canadian Broadcasting Corporation, 1984—, and MTV/Nickelodeon (United States), 1989—. Oak Street Music (music publishing and recording label), Winnipeg, president, 1987. Guest on numerous television specials, telethons, and concert broadcasts, 1977—. Performs in festivals and concerts throughout the United States and Canada, including the Philadelphia International Theatre Festival for Children, 1987, Concert for Kids, Centennial Concert Hall, 1988, Universal Amphitheater, Wolf Trap Farm, and Lehman Centre for the Performing Arts. Keynote speaker for early childhood education conferences in the United States and Canada.

Recorded original compositions as well as traditional children's songs on albums, including *The Cat Came Back,* 1979; *Polka Dot Pony,* 1981; *Special Delivery,* 1983; *A House for Me,* 1985; *Fred Penner's Place,* 1988; *Collections,* 1989; *The Season,* 1990; and *Happy Feet,* 1991. Also performed on videos, including *The Cat Came Back* (live concert with the Cat's Meow Band), 1990, and *A Circle of Songs* (with Len Udow and others), 1991.

MEMBER: Actors Equity, American Federation of Musicians, Association of Canadian Television and Radio Artists.

AWARDS, HONORS: Juno award nominations (Canada), 1979 for *The Cat Came Back,* 1981 for *Polka Dot Pony,* 1983 for *Special Delivery,* 1986 for *A House for Me,* and 1990 for *The Season;* Juno award, 1988, for *Fred Penner's Place;* Parent's Choice Awards, Parent's Choice Foundation, 1983 for *Special Delivery,* 1986 for *A House for Me,* and 1989 for *Collections; The Cat Came Back* achieved Canadian gold certification status, 1985.

Philippa Pearce's *A Dog So Small* includes Antony Maitland's illustration of the West End on the afternoon of Christmas Eve.

FRED PENNER

WRITINGS:

BASED ON PENNER'S SONGS; INCLUDE MUSIC AND
  LYRICS

The Bump, illustrated by Barbara Hicks, Hyperion Press,
  1984.
Ebeneezer Sneezer, illustrated by Hicks, Hyperion Press,
  1985.
Rollerskating, illustrated by Hicks, Hyperion Press, 1987.
(With Sheldon Oberman) *Julie Gerond and the Polka Dot
  Pony,* illustrated by Alan Pakarnyk, Hyperion Press,
  1988.
Sing Along Play Along (contains songs from Penner's first
  four albums), illustrated by Hicks, McGraw, 1990.

SIDELIGHTS: Blending song, conversation, comedy, stories, and fun, Fred Penner entertains both children and adults
with his energetic musical performances. Music is a form of
communication for Penner; through it he spreads not only
joy but also knowledge about the world. He intermixes
different styles of music with tidbits on everything from the
habitats of animals to methods of fending off colds. "As a
parent and performer for young children," Penner remarked,
"I feel it is important to take advantage of the love that
children naturally have for music. It can be so much more
than simply background music; movement and song provide
a powerful impetus for learning."

Born in 1946 in the Canadian city of Winnipeg, Penner began
playing the guitar and singing as a high school student.
Thereafter he sang in choirs and folk groups and performed
in theatre while studying at the University of Winnipeg. After
graduating with a bachelor's degree in economics and psychology in 1970, Penner began working in residential treatment centers for children. Though many youths in the centers
were socially withdrawn, they came to life when Penner
played his guitar. "Music was able to cut through any of the
problems they were having," Penner told Jonathan Takiff in
the *Philadelphia Daily News.*

Penner was not wholly unfamiliar with using music as a form
of communication. His sister Susie, who had a form of mental
retardation called Down's syndrome and died at age twelve,
responded quite readily to music. As Penner related to
Starweek, "I gained more understanding about the importance of music through her than through any other human
being, because she loved music in the purest sense."

In search of the best way to use his talents, Penner began his
professional performing career as an actor in musicals and
dramas. He also toured with Kornstock, a musical comedy
troupe, and later became a musician in Sundance, his wife's
dance company for children. Beginning in 1977 Penner appeared on many television specials and concert broadcasts,
and in 1979 the music he created for a Sundance production
led to his first album, *The Cat Came Back.* Seven other
children's albums have followed, including 1983's *Special
Delivery* and 1985's *A House for Me,* all combining traditional music along with original songs. "Penner's picks all
have hummable tunes, focused lyrics with memorable cho-
ruses, and most display a positive moral tone—delivering
lessons about perseverance, self-confidence, tolerance, and
honest patriotism—without talking down to the listeners,"
judged Takiff in the *Philadelphia Daily News.*

Soon Penner was performing for capacity crowds throughout the United States and Canada and gaining recognition
for his exuberance, originality, and spontaneity. He frequently surprises his audiences with imaginative en-
trances—by speeding out atop a skateboard or by tossing a
series of frisbees across the stage before entering. Gaining full
audience participation is of prime importance to Penner, so
he mixes favorite sing-a-long tunes such as "Michael, Row
the Boat Ashore" and "Zip-a-dee-doo-dah" with well-
known original selections, including "Poco" and "A House
Is a House for Me." Between songs Penner engages everyone
in lively activities such as stretching exercises and audito-
rium-wide "waves." He also supervises unique projects—during one show he and his Cat's Meow Band formed
chickens from folded towels. "There is no doubt Penner
knows how to entertain kids in fine style," declared Gloria
Kelly in the *Halifax Herald* about one of Penner's concerts.
"They cheered when he came on stage and were still cheering
and clapping when his hour long show was finished."

Even more important to Penner, though, is sharing lessons
on values and morals with the children. This concern for his
young audience seems to influence his entire life. "The bottom line when working with children is the honesty and
integrity that you present an audience," Penner said in *TV
Guide,* "You must realize that a child learns from everything
you do. It's easy enough to get up on-stage and sing a couple
of songs, but that is not where it stops; it's a life commit-
ment."

In 1984 the Canadian Broadcasting Company asked Penner
to host its first children's television production in almost
twenty years. Penner, seeing an opportunity to provide an
alternative to the advertisement- and violence-filled programs often aired on children's television, accepted. Five
times a week on *Fred Penner's Place,* the host sings, plays his
guitar, and tells stories, all from his secret hiding place in the
woods. According to Sandy Greer in *Starweek,* Penner
travels to this secluded setting each program because children
like to have secret places where they feel protected. "That
journey captures the imagination," said Penner, "which is a
vital quality and feeling that I attempt to spark with children."

Although Penner considers himself primarily an entertainer, he has also branched out into writing. Since 1984 he has written four books for children, each based on an original song, and a song and activity book, *Sing Along Play Along.* Such books help children understand themselves and their individual potentials. Two works in particular, *Julie Gerond and the Polka Dot Pony* and *The Bump,* focus on inventiveness and self-worth. In the former, Julie Gerond thinks of a way to help her pony friend escape the spell of an evil woman. And the title character of *The Bump*—a knoll on the prairie—realizes his importance when a family chooses to build its home over him. "Many people I know including myself sort of feel like bumps, sometimes," Penner told Bradley Bird in the *Winnipeg Free Press.* "But we all aspire to other things, and until you find out where you are and what your foundation is, all those dreams will never be realized."

Through his albums, books, television show, and concerts, Penner inspires children to discover their dreams. He stimulates their imaginations by encouraging them to join with him—to sing along, solve his riddles, or act out lyrics to a song. And Penner never forgets that having fun is an integral part of learning, especially during his concerts. "The base is enjoyment and part of the fun is sharing a musical moment," Penner told Barbara S. Rothschild in the *New Jersey Courier-Post.* "At the end of the show, parents and children alike feel they've shared a positive musical experience."

Penner told *SATA:* "We all have opinions, thoughts, and ideas that turn around and around in our minds and sometimes come out in many wonderful ways: stories, music, pictures, etc. When someone sings you a song or reads you a book, that can help your feelings to start to grow and give your imagination an extra nudge.

"Sharing thoughts and ideas with others is what I do in my life. My own family helps me to discover new feelings all the time, and that way I learn what is important to me and what I would like to share with others. Through radio and TV we are able to see and hear people trying to express themselves to us. But there is so much to choose from; the hard part is deciding what we want to be part of our lives. That is where parents come in; our job is to make choices that will enrich the lives of our children."

WORKS CITED:

Bird, Bradley, "Actor-Musician Penner Writes Fantasy for Children," *Winnipeg Free Press,* December 12, 1984.
Greer, Sandy, "Fred's Music Hath Charms for Children: Fred Penner Takes Children to a Magical World Where He Believes in the Healing Power of Music," *Starweek* (Toronto), April 5-12, 1986.
Kelly, Gloria, "Penner Delights at Cohn," *Halifax Herald,* January 20, 1986.
"On the Town with Les Wiseman," *TV Guide* (Vancouver), October 31-November 6, 1987, p. 2.
Rothschild, Barbara S., "An Act for the Child in All of Us: Canadian Fred Penner Entertaining to Adults, Too," *New Jersey Courier-Post,* May 17, 1987.
Takiff, Jonathan, "Fred Penner: A Music Man for All Ages; Children's Festival Brings Him Here," *Philadelphia Daily News,* May, 1987.

FOR MORE INFORMATION SEE:

PERIODICALS

Ottawa Citizen, February 20, 1987; February 23, 1987.
Winnipeg Free Press, March 14, 1988.

Sketch by Denise E. Kasinec

*   *   *

PETRUCCIO, Steven James 1961-

PERSONAL: Born April 17, 1961, in Brooklyn, NY; son of Albert (an art director) and Marie (a secretary; maiden name, Trimboli) Petruccio; married Kathy Ann (a designer), September 13, 1986; children: Stephanie Marie. *Education:* School of Visual Arts, B.F.A., 1983. *Religion:* Roman Catholic. *Hobbies and other interests:* Fine art paintings, playing the guitar.

ADDRESSES: Home—6 Sycamore Ct., Fishkill, NY 12524.

CAREER: Free-lance illustrator for various clients.

MEMBER: Dutchess County Arts Association.

ILLUSTRATOR:

Mabel Watts, *Dr. Hilda Makes House Calls,* Golden Books, 1988.

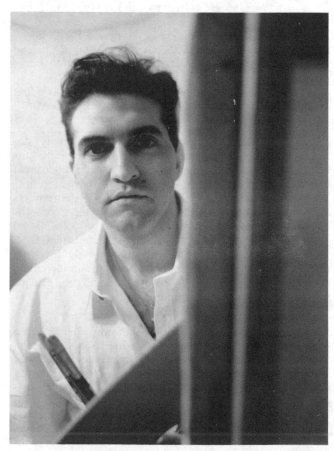

STEVEN JAMES PETRUCCIO

Marguerite Henry, *Misty: The Big Race,* Checkerboard
    Press, 1988.
Henry, *Misty: Going Home,* Checkerboard Press, 1988.
Henry, *Battle of the Stallions,* Checkerboard Press, 1988.
Henry, *Sire of Champions,* Checkerboard Press, 1988.
Elizabeth Smith, *A Service Dog Goes to School: The Story of a
    Dog Trained to Help the Disabled,* Morrow, 1988.
Rose Wyler, *Grass and Grasshoppers,* edited by Jane
    Steltenpohl, Silver Burdett, 1989.
Wyler, *Raindrops and Rainbows,* edited by J. Steltenpohl,
    Silver Burdett, 1989.
Wyler, *The Starry Sky,* edited by J. Steltenpohl, Silver
    Burdett, 1989.
Wyler, *Puddles and Ponds,* Silver Burdett, 1990.
Wyler, *Wonderful Woods,* Silver Burdett, 1990.
Wyler, *Seashore Surprises,* Silver Burdett, 1990.
Cathy East Dubowski, *Squanto: First Friend To the Pilgrims,*
    Dell, 1990.
Kate McMullan, *Harriet Tubman: Conductor of the Un-
    derground Railroad,* Dell, 1990.

WORK IN PROGRESS: A book about sea creatures for
Checkerboard Press; "working on four books I have written
and plan to illustrate, using Hudson Valley settings."

SIDELIGHTS: Steven James Petruccio told *SATA:* "I remember as a child in Brooklyn, sitting in front of my house
and drawing the tree that grew there. Drawing was a natural
way to pass the time in my home. My father would often work
at home at his drawing board and I would be there watching
as he did. He would show me how to draw something and I
would practice it. My brothers and I were often given pencil
and paper, and I recall filling page after page with drawings. I
would copy comic book characters and study anatomical
drawings until each detail was perfect.

"This process went on for years. In grammar school, my
older brother and I were always chosen to do school posters
and this was expected of my younger brother also. Throughout those years and in high school, I'd done many drawings
and had gotten very good at it. The high school which I
attended offered no art education courses, so I continued to
draw on my own. I would look at books about various artists
and study their works. Michelangelo was most inspiring and
I'd pour over the large reproductions of his paintings for the
Sistine Chapel. When my older brother entered college, he
would bring home books on many artists and illustrators. I
then discovered an outlet for my talent.

"N. C. Wyeth was, and still is, the biggest influence on my
work and what goes into the thought process of illustration. I
compiled a portfolio of my drawings and tried to get into the
School of Visual Arts. Luckily, my talent was recognized,
and I was accepted to the school. I found it to be a place where
I could practice my drawing and painting skills in the midst of
valuable critics—other artists! I graduated four years later
with a portfolio of illustrations and confidence instilled by
some special instructors.

"I began landing free-lance assignments immediately and
became very busy doing what I'd always wanted to do.
Eventually I began illustrating childrens' books, and over the
past four years have arrived at a comfortable and intelligent
way of working. I say intelligent not referring to myself, but
to my painting and drawing. I believe that children should

**Petruccio's drawing from *Squanto: First Friend to the
Indians,* by Cathy East Dubowski, illustrates his realistic style and attention to anatomical detail.**

not be talked down to in illustrations. They don't need to see
something cute to get the point across. So my work tends
toward the more realistic side but with a style that is pleasing
and interesting to look at. I have never lost the love for detail
that I had as a child doing anatomical studies and that comes
through in my work. Having the opportunity to speak with
children about my work and hear their comments about my
paintings only reinforces the case. I feel that I have inherited a
certain sensitivity from my mother that adds to the elements I
put into my work and making sure the right feeling comes
through each time.

"I also have the ability to put feelings and pictures into
words, and so I have written four children's books which I
plan to illustrate and present to publishers. Hopefully this
will open another outlet through which I can reach others
and share my talents. The special paintings I do of the
Hudson Valley have gained recognition at the Dutchess
County Arts Association and the Northeast Watercolor
Society. I hope to bring the unique quality of this work to
childrens' books.

PIERCE, Meredith Ann 1958-

PERSONAL: Born July 5, 1958, in Seattle, WA; daughter of Frank N. (a professor of advertising) and Jo Ann (an editor and professor of agriculture; maiden name, Bell) Pierce. *Education:* University of Florida, B.A., 1978, M.A., 1980. *Hobbies and other interests:* Music (composition, harp, and voice), picturebook collecting, film and theater, anthropology, archaeology, languages, folklore and mythology, cats, science fiction, fantasy, and children's literature.

ADDRESSES: Home—424-H Northeast Sixth St., Gainesville, FL 32601.

CAREER: Writer. Bookland, Gainesville, FL, clerk, 1981; Waldenbooks, Gainesville, clerk, 1981-87; Alachua County (FL) Library District, library assistant, 1987—. Treasurer, Children's Literature Association Conference, Gainesville, 1982; University of Florida, instructor of creative writing, 1978-80, 1984.

MEMBER: Phi Beta Kappa.

AWARDS, HONORS: First prize, *Scholastic*/Hallmark Cards creative writing contest, 1973; Best Books for Young Adults citation, American Library Association (ALA), Best of the Best Books 1970-1982 citation, ALA, *New York Times* Notable Children's Book citation, and Parents' Choice Award Superbook citation, all 1982, Children's Book Award, International Reading Association, 1983, California Young Reader Medal, 1986, and *Booklist* Best Books of the Decade (1980-89) list, all for *The Darkangel;* Jane Tinkham Broughton Fellow in writing for children, Bread Loaf Writ-

MEREDITH ANN PIERCE

ers' Conference, 1984; Best Books for Young Adults semi-finalist, ALA, 1985, for *A Gathering of Gargoyles;* Best Books for Young Adults citation, ALA, 1985, Parents' Choice Award for Literature citation, 1985, and New York Public Library Books for the Teen Age exhibit citation, 1986, all for *The Woman Who Loved Reindeer;* Individual Artist Fellowship Special Award for Children's Literature, Florida Department of State, Division of Cultural Affairs, 1987; Best Books for Young Adults citation, ALA, 1991, for *The Pearl of the Soul of the World.*

WRITINGS:

YOUNG ADULT FANTASY NOVELS

The Darkangel (first novel in the "Darkangel" trilogy), Little, Brown, 1982.
A Gathering of Gargoyles (second novel in the "Darkangel" trilogy), Little, Brown, 1984.
Birth of the Firebringer (first novel of the proposed "Firebringer" trilogy), Macmillan, 1985.
The Woman Who Loved Reindeer, Little, Brown, 1985.
The Pearl of the Soul of the World (third novel in the "Darkangel" trilogy), Little, Brown, 1990.

OTHER

Where the Wild Geese Go (picturebook), illustrated by Jamichael Henterly, Dutton, 1988.
(Contributor) *Four from the Witch World* (contains novella "Rampion"), edited by Andre Norton, Tor Books, 1989.

Contributor to anthologies and to periodicals, including *Mythlore, Horn Book, ALAN Review, Voice of Youth Advocates (VOYA),* and *New Advocate.*

WORK IN PROGRESS: Dark Moon, the second novel in the proposed "Firebringer" trilogy.

SIDELIGHTS: Meredith Ann Pierce's novels are highlighted by their imaginative plots and settings, poetic language, and determined, independent characters. Her most noted work, the "Darkangel" fantasy trilogy, relates a young girl's struggle to free herself, her friends, and her world from an evil witch's power. Pierce's work "combines a mythic inventiveness with such elemental themes as love, conflict and quest," Joan Nist observes in the *ALAN Review,* and adds that Pierce "is one of the foremost young authors of fantasy today." As a *Publishers Weekly* reviewer writes, "The author's imagination seems boundless and she writes with such assurance that readers believe in every magic being and occurrence."

Pierce used considerable imagination to entertain herself when she was young, she related in an interview with *Something about the Author (SATA):* "I was a great collector of stuffed animals and had several entire imaginary lives." She would spend hours talking and playing with her unseen companions and also joined her brothers and sister in their own make-believe games. "I would play with anything that was available whether it was animate or not," Pierce recounted. "It would always be some sort of imagined environment—it was like role-playing games (i.e. Dungeons and Dragons) before role-playing games were invented."

Pierce also indulged her imagination with books. She made trips to the library with her parents, who frequently read aloud to her. With their encouragement, she began to read by herself around age three. "I was extremely self-contained," she said. "Since I could read real young, I could get my hands

The award-winning *The Darkangel Trilogy* focuses on Aerial's struggle to free herself and her people from the power of the darkangels. (Jacket illustration by Dawn Wilson.)

on all this information—a book. A lot of kids need an adult or somebody older around to feed them information, because they don't have access to it themselves. But I could read so young that I could feed myself information."

One book that Pierce remembers fondly is Lewis Carroll's classic *Alice in Wonderland.* Her version included records to read along with, and reading it over and over made a great impression on her. "*Alice in Wonderland* is like my religion," Pierce remarked in her interview. "It was introduced into my system before my immune system was complete, so it's wired into my psyche. I can't distinguish between my own mythology and early influences like *Alice in Wonderland* or the movie *The Wizard of Oz.* Some of the stuff that I saw really impressed me when I was very little and just went straight into my neurons—it's inseparable from my way of thinking."

By the time she was in sixth grade, Pierce was reading from the "adult" section of the library. School was fairly easy for her, due to the knowledge she had gained from reading. "To be at school was to be in an environment where you can be reasonably successful—you can answer all the questions, you don't really have to study, you can do all the stuff that you know already—and the teachers like you." She also demonstrated her independence by remaining outside the usual school cliques. "I wasn't the popular cheerleader type," she related. "I didn't have this need to belong to a group—a group where you all dress alike and you all think alike and you all giggle exactly the same—that's not my scene."

Pierce constantly wrote down ideas and stories when she was a student, but she didn't realize that people could actually make a living writing novels, she said in her interview. "My parents always treated my writing as another one of those obsessive little hobbies; 'Why would you rather be writing a novel than doing something else normal?' Since they were the authority figures I had to pretend that this wasn't the most important thing in my life and find some other career." But at the University of Florida Pierce met Joy Anderson, a professor and children's writer who showed her that writing could be a potential career. "Through her I got a much better idea of what writing is all about. She taught not just the craft of writing, but also the marketing aspect."

Anderson was instrumental in helping develop Pierce's talent. As part of their class assignments, Anderson's students would prepare a manuscript to be submitted to a publisher. In addition, Pierce noted, "Joy was very good about shoring up my confidence and giving me real specific criticism. If someone says 'Oh that's good, oh what a good writer you are, oh that's nice,' that's emotional stroking and I just hate that. But if someone will say, 'I like the opening, the opening was strong, but in the second paragraph when we get to this sentence my mind wandered. What are you going to do to fix it?,' that's something very narrow and focused and precise. Joy would give me very precise suggestions and comments that would leave the solution up to me."

Pierce developed her first novel, *The Darkangel,* in this fashion. The story takes place on the moon and follows the journey of Aeriel, a servant girl who sets out to rescue her mistress from a vampire who is evil but strangely attractive. Finding a publisher for the novel wasn't daunting for Pierce because of her experience in college. "I was very confident by the time I sent off *Darkangel* that Joy had given me not only positive feedback but accurate feedback and that the manuscript was good and that it would be accepted," the author said in her interview. Pierce's intuition was correct, for *The Darkangel* was soon accepted by Little, Brown and was published in 1982 to much critical praise.

Nancy Willard, for instance, calls *The Darkangel* "one of the best fantasies I've read in a long time." She adds in the *New York Times Book Review* that it is "written with plenty of skill and elvish craft." *Magazine of Fantasy and Science Fiction* critic Algis Budrys likewise admires Pierce's "golden, life-repleted universe full of amazing, often charming creatures." He also states that *The Darkangel* "is a marvelous tissue of allusions and evocations." Aeriel's quest to find the starhorse that can defeat the vampire resembles many classic fairy tales and fantasies. Nevertheless, "the author has her own personal vision, creating a sense of place through powerful images in a haunting, provocative novel," *Horn Book* reviewer Mary M. Burns notes. "Like the best fairy tales," Willard concludes, "*The Darkangel* will last and be loved by readers of all ages."

One outstanding feature of *The Darkangel* is Aeriel's determination to stand her ground in the face of danger. Although she is threatened by the vampire Irrylath, she frees his gargoyles and returns to his castle to confront him. Aeriel's courage and persistence grew out of one of the author's childhood experiences. As a young child Pierce was forced to deal with an alcoholic and abusive relative who was much older and stronger than she. "One day I found myself in the absurd position of facing someone twice my size who, for no cause, had made up his mind to do me violence," Pierce related in a *Horn Book* article. Tired of living with her fear of this person, Pierce continued, "I found myself being filled by the most supernal fury. How dare this person believe I was just going to stand there and take this?" At that point Pierce determined not to give in, whatever the consequences, and the relative left her alone. This showdown was "a little bit of a revelation—that a lot of human relationships are bluff, and that's an important thing to know," the author stated in her *SATA* interview. "Just because somebody tells you a thing is so, that 'This is the situation and I have great power over you,' doesn't mean it's true."

Although *The Darkangel* concludes with Aeriel marrying Irrylath and making him human by exchanging her heart for his, she is left his bride in name only. In the second volume of Pierce's trilogy, *A Gathering of Gargoyles,* Aeriel discovers Irrylath is still bound to the evil White Witch and cannot love another. To release him, Aeriel searches the moon to find their world's lost lons, ancient animal guardians who will help lead the battle against the Witch's forces.

Critics have responded favorably to this sequel as well. "Pierce is intensely visual, even poetic, in her descriptions and imaginative in her surprising plot turns," Eleanor Cameron reports in the *New York Times Book Review. Fantasy Review* contributor Walter Albert calls *A Gathering of Gargoyles* "perhaps an even finer work" than *The Darkangel,* and praises Pierce for her "stylistic growth." The critic concludes: "If Pierce does no more than equal her achievement in *A Gathering of Gargoyles* in the third volume, the three novels

At age nine, Pierce wrote the first sentence to what later became *Birth of the Firebringer,* the coming-of-age story of a rebellious young unicorn. (Jacket illustration by Dale Gottlieb.)

will surely be ranked with the small number of enduring fantasy classics."

In the last novel of the series, *The Pearl of the Soul of the World,* Aeriel takes on yet another urgent task: to bring the White Witch a gift and persuade her to renounce evil. This results in a showdown between good and evil, something that has fascinated Pierce for many years—ever since she discovered the comic *Prince Valiant.* "I love the whole medieval ethos," the author said in her *SATA* interview. "I know they were all starving to death and had all these diseases and their teeth were falling out and all that. But in a lot of the medieval legends, people were intensely religious and everything was important, everything was a struggle between heaven and hell. Good and evil has influenced my writing even though I'm not a Christian and don't belong to an organized religion. This sort of spirituality pervades the books whether I want it to or not."

A *Kirkus Reviews* writer remarks that in *The Pearl of the Soul of the World* Pierce gives her struggle of good-versus-evil "a symbolic life of unusual complexity and is notably inventive in creating" her world. But the critic also faults the author for her intricate, sometimes "laughably lush" descriptions. On the other hand, *Horn Book* critic Ann A. Flowers believes Pierce's style is one of the story's great strengths, with its "shimmering, fragile textures and delicate, shadowy descriptions." And a *Publishers Weekly* reviewer praises Pierce's "meticulous, creative use of language" for giving "form and substance to a fascinating mythic world." "Pierce continues to have the power to capture the imagination of her readers," Ruth S. Vose states in *School Library Journal.* "Her creativity never falters."

In her *SATA* interview, Pierce responded to the criticism that her language is too complex: "Should I dumb it down? Should I pretend that I don't speak English? Should I pretend that I speak baby talk? The conclusion that I've come to is that I can't change the way I think and I can't change my vocabulary and pretend that I don't know words that I know. Word use is not throwing down big words and saying, 'I can spell supercalifragilisticexpialidocious—aren't I smart?' It's saying, 'I know exactly when to use that word and I know exactly when not to use it.' There are a lot of word games in my stories, coined words and made up words, compound words, because I like doing that, it's very enjoyable."

Besides, the author added, she doesn't have a specific audience in mind when she writes. "I know that my books are marketed officially in hardcover as children's or young adult books, but when I write them I don't think of the audience at all, because the author and the audience are one entity. It's like lying down and going to sleep and having a dream. If somebody wants to sneak up while you're asleep and peek in your ear and see what dream is running around inside your head, that's fine. Just like if I want to write this story down and somebody else wants to pay me to read it, that's fine, but I don't think of the audience because the audience is me."

Pierce does recognize that her work, like most fantasy and science fiction, has special appeal for young people. "Adolescents are just getting ready to turn into adults," she explained to *SATA* in her interview. "Lots of fantasy and science fiction stories are about metamorphosis or about transporting you from one environment, a familiar environment, into an unknown environment. So what I write lends itself naturally to young adults—but it's also enjoyed by younger kids. I get fan mail from as young as fourth grade all the way up to adults."

Birth of the Firebringer, the first book in a proposed trilogy, also features a young protagonist struggling to overcome evil. Jan is the impulsive, outspoken son of the Prince of Unicorns, and wants to prove his worth to his father. He joins the unicorns' annual pilgrimage to a sacred lake, but finds himself challenged by an ancient enemy. "Jan is a dramatic hero," Hazel Rochman comments in a *Booklist* review, and "his coming-of-age from uncertain child to a leader who has grown beyond his father will have strong appeal for many young people." While rite-of-passage stories are common to fantasy, *Birth of the Firebringer*'s "vital characters and the unique device of a narrator whose identity remains hidden until story's end give it a fresh appeal," Holly Sanhuber notes in *School Library Journal.* "The language here is as elegant as the unicorn people it chronicles," a *Kirkus Reviews* writer concludes, and the herd's mythology and rituals "are woven skillfully into the story."

Inventing a new society like that of the unicorns' is another aspect of writing fantasy that Pierce enjoys. "I'm very interested in environments, in worlds, civilizations, belief systems, societies, rules of society or religions. Both fantasy and science fiction tend to do a whole lot of world-building because they will build the environment, they will build the world, they'll get it all set up and then they'll say, 'What if?' Then they'll run with that idea." To develop all the details of a new world, Pierce draws on her wide reading experience. "I read lots of anthropology and mythology, religion and alternate cultures and books about animal behavior. All of that I read for pleasure, but it's also my research because it comes back in my stories, in shadows and echoes, distortions and amalgams. It refigures itself into a fantasy."

The Woman Who Loved Reindeer, for instance, makes use of "traditional elements in fresh ways," Patty Campbell comments in *Wilson Library Bulletin.* Pierce uses traces of Arctic folklore in this tale of Caribou, a young woman who raises an orphaned baby only to find he is a *trangl*—a demon who can take human or reindeer form. Through her love and determination, Caribou earns the trust of the changeling Reindeer and is able to lead her tribe away from danger. This is "a haunting story of great beauty," Campbell writes, intensified by "a style both simple and poetic." "The author's imaginary world is an intriguing combination of realistic, folkloric, and fantastic elements," *Horn Book* writer Flowers remarks; "her style is smooth, clear and elegant, with never a word in the wrong place." *The Woman Who Loved Reindeer,* the critic concludes, is "a remarkably fine fantasy by an emerging master of the genre."

Keeping all the details of a world uniform and reliable is an essential part of any fantasy, Pierce maintained in her *SATA* interview. "You have to be self-consistent. The whole point of fantasy is that it's a shadow game; you are casting shadows on the wall and convincing the viewer that the shadow is reality. If you ever jar the viewer into thinking 'Wait a minute, that can't happen,' you break their suspension of disbelief and you ruin the shadow game. When I write I don't ever want my reader to wake up. I want my reader to remain immersed in the world, and so I try to make everything very consistent so that I won't ever wake the dreamer before the dream is finished."

Although she compares reading about new worlds to dreaming, Pierce challenges the idea that fantasy and science fiction are escapist. "Actually, science fiction and fantasy examine the real world we live in, but they do it in mask," she commented. "They pretend that we're talking about a different culture, pretend we're talking about an imaginary people,

A young woman embarks on an epic journey with a trangl—part human, part stag—in *The Woman Who Loved Reindeer.* (Jacket illustration by Dennis Nolan.)

but really we're talking about ourselves. That in some ways defeats the mind's censor which says certain ideas are forbidden and allows you to think of thoughts that you might not have thought before and examine possibilities that you might not have allowed yourself to examine. When you close the fantasy or science fiction book and come back to real life you still may have some of the things that you've learned—and I don't mean little didactic lessons, but ways of thinking."

Opening her own mind to new ideas is an important part of developing stories, Pierce said. "I constantly gather ideas and I fling them into this little hopper. All of them are in there, jumping and moving around and seething and massing, and some of them will start sticking to each other and connecting themselves, like little legos, building little plots. When one of those little lego conglomerations gets big enough, it will start rattling around inside of my skull saying 'Write me, write me, write me, write me.' It may not be big enough for a story yet, but it's usually big enough for a start."

In addition, Pierce uses pictures and images to inspire her. "When I was little I used to look through magazines and find advertisements and pictures that were interesting and I would tear them out and collect them in a photograph album. The image would inspire me with an idea to make a story. So if somebody gives me a bundle of photographs or a collection of images or hands me an object and says 'there's a story in this,' I'll sit there and I'll think of a story."

Pierce's one picturebook, *Where the Wild Geese Go,* evolved in this way. An editor at Dutton was eager to work with Pierce and sent her a set of pictures, suggesting Pierce could find a story in them. The illustrations, by Jamichael Henterly, featured a little girl with several animals, most in snowy settings. "I took about three seconds worth of a look at the pictures and said, 'Yes, there is a story,'" Pierce related. "They each have this young girl in them, each is in a wintry setting except for one with sheep in it, and here's the way the story goes. I laid the pictures out, this happens and this and this, and I sent her an outline of it."

Where the Wild Geese Go tells of Truzjka, a young girl who sets out to save her ill grandmother by searching for the home of the wild geese. Truzjka is a careless girl who is easily distracted from chores. Her journey includes a series of challenges that force her to overcome her thoughtless nature. She returns home to find she has been ill, not her grandmother, and may have only dreamed her journey. Nevertheless, she keeps the memories and the knowledge she has learned from her visit. A *Publishers Weekly* reviewer applauds the story: "Pierce's narrative weaves an enchanting aura, full of descriptive imagery and mysterious allusions, all of which fit together into a cohesive whole."

Learning to become independent and take responsibility for oneself, as Truzjka does, is an important theme in Pierce's work. "A lot of my characters are in a situation where they are very controlled," the author said in her *SATA* interview. "Aeriel in the 'Darkangel' trilogy is a slave; that's about as controlled as you can get. Jan, the hero in *Birth of the Fire Bringer,* is a young adolescent and so he's controlled by his parents, controlled by his society, controlled by adults. Truzjka, the heroine in *Where the Wild Geese Go,* is a child controlled by her grandmother, controlled by her fears, by her ineptitude. In my stories the characters think of ways to escape this external control and be in charge of their own lives, make their own decisions. Usually the confrontation cannot be direct, because often in real life you don't have the opportunity or there are reasons why a direct confrontation would be very dangerous and disastrous. But there are other ways around that have the same effect, that can free you from restraints and restrictions and the control of others."

But Pierce isn't out to promote a specific point of view or moral when she writes. Instead, she commented, "I hope that readers will enjoy my books and will have their imaginations excited. I hope that people will want to read more, that reading one book will inspire them to read another, because reading is still the primary means of getting information. The more information you have the more powerful you are; the more power you have the more options you have, so information is very, very important." She explained: "It seems to me that reading is a vicarious experience where you get to run a 'what if' scenario. If you can learn through a vicarious experience you're that much ahead of the game."

WORKS CITED:

Albert, Walter, "One of a Small Number of Fantasy Classics," *Fantasy Review,* May, 1985, p. 20.

Review of *Birth of the Firebringer, Kirkus Reviews,* October 1, 1985, p. 1090.

Budrys, Algis, review of *The Darkangel, Magazine of Fantasy and Science Fiction,* November, 1984, p. 38.

Burns, Mary M., review of *The Darkangel, Horn Book,* August, 1982, p. 416.

Cameron, Eleanor, review of *A Gathering of Gargoyles, New York Times Book Review,* December 30, 1984, p. 19.

Campbell, Patty, "The Young Adult Perplex," *Wilson Library Bulletin,* March, 1986, pp. 50-51.

Flowers, Ann A., review of *The Woman Who Loved Reindeer, Horn Book,* March-April, 1986, pp. 208-209.

Flowers, Ann A., review of *The Pearl of the Soul of the World, Horn Book,* May, 1990, p. 340.

Review of *A Gathering of Gargoyles, Publishers Weekly,* November 30, 1984, p. 92.

Nist, Joan, review of *The Woman Who Loved Reindeer, ALAN Review,* winter, 1985, p. 31.

Review of *The Pearl of the Soul of the World, Kirkus Reviews,* January 1, 1990, p. 49.

Review of *The Pearl of the Soul of the World, Publishers Weekly,* February 9, 1990, p. 63.

Pierce, Meredith Ann, "A Lion in the Room," *Horn Book,* January-February, 1988, pp. 35-41.

Pierce, Meredith Ann, telephone interview for *Something about the Author* conducted by Diane Telgen, June 4, 1991.

Rochman, Hazel, review of *Birth of the Firebringer, Booklist,* February 15, 1986, p. 870.

Sanhuber, Holly, review of *Birth of the Firebringer, School Library Journal,* January, 1986, p. 70.

Vose, Ruth S., review of *The Pearl of the Soul of the World, School Library Journal,* April, 1990, p. 145.

Review of *Where the Wild Geese Go, Publishers Weekly,* February 12, 1988, p. 82.

Willard, Nancy, "Vampire on the Moon," *New York Times Book Review,* April 25, 1982, pp. 35, 47.

Pierce with a fifteen-string Nordic lyre she acquired on a trip to England.

FOR MORE INFORMATION SEE:

BOOKS

Children's Literature Review, Volume 20, Gale, 1990.

PERIODICALS

Bulletin for the Center of Children's Books, July-August, 1982; December, 1985.
English Journal, April, 1985.
Horn Book, May-June, 1988.
New York Times, November 30, 1982.
School Library Journal, June-July, 1988.

Sketch by Diane Telgen

*   *   *

POHRT, Tom

ADDRESSES: Home—Ann Arbor, MI. *Office*—c/o Farrar, Straus, & Giroux Inc., 19 Union Square W., New York, NY 10003.

CAREER: Illustrator.

AWARDS, HONORS: Off-the-Cuff Award for most promising new artist, *Publishers Weekly,* 1990.

ILLUSTRATOR:

James Heynen, *The Man Who Kept Cigars in His Cap,* Graywolf, 1979.
Bruce Donehower, *Miko: Little Hunter of the North,* Farrar, Straus, 1990.
Barry Lopez, *Crow and Weasel* (Book-of-the-Month Club selection), North Point Press, 1990.

SIDELIGHTS: Tom Pohrt is a self-taught artist who received much critical recognition after illustrating Barry Lopez's 1990 book, *Crow and Weasel.* It was Pohrt's unique style of art, especially the way he draws animals, that caught Lopez's attention some ten years before the pair worked together on the project. "When I first came across Tom's line drawings," Lopez told *Publishers Weekly* contributor Michael Coffey, "I could see that he saw animals in a different way than any artist ever had. I was intrigued."

Lopez, primarily known for his books for adults on natural history and the environment, teamed with Pohrt on *Crow and Weasel* to create a story that reviewers claim is of interest to readers of all ages, including children. Called a "novella-length fable" by publicists, the tale is set in a mythical time when animals and humans lived together and spoke one language. Lopez and Pohrt created this phenomenon by describing the book's two main characters as human in the text, while showing them as a crow and weasel dressed in Indian attire in the story's illustrations.

Crow and Weasel follows the adventures of the two youths as they seek to discover themselves and the world around them. According to the tale, the pair plan to journey "farther north than anyone had ever gone, farther north than their people's stories went." The book is similar to traditional native American folk stories as it shows the lessons the boys learn about people, the land, and nature through their own self-discovery.

Illustrator Tom Pohrt (right), with his dog and author Barry Lopez.

The work was hailed by various critics for the morals explored in the story line and its imaginative and stunning artwork. Some reviewers remarked that Pohrt's color paintings authentically captured the dress, lifestyle, and culture of the Indians of the past, particularly the Plains Indians. Coffey noted that Pohrt was able to craft such realistic pictures because he researched Indian clothing, weapons, and other artifacts for the project.

WORKS CITED:

Coffey, Michael, and others, "Coming Attractions: A Variety of Authors and Artists Discuss Their Projects for the Fall Season," *Publishers Weekly,* July 27, 1990, p. 138.
Lopez, Barry, *Crow and Weasel,* North Point Press, 1990.

FOR MORE INFORMATION SEE:

PERIODICALS

Booklist, November 15, 1979; May 15, 1990.
Kirkus Reviews, August 15, 1990.
Los Angeles Times Book Review, November 25, 1990.
New Yorker, November 26, 1990.
New York Times Book Review, November 25, 1990.
Publishers Weekly, July 27, 1990.
Washington Post Book World, December 9, 1990; December 12, 1990.*

*   *   *

POPLOFF, Michelle 1956-

PERSONAL: Born July 25, 1956, in Brooklyn, NY; daughter of Alvin (a publishing sales representative) and Elaine (a social services case worker; maiden name, Kolbrenner) Wrobel; married Jeff Poploff (president of a computer software firm), July 12, 1981; children: Daniel and Leanne. *Education:* Queens College, B.A., 1974-78. *Religion:* Jewish.

ADDRESSES: c/o Publicity Director, Walker Books, 720 Fifth Ave., New York, NY 10019.

CAREER: Affiliated with Bantam, Doubleday, and Dell Publishing Co., New York, NY, 1979—, currently executive editor, Dell Books for Young Readers.

MEMBER: Society of Children's Book Writers.

WRITINGS:

Busy O'Brien and the Great Bubble Gum Blowout, Walker Books, 1990.

WORK IN PROGRESS: Busy O'Brien and the Caterpillar Punch Bunch, 1992.

SIDELIGHTS: Michelle Poploff writes: "As far back as I can remember, I've enjoyed reading and writing. As a child I wrote many poems and short stories. Now I wish I'd saved them. I very much enjoy hearing stories about the childhood experiences of family members from previous generations. I used some of their stories and anecdotes and turned them into stories that were published in 'nostalgia type' magazines.

"I've also written short stories for children that take place during some of the Jewish holidays. While some of the holiday traditions are blended into the stories, they are for all children.

MICHELLE POPLOFF

"I keep a pad and pen on the table next to our bed and write down thoughts and ideas that might work for a story or a book. When I hear a funny line or an interesting name I write that down. Who knows where it will end up.

"A number of years ago, my sister worked for the mayor of her town. She happened to be a woman. I filed that notion away. What would it be like to be the mayor's daughter? Anything could happen and for Busy, it usually does. When I was in sixth grade, I was the monitor for a kindergarten class. There was a little freckle-faced girl in the class, named Elizabeth, but everyone called her Busy. I guess that name stayed with me through the years. The second book about Busy and her friends will be published next spring.

"My son and daughter love when I read to them. My son who is five has a hard time coming to grips with the fact that I actually wrote a book. I think—in fact, I know—that there's a lot of Daniel in the Gilbert Bratski character in the book. The funny thing is that I wrote the first draft for Busy before Daniel was born."

*   *   *

PROYSEN, Alf 1914-1970

PERSONAL: Born 1914 in Norway; died 1970.

WRITINGS:

JUVENILE; IN ENGLISH TRANSLATION

Little Old Mrs. Pepperpot and Other Stories, translated by Marianne Helwig, Helene Obolensky, 1959.
Little Old Mrs. Pepperpot Again and Other Stories, translated by Helwig, Helene Obolensky, 1960.
The Town that Forgot It Was Christmas, adapted by Kay Ware and Lucille Sutherland, McGraw, 1961.
The Goat that Learned to Count, adapted by Ware and Sutherland, McGraw, 1961.
Down the Mole Hole, adapted by Ware and Sutherland, McGraw, 1964.
Mrs. Pepperpot to the Rescue, translated by Helwig, Pantheon, 1964.
Mrs. Pepperpot in the Magic Wood, translated by Helwig, Pantheon, 1968.
Mrs. Pepperpot's Outing, translated by Helwig, Pantheon, 1971.
Mrs. Pepperpot's Year, translated by Helwig, Hutchinson, 1973.
Mrs. Pepperpot's Busy Day, translated by Helwig, Puffin, 1975.

OTHER

Utpa Livets vei: Kjaerlighet pa rundpinne (short stories), Tiden Norsk Forlag, 1958.
To Pinner i Kors: Komedie i Seks Bilder, au Alf Proysen og Asbjorn Toms (play), Tiden Norsk Forleg, 1961.

Also author of untranslated children's books, including *Trost i Taklampa,* Tiden Norsk Forleg, 1950.

ADAPTATIONS: Many of the "Mrs. Pepperpot" stories have been adapted for Swedish television.*

RENNERT, Richard Scott 1956-
(Richard Scott)

PERSONAL: Born February 11, 1956, in Queens, NY; son of Fred (an importer) and Corinne (Hausman) Rennert. *Education:* Haverford College, B.A. 1978.

ADDRESSES: Home—245 Martling Ave., Tarrytown, NY 10591. *Office*—Chelsea House, 95 Madison Ave., New York, NY 10016.

CAREER: Writer. Franklin Library, New York City, editor, 1978-82; Charles Scribner's Sons, New York City, editor, 1982-85; Harper & Row, New York City, editor, 1985-87; Chelsea House, New York City, senior editor, 1987—.

WRITINGS:

UNDER PSEUDONYM RICHARD SCOTT

Jackie Robinson, introductory essay by Coretta Scott King, Chelsea House, 1987.
Jesse Owens, Chelsea House, 1991.

Editor of "Black Americans of Achievement" series for Chelsea House.

WORK IN PROGRESS: A sports biography to be illustrated by Margaret Tolbert.

SIDELIGHTS: Richard Scott Rennert told *SATA:* "I have edited a wide variety of books for children, young adults, and adults, all of which have helped me grow as a writer. I especially enjoy editing and writing books about sports."

FOR MORE INFORMATION SEE:

PERIODICALS

Booklist, September 1, 1987.
School Library Journal, September, 1987.

*　　*　　*

RICH, Louise Dickinson 1903-1991

OBITUARY NOTICE—See index for *SATA* sketch: Born June 14, 1903, in Huntington, MA; died of congestive heart failure, April 9, 1991, in Mattapoisett, MA. Author. Louise Dickinson Rich's intense love of the outdoors was reflected in her 1943 best-selling book *We Took to the Woods,* a Thoreau-like account of her backwoods lifestyle in northwestern Maine. Rich and her husband Ralph lived in a camp on the Rapid River from their marriage until Ralph died in 1945. Rich then turned to supporting herself and her children through her writing. Besides the autobiographical *We Took*

to the Woods and *My Neck of the Woods,* her works include the young adult novels *Trail to the North, Start of the Trail,* and *Summer at High Kingdom,* and many books of history for children.

OBITUARIES AND OTHER SOURCES:

PERIODICALS

New York Times, April 11, 1991, p. B14.

*　　*　　*

ROCKWOOD, Roy
[Collective pseudonym]

WRITINGS:

A Schoolboy's Pluck; or, The Career of a Nobody, Mershon, 1900.
The Wizard of the Sea; or, A Trip under the Ocean, Mershon, 1900.
The Cruise of the Treasure Ship; or, The Castaways of Floating Island (also see below), Mershon, 1906.
Jack North's Treasure Hunt; or, Daring Adventures in South America (also see below), Chatterton-Peck, 1907.
(Contributor) *Popular Stories for Boys* (includes *Bomba the Jungle Boy; or, The Old Naturalist's Secret*), Cupples & Leon, 1934.

"BOMBA THE JUNGLE BOY" SERIES

Bomba the Jungle Boy; or, The Old Naturalist's Secret, Cupples & Leon, 1926, reprinted, Grosset & Dunlap, 1953, published as *Bomba the Jungle Boy,* 1978.
Bomba the Jungle Boy at the Moving Mountain; or, The Mystery of the Caves of Fire, Cupples & Leon, 1926, reprinted, Grosset & Dunlap, 1953, published as *Bomba the Jungle Boy: The Moving Mountain,* 1978.
Bomba the Jungle Boy at the Giant Cataract; or, Chief Nascanora and His Captives, Cupples & Leon, 1926, reprinted, Grosset & Dunlap, 1953.
Bomba the Jungle Boy on Jaguar Island; or, Adrift on the River of Mystery, Cupples & Leon, 1927, reprinted, Grosset & Dunlap, 1953.
Bomba the Jungle Boy in the Abandoned City; or, A Treasure 10,000 Years Old, Cupples & Leon, 1927, reprinted, Grosset & Dunlap, 1953.
Bomba the Jungle Boy on Terror Trail; or, The Mysterious Men from the Sky, Cupples & Leon, 1928, reprinted, Grosset & Dunlap, 1953.
Bomba the Jungle Boy in the Swamp of Death; or, The Sacred Alligators of Abarago, Cupples & Leon, 1929, reprinted, Grosset & Dunlap, 1953.
Bomba the Jungle Boy among the Slaves; or, Daring Adventures in the Valley of Skulls, Cupples & Leon, 1929, reprinted, Grosset & Dunlap, 1953.
Bomba the Jungle Boy on the Underground River; or, The Cave of Bottomless Pits, Cupples & Leon, 1930, reprinted, Grosset & Dunlap, 1953.
Bomba the Jungle Boy and the Lost Explorers; or, A Wonderful Revelation, Cupples & Leon, 1930, reprinted, Grosset & Dunlap, 1953.
Bomba the Jungle Boy in a Strange Land; or, Facing the Unknown, Cupples & Leon, 1931.
Bomba the Jungle Boy among the Pygmies; or, Battling with Stealthy Foes, Cupples & Leon, 1931.
Bomba the Jungle Boy and the Cannibals; or, Winning against Native Dangers, Cupples & Leon, 1932.

Bomba brought the paddle down with all his force. (From *Bomba the Jungle Boy* by Roy Rockwood, illustrated by W. S. Rogers.)

Bomba the Jungle Boy and the Painted Hunters; or, A Long Search Rewarded, Cupples & Leon, 1932.

Bomba the Jungle Boy and the River Demons; or, Outwitting the Savage Medicine Man, Cupples & Leon, 1933.

Bomba the Jungle Boy and the Hostile Chieftain; or, A Hazardous Trek to the Sea, Cupples & Leon, 1934.

Bomba the Jungle Boy Trapped by the Cyclone; or, Shipwrecked on the Swirling Seas, Cupples & Leon, 1935.

Bomba the Jungle Boy in the Land of Burning Lava; or, Outwitting Superstitious Natives, Cupples & Leon, 1936.

Bomba the Jungle Boy in the Perilous Kingdom; or, Braving Strange Hazards, Cupples & Leon, 1937.

Bomba the Jungle Boy in the Steaming Grotto; or, Victorious through Flame and Fury, Cupples & Leon, 1938.

"DAVE DASHAWAY" SERIES

Dave Dashaway, the Young Aviator; or, In the Clouds for Fame and Fortune, Cupples & Leon, 1913.

Dave Dashaway and His Hydroplane; or, Daring Adventures over the Great Lakes, Cupples & Leon, 1913.

Dave Dashaway and His Giant Airship; or, A Marvelous Trip across the Atlantic, Cupples & Leon, 1913.

Dave Dashaway around the World; or, A Young Yankee Aviator among Many Nations, Cupples & Leon, 1913.

Dave Dashaway, Air Champion; or, Wizard Work in the Clouds, Cupples & Leon, 1915.

"DAVE FEARLESS" SERIES

Dave Fearless after a Sunken Treasure; or, The Rival Ocean Divers (originally published as *The Rival Ocean Divers; or, The Search for a Sunken Treasure;* also see below), G. Sully, 1918.

Dave Fearless on a Floating Island; or, The Cruise of the Treasure Ship (originally published as *The Cruise of the Treasure Ship; or, The Castaways of Floating Island;* also see below), G. Sully, 1918.

Dave Fearless and the Cave of Mystery; or, Adrift on the Pacific (originally published as *Adrift on the Pacific; or, The Secret of the Island Cave;* also see below), G. Sully, 1918.

Dave Fearless among the Icebergs; or, The Secret of the Eskimo Igloo, Garden City, 1926.

Dave Fearless Wrecked among Savages; or, The Captives of the Headhunters, Garden City, 1926.

Dave Fearless and His Big Raft; or, Alone on the Broad Pacific, Garden City, 1926.

Dave Fearless on Volcano Island; or, The Magic Cave of Blue Fire, Garden City, 1926.

Dave Fearless Captured by Apes; or, In Gorilla Land, Garden City, 1926.

Dave Fearless and the Mutineers; or, Prisoners on the Ship of Death, Garden City, 1926.

Dave Fearless under the Ocean; or, The Treasure of the Lost Submarine, Garden City, 1926.

Dave Fearless in the Black Jungle; or, Lost among the Cannibals, Garden City, 1926.

Dave Fearless near the South Pole; or, The Giant Whales of Snow Island, Garden City, 1926.

Dave Fearless Caught by Malay Pirates; or, The Secret of Bamboo Island, Garden City, 1926.

Dave Fearless on the Ship of Mystery; or, The Strange Hermit of Shark Cove, Garden City, 1927.

Dave Fearless on the Lost Brig; or, Abandoned in the Big Hurricane, Garden City, 1927.

Dave Fearless at Whirlpool Point; or, The Mystery of the Water Cave, Garden City, 1927.

Dave Fearless among the Cannibals; or, The Defense of the Hut in the Swamp, Garden City, 1927.

"DEEP SEA" SERIES

The Rival Ocean Divers; or, The Search for a Sunken Treasure, Stitt, 1905.

The Cruise of the Treasure Ship; or, The Castaways of Floating Island, Stitt, 1907.

Adrift on the Pacific; or, The Secret of the Island Cave, Grosset & Dunlap, 1908.

Jack North's Treasure Hunt; or, Daring Adventures in South America, Grosset & Dunlap, 1908.

"GREAT MARVEL" SERIES

Through the Air to the North Pole; or, The Wonderful Cruise of the Electric Monarch, Cupples & Leon, 1906.

Under the Ocean to the South Pole; or, The Strange Cruise of the Submarine Wonder, Cupples & Leon, 1907.

Five Thousand Miles Underground; or, The Mystery of the Center of the Earth, Cupples & Leon, 1908.

Through Space to Mars; or, The Most Wonderful Trip on Record, Cupples & Leon, 1910.

Lost on the Moon; or, In Quest of the Field of Diamonds, Cupples & Leon, 1911.

On a Torn-Away World; or, Captives of the Great Earthquake, Cupples & Leon, 1913.

Johnny Sheffield as Bomba in the 1954 Allied Artists release *The Golden Idol,* one of twelve films made between 1949 and 1955 based on the "Bomba the Jungle Boy" series.

The City beyond the Clouds; or, Captured by the Red Dwarfs, Cupples & Leon, 1925.

By Air Express to Venus; or, Captives of a Strange People, Cupples & Leon, 1929.

By Space Ship to Saturn; or, Exploring the Ringed Planet, Cupples & Leon, 1935.

"SEA TREASURE" SERIES

Adrift on the Pacific; or, The Secret of the Island Cave, Grosset & Dunlap, 1908.

The Cruise of the Treasure Ship; or, The Castaways of Floating Island, Grosset & Dunlap, 1908.

The Rival Ocean Divers; or, The Search for a Sunken Treasure, Grosset & Dunlap, 1908.

Jack North's Treasure Hunt; or, Daring Adventures in South America, Grosset & Dunlap, 1908.

"SPEEDWELL BOYS" SERIES

The Speedwell Boys on Motorcycles; or, The Mystery of a Great Conflagration, Cupples & Leon, 1913.

The Speedwell Boys and Their Racing Auto; or, A Run for the Golden Cup, Cupples & Leon, 1913.

The Speedwell Boys and Their Power Launch; or, To the Rescue of the Castaways, Cupples & Leon, 1913.

The Speedwell Boys in a Submarine; or, The Treasure of Rocky Cove, Cupples & Leon, 1913.

The Speedwell Boys and Their Ice Racer; or, Lost in the Great Blizzard, Cupples & Leon, 1915.

OTHER

Also author of *Flyer Fred, the Cyclist Ferret; or, Running Down the Rough and Ready Rascals,* for the dime novel series Half-Dime Library. Contributor to periodicals, including *Golden Hours, Banner Weekly, Young Sports of America,* and *Bright Days.*

ADAPTATIONS: Twelve black-and-white films loosely based on the "Bomba the Jungle Boy" series were made between 1949 and 1955. All were directed by Ford Beebe and starred Johnny Sheffield (who also played "Boy" in the Tarzan films) as Bomba: "Bomba, the Jungle Boy," Allied Artists, 1949; "Bomba on Panther Island," Allied Artists, 1949; "Bomba and the Hidden City," Allied Artists, 1950; "The Lost Volcano," Allied Artists, 1950; "Elephant Stampede," Allied Artists, 1951; "The Lion Hunters," Allied Artists, 1951; "African Treasure," Allied Artists, 1952; "Bomba and the Jungle Girl," Allied Artists, 1952; "Safari Drums," Allied Artists, 1953; "The Golden Idol," Allied Artists, 1954; "Killer Leopard," Allied Artists, 1954; and "Lord of the Jungle," Allied Artists, 1955.

SIDELIGHTS: Roy Rockwood was the pseudonym used by the Stratemeyer Syndicate for some of its most popular boys' series. Edward Stratemeyer, Howard R. Garis, and Leslie McFarlane are known to have used this pseudonym to produce stories in various genres ranging from jungle and racing adventure to science fiction.

The most prominent of these adventure series was "Bomba the Jungle Boy," "whose adventures in many volumes provided an endless survival course for thousands of youngsters who were never likely to find themselves within miles of a jungle," remembers Leslie McFarlane in his autobiography *Ghost of the Hardy Boys.* Bomba was described by Arthur Prager in *Rascals at Large: or, The Clue in the Old Nostalgia* as "Stratemeyer's answer to Tarzan." Like Tarzan, Bomba was a foundling, raised from childhood in the jungles of the upper Amazon basin by the half-demented naturalist Cody Casson. The resemblances were not exact; Prager states that while Tarzan "spoke like a true English gentleman, and conversed easily in French as well," the Jungle Boy "usually referred to himself in the third person." Also, while Tarzan's exploits explore themes of sex and violence, Bomba's adventures center around his search for his parents, Andrew and Laura Bartow. Prager points out that a strain of racism ran through both series, but indicates that Bomba's was more overt "until the jungle lad got to civilization and found that all men are vile and only the virgin jungle is pure. By the end of the series he had found out that you can't trust anybody, regardless of color."

The Rockwood pseudonym was also used for the "Speedwell Boys" series, which Prager compares to the later "Hardy Boys" novels, and for the "Dave Fearless" diving adventures. Dan and Billy Speedwell "were mechanically inclined, and could break down an automobile engine and repair it in no time at all," reports Prager. The brothers and their girl friends, Mildred and Lettie, built racing machines that they crashed periodically. Leslie McFarlane, who contributed at least three volumes to Dave Fearless's adventures, recalls that Dave "was no novice in the diving business"; at the age of twenty-one, he was a fully qualified diver. With his friend Bob Vilett, a marine engineer, he braved dangers below and above the ocean waves.

One of the best remembered of all series produced under this pseudonym, however, was the "Great Marvel" series, described by Prager as "a mixture of Jules Verne and Edgar Rice Burroughs (in his science fiction period), toned [down] to subteen level." In some ways, the series was very innovative; Prager remarks that in one volume of the series Stratemeyer "invented jet propulsion." He concludes that the series "was fun to read, and omitted much of the corn that was chronic in similar series of the pre-war era." See the *SATA* index for more information on Howard R. Garis, Leslie McFarlane, and Edward L. Stratemeyer.

WORKS CITED:

McFarlane, Leslie, *Ghost of the Hardy Boys,* Two Continents, 1976.
Prager, Arthur, "The Superboys," *Rascals at Large; or, The Clue in the Old Nostalgia,* Doubleday, 1971, pp. 307-34.

FOR MORE INFORMATION SEE:

BOOKS

Dizer, John T., Jr., *Tom Swift & Company: "Boys' Books" by Stratemeyer and Others,* McFarland & Co., 1982.
Garis, Roger, *My Father Was Uncle Wiggly,* McGraw-Hill, 1966.
Johnson, Deidre, editor and compiler, *Stratemeyer Pseudonyms and Series Books: An Annotated Checklist of Stratemeyer and Stratemeyer Syndicate Publications,* Greenwood Press, 1982.

PERIODICALS

Journal of Popular Culture, winter, 1974.

* * *

ROEHRIG, Catharine H. 1949-

PERSONAL: Surname is pronounced "Re-rig"; born July 8, 1949, in Newton, MA; daughter of Albert Karl (a psychologist) and Ruth (an audiovisual technician; maiden name, Matthews) Roehrig. *Education:* Hollins College, B.A., 1971; Bryn Mawr College, M.A., 1977; University of California, Berkeley, Ph.D., 1990.

ADDRESSES: Office—Department of Egyptian Art, Metropolitan Museum of Art, New York, NY 10028.

CAREER: Peace Corps, Washington, D.C., English teacher in Tunisia, 1971-73; University of California, Berkeley, research assistant, 1979-85, teaching assistant, 1982-85; assistant director of Berkeley Theban Mapping Project, 1980-88; Museum of Fine Arts, Boston, MA, research assistant, 1985-88; Metropolitan Museum of Art, New York City, assistant curator, 1989—.

WRITINGS:

Mummies and Magic: An Introduction to Egyptian Funerary Beliefs, Museum of Fine Arts (Boston), 1988.
Fun with Hieroglyphs, Metropolitan Museum of Art/Viking, 1990.

SIDELIGHTS: Catharine Roehrig's *Fun with Hieroglyphs* explains the writing system of ancient Egypt and, in a unusual move, includes a set of rubber stamps so that young readers can create hieroglyphic messages of their own. A reviewer for *Publishers Weekly* called the work "an intriguing glimpse at one of the most influential legacies of ancient cultures."

Roehrig told *SATA:* "My mother is fond of saying that I fell in love with a five thousand-year-old pharaoh at the age of twelve and that's why I'm an Egyptologist today. In some ways that's true. Like most children, I was fascinated by the ancient Egyptians. But it was my parents who really got me started. I have slight dyslexia, a learning problem that made it hard for me to learn to read well (I still don't read out loud well). In seventh grade, I had to do an oral report. We were supposed to study some topic (to be chosen by us), write a report, and present it in front of an eighth-grade class. The whole idea terrified me. My mom and dad knew I loved Egypt, so they gave me a book on the tomb of pharaoh Tutankhamun (they were both small children when the tomb was discovered in 1922, and they remembered how excited everyone had been at the time). I thought that the gold mask of Tutankhamun was the most beautiful thing ever made. It still ranks pretty high on my list of favorite things."

WORKS CITED:

Review of *Fun with Hieroglyphs, Publishers Weekly,* November 2, 1990, pp. 74-5.

S., Svend Otto
See SOERENSEN, Svend Otto

*   *   *

SALINGER, J(erome) D(avid) 1919-

PERSONAL: Born January 1, 1919, in New York, NY; son of Sol (an importer) and Miriam (Jillich) Salinger; allegedly married Sylvia (a French physician; maiden name unknown), September, 1945, (divorced, 1947); married Claire Douglas, February 17, 1955 (divorced, October, 1967); children: (second marriage) Margaret Ann, Matthew. *Education:* Graduated from Valley Forge Military Academy, 1936; attended New York University, Ursinus College, and Columbia University (where he studied with Whit Burnett).

ADDRESSES: Home and office—Cornish, NH. *Agent*—Harold Ober Associates, Inc., 425 Madison Ave., New York, NY 10017.

CAREER: Writer. Worked as an entertainer on the Swedish liner *M.S. Kungsholm* in the Caribbean, 1941. *Military service:* U.S. Army, 1942-46; served in Europe; became staff sergeant; received five battle stars.

WRITINGS:

The Catcher in the Rye (novel; Book-of-the-Month Club selection), Little, Brown, 1951.

J. D. SALINGER

Nine Stories, Little, Brown, 1953 (published in England as *For Esme—With Love and Squalor, and Other Stories,* Hamish Hamilton, 1953).
Franny and Zooey (two stories; "Franny" first published in *New Yorker,* January 29, 1955, "Zooey," *New Yorker,* May 4, 1957), Little, Brown, 1961.
Raise High the Roof Beam, Carpenters; and, Seymour: An Introduction (two stories; "Raise High the Roof Beam, Carpenters" first published in *New Yorker,* November 19, 1955, "Seymour," *New Yorker,* June 6, 1959), Little, 1963.
The Complete Uncollected Short Stories of J. D. Salinger, two volumes, unauthorized edition, [California], 1974.

Contributor to *Harper's, Story, Collier's, Saturday Evening Post, Cosmopolitan,* and *Esquire.*

ADAPTATIONS: "Uncle Wiggily in Connecticut" (published in *Nine Stories*) was made into the motion picture *My Foolish Heart,* 1950.

SIDELIGHTS: With the publication of *The Catcher in the Rye* in 1951, J. D. Salinger not only defined a generation, but also gave young adults a character in whom they could see themselves—Holden Caulfield, "the innocent child in the evil and hostile universe, the child who can never grow up," writes Maxwell Geismar in his *American Moderns: From Rebellion to Conformity.* Its more than ten million copies have been translated into many languages; both a classic and an object of debate, the book made Salinger a literary phenomenon. Although his reputation and readership were unmatched by any other living writer of the time, he retreated to a primitive country house in Cornish, New Hampshire only a few years after the appearance of his novel; he signed no autographs and refused to give lectures or interviews. "No one else has ever been known in quite the way that Salinger has—first as the creator of a voice and a consciousness in which a vast number of very different readers have recognized themselves, second as an elusive figure uneasy with his audience and distrustful of his public, and finally as a kind of living ghost, fiercely protective of his isolation," asserts Philip Stevick in the *Dictionary of Literary Biography.* A fence was eventually built around Salinger's house, and a *Newsweek* contributor explains that the only way to reach the residence is by way of a dog-patrolled fifty-foot cement tunnel from the garage. In his *J. D. Salinger,* Warren French quotes Salinger as having said: "I feel tremendously relieved that the season for success for *The Catcher in the Rye* is nearly over. I enjoyed a small part of it, but most of it I found hectic and professionally and personally demoralizing." Since 1965 Salinger has published nothing, but his voice continues to speak to countless readers of all ages.

Very little is known about Salinger's childhood. His father was a Jewish importer of hams and cheeses, his mother a Scotch-Irish gentile. Stevick maintains that the family's address indicates they led a prosperous life. Salinger attended several New York public schools before being enrolled in his first private school. In 1934, Salinger entered Valley Forge Military Academy in Pennsylvania, graduating two years later. Soon after, he briefly attended New York University and traveled in Europe. During this time, adds Stevick, Salinger was constantly writing and sending his stories to

With *The Catcher in the Rye*, Salinger not only defined a generation, but gave young adults a character in whom they could see themselves—Holden Caulfield. (Rendition of Caulfield by James McMullan for *Esquire*.)

numerous magazines; and was first published in *Story* in 1940. Twenty-three stories appeared in "middle-range" magazines such as the *Saturday Evening Post, Mademoiselle, Good Housekeeping,* and *Collier's,* and were pirated for an unauthorized collection in 1974. "Salinger has disavowed those early stories and, on one occasion," observes Stevick, "took legal steps to enjoin their unauthorized publication."

Salinger first appeared in the *New Yorker* in 1946, and by 1948 he was publishing almost exclusively for this magazine. "He soon became 'a *New Yorker* writer' and a friend of its major editorial figures," observes Stevick, adding that Salinger "was honored by his presence in its elegant pages and by its high standards for fiction." The stories included in *Franny and Zooey* and *Raise High the Roof Beam, Carpenters; and, Seymour: An Introduction* first appeared in the *New Yorker,* and all exhibit a similarity of character. "Salinger discovered a focus that was to continue through a large portion of his fiction, namely the use of childhood, adolescence, or youth as both an object of interest in itself and as a thematic lever by means of which the nature of the wider world could be pried open," maintains Stevick, adding: "Sensitive and perceptive, Salinger's younger characters are unable to prevail against the hypocrisy around them. Or,

authentic and bright on the one hand, fatally naive on the other, they conspire in their own failures."

The Catcher in the Rye continues this focus through the character of Holden Caulfield. The novel opens with Holden in a psychiatric hospital, recovering from some sort of breakdown. It is written in the first person, and describes the two days Holden spent in New York after being expelled from his third prep school. Holden's age dictates the type of language used in the novel, so all the slang and four-letter words used by adolescents are included. The novel has experienced a controversial history, focusing primarily on this raw language. French points out that the book was temporarily banned in both South Africa and Australia because it was thought to be immoral. And in 1956, adds French, the National Organization for Decent Literature in Nevada found the novel to be "objectional." It was also banned from an eleventh-grade English class in Oklahoma in 1961, and, in 1970, it was prohibited in one Carolina county for its obscenity. Many small-town libraries even kept their copy of *The Catcher in the Rye* on a restricted shelf after it had become a part of many high school and college courses. "There is probably not one phrase in the whole book that Holden Caulfield would not have used upon occasion, but when they are piled upon each other in cumulative monotony, the ear refuses to believe," explains Virgilia Peterson in the *New*

York Herald Tribune Book Review. Edward P. J. Corbett, though, argues in *America* that "Holden's swearing is so habitual, so unintentional, so ritualistic that it takes on a quality of innocence." Corbett also contends that "all of the scenes about sexual matters are tastefully, even beautifully, treated." Holden has fundamentally sound values, concludes Corbett, adding that "future controversy will probably center on just what age an adolescent must be before he is ready for this book."

J. D. Salinger is reported to have said he regretted that *The Catcher in the Rye* "might be kept out of the reach of children," states Peter J. Seng in *College English.* "It is hard to guess at the motives behind his remark," continues Seng, "but one of them may have been that he was trying to tell young people how difficult it was to move from their world into the world of adults. He may have been trying to warn them against the pitfalls of the transition." Throughout the novel, Holden is trying to deal with just such a transition and is presented as "the fumbling adolescent nauseated by the grossness of the world's body," asserts James E. Miller, Jr. in his *J. D. Salinger.* "Phoniness" is the word that Holden uses to describe almost everything in the world around him, says Seng, and he wants to protect children from all of these evils. But, as his sister Phoebe points out, Holden doesn't "like" anything—he is unwilling to compromise and this is why he is telling his story from a psychiatric hospital. "Holden will survive," continues Seng, "but first he must learn to love other human beings as well as he loves children. He must acquire a sense of proportion, a sense of humor. He must learn compassion for the human, the pompous, the phoney, the perverse; such people are the fellow inhabitants of his world, and behind their pitiful masks are the faces of the children in the rye."

The problems presented in *The Catcher in the Rye* seem to have a universal relevance. "For many young adults it is the most honest and human story they know about someone they recognize—even in themselves—a young man caught between childhood and maturity and unsure which way to go," point out Kenneth L. Donelson and Alleen Pace Nilsen in *Literature for Today's Young Adults.* "There is no question that Salinger's book captured—and continues to capture—the hearts and minds of countless young adults as no other book has," conclude Donelson and Nilsen. "I have no idea why Salinger has not in recent years graced us with more stories," states *New Republic* contributor Robert Coles. "It is no one's business, really. He has already given us enough," continues Coles, "maybe too much: we so far have not shown ourselves able to absorb and use the wisdom he has offered us."

WORKS CITED:

Coles, Robert, "J. D. Salinger," *New Republic,* April 28, 1973, pp. 30-32.
Corbett, Edward P. J., "Raise High the Barriers Censors," *America,* January 7, 1961, pp. 441-443.
Dictionary of Literary Biography, Volume 102: *American Short-Story Writers, 1910-1945,* Gale, 1991, pp. 258-265.
Donelson, Kenneth L., and Alleen Pace Nilsen, *Literature for Today's Young Adults,* Scott, Foresman, 1980, pp. 163-165.
French, Warren, *J. D. Salinger,* Twayne, 1963.
Geismar, Maxwell, "J. D. Salinger: The Wise Child and the 'New Yorker' School of Fiction," *American Moderns:*

Salinger's second book, *Nine Stories,* appeared in Britain under the title *For Esme—With Love and Squalor.*

From Rebellion to Conformity, Hill and Wang, 1958, pp. 195-209.
Miller, James E., Jr., *J. D. Salinger,* University of Minnesota Press, 1965, p. 48.
Newsweek, July 30, 1979.
Peterson, Virgilia, "Three Days in the Bewildering World of an Adolescent," *New York Herald Tribune Book Review,* July 15, 1951, p. 3.
Seng, Peter J., "The Fallen Idol: The Immature World of Holden Caulfield," *College English,* December, 1961, pp. 203-209.

FOR MORE INFORMATION SEE:

BOOKS

Allen, Walter, *The Modern Novel,* Dutton, 1965.
Alsen, Everhard, *Salinger's Glass Stories as a Composite Novel,* Whitston, 1983.
Authors and Artists for Young Adults, Volume 2, Gale, 1989.
Belcher, W. F., and J. W. Lee, editors, *J. D. Salinger and the Critics,* Wadsworth, 1962.
Bloom, Harold, editor, *J. D. Salinger: Modern Critical Views,* Chelsea, 1987.
Burnett, Hallie and Whit, *Fiction Writer's Handbook,* Harper, 1975.

Carpenter, Humphrey, *Secret Gardens: A Study of the Golden Age of Children's Literature,* Houghton, 1985.
Children's Literature Review, Volume 18, Gale, 1989.
Concise Dictionary of American Literary Biography: The New Consciousness, 1941-1968, Gale, 1987.
Contemporary Literary Criticism, Gale, Volume 1, 1973, Volume 3, 1975, Volume 8, 1978, Volume 12, 1980, Volume 56, 1989.
Dictionary of Literary Biography, Volume 2: *American Novelists since World War II,* Gale, 1978.
Filler, Louis, editor, *Seasoned "Authors" for a New Season: The Search for Standards in Popular Writing,* Bowling Green University Popular Press, 1980.
French, Warren *J. D. Salinger, Revisited,* Twayne, 1988.
French, *The Fifties: Fiction, Poetry, Drama,* Everett/Edwards, 1970.
Grunwald, Henry Anatole, editor, *Salinger: A Critical and Personal Portrait,* Harper, 1962.
Gwynn, F. L., and J. L. Blotner, *The Fiction of J. D. Salinger,* University of Pittsburgh Press, 1958.
Hamilton, Ian, *In Search of J. D. Salinger,* Random House, 1988.
Hamilton, Kenneth, *Jerome David Salinger: A Critical Essay,* Eerdmans, 1967.
Hasson, Ihab, *Radical Innocence: Studies in the Contemporary American Novel,* Princeton University Press, 1961.
Kazin, Alfred, *Contemporaries,* Atlantic Monthly Press, 1962.
Kermode, Frank, *Puzzles and Epiphanies,* Chilmark, 1962.
Laser, Marvin, and Norman Fruman, editors, *Studies in J. D. Salinger,* Odyssey, 1963.
Lundquist, James, *J. D. Salinger,* Ungar, 1979.
Marsden, Malcolm M., editor, *If You Really Want to Know: A Catcher Casebook,* Scott, 1963.
Rosen, Gerald, *Zen in the Art of J. D. Salinger,* Creative Arts, 1977.
Sadker, Myra Pollack, and David Miller Sadker, *Now Upon a Time: A Contemporary View of Children's Literature,* Harper, 1977.
Short Story Criticism, Volume 2, Gale, 1989.
Sublette, Jack R., *J. D. Salinger: An Annotated Bibliography, 1938-1981,* Garland, 1984.

PERIODICALS

America, January 26, 1963.
American Book Collector, May-June, 1981.
American Literature, November, 1968.
Atlantic, August, 1961.
Book Week, September 26, 1965.
Catholic World, February, 1962.
College English, January, 1961.
Commentary, September, 1987.
Crawdaddy, March, 1975.
Criticism, summer, 1967.
Critique, spring-summer, 1965.
Daily Eagle (Claremont, NH), November 13, 1953.
Dalhousie Review, autumn, 1967.
English Journal, March, 1964; April, 1983.
Harper's, February, 1959; October, 1962; December, 1962.
Horizon, May, 1962.
Library Journal, July, 1951.
Life, November 3, 1961.
Mademoiselle, August, 1961.
Minnesota Review, May-July, 1965.
Modern Fiction Studies, autumn, 1966.
Newsweek, May 30, 1960; January 28, 1963.
New York Post Weekend Magazine, April 30, 1961.
New York Times, November 3, 1974.
Partisan Review, fall, 1962.
People, October 31, 1983.
Ramparts, May, 1962.
Saturday Review, September 16, 1961; November 4, 1961.
Studies in Short Fiction, spring, 1967; spring, 1970; winter, 1973; summer, 1981; winter, 1981.
Time, September 15, 1961.
Village Voice, August 22, 1974.
Western Humanities Review, winter, 1955-56.*

Sketch by Susan M. Reicha

* * *

SCHINDELMAN, Joseph 1923-

PERSONAL: Born July 4, 1923, in New York, NY; married Ida Zager, 1944; children: Dale, Laurel, Maxine, Michael. *Education:* Attended Art Students' League and City College (now of the City University of New York). *Hobbies and other interests:* Fishing.

CAREER: Illustrator. Columbia Broadcasting System, New York City, associate art director; Papert, Koenig, Lois (advertising agency), promotion art director. *Exhibitions:* Work has been exhibited at American Institute of Graphic Arts. *Military service:* U.S. Army, 15th Air Force; served as gunner during World War II.

AWARDS, HONORS: The Great Picture Robbery was chosen one of the *New York Times*'s Best Illustrated Children's Books of the Year, 1963; *Maurice Goes to Sea* and *The Six Who Were Left in a Shoe* were each chosen one of the American Institute of Graphic Arts Children's Books, 1967-68.

ILLUSTRATOR:

Eve Merriam, *There Is No Rhyme for Silver* (poems; Junior Literary Guild selection), Atheneum, 1962.
Leon A. Harris, *The Great Picture Robbery,* Atheneum, 1963.
J. Allan Bosworth, *Voices in the Meadow* (Junior Literary Guild selection), Doubleday, 1964.
Roald Dahl, *Charlie and the Chocolate Factory,* Knopf, 1964.
John F. Raymond, *The Marvelous March of Jean Francois,* Doubleday, 1965.
Beryl Netherclift, *Snowstorm,* Knopf, 1968.
Harris, *Maurice Goes to Sea,* Norton, 1968.
Padraic Colum, *The Six Who Were Left in a Shoe,* McGraw, 1968.
Mike Thaler, *The Staff,* Knopf, 1971.
Dahl, *Charlie and the Great Glass Elevator: The Further Adventures of Charlie Bucket and Willy Wonka, Chocolate-Maker Extraordinaire,* Knopf, 1972.
Harris, *The Great Diamond Robbery,* Atheneum, 1985.*

* * *

SCHMIDT, Annie M. G. 1911-

PERSONAL: Born May 20, 1911, in Kapelle, South Beveland, Holland; daughter of a vicar.

CAREER: Librarian in Holland, 1932-46; *Het Parool,* Holland, documentation office manager, beginning in 1946; writer.

ANNIE M. G. SCHMIDT

AWARDS, HONORS: Staatsprijs voor kinder- en jeugdliteratuur, c. 1964; runner-up, Hans Christian Andersen Award, 1968, for *Wiplala;* Australian State Prize, 1968; Constantijin Huygens Award, 1987; Hans Christian Andersen Award, 1988.

WRITINGS:

TRANSLATED WORKS FOR CHILDREN

Wiplala, translated by Henrietta Anthony, illustrated by Jenny Dalenoord, Abelard-Schuman, 1962 (originally published under same title, Arbeiderspers, 1960).

Good Luck, Mick and Mandy, translated by Rose E. Pool, Odhams Books, 1961 (originally published as *Daar gaan Jip en Janneke*).

Love from Mick and Mandy, translated by Pool, Odhams Books, 1961 (originally published as *Een zoentje van Jip en Janneke*).

Take Care, Mick and Mandy, translated by Pool, Odhams Books, 1961 (originally published as *Pas op, Jip en Janneke*).

Bob and Jilly, translated by Lance Salway, illustrated by Carolyn Dinan, Methuen Children's Books, 1976 (originally published as *Jip en Janneke,* 1963).

Bob and Jilly Are Friends, translated by Salway, illustrated by Carolyn Dinan, Methuen Children's Books, 1977 (originally published in *Jip en Janneke,* 1963).

Bob and Jilly in Trouble, translated by Salway, illustrated by Dinan, Methuen Children's Books, 1980 (originally published in *Jip en Janneke,* 1963).

(With Fiep Westendorp) *Frizzlycurl,* translated by Elizabeth Willems-Treeman, Enschede, 1966 (originally published as *Kroezebetje,* Arbeiderspers, 1966).

Dusty and Smudge and the Bride, translated by Salway, illustrated by Westendorp, Methuen Children's Books, 1977 (originally published as *Floddertje en de bruid,* 1973).

Dusty and Smudge and the Soap Suds, translated by Salway, illustrated by Westendorp, Methuen Children's Books, 1977 (originally published as *Schuim,* 1973).

Dusty and Smudge Spill the Paint, translated by Salway, illustrated by Westendorp, Methuen Children's Books, 1977 (originally published as *Opgesloten,* 1973).

Dusty and Smudge Keep Cool, translated by Salway, illustrated by Westendorp, Methuen Children's Books, 1977 (originally published as *Allemaal kaal,* 1973).

Dusty and Smudge Splash the Soup, translated by Salway, illustrated by Westendorp, Methuen Children's Books, 1979 (originally published as *Moeder is ziek,* 1973).

Dusty and Smudge and the Cake, translated by Salway, illustrated by Westendorp, Methuen Children's Books, 1979 (originally published as *Tante is jarig,* 1973).

The Empty House, translated by Margo Logan, Jacaranda Press, 1977 (originally published as *Het lege huis,* 1974).

Grandpa's Glasses, translated by Logan, Jacaranda Press, 1977 (originally published as *De bril van opa,* 1974).

Highland Low, translated by Logan, Jacaranda Press, 1977 (originally published as *Hoog en laag,* 1974).

The Tunnel, translated by Logan, Jacaranda Press, 1977 (originally published as *De tunnels,* 1974).

The Island of Nose, translated by Salway, illustrated by Jan Marinus Verburg, Methuen, 1977 (originally published as *Tom Tippelaar,* Querido's, 1977).

Pink Lemonade: Poems for Children, translated and adapted by Henrietta ten Harmsel, illustrated by Linda Cares, Eerdmans, 1981.

UNTRANSLATED WORKS

Het fluitketeltje en andere versjes (title means "The Little Teakettle and Other Rhymes"), Arbeiderspers, 1950.

En wat dan nog?, Arbeiderspers, 1950.

De spin Sebastiaan, Arbeiderspers, 1951.

Impressies van een simpele ziel, Querido's, 1951.

Kom, zei het schaap Veronica (also see below), Arbeiderspers, 1953.

Abeltje (title means "Little Abel"), [Netherlands], 1953.

De A van Abeltje (title means "Abel's A"), [Netherlands], 1955.

In Holland staat mijn huis, Querido's, 1955.

De ark van mensen, illustrated by Jenny Dalenoord, Amsterdamsche Boeken Courantmij, 1956.

Doorsnee in doorsnee, Arbeiderspers, 1956.

De groeten van Jip en Janneke, illustrated by Westendorp, Arbeiderspers, 1957.

Nieuwe impressies van een simpele ziel, Querido's, 1957.

Tijs en Lapje, Damesweekblad Eva, 1960.

(With Henri Knap) *Meneer recht, mevrouw averecht,* Arbeiderspers, 1963.

Heksen en zo (title means "Witches and So on"), Arbeiderspers, 1964.

Heerlijk duurt het langst, Arbeiderspers, 1967.

Ja zuster, nee zuster (title means "Yes Nurse, No Nurse"; also see below), Arbeiderspers, 1967.

Vingertje Lik en een heleboel andere versjes, illustrated by Wim Bijmoer, Arbeiderspers, 1967.

In a beautiful garden in faraway France
Cool paths curve along in the shade,
And tulips and lilies and roses surround
A pond full of pink lemonade.

The children go rowing around in a boat —
It's never against the law —
And when they're not singing, they take a cool sip
Through a very long, elegant straw.

The pond is bright pink, almost raspberry red,
And sometimes the children may wade
With trousers and dresses pulled up very high
In the pond full of pink lemonade.

If one of the children flops out of the boat,
They rescue him quick as a wink,
And then they start licking so that he won't stay
So terribly sticky and pink!

It really is charming, that garden in France —
The flowers, the paths in the shade —
But still you'll agree that the nicest of all
Is the pond full of pink lemonade.

Title poem from Schmidt's collection of well-loved children's verse. (Translation of *Pink Lemonade* by Henrietta ten Harmsel, illustration by Linda Cares.)

Het beest met de achternaam, edited by Wim Hora Adema, Arbeiderspers, 1968.
Troost voor dames: Een keuze uit de impressies van een sipele ziel, Querido's, 1968.
En ik dan?, Arbeiderspers, 1969.
(With others) *Fluitje van 'n cent,* Ring, 1969.
(With Bloed Kwaad, Harriet Freezar, Marjolein Heijermans, and others) *Reacties van tien vrouwen op het studentenverzet,* illustrated by Westendorp, Arbeiderspers, 1969.
Minoes, illustrated by Carl Hollander, Arbeiderspers, 1970.
Pluk van de Petteflet, illustrated by Westendorp, Arbeiderspers, 1971.
Het hele schaap Veronica (contains *Het schaap Veronica, Kom, zei het schaap Veronica,* and *Het schaap Veronica haar staart*), illustrated by Westendorp, Querido's, 1972.
(With Westendorp) *Floddertje,* Querido's, 1973.
Het beertje Pippeloentje: Niet met de deuren slaan, Arbeiderspers, 1973.
Water bij de wijn, Querido's, 1973.
Er valt een traan op de tompoes, Querido's, 1980.
Otje, illustrated by Westendorp, Querido's, 1980.
(With Mance Post) *Waaidorp,* Querido's, 1980.
Een visje bij de thee: Drieentwintig verhalen en achtenzestig versjes uit eenentwintig boeken, Querido's, 1983.
Simpele zielen en nog wat, Querido's, 1989.
Altijd acht gebkeven over de kinderliteratuur, Querido's, 1991.

Also author of musicals and cabaret texts. Creator of television series, including *Ja zuster, nee zuster,* based on Schmidt's book of the same title, and *Pension Hommeles;* and of radio programs, including *In Holland staat een huis.* Contributor to *Nieuw cabaret,* compiled by Guus Dijkhuizen, Bruna en Zoon's, 1962, and to periodicals, including *Het Parool.*

SIDELIGHTS: In 1988 Annie M. G. Schmidt became the first Dutch author to receive the Hans Christian Andersen Award for her many contributions to children's literature. Her well-loved rhymes and verse as well as her "Jip en Janneke" (translated as "Bob and Jilly" or "Mick and Mandy") books, which relate the adventures of two playful and strong-willed children, have been translated into several languages. Born in 1911, Schmidt grew up on an island in Holland where her father was a vicar. Upon completing her secondary education, she spent a short stint at a notarial school before deciding to work as a librarian in a children's reading-room, a vocation that lasted nearly fifteen years. Schmidt's career as a writer began when her first children's poems were published in *Het Parool,* a newspaper for which she had been employed as a documentation office manager. Since then the author has produced numerous works in a variety of genres though she remains best known for her children's poetry. Some of her poems appear in English translation in the anthology titled *Pink Lemonade.*

In a 1970 speech quoted in *Bookbird,* Schmidt commented on her transition from librarian to writer: "To me the essence of working in a library for young people was being able to say: 'Dinner is ready, come in, there is a lot to eat, there are delicious things. Sausages and cheese, but also crisps and sweets. Try this and try that. . . . That was what I felt to be the essence. It was the feeling: Share my food. Come and look at everything that's here.

"Writing for children is essentially the same thing. Why does a person take up writing for children? I am talking about the *real* writers now, not about the false ones. The false ones think: 'Well, writing for children is not difficult . . . let's see

. . . children like adventure and suspense, I'll make something up.' Other false writers think: 'You must teach children something, morals, ethics and culture; I will place myself on this platform and from this height I will give them something to help them along their path of life.'

"The real writer does not go in for all this. He only does what the librarian does: Share my food, share my imagination . . . share my truth, come with me, I'll show you a great many things that have made a great impression on me, share my experience.

"Share my imagination, share my truth. And by truth I don't mean reality, for *that* is something quite different. An absurd fairy-tale can contain more truth than a documentary."

Most of Schmidt's stories and poems display elements of fantasy and reality and highlight differences in the realms of the child and the adult. "What the writer wants is to share his world with the child," Schmidt stated, as quoted in *Bookbird.* "His world? The world of a grown-up? No, his child's world. The real writer of children's books has, in a way, remained a child. He still has his wings. He has never lost them." In Schmidt's works, the idealism and vivid imagination of the young prevail, and she often portrays her youthful characters shunning the restrictions and seriousness of adults. In her Bob and Jilly stories, for example, a little girl and boy amuse themselves with such rebellious antics as sliding down banisters, scaring birds from cherry trees, walking in puddles, and eating excessive amounts of ice cream. Although some critics have found the behavior of Schmidt's characters reproachable, the author has been lauded for her accurate depiction of the five-year-old child's world.

Schmidt's poems and stories are also characterized by their playful plots. The author believes that children's literature must above all be entertaining, an attitude she acquired while working as a librarian. "One day when she was attempting to inspire [the children] by reading something very 'uplifting,' they staged a noisy rebellion, demanded the return of the two cents apiece they had paid, and finally had to be dismissed by a concierge," related Henrietta Ten Harmsel in *Children's Literature: An Annual of the Modern Language Association Seminar on Children's Literature and the Children's Literature Association.* "When Annie Schmidt left the library that day, several children again accosted her for their two cents, for money was precious to them in that depression era. 'They taught me a lesson I never forgot,' she says. 'After that I began to read and tell only stories and poems which would genuinely appeal to children, even including some of my own things, which I had then never considered publishing.'"

Because she was "extremely critical of her own writing," noted Ten Harmsel, Schmidt was reluctant about publishing her first writings until persuaded by friends. The author eventually became one of the most prominent children's writers in Holland and the creator of well-liked radio and television programs. Her philosophy concerning authorship is perhaps one reason for her immense popularity in her native country. "The writer of children's books," Schmidt asserted in *Bookbird,* "has . . . retained the child's way of looking at things; he can laugh at things children laugh at, cry about things children cry about and feel their suspense. All this he wants to share with them. That's why he sits down to write his story or his book. Not to make money, not to instruct or to moralize, not even to amuse. No, just to share."

WORKS CITED:

Schmidt, Annie M. G., "Some Questions Facing the Author," *Bookbird,* September 15, 1971, pp. 3-10.
Ten Harmsel, Henrietta, "Annie M. G. Schmidt: Dutch Children's Poet," *Children's Literature: An Annual of the Modern Language Association Seminar on Children's Literature and the Children's Literature Association,* Volume 11, 1983, pp. 135-44.

FOR MORE INFORMATION SEE:

BOOKS

Children's Literature Review, Volume 22, Gale, 1991.

PERIODICALS

Bookbird, September 15, 1988.*

*   *   *

SCOTT, Richard
See RENNERT, Richard Scott

*   *   *

SEUSS, Dr.
See GEISEL, Theodor Seuss

*   *   *

SHARP, Margery 1905-1991

OBITUARY NOTICE—See index for *SATA* sketch: Born January 25, 1905; died March 14, 1991. Author. Sharp's stories and novels reached both reading and theatrical audiences through the many filmed adaptations of her work. One of her most popular books, *The Nutmeg Tree,* was filmed as *Julia Misbehaves* in 1948. She was best known in the United States, however, as the author of the "Miss Bianca" series of children's stories, featuring a small mouse who works for the Rescue Aid Society, an animal organization that helps people in distress. *The Rescuers* and *Miss Bianca,* Sharp's first two books about Miss Bianca's adventures, were adapted and animated by Walt Disney Productions in 1977 as *The Rescuers.*

OBITUARIES AND OTHER SOURCES:

BOOKS

Who's Who, 143rd edition, St. Martin's, 1991.

PERIODICALS

Times (London), March 15, 1991, p. 16.

*   *   *

SHELDON, Ann
[Collective pseudonym]

WRITINGS:

"LINDA CRAIG" SERIES

Linda Craig and the Palomino Mystery, Doubleday, 1962, reprinted under title *Linda Craig: The Palomino Mystery,* Wanderer, 1981.

Linda Craig and the Clue on the Desert Trail, Doubleday, 1962, reprinted under title *Linda Craig: The Clue on the Desert Trail,* Wanderer, 1981.

Linda Craig and the Secret of Rancho del Sol, Doubleday, 1963, reprinted under title *Linda Craig: The Secret of Rancho del Sol,* Wanderer, 1981.

Linda Craig and the Mystery of Horseshoe Canyon, Doubleday, 1963, reprinted under title *Linda Craig: The Mystery of Horseshoe Canyon,* Wanderer, 1981.

Linda Craig and the Ghost Town Treasure, Doubleday, 1964, reprinted under title *Linda Craig: The Ghost Town Treasure,* Wanderer, 1982.

Linda Craig and the Mystery in Mexico, Doubleday, 1964, reprinted under title *Linda Craig: The Mystery in Mexico,* Wanderer, 1981.

Linda Craig: The Haunted Valley, Wanderer, 1982.
Linda Craig: The Secret of the Old Sleigh, Wanderer, 1983.
Linda Craig: The Emperor's Pony, Wanderer, 1983.
Linda Craig: The Phantom of Dark Oaks, Wanderer, 1984.
Linda Craig: Search for Scorpio, Wanderer, 1984.

"LINDA CRAIG ADVENTURES" SERIES

The Golden Secret, Minstrel, 1988.
A Star for Linda, Minstrel, 1988.
The Silver Stallion, Minstrel, 1988.
The Crystal Trail, Minstrel, 1988.
The Glimmering Ghost, Minstrel, 1989.

The **"Linda Craig" series features a young female detective once described as "Nancy Drew on horseback."** (From *Linda Craig: The Secret of Rancho del Sol,* by Ann Sheldon, cover illustration by John Speirs.)

The Ride to Gold Canyon, Minstrel, 1989.
A Horse for Jackie, Minstrel, 1989.
A Star in the Saddle, Minstrel, 1989.
The Riding Club, Minstrel, 1989.
Anything for Kelly, Minstrel, 1989.
Everybody's Favorite, Minstrel, 1990.
Kathy in Charge, Minstrel, 1990.

ADAPTATIONS: "The Tom Swift and Linda Craig Mystery Hour" was produced by Paramount and aired by ABC-TV on July 3, 1983. It starred Willie Aames as Tom and Lori Loughlin as Linda.

SIDELIGHTS: Ann Sheldon is the collective pseudonym used to write the "Linda Craig" series, which featured Linda Craig and her prize-winning palomino Chica d'Oro. Linda and her brother Bob were orphans, having lost their parents—a military officer and his wife—in an accident in Hawaii. They lived on their grandparents' ranch, Rancho del Sol, in the San Quinto valley of southern California. With the help of their friends they solved mysteries, an association Arthur Prager described in *Rascals at Large; or, The Clue in the Old Nostalgia* as "Nancy Drew on horseback."

Carol Billman, in her *The Secret of the Stratemeyer Syndicate,* echoes Prager's assessment. She points out that the many Gothic elements which characterize Nancy Drew's adventures are present in the Linda Craig stories: *The Phantom of Dark Oaks,* for instance, is "a story full of spiral staircases, a stately plantation, supernatural noises, and the threat of ghosts—Nancy Drew in western drag." In 1988 a new series of "Linda Craig" adventures appeared. Among other changes, Linda's horse was renamed Amber. Harriet Adams initiated the Linda Craig series. See the *SATA* index for more information on Harriet S. Adams, Edward L. Stratemeyer, and Andrew E. Svenson.

WORKS CITED:

Billman, Carol, "Stratemeyer's Success: Further Investigation," *The Secret of the Stratemeyer Syndicate: Nancy Drew, the Hardy Boys, and the Million Dollar Fiction Factory,* Ungar, 1986, pp. 141-55.

Prager, Arthur, "The Secret of Nancy Drew: Pushing Forty and Going Strong," *Rascals at Large; or, The Clue in the Old Nostalgia,* Doubleday, 1971, pp. 73-95.

FOR MORE INFORMATION SEE:

BOOKS

Johnson, Deidre, editor and compiler, *Stratemeyer Pseudonyms and Series Books: An Annotated Checklist of Stratemeyer and Stratemeyer Syndicate Publications,* Greenwood Press, 1982.

*   *   *

SIS, Peter 1949-

PERSONAL: Born May 11, 1949, in Brno, Moravia, Czechoslovakia; immigrated to United States, 1982, naturalized citizen, 1989; son of Vladimir (a filmmaker and explorer) and Alena (an artist; maiden name, Petrvalska) Sis; married Terry Lajtha (a film editor), October 28, 1990. *Education:* Academy of Applied Arts, Prague, Czechoslovakia, M.A., 1974; attended Royal College of Art, London, England,

PETER SIS

1977-79. *Religion:* Roman Catholic. *Hobbies and other interests:* Horseback riding, music, mime, and travel.

ADDRESSES: Home—10 Bleeker St., #7B, New York, NY 10012.

CAREER: Artist, animator, illustrator, and writer. Worked as a disc jockey while in art school. Teacher of art classes at schools in Los Angeles, CA, and New York City. *Military service:* Czechoslovak Army, graphic designer with army's symphony orchestra, 1975-76.

EXHIBITIONS: Group shows include Interama, Berlin, 1975; Best of British Illustrators, London, 1979; Magical Mystery Tour, Los Angeles, 1982; Expo Art and Metropole, Montreal, 1984; Bienalle of Illustrations, Japan, 1985; University of Oregon School of Art, Portland, 1986; and International Gallery, San Diego, CA, 1986. One-man shows at Gallery Klostermauer, St. Gallen, Switzerland, 1975; Gallery Ploem, Delft, Netherlands, 1977; Gallery Martinska, 1977, Gallery Nerudova, 1978, and Gallery Rubin, 1979, all in Prague, Czechoslovakia; Gallery Vista Nova, Zurich, Switzerland, 1980; Gallery Medici, London, 1981; and Ohio University School of Art, Athens, Ohio, 1990.

MEMBER: Association Internationale du Film d'Animation, American Institute of Graphic Arts, Graphic Artists Guild.

AWARDS, HONORS: Golden Berlin Bear for best short film, Berlin International Film Festival, 1980, for *Heads;* Grand Prix Toronto, 1981, for short film *Players;* CINE Golden Eagle Award, Council on International Non-Theatrical Events, 1983, for *You Gotta Serve Somebody; Rainbow Rhino* and *Beach Ball* were listed among the *New York Times*

"ten best illustrated children's books for the year," 1987 and 1990, respectively.

WRITINGS:

SELF-ILLUSTRATED

Rainbow Rhino, Random House, 1987.
Waving: A Counting Book, Greenwillow, 1988.
Going Up!: A Color Counting Book, Greenwillow, 1989.
Beach Ball, Greenwillow, 1990.
Follow the Dream: The Story of Christopher Columbus, Knopf, 1991.
Whale's Tail, Greenwillow, in press.

ILLUSTRATOR

Eveline Hasler, *Hexe Lakritze und der Buchstabenkoenig,* Benziger (Zurich, Switzerland), 1977.
Hasler, *Hexe Lakritze und Rhino Rhinoceros,* Benziger, 1979.
Milos Maly, reteller, *Tales of the Amber Ring* (Baltic fairy tales), Artia (Prague), 1981, Orbis, 1985.
Max Bolliger, *Eine Zwergengeschichte* (title means "Little Singer"), Bohem (Zurich), 1982.
George Shannon, *Bean Boy,* Greenwillow, 1983.
Shannon, *Stories to Solve: Folktales from around the World,* Greenwillow, 1984.
Sid Fleischman, *The Whipping Boy,* Greenwillow, 1985.
Julia Cunningham, *Oaf,* Knopf, 1986.
Caron Lee Cohen, *Three Yellow Dogs,* Greenwillow, 1986.
Myra Cohn Livingston, *Higgledy-Piggledy,* Atheneum, 1986.

Illustrator Peter Sis attributes his "soft technique" to his traditional art training in Europe. (Postcard illustration from *The Midnight Horse* by Sid Fleischman, illustrated by Sis.)

Jean Marzollo and Claudio Marzollo, *Jed and the Space Bandits,* Dutton, 1987.

Monica Mayper, *After Good-Night,* Harper, 1987.

Eve Rice, *City Night,* Greenwillow, 1987.

Fleischman, *The Scarebird,* Greenwillow, 1988.

Kate Banks, *Alphabet Soup,* Knopf, 1988.

Caroline Feller Bauer, editor, *Halloween: Stories and Poems,* Harper, 1989.

Fleischman, *The Ghost in the Noonday Sun,* Greenwillow, 1989.

Fleischman, *Midnight Horse,* Greenwillow, 1990.

Shannon, *More Stories to Solve,* Greenwillow, 1991.

Also illustrator of *Fairy Tales of the Brothers Grimm,* Albatros (Prague), Volume 1, 1976, Volume 2, 1977; *Zizkov Romances,* CSS (Prague), 1978; and *Poetry,* CSS, 1980. Contributor of illustrations to *American Illustration, New York Times, New York Times Books Review, Atlantic Monthly, Time, Newsweek, House & Garden, Esquire, Forbes, Connoisseur,* and *Print.*

SHORT FILMS

Mimikry, Academy of Applied Arts (Prague), 1975.

Island for 6,000 Alarm Clocks, Kratky Film, 1977.

Heads, Kratky Film, 1979.

Players, Halas & Batchelor (London), 1981.

Hexe Lakritze (ten parts; title means "Little Witch Licorice"), televised in Zurich, Switzerland, 1982.

You Gotta Serve Somebody, Fine Arts (Los Angeles), 1983.

Aesop's Fables, (two films), Helicon Video, 1984.

Twelve Months, Billy Budd Films, 1985.

Heads and *Island for 6,000 Alarm Clocks* are part of the permanent film collection of the Museum of Modern Art in New York City.

WORK IN PROGRESS: Working on a video adaptation of *Rumpelstilskin,* to be produced by Rabbit Ears, and on books about the komodo dragon, astronomy, and the golem. (According to legend, golems are artificial human-like figures made out of clay and brought to life by magical means.)

SIDELIGHTS: Peter Sis is a distinguished illustrator and writer who is recognized internationally for his contributions to children's literature. Since the mid-1970s, he has made more than half a dozen short films, illustrated nearly twenty books for other authors, and written six of his own self-illustrated children's books.

Sis was born into an artistic family, and his parents had a profound influence on his growth as an artist. During most of the 1950s and 1960s, his native country of Czechoslovakia was dominated by the Soviet government, and citizens had limited political and cultural freedoms. Reflecting on his youth in an interview with *Something about the Author* (*SATA*), Sis recounted, "I grew up in the city of Prague, Czechoslovakia, in the time of the strong hand of the Communist rule, which completely shaped my parents' lives. But people can't choose if they live in the time of war or peace or anything. It's amazing, though, that even within that very undesirable world we had time to play our games and have fun and everything as children always do. So now, in retrospect, I think I had a wonderful childhood, mostly thanks to my parents."

As early as age four or five, Sis began drawing pictures, and within a few years he became quite serious about his craft. "I was already illustrating regularly by the time I was eight or nine. My father and my mother would give me certain assignments, and I remember I would even have deadlines." When he had reached his early teens, Sis was convinced that he wanted to pursue a career as a professional artist. He began discussing his ambitions with his father, a filmmaker and explorer, who told him that an artist's life can be very lonely, isolated, and demanding. Sis told *SATA,* "I replied to him, Oh sure, of course, without realizing what it meant."

Sis credits his parents with providing an appropriate environment to foster his growth as an artist. His talents flourished in an atmosphere that balanced creative freedom with a certain amount of structure and discipline. Above all, he was challenged intellectually as a youth by his parents. "I think if parents can make sure that kids have a sort of extended period of childhood and of creativity and of dreaming, it's wonderful. I know it's hard sometimes with peer pressure and fashion and music and everything, but there is so much time for that in the future. There's no way back to childhood, though."

Once in formal art school, however, Sis began to experience some frustration in his quest to be an artist. The abstract upbringing he received from his parents clashed with the traditional ideals of formal artistic training. "Art school, at times, wasn't enjoyable at all," Sis recalled in the *SATA* interview. "The teachers were very academically educated, and they wanted us to draw absolutely according to the style of nineteenth-century type paintings. It was very hard because there was really no space for fantasy or individuality." There were about fifteen young artists in Sis's class, and each assignment turned in by the students was ranked from best to worst. "I don't think it was quite fair," he mused, "because of course two girls in class were always the best, and my friend and I were always the worst. It was quite painful for me, but I think it's very good now when I teach that I remember how frustrated I was. I would never say, This is good, or This is bad, because I think everybody has a completely different angle on their work." Sis received his master's degree from the Academy of Applied Arts in Prague in 1974 and later attended the Royal College of Art in London, England. In spite of the difficulties he faced earlier as a young student in different art schools, he attributes his so-called "soft technique," which is still evident in his works, to his traditional art education.

Sis first became involved with animated films in the 1960s, and he considers famous Czechoslovakian illustrator, animator, and teacher Jiri Trnka to have been an important role model. By the early 1980s, Sis was already a popular artist and filmmaker in Europe. "Film for me was the passport to the whole world," he told *SATA.* His short animated film *Heads* earned the Golden Bear at the 1980 Berlin International Film Festival. He was then invited to design and paint illustrations for a Swiss television series called *Hexe Lakritze* ("Little Witch Licorice"). Sis also worked on another film in London. Then, in 1982, he traveled to Los Angeles, California—the site of the 1984 Olympic Games—to do a film that tied in the theme of the liberation of humanity with the Olympics. However, following the Soviet Union's decision to boycott the 1984 Olympics because of supposed anti-Soviet activity in the United States, other eastern and central European countries, including Czechoslovakia, also withdrew from the competition. The Olympic film project was canceled, but Sis remained in Los Angeles to pursue his career in art.

"It was very hard to find my way around in Los Angeles," Sis explained to *SATA,* "because all of a sudden things were

Sis's first venture as both author and illustrator, *Rainbow Rhino*, drew praise for its spacious depiction of distant stretches of land.

completely different than what I was used to in Europe—the palm trees and lifestyle and everything. I felt completely misplaced and strange. I couldn't admit that I had lost and then go back to Prague. I went through a very strange emotional state of immigration. I felt like a door had slammed on me. I just couldn't figure out how things worked. And most of the illustrators I admired were on the East Coast anyway. I was in Los Angeles showing my things to people from the galleries who commission art, and they kept saying, 'It's too European, it's too dark. You would have to lighten the sky and come up with some bright colors and some people on roller skates.' I was confused by it all."

Although Sis had difficulty obtaining film and illustration jobs during his first years in the United States, he did find work teaching classes in illustration in Los Angeles. In addition, he illustrated two of Aesop's fables for television. Sis also kept up contact with a woman in Switzerland who commissioned artists to paint eggs for her. He found the job difficult "because of course you cannot paint on regular chicken eggs. They're too small, so you need like goose or duck eggs. Where do you get goose and duck eggs in Los Angeles unless you go to Chinatown?" Sis had trouble buying the large eggs, since they weren't readily available—even from merchants in Chinatown. "I tried to explain that I didn't want to eat them. I just needed the shells. It was kind of funny."

At about the same time, Sis took the advice of a friend who suggested that he send a sample of his work to famous American children's writer and illustrator Maurice Sendak. Sis never expected to get a response, but Sendak was impressed enough with the young artist's work to call him personally and discuss his career aspirations. Several months

later, Sendak called again while attending the 1984 American Library Association convention, which was held in Los Angeles. He invited Sis to join him at the convention and introduced him to Ava Weiss, art director of Greenwillow Books, a New York City-based publisher. Sis broke into the American book illustration market on the spot, agreeing to illustrate George Shannon's *Bean Boy*. "It was just like a fairy tale, because it all happened in one afternoon," he told *SATA.*

It had become increasingly clear that Sis needed to move to New York, the U.S. publishing center, in order to widen his sphere of job possibilities. In fact, he was in the process of relocating to the East Coast when *Bean Boy* was published. Still, after arriving in New York in 1985, Sis found it hard to obtain enough work to pay his bills. He admitted to *SATA,* "It's difficult being on your own and beginning somewhere without really a penny," but added that his eagerness to prove himself motivated him to "work day and night."

Following *Bean Boy,* Sis illustrated two more books for Greenwillow, Sid Fleischman's juvenile novel *The Whipping Boy,* which won the Newbery Medal in 1985, and *Stories to Solve: Folktales from around the World,* by Shannon. The pictures in both books are black and white. Sis informed *SATA* that it is common practice for publishers to restrict new artists to black and white illustrations for a while, until they have demonstrated solid skills in basic sketch technique. "Gradually I worked through three or four books to get to color." Sis also had to Americanize his drawing style by modifying his portrayal of the human face. His initial drawings for *Bean Boy* were considered too foreign by American publishing standards. According Sis's art director, the features of the title character needed softening—especially the little pointed nose. He quoted her as saying, "The face looks too European. Make it more American with the nose." Sis made the necessary adjustments and received national acclaim for his contributions to the book.

The artist's hard work paid off. Sis became a regular contributor of illustrations to the *New York Times Book Review* and, over the next five years, he illustrated nearly a dozen books for various authors and published his first four self-illustrated children's books. His varied experiences as an illustrator have provided him with some broad insights into the world of book illustration. The job of a professional illustrator, Sis suggested in his *SATA* interview, is to provide pictures that will complement an author's story and capture the spirit of the text. But when designing artwork for other authors' books, illustrators are not given considerable freedom in determining which scenes to draw. "If somebody writes about a forest or something, I'm forced to do fifty thousand trees, even if I don't feel like doing trees," he explained. "The advantage of being my own writer is that I can always write about a desert and one palm tree or something. That's a great thing—if I don't want to deal with something, I don't have to do it."

Despite his preference for working on self-illustrated children's books, Sis has received rave reviews for the books he illustrates for other authors. Many critics consider Sis a master craftsman who possesses an uncanny ability to create artwork that heightens the mood established in an author's story. The dreamy, magical quality of his oil paintings for Fleischman's 1987 book *The Scarebird,* for instance, parallels the development of an enduring bond between the two main characters—an old, lonely farmer and his young hired hand. Some reviewers have noted that the old man's solitude is mirrored in the illustrator's depiction of the vast, expansive, sweeping sky. "As the intensity of the sky and the colors build up through the book," asserted Sis, "the relationship between the man and the boy is building up." Liz Rosenberg, writing in the *New York Times Book Review,* commented that Sis's illustrations for *The Scarebird* "have a luminous, stark, cartoony quality, an awkward loveliness that, like the prose, conveys much by what is left unsaid."

Sis enjoys the opportunities afforded him by the American book publishing market. "In Central Europe," he told *SATA,* "artists develop a certain style and stick to it throughout their entire careers." But in the United States, Sis is given more freedom to vary his style, work on different types of projects, and experiment with assorted illustration techniques. "I'm grateful that I can sort of play around and try new things. It's great that I can approach each project differently." When designing his own self-illustrated books, Sis says he trusts "in inspiration, instinct, and impulse, rather than having figured things out completely from the beginning. I am always tempted by some image. I see images and then start to make a story around them."

Two of Sis's books developed from little ideas that sprang from his observations of situations around him—like the way the elevators work in the *New York Times* building or the way people hail cabs in New York City. "One of the first things that happened to me in New York was that I saw this person waving," he related to *SATA.* "I thought, great, nobody I know—just a friendly person. Then I realized that person was waving at a cab. Later, I read in the *New York Times* about this woman who was waving at a cab. At the same time, a bus with out of town tourists was passing by, and they thought she was waving at them, so they started waving at her. They happened to be passing a cafe on Seventh

Avenue where people sit outside, and they thought the bus was waving at them, so the people in the cafe started waving at the bus. For three minutes the whole street was waving!" That story grew into *Waving: A Counting Book,* which was published in 1988.

Waving was followed by *Going Up!: A Color Counting Book,* about the people a little girl encounters on an elevator, and *Beach Ball,* which traces a girl's romp through the sand after her elusive ball. All three books—*Waving, Going Up,* and *Beach Ball*—feature the same little girl, Mary, as a main character. She is an innocent character that Sis based in combination on his mother, who lived for a time in the United States as a child, and her mother, who was called by the American name Mary.

Sis's 1991 book *Follow the Dream: The Story of Christopher Columbus* retells the tale of the Italian explorer's accidental discovery of the new world while trying to reach the Orient by a westward route from Europe in 1492. The book was inspired in part by Sis's continuing fascination with his father's exploration and travels and his own journey from a Soviet-dominated country to the new world. "Columbus didn't let the walls hold him back. For him, the outside world was not to be feared but *explored,*" wrote Sis in his introduction to the book. "With the Columbus story," he explained to *SATA,* "I realized coincidental things with my own life or with somebody who wants to break free from certain situations. With determination and persistence, a person can do it." In 1989, seven years after his arrival in America, Sis obtained U.S. citizenship. He further expressed to *SATA* a desire to share his attainment of freedom with other people who feel repressed or imprisoned in some way. "I also thought this might be a wonderful story for kids who live in urban ghettos or something."

Sis considers *Follow the Dream* his "biggest and best book so far." Experimenting with both color and composition, he used oil colors on special plaster-like backgrounds to achieve the textured, old-world look of fifteenth-century paintings. In addition, the nature of the subject matter gave Sis the freedom to create otherworldly images and creatures. For instance, the book's end papers show monsters outside the walls of Europe. There is a man with one foot, a man with a dog face, a cyclops, and a man with no head. In classic old books these beasts represented to Europeans what people looked like outside the continent's boundaries.

It took Sis about seven or eight months to complete the artwork for *Follow the Dream.* The original illustrations are about three times larger than the copies that appear in the book, and Sis reportedly spread the huge pictures out on the walls and floors of his New York City loft. "I was trying to achieve some continuity. It was intense. I thought it would never end, but I had wonderful help from Terry Lajtha, who is now my wife. We said that when I finished with it we would go to Padua in Italy for our wedding. Everything was arranged for the wedding, so she said that I had better make sure it's finished."

Sis actually developed the idea for his next book, *The Whale's Tail,* before he started work on *Follow the Dream.* "The Whale's Tail* is based on a true story I'd seen on public television about the whale that was captured as a little baby and kept in San Diego Zoo for a year," Sis explained in his *SATA* interview. "The whale grew up so much that the zoo couldn't possibly keep her. It was a sad film. The zookeepers released the whale, expecting that she would join the other whales. But she liked children, so when they would take a

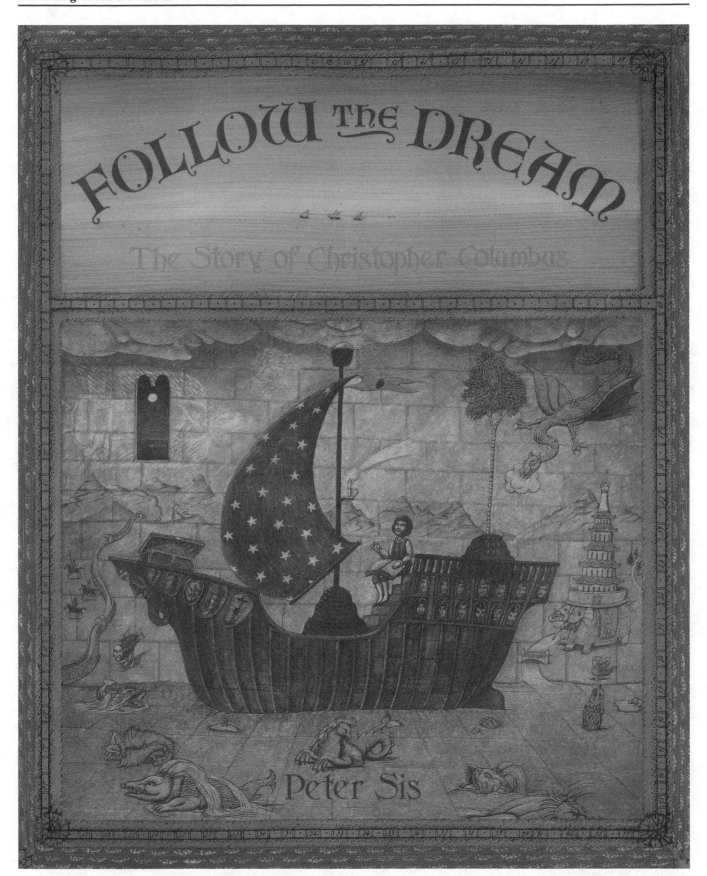

Sis's 1991 book, *Follow the Dream: The Story of Christopher Columbus,* was inspired in part by his own journey from a Soviet-dominated country to the new world.

In *Follow the Dream*, Sis used watercolors on special plaster-like backgrounds to achieve the textured look of fifteenth-century paintings.

walk on the shore she would come very close like she wanted to play. I wrote the book from the perspective of the whale. She was with people since she was a little, little whale and had never seen any other whales, so she didn't even know what they looked like. The whole book is a sort of visual poetry. There's lots of water and one whale always lonely in the middle of it. It's a very spacious book.''

The loneliness that pervades *The Whale's Tail* hearkens back to Sis's 1987 self-illustrated book for children titled *Rainbow Rhino*. The book tells the story of Rainbow Rhinoceros and his friends, the three rainbow birds, who live together ''somewhere behind the mountains in the middle of a deep valley.'' One day they all venture up the mountain to explore the unknown land that lies beyond the mysterious forest. First one bird, then another, and finally the last is lured away from the group by the overpowering beauty of their new and wondrous surroundings, until the rhino is left alone to wan-

der the mountainside. But the rhino and the three birds soon learn of the perils of the forest, find one another once more, and return to the safety and serenity of the valley. The story proves that ''no one . . . can content himself with mere bliss that is too easily available,'' noted Janwillem van de Wetering in the *New York Times Book Review*.

''*Rainbow Rhino* is the story of the immigration in a sense,'' Sis told *SATA*, ''even though it is like a contradiction in that the rhino goes back home after seeing the outside world because it's dangerous out there.'' At one point it looked like a Czechoslovakian film company was interested in making a film out of the book. But Sis maintains that he ''won't allow it because it would be like telling people not to go out and explore because of the dangers.'' Sis did not intend for *Rainbow Rhino* to be interpreted in a political context. His original intent, he confided to *SATA*, was simply to create a book that would make children happy.

Sis's art reflects his upbringing in an atmosphere that balanced creative freedom with structure and discipline. (Postcard of "Channeling," by Sis.)

Rainbow Rhino was listed among the *New York Times* ten best illustrated children's books of 1987. Many critics praised Sis for his harmonious blend of straightforward text and enchanting paintings, noting especially his refined and soulful characterization of the rhino, his ability to portray changes in mood and emotions through the use of color, and his hazy, spacious depictions of distant stretches of land. Commenting on both the beauty and simplicity of Sis's words and pictures, van de Wetering declared that in *Rainbow Rhino*, the artist comes "close to true innocence through a variety of skillful techniques."

Through his work, Sis aims to cultivate free and open thought among children. In his *SATA* interview, he expressed his belief that an artist's works should challenge a child's imagination. He is especially intrigued by the wonder and innocence of early elementary school students. "I really like talking to second graders. The young kids are wonderful because their minds are completely open. And the feelings children have here are probably the same as children have all over the world. It's amazing to see—in Asia, Thailand, Indonesia, or wherever—how similar the children are, whether they play with a piece of wood, or they play with very sophisticated computer."

To exemplify his ideas about the development of young people's imaginations, Sis alluded to a short story by German novelist Thomas Mann called "A Man and His Dog." "It takes place in Venice and one of the characters is a very rich woman," explained Sis. "She has a dog that only eats certain food and sleeps on a silk pillow. After midnight, while the narrator of the story is taking a walk, he meets up with the woman's dog. He sees that this creature is completely dirty and actually eats from the garbage cans at night." Sis warns against children being brought up in a very narrow world with only the best of everything and feels that young people should be exposed to alternative cultures, viewpoints, and ways of life to achieve a balanced perspective of the world around them. "I think children should have choices, and I would like to participate in their growth." Indeed, Sis advises young readers who aspire to a career as an artist to persevere and "not be intimidated by anybody." He believes that artistic talent should develop naturally, and a child should be left to "create freely—without any pressure to achieve commercial success."

"I hope I have some children soon because then, I think, a completely new door would open to me. I can see the importance of education and reading, and I want to do much more about it," Sis revealed in his *SATA* interview. He would like to continue sharing his experiences with young people, and he feels that the best way to do it is through pictures and books. "I still think I might be able, in the future, to come up with some combination of books and films, something that would let me use both my educational upbringing as an animator and filmmaker and my experience as a children's book writer. It's a sort of civic responsibility, but it's also a romantic thing. I would like to recreate something from childhood—create something wonderful, some sort of magic."

WORKS CITED:

Rosenberg, Liz, "Lonesome John Finds a Friend," *New York Times Book Review,* November 13, 1988, p. 56.

Sis, Peter, *Rainbow Rhino,* Random House, 1987.

Sis, Peter, *Follow the Dream: The Story of Christopher Columbus,* Knopf, 1991.

Sis, Peter, telephone interview with Barbara Carlisle Bigelow for *Something about the Author,* conducted June 6, 1991.

van de Wetering, Janwillem, review of *Rainbow Rhino, New York Times Book Review,* November 8, 1987, p. 42.

FOR MORE INFORMATION SEE:

PERIODICALS

Horn Book, July/August, 1987.

Kirkus Reviews, August 15, 1989.

New York Times Book Review, May 8, 1988.

Publishers Weekly, June 12, 1987; February 26, 1988; September 9, 1988; March 24, 1989; August 10, 1990.

Teaching K-8, April, 1988.

Time, December 14, 1987.

Wilson Library Bulletin, June, 1989.

Sketch by Barbara Carlisle Bigelow

*   *   *

SMITH, Jessie
See KUNHARDT, Edith

SVEND OTTO SOERENSEN

SOERENSEN, Svend Otto 1916-
(Svend Otto; Svend Otto S.)

PERSONAL: Born June 2, 1916, in Copenhagen, Denmark; son of Conrad and Anna Kristine (Pedersen) Soerensen; married Eva Wiborg, March 1, 1947; divorced, 1984; children: Kristin, Annette, Tine. *Education:* Attended Danish State Arts and Craft School, Bizzie Hoeyers Malerskole, and St. Martin's School of Art, London. *Religion:* Protestant. *Hobbies and other interests:* Travel (Europe, China, Africa, Mexico); "I always visit and stay in the countries I draw and write about in my books."

ADDRESSES: Home—Orehoejvei 26, 4320 Lejre, Denmark.

CAREER: Children's book author and illustrator.

AWARDS, HONORS: Highly commended Hans Christian Andersen Medal nominee, 1976; Hans Christian Andersen Medal, 1978; Golden Plaquette Prag, 1981; *The Runaway Pancake* was named a Children's Choice Book, International Reading Association and Children's Book Council, 1981; Danish Illustration Prize from Culture Ministry, 1982; Nordic Children's Book Prize, 1989.

WRITINGS:

AUTHOR AND ILLUSTRATOR UNDER NAME SVEND OTTO; IN ENGLISH TRANSLATION

Tim and Trisha, translation by Joan Tate, M. Joseph, 1977 (originally published in Denmark as *Tim og Trine,* 1976).

Taxi Dog, Parents' Magazine Press, 1978 (published in England as *Jasper the Taxi Dog;* originally published in Denmark as *Taxa-hunden Jesper,* 1977).

Inuk and His Sledge-Dog (also see below), translation by Tate, Pelham, 1979 (originally published in Denmark as *Mads og Millalik*).

Jon's Big Day (also see below), translation by Tate, Pelham, 1981 (originally published in Denmark as *Helgis store dag*).

The Giant Fish (also see below), translation by Tate, Pelham, 1981 (originally published in Denmark as *Kaempefisken*).

The Giant Fish and Other Stories (includes *Inuk and His Sledge Dog* and *Jon's Big Day*), translation from Danish by Tate, Larousse, 1982.

Children of the Yangtze River, translation by Tate, Pelham, 1982 (originally published in Denmark as *Boernene ved Yangtze Kiang*).

AUTHOR AND ILLUSTRATOR UNDER NAME SVEND OTTO S.; IN ENGLISH TRANSLATION

Ling and the Little Devils, translation by Tate, Pelham, 1984 (originally published in Denmark as *Ling og de sma djaevle*).

Small in a Big World, Gyldendal, 1987 (originally published in Denmark as *Lille i den store verden*).

The Flood, Gyldendal, 1988 (originally published in Denmark as *Stormfloden*).

The Kamelrider, Gyldendal, 1989 (originally published in Denmark as *Kamelrytteren*).

The Dragon and the Small Lake Trolls, Gyldendal, 1990 (originally published in Denmark as *Dragen og de sma soetrolde*).

ILLUSTRATOR UNDER NAME SVEND OTTO; IN ENGLISH TRANSLATION

Lennart Hellsing, *The Wonderful Pumpkin,* Atheneum, 1976 (published in Sweden as *Der underbara pumpan,* Raben & Sjoegren [Stockholm], 1975).

Joan Tate, *The Fox and the Stork,* Pelham, 1985.

Astrid Lindgren, *My Nightingale Is Singing,* translation by Crampton, Viking, 1986 (originally published in Denmark as *Spelar min lind sjunger min naektergal*).

Also illustrator of *Avalanche!,* translation by Tate, 1987 (originally published in Denmark as *Lawinegevaar!*), *The Camel Rider,* 1989, *Old Danish Trees,* 1990, *Mother Holle,* and Aesop's *The Donkey and His Dog.*

ILLUSTRATOR UNDER NAME SVEND OTTO S.; IN ENGLISH TRANSLATION

Hans Christian Andersen, *The Tinder Box,* translation from Danish by M. R. James, Van Nostrand, 1971.

Andersen, *The Fir Tree,* translation by M. R. James, Van Nostrand, 1971 (originally published in Denmark as *Grantraet*).

Puss in Boots, Ward Lock, 1973.

Jakob Ludwig Karl and Wilhelm Karl Grimm, *The Musicians of Bremen,* translation from Danish by Anne Rogers, Larousse, 1974.

J. and W. Grimm, *Snow White and the Seven Dwarfs,* translation from Danish by Rogers, Larousse, 1975.

J. and W. Grimm, *Briar Rose, the Sleeping Beauty,* translation by Rogers, Larousse, 1975 (published in Denmark as *Dornroschen*).

J. and W. Grimm, *Tom Thumb,* translation from Danish by Anthea Bell, Larousse, 1976.

J. and W. Grimm, *The Wolf and the Seven Little Kids,* translation from Danish by Rogers, Pelham, 1977.

J. and W. Grimm, *Cinderella,* translation by Rogers, Larousse, 1978 (published in Denmark as *Aschenputtel*).

Peter Faber, *A Christmas Book,* translation by Tate, Pelham Books, 1978 (originally published in Denmark as *Sikken voldsom traengsel og alarm*).

J. and W. Grimm, *The Best of Grimm's Fairy Tales,* translation from Danish by Bell and Rogers, Larousse, 1979 (published in England as *Favourite Tales from Grimm,* Pelham, 1979).

J. and W. Grimm, *The Brave Little Tailor,* translation from Danish by Bell, Larousse, 1979.

Andersen, *The Ugly Duckling,* translation from Danish by Bell, Kaye & Ward, 1979.

Kirsten Hare, *Karen and the Space Machine,* translation from Danish by Tate, Pelham, 1979.

Peter Christen Asbjoernsen and Joergen Moe, *The Runaway Pancake,* translation by Tate, Pelham, 1980 (originally published in Denmark as *Pandekagen*).

Robert Fisker, *Sparrow Flies Away,* translation from Danish by Tate, Pelham, 1980.

Fisker, *Sparrow Falls Out of the Nest,* translation from Danish by Tate, Pelham, 1981.

Hans Hansen, *Jenny Moves House,* translation from Danish by Tate, Pelham, 1981.

J. and W. Grimm, *Hansel and Gretel,* translation from Danish by Bell, Larousse, 1983 (published in Denmark as *Hans og Grete*).

J. and W. Grimm, *More Favourite Tales from Grimm,* translation from Danish by Bell and Rogers, Pelham, 1983.

Gunnel Linde, *Bicycles Don't Grow on Trees,* translation from Swedish by Patricia Crampton, Dent, 1984.

Linde, *Trust in the Unexpected,* translation by Crampton, Atheneum, 1984 (originally published in Sweden as *Lita pae det ovaentade*).

Bjarne Reuter, *The Princess and the Sun, Moon and Stars,* translation by Tate, Pelham, 1986 (originally published in Denmark as *Da solen skulle saegles*).

P. Asbjoernsen, *The Three Billy Goats Gruff: A Retelling of a Classic Tale,* Heath, c. 1989 (published in Norway as *Tre bukkene bruse*).

Also illustrator of Arthur Conan Doyle's *Silver.*

AUTHOR AND ILLUSTRATOR OF UNTRANSLATED WORKS UNDER NAME SVEND OTTO S.

I en fynsk Hoestak, Aschehoug (Copenhagen), 1946.

Also author and illustrator of *Boernene i Nordatlanten,* 1981; *Lavinen kommer,* 1986.

ILLUSTRATOR OF UNTRANSLATED WORKS UNDER NAME SVEND OTTO

Hans Christian Andersen, *Boernenes,* Carlsen (Copenhagen), 1972.

Soeren Christensen, *Tornerose i eventyrskoven og andre kapitler om folkeeventyr,* Gyldendal (Copenhagen), 1976.

ILLUSTRATOR OF UNTRANSLATED WORKS UNDER NAME SVEND OTTO S.

Herman Bang, *Sommerglaeder,* Lademann (Copenhagen), 1970.

Andersen, *Bornenes H. C. Andersen,* Carlsen, 1972.

J. and W. Grimm, *Gweneira,* Gwaag y Dref Wan (Cardiff), 1975.

Anine Rud, *Pigen der var klogere end kejseren og andre folkeeventyr om kloge kvinder,* Gyldendal, 1976.

Maria Kirstine Dorothea Jensen, *Stygge Krumpen,* Lademann, 1976.

Ebbe Klovedal Reich, *Nissen fra Nuernberg,* Gyldendal, 1979.

Mada agus Millalik, Oifig an tSolathair (Dublin), 1979.

Lars-Henrik Olsen, *Landet pae den anden side,* Mallings (Copenhagen), c. 1982.

Also illustrator of numerous other untranslated works including Aesop's *Aeselet og hunden* and *Storken og reven;* Jette Ahm's *Ahasveris—Jerusalems skomager* and *Fredloes—i Haraldsted skov;* Julens Ander's *Et juleeventyr;* Hans Christian Andersen's *Den grimme aelling* and *Eventyr;* Franz Berliner's *Hestestormen;* Christian Bernhardsen's *Lille Ven;* Cecil Boedker's *Flugten fra Farao* and *Maria's kind;* Aage Brandt's *Filippo og friheden;* Hanne Brandt's *Min soester Linda;* Onelio Jorge Cardoso's *Negrita;* Gustav Christiansen's *Daen levene tsid;* Ole E. Christiansen's *Greve Arres kiste* Soeren Christensen's *Prins Karl og den gyldne fugl;* J. F. Cooper's *Stifinder;* Robert Fisker's *Mikkel Ravn i den doede by, Mikkel Ravn i Skanoer, Mikkel Ravn pae Haervejen, Mikkel Ravn ved Skanderborg, Piita-Tukak namminiilerpog,* and *Sparvungens foersta aer;* Grimms' *Bord daek dig, Den store eventyrbog, Den tapre skraedder, Mor Hulda, Roedhaette,* and *Tornerose;* Hans Hansen's *Vi er flyttet, Nuukkatta;* Martin Hansen's *Synden;* Kirsten Hare's *Bomber*

Soerensen, who has illustrated many stories by Hans Christian Andersen, was first introduced to the tales when he was four. (Illustration by Soerensen from Andersen's *The Ugly Duckling*.)

mod Koebenhavn, Det beqyndte pae et marked, Mystik i Tunesien, and *Rufo og Helia;* Knud Hermansen's *Aret rundt, De smae blokke, Opgaver S og M boegerne, Soeren og mette, Soeren og Mette og deres kammerater, Soeren og Mette og dyrene, Soren og Mette laeser historier,* and *Vi loeser opgaver;* Knud Holst's *Laerken;* Folke Barker Joergensen's *Den store gevinst;* Helga Joergensen's *Den lille bonde;* Kurt Juul's *Oernens Klo;* Ole Lund Kirkegaard's *Jeq og bestefar—og Nisse-Nils* and *Mig og bedstefar—og sae Nisse Pok;* Ebbe Kloevedal Reich's *David—de fredloeses konge, David—Guds udvalgte konge,* and *David—slaegtens konge;* Goesta Knutsson's *Hvordan skal det gae Pelle Haleloes?, Pelle Haleloes i skolen,* and *Pelle Haleloes og gravhunden Max;* Gunnel Linde's *Hur natten ser ut pae mitten, Midt pae natta,* and *Tro altid pae det uventede;* Astrid Lindgren's *Alle vi boern i Bulderby, Bulderbybogen, Jonas og Lotte og jeg, Mere om os boern i Bulderby,* and *Suser min lind;* Vilhelm Lytken's *Trofast skal ikke doe;* Martin Miehe-Renard's *Jul pae slottet;* Torben Olsen's *Den dumme trold;* Iva Prochazkova's *Sommeren med Amos* and *Der sommer hat Eselohren;* Bent Rasmussen's *Drengen fra Afu Afu;* and *Greve Arres skat;* Bjarne Reuter's *De man die de zon wilde kopen* and *Ta i solin skuldi seljast;* Robert Louis Stevenson's *Dr. Jekyll og Mr.*

Hyde; Renate Welsh's *Nina—og de andre;* and K. H. With's *Musebogen.*

OTHER

Also illustrator of *Ein Tag im Land der Trolle, Dagur viku, Flundran, Mass og Milalikkur,* and *Hesten uden hoved* (title means "The Horse without a Head") by Berna. Also illustrator of books for adults, including Thomas Mann's *Buddenbrook,* Franz Kafka's *The Process,* Alain Fournier's *Le Grand Meaulnes,* Charles Dickens' *A Christmas Carol,* and Richard Llewellyn's *How Green Was My Valley.* Author and illustrator under name Svend Otto of *Helgis store dag,* 1980, *Kaempefisken,* 1981. Also illustrator of the covers of approximately 1,500 books.

SIDELIGHTS: Under the name Svend Otto S., internationally renowned illustrator Svend Otto Soerensen has provided the artwork for hundreds of books by other authors in addition to illustrating many of his own texts. His books, primarily intended for children, have been published in his native Denmark, as well as Sweden, Norway, Finland, France, Germany, Greenland, Greece, Holland, Faero Islands, Iceland, Ireland, Wales, Portugal, Japan, China,

South Africa, and the United States. "Svend Otto's special quality as an artist is an enormous desire to make things come alive," states Gunnar Jakobsen in *Bookbird.* "His art work is meant to communicate what he sees. He absorbs the text and creates a parallel to it, thus rendering the text intelligible by directing attention to it."

Born in Copenhagen in 1916, Svend Otto S. grew up in the working-class community of Falster. In an interview with Jakob Gormsen in *Bookbird,* he recalls that when he was four, his mother introduced him to the tales of Hans Christian Andersen; and although the stories were frequently beyond his age, he was able to understand them by intuition. He remembers being struck by how much he was able to understand from the illustrations by Wilhelm Pedersen and Froehlich. "In our circles no one knew that you could make a living by drawing," he tells Gormsen, adding, "In school I read about the possibility of becoming an illustrator but the only thing that was said about this vocation was that you had to tighten your belt for seven years." He recently remarked, "But I did not have to wait so long!"

Svend Otto S. drew his first picture at the age of three as "a protest against being so bundled up," he tells Gormsen: "I drew a picture of myself in a giant coat in rainy weather. I still have this picture and it's not so bad." After studying art under Bizzie Hoeyer and at the St. Martin's School of Art in London, he made book covers, posters, and magazine illustrations. Later on, he illustrated books and children's books for Gyldendal and other publishers. Illustrations "should be a visual extension to the text," Svend Otto S. tells Gormsen, explaining that "you can, for example, show readers an environment which they otherwise wouldn't know or the

atmosphere in which the action occurs." In his Hans Christian Andersen Medal acceptance speech, he delineates the lofty goals he has for his illustrations: "I would like to make everyday things fantastic and fantastic things realistic. . . . I want to stimulate children's feelings for poetry. . . . I want to arouse compassion and warmth between people."

WORKS CITED:

Gormsen, Jakob, "An Interview with Svend Otto S., the Famous Danish Illustrator," *Bookbird,* January, 1979, pp. 6-12.
Jakobsen, Gunnar, *Bookbird,* November, 1989, pp. 13-22.
S., Svend Otto, "Acceptance Speech—1978 H. C. Andersen Illustrator's Medal," *Bookbird,* April, 1978.

FOR MORE INFORMATION SEE:

PERIODICALS

Bulletin of the Center for Children's Books, June, 1978; September, 1978; May, 1983.
New Statesman, December 7, 1984.
New Yorker, December 6, 1982.
New York Times Book Review, December 14, 1980.
School Library Journal, September, 1978; November, 1981; October, 1982; August, 1983.
Times Educational Supplement, November 17, 1978; May 1, 1981; May 15, 1987.
Times Literary Supplement, March 27, 1981; March 26, 1982.

*   *   *

SORENSEN, Svend Otto
See SOERENSEN, Svend Otto

*   *   *

STANGL, (Mary) Jean 1928-

PERSONAL: Born May 14, 1928, in Irondale, MO; daughter of Joseph (a rancher) and Cecil (Parrack) Green; married Herbert Stangl (with Naval Office), August 14, 1946; children: Steve, Kenneth, Bruce. *Education:* University of La Verne, B.A., 1975; California State University, Northridge, M.A., 1977. *Politics:* Democrat. *Religion:* Protestant. *Hobbies and other interests:* Flower gardening, swimming, hiking, traveling, reading, and collecting old children's books and lead crystal vases and animals.

ADDRESSES: Home—1658 Calle La Cumbre, Camarillo, CA 93010.

CAREER: Ventura Community College, Ventura, CA, instructor in early childhood education, 1975-85; University of California, Santa Barbara, CA, instructor in extension department, 1976-85.

MEMBER: Society of Children's Book Writers (regional advisor), Southern California Council on Literature for Children and Young People, National Association for the Education of Young Children, Friends of the Library.

WRITINGS:

Finger Painting Is Fun, privately printed, 1975.

Self-illustrated notecard from Soerensen.

JEAN STANGL

The No-Cook Cookery Cookbook, privately printed, 1976.
Paper Stories, Pitman Learning, 1984.
Holiday Movement Activities, Front Row Experience, 1984.
Flannelgraphs: Flannel Board Fun for Little Ones, Pitman Learning, 1986.
Magic Mixtures: Creative Fun for Little Ones, Pitman Learning, 1986.
Fingerlings: Finger Puppet Fun for Little Ones, Pitman Learning, 1986.
Cut and Tell Bible Stories: Old Testament, Standard Publishing, 1987.
Cut and Tell Bible Stories: New Testament, Standard Publishing, 1987.
The Tools of Science, Dodd, Mead, 1987.
Is Your Storytale Dragging?, Fearon, 1987.
Hats, Hats, and More Hats: 70 Hats Kids Can Make and Wear, Fearon, 1989.
Crystals and Crystal Gardens You Can Grow, F. Watts, 1990.
H2O Science: Water Science Activities, Fearon, 1990.
Gardening Fun for Little Ones, Fearon, 1991.
Movement Fun for Little Ones, Fearon, 1991.
Mother Goose Fun for Little Ones, Fearon, 1991.
A Treasure Chest of Patterns, Fearon, 1991.
A Treasure Chest of Pattern Ideas, Fearon, 1991.
Story Sparklers, Denison, 1991.
Recycle-Saurus, Fearon, 1992.

Also author of Bible stories, activities, take-home story papers, crafts, and Bible school materials for Gospel Light Publishers. Contributor to *Children, Ranger Rick Nature Magazine, Ebony, Jr., Friend, On the Line, First Teacher,* *Instructor, Learning, Early Years, Living with Preschoolers, Mother Earth News, Mature Living,* and *Women's Circle.*

* * *

STEINBERG, Saul 1914-

PERSONAL: Born June 15, 1914, in Ramnicul-Sarat, Romania; came to the United States, 1942; naturalized U.S. citizen, 1943; son of Moritz (a box manufacturer) and Rosa (a cakemaker; maiden name, Jacobson) Steinberg; married Hedda Lindenberg Sterne (a painter), October 11, 1943. *Education:* Attended University of Bucharest, 1932; Reggio Politecnico (Milan), Dottore Architettura, 1940.

CAREER: Artist. Worked as cartoonist in Milan, Italy, for *Bertoldo,* 1936-39; practicing architect in Milan, 1939-41; free-lance cartoonist and illustrator, 1941—; writer, 1949—. Artist-in-residence, Smithsonian Institution, 1966-67. *Military service:* U.S. Naval Reserve, 1943-46; became lieutenant.

EXHIBITIONS: One-man: Wakefield Gallery, New York City, 1943; Young Books, Inc., New York City, 1945; Institute of Design, Chicago, Ill., 1948; Museum of Art, Rhode Island School of Design, Providence, 1950; Betty Parsons Gallery, New York City, 1950, 1952, 1966, 1969, 1973, 1976; Galleria l'Obelisco, Rome, Italy, 1951, 1952, 1957; Galeria de Arte, Sao Paulo, Brazil, 1952; Museu de Arte, Sao Paulo, 1952; Gump's Gallery, San Francisco, Calif., 1952; Institute of Contemporary Arts, London, England, 1952, 1957; Sidney Janis Gallery, New York City, 1952, 1966, 1969, 1973, 1976; Kunsthalle, Wuppertal-Barmen, West Germany, 1952; Leopold-Hoesch-Museum, Dueren, West Germany, 1952; Frank Perls Gallery, Beverly Hills, Calif., 1952; Arts Clubs of Chicago, 1953; Galerie Blanche, Stockholm, Sweden, 1953; Galerie Maeght, Paris, 1953, 1966, 1971, 1973, 1974, 1977; Stedelijk Museum, Amsterdam, Netherlands, 1953; Virginia Museum of Fine Arts, Richmond, 1953; Corcoran Gallery of Art, Washington, D.C., 1954; Dallas Museum of Fine Arts, Texas, 1954; Museum am Ostwall, Dortmund, West Germany, 1954; Frankfurter Kunstkabinett, Frankfurt, West Germany, 1954; Kestner-Gesellschaft, Hannover, West Germany, 1954; Kunstmuseum, Basel, Switzerland, 1954; Santa Barbara Museum, Calif., 1954; Harvard School of Design, Cambridge, Mass., 1955; Allan Frumkin Gallery, Chicago, 1956; Musee d'Art Moderne, Brussels, Belgium, 1959, 1967.

The Art Gallery, University of California, Santa Barbara, 1962; Davison Art Center, Wesleyan University, Middletown, Conn., 1965; Wallraf-Richartz-Museum, Cologne, West Germany, 1966; B. C. Holland Gallery, Chicago, Ill., 1967; Museum Boymans-van Beuningen, Rotterdam, Netherlands, 1967; Obelisk Gallery, Boston, Mass., 1967; Musees Royaux des Beaux-Arts de Belgique, Brussels, 1967; Museo de Bellas Artes, Caracas, Venezuela, 1968; Hamburger Kunsthalle, Hamburg, West Germany, 1968; Irving Galleries, Milwaukee, Wis., 1968; Louisiana Museum, Humbleback, Denmark, 1968; Moderna Museet, Stockholm, 1968; J. L. Hudson Gallery, Detroit, Mich., 1969; Felix Landau Gallery, Los Angeles, Calif., 1970; Galerie Maeght, Zurich, Switzerland, 1971, 1977; Richard Gray Gallery, Chicago, 1971; Galleria Galatea, Milan, Italy, 1973; National Collection of Fine Arts, Smithsonian Institution, Washington, D.C., 1973-74; Institute of Contemporary Arts, Boston, Mass., 1974; traveling exhibition organized by Koelnischer Kunstverein, Cologne, exhibited at Wuerttembergischer

Kunstverein, Stuttgart, Kestner-Gesellschaft, Hannover, Kulturhaus der Stadt Graz, and Museum des 20, Jahrhunderts, Vienna, 1974-75, Whitney Museum, New York City, 1978.

Group shows: Museum of Modern Art, New York City, 1946, 1949; Detroit Institute of Arts, Mich., 1949; Whitney Museum of American Art, New York City, 1949, 1954-56, 1965, 1974; Art Institute of Chicago, Ill., 1949, 1952, 1971; Walker Art Center, Minneapolis, Minn., 1952; Institute of Contemporary Arts, London, 1952; American Federation of Arts, New York City, 1953, 1970; Brandeis University, Waltham, Mass., 1953; "X Triennale in Milano," Milan, 1954; Brooklyn Museum, N.Y., 1957; Fort Worth Art Center, Tex., 1958, 1969; Frederiksberg Town Hall, Copenhagen, Denmark, 1958; United States Pavilion, World's Fair, Brussels, 1958.

Horace Mann School, Riverdale, New York City, 1962; Norfolk Museum of Arts and Sciences, Va., 1962; "Die Kunst der Schrift," UNESCO (traveling exhibition), 1964; New School Art Center, New York City, 1965, 1969-70; The Art Gallery, University of California, Santa Barbara, 1966; Kunstverein und Akademie der Kuenste, Berlin, West Germany, 1966; Musee d' Art Moderne, Paris, 1966; Kunsthalle, Darmstadt, West Germany, 1967; Finch College Museum of Art, New York City, 1968; Kunstverein, Frankfurt, 1968; Museum of Art, Rhode Island School of Design, Providence, 1968.

Museum of Art, Carnegie Institute, Pittsburgh, Pa., 1970; Fondation Maeght, St.-Paul-de-Vence, France, 1970; Sidney Janis Gallery, New York City, 1970, 1975-76; Bibliotheque Nationale, Paris, 1971; Corcoran Gallery of Art, Washington, D.C., 1971; Kunsthalle, Recklinghausen, West Germany, 1972; Kunsthaus, Zurich, 1972; Yale University Art Gallery, New Haven, Conn., 1973; Galerie Beyeler, Basel,

Artist Saul Steinberg with cutout of himself as a boy.

1974; Cleveland Museum of Art, Ohio, 1974, 1975; Akron Art Institute, Ohio, 1976; Hamilton Gallery of Contemporary Art, New York City, 1977; Documenta Druck Verlag GmbH, Kassel, West Germany, 1977; Minnesota Museum of Art, St. Paul, 1977; Renwick Gallery, Smithsonian Institution, Washington, D.C., 1977.

Executed murals, including Terrace Plaza Hotel, Cincinnati, Ohio, 1947; United States Pavillion at Brussels World Fair, 1958. Work in collections, including Museum of Modern Art, N.Y.; Metropolitan Museum of Art, N.Y.; Detroit Institute of Art, Mich.; Victoria and Albert Museum, London, England; Albright-Knox Art Gallery, Buffalo, N.Y.; Fogg Museum, Harvard University, Cambridge, Mass.

AWARDS, HONORS: Gold Medal from American Academy and Institute of Arts and Letters, 1974.

WRITINGS:

ALL SELF-ILLUSTRATED

All in Line, Duell, Sloan & Pearce, 1945.
The Art of Living, Harper, 1949.
(Compiler) *The Cartoons of Cobean,* Harper, 1952.
The Passport, Harper, 1954, reissued, Random House, 1979.
Steinberg's Umgang mit Menschen, Rowohlt Verlag (West Germany), 1954.
Dessins, Gallimard (France), 1956.
The Labyrinth, Harper, 1960.
The Catalogue: A Selection of Drawings Reprinted from the Art of Living, the Passport, and the Labyrinth, World Publishing, 1962.
Steinberg's Paperback, Rowohlt Taschenbuch Verlag GmbH, 1964.
The New World, Harper, 1965.
The Inspector, Viking, 1973.

ILLUSTRATOR

Margaret Scoggin, editor, *Chucklebait: Funny Stories for Everyone,* Knopf, 1947.
M. Scoggin, editor, *More Chucklebait: Funny Stories for Everyone,* Knopf, 1949.
S. N. Behrman, *Duveen,* Random House, 1952.
Michel Butor and Harold Rosenberg, *Le Masque* (also illustrated with photographs by Inge Morath), Maeght Editeur (France), 1966.

Artwork represented in numerous collections, including *Drawings,* R. Piper [Munich], 1958, and *Saul Steinberg: Zeichnungen, Aquarelle, Collagen, Gemaelde, Reliefs, 1963-1974,* Koelnischer Kunstverein, 1974. Contributor of writings and artwork to periodicals, including *Harper's Bazaar, Life, PM,* and *New Yorker.*

SIDELIGHTS: Saul Steinberg was born in Ramnicul-Sarat, near Bucharest, Romania, on June 15, 1914. His father was a box manufacturer while his mother baked "wonderful cakes with all sorts of decorations. . . . ," Steinberg tells *People.* "My childhood still remains close to me. I can't understand the affliction called amnesia. I seem to remember everything from those times."

Sent to a local school where he felt himself to be a misfit, Steinberg found consolation in literature. An autobiographical story by Russian writer Maxim Gorky made a deep impression on the young boy. Steinberg tells *Time* that the story was "an excellent metaphor for how I felt. One must consider the idea of the artist as orphan, an orphaned prodigy, whose parents find him somewhere—the bulrushes, perhaps. To pretend to be an orphan, alone, is a form of narcissism. I suppose all children have this disgusting form of self-pity; but more so the artist, who is Robinson Crusoe. He must invent his stories, his pleasures; he succeeds in reconstructing a parody of civilization from scratch. He *makes* himself by education, by survival, by constantly paying attention to himself, but also by creating a world around himself that hadn't existed before. The corollary of this is the desire not to end childhood. Which in turn makes for a desire not to stop growing."

In 1933, after one year of studies at the University of Bucharest, Steinberg enrolled in the Reggio Politechnico in Milan, Italy, to study architecture. The school was heavily influenced by the Cubist art movement, Steinberg claims in *Time:* "You learn all the cliches of your time. My time was late cubism, via Bauhaus; our clouds came straight out of Arp [French sculptor], complete with a hole in the middle, even our trees were influenced by the mania for the kidney shape."

In 1936 Steinberg began selling his cartoons to *Bertoldo,* a satirical biweekly magazine in Milan. His first published drawing took only ten minutes to draw, but Steinberg gazed at it in the magazine for hours, amazed that he could make money from doing something he enjoyed.

Steinberg graduated as Dottore in Architettura in 1940. On his diploma was written: "Steinberg Saul . . . di razza Ebraica [of the Jewish race]." The notation was meant to identify Jewish graduates at a time of widespread antiSemitism. With the outbreak of World War II, Steinberg left Italy for neutral Portugal, where he boarded a boat to America. At Ellis Island he was met by immigration officials who asked questions. "But not hostile ones," Steinberg explains in *People.* "They were motherly. I found people who wanted to help."

Unfortunately, the small quota for Romanian immigrants had been filled and Steinberg was not allowed to enter the country. He found himself deported to Santo Domingo in the Caribbean. Even though he was not in the United States, he was able to begin publishing drawings in the *New Yorker* and in American newspapers. In July, 1942, sponsored by the *New Yorker,* he was able to immigrate to America, arriving in Miami, where he caught a bus to New York City.

Steinberg was soon drawing the American landscape, especially baseball games, small towns, and diners. His drawings were meant to serve as documents of a particular time and place. Some of the drawings influenced later artists to create Pop Art, which focuses exclusively on elements of popular culture.

In 1943 Steinberg enlisted in the U.S. Navy and participated in various World War II operations in India, China, North Africa, and Italy. In China he served as a kind of interpreter between the American and Chinese troops, his pictures illustrating what needed to be said. Writing in his book *Saul Steinberg,* Harold Rosenberg claims that "while [Steinberg] and the Chinese understood each other perfectly, he could not communicate with the Americans since he knew no English. His theory is that his real mission was to confuse enemy intelligence agents by compelling them to wonder what this foreigner was doing with the United States Navy in China."

In 1978 *Time* chronicled Steinberg's career as cartoonist and artist.

All in Line, Steinberg's first book of drawings, was published in 1945. A *Time* magazine critic reported: "The book is a collection of 210 acidulous, weavy, relaxed drawings, some of which look as though they had been made by dropping black thread on a white-washed floor . . . dozens of sharply observed, deftly reported spot scenes of U.S. military life superimposed on the life of China, India, Italy, North Africa. . . . His travel impressions (half the book) are vaguely intended to be geographical notes on the world as a G.I. sees it."

After the war Steinberg resumed his traveling. He enjoyed driving the roads of western America, touring according to a whimsical itinerary which allowed him to see the untouched backwoods of the country. In 1955, Steinberg's love of travel led to his being hired by *Life* magazine to do a series of baseball drawings. He travelled with the Milwaukee Braves to towns all over the Midwest. "Baseball," Steinberg explains in Rosenberg's book, "is an allegorical play about America, a poetic, complex and subtle play of courage, fear, good luck, mistakes, patience about fate and sober self-esteem (batting average). It is impossible to understand America without a thorough knowledge of baseball."

Steinberg has been influenced by a wide range of artistic styles, from ancient Egyptian paintings to advertising art. His study of architecture in particular has given him a respect for precision and draftsmanship. "I have to try everything," Steinberg tells *Art in America,* "and right now I'm going to go through painting for a while."

The variety of Steinberg's artwork was evident in his first American retrospective at the Whitney Museum in 1978.

Speaking of the show, Steinberg remarked in *Artnews:* "Seeing the retrospective is like looking at a group show. It has to be. It's the nature of my work. What I can see clearly is the evolution."

Steinberg's versatility has defied categorization. "I don't quite belong to the art, cartoon or magazine world," he notes in *Life,* "so the art world doesn't quite know where to place me." His place in the art world is less important to Steinberg than his standing with other artists. "Good artists have always accepted me. Lousy artists haven't," he remarks in *Art in America.* Steinberg's own evaluation of his work emphasizes his uniqueness, although not a uniqueness of technique. "My technique doesn't mean a thing," he explains in *Art in America.* "It's simple; it can be copied by anybody and I myself don't think of it as being original. I'm not looking for originality in a technique. I would say the same thing about Mozart, for example.... What's immediately recognizable about him is the unmistakable combination of sadness and gaiety, happiness plus a very active, very energetic melancholy. And I guess I have, and every artist has, something like this specific thing that I call either taste or aroma, that you can detect, before looking, from a distance. I guess if I want to compare myself to Mozart, I have the same thing—this sort of seriousness or melancholy, if you want, camouflaged as gaiety."

WORKS CITED:

Art in America, November-December, 1970, pp. 110-117.
Artnews, May, 1978, pp. 132-138.
Life, December 10, 1965, p. 59ff.
People, May 29, 1978, pp. 79-83.
Rosenberg, Harold, *Saul Steinberg,* Knopf, 1978, pp. 235-245.
Time, April 15, 1966, April 17, 1978, pp. 93-96.

FOR MORE INFORMATION SEE:

BOOKS

Current Biography 1957, H. W. Wilson, 1958.
Selden Rodman, *Conversations with Artists,* Devin-Adair, 1957.
Harold Rosenberg, *The Anxious Object,* Mentor Books, 1969.

PERIODICALS

American Artist, February, 1951.
Architectural Digest, December, 1982.
Architectural Forum, April, 1948.
Art Digest, August, 23, 1945.
Art in America, September/October, 1978.
Artnews, January, 1955; March, 1966; November, 1969.
Artnews Annual, [New York], 1970.
Commentary, October, 1947.
Daedalus, winter, 1960.
English Journal, November, 1971.
Esquire, April 25, 1978.
Forbes, December 25, 1978.
Harper's, April, 1952; August, 1954.
Horizon, April, 1978.
Jewish Observer and Middle East Review, May 30, 1952.
Life, August 27, 1951.
Nation, December 19, 1966.
Newsweek, February 11, 1952; April 28, 1958; December 12, 1966; April 17, 1978.
New Yorker, December 26, 1970.
New York Times, February 3, 1952; November 9, 1969; November 9, 1978.
New York Times Magazine, November 13, 1966; April 16, 1978.
Publishers Weekly, May 7, 1973.
Saturday Review, December 4, 1954; January 7, 1961.
Time, June 18, 1945; February 11, 1952; October 18, 1954; April 15, 1966; April 17, 1978.
Village Voice, December 10, 1980; May 13, 1981; May 22, 1984.*

*   *   *

STEVENS, Leonard A. 1920-

PERSONAL: Born November 7, 1920, in Lisbon, NH; son of Lawrence A. and Margaret (Healy) Stevens; married Carla McBride (a teacher of writing), December 18, 1954; children: Timothy, Brooke, Sara, April. *Education:* Attended St. Anselm College; University of Iowa, B.A., 1947, M.A., 1949. *Politics:* Democrat.

ADDRESSES: Home—Christian St., Bridgewater, CT 06752. *Office*—Box 38, New Milford, CT.

CAREER: Writer. Executive director of Housatonic Valley Association, CT, 1973-74; speech maker for Citizens Committee for the Hoover Report, New York, NY; news editor at Radio Station WSUI, Iowa City, IA, for two years. Former chairman, Bridgewater Board of Education; member, Bridgewater Conservation Commission. Delegate, National Democratic Convention, 1968, 1972; chairman, Bridgewater Democratic Town Committee. *Military service:* U.S. Army Air Forces, World War II; served in Guam with 20th Air Force; became captain.

AWARDS, HONORS: Equal: The Case of Integration vs. Jim Crow was listed as a children's book of the year, 1976, by Child Study Association.

WRITINGS:

FOR YOUNG PEOPLE

Old Peppersass: The Locomotive that Climbed Mount Washington, Dodd, 1959.
The Trucks that Haul by Night, Crowell, 1966.
The Elizabeth: Passage of a Queen, Knopf, 1968.
North Atlantic Jet Flight, Crowell, 1968.
How a Law Is Made: The Story of a Bill against Air Pollution, Crowell, 1970.
The Town that Launders Its Water: How a California Town Learned to Reclaim and Reuse Its Water, Coward, 1971.
Salute! The Case of the Bible vs. the Flag, Coward, 1973.
Clean Water: Nature's Way to Stop Pollution, Dutton, 1974.
Neurons: Building Blocks of the Brain, Crowell, 1974.
Equal!: The Case of Integration vs. Jim Crow, Coward, 1976.
Trespass!: The People's Privacy vs. the Power of the Police, Coward, 1977.
Death Penalty: The Case of Life vs. Death in the United States, Coward, 1978.
(With Joe Shoemaker) *Returning the Platte to the People: A Story of a Unique Committee, the Platte River Development Committee,* Greenway Foundation, 1981.

OTHER

(With Ralph G. Nichols) *Are You Listening?,* McGraw, 1957.
New York to Rome: Jet Flight 808, Harper, 1962.

On Growing Older, U.S. Government Printing Office, 1964.
The Ill-Spoken Word: The Decline of Speech in America, McGraw, 1966.
(Photographic illustrator) Carla M. Stevens, *The Birth of Sunset's Kittens,* Addison-Wesley, 1969.
Explorers of the Brain, Knopf, 1971.
(With Charly Baumann) *Tiger, Tiger: My Twenty-five Years with the Big Cats,* Playboy Press, 1975.
(With John Richard Sheaffer) *Future Water: An Exciting Solution to America's Most Serious Resource Crisis,* Morrow, 1983.

Also author of booklets and newspapers for the Citizens Committee for the Hoover Report. Contributor to magazines, including *Saturday Evening Post, Collier's, Nation, Reader's Digest, Nation's Business,* and *Catholic Digest.**

*   *   *

STONE, Rosetta
See GEISEL, Theodor Seuss

*   *   *

STOTT, Dorothy (M.) 1958-
(Dot Stott)

PERSONAL: Born October 24, 1958, in Norwich, CT. *Education:* Graduated from Paier School of Art, 1981.

ADDRESSES: Home—Mt. Antone View, Rupert, VT 05768. *Agent*—Kirchoff/Wohlberg, 866 United Nations Plaza, New York, NY 10017.

CAREER: Author and illustrator, 1981—.

MEMBER: Society of Illustrators, Society of Children's Book Writers.

WRITINGS:

FOR CHILDREN

(Under name Dot Stott) *The Three Little Kittens* (self-illustrated), Grosset & Dunlap, 1984.
(Illustrator under name Dot Stott) Carey Timm, *My Little Pony Learns to Count,* Random House, 1985.
(Illustrator) Anne Miranda, *Baby Talk,* Dutton, 1987.
(Illustrator) Miranda, *Baby Walk,* Dutton, 1988.
(Illustrator) Miranda, *Baby-Sit,* Little, Brown, 1990.
Too Much (self-illustrated), Dutton, 1990.
Little Duck's Bicycle Ride (self-illustrated), Dutton, 1991.
A Christmas Book, Dutton, 1991.
Zip/Whiz/Zoom, Little, Brown, in press.

Contributor of illustrations to textbooks.

WORK IN PROGRESS: The Christmas Troll, for Dutton.

SIDELIGHTS: Dorothy Stott told *SATA:* "Moving to Vermont from Connecticut has enhanced the quality of my life and my work. I live alone on the side of a peaceful mountain with beautiful views from my studio."

STOTT, Dot
See STOTT, Dorothy (M.)

*   *   *

STRATEMEYER, Edward L. 1862-1930
(Horatio Alger, Jr., Captain Ralph Bonehill, Oliver Optic, E. Ward Strayer, Arthur M. Winfield; joint pseudonym: Louis Charles; house pseudonyms: Nick Carter, Julia Edwards, Harvey Hicks)

PERSONAL: Born October 4, 1862, in Elizabeth, NJ; died of lobar pneumonia, May 10, 1930, in Newark, NJ; son of Henry Julius (a tobacconist and dry goods dealer) and Anna (Siegal) Stratemeyer; married Magdalene Baker Van Camp, March 25, 1891; children: Harriet Stratemeyer Adams, Edna Camilla Stratemeyer Squier. *Education:* Attended public schools in Elizabeth, NJ.

CAREER: Worked in family's tobacco shop in Elizabeth, NJ, until 1889; briefly owned and managed a stationery store; free-lance writer, 1889-1930. Founder and chief executive of Stratemeyer Literary Syndicate, New York, NY, ca. 1906-30.

WRITINGS:

The Minute Boys of Lexington, Estes & Lauriat, 1898.
(With William Taylor Adams, under pseudonym Oliver Optic) *An Undivided Union,* Lee & Shepard, 1899.
The Minute Boys of Bunker Hill, Estes & Lauriat, 1899.
(Under pseudonym Captain Ralph Bonehill) *Young Hunters in Puerto Rico; or, The Search for a Lost Treasure,* Donohue, 1900.

EDWARD L. STRATEMEYER

Between Boer and Briton; or, Two Boys' Adventures in South Africa, Lee & Shepard, 1900, published as Volume 13 of "Stratemeyer Popular Series," Lothrop, Lee & Shepard, published as *The Young Ranchman; or, Between Boer and Briton,* Street & Smith, 1920.

(With brother, Louis Stratemeyer, under joint pseudonym Louis Charles) *Fortune Hunters of the Philippines; or, The Treasure of the Burning Mountain,* Mershon, 1900.

(With L. Stratemeyer, under joint pseudonym Louis Charles) *The Land of Fire; or, Adventures in Underground Africa,* Mershon, 1900.

American Boys' Life of William McKinley, Lee & Shepard, 1901.

(Under pseudonym Captain Ralph Bonehill) *Three Young Ranchmen; or, Daring Adventures in the Great West,* Saalfield, 1901.

(Under pseudonym Arthur M. Winfield) *Larry Barlow's Ambition; or, The Adventures of a Young Fireman,* Saalfield, 1902.

(Under pseudonym Captain Ralph Bonehill) *The Boy Land Boomer; or, Dick Arbuckle's Adventures in Oklahoma,* Saalfield, 1902.

(Under pseudonym Arthur M. Winfield) *Bob the Photographer; or, A Hero in Spite of Himself,* Wessels, 1902.

(Under pseudonym Captain Ralph Bonehill) *The Young Naval Captain; or, The War of All Nations,* Thompson & Thomas, 1902, published as *Oscar, the Naval Cadet; or, Under the Sea,* Donohue.

(Under pseudonym Arthur M. Winfield) *Mark Dale's Stage Adventure; or, Bound to Be an Actor,* McKay, 1902.

(Under pseudonym Captain Ralph Bonehill) *Neka, the Boy Conjurer; or, A Mystery of the Stage,* McKay, 1902.

(Under pseudonym Arthur M. Winfield) *The Young Bank Clerk; or, Mark Vincent's Strange Discovery,* McKay, 1902.

(Under pseudonym Captain Ralph Bonehill) *Lost in the Land of Ice; or, Daring Adventures around the South Pole,* Wessels, 1902.

(Under pseudonym Arthur M. Winfield) *The Young Bridge-Tender; or, Ralph Nelson's Upward Struggle,* by Harvey Hicks), McKay, 1902.

(Under pseudonym Captain Ralph Bonehill) *The Tour of the Zero Club; or, Adventures amid Ice and Snow,* Street & Smith, 1902.

(Under pseudonym Arthur M. Winfield) *A Young Inventor's Pluck; or, The Mystery of the Wellington Legacy,* Saalfield, 1902.

Two Young Lumbermen; or, From Maine to Oregon for Fortune, Lee & Shepard, 1903, published as Volume 14 of "Stratemeyer Popular Series," Lothrop, Lee & Shepard.

Joe the Surveyor; or, The Value of a Lost Claim, Lee & Shepard, 1903, published as Volume 11 of "Stratemeyer Popular Series," Lothrop, Lee & Shepard.

Larry the Wanderer; or, The Rise of a Nobody, Lee & Shepard, 1904, published as Volume 12 of "Stratemeyer Popular Series," Lothrop, Lee & Shepard.

(Under pseudonym Captain Ralph Bonehill) *The Island Camp; or, The Young Hunters of Lakeport,* A. S. Barnes, 1904.

American Boys' Life of Theodore Roosevelt, Lee & Shepard, 1904.

(Under pseudonym Captain Ralph Bonehill) *The Winning Run; or, The Baseball Boys of Lakeport* (also see below), A. S. Barnes, 1905.

(Under pseudonym Horatio Alger, Jr.) *Joe the Hotel Boy; or, Winning out by Pluck* (also see below), Cupples & Leon, 1906.

Defending His Flag; or, A Boy in Blue and a Boy in Gray, Lothrop, Lee & Shepard, 1907.

(Under pseudonym Horatio Alger, Jr.) *Ben Logan's Triumph; or, The Boys of Boxwood Academy* (also see below), Cupples & Leon, 1908.

First at the North Pole; or, Two Boys in the Arctic Circle, Lothrop, Lee & Shepard, 1909, published as Volume 15 of "Stratemeyer Popular Series," published as *The Young Explorers; or, Adventures above the Arctic Circle,* Street & Smith, 1920.

(Under pseudonym E. Ward Strayer) *Making Good with Margaret,* G. Sully, 1918.

"SHIP AND SHORE" SERIES

The Last Cruise of the Spitfire; or, Luke Foster's Strange Voyage, Merriam, 1894, published as Volume 1 of "Stratemeyer Popular Series," Lothrop, Lee & Shepard.

Reuben Stone's Discovery; or, The Young Miller of Torrent Bend, Merriam, 1895, published as Volume 2 of "Stratemeyer Popular Series," Lothrop, Lee & Shepard.

True to Himself; or, Roger Strong's Struggle for Place, Lee & Shepard, 1900, published as Volume 3 of "Stratemeyer Popular Series," Lothrop, Lee & Shepard.

"BOUND TO SUCCEED" SERIES

Richard Dare's Venture; or, Striking out for Himself, Merriam, 1894, revised edition, Lee & Shepard, 1899.

Oliver Bright's Search; or, The Mystery of a Mine, Merriam, 1895, revised edition, Lee & Shepard, 1899.

To Alaska for Gold; or, The Fortune Hunters of the Yukon, Lee & Shepard, 1899, published as Volume 6 of "Stratemeyer Popular Series," Lothrop, Lee & Shepard.

"BOUND TO WIN" SERIES

Bound to Be an Electrician; or, Franklin Bell's Road to Success, Allison, 1897.

(Under pseudonym Arthur M. Winfield) *The Schooldays of Fred Harley; or, Rivals for All Honors,* Allison, 1897.

(Under pseudonym Captain Ralph Bonehill) *Gun and Sled; or, The Young Hunters of Snow-Top Island,* Allison, 1897.

Shorthand Tom; or, The Exploits of a Young Reporter, Allison, 1897.

(Under pseudonym Arthur M. Winfield) *The Missing Tin Box; or, The Stolen Railroad Bonds,* Allison, 1897.

(Under pseudonym Captain Ralph Bonehill) *Young Oarsmen of Lakeview; or, The Mystery of Hermit Island,* Allison, 1897.

The Young Auctioneers; or, The Polishing of a Rolling Stone, Allison, 1897.

(Under pseudonym Arthur M. Winfield) *Poor but Plucky; or, The Mystery of a Flood,* Allison, 1897.

(Under pseudonym Captain Ralph Bonehill) *The Rival Bicyclists; or, Fun and Adventures on the Wheel,* Donohue, 1897, reprinted as part of the "Boys' Liberty" series under title *Rival Cyclists* by Donohue.

Fighting for His Own; or, The Fortunes of a Young Artist, Allison, 1897.

(Under pseudonym Arthur M. Winfield) *By Pluck, not Luck; or, Dan Granbury's Struggle to Rise,* Allison, 1897.

(Under pseudonym Captain Ralph Bonehill) *Leo the Circus Boy; or, Life under the Great White Canvas,* Allison, 1897.

"OLD GLORY" SERIES

Under Dewey at Manila; or, The War Fortunes of a Castaway, Lee & Shepard, 1898.

A Young Volunteer in Cuba; or, Fighting for the Single Star, Lee & Shepard, 1898.

Fighting in Cuban Waters; or, Under Schley on the Brooklyn, Lee & Shepard, 1899.

"Oh, you will not harm little Muro and myself?"
(Frontispiece from 1930 edition of *Under MacArthur in Luzon,* from Stratemeyer's "Old Glory" series, illustration by A. B. Shute.)

Under Otis in the Philippines; or, A Young Officer in the Tropics, Lee & Shepard, 1899.

The Campaign of the Jungle; or, Under Lawton through Luzon, Lee & Shepard, 1900.

Under MacArthur in Luzon; or, Last Battles in the Philippines, Lee & Shepard, 1901.

"ROVER BOYS SERIES FOR YOUNG AMERICANS"; UNDER PSEUDONYM ARTHUR M. WINFIELD

The Rover Boys at School; or, The Cadets of Putnam Hall, Mershon, 1899.

The Rover Boys on the Ocean; or, A Chase for Fortune, Mershon, 1899.

The Rover Boys in the Jungle; or, Stirring Adventures in Africa, Mershon, 1899.

The Rover Boys out West; or, The Search for a Lost Mine, Mershon, 1900.

The Rover Boys on the Great Lakes; or, The Secret of the Island Cave, Mershon, 1901.

The Rover Boys in the Mountains; or, A Hunt for Fun and Fortune, Mershon, 1902.

The Rover Boys on Land and Sea; or, The Crusoes of Seven Islands, Mershon, 1903.

The Rover Boys in Camp; or, The Rivals of Pine Island, Mershon, 1904.

The Rover Boys on the River; or, The Search for the Missing Houseboat, Stitt, 1905.

The Rover Boys on the Plains; or, The Mystery of Red Rock, Mershon, 1906.

The Rover Boys in Southern Waters; or, The Deserted Steam Yacht, Mershon, 1907.

The Rover Boys on the Farm; or, Last Days at Putnam Hall, Grosset & Dunlap, 1908.

The Rover Boys on Treasure Isle; or, The Strange Cruise of the Steam Yacht, Grosset & Dunlap, 1909.

The Rover Boys at College; or, The Right Road and the Wrong, Grosset & Dunlap, 1910.

The Rover Boys Down East; or, The Struggle for the Stanhope Fortune, Grosset & Dunlap, 1911.

The Rover Boys in the Air; or, From College Campus to Clouds, Grosset & Dunlap, 1912.

The Rover Boys in New York; or, Saving Their Father's Honor, Grosset & Dunlap, 1913.

The Rover Boys in Alaska; or, Lost in the Fields of Ice, Grosset & Dunlap, 1914.

The Rover Boys in Business; or, The Search for the Missing Bonds, Grosset & Dunlap, 1915.

The Rover Boys on a Tour; or, Last Days at Brill College, Grosset & Dunlap, 1916.

"FLAG OF FREEDOM" SERIES; UNDER PSEUDONYM CAPTAIN RALPH BONEHILL

When Santiago Fell; or, The War Adventures of Two Chums (also see below), Mershon, 1899, published as *For His Country; or, The Adventures of Two Chums* by Edward Stratemeyer, Street & Smith, 1920.

A Sailor Boy with Dewey; or, Afloat in the Philippines (also see below), Mershon, 1899, published as *Comrades in Peril; or, Afloat on a Battleship* by Edward Stratemeyer, Street & Smith, 1920.

Off for Hawaii; or, The Mystery of a Great Volcano (also see below), Mershon, 1899, published as *The Young Pearl Hunters; or, In Hawaiian Waters* by Edward Stratemeyer, Street & Smith, 1920.

The Young Bandmaster; or, Concert, Stage, and Battlefield, Mershon, 1900.

Boys of the Fort; or, A Young Captain's Pluck (also see below), Mershon, 1901, published as *Boys of the Fort; or, True Courage Wins* by Edward Stratemeyer, Street & Smith, 1920.

With Custer in the Black Hills; or, A Young Scout among the Indians (also see below), Mershon, 1902, published as *On Fortune's Trail; or, The Heroes of the Black Hills* by Edward Stratemeyer, Street & Smith, 1920.

"MEXICAN WAR" SERIES; UNDER PSEUDONYM CAPTAIN RALPH BONEHILL

For the Liberty of Texas, Estes, 1900, reprinted under name Edward Stratemeyer, Lothrop, Lee & Shepard, 1909, reprinted, 1930.

With Taylor on the Rio Grande, Estes, 1901, reprinted under name Edward Stratemeyer, Lothrop, Lee & Shepard, 1909, reprinted, 1930.

Under Scott in Mexico, Estes, 1902, reprinted under name Edward Stratemeyer, Lothrop, Lee & Shepard, 1909, reprinted, 1930.

"SOLDIERS OF FORTUNE" SERIES

On to Pekin; or, Old Glory in China, Lee & Shepard, 1900.

Under the Mikado's Flag; or, Young Soldiers of Fortune, Lee & Shepard, 1904.

At the Fall of Port Arthur; or, A Young American in the Japanese Navy, Lothrop, Lee & Shepard, 1905.

Under Togo for Japan; or, Three Young Americans on Land and Sea, Lothrop, Lee & Shepard, 1906.

"RISE IN LIFE" SERIES; UNDER PSEUDONYM HORATIO ALGER, JR.

Out for Business; or, Robert Frost's Strange Career, Mershon, 1900.

Falling in with Fortune; or, The Experiences of a Young Secretary, Mershon, 1900.

Young Captain Jack; or, The Son of a Soldier, Mershon, 1901.

Nelson the Newsboy; or, Afloat in New York, Mershon, 1901.

Jerry the Backwoods Boy; or, The Parkhurst Treasure, Mershon, 1904.

Lost at Sea; or, Robert Roscoe's Strange Cruise, Mershon, 1904.

From Farm to Fortune; or, Nat Nason's Strange Experience, Stitt, 1905.

The Young Book Agent; or, Frank Hardy's Road to Success, Stitt, 1905.

Randy of the River; or, The Adventures of a Young Deck Hand, Chatterton-Peck, 1906.

Joe, the Hotel Boy; or, Winning out by Pluck, Grosset & Dunlap, 1912.

Ben Logan's Triumph; or, The Boys of Boxwood Academy, Grosset & Dunlap, 1912.

Cover from the original 1900 edition of *Fortune Hunters of the Philippines*, the first book written by Edward L. Stratemeyer and his brother, Louis, under the pseudonym Louis Charles.

"COLONIAL" SERIES

With Washington in the West; or, A Soldier Boy's Battles in the Wilderness, Lee & Shepard, 1901.

Marching on Niagara; or, The Soldier Boys of the Old Frontier, Lee & Shepard, 1902.

At the Fall of Montreal; or, A Soldier Boy's Final Victory, Lee & Shepard, 1903.

On the Trail of Pontiac; or, The Pioneer Boys of the Ohio, Lee & Shepard, 1904.

The Fort in the Wilderness; or, The Soldier Boys of the Indian Trails, Lee & Shepard, 1905.

Trail and Trading Post; or, The Young Hunters of the Ohio, Lothrop, Lee & Shepard, 1906.

"PUTNAM HALL" SERIES; UNDER PSEUDONYM ARTHUR M. WINFIELD

The Putnam Hall Cadets; or, Good Times in School and Out, Mershon, 1901, reprinted as Volume 5 of series under title *The Cadets of Putnam Hall; or, Good Times in School and Out,* Grosset & Dunlap, 1921.

The Putnam Hall Rivals; or, Fun and Sport Afloat and Ashore, Mershon, 1906, reprinted as Volume 6 of series under title *The Rivals of Putnam Hall; or, Fun and Sport Afloat and Ashore,* Grosset & Dunlap, 1921.

The Putnam Hall Champions; or, Bound to Win Out, Grosset & Dunlap, 1908, reprinted as Volume 4 of series under title *The Champions of Putnam Hall; or, Bound to Win Out,* 1921.

The Putnam Hall Rebellion; or, The Rival Runaways, Grosset & Dunlap, 1909, reprinted as Volume 3 of series under title *The Rebellion at Putnam Hall; or, The Rival Runaways,* 1921.

The Putnam Hall Encampment; or, The Secret of the Old Mill, Grosset & Dunlap, 1910, reprinted as Volume 2 of series under title *Camping Out Days at Putnam Hall; or, The Secret of the Old Mill,* 1921.

The Putnam Hall Mystery; or, The School Chums' Strange Discovery, Grosset & Dunlap, 1911, reprinted as Volume 1 of series under title *The Mystery at Putnam Hall; or, The School Chums' Strange Discovery,* 1921.

"PAN-AMERICAN" SERIES

Lost on the Orinoco; or, American Boys in Venezuela, Lee & Shepard, 1902.

The Young Volcano Explorers; or, American Boys in the West Indies, Lee & Shepard, 1902.

Young Explorers of the Isthmus; or, American Boys in Central America, Lee & Shepard, 1903.

Young Explorers of the Amazon; or, American Boys in Brazil, Lee & Shepard, 1904.

Treasure Seekers of the Andes; or, American Boys in Peru, Lothrop, Lee & Shepard, 1907.

Chased across the Pampas; or, American Boys in Argentina and Homeward Bound, Lothrop, Lee & Shepard, 1911.

"WORKING UPWARD" SERIES

The Young Auctioneers; or, The Polishing of a Rolling Stone, Lee & Shepard, 1903, published as Volume 7 of "Stratemeyer Popular Series," Lothrop, Lee & Shepard.

Bound to Be an Electrician; or, Franklin Bell's Road to Success, Lee & Shepard, 1903, published as Volume 8 of "Stratemeyer Popular Series," Lothrop, Lee & Shepard.

Shorthand Tom, the Reporter; or, The Exploits of a Bright Boy (originally published as *Shorthand Tom; or, The Exploits of a Young Reporter*), Lee & Shepard, 1903, published as Volume 9 of "Stratemeyer Popular Series," Lothrop, Lee & Shepard.

They made a splendid dinner of some baked maskalonge. (Frontispiece from the original 1906 edition of *Four Boy Hunters,* by Captain Ralph Bonehill.)

Fighting for His Own; or, The Fortunes of a Young Artist, Lee & Shepard, 1903, published as Volume 10 of "Stratemeyer Popular Series," Lothrop, Lee & Shepard.

Oliver Bright's Search; or, The Mystery of a Mine, Lee & Shepard, 1903, published as Volume 5 of "Stratemeyer Popular Series," Lothrop, Lee & Shepard.

Richard Dare's Venture; or, Striking out for Himself, Lee & Shepard, 1903, published as Volume 4 of "Stratemeyer Popular Series," Lothrop, Lee & Shepard.

"FRONTIER" SERIES; UNDER PSEUDONYM CAPTAIN RALPH BONEHILL

With Boone on the Frontier; or, The Pioneer Boys of Old Kentucky (also see below), Mershon, 1903, published as *Boys of the Wilderness; or, Down in Old Kentucky* by Edward Stratemeyer, Street & Smith, 1932.

Pioneer Boys of the Great Northwest; or, With Lewis and Clark across the Rockies (also see below), Mershon, 1904, published as *Boys of the Great Northwest; or, Across the Rockies* by Edward Stratemeyer, Street & Smith, 1932.

Pioneer Boys of the Gold Fields; or, The Nugget Hunters of '49 (also see below), Stitt, 1906, published as *Boys of the Gold Fields; or, The Nugget Hunters* by Edward Stratemeyer, Street & Smith, 1932.

"BRIGHT AND BOLD" SERIES; UNDER PSEUDONYM ARTHUR M. WINFIELD

Poor but Plucky; or, The Mystery of a Flood, Donohue, 1905.

The Schooldays of Fred Harley; or, Rivals for All Honors, Donohue, 1905.

By Pluck, not Luck; or, Dan Granbury's Struggle to Rise, Donohue, 1905.

The Missing Tin Box; or, The Stolen Railroad Bonds, Donohue, 1905.

"DAVE PORTER" SERIES

Dave Porter at Oak Hall; or, The Schooldays of an American Boy, Lee & Shepard, 1905.

Dave Porter in the South Seas; or, The Strange Cruise of the Stormy Petrel, Lothrop, Lee & Shepard, 1906.

Dave Porter's Return to School; or, Winning the Medal of Honor, Lothrop, Lee & Shepard, 1907.

Dave Porter in the Far North; or, The Pluck of an American Schoolboy, Lothrop, Lee & Shepard, 1908.

Dave Porter and His Classmates; or, For the Honor of Oak Hall, Lothrop, Lee & Shepard, 1909.

Dave Porter at Star Ranch; or, The Cowboy's Secret, Lothrop, Lee & Shepard, 1910.

Dave Porter and His Rivals; or, The Chums and Foes of Oak Hall, Lothrop, Lee & Shepard, 1911.

Dave Porter on Cave Island; or, A Schoolboy's Mysterious Mission, Lothrop, Lee & Shepard, 1912.

Dave Porter and the Runaways; or, Last Days at Oak Hall, Lothrop, Lee & Shepard, 1913.

Dave Porter in the Gold Fields; or, The Search for the Land-slide Mine, Lothrop, Lee & Shepard, 1914.

Dave Porter at Bear Camp; or, The Wild Man of Mirror Lake, Lothrop, Lee & Shepard, 1915.

Dave Porter and His Double; or, The Disappearance of the Basswood Fortune, Lothrop, Lee & Shepard, 1916.

Dave Porter's Great Search; or, The Perils of a Young Civil Engineer, Lothrop, Lee & Shepard, 1917.

Dave Porter under Fire; or, A Young Army Engineer in France, Lothrop, Lee & Shepard, 1918.

Dave Porter's War Honors; or, At the Front with the Flying Engineers, Lothrop, Lee & Shepard, 1919.

"BOY HUNTERS" SERIES; UNDER PSEUDONYM CAPTAIN RALPH BONEHILL

Four Boy Hunters; or, The Outing of the Gun Club, Cupples & Leon, 1906.

Guns and Snowshoes; or, The Winter Outing of the Young Hunters, Cupples & Leon, 1907.

Young Hunters of the Lake; or, Out with Rod and Gun, Cupples & Leon, 1908.

Out with Gun and Camera; or, The Boy Hunters in the Mountains, Cupples & Leon, 1910.

"LAKEPORT" SERIES

The Gun Club Boys of Lakeport; or, The Island Camp, (originally published as *The Island Camp; or, The Young Hunters of Lakeport* by Captain Ralph Bonehill), Lothrop, Lee & Shepard, 1908.

The Baseball Boys of Lakeport; or, The Winning Run (originally published as *The Winning Run; or, The Baseball Boys of Lakeport* by Captain Ralph Bonehill), Lothrop, Lee & Shepard, 1908.

The Boat Club Boys of Lakeport; or, The Water Champions, Lothrop, Lee & Shepard, 1908.

The Football Boys of Lakeport; or, More Goals Than One, Lothrop, Lee & Shepard, 1909.

The Automobile Boys of Lakeport; or, A Run for Fun and Fame, Lothrop, Lee & Shepard, 1910.

The Aircraft Boys of Lakeport; or, Rivals of the Clouds, Lothrop, Lee & Shepard, 1912.

"FLAG AND FRONTIER" SERIES; UNDER PSEUDONYM CAPTAIN RALPH BONEHILL

With Boone on the Frontier; or, The Pioneer Boys of Old Kentucky, Grosset & Dunlap, 1912.

Pioneer Boys of the Great Northwest; or, With Lewis and Clark across the Rockies, Grosset & Dunlap, 1912.

Pioneer Boys of the Gold Fields; or, The Nugget Hunters of '49, Grosset & Dunlap, 1912.

With Custer in the Black Hills; or, A Young Scout among the Indians, Grosset & Dunlap, 1912.

Boys of the Fort; or, A Young Captain's Pluck, Grosset & Dunlap, 1912.

The Young Bandmaster; or, Concert, Stage, and Battlefield, Grosset & Dunlap, 1912.

Off for Hawaii; or, The Mystery of a Great Volcano, Grosset & Dunlap, 1912.

A Sailor Boy with Dewey; or, Afloat in the Philippines, Grosset & Dunlap, 1912.

When Santiago Fell; or, The War Adventures of Two Chums, Grosset & Dunlap, 1912.

"SECOND ROVER BOYS SERIES FOR YOUNG AMERICANS"; UNDER PSEUDONYM ARTHUR M. WINFIELD

The Rover Boys at Colby Hall; or, The Struggles of the Young Cadets, Grosset & Dunlap, 1917.

The Rover Boys on Snowshoe Island; or, The Old Lumberman's Treasure Box, Grosset & Dunlap, 1918.

THE ROVER BOYS
AT SCHOOL

OR

THE CADETS OF PUTNAM HALL

BY

ARTHUR M. WINFIELD

(Edward Stratemeyer)

AUTHOR OF THE ROVER BOYS IN CAMP, THE ROVER BOYS ON THE OCEAN, THE PUTNAM HALL SERIES, ETC.

ILLUSTRATED

NEW YORK
GROSSET & DUNLAP
PUBLISHERS
Made in the United States of America

In the first "Rover Boys" title, prolific author Edward Stratemeyer is credited on the title page, beneath his pseudonym. (From the 1899 edition of *The Rover Boys at School.*)

The Rover Boys under Canvas; or, The Mystery of the Wrecked Submarine, Grosset & Dunlap, 1919.

The Rover Boys on a Hunt; or, The Mysterious House in the Woods, Grosset & Dunlap, 1920.

The Rover Boys in the Land of Luck; or, Stirring Adventures in the Oilfields, Grosset & Dunlap, 1921.

The Rover Boys at Big Horn Ranch; or, The Cowboys' Double Roundup, Grosset & Dunlap, 1922.

The Rover Boys at Big Bear Lake; or, The Camps of the Rival Cadets, Grosset & Dunlap, 1923.

The Rover Boys Shipwrecked; or, A Thrilling Hunt for Pirates' Gold, Grosset & Dunlap, 1924.

The Rover Boys on Sunset Trail; or, The Old Miner's Mysterious Message, Grosset & Dunlap, 1925.

The Rover Boys Winning a Fortune; or, Strenuous Days Afloat and Ashore, Grosset & Dunlap, 1926.

OTHER

Also author of *Dave Porter on the Atlantic; or, The Castaways of the Menagerie Ship.* Contributor of stories to magazines, including *Golden Days, Argosy, Good News, Boys of America, Bright Days, Young Sports of America,* and *Young People of America,* under a variety of pseudonyms, including Horatio Alger, Jr., Captain Ralph Bonehill, Roy Rockwood, and Arthur M. Winfield; contributor of stories to dime novel series, under a variety of pseudonyms, including Horatio Alger, Jr., Nick Carter, and Julia Edwards. Plotter and editor of books for Stratemeyer Literary Syndicate. Editor, *Good News;* founder and editor, *Bright Days.*

SIDELIGHTS: "If anyone ever deserved a bronze statue in Central Park, somewhere between Hans Christian Anderson and Alice in Wonderland," declares Arthur Prager in *Saturday Review,* "it is Edward Stratemeyer, incomparable king of juveniles." Between 1886, when he wrote his first story on wrapping paper in his family's tobacco shop, and his death in 1930, Stratemeyer wrote, outlined, and edited more than 800 books under sixty-five pseudonyms, plus myriad short stories. His beloved creations include Dick, Tom, and Sam Rover (the Rover Boys), Bert, Nan, Freddie, and Flossie Bobbsey (the Bobbsey Twins), Tom Swift, Bomba the Jungle Boy, Frank and Joe Hardy, and Nancy Drew. John T. Dizer, writing in *Tom Swift & Company: "Boys' Books" by Stratemeyer and Others,* calls the literary syndicate that he founded "the most important single influence in American juvenile literature." "As oil had its Rockefeller, literature had its Stratemeyer," eulogized *Fortune* magazine shortly after his death.

"The bulk of Stratemeyer's literary apprenticeship was served in writing and editing for periodicals," explains *Dictionary of Literary Biography* contributor Mary-Agnes Taylor. His initial success—his first story sold to *Golden Days,* a Philadelphia weekly paper for boys, for $75—encouraged the young author to write more stories. He soon became a regular contributor to Frank Munsey's periodical *Golden Argosy* and, in 1893, the magazine and dime novel publishers Street & Smith offered him the editorship of their journal *Good News.* By 1896 he was also editing the Street & Smith periodicals *Young Sports of America* (which became *Young People of America*) and *Bright Days,* as well as contributing women's serials to the *New York Weekly* under the pseudonym Julia Edwards, and dime novels under the pseudonyms Captain Ralph Bonehill and Allen Chapman, as well as under his own name. "Perhaps the greatest advantage of his association with Street and Smith, however," continues Taylor, "was his exposure to the literary idols of his time," including Frederic Van Rensselaer Dey, "creator of dime novel detective hero Nick Carter; Upton Sinclair, who wrote the True Blue series as Ensign Clark Fitch, USN; prolific dime novelist Edward S. Ellis; William Taylor Adams; and Horatio Alger himself." After the deaths of Adams and Alger, Stratemeyer was chosen to complete some of their unfinished manuscripts, using the pseudonyms Oliver Optic and Horatio Alger, Jr.

Stratemeyer's success as a novelist came in 1898, during the Spanish-American War. "War was glamour in those days. Uniforms were splendid, and battles were glorious," explains Prager. The author had recently submitted a novel about several young men serving on a battleship to Lothrop, Lee & Shepard, a publishing house in Boston, when news of Admiral Dewey's victory over the Spanish fleet at Manila Bay reached the U.S. The publishers wrote the author, inquiring if he could revise his story to reflect Dewey's victory. Stratemeyer did, and *Under Dewey at Manila; or, The War Fortunes of a Castaway,* featuring Larry and Ben Russell and their chum Gilbert Pennington, became "the financial hit of the juvenile publishing industry in 1899," according to Prager. Popular demand brought the boys back for many more adventures in the "Old Glory" and the "Soldiers of Fortune" series, and Stratemeyer further exploited the market for war stories with books featuring boys in the French and Indian War, the American Revolution, and the Mexican War. Many were well-received by critics, including parents, teachers, and churchmen as well as the readers themselves.

"These early books are important in two respects," declares Taylor. "They are crammed with well-researched facts and they make use of some literary techniques that mark virtually all of the author's later works." Stratemeyer directly addressed the reader in the introductions of his books, and his voice often interrupted the text. Frequently the story's action paused near the beginning of the volume to allow the narrator to recap the hero's previous adventures, and each account included an advertisement for the next volume in the series. Stratemeyer's prose was also rather stilted, reflecting his early association with Alger and Adams at Street & Smith, and he often relied on stereotyped views of various ethnic groups. "Except for Alger himself," declares Russel B. Nye in *The Unembarrassed Muse: The Popular Arts in America,* "no writer of juvenile fiction had a more unerring sense of the hackneyed."

Whatever the drawbacks of Stratemeyer's prose, his work became highly popular with young readers. Late in 1899, realizing that the attraction of contemporary war stories was likely to be temporary, he introduced the "Rover Boys Series for Young Americans" under the pen name Arthur M. Winfield. These books chronicled the adventures of three brothers—Dick, Tom, and Sam Rover—at Putnam Hall, a military boarding school, and later at midwestern Brill College, and they captured the imaginations of turn-of-the-century adolescent Americans in a way no other series heroes had before. "Between the publication of the first three volumes late in 1899 and the publication of the last volume in 1926," reports Taylor, "sales ran somewhere between five and six millions of copies." The brothers, described as "lively, wide-awake American boys" by the author, were supported by a memorable cast of characters, including Dora Stanhope, and Grace and Nellie Laning, their sweethearts, their chums John "Songbird" Powell and William Philander Tubbs, and assorted bullies and other villains: Josiah Crabtree, Tad Sobber, Jesse Pelter, and Dan Baxter, among others.

The horse managed to crawl to a place of safety, but Dick lost his balance and went crashing down. (Frontispiece from the 1905 edition of *The Rover Boys Out West,* by Edward L. Stratemeyer writing as Arthur M. Winfield.)

Stratemeyer originally conceived the "Rover Boys" series in the vein of *Tom Brown's Schooldays,* depicting youthful adventures, games and hijinks, but he also featured elements of melodrama and detective fiction, claims Carol Billman in *The Secret of the Stratemeyer Syndicate: Nancy Drew, the Hardy Boys, and the Million Dollar Fiction Factory.* Many volumes featured searches for missing people or buried treasure; *The Rover Boys in the Jungle,* for instance, took our heroes to Africa in search of their father. The Rovers and their friends "faced unprecedented dangers," explains the *Literary Digest.* "As the fun-loving Tom expressed it, on the historic occasion when an avalanche was rolling down on them from above, their cabin was in flames, Dan Baxter and his cronies were taking pot-shots at them from across the canyon, Dora Stanhope was clinging to the edge of the cliff, and the battle-ship *Oregon* was still ten miles away, 'Well, we're in a pretty pickle, and no mistake!'" "But always, to our immense surprise," the *Digest* concludes, "they would emerge unscathed, restore the missing fortune, and be rewarded by three rousing cheers and—a sop to the feminine trade—an arch look from Dora and Nellie and Grace; while the discomfited bullies, outwitted again, began plotting at once their future conspiracies, to be related in the next volume of the Rover Boys Series for Young Americans."

Eventually Stratemeyer permitted Dick, Tom and Sam to graduate and to start a business together, pooling their resources to form the Rover Company. They married their girls and settled down to raise families in adjoining houses on New York's Riverside Drive. Stratemeyer went on to chronicle their children's adventures in the "Second Rover Boys Series for Young Americans," which lasted for ten volumes. However, the younger Rovers never achieved the success their fathers had, explains Prager, writing in *Rascals at Large; or, The Clue in the Old Nostalgia.* "The generation that had loved the Rover Boys moved on to new things. Did the Crash wipe out the Rover Company? Did their Riverside Drive houses succumb to high taxes and urban blight? We never found out."

The Rovers' success encouraged Stratemeyer to create other series. "Almost as soon as the first sales figures came in," reports Prager in *Saturday Review,* "he was designing a dozen similar series and concocting pseudonyms. He took his basic Rover figures, changed the names, associated them with some kind of speedy vehicle or popular scientific device, and slipped them into his formula." Stratemeyer soon found that his ideas outstripped his writing capacity and began to hire independent writers to fill in his outlines. Working with "Uncle Wiggily" creator Howard R. Garis under the pseudonym Clarence Young, Stratemeyer created the "Motor Boys" series; as Allen Chapman, he devised the adventures of the "Radio Boys" and "Ralph of the Railroad" series; as Victor Appleton, the "Motion Picture Boys" and "Tom Swift" series; as Franklin W. Dixon, the "Hardy Boys" and "Ted Scott Flying Stories" series, and many others. For sports enthusiasts he produced the "Baseball Joe" books under the pseudonym Lester Chadwick, and as Roy Rockwood he created Bomba the Jungle Boy, a teen-aged Tarzan. For girls and younger readers, he introduced the "Moving Picture Girls," the "Outdoor Girls," and the "Bobbsey Twins" series, using the pseudonym Laura Lee Hope; as Alice B. Emerson he developed the "Betty Gordon" and "Ruth Fielding" series, and as Carolyn Keene he invented Nancy Drew.

Stratemeyer engaged in innovative publishing strategies in order to get his many series published. "Using the kind of reasoning that would later make Henry Ford a billionaire," Prager declares in *Saturday Review,* "he talked his publishers into slashing the prices of the 'Rover' and 'Motor Boys' series from a dollar to 50 cents, relying on volume sales to make up and exceed lost profit. The plan was a smashing success. At half a dollar, kids could buy the books without going through the parent-middleman." By around 1906 demand had increased so much that Stratemeyer had to systematize his production by setting up the Stratemeyer Syndicate, "a kind of literary assembly line," Prager calls it, resembling in some ways the syndicate devised by the French writer Alexandre Dumas half a century before. Stratemeyer created plot outlines for series titles and sent them to contract writers, who wrote the actual stories. They then returned the manuscript to Stratemeyer, who edited it and had it put on electrotype plates, which were then leased to the publishers. Stratemeyer retained all rights to the stories, paying his contract writers an average of one hundred dollars a book. "The whole process," Prager explains, "took a month to six weeks."

Stratemeyer's success and his factory-like writing process made enemies among those who considered themselves guardians of the juvenile mind. A few years after the Boy Scouts of America were established Franklin K. Mathiews, the Chief Scout Librarian, and James E. West, the Chief Scout Executive, contacted Grosset & Dunlap, one of Stratemeyer's chief publishers, and proposed a mass reprinting of a list of Boy Scouts Approved Books in inexpensive editions. Somewhat later, Mathiews published an article in *Outlook* magazine savagely denouncing juvenile fiction that did not meet his standards, although he never mentioned the Stratemeyer Syndicate by name. "Mathiews began by noting that in most surveys of children's reading, inferior books, (defined as those not found in libraries), were widely read and probably as influential as the better books," reports Ken Donelson in *Children's Literature.* Mathiews suggested that the poor quality of Syndicate-type fiction, revealed in the lack of moral purpose and uncontrolled excitement of the stories, could cripple a young reader's imagination "as though by some material explosion they had lost a hand or foot." "I wish I could label each one of these books: 'Explosives! Guaranteed to Blow Your Boy's Brains Out,'" he declared. The Chief Scout Librarian backed up his accusations with statements from other librarians testifying to the poor quality of series books and encouraged other authors, especially Percy Keese Fitzhugh, to write series fiction, but Stratemeyer's sales remained high. He had, however, learned something from the encounter: future Syndicate series "toned down danger, thrills, and violence in favor of well-researched instruction," says Prager in *Saturday Review.*

One measure of Stratemeyer's success lies in the fact that now, more than half a century after his death, new volumes are added yearly to series he created. The "Bobbsey Twins," "Hardy Boys" and "Nancy Drew" books continue to captivate readers, and sales are as high as ever. Despite critic's misgivings, states Prager in *Rascals at Large,* the books "are well worth a reappraisal in the light of current taste, and like most items handcrafted in those days, they wear like iron and last for years." "Stratemeyer's legacy—respectable or not—is read on," declares Billman, "night after night, reader after reader, generation after generation."

Upon Stratemeyer's death in 1930, the Syndicate was administered by his daughters, Harriet Adams and Edna Squier. Adams remained in control of the Syndicate until her death in 1982. See the *SATA* index for more information on Stratemeyer, his Syndicate and its pseudonyms, including the entries for Harriet S. Adams, Mildred Benson, Howard R. Garis, and Andrew E. Svenson, and for the following pseudonyms: Victor Appleton, Lester Chadwick, Allen Chapman, Elmer A. Dawson, Franklin W. Dixon, Julia K. Duncan, Alice B. Emerson, James Cody Ferris, Graham B. Forbes, Laura Lee Hope, Francis K. Judd, Carolyn Keene, Margaret Penrose, Roy Rockwood, Helen Louise Thorndyke, Frank V. Webster, and Clarence Young.

WORKS CITED:

"Age Does Not Dim the Glory of the Rover Boys," *Literary Digest,* April 21, 1928, p. 38.

Billman, Carol, *The Secret of the Stratemeyer Syndicate: Nancy Drew, the Hardy Boys, and the Million Dollar Fiction Factory,* Ungar, 1986, pp. 17-35, 37-54.

Dizer, John T., Jr., *Tom Swift & Company: "Boys' Books" by Stratemeyer and Others,* McFarland & Co., 1982.

Donelson, Ken, "Nancy, Tom, and Assorted Friends in the Stratemeyer Syndicate Then and Now," *Children's Literature,* Volume 7, 1978, pp. 17-44.

"For It Was Indeed He," *Fortune,* April, 1934, pp. 86-90.

Mathiews, Franklin K., "Blowing Out the Boy's Brains," *Outlook,* November 18, 1914, pp. 652-54.

Nye, Russel B., "For It Was Indeed He: Books for the Young," *The Unembarrassed Muse: The Popular Arts in America,* Dial, 1970, pp. 60-87.

Prager, Arthur, "Edward Stratemeyer and His Book Machine," *Saturday Review,* July 10, 1971, pp. 15-53.

Prager, Arthur, *Rascals at Large; or, The Clue in the Old Nostalgia,* Doubleday, 1971, pp. 7-12, 217-64.

Taylor, Mary-Agnes, "Edward Stratemeyer," *Dictionary of Literary Biography,* Volume 42: *American Writers for Children before 1900,* edited by Glenn E. Estes, Gale, 1985, pp. 351-62.

FOR MORE INFORMATION SEE:

BOOKS

Garis, Roger, *My Father Was Uncle Wiggily,* McGraw-Hill, 1966.

Johnson, Deidre, editor and compiler, *Stratemeyer Pseudonyms and Series Books: An Annotated Checklist of Stratemeyer and Stratemeyer Syndicate Publications,* Greenwood Press, 1982.

McFarlane, Leslie, *Ghost of the Hardy Boys,* Two Continents, 1976.

Reynolds, Quentin, *The Fiction Factory; or, From Pulp Row to Quality Street,* Random House, 1955.

PERIODICALS

American Heritage, December, 1976.
Journal of Popular Culture, spring, 1974.
Midwest Quarterly, October, 1972.
Outlook, November 18, 1914.
Saturday Review, January 25, 1969.
Smithsonian, October, 1991.

OBITUARIES:

PERIODICALS

New York Times, May 13, 1930.*

*   *   *

STRAYER, E. Ward
See STRATEMEYER, Edward L.

*   *   *

SWEDE, George 1940-

PERSONAL: Original name, Juris Purins; name legally changed; born November 20, 1940, in Riga, Latvia; son of Virgo Purins Swede Paynter and Janis Purins; married Anita Krumins (an educator in business and technical communications); children: Juris Krumins, Andris Krumins. *Education:* University of British Columbia, B.A., 1964; Dalhousie University, M.A., 1965.

ADDRESSES: Home—70 London St., Toronto, Ontario M6G 1N3, Canada. *Office*— P.O. Box 279, Station P, Toronto, Ontario M5S 2S8, Canada.

CAREER: Vancouver City College, Vancouver, British Columbia, instructor in psychology, 1966-67; psychologist for public schools in Toronto, Ontario, 1967-68; Ryerson Polytechnical Institute, Toronto, instructor, 1968-73, professor of psychology, 1973—, chairman of department, 1974-75.

Director of developmental psychology at Open College, Toronto, 1973-75.

MEMBER: International PEN, Canadian Society of Children's Authors, Illustrators, and Performers (member of executive committee, 1981-84), League of Canadian Poets, Writers Union of Canada, Haiku Canada (co-founder, 1977), Haiku Society of America.

AWARDS, HONORS: Special mention and honorable mention from *Modern Haiku,* 1977; awards from *Bonsai,* 1977, *Dragonfly,* 1977, 1978, 1979, and *Gusto,* 1979, all for haiku; Golden State Bank Award, 1979, and Yuki Teikei Haiku Society Award, 1980, both from Yuki Teikei Haiku Society; honorable mention from Haiku Society of America, 1980, for *Wingbeats;* winner of High/Coo Press Mini-Chapbook Competition, 1982, for *All Her Shadows;* Museum of Haiku Literature Award from *Frogpond,* 1983, 1985, and 1987; Children's Book Centre "Our Choice" Award, 1984, for *Tick Bird;* honorable mention, World Haiku Contest, 1989; Mirrors International Tanka Award, 1990. Grants from Ontario Arts Council, 1978, 1979, 1980, 1984, 1985, 1986, 1988, and 1989.

WRITINGS:

JUVENILE FICTION

(With wife, Anita Krumins) *Quilby, the Porcupine Who Lost His Quills,* Three Trees Press, 1979.
The Case of the Moonlit Gold Dust, Three Trees Press, 1979.
The Case of the Missing Heirloom, Three Trees Press, 1980.
The Case of the Seaside Burglaries, Three Trees Press, 1981.
The Case of the Downhill Theft, Three Trees Press, 1982.
Undertow, Three Trees Press, 1982.
Dudley and the Birdmen, Three Trees Press, 1985.

GEORGE SWEDE

Dudley and the Christmas Thief, Three Trees Press, 1986.
Leaping Lizard, Three Trees Press, 1988.

POETRY

Unwinding, Missing Link Press, 1974.
Tell-Tale Feathers, Fiddlehead Poetry Books, 1978.
Endless Jigsaw, Three Trees Press, 1978.
A Snowman, Headless, Fiddlehead Poetry Books, 1979.
Wingbeats, Juniper Press, 1979.
As Far as the Sea Can Eye, York Publishing, 1979.
(Editor) *Canadian Haiku Anthology,* Three Trees Press, 1979.
This Morning's Mockingbird, High/Coo Press, 1980.
Eye to Eye with a Frog, Juniper Press, 1981.
All of Her Shadows, High/Coo Press, 1982.
Flaking Paint, Underwhich Editions, 1983.
Frozen Breaths, Wind Chimes Press, 1983.
(Editor) *Cicada Voices,* High/Coo Press, 1983.
Tick Bird, Three Trees Press, 1983.
Time is Flies , Three Trees Press, 1984.
Bifids, Curvd H & Z Press, 1984.
Night Tides, South Western Ontario Poetry, 1984.
(With LeRoy Gorman and Eric Amann) *The Space Between,* Wind Chimes Press, 1984.
High Wire Spider, Three Trees Press, 1986.
(With J. W. Curry) *Where Even the Factories Have Lawns,* Gesture Press, 1988.
I Throw Stones at the Mountains, Wind Chimes Press, 1988.
Holes in My Cage, Three Trees Press, 1989.
I Want to Lasso Time, Simon & Pierre, 1991.

OTHER

The Modern English Haiku (essays), Columbine Edition, 1981.
(Editor) *The Universe is One Poem* (essays and instructional materials), Simon & Pierre, 1990.

Contributor of poems to over 100 periodicals. Work represented in numerous anthologies. *Writer's Quarterly,* children's book review editor, 1982-84, poetry review editor, 1984-86, poetry editor, 1986-90; *Poetry Toronto,* poetry editor, 1986-90; *Brussel Sprouts,* guest editor, 1988.

SIDELIGHTS: George Swede told *SATA:* "I have found that an idea for a poem (or the entire poem itself) can occur at any time (riding on the subway or raking leaves). For this reason, I always carry a pen and a small notebook in my shirt pocket. When ideas come, I can then write them down immediately. Before I began this practice, I tried to keep the thoughts in my head and, of course, forgot most of them.

"To get enough poems for a book usually takes a while. For example, one of the poems in *Time is Flies* was written ten years before the book was published (October, 1984) and a few were written only several months earlier. During the ten year period I wrote hundreds of poems (most of them very short). But I sent to the publisher only those (about sixty) I thought he would like. Then he chose the thirty-seven poems that actually appear in *Time is Flies.*"

*   *   *

TAMES, Richard (Lawrence) 1946-

PERSONAL: Born January 30, 1946, in Ilford, England; son of Albert Edward (a company director) and Phyllis (Amos) Tames; married Elizabeth Elliston, April 15, 1968 (separated, 1980). *Education:* Pembroke College, Cambridge, B.A.,

1967; Birkbeck College, London, M.Sc., 1974. *Hobbies and other interests:* Photography, travel, London.

ADDRESSES: Home—76 Regent Sq., Bruce Rd., London E3 3HW, England; and 25 Wisdom's Green, Coggeshall, Essex, C06 1SG England. *Agent*—c/o The Watts Group, 96 Leonard St., London EC2A 4RH, England.

CAREER: Haberdashers' Aske's School, Elstree, England, master, 1967-70; Chiswick Polytechnic, London, England, lecturer, 1970-71; researcher for Granada Television, 1972; secretary to the council of the Hansard Society for Parliamentary Government, 1973-74; University of London, School of Oriental and African Studies, London, assistant organizer of extramural studies, 1975-78, deputy organizer, 1978-83, organizer, 1983-85, head of external services, 1985-90. History teacher on adjunct faculty of Syracuse University, London campus, 1974—. Board member, U.K. committee for UNICEF. Senior consultant, University Consultants, Ltd. (Japan).

MEMBER: British Association of Japanese Studies.

WRITINGS:

The Transport Revolution in the Nineteenth Century, Oxford University Press, 1970.
Documents of the Industrial Revolution, 1750-1850, Hutchinson Educational, 1971.
Towards the Welfare State, 1700 to the Present Day, Nelson, 1971.
Economy and Society in Nineteenth-Century Britain, Allen & Unwin, 1972, Beekman, 1976.
William Morris, 1834-1896: An Illustrated Life of William Morris, Shire, 1972.
The General Strike, Jackdaw/Grossman, 1972.
Last of the Tzars: The Life and Death of of Nicholas and Alexandra, Pan Books, 1972.
Josiah Wedgwood, 1730-1795: An Illustrated Life of Josiah Wedgwood, Shire, 1972, Newbury Books, 1973.
Isambard Kingdom Brunel, 1806-1859: An Illustrated Life of Isambard Kingdom Brunel, Shire, 1972, published as *Isambard Brunel,* Newbury Books, 1973.
General Gordon, 1833-1885: An Illustrated Life of Charles George Gordon, Shire, 1972, Newbury Books, 1973.
Mungo Park: An Illustrated Life of Mungo Park, 1770-1806, Newbury Books, 1973.
Henry Morton Stanley: An Illustrated Life of Henry Morton Stanley, 1841-1904, Shire, 1973.
Our Daily Bread, Penguin, 1973.
Ernest Bevin, Newbury Books, 1974.
Hitler, Shire, 1974.
The Conquest of South America, Methuen, 1974.
Sir Winston Churchill, Shire, 1974.
People and Politics: An Introductory Reader, C. Knight, 1975.
Japan Today, Kaye & Ward, 1976.
Modern France: State and Society, Harrap, 1977.
The World of Islam: A Teacher's Handbook, School of Oriental and African Studies, University of London, 1977.
Buildings in Spain, Harrap, 1977.
China Today, Kaye & Ward, 1978.
People, Power, and Politics, Thomas Nelson, 1978.
Japan: A Teacher's Handbook, Paul Norbury Publications, 1978, 2nd revised edition published as *The Japan Handbook: A Guide for Teachers,* 1981.
Cities, Greenhaven Press, 1980.
The French Revolution, Greenhaven Press, 1980.
Napoleon, Greenhaven Press, 1980.

The Arab World Today, Kaye & Ward, 1980.
Japan in the Twentieth Century, Batsford, 1981.
India and Pakistan in the Twentieth Century, Batsford, 1981.
Emergent Nations: Strategies for Development, Blackie & Son, 1981.
Servant of the Shogun: Being the True Story of William Adams, Pilot and Samurai, First Englishman in Japan, P. Norbury, 1981, State Mutual Book & Periodical Service, 1985.
The Muslim World, Silver Burdett, 1982.
Approaches to Islam, John Murray, 1982.
Makers of Modern Britain, Batsford, 1982.
The Japanese, Trafalgar Square, 1982.
Knowing British History: Food, Evans, 1982.
Growing Up in the 1960s, Batsford, 1983.
Victorian London, Batsford, 1984.
The Great War, David & Charles, 1984.
Nazi Germany, Trafalgar Square, 1985.
Islam, Batsford, 1985.
Japan, the Land and its People, Silver Burdett, 1986, revised edition, 1987.
Exploring Other Civilizations, Dufour, 1987.
Patterns, Pilgrims and Puritans, Trafalgar Square, 1987.
Radicals, Reformers and Railways, 1815-1851, Trafalgar Square, 1987.
The American West, Trafalgar Square, 1988.
Passport to Japan, Watts, 1988.
Japan since 1945, Watts, 1989.
Take a Trip to Lebanon, Watts, 1989.
Take a Trip to Lybia, Watts, 1989.
Take a Trip to Iran, Watts, 1989.
Take a Trip to Iraq, Watts, 1989.
Hellen Keller, Watts, 1989.
Marie Curie, Watts, 1989.
Mother Theresa, Watts, 1989.
Amelia Earhart, Watts, 1989.
Anne Frank, Watts, 1989.
Florence Nightingale, Watts, 1989.
The First Day of the Somme, Trafalgar Square, 1990.
Journey Through Canada, Troll Associates, 1990.
Journey Through Japan, Troll Associates, 1990.
The Nineteen Fifties, Watts, 1990.
The Nineteen Eighties, Watts, 1990.
Alexander Fleming, Watts, 1990.
Alexander Graham Bell, Watts, 1990.
Thomas Edison, Watts, 1990.
The Wright Brothers, Watts, 1990.
Louis Pasteur, Watts, 1990.
Guglielmo Marconi, Watts, 1990.
Mozart, Watts, 1991.
Tchaikovsky, Watts, 1991.
Verdi, Watts, 1991.
Beethoven, Watts, 1991.
Nelson Mandela, Watts, 1991.
The Nineteen Thirties, Watts, 1991.
The Nineteen Twenties, Watts, 1991.

Author of television scripts for BBC-Schools Television and Radio and Inner London Education Authority Schools Television.

ADAPTATIONS: Servant of the Shogun: Being the True Story of William Adams, Pilot and Samurai, First Englishman in Japan, was dramatized for radio and broadcast on BBC Radio in England.

WORK IN PROGRESS: Biographies and histories illustrated with his own photos.

SIDELIGHTS: Richard Tames once wrote, "For the past seventeen years I have served as a member of the adjunct faculty of Syracuse University's London campus, teaching British history. It's a stimulating experience in inter-cultural communication. Most of my working time, however, has been spent in trying to assist British teachers in coming to terms with the curricular challenge of our multicultural society in an increasingly interdependent world. Recent years have surely shown the importance of understanding the achievements of the Japanese and the aspirations of the Muslims, whose cultures represent two of my major areas of interest."

More recently, he wrote, "My writing interests began in the field of British history and, although I have since developed wider interests, I do try to keep up this side of my work. I am particularly keen to write about areas I know well at first hand, like London and East Anglia. Centenaries and anniversaries often suggest new subjects for writing and sometimes revive interest in existing books. In 1985 the 150th anniversary of the Great Western Railway led to the sixth printing of my short biography of Isambard Brunel, its builder. With its long and crowded history, Britain is always able to come up with an anniversary of some kind every year. Knowing this helps a writer plan ahead and take account of the public interest in a subject that is more or less bound to arise.

"One of my constant concerns has been to try to get across to the reader the very basic point that history is about *real* people who have *actually* lived. Perhaps that's why so much of my writing has been biographical. I particularly enjoyed researching and writing the true story of William Adams, the first Englishman to visit Japan. Many people will have read about John Blackthorne, the hero of James Clavell's novel *Shogun* or seen Richard Chamberlain play this part in the television mini-series based on the novel. But not many people perhaps realize that the essence of this story really happened. This is what I have tried to show in *Servant of the Shogun.* I hope that people who see the TV series will want to read the novel and then, when they have read the novel, will want to know the real story. Thanks to BBC Radio I also had the opportunity to present this story to the public as a drama documentary.

"Over the last four years I have developed an interest in photography which enables me to illustrate my work with my own pictures. I was able to take about half of the sixty photographs in my book on *Victorian London* and the same proportion in my *Dictionary of Islam* which uses pictures I took in Tunisia, Turkey and India. More and more I find I'm looking for subjects I can photograph as well as write about.

"In the past year I have qualified as a London Tourist Board 'Blue Badge' Registered Guide. This has involved acquiring a very detailed knowledge of such familiar landmarks as Westminster Abbey, the Tower of London and St. Paul's Cathedral as well as a general familiarity with one of the most complex cities in the world. I am developing a particular interest in American connections with London and hope to write more about my native city in the future."

"I smell the ocean!" Honey Bunch said. (Frontispiece from *Honey Bunch: Her First Trip on the Ocean,* by Helen Louise Thorndyke.)

THORNDYKE, Helen Louise
[Collective pseudonym]

WRITINGS:

"HONEY BUNCH" SERIES

Honey Bunch: Just a Little Girl, Grosset & Dunlap, 1923.
Honey Bunch: Her First Visit to the City Grosset & Dunlap, 1923.
Honey Bunch: Her First Days on the Farm, Grosset & Dunlap, 1923.
Honey Bunch: Her First Visit to the Seashore, Grosset & Dunlap, 1924.
Honey Bunch: Her First Little Garden, Grosset & Dunlap, 1924.
Honey Bunch: Her First Days in Camp, Grosset & Dunlap, 1925.
Honey Bunch: Her First Auto Tour, Grosset & Dunlap, 1926.
Honey Bunch: Her First Trip on the Ocean, Grosset & Dunlap, 1927.
Honey Bunch: Her First Trip West, Grosset & Dunlap, 1928.
Honey Bunch: Her First Summer on an Island, Grosset & Dunlap, 1929.
Honey Bunch: Her First Trip on the Great Lakes, Grosset & Dunlap, 1930.

Honey Bunch: Her First Trip in an Airplane, Grosset & Dunlap, 1931.
Honey Bunch: Her First Visit to the Zoo, Grosset & Dunlap, 1932.
Honey Bunch: Her First Big Adventure, Grosset & Dunlap, 1933.
Honey Bunch: Her First Big Parade, Grosset & Dunlap, 1934.
Honey Bunch: Her First Little Mystery, Grosset & Dunlap, 1935.
Honey Bunch: Her First Little Circus, Grosset & Dunlap, 1936.
Honey Bunch: Her First Little Treasure Hunt, Grosset & Dunlap, 1937.
Honey Bunch: Her First Little Club, Grosset & Dunlap, 1938.
Honey Bunch: Her First Trip in a Trailer, Grosset & Dunlap, 1939.
Honey Bunch: Her First Trip to a Big Fair, Grosset & Dunlap, 1940.
Honey Bunch: Her First Twin Playmates, Grosset & Dunlap, 1941.
Honey Bunch: Her First Costume Party, Grosset & Dunlap, 1943.
Honey Bunch: Her First Trip on a Houseboat, Grosset & Dunlap, 1945.
Honey Bunch: Her First Winter at Snowtop, Grosset & Dunlap, 1946.
Honey Bunch: Her First Trip to the Big Woods, Grosset & Dunlap, 1947.
Honey Bunch: Her First Little Pet Show, Grosset & Dunlap, 1948.
Honey Bunch: Her First Trip to a Lighthouse (also see below), Grosset & Dunlap, 1949.
Honey Bunch: Her First Visit to a Pony Ranch, Grosset & Dunlap, 1950.
Honey Bunch: Her First Tour of Toy Town (also see below), Grosset & Dunlap, 1951.
Honey Bunch: Her First Visit to Puppyland, Grosset & Dunlap, 1952.
Honey Bunch: Her First Trip to Reindeer Farm (also see below), Grosset & Dunlap, 1953.
Honey Bunch and Norman Ride with the Sky Mailman (also see below), Grosset & Dunlap, 1954.
Honey Bunch and Norman Visit Beaver Lodge (also see below), Grosset & Dunlap, 1955.

"HONEY BUNCH AND NORMAN" SERIES

Honey Bunch and Norman, Grosset & Dunlap, 1957.
Honey Bunch and Norman on Lighthouse Island (originally published as part of the "Honey Bunch" series under title *Honey Bunch: Her First Trip to a Lighthouse*), Grosset & Dunlap, 1957.
Honey Bunch and Norman Tour Toy Town (originally published as part of the "Honey Bunch" series under title *Honey Bunch: Her First Tour of Toy Town*), Grosset & Dunlap, 1957.
Honey Bunch and Norman Play Detective at Niagara Falls, Grosset & Dunlap, 1957.
Honey Bunch and Norman Ride with the Sky Mailman (originally published as part of the "Honey Bunch" series), Grosset & Dunlap, 1958.
Honey Bunch and Norman Visit Beaver Lodge, Grosset & Dunlap, 1958.
Honey Bunch and Norman Visit Reindeer Farm (originally published as part of the "Honey Bunch" series under title *Honey Bunch: Her First Trip to Reindeer Farm*), Grosset & Dunlap, 1958.
Honey Bunch and Norman in the Castle of Magic, Grosset & Dunlap, 1959.

Honey Bunch and Norman Solve the Pine Cone Mystery, Grosset & Dunlap, 1960.
Honey Bunch and Norman and the Paper Lantern Mystery, Grosset & Dunlap, 1961.
Honey Bunch and Norman and the Painted Pony, Grosset & Dunlap, 1962.
Honey Bunch and Norman and the Walnut Tree Mystery, Grosset & Dunlap, 1963.

SIDELIGHTS: Grosset & Dunlap's advertisements for these series, which were intended for children ages four to eight, described Honey Bunch Morton as "a dainty, thoughtful little girl who keeps one wondering what she is going to do next." She was occasionally joined in her escapades by her friend Norman who, as the series progressed, became a more active participant in her adventures. Eventually, the Stratemeyer Syndicate began a new series co-starring Norman with Honey Bunch.

Bobbie Ann Mason, in her book *The Girl Sleuth: A Feminist Guide,* calls Honey Bunch Morton "Shirley Temple's literary precursor, portrayed and illustrated as a dainty stereotype—clean, obedient, cute, talented." While Norman and Stub, Honey Bunch's tomboy friend, occasionally indulged in mischief, Honey Bunch herself was always well-behaved, says Mason: "She learned to be, in fact, a juvenile Victorian matron." The stories themselves, the reviewer continues, focus on comfortable home-centered values; Honey Bunch's world is cozy, and her favorite spot is the "kitty corner," a "perfect world in miniature, a little elf nook, a playhouse, a gingerbread cottage, an English garden in a terrarium, a hideaway in an attic."

Harriet Adams and Andrew Svenson both worked on these series; Adams produced at least seven volumes herself. Another five volumes in the "Honey Bunch" series are credited to Mildred Augustine Wirt Benson. See the *SATA* index for more information on Harriet S. Adams, Mildred Benson, Edward L. Stratemeyer, and Andrew E. Svenson.

WORKS CITED:

Johnson, Deidre, editor and compiler, *Stratemeyer Pseudonyms and Series Books: An Annotated Checklist of Stratemeyer and Stratemeyer Syndicate Publications,* Greenwood Press, 1982, p. 252.
Mason, Bobbie Ann, "The Land of Milk and Honey Bunch," *The Girl Sleuth: A Feminist Guide,* Feminist Press, 1975, pp. 19-28.

FOR MORE INFORMATION SEE:

BOOKS

Paluka, Frank, *Iowa Authors: A Bio-Bibliography of Sixty Native Writers,* Friends of the University of Iowa Libraries, 1967.

*   *   *

TIBO, Gilles 1951-

PERSONAL: Born in 1951, in Nicolet, Quebec, Canada; married; children: Simon.

CAREER: Author and illustrator.

WRITINGS:

IN ENGLISH TRANSLATION; SELF-ILLUSTRATED

Simon and the Snowflakes, Tundra Books, 1988 (originally published as *Simone et les flocons de neige,* Livres Toundra, 1988).
Simon and the Wind, Tundra Books, 1989 (originally published as *Simon et le vent d'automne,* Livres Toundra, 1989).
Simon Welcomes Spring, Tundra Books, 1990 (originally published as *Simon fete le printemps,* Livres Toundra, 1990).

UNTRANSLATED WORKS; SELF-ILLUSTRATED

L'Oeil Voyeur, Les Editions du Cri, 1970.
Monsieur Quidam, l'apres-midi dernier: Un conte a lire tranquillement, Le Tamanoir, 1976.
La Nuit du grand coucou, Courte Echelle, 1984.

Also author and illustrator of *Le Roi du sommeil.*

ILLUSTRATOR

Louis Philippe Cote, *Le Prince sourire et le lys bleu,* Le Tamanoir, 1975.
Andre Cailloux, *Je te laisse une caresse,* Le Tamanoir, 1976.
Felix Leclerc, *Le Tour de l'ile,* Editions la courte echelle, 1980.
Helene Vachon and Arlette Lefroncois, *Livres a fabriquer soi-meme,* La Pocatiere, 1985.
Edgar Allan Poe, *Annabel Lee: The Poem,* Tundra Books, 1987.
Louis Hemon, *Maria Chapdelaine,* translated by Alan Brown, Tundra Books, 1989.
Robert Munsch, *Giant,* Firefly Books, 1989.
Alice Bartels, *The Beast,* Firefly Books, 1990.

Gilles Tibo and his son Simon.

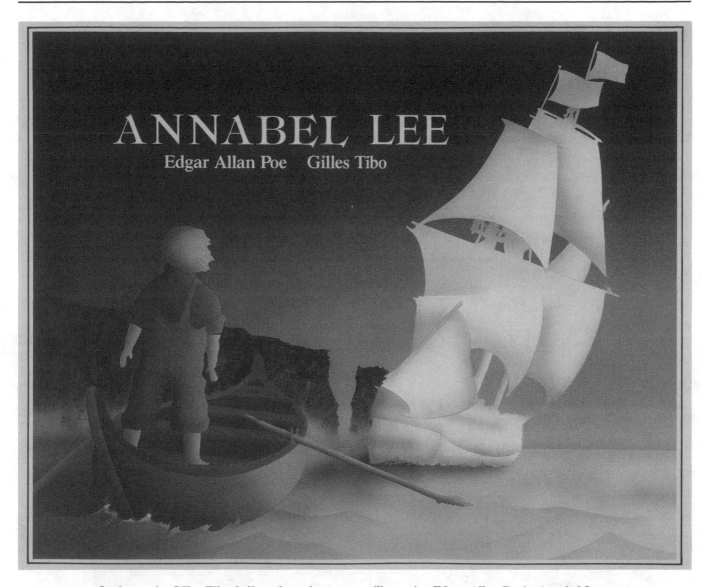

Quebec artist Gilles Tibo dedicated nearly a year to illustrating Edgar Allan Poe's *Annabel Lee*.

SIDELIGHTS: Gilles Tibo taught himself to draw and his first work was published when he was only seventeen years old. He has written and illustrated books and provided drawings for newspapers, magazines, record albums, and movie posters.*

*   *   *

UNGER, Jim 1937-

PERSONAL: Born January 21, 1937, in London, England; moved to Canada, 1968; son of Cecil James (an electronics engineer) and Lillian Maud Unger; married Patricia M. Smith, November, 1969 (divorced, 1975). *Education:* Attended art schools, 1952-59. *Politics:* "A-political."

CAREER: Minto Construction Co., Ottawa, Ontario, graphic artist in advertising department, 1968-71; *Mississauga Times,* Mississauga, Ontario, art director, 1971-74; Jim Unger, Inc., Ottawa, syndicated cartoonist, 1974—. Worked previously as an insurance clerk, police officer, driving instructor, taxi driver, and office manager. *Military service:* British Army, surveyor, 1955-57.

AWARDS, HONORS: Named cartoonist of the year, Ontario Weekly Newspapers Association, 1972, 1973, and 1974; Reuben Award, National Cartoonists Society, 1988, for syndicated cartoon panel Herman.

WRITINGS:

SELF-ILLUSTRATED; PUBLISHED BY ANDREWS & McMEEL

"And You Wonder, Herman, Why I Never Want to Go to Italian Restaurants, 1977.
First Treasury of Herman, 1979.
The Second Herman Treasury, 1980.
The Latest Herman, 1981.
Herman Sundays: The First Seventy-seven Weekend Herman Comics in Full Color, 1982.
Herman, the Third Treasury, 1982.
Herman, You Were a Much Stronger Man on Our First Honeymoon: A Collection of Herman Daily Panel, 1983.
Herman and the Extraterrestrials, 1983.
Herman, M.D., 1983.
Herman out to Lunch, 1983.
A Collection of Herman Color Comics, 1983.
Herman, Dinner's Served . . . As Soon As the Smoke Clears!, 1985.

JIM UNGER

Herman Treasury Five, 1986.
Herman: The Sixth Treasury, 1988.
They're Gonna Settle out of Court, Herman, 1989.
Herman over the Wall: The Seventh Treasury, 1990.

Also author of *It's Called "Midnight Surrender," Herman;*
Feeling Run down Again, Herman?; and *The Cat's Got Your*
Teeth Again.

"Here, Kitty, Kitty." (From *Herman, Dinner's*
Served ... As Soon As the Smoke Clears!, written
and illustrated by Unger.)

SELF-ILLUSTRATED; OTHER

Apart from a Little Dampness, Herman, How's Everything
Else?, Sheed & Ward, 1975.
Herman the Fourth Treasury, Andrews, McMeel & Parker,
1984.
People Are Starting to Complain, Herman: A Collection of
Sunday Comics, McMeel & Parker, 1984.
Any Other Complaints, Herman?, New American Library of
Canada, 1985.
Herman, You Can Get in the Bathroom Now, Andrews, Mc-
Meel & Parker, 1987.

SIDELIGHTS: Jim Unger is best known for his cartoon
strip, *Herman,* which appears in newspapers throughout the
United States and Canada. Explaining the reason for
Herman's popularity, Unger once commented, "I have a
great love of humanity which I think is the strength of my
humor." Unger's cast of characters, led by Herman, are not
usually beautiful or successful, but they are still good people
even though they slouch, have wrinkled clothes, and make a
lot of mistakes in their everyday lives. The author believes
that showing these types of characteristics and failures in his
subjects is important because such shortcomings are common. In the introduction to *Herman the Fourth Treasury* he
remarked, "Whether we are sixteen or sixty, . . . the more
natural we are, the more attractive we are to others. Sadly, we
are very often led to believe the exact opposite." He continued, "When I draw *Herman,* I draw funny-looking people,
saying and doing very natural things. I know why you laugh
and I think you know why you laugh. It may be a comfort to
you to know that millions of other people around the world
are laughing too. It's certainly a comfort to me. I was
beginning to think I was on the wrong planet."

WORKS CITED:

Unger, Jim, *Herman the Fourth Treasury,* Andrews, McMeel
& Parker, 1984, p. 10.*

        *   *   · *

Van ZWIENEN, Ilse Charlotte Koehn 1929-1991
(Ilse Koehn)

OBITUARY NOTICE—See index for *SATA* sketch: Born
August 6, 1929, in Berlin, Germany; died of a heart attack,
May 8, 1991, at home in Greenwich, CT. Graphic artist and
author. Ilse Charlotte Koehn Van Zwienen, who wrote under
the name Ilse Koehn, chronicled her early life in *Mischling,*
Second Degree: My Childhood in Nazi Germany. In the book,
she described the experience of living in evacuation camps
during most of World War II. The volume received many
awards, including a nomination for the National Book
Award for children's literature in 1978. Van Zwienen was
also an illustrator who graduated from Berlin Art Academy.

OBITUARIES AND OTHER SOURCES:

BOOKS

International Authors and Writers Who's Who, 11th edition,
International Biographical Centre, 1989.

PERIODICALS

New York Times, May 16, 1991.

VERR, Harry Coe
See KUNHARDT, Edith

*   *   *

WARNER, Frank A.
[Collective pseudonym]

WRITINGS:

"BOB CHASE BIG GAME" SERIES

Bob Chase with the Big Moose Hunters, Barse & Co., 1929.
Bob Chase after Grizzly Bears, Barse & Co., 1929.
Bob Chase in the Tiger's Lair, Barse & Co., 1929.
Bob Chase with the Lion Hunters, Barse & Co., 1930.

"BOBBY BLAKE" SERIES

Bobby Blake at Rockledge School; or, Winning the Medal of Honor, Barse & Hopkins, 1915.
Bobby Blake at Bass Cove; or, The Hunt for the Motor Boat Gem, Barse & Hopkins, 1915.
Bobby Blake on a Cruise; or, The Castaways of Volcano Island, Barse & Hopkins, 1915.
Bobby Blake and His School Chums; or, The Rivals of Rockledge, Barse & Hopkins, 1916.
Bobby Blake at Snowtop Camp; or, Winter Holidays in the Big Woods, Barse & Hopkins, 1916.
Bobby Blake on the School Nine; or, The Champions of Monotook Lake League, Barse & Hopkins, 1917.
Bobby Blake on a Ranch; or, The Secret of the Mountain Cave, Barse & Hopkins, 1918.
Bobby Blake on an Auto Tour; or, The Mystery of the Deserted House, Barse & Hopkins, 1920.
Bobby Blake on the School Eleven; or, Winning the Banner of Blue and Gold, Barse & Hopkins, 1921.
Bobby Blake on a Plantation; or, Lost in the Great Swamp, Barse & Hopkins, 1922.
Bobby Blake in the Frozen North; or, The Old Eskimo's Last Message, Barse & Hopkins, 1923.
Bobby Blake on Mystery Mountain, Barse & Hopkins, 1926.

SIDELIGHTS: Two Stratemeyer Syndicate series were released under this pseudonym. Bob Chase, according to the publisher's advertisements, was "a young lumberjack who is a crack shot. While tracking game in the wilds of Maine he does some rich hunters a great service," and he becomes their companion, travelling around the world with them on hunting expeditions. The stories contained "much valuable data on animal life as lived in the wilderness." The Bobby Blake books were intended for boys from eight to twelve years old. They were advertised as "true stories of life at a modern American boarding school." See the *SATA* index for more information on Harriet S. Adams, Edward L. Stratemeyer, and Andrew E. Svenson, who wrote under this collective pseudonym.

WORKS CITED:

Johnson, Deidre, editor and compiler, *Stratemeyer Pseudonyms and Series Books: An Annotated Checklist of Stratemeyer and Stratemeyer Syndicate Publications,* Greenwood Press, 1982, p. 258.

*   *   *

WATLING, James 1933-

PERSONAL: Born February 7, 1933, in Newcastle-upon-Tyne, England. *Education:* Barrow-in-Furness School of

JAMES WATLING

Art, 1945-53; Leeds School of Art, A.T.C., 1954; post-graduate study. *Hobbies and other interests:* Birds, outdoors, cabinet making, home construction.

ADDRESSES: Home—Box 1084, Rawdon, Quebec, Canada J0K 150. *Office*—c/o Random House, 225 Park Ave. S., New York, NY 10003. *Agent*—Publishers Graphics, 251 Greenwood Ave., Bethel, CT 06801.

CAREER: Illustrator. McGill University, Montreal, Quebec, associate professor and art program director, faculty of education, 1963—.

ILLUSTRATOR:

Hans Christian Andersen, *The Emperor and the Nightingale,* Troll Associates, 1979.
Corinne Denan, *Tales of Magic and Spells,* Troll Associates, 1980.
Keith Brandt, *Wonders of the Seasons,* Troll Associates, 1982.
Susan Gold Purdy, *Eskimos,* Watts, 1982.
Laurence Santrey, *Discovering the Stars,* Troll Associates, 1982.
Raymond Harris, *Best Short Stories,* Jamestown Publishers, 1983.
Peter Zachary Cohen, *The Great Red River Raft,* A. Whitman, 1984.
Brandt, *Deserts,* Troll Associates, 1985.
Louis Sabin, *Grasslands,* Troll Associates, 1985.
Eileen Curran, *Life in the Meadow,* Troll Associates, 1985.
Curran, *Mountains and Volcanoes,* Troll Associates, 1985.
Kim Jackson, *The Planets,* Troll Associates, 1985.
Linda Walvoord Girard, *Earth, Sea, and Sky: The Work of Edmond Halley,* A. Whitman, 1985.

Story by Robert McConnell   Paintings by James Watling   Napoleon Publishing

The paintings for Robert McConnell's *Nip and Tuck* were created from Watling's observations of animals and birds in their natural habitat.

Drollene P. Brown, *Belva Lockwood Wins Her Case,* A. Whitman, 1987.

David Cutts, *King of the Golden Mountain,* Troll Associates, 1988.

Judy Donnelly, *Tut's Mummy: Lost and Found,* Random House, 1988.

Stephen Krensky, *Witch Hunt: It Happened in Salem Village,* Random House, 1989.

Janet Palazzo-Craig, *Discovering Prehistoric Animals,* Troll Associates, 1990.

Stephen Caitlin, *Wonders of Swamps and Marshes,* Troll Associates, 1990.

Linda Hayward, *The First Thanksgiving,* McKay, 1990.

Richard Berleth, *Samuel's Choice,* A. Whitman, 1990.

Robert McConnell, *Nip and Tuck,* Napoleon (Toronto), 1990.

Krensky, *Children of the Earth and Sky,* Scholastic Inc., 1991.

Anita Larsen, *Histories Mysteries: The Roanoke Missing Persons Case,* Crestwood, in press.

SIDELIGHTS: James Watling told *SATA* that he is "particularly interested in historical illustration and illustration of nature/wildlife."

*   *   *

WEBB, Margot 1934-

PERSONAL: Born August 28, 1934, in Halle, Germany; daughter of Egmont and Ilse (a homemaker; maiden name, Ambach) Lewin; married Pritam Dave, February 24, 1949 (died, 1984); married Marcus Webb (a chief editor), May 3, 1987; children: Robert Dave, Peter Dave, Sandra Lynne Kyte. *Education:* Received master's degree from University of Southern California, 1979, doctoral study, 1983. *Politics:* Democrat. *Religion:* Jewish. *Hobbies and other interests:* Classical music, poetry, philosophy.

ADDRESSES: Home—15612 San Moritz Dr., P.O. Box 6505, Pine Mountain Club, CA 93222.

CAREER: Teacher, counselor, translator, and writer. Translator in Bombay, India, 1949; teacher and counselor in elementary schools in Los Angeles, CA, 1961-89; counselor for Program for Integration of Institute for Teacher Leadership, 1984-86; full-time writer, 1989—.

MEMBER: Child Survivors of the Holocaust; head of professional writers' group in Pine Mountain Club, CA.

WRITINGS:

Coping with Street Gangs, Rosen Publishing, 1990.
Coping with Overprotective Parents, Rosen Publishing, 1990.
The Value of Loyalty, Rosen Publishing, 1991.
Coping When Your Parents Are Activists, Rosen Publishing, in press.
Shadows at Noon (novel), Lerner Publications, in press.

Contributor of articles to periodicals, including *Christian Home and School, Emergency Medical Services, Options for Physicians in Transition,* and *Rosicrucian Digest.*

WORK IN PROGRESS: Jose at Risk, a novel about a gang member and his efforts to amend his life; and *Monsoon,* a novel about India.

SIDELIGHTS: Margot Webb told *SATA:* "I was born in Germany. The Holocaust began soon afterwards. This has colored my life and my writing. My main thrust is to have readers understand the importance of good over evil, which can only be accomplished by action. I feel blaming others is not the way to have a fair world. Having a goal and working toward it, especially in race relations, is one of the most worthwhile activities one can do.

"I like to write for young adults. Having worked with them for many years, I feel I understand their problems. I certainly haven't forgotten the frustrations of teen years . . . nor the fun. I hope my readers will feel that life is a big adventure. The more they try to do, the more exciting the journey becomes.

"I'd like young people to realize that there are solutions to problems . . . solutions they can work out with help from people they trust. Perhaps I write about problematic situations because I, too, had to find my way and make my path.

"I have tremendous confidence in today's youth and I'd like to congratulate them on their questioning, their searching, and their growing in *their* own way."

FOR MORE INFORMATION SEE:

PERIODICALS

Bakersfield Californian, March 12, 1990.
Booklist, September 1, 1990.
School Library Journal, October, 1990.

WEBSTER, Frank V.
[Collective pseudonym]

WRITINGS:

Only a Farm Boy; or, Dan Hardy's Rise in Life, Cupples & Leon, 1909.
Tom the Telephone Boy; or, The Mystery of a Message, Cupples & Leon, 1909.
The Boy from the Ranch; or, Roy Bradner's City Experiences, Cupples & Leon, 1909.
The Young Treasure Hunter; or, Fred Stanley's Trip to Alaska, Cupples & Leon, 1909, reprinted, Saalfield, 1938.
Bob the Castaway; or, The Wreck of the Eagle, Cupples & Leon, 1909, reprinted, Saalfield, 1938.
The Young Firemen of Lakeville; or, Herbert Dare's Pluck, Cupples & Leon, 1909, reprinted, Saalfield, 1938.
The Newsboy Partners; or, Who Was Dick Box?, Cupples & Leon, 1909.
The Boy Pilot of the Lakes; or, Nat Morton's Perils, Cupples & Leon, 1909.
Two Boy Gold Miners; or, Lost in the Mountains, Cupples & Leon, 1909, reprinted, Saalfield, 1938.
Jack the Runaway; or, On the Road with a Circus, Cupples & Leon, 1909, reprinted, Saalfield, 1938.
Comrades of the Saddle; or, The Young Rough Riders of the Plains, Cupples & Leon, 1910, reprinted, Saalfield, 1938.
The Boys of Bellwood School; or, Frank Jordan's Triumph, Cupples & Leon, 1910, reprinted, Saalfield, 1938.
Bob Chester's Grit; or, From Ranch to Riches, Cupples & Leon, 1911, reprinted, Saalfield, 1938.
Airship Andy; or, The Luck of a Brave Boy, Cupples & Leon, 1911.
The High School Rivals; or, Fred Markham's Struggles, Cupples & Leon, 1911.
Darry the Life Saver; or, The Heroes of the Coast, Cupples & Leon, 1911, reprinted, Saalfield, 1938.
Dick the Bank Boy; or, The Missing Fortune, Cupples & Leon, 1911.
Ben Hardy's Flying Machine; or, Making a Record for Himself, Cupples & Leon, 1911.
The Boys of the Wireless; or, A Stirring Rescue from the Deep, Cupples & Leon, 1912, reprinted, Saalfield, 1938.
Harry Watson's High School Days; or, The Rivals of Rivertown, Cupples & Leon, 1912.
The Boy Scouts of Lenox; or, Hiking over Big Bear Mountain, Cupples & Leon, 1915.
Tom Taylor at West Point; or, The Old Army Officer's Secret, Cupples & Leon, 1915.
Cowboy Dave; or, The Round Up at Rolling River, Cupples & Leon, 1915, reprinted, Saalfield, 1938.
Two Boys of the Battleship; or, For the Honor of Uncle Sam, Cupples & Leon, 1915.
Jack of the Pony Express; or, The Young Rider of the Mountain Trails, Cupples & Leon, 1915, reprinted, Saalfield, 1938.

SIDELIGHTS: Some sources group all the books published under the pseudonym Frank V. Webster as a single series even though they did not share the same characters, themes, or settings. Cupples & Leon's advertisements described them as very much like those "of the boys' favorite author, the late lamented Horatio Alger, Jr." See the *SATA* index for more information on Harriet S. Adams, Edward L. Stratemeyer, and Andrew E. Svenson, who shared this collective pseudonym.

WORKS CITED:

Johnson, Deidre, editor and compiler, *Stratemeyer Pseudonyms and Series Books: An Annotated Checklist of Stratemeyer and Stratemeyer Syndicate Publications,* Greenwood Press, 1982, p. 260.

* * *

WELLINGTON, Monica 1957-

PERSONAL: Born June 17, 1957, in London, England; daughter of Roger (a business executive) and Diana (Guerin) Wellington; married; children: Lydia. *Education:* University of Michigan, B.F.A., 1978; additional study at School of Visual Arts, 1986. *Hobbies and other interests:* Travel, ballet, sewing, quilting.

ADDRESSES: Home—251 East 32nd St., New York, NY 10016.

CAREER: Artist; free-lance writer and illustrator of children's books, 1987—. Worked in antique gallery and in the ceramics department of the Victoria and Albert Musuem, London, England.

MEMBER: Society of Children's Book Writers.

WRITINGS:

SELF-ILLUSTRATED

Molly Chelsea and Her Calico Cat, Dutton, 1988.
All My Little Ducklings, Dutton, 1989.
Seasons of Swans, Dutton, 1990.
The Sheep Follow, Dutton, 1992.

ILLUSTRATOR

A. G. Deming, *Who Is Tapping at My Window?,* Dutton, 1988.
Virginia Griest, *In Between,* Dutton, 1989.

MONICA WELLINGTON

Arnold Shapiro, *Who Says That?,* Dutton, 1991.

WORK IN PROGRESS: The Cookie Baker.

SIDELIGHTS: Monica Wellington told *SATA:* "As a young child, until the age of seven, I lived in England, Germany and Switzerland. I think my early childhood has a big influence on my books. In Switzerland we lived close to a small town. We were surrounded by mountains, woods, lakes, orchards, fields, and farms. Again in my books, I find myself doing pictures of these kinds of places.

"The Idea for *All My Little Ducklings* came from a German song I remembered: 'Alle Meine Entchen'—'All my little ducklings, swimming in the sea, heads are in the water, tails are to the sun.' I took this image as a starting point and it grew into a book about a day in the life of this family of ducks.

"*Molly Chelsea and Her Calico Cat* is about going to shops in the little towns we lived close to and also about the cats we always have had. Molly goes out to the shops to get treats for her special cat. Everyday my sister and I went out with my mother to do errands at various little shops. We bought bread at the bakery, meat at the butcher, cheese at the dairy. Then there weren't big supermarkets where you could get everything at once.

"I always loved to draw as a child. I recently found some of the first pictures I did when we were living in Europe and they are not that different from what I am doing now! I still like to do pictures of the same things! I didn't know then that I wanted to write and illustrate children's books—that I didn't know for a long time, not until I was almost thirty.

"In the meantime, we moved to the United States. I lived in New York, Massachusetts, Rhode Island, and Vermont. I went to college at the School of Art at the University of Michigan. There I did pottery, painting, and printmaking. I had no idea yet of doing children's books. After college I lived in London where I studied the history of decorative arts and then worked in an antique gallery specializing in English porcelain and also the Victoria and Albert Museum in the ceramics department. After several years of that, I realized I wanted to do and make art again. I moved to New York City in 1981 and have been working ever since as a free-lance artist. For about three years I worked in a pottery studio. Then gradually I started to do more painting projects. The more pictures I did, because of the style and images that were developing, the more I thought of doing children's books. I kind of wandered into the field before I decided that this was what I really wanted to do.

"In 1986, I took a course at the School of Visual Arts with Bruce Degen and this was a big help. After that I went to publishers with my portfolio and I soon met Lucia Monfried at Dutton who has been my editor for all my books.

"One of the pictures in my portfolio had been a class assignment—illustrating a poem by A. G. Deming, first published over twenty years ago. My editor had the idea to use this picture as a starting point and to make this poem into *Who Is Tapping at My Window?*

"I have both written and illustrated about half of my books; the other half I have illustrated a story written by another author. My own books usually start with an idea of what I want to paint pictures about. The pictures come before the words for me. I am usually still working on the words after I finish the pictures. My books so far are all picture books for very young children—perhaps because that was such a wonderful and idyllic time in my own childhood."

* * *

WHITE, Ramy Allison [Collective pseudonym]

WRITINGS:

"SUNNY BOY" SERIES

Sunny Boy in the Country, Barse & Hopkins, 1920.
Sunny Boy at the Seashore, Barse & Hopkins, 1920.
Sunny Boy in the Big City, Barse & Hopkins, 1920.
Sunny Boy in School and Out, Barse & Hopkins, 1921.
Sunny Boy and His Playmates, Barse & Hopkins, 1922.
Sunny Boy and His Games, Barse & Hopkins, 1923.
Sunny Boy in the Far West, Barse & Hopkins, 1924.
Sunny Boy on the Ocean, Barse & Hopkins, 1925.
Sunny Boy with the Circus, Barse & Hopkins, 1926.
Sunny Boy and His Big Dog, Barse & Hopkins, 1927.
Sunny Boy in the Snow, Barse & Co., 1929.
Sunny Boy at Willow Farm, Barse & Co., 1929.
Sunny Boy and His Cave, Barse & Co., 1930.
Sunny Boy at Rainbow Lake, Grosset & Dunlap, 1931.

SIDELIGHTS: The "Sunny Boy" series, intended for young children, chronicled the adventures of Sunny, described by the publishers as "a little fellow with big eyes and an inquiring disposition." See the *SATA* index for more information on Harriet S. Adams, Edward L. Stratemeyer, and Andrew E. Svenson, who contributed to this series under the pseudonym of Ramy Allison White.

WORKS CITED:

Johnson, Deidre, editor and compiler, *Stratemeyer Pseudonyms and Series Books: An Annotated Checklist of Stratemeyer ands Stratemeyer Syndicate Publications,* Greenwood Press, 1982, p. 267.

FOR MORE INFORMATION SEE:

BOOKS

Mason, Bobbie Ann, *The Girl Sleuth: A Feminist Guide,* Feminist Press, 1975.

PERIODICALS

Journal of Popular Culture, winter, 1974.

* * *

WINFIELD, Arthur M. See STRATEMEYER, Edward L.

* * *

WREDE, Patricia C(ollins) 1953-

PERSONAL: Surname is pronounced "Reedy"; born March 27, 1953, in Chicago, IL; daughter of David Merrill (a mechanical engineer) and Monica Marie (an executive; maiden name, Buerglar) Collins; married James M. Wrede (a financial consultant), July 24, 1976 (divorced, 1992). *Education:* Carleton College, A.B., 1974; University of Min-

PATRICIA C. WREDE

nesota, M.B.A., 1977. *Politics:* Independent. *Religion:* Roman Catholic.

ADDRESSES: Home and office—4900 West 60th St., Edina, MN 55424-1709. *Agent*—Valerie Smith, Route 44-55, RR Box 160, Modena, NY 12548.

CAREER: Minnesota Hospital Association, Minneapolis, MN, rate review analyst, 1977-78; B. Dalton Bookseller, Minneapolis, MN, financial analyst, 1978-80; Dayton-Hudson Corporation, Minneapolis, MN, financial analyst, 1980-81, senior financial analyst, 1981-83, senior accountant, 1983-85; full-time writer, 1985—. Laubach reading tutor.

MEMBER: Science Fiction Writers of America, Novelists, Inc.

AWARDS, HONORS: "Books for Young Adults" Recommended Reading List citation, 1984, for *Daughter of Witches,* and 1985, for *The Seven Towers;* Minnesota Book Award for Fantasy and Science Fiction, 1991, for *Dealing with Dragons.*

WRITINGS:

Shadow Magic, Ace Books, 1982.
Daughter of Witches, Ace Books, 1983.
The Seven Towers, Ace Books, 1984.
Talking to Dragons, Tempo/MagicQuest Books, 1985.
The Harp of Imach Thyssel, Ace Books, 1985.
(Contributor) Will Shetterly and Emma Bull, editors, *Liavek,* Ace Books, 1985.
(Contributor) Shetterly and Bull, editors, *Liavek: The Players of Luck,* Ace Books, 1986.
Caught in Crystal, Ace Books, 1987.

(Contributor) Jane Yolen, editor, *Spaceships and Spells,* Harper & Row, 1987.

(With Caroline Stevermer) *Sorcery and Cecelia,* Ace Books, 1988.

(Contributor) Bruce Coville, editor, *The Unicorn Treasury,* Doubleday, 1988.

(Contributor) Shetterly and Bull, editors, *Liavek: Spells of Binding,* Ace Books, 1988.

Snow White and Rose Red ("Fairy Tales" series), Tor Books, 1989.

(Contributor) Shetterly and Bull, editors, *Liavek: Festival Week,* Ace Books, 1990.

(Contributor) Andre Norton, editor, *Tales of the Witch World 3,* Tor Books, 1990.

Dealing with Dragons ("Chronicles of the Enchanted Forest" series, Volume 1; prequel to *Talking to Dragons*), Harcourt, 1990.

Mairelon the Magician, Tor Books, 1991.

Searching for Dragons ("Chronicles of the Enchanted Forest" series, Volume 2), Harcourt, 1991.

WORK IN PROGRESS: A third volume in the "Chronicles of the Enchanted Forest"; a revised version of *Talking to Dragons,* the fourth volume of the "Chronicles of the Enchanted Forest."

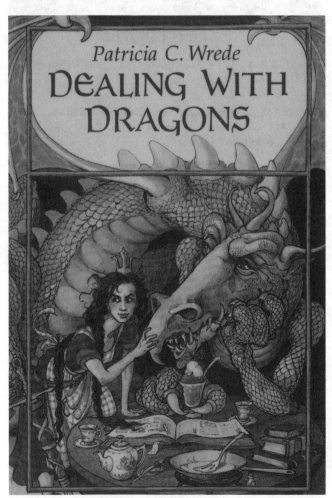

Dealing with Dragons **developed out of a short story Wrede wrote for an anthology.** (Cover illustration by Trina Schart Hyman.)

SIDELIGHTS: Patricia C. Wrede writes, "I started writing fiction in the seventh grade and never really stopped in spite of the fact that for many years I did not really expect writing to be more than a hobby. My mother aided and abetted me by typing out the pages I wrote longhand during class, and my father read them and told me they were great (he still thinks I should try to publish the book I was trying to write back then). I also told stories to my younger siblings (I am the eldest of five) and to any of my friends who would listen.

"In college, I placed out of the required Freshman English class and never got around to taking any others. Instead, I majored in biology and filled in the college distribution requirement with history and art.

"After I graduated in 1974, I began work on my first novel, *Shadow Magic.* It took me five years to finish it, during which time I married, earned an M.B.A., and changed jobs several times. In 1980, three months before the book sold, I joined a group of friends who were starting a critique group which later became known as the Scribblies. It turned out to be very successful; of the seven members, none of whom had been professionally published when the group began, all seven eventually sold something, and at least four members, as of this writing, are supporting themselves writing fiction. The group taught me a great deal about good writing, and I remain infinitely grateful to them all.

"In 1985, shortly before the publication of my fifth book, I left both my job and the Scribblies. About a year later, Jane Yolen asked me to contribute a short story to an anthology she was planning to edit. Normally, I find short fiction very difficult (my natural length is the novel), but I had an idea that seemed to suit her requirements, so I wrote 'The Improper Princess,' a short 'prequel' to *Talking to Dragons.* Jane loved it and bought it, but said several times that she thought there was more to it than that.

"When Harcourt, Brace, Jovanovich asked Jane to edit a line of children's books for them a few years later, she remembered me and the story and urged me to expand it. I agreed, and the result was *Dealing with Dragons.* Jane still wasn't satisfied, and talked me into continuing the series, which is currently in progress.

"I still tell stories to my young nieces, and to any of my friends who will listen, though most of them have learned to say sternly, 'Go home and write that down! I don't want to hear it, I want to read it.'"

*   *   *

WYNNE-JONES, Tim(othy) 1948-

PERSONAL: Born August 12, 1948, in Bromborough, Cheshire, England; son of Sydney Thomas (an engineer) and Sheila Beryl (a homemaker; maiden name, Hodgson) Wynne-Jones; married Amanda West Lewis (a writer, calligrapher, and teacher), in September, 1980; children: Alexander, Magdalene, Lewis. *Education:* University of Waterloo, B.F.A., 1974; York University, M.F.A., 1979.

ADDRESSES: Home and office—Rural Route No. 4, Perth, Ontario K7H 3C6, Canada. *Agent*—Lucinda Vardey, 297 Seaton St., Toronto, Ontario M5A 2T6, Canada.

CAREER: Writer, teacher, and editor.

TIM WYNNE-JONES

MEMBER: International P.E.N., Writers Union of Canada, Crime Writers of Canada, Association of Canadian Television and Radio Artists, Society of Composers, Authors, and Music Publishers of Canada.

AWARDS, HONORS: Seal First Novel Award, Bantam/ Seal Books, 1980, for *Odd's End,* Ruth Schwartz Children's Award, 1983, for *Zoom at Sea;* O.I.D.E. Award, 1983, for *Zoom at Sea;* Author's Award, The Foundation for the Advancement of Canadian Letters, 1990, for *Fastyngange.*

WRITINGS:

Odd's End, Little, Brown, 1980.
The Knot, McClelland & Stewart, 1982.
Zoom at Sea, Douglas & McIntyre, 1983.
Zoom Away, Douglas & McIntyre, 1985.
I'll Make You Small, Douglas & McIntyre, 1986.
Mischief City, Douglas & McIntyre, 1986.
Fastyngange, Lester & Orpen Dennys (Toronto), 1988, published in England as *Voices.*
Builder of the Moon, Macmillan, 1989, published in Canada as *Architect of the Moon.*
Hour of the Frog, Little Brown, 1990.

Also author of a children's opera titled *A Midwinter Night's Dream* and a musical version of *Mischief City.* Author of regular column of children's book reviews for the Toronto *Globe and Mail,* 1985-88.

WORK IN PROGRESS: The Mouse in the Manger, publication expected in 1992; *Zoom Downstream,* publication expected in 1992; *The Last Piece of Sky,* publication expected in 1993.

SIDELIGHTS: Tim Wynne-Jones told *SATA:* "I see the world as something which must be identified, over and over again, in words. I see fiction as the only sense in a world gone mad. Fiction, even bad fiction, aspires to form and to cosmos. The world—the facts of existence—is, as Italian writer Italo Calvino calls it, a 'shapeless avalanche of events.' I sign my letters 'yours in fiction' remembering the canon at my old church who signed his letters 'yours in Christ.' I believe in fiction, in its redemptive powers, in its mysterious working upon us as we read, freed to think in the very action of following the written word."

*   *   *

YEE, Paul (R.) 1956-

PERSONAL: Born October 1, 1956, in Spalding, Saskatchewan, Canada; son of Gordon and Gim May Yee. *Education:* University of British Columbia, B.A., 1978, M.A., 1983.

ADDRESSES: Home—125 Aldwych Ave., Toronto, Ontario, Canada M4J 1X8.

CAREER: City of Vancouver Archives, Vancouver, British Columbia, assistant city archivist, 1980-88; Archives of Ontario, Toronto, Ontario, portfolio manager, 1988—.

AWARDS, HONORS: British Columbia Book Prize for Children's Literature, National I.O.D.E. Book Award, and Parents' Choice Honor, all 1990, all for *Tales from Gold Mountain.*

WRITINGS:

Teach Me to Fly, Skyfighter! (stories), illustrations by Sky Lee, Lorimer (Toronto), 1983.
The Curses of Third Uncle (novel), Lorimer, 1986.
Saltwater City: An Illustrated History of the Chinese in Vancouver, Douglas & McIntyre (Vancouver), 1988, University of Washington, 1989.

PAUL YEE

Tales from Gold Mountain: Stories of the Chinese in the New World, illustrations by Simon Ng, Groundwood (Toronto), 1989, Macmillan (New York), 1990.

WORK IN PROGRESS: Roses on Fresh Snow, another "New World folk tale," for Macmillan; *Call Me Clark,* a juvenile novel, for Groundwood.

FOR MORE INFORMATION SEE:

PERIODICALS

Books in Canada, December, 1986.
Horn Book, July, 1990.
Quill and Quire, December, 1986; October, 1988; December, 1989.

*   *   *

YOUNG, Clarence
[Collective pseudonym]

WRITINGS:

"JACK RANGER" SERIES

Jack Ranger's Schooldays; or, The Rivals of Washington Hall, Cupples & Leon, 1907.
Jack Ranger's Western Trip; or, From Boarding School to Ranch and Range, Cupples & Leon, 1908.
Jack Ranger's School Victories; or, Track, Gridiron and Diamond, Cupples & Leon, 1908.
Jack Ranger's Ocean Cruise; or, The Wreck of the Polly Ann, Cupples & Leon, 1909.
Jack Ranger's Gun Club; or, From Schoolroom to Camp and Trail, Cupples & Leon, 1910.
Jack Ranger's Treasure Box; or, The Outing of the Schoolboy Yachtsmen, Cupples & Leon, 1911.

"MOTOR BOYS" SERIES

The Motor Boys; or, Chums through Thick and Thin, Cupples & Leon, 1906.
The Motor Boys Overland; or, A Long Trip for Fun and Fortune, Cupples & Leon, 1906.
The Motor Boys in Mexico; or, The Secret of the Buried City, Cupples & Leon, 1906.
The Motor Boys across the Plains; or, The Hermit of Lost Lake, Cupples & Leon, 1907.
The Motor Boys Afloat; or, The Stirring Cruise of the Dartaway, Cupples & Leon, 1908.
The Motor Boys on the Atlantic; or, The Mystery of the Lighthouse, Cupples & Leon, 1908.
The Motor Boys in Strange Waters; or, Lost in a Floating Forest, Cupples & Leon, 1909.
The Motor Boys on the Pacific; or, The Young Derelict Hunters, Cupples & Leon, 1909.
The Motor Boys in the Clouds; or, A Trip for Fame and Fortune, Cupples & Leon, 1910.
The Motor Boys over the Rockies; or, A Mystery of the Air, Cupples & Leon, 1911.
The Motor Boys over the Ocean; or, A Marvelous Rescue in Mid-Air, Cupples & Leon, 1911.
The Motor Boys on the Wing; or, Seeking the Airship Treasure, Cupples & Leon, 1912.
The Motor Boys after a Fortune; or, The Hut on Snake Island, Cupples & Leon, 1912.
The Motor Boys on the Border; or, Sixty Nuggets of Gold, Cupples & Leon, 1913.

The great race was under way. (Frontispiece from *The Motor Boys in the Clouds,* by Clarence Young.)

The Motor Boys under the Sea; or, From Airship to Submarine, Cupples & Leon, 1914.
The Motor Boys on Road and River; or, Racing to Save a Life, Cupples & Leon, 1915.
Ned, Bob and Jerry at Boxwood Hall; or, The Motor Boys as Freshmen, Cupples & Leon, 1916, reprinted as *The Motor Boys at Boxwood Hall; or, Ned, Bob and Jerry as Freshmen,* 1916.
Ned, Bob and Jerry on a Ranch; or, The Motor Boys among the Cowboys, Cupples & Leon, 1917, reprinted as *The Motor Boys on a Ranch; or Ned, Bob and Jerry among the Cowboys,* 1917.
Ned, Bob and Jerry in the Army; or, The Motor Boys as Volunteers, Cupples & Leon, 1918, reprinted as *The Motor Boys in the Army; or, Ned, Bob and Jerry as Volunteers,* 1918.
Ned, Bob and Jerry on the Firing Line; or, The Motor Boys Fighting for Uncle Sam, Cupples & Leon, 1919, reprinted as *The Motor Boys on the Firing Line; or, Ned, Bob and Jerry Fighting for Uncle Sam,* 1919.
Ned, Bob and Jerry Bound for Home; or, The Motor Boys on the Wrecked Troopship, Cupples & Leon, 1920, reprinted as *The Motor Boys Bound for Home; or, Ned, Bob, and Jerry on the Wrecked Troopship,* 1920.
The Motor Boys on Thunder Mountain; or, The Treasure Chest of Blue Rock, Cupples & Leon, 1924.

"RACER BOYS" SERIES

The Racer Boys; or, The Mystery of the Wreck, Cupples & Leon, 1912, reprinted under pseudonym Vance Barnum as *Frank and Andy Afloat; or, The Cave on the Island,* G. Sully, 1921.

The Racer Boys at Boarding School; or, Striving for the Championship, Cupples & Leon, 1912, reprinted under pseudonym Vance Barnum as *Frank and Andy at Boarding School; or, Rivals for Many Honors,* G. Sully, 1921.

The Racer Boys to the Rescue; or, Stirring Days in a Winter Camp, Cupples & Leon, 1912, reprinted under pseudonym Vance Barnum as *Frank and Andy in a Winter Camp; or, The Young Hunters' Strange Discovery,* G. Sully, 1921.

The Racer Boys on the Prairies; or, The Treasure of Golden Peak, Cupples & Leon, 1913.

The Racer Boys on Guard; or, The Rebellion at Riverview Hall, Cupples & Leon, 1913.

The Racer Boys Forging Ahead; or, The Rivals of the School League, Cupples & Leon, 1914.

OTHER

Also contributor of short stories to periodicals *Bright Days* and *Young Sports of America* (which became *Young People of America*), replacing earlier pseudonym Captain Young of Yale.

The travelers saw below them a long narrow valley. (Frontispiece from *The Motor Boys over the Rockies,* by Young.)

SIDELIGHTS: The "Motor Boys" series, published under the pseudonym Clarence Young, was the first Stratemeyer Syndicate series produced by Edward L. Stratemeyer and Howard R. Garis working together. Garis, best known as the author of the "Uncle Wiggily" stories, did much of the writing for the series while Stratemeyer provided detailed plot outlines.

Roger Garis, in *My Father Was Uncle Wiggily,* an account of his family's adventures in writing, says that the Motor Boys were enormously popular, and explains why: "To visualize a series based on travels in an auto would, today, be rather difficult. But at the time my father wrote [the Motor Boys series] the automobile, while not exactly a rarity, was nevertheless a symbol of adventure. Anyone who set forth for an extended trip in an auto had to consider the possibility of motor breakdowns, punctures, explosions, fire, accidents with other cars or with horse-drawn wagons, and in general hazards which, while present to a degree today, were then more or less expected. So the very idea of The Motor Boys—boys who were courageous enough to speed over mountains and through valleys and across dangerous terrain in one of those newfangled horseless carriages—was one to create excitement."

The "Motor Boys" were also popular for reasons other than their story lines. In an innovative publishing move, Stratemeyer and Cupples & Leon priced them at fifty cents each, considerably lower than any other hardback books on the market. The low price enabled young readers to buy the books themselves without having to turn to their parents. Leslie McFarlane, in his autobiography *Ghost of the Hardy Boys,* describes the buyers' reaction to the series: "'The Motor Boys' took off like Barney Oldfield. The magic of the internal combustion engine had a good deal to do with it, of course, but the fifty cent price actually did the trick! Over the next few years 'The Motor Boys' added nineteen new titles, went through thirty-five editions and sold five million copies before they ran out of gas." See the *SATA* index for more information on Harriet S. Adams, Howard R. Garis, Edward L. Stratemeyer, and Andrew E. Svenson.

WORKS CITED:

Garis, Roger, *My Father Was Uncle Wiggily,* McGraw-Hill, 1966.

McFarlane, Leslie, *Ghost of the Hardy Boys,* Two Continents, 1976.

FOR MORE INFORMATION SEE:

BOOKS

Johnson, Deidre, editor and compiler, *Stratemeyer Pseudonyms and Series Books: An Annotated Checklist of Stratemeyer and Stratemeyer Syndicate Publications,* Greenwood, 1982.

Prager, Arthur, *Rascals at Large; or, The Clue in the Old Nostalgia,* Doubleday, 1971.

*   *   *

YOUNG, Ruth 1946-

PERSONAL: Born May 22, 1946, in New York, NY; daughter of Philip Kirschner (an auto parts exporter) and Leona Goldberg; married George Young, 1983; children: Lucia

Grace. *Education:* Connecticut College for Women, B.A., 1968; graduate study at Bank Street College, 1968-70.

ADDRESSES: Home—1443 Willard St., San Francisco, CA 94117.

CAREER: Author, artist, composer, and playwright, in San Francisco, CA, 1975—. Script and story consultant; character designer; film and computer animator. Taught kindergarten and pre-school in Manhattan and Connecticut.

WRITINGS:

JUVENILE

The Great-Catsby, illustrated by Mitchell Rose, St. Martin's Press, 1985.
My Blanket, self-illustrated, Viking Kestrel, 1987.
My Babysitter, self-illustrated, Viking Kestrel, 1987.
My New Baby, self-illustrated, Viking Kestrel, 1987.
My Potty Chair, self-illustrated, Viking Kestrel, 1987.
Starring Francine and Dave (three one-act plays; contains *Peanut Butter and Jelly, Lemonade,* and *Chocolate Cake*), Orchard Books, 1988.
A Trip to Mars, illustrated by Maryann Cocca-Leffler, Orchard Books, 1990.
Daisy's Taxi, illustrated by Marcia Sewall, Orchard Books, 1991.
Golden Bear, illustrated by Rachel Isadora, Viking, in press.

ILLUSTRATOR

Lorle Harris, *Biography of a River Otter,* Putnam, 1976.
Jim Aylesworth, *One Crow,* Lippincott, 1987.
Ann Morris, *Eleanora Mousie Catches a Cold,* Macmillan, 1987.
Morris, *Eleanora Mousie Makes a Mess,* Macmillan, 1987.
Morris, *Eleanora Mousie's Gray Day,* Macmillan, 1987.
Morris, *Eleanora Mousie in the Dark,* Macmillan, 1987.

OTHER

(With Rose) *To Grill a Mockingbird and Other Tasty Titles* (self-illustrated humor and cookbook), Penguin Books, 1985.

WORK IN PROGRESS: A two-act play, *Picasso's Door.*

SIDELIGHTS: Ruth Young told *SATA:* "When I was four years old, my father bought a piano. That was an important event in my life. To me, this piano had a life of its own—the notes themselves and their personalities, the stormy, deep ones with their big feet, the magical skittery high ones, and of course, the everyday sturdy, dependable ones toward the middle of the keyboard. They all kept me company during childhood and coaxed out the storymaker.

"I had just one book as a child, Lewis Carroll's *Alice in Wonderland,* which went way beyond my comprehension at the time, though the illustrations intrigued me. I find, when I look at them now, that I know their details intimately. The world of children's books opened to me later as a kindergarten teacher, and I discovered—reading so many books aloud and repeatedly—that this world was a close neighbor to my earlier musical habitat. I hear my books before I write them, and then I write quickly, before the music gets lost in the soundwash of ticking clocks, telephones, and teapots."

GEORGE ZEBROWSKI

ZEBROWSKI, George 1945-

PERSONAL: Born December 28, 1945, in Villach, Austria; brought to the United States, 1951; naturalized citizen, 1964; son of Antoni and Anna (Popowicz) Zebrowski. *Education:* Attended State University of New York at Binghamton, 1964-69. *Hobbies and other interests:* Future studies, chess, classical music, films, tennis, swimming, philosophy of science.

ADDRESSES: Home—P.O. Box 486, Johnson City, NY 13790. *Agent*—Joseph Elder Agency, 150 West 87th St., New York, NY 10024; P.O. Box 298, Warwick, NY 10990.

CAREER: Science fiction writer and editor. Binghamton *Evening Press,* Binghamton, NY, copyeditor, 1967; filtration plant operator, New York City, 1969-70; State University of New York at Binghamton, lecturer in science fiction, 1971. Crown Publishers, general editor and consultant, 1983-85; Science Fiction Writers Speakers Bureaus, lecturer.

MEMBER: Science Fiction Writers of America, H. G. Wells Society.

AWARDS, HONORS: Nebula Award finalist, 1971, for short story, "Heathen God," and 1984, for short story, "The Eichmann Variations"; *Sunspacer* was named an outstanding book of the year by *Books for Teens,* 1984, and named a core collection book by *Anatomy of Wonder;* Theodore Sturgeon Award nomination, 1986, for short story, "The Idea Trap"; *Macrolife* was named one of the one hundred all-time best works of science fiction by *Library Journal.*

WRITINGS:

The Omega Point (second book in trilogy; also see below), Ace Books, 1972.

The Star Web, Laser Books, 1975.

The Monadic Universe and Other Stories, introduction by Thomas N. Scortia, Ace Books, 1977, 2nd edition, additional introduction by Howard Waldrop, 1985.

Ashes and Stars (first book in trilogy; also see below), Ace Books, 1977.

Macrolife (novel), Harper, 1979, reissued with an introduction by Ian Watson, Easton Press, 1990.

The Omega Point Trilogy (contain *Ashes and Stars, The Omega Point,* and *Mirror of Minds*), Ace Books, 1983.

Sunspacer (juvenile), Harper, 1985.

The Stars Will Speak, (juvenile), Harper, 1985.

Stranger Suns, Bantam, 1991.

EDITOR

Planet One: Tomorrow Today (anthology), Unity Press, 1975.

(With Thomas N. Scortia) *Human Machines: An Anthology of Stories about Cyborgs,* Random House, 1975.

(With Jack Dann) *Faster Than Light: An Anthology of Stories about Interstellar Travel,* Harper, 1976.

The Best of Thomas N. Scortia, Doubleday, 1981.

Zebrowski's futuristic young adult novel tells the story of Lissa, a teenager from a distant man-made planet who comes to Earth to study at a space institute. (Cover illustration by Ivan Powell.)

(With Isaac Asimov and Martin H. Greenberg) *Creations: The Quest for Origins in Story and Science* (anthology), Crown, 1983.

Nebula Awards 20, Harcourt, 1986.

Nebula Awards 21, Harcourt, 1987.

Synergy 1, Harcourt, 1987.

Nebula Awards 22, Harcourt, 1988.

Synergy 2, Harcourt, 1988.

Synergy 3, Harcourt, 1988.

Synergy 4, Harcourt, 1989.

Editor of ten-volume "Classics of Modern Science Fiction" series. Editor, *Bulletin of the Science Fiction Writers of America,* 1970-75 and 1983— .

OTHER

Contributor to books, including Strange Gods, edited by Roger Elwood, Pocket Books, 1974; *Science Fiction: Contemporary Mythology,* edited by Patricia Warrick, Martin H. Greenbert, and Joseph D. Olander, Harper, 1978; *Light Years and Dark,* edited by Michael Bishop, Berkley Publishing, 1984; and *Universe 16,* edited by Terry Carr, Doubleday, 1986. Contributor of short stories, reviews, and translations to periodicals, including *Isaac Asimov's Science Fiction Magazine, Fantasy & Science Fiction, Personal Computing, Science Fiction Review,* and *Washington Post Book World.*

Zebrowski's works have been translated into French, Dutch, Portuguese, Japanese, Italian, Spanish, Swedish, and German.

ADAPTATIONS: The short story "The Heathen God" was produced as a play by Readers Theater, University of Nebraska, Lincoln, in April, 1983.

SIDELIGHTS: George Zebrowski, a prominent science fiction writer, was born in Austria in 1945, while World War II was still raging in Europe. When he was young, Zebrowski lived in several European countries, moved to England, and eventually came to the United States in 1951, when he was six years old. The author uses his childhood experiences as a foundation for many of his works. Often his characters go on adventures that take them far away from their homes, and they must adapt to new surroundings. Zebrowski's characters have an added challenge because frequently the action takes place in the future or on a different planet.

Zebrowski's has produced two books for young readers, *Sunspacer* and *The Stars Will Speak.* In *Sunspacer,* Joe Sorby has just graduated from high school in New York and plans to study physics at a space station near the moon. However, he must deal with problems, including a girlfriend who is angry with him, the break up of his parents, and his fear of going away from home for the first time. In *The Stars Will Speak,* teenager Lissa Quintana-Greene-Wolfe leaves her home on a far-away man-made planet to study space messages at an institute on Earth. For twenty years, there has been a signal thought to be from an alien civilization that no one can understand. Lissa dreams of being the one to decode the message and communicate with the aliens. Lissa must make a decision about her career after she falls in love with a coworker.

Zebrowski told *SATA:* "My experience in writing for young adults is that they dislike books that are labeled as being for children or young adults. This is especially true of young science fiction readers who quickly move on to so-called adult works. (That's what I did when I started reading). After writing many stories and three novels for young adults, I now believe that such stories should be written just like any others, except that the main characters happen to be youthful. Books that are written down to young people, so they may understand them better, are often rejected by those same young readers. This does not mean that an author has to make books hard to understand, only that he should trust his readers and respect their intelligence. Books that are aimed at young readers by publishers, librarians, and teachers, come across as "lessons," and kids quickly spot these as phony, pre-censored insults. The only test of a book for young adults should be that it is a good book that anyone can read—regardless of age."

FOR MORE INFORMATION SEE:

BOOKS

Dictionary of Literary Biography, Volume 8: *Twentieth-Century American Science Fiction Writers,* Gale, 1981.

Elliot, Jeffrey M. and R. Reginald, *The Work of George Zebrowski: An Annotated Bibliography and Guide,* Borgo, 1986, 2nd edition, 1990.

Gunn, James, editor, *The New Encyclopedia of Science Fiction,* Viking, 1988.

Twentieth Century Science Fiction Writers, St. James Press, 1981, 2nd edition, 1986.

Cumulative Indexes

Illustrations Index

(In the following index, the number of the volume in which an illustrator's work appears is given *before* the colon, and the page number on which it appears is given *after* the colon. For example, a drawing by Adams, Adrienne appears in Volume 2 on page 6, another drawing by her appears in Volume 3 on page 80, another drawing in Volume 8 on page 1, and another drawing in Volume 15 on page 107.)

YABC

Index citations including this abbreviation refer to listings appearing in *Yesterday's Authors of Books for Children,* also published by Gale Research Inc., which covers authors who died prior to 1960.

S

Author Index

The following index gives the number of the volume in which an author's biographical sketch, Brief Entry, or Obituary appears.

This index includes references to all entries in the following series, which are also published by Gale Research Inc.

YABC—*Yesterday's Authors of Books for Children: Facts and Pictures about Authors and Illustrators of Books for Young People from Early Times to 1960*, Volumes 1-2

CLR—*Children's Literature Review: Excerpts from Reviews, Criticism, and Commentary on Books for Children*, Volumes 1-25

SAAS—*Something about the Author Autobiography Series*, Volumes 1-13